Church, Faith and Culture in the Medieval West

General Editor: Brenda Bolton

About the series

In the last generation an important transformation has taken place in the study of the Medieval Church in the Latin West. This new focus has moved away from a narrow concentration on single religious themes to introduce a greater cultural awareness. Recent cross-disciplinary studies on the Church's rules on consanguinity provide a case in point while other research has benefited from theological, political or literary perspectives.

The new Ashgate series *Church, Faith and Culture in the Medieval West* will contain some of the most innovative work from this area of current research and will be drawn not only from more established scholars but also from those who are younger. The series, therefore, will contribute much new work, approaching the subject with vertically throughout the period from *c.* 400 to *c.* 1500 or horizontally throughout the whole of Christendom. The series is conceived as primarily monographic but may also include some collected essays on themes of particular relevance and the significant of individuals. The aim will be to draw authors from a range of disciplinary backgrounds, but all will share are commitment to innovation, analysis and historical accuracy.

About the book

Never before had France had a church council so large: almost 1000 churchmen assembled at Bourges on 29 November 1225 to authorize a tax on their incomes in support of the Second Albigensian Crusade. About one third of the participants were representatives sent by corporate bodies, in accordance with a new provision of canon law that insisted, for the first time ever, that there should be no taxation without representation.

Basing himself on the rich surviving records, Professor Kay paints a skilful portrait of this council: the political manoeuvering by the papal legate to ensure the tax went through, and his use of this highly public occasion to humiliate members of the University of Paris; and, on the other hand, his failure to win a permanent endowment to support the papal bureaucracy, the bishops' effective protests against the pope's threat to diminish their jurisdiction over monasteries, and a subsequent 'taxpayers' revolt' that challenged the validity of the tax. The book also draws out the importance and implications of what took place, highlighting the council's place at the fountainhead of European representative democracy, the impact of the decisions made on the course of the Albigensian Crusade, the reform of monasticism, and the funding of the papal government which was left to rely on stop-gap expedients, such as the sale of indulgences. In addition, the author suggests that the corpus of texts, newly edited from the original manuscripts and with English translation, could be seen as a model for the revision of the conciliar corpus, most of which still remains based on eighteenth-century scholarship that challenged the validity of the tax. The book also draws out the importance and implications of what took place, highlighting the council's place at the fountainhead of European representative democracy, the impact of the decisions made on the course of the Albigensian Crusade, the reform of monasticism, and the funding of the papal government which was left to rely on stop-gap expedients, such as the sale of indulgences. In addition, the author suggests that the corpus of texts, newly edited from the original manuscripts and with English translation, could be seen as a model for the revision of the conciliar corpus, most of which still remains based on eighteenth-century scholarship.

Church, Faith and Culture in the Medieval West

General Editor: Brenda Bolton

Other titles in the series:

Michelle Still
The Abbot and the Rule
Religious life at St Albans, 1290–1349

Gillian R. Knight
The Correspondence between Peter the
Venerable and Bernard of Clairvaux
A semantic and structural analysis

Sylvia Schein
Gateway to the Heavenly City
Crusader Jerusalem and the Catholic West (1099–1187)

Edited by Brenda Bolton and Anne Duggan
Adrian IV, the English Pope (1154–1159)

Edited by Robert C. Figueira
Plenitude of Power
The doctrines and exercise of authority in the Middle Ages

The Council of Bourges, 1225

To my wife
Sherry Needham Kay

A papal legate presides over a council: Otto of Tonengo at the Council of London in 1237 (see chap. 7, n. 31). Drawing by Matthew Paris in his *Chronica majora*, made in the 1240s (see Doc. 43.pr.), from Cambridge, Corpus Christi College, MS. 16, fol. 109r, by the kind permission of the Parker Library.

The Council of Bourges, 1225

A documentary history

Richard Kay

Ashgate

Published by
Ashgate Publishing Ltd.
Gower House, Croft Road,
Aldershot, Hampshire GU11 3HR
England

Ashgate Publishing Company
131 Main Street
Burlington, VT 05401-5600
USA

Ashgate website: http://www.ashgate.com

British Library Cataloguing-in-Publication Data
Kay, Richard
   The Council of Bourges, 1225 : a documentary history. –
   (Church, faith and culture in the medieval West)
   1. Council of Bourges 2. Catholic Church – France – History – To 1500
   3. France – Church history – 987–1515
   I. Title
   282.4′4′09022

Library of Congress Cataloging-in-Publication Data
Kay, Richard, 1931–
   The Council of Bourges, 1225 : a documentary history / Richard Kay.
      p.   cm. — (Church, faith, and culture in the Medieval West)
   Includes bibliographical references and index. (alk. paper)
      1. Catholic Church. Council of Bourges (1225)   I. Title.   II. Series.
   BX1529 .K39 2002
   262′52—dc21

                                                                         2001053596

This volume is printed on acid-free paper.

ISBN 0 7546 0803 4

Printed and bound in Great Britain by MPG Books Ltd, Bodmin, Cornwall

CONTENTS

List of figures and tables   vii
Foreword   ix
List of abbreviations   xv

CHAPTER 1
The Second Albigensian Crusade before 1225   1

CHAPTER 2
Cardinal Romanus and his legation to France 1225   39

CHAPTER 3
Organization of the council   77

CHAPTER 4
Granting the Albigensian tenth   115

CHAPTER 5
Collecting the Albigensian tenth   147

CHAPTER 6
A proposal for financing papal government   175

CHAPTER 7
The rejection of fiscal reform   201

CHAPTER 8
Monastic reform and repentant masters   233

Afterword   255

Documents

List of documents   263
Introduction to the documents   265

SECTION I
Narrative accounts of the council   269

SECTION 2
Franco–papal negotiations preliminary to the crusade   325

SECTION 3
Collection of the tenth for the crusade   399

SECTION 4
Proposals for financing papal government   457

SECTION 5
Monastic provincial chapters   519

SECTION 6
Miscellaneous   537

Bibliography   567
Index   589

LIST OF FIGURES AND TABLES

FIGURES

1   The legation of Cardinal Romanus 1225-1227   86
2   Stemma of *Relatio de concilio Bituricensi*   275
3   Stemma of *Super muros Jerusalem*   471
4   The manuscript tradition of Document 43   496
5   Stemma of "Walter of Coventry" (C) and related manuscripts   512

TABLES

1   The provinces of Cardinal Romanus' legation   87

FOREWORD

A monograph the size and complexity of the present one would require no justification if its subject were the Fourth Lateran Council, which is already famous as a significant event in the history of Latin Christendom. The importance of the Council of Bourges, however, is not widely recognized and consequently should be explained at the outset.

Size is a convenient initial indicator of this council's importance, for the meeting at Bourges in 1225 was the largest clerical assembly ever held in France up to that time, and indeed in the Latin West only the Fourth Lateran Council had been bigger. Sheer size, however, is not as important as the reason for it, which in both cases was due to a fateful innovation: representative government. In addition to the bishops, abbots, and other prelates who attended in person, certain ecclesiastical corporations, such as cathedral chapters, sent agents, legally termed "proctors," to represent their interests, and especially their property rights, which would be affected by any tax imposed by the council. Today, when government by elected representatives is commonplace in all but the smallest assemblies, this practice is taken for granted; but in 1225 it was a novelty with an uncertain future. Although proctors attended the Fourth Lateran Council, we have no record of what role, if any, they played in the proceedings; in fact, the Council of Bourges is the first assembly for which their participation is documented. What is more, the record for Bourges is an extensive one in which the decision-making process can be traced in more detail than for any other assembly for decades. Hence the Council of Bourges deserves careful attention as the earliest recorded instance of representative government in practice.

In 1225 consent to taxation could be of two kinds, either voluntary or involuntary,[1] and the proctors at Bourges were asked to consent in both ways. Their greatest victory was to refuse the pope's request for voluntary taxation, made in the bull *Super muros Jerusalem*, for a permanent subsidy to support the papal bureaucracy. The proctors at Bourges were so elated at the effectiveness of their resistance that one of them recorded their arguments at length in the unique *Relatio de concilio Bituricensi*, which was sent to their counterparts in

---

1. For the distinction, see Gaines Post, *Studies in Medieval Legal Thought* (Princeton, 1964), pp. 171 and 226.

England, where it provided a model for the first representative assembly in English history. Involuntary, or procedural, consent to taxation is a more difficult concept for present-day readers to understand, particularly because contemporary sources rarely discuss decisions involving this kind of consent; but its operation at Bourges can be examined in detail, thanks to the *Relatio* and a subsequent tax revolt, which was well documented.

The main purpose of the Council of Bourges was to commit the churches of France and adjacent provinces to a ten-percent tax on clerical incomes for five years, which was the king of France's price for conducting the Second Albigensian Crusade. The history of the council is accordingly part of the larger story of that crusade, which is most important as the first step towards the absorption of Languedoc into the French royal desmesne. It has long been debated whether the crusade was inspired by French royal aggression or by papal zeal to destroy the Catharist heresy and, contrary to the current tendency to blame the papacy, the present study argues that the curia favored a peaceful solution to the Albigensian question and, when it could not prevent French aggression, managed to moderate it and eventually, by skillful diplomacy, to achieve a negotiated settlement in the Peace of Paris of 1229.

These highlights are enough to justify an intensive study of the Council of Bourges, but there are incidental benefits as well. The crusade and its aftermath were arranged by the papal legate to France, Romanus Bonaventura, who consequently is the principal figure (not to say hero) of our story. The portrait of him that emerges from our study reveals many facets of a complex character: an arrogant aristocrat, a clever canonist, an adroit diplomat, a lover of learning hated by the University of Paris, and above all a single-minded servant of the Roman church. His is the first generation of cardinals who can be known in such detail, and Romanus can now take his place alongside Conrad von Urach and Guala Bicchieri, who both have recently received comprehensive studies.

This monograph also illuminates many other topics of less general interest: the procedure of church councils, the theory and practice of papal legation, the chapters-general of Benedictine monks, Anglo-French diplomacy, and the hesitant growth of papal monarchy.

Finally, one unusual feature of this study requires some explanation: almost half the work consists of original documents, for the most part Latin texts in new editions, accompanied by interpretative introductions and English translations. Although a few of these texts have never been published before, most of them have been well known for over a century, and many of them for almost two. I decided to re-edit the sources for this study as another step towards the modernization of the conciliar corpus—a slow process which has only been done for England by Powicke's *Councils & Synods* and for a few individual councils elsewhere. It will be a long time before anyone can undertake a "new Mansi," and in the meantime the way must be prepared by interim studies of specific councils, for which the present work is offered as a model.

★   ★   ★

For the reader who, although now satisfied that this work is worthwhile, may still be curious about its origins, I venture to add a few lines of autobiography. The Council of Bourges was suggested to me in 1953 by Gaines Post as the subject for a master's thesis. At the time I was content to work from the traditional texts, but I became progressively wary—even appalled—at the ramshackle state of the conciliar corpus as, in preparation for a doctoral dissertation, I read through six folio volumes of Mansi's *Amplissima collectio* with Hefele and Leclercq's *Histoire des conciles* as my principal guide. It all had to be done over again—but how? The French materials were too scattered and disparate to permit a single, coordinated effort, such as Powicke and his collaborators were making in England; at best a single French province was a lifetime project, so studies of individual councils seemed the most feasible place to begin. What was needed, I thought, was a model for such studies, and in 1965 I resolved to provide one by enlarging my master's thesis to include new editions of all the original sources. A decade of uninterrupted work would have sufficed, but such long-term projects were discouraged by the publish-or-perish policies of American universities, with the result that half the work was completed only after I had retired in 1998. In the process, my old master's thesis has been completely rewritten—hardly a sentence survives in the present narrative—although my early concerns with conciliar procedure, and especially the mechanisms of counsel and consent, are still very much in evidence.

★   ★   ★

A word needs to be said about the citation of my authorities, because the system I have adopted is not altogether conventional. First, the documentary section of the book is usually cited parenthetically in the text by a reference to a given document (e.g. Doc. 4), often adding the relevant section (e.g. Doc. 4.7) or referring to the prolegomena, or introductory material (e.g. Doc. 4.pr.).

To make fullest use of all other references, it should be understood that the *most complete* bibliographical details are given in the Bibliography. In each chapter, the first time a work is cited, I give the basic facts—author, title, place and date of publication—but one must turn to the Bibliography for peripheral data, such as the subtitle, series title, reprintings, and descriptions of multivolume works.

After the first reference in each chapter, a condensed form of citation is used for most works, consisting of the last name of the author(s) plus a short form of the title. A few works, however, are always cited in an abbreviated form that is explained in the List of Abbreviations.

Note, however, that these principles apply only to the narrative chapters; a different system of citation has been used in connection with the documents. The bibliographic references provided for each document are rarely repeated in the general bibliography, which otherwise would be cluttered with scattered materials on a given author—e.g. Gerald of Wales—that have already been given together at the place where they are both needed and expected, in the introduction to the document itself (e.g. Doc. 40).

A separate Introduction to the Documents explains the rationale for that somewhat unusual feature of this book and also describes my editorial principles and methods in detail.

★   ★   ★

It remains to acknowledge the help I have received over the past forty-seven years. Foremost among my benefactors, of course, is Gaines Post, whose influence pervades the work that he originally suggested and directed. Subsequently a number of other scholars have answered specific questions and offered useful suggestions: Malcolm Barber, C. R. Cheney, Anthony P. Corbeill, Robert C. Figueira, David Heimann, John C. Holt, Caroline A. Jewers, Norris J. Lacy, Adriana Marucchi, Alexandra Mason, James M. Powell, Kathryn L. Reyerson, Richard R. Ring, David S. Spear, Jeanne Vielliard, Dorothea Weber, and Schafer Williams. Joseph R. Strayer read the first version of this study; all of the final version was read by Casey Law and parts of it by James A. Brundage and John C. Moore. Among my former students, who discussed some of the documents in seminars, I am particularly indebted to Howard Felber, Casey Law, John Lomax, and Dudley Stutz. The figures and tables were prepared by Paul Hotvedt.

Many institutions made this work possible. Financial support was provided by a postdoctoral fellowship at the Johns Hopkins University and a variety of grants from the University of Kansas. Moreover, their libraries were an invaluable resource, as were those of the Universities of Colorado, Kentucky, and Wisconsin. I am particularly grateful to the repositories of the manuscript materials that were essential for this study, not only for access to the originals and for photocopies, but also for permission to publish these texts: in France, the Archives de France and Bibliothèque nationale de France; in England, the British Library, the Public Record Office, and the Parker Library of Corpus Christi College, Cambridge; and of course the Biblioteca Apostolica Vaticana. Microfilms were also provided by two centers of documentation: the Institut de recherche et d'histoire des textes (Paris) and the Stephan Kuttner Institute of Medieval Canon Law (Munich).

Finally, and however inadequately, I wish to thank my wife, Sherry, to whom this book is dedicated, for the cheerful companionship and patient forbearance with which she has supported me, both in the completion of this work and in all else.

Richard Kay

Lawrence, Kansas
30 November 2000

LIST OF ABBREVIATIONS

ad an. = ad annum.

Arch. nat. = Archives nationales (Paris).

Arch. Vat. = Archivio Segreto Vaticano

arr. = arrondissement.

Auvray = *Les Registres de Gregoire IX (1227–1241)*, ed. L. Auvray et al., Bibliothèque des écoles françaises d'Athènes et de Rome, 2nd ser., no. 9, 4 vols. (Paris, 1890–1955).

AV = *The* [Authorized Version of the] *Holy Bible containing the Old and New Testaments and the Apocrypha, translated by His Majesty's special command* [King James I, A.D. 1611].

Barbiche = *Les Actes pontificaux originaux des Archives nationales de Paris*, vol. I: *1198–1261*, ed. B. Barbiche, Commission internationale de diplomatique (CISH), Index actorum Romanorum pontificum ab Innocentio III ad Martinum V electum, vol. I (Vatican City, 1975).

Baronio–Theiner = *Annales ecclesiastici a Christo nato ad annum 1571*, ed. C. Baronius (Baronio) et al., new ed. by A. Theiner, 37 vols. (Bar-le-Duc, 1864–1874).

Bibl. mun. = Bibliothèque municipale.

BL = British Library (formerly British Museum).

BnF = Bibliothèque nationale de France (Paris).

Böhmer–Ficker–Winkelmann = *Regesta Imperii,* ed. J. F. Böhmer, Bd. V: *Jüngere Staufer: 1198–1272*, ed. J. Ficker, E. Winkelmann, and F. Wilhelm, 3 vols. (Innsbruck, 1881–1901).

Bossuat, *Manuel* = R. Bossuat, *Manuel bibliographique de la littérature française du Moyen Age* (Melun, 1951).—*Supplément (1949–1953)* (Paris, 1955).—*Second supplément (1954–1961)* (Paris, 1961).

Chevalier, *Bio-bibliographie* = *Répertoire des sources historiques du Moyen Age: Bio-bibliographie,* ed. C. U. J. Chevalier, 2nd ed., 2 vols. (Paris, 1905–1907).

Chevalier, *Topo-bibliographie* = *Répertoire des sources historiques du Moyen Age: Topo-bibliographie,* ed. C. U. J. Chevalier, 2 vols. (Montbéliard, 1894–1903).

Cottineau, *Répertoire* = *Répertoire topo-bibliographique des abbayes et prieurés,* ed. L. H. Cottineau and G. Poras, 3 vols. (Macon, 1935–1970).

Denifle–Châtelain = *Chartularium Universitatis Parisiensis,* ed. H. Denifle and E. Châtelain, 4 vols. (Paris, 1891–1899).

dép. = département.

Devic-Vaissète = *Histoire générale de Languedoc*, ed. C. Devic and J. Vaissète, 3rd ed. [by A. Molinier et al.], 16 vols. (Toulouse, 1872-1904).

DHGE = *Dictionnaire d'histoire et de géographie ecclésiastiques.*

Douay-Rheims = *The Holy Bible Translated from the Latin Vulgate*, revised by R. Challoner (New York, 1899).

ed. = edition, edited by.

Eubel, *Hierarchia* = *Hierarchia Catholica Medii Aevi (1198–1431)* ed. C. Eubel, vol. I, 2nd ed. (Munster i. W., 1898).

Fabre-Duchesne, *Liber censuum* = *Le "Liber censuum" de l'église romaine*, ed. P. Fabre and L. Duchesne, Bibliothèque des écoles françaises d'Athènes et de Rome, 2nd ser., no. 6, 3 vols. (Paris, 1889-1952).

Friedberg = *Corpus iuris canonici*, ed. E. Friedberg, 2 vols. (Leipzig, 1879-1881).

Gallia Christiana = *Gallia Christiana in ecclesiasticas provincias distributa*, edited by the Benedictines of the Congregation of St-Maur and (vols. XIV–XVI) by B. Hauréau, 16 vols. (Paris, 1715-1865).

Hist. litt. Fr. = *Histoire lit(t)éraire de la France*, ed. A. Rivet et al., 42 vols. to date (Paris, 1733–).

Horoy = *Honorii III Romani pontificis opera omnia*, ed. C. A. Horoy, 5 vols., Medii Aevi bibliotheca patristica, vols. 1-5 (Paris, 1879-1882).

inc. = incipit.

Labbe-Cossart = *Sacrosancta concilia*, ed. P. Labbe and G. Cossart, 18 vols. (Paris, 1671-1672).

Latham = *Revised Medieval Latin Word-list from British and Irish Sources*, ed. R. E. Latham (London, 1965).

Maleczek, *Kardinalskolleg* = W. Maleczek, *Papst und Kardinalskolleg von 1191 bis 1216: Die Kardinäle unter Coelestin III. und Innocenz III.*, Publikationen des historischen Instituts beim österreichischen Kulturinstitut in Rom, Abt. 1, Bd. 6. (Vienna, 1984).

Mansi = *Sacrorum conciliorum nova et amplissima collectio*, ed. G. D. Mansi, 31 vols. (Florence/Venice, 1759-1798); reprint with continuation (vols. 0 + XXXII–LIII) ed. L. Petit and J. B. Martin (Paris/Arnhem: Welter, 1901-1927).

Martène-Durand, *Thesaurus* = *Thesaurus novus anecdotorum*, ed. E. Martène and U. Durand, 5 vols. (Paris, 1717).

Martène-Durand, *Vet. script. coll.* = *Veterum scriptorum et monumentorum historicorum, dogmaticorum, moralium amplissima collectio*, ed. E. Martène and U. Durand, 9 vols. (Paris, 1724-1733).

Mas Latrie, *Trésor de chronologie* = L. de Mas Latrie, *Trésor de chronologie d'histoire et de géographie pour l'étude et l'emploi des documents du Moyen Age* (Paris, 1889).

MGH = Monumenta Germaniae historica.

Migne, *Pat. Lat.* = *Patrologiae cursus completus . . . series Latina*, ed. J. P. Migne, 221 vols. (Paris, 1841-1864).

Molinier, "Catalogue . . . Montfort" = A. Molinier, "Catalogue des actes de Simon et d'Amauri de Montfort," *Bibliothèque de l'Ecole des chartes*, XXXIV (1873), 153-203, 445-501.

Molinier, "Catalogue . . . Raimond" = A. Molinier, "Catalogue des actes de Raimond VI & de Raimond VII," in Devic-Vaissète, VIII (1879), 1940-2008.

Molinier, *Sources* = A. Molinier, *Les Sources de l'histoire de France dès origines aux guerres d'Italie (1494)*, Les Sources de l'histoire de France depuis les origines jusqu'en 1815, ed. A. Molinier et al., Part I = Manuels de bibliographie historique, 3-5, 6 vols. (Paris, 1901-1906).

MS = manuscript.

Niermeyer, *Lexicon* = J. F. Niermeyer, *Mediae Latinitatis lexicon minus* (Leiden, 1984).

n.s. = new series, new style.

o.s. = old series, old style.

Petit-Dutaillis, *Louis* = C. Petit-Dutaillis, *Etude sur la vie et le règne de Louis VIII (1187–1226)*, Bibliothèque de l'Ecole des hautes études, fasc. 101 (Paris, 1894).

Potthast = *Regesta pontificum Romanorum inde ab a. post Christum natum MCX-CVIII ad a. MCCCIV*, ed. A. Potthast, 2 vols. (Berlin, 1874-1875).

Potthast, *Wegweiser* = *Bibliotheca historica Medii Aevi: Wegweiser durch die Geschichtswerke des europäischen Mittelalters bis 1500*, ed. A. Potthast, 2nd ed., 2 vols. (Berlin, 1896).

Powicke-Cheney, *Councils & Synods*, II.i = *Councils & Synods, with Other Documents Relating to the English Church*, vol. II: *A.D. 1205–1313*, part i: *1205–1265*, ed. F. M. Powicke and C. R. Cheney (Oxford, 1964).

pr. = principium, proem.

Pressutti = *Regesta Honorii Papae III*, ed. P. Pressutti, 2 vols. (Rome, 1888-1895).

PRO = Public Record Office (London).

Rec. hist. Gaules = *Recueil des historiens des Gaules et de la France; Rerum Gallicarum et Francicarum scriptores*, ed. M. Bouquet et al., 24 vols. (Paris, 1738-1904).

ref. = reference.

Rolls Series = *Rerum Britannicarum Medii Aevi scriptores, or Chronicles and memorials of Great Britain and Ireland during the Middle Ages*, published . . . under the direction of the Master of the Rolls, 99 titles (London, 1858-1896).

Rymer, *Foedera* = *Foedera, conventiones, literae, et cujuscunque generis acta publica, inter reges Angliae et alios quosvis imperatores, reges, pontifices, principes, vel communitates*, ed. T. Rymer et al., 2nd ed., 20 vols. (London, 1726-1735); 3rd ed. by G. Holmes, 10 vols. (The Hague, 1739-1745); 4th ed., 4 vols. (London, 1816-1869).

s. a. = sine anno.

Shirley, *Royal Letters* = *Royal and Other Historical Letters Illustrative of the Reign of Henry III*, ed. W. W. Shirley, Rolls Series, no. 27, 2 vols. (London, 1862-1866).

Teulet = *Layettes du Trésor des chartes*, ed. A. Teulet et al., 5 vols., Archives nationales, Inventaires et documents (Paris, 1863-1909).

Wilkins, *Concilia* = *Concilia Magnae Britanniae et Hiberniae*, ed. D. Wilkins, 4 vols. (London, 1737).

~ = between (two numbers): e.g. 1~10 = "between one and ten."

CHAPTER I

THE SECOND ALBIGENSIAN CRUSADE
BEFORE 1225

In November 1225, Romanus, the papal legate to France, was trying to induce the king to join the Second Albigensian Crusade. Louis VIII had set two main conditions as the price of his participation: first, he wanted a clear title to the county of Toulouse; second, he wanted a financial subsidy from the French church. The legate was willing to meet both these conditions in the pope's name, but if they were to be legally binding, he had to consult the churches of his legation before making the decision. For this reason Romanus summoned representatives from fifteen ecclesiastical provinces to meet with him in council at Bourges on 30 November 1225. To understand the questions that were considered there, we must survey in this chapter the origin and progress of the Second Albigensian Crusade during the decade prior to 1225. We shall pay particular attention to Raymond VII and Amaury de Montfort, the two claimants to the county of Toulouse, who both appeared before the Council of Bourges to be heard and judged. We shall also follow the vacillations of Pope Honorius III, who declared the crusade but could not decide how to use it. Most especially, we must trace in detail his negotiations with the king of France, which culminated in the legation of Romanus and the Council of Bourges.

The Catharist "heresy" was the source of all these problems. In the twelfth century, this Manichaean alternative to Catholic Christianity had spread widely through western Europe. By the end of the century, the center of the infection was clearly in Languedoc, where the city of Albi lent its name to the heretics, who were commonly called "Albigensians." As the local clergy proved ineffective against the heretics, Pope Innocent III (1198-1216) attempted to cure the disease by extraordinary remedies. Competent preachers, such as the future St Dominic, combated the heretics through popular preaching, learned disputation, and exemplary living. Papal legates replaced incompetent prelates and urged the feudal lords of Languedoc to repress the heretics; the least cooperative and most important ones they excommunicated, including the overlord of the area, Raymond VI de St-Gilles, count of Toulouse. Finally, when the pope's legate was murdered in January 1208, Innocent became convinced that the lords of Languedoc were as incompetent as the local clergy, since they were either unwilling or unable to maintain law and order. Therefore the pope proclaimed a crusade against the Christian land of Languedoc: heresy was to be uprooted, and those local lords who did not cooperate were to lose their lands to the crusaders.[1]

Exposition en proie was a powerful incentive. The lure of land quickly brought an army of volunteers from the north of France, who chose as their leader Simon de Montfort. During the first phase of the conquest, Raymond VI of Toulouse cooperated with the crusaders, but papal legates kept raising the price of appeasement until, at the Council of Montpellier in 1211, the demands became ruinous. The count was expected to apprehend heretics and either expel them from his lands or turn them over to the Church, which would often mean that he would have to wage war on his vassals. Moreover, he was held responsible for the maintenance of law and order in his county. Paradoxically, the council also required Raymond to disarm: he was to dismiss the mercenary troops on whom he relied in any war against his vassals, and he was even expected to destroy his own fortifications. Finally, he was deprived of the last vestige of control by the requirement that he join the Templars or Hospitallers and go crusading in the Holy Land.[2]

Little wonder that Raymond VI refused to comply and began to oppose the crusaders. His resistance was shattered, however, at the battle of Muret (12 September 1213), and Simon took possession of the county of Toulouse. The Roman church reserved the right to divide the spoils, for which purpose the Fourth Lateran Council heard the respective claims of Raymond and Simon and voted by a three-quarters majority in favor of de Montfort (November 1215). In accordance with this judgment, Innocent III passed sentence on 14 December 1215.[3] Raymond VI was condemned as incompetent, because he could maintain neither the peace nor the faith in his lands, and therefore was deposed from

1. Potthast, no. 3323 (9 Mar. 1208). H. Pissard, *La Guerre sainte en pays chrétien* (Paris, 1912). Only in the next generation did canonists provide a theoretical basis for Innocent's unprecedented action: F. H. Russell, *The Just War in the Middle Ages* (Cambridge, Eng., 1975), pp. 202, 206-207, 209. Innocent, no doubt, acted in the belief that the papal *plenitudo potestatis* gave him unlimited power to devise new remedies. For an overview, see A. P. Evans, "The Albigensian Crusade," in *A History of the Crusades*, ed. K. M. Setton, II, 2nd ed. (Madison, 1969), 277-324, preceded by a helpful map of Languedoc and central France.

2. The precise terms of the ultimatum are not known with certainty: J. R. Strayer, *The Albigensian Crusades* (New York, 1971), p. 78; J. Sumption, *The Albigensian Crusade* (London, 1978), pp. 126-127.

3. R. Foreville, *Latran I, II, III et Latran IV* (Paris, 1965), pp. 241, 265-268. Incompetence was the principal ground for Raymond VI's deposition (see text cited in the next note). Canonists based the pope's power to depose incompetent rulers on the case of Childeric III: Gratian, *Decretum* C.15 q.6 c.3 *Alias item*, ed. Friedberg, I, 756. See E. Peters, *The Shadow King* (New Haven, 1970), index s.v. "Childeric."

all his offices and sent to do penance in exile. He was to receive an annual pen-sion as long as he humbly obeyed the Church. Simon de Montfort received all the lands that the crusaders had conquered from the heretics, together with the cities of Toulouse and Montauban, which were identified as the chief centers of the heresy. Unconquered parts of the St-Gilles domains were held in custody by the papacy on the understanding that they were reserved for Raymond's son and heir, Raymond VII, who was then eighteen, "after he becomes of legal age, if he shows himself worthy to obtain the whole or only a portion, just as shall seem more expedient."[4]

Although the decree does not specify precisely what lands had been con-quered, it would seem that the fiefs that Raymond had held from the French crown were intended, or at least this was how the French crown implemented the pope's decree, for at Melun on 10 April 1216, King Philip II Augustus in-vested Simon with them all: "Know that we have received as our liege man our dear and faithful Simon, count of Montfort, for the duchy of Narbonne, the county of Toulouse, the viscounties of Béziers and of Carcassonne; namely, for the fiefs and lands that Raymond, former count of Toulouse, held of us. . . ."[5] What was left for young Raymond were apparently some of his father's lands that lay in the Empire, or as the pope put it in December 1217, "a part of the lands your father possessed on this side of the Rhone," that is, on the east bank.[6] The papacy did not specify, however, what portion it had reserved for Raymond

4. Potthast, no. 5009, ed. Devic-Vaissète, VI, 474. This decretal was incorporated in the *Compilatio quarta* 5.5.1 (X –), ed. E. Friedberg, *Quinque compilationes antiquae* (Leipzig, 1882), pp. 147-148: "Residua terra, que non fuit a cruce signatis obtenta, custodiatur ad mandatum ecclesiae per uiros idoneos, qui negotium pacis et fidei manu teneant et defendant, ut prouideri possit unico filio comitis prefati Tolosani postquam ad legitimam etatem peruenerit, si talem se studuerit exhibere, quod in toto uel in parte ipsi merito debeat prouideri, pro ut magis uidebitur expedire" (p. 147). Honorius III considered this to be a statute made in the Fourth Lateran Council: on 20 May 1222, when he quoted it in letters addressed to his legate in France and to Philip Augustus, the pope described it as "statutum quod super hoc factum fuit in concilio generali" (Pressutti, no. 3977 [cf. 4369], ed. *Rec. hist. Gaules*, XIX, 722-723).

5. *Rec. hist. Gaules*, XIX, 646 n. See also P. Belperron, *La Croisade contre les Albigeois et l'union du Languedoc à la France (1209–1249)*, 2nd ed. (Paris, 1967), pp. 335-336; M. Roquebert, *L'Epopée cathare*, III (Toulouse, 1986), pp. 21-22, 503 (10-30 April 1216). For slight differences in the royal charters, see J. W. Baldwin, *The Government of Philip Augustus* (Berkeley and Los Ange-les, 1986), p. 562, n. 15.

6. Devic-Vaissète, VI, 513; Pressutti, no. 945, and Potthast, no. 5645. Belperron, *Croisade*, p. 331, preferred to consider the Rhone as the boundary but admitted that the division be-tween Simon and Raymond VII must remain uncertain, especially the status of the city of Beaucaire, on the west bank of the Rhone, and the duchy of Narbonne. Strayer, *Albigensian Crusades*, argues that Beaucaire "could be considered part of Provence" (p. 109 n).

VII; at most, the possibilities included the marquisate of Provence, the county of Venaissin, and the eastern part of the duchy of Narbonne.[7]

This settlement, which seemed to end the affair, was soon shattered by young Raymond VII, who in May 1216 crossed the Rhone, took the city of Beaucaire on the west bank, and held it all summer against the unsuccessful attacks of Simon de Montfort.[8] The next year both Church and crown sent slight assistance to Simon. The new pope, an octogenarian who had been consecrated as Honorius III on 25 July 1216, sent Cardinal Bertrand to reestablish peace on 19 January 1217; while Philip Augustus, on his part, sent a hundred knights for six months' service with Simon in the summer of 1217.[9] Despite these reinforcements, Montfort suffered a far more crushing blow from another direction. Old Raymond VI had spent the previous year in Spain; now he marched across the Pyrenees with an army of Aragonese and Catalan mercenaries, rallied his old vassals, the counts of Foix and Comminges, and recaptured Toulouse itself on 13 September 1217.[10] Again Simon de Montfort besieged his enemies, this time with more disastrous results, for not only was a ten months' siege of no avail, but on 25 June 1218 Simon himself was ignominiously killed by a stone that was thrown from a mangonel operated by the women of Toulouse.[11] His son, Amaury de Montfort, inherited the county of Toulouse.

The Second Albigensian Crusade: early years, 1218–1221

During the siege of Toulouse, the papacy had supported Simon with an epistolary campaign that was no more effective against the Raymonds than were military operations. No sooner had the news of the capture of Toulouse reached Rome than Honorius directed his legate in Occitania to warn King James of Aragon that he should recall those mercenaries whom Raymond VI had brought from Aragon. When no action was taken, the request was made again on 27 December 1217,

---

7. Devic-Vaissète, VI, 474-475. J. Madaule, *The Albigensian Crusade* (New York, 1967), pp. 76, 78, mentions only the marquisate of Provence; cf. Sumption, *Albigensian Crusade*, p. 181.

8. Belperron, *Croisade*, p. 339; Madaule, *Albigensian Crusade*, pp. 78-79; Strayer, *Albigensian Crusades*, pp. 108-109; W. L. Wakefield, *Heresy, Crusade and Inquisition in Southern France, 1100–1250* (London, 1974), p. 117; Sumption, *Albigensian Crusade*, pp. 182-185; Roquebert, *Epopée cathare*, III, 15-34.

9. Devic-Vaissète, VI, 478; Belperron, *Croisade*, p. 348; Roquebert, *Epopée cathare*, III, 76, 80.

10. Belperron, *Croisade*, p. 349; Madaule, *Albigensian Crusade*, pp. 79-84; Strayer, *Albigensian Crusades*, pp. 110-112; Wakefield, *Heresy*, p. 118; Sumption, *Albigensian Crusade*, pp. 191-192; Roquebert, *Epopée cathare*, III, 82-90.

11. Belperron, *Croisade*, pp. 351-359; Madaule, *Albigensian Crusade*, pp. 84-86; Strayer, *Albigensian Crusades*, pp. 113-115; Wakefield, *Heresy*, pp. 119-121; Sumption, *Albigensian Crusade*, pp. 192-198; Roquebert, *Epopée cathare*, III, 130-141.

this time not only to the king but also to the real power in the kingdom, the regent Don Sancho.[12] Since Raymond's forces continued to be more than a match for Simon's, we may infer that these demands had no practical effect.

During the three weeks after Christmas 1217, a series of letters issued from the papal chancery in rapid succession. The consuls and citizens of Toulouse, Avignon, Marseilles, and St-Gilles, together with the inhabitants of Tarascon and Beaucaire, were ordered to abandon the cause of Raymond unless they wished to remain excommunicate and suffer *exposition en proie*. Raymond VII was admonished for imitating his father and for not waiting to inherit the portion that Innocent had reserved for him. The count of Foix, the people of Montpellier, and various rebel barons were enjoined to lay down their arms. Philip Augustus was urged to aid Simon de Montfort, and those who were already supporting Simon were praised and encouraged. The bishops of Occitania were asked to send Simon men and money and to give his enemies neither aid nor counsel.[13] Finally, on 3 January 1218 the archbishops of Reims, Sens, Tours, Rouen, Bourges, Lyon, and Bordeaux, and their suffragans, were ordered to urge all those who had not taken the Cross for the Holy Land to aid Simon, for which the bishops were authorized to grant a suitable indulgence.[14]

Thus Honorius at this point stopped short of renewing the crusade, but the failure of the siege of Toulouse six months later led him to take the final step. On 11 August 1218 the pope repeated the request to the French episcopate that he had made in January, but this time he added a plenary papal indulgence to all who undertook to assist Simon, which was more attractive than the one offered earlier by the French prelates. This new appeal was made not only to the provinces of France listed above, but also to those of Besançon, Tarentaise, Embrun, Aix, Arles, and Vienne—all six of which were later to be represented at Bourges—and of Cologne, Trier, Mainz, and Salzburg, and to the Cistercian abbots as well.[15] In effect, the Second Albigensian Crusade had been declared.

Like its predecessor, this was to be a papal crusade, but with an important difference: Capetian participation. The French crown had not taken part in the

12. Pressutti, no. 842, and Potthast, no. 5610 (23 Oct. 1217); Pressutti, nos. 941, 943, and Potthast, nos. 5643-5644 (27 and 29 Dec. 1217); Belperron, *Croisade*, p. 355, where the December letter is inexplicably dated the 28th; Roquebert, *Epopée cathare*, III, 112-113.

13. Pressutti, nos. 940, 944-946, 949-950, 1006; Potthast, nos. 5642, 5645-5648, 5650, 5670; Belperron, *Croisade*, p. 355; Roquebert, *Epopée cathare*, III, 113.

14. Pressutti, no. 959, and Potthast, no. 5657 (cf. no. 5648), ed. *Rec. hist. Gaules*, XIX, 645-646.

15. Pressutti, no. 1577, and Potthast, no. 5888 (30 July 1218), ed. *Rec. hist. Gaules*, XIX, 664-665; cf. Teulet, no. 1301; Barbiche, no. 183 (11 Aug. 1218); Belperron, *Croisade*, p. 364; Roquebert, *Epopée cathare*, III, 162.

First Albigensian Crusade as long as John of England remained a threat to France. Only after John and his allies had been defeated decisively at Bouvines and La Roche au Moine in July 1214 did Philip Augustus authorize a royal expedition into Languedoc, which his heir-apparent, Prince Louis, who had taken the Cross in 1213, finally led in 1215.[16] By then, of course, the crusade was over, so royal intervention had merely helped Simon de Montfort to consolidate his position in the lands he had already conquered.[17] Now in 1218 Honorius hoped that Philip Augustus would lend more timely aid to the Second Albigensian Crusade, and on 12 August the pope exhorted the king to send an army into Albigeois. At this point Honorius still regarded the house of Montfort as the Church's bulwark against heresy in Occitania; to maintain it, he confirmed the title of Simon's son and heir, Amaury de Montfort, to all the lands that Innocent III had assigned to Simon after the Lateran council.[18] Thus the papacy could not attract Philip with an *exposition en proie*, but other powerful inducements were available if the king would fight as a crusader rather than simply as de Montfort's suzerain.

Early in September, Honorius wrote two letters that were calculated to involve the king in the crusade. One guaranteed special papal protection for the persons and lands of all who would crusade in Albigeois, but especially for the king and kingdom of France.[19] Previously he had offered them the spiritual privileges of a crusade, notably indulgences, but now he added to this the protected status for crusaders and their families and possessions that was one of the most valued temporal privileges that canon law conferred on a crusader.[20] By stating the terms explicitly in writing, Honorius assured the king and his vassals that the usual privileges, temporal as well as spiritual, were available to them in this unusual crusade against Christian lands. This papal guarantee in itself was hardly enough to persuade the king to take the Cross, however; the real incentive was contained in the other letter, dated 5 September 1218, which promised Philip

16. Philip's involvement with the crusade from 1214 until his death is summarized by Baldwin, *Government*, pp. 336-339.

17. Petit-Dutaillis, *Louis*, pp. 186-193; this in no way is replaced by the most recent biography: *Louis VIII le Lion: Roi de France méconnu, roi d'Angleterre ignoré*, by J. Choffel (Paris, 1983), an impressionistic account that stresses Anglo-French relations and lacks documentation. Madaule, *Albigensian Crusade*, pp. 74-76; Wakefield, *Heresy*, pp. 110, 112; Sumption, *Albigensian Crusade*, pp. 178-179.

18. Pressutti, nos. 1578, 1582, 1583; Potthast, nos. 5889, 5890, 5893; Molinier, "Catalogue . . . Montfort," no. 164; Belperron, *Croisade*, p. 364; Wakefield, *Heresy*, p. 122; Roquebert, *Epopée cathare*, III, 162.

19. Pressutti, no. 1614, and Potthast, no. 5900 (5 Sept. 1218); ed. *Rec. hist. Gaules*, XIX, 671; Roquebert, *Epopée cathare*, III, 162.

20. J. A. Brundage, *Medieval Canon Law and the Crusader* (Madison, 1969), pp. 160-168.

that, if he would undertake the crusade, he would receive, among other financial benefits, half of the tax that Honorius was then collecting from the French clergy.[21]

The idea was a stroke of genius. Even more than most feudal monarchs, Philip Augustus was always eager to supplement his cash income, and the proceeds of the Saladin tithe of 1188 had shown him how lucrative a general tax on the clergy could be for the crown. Since 1188 such taxes had occasionally been levied on the clergy to support a crusade in the Holy Land—indeed, the money being collected in 1218 was levied to support the Fifth Crusade[22]—but neither the Albigensian Crusades nor the French crown had benefited from them. Now both could profit, thanks to the financial dexterity of Honorius III, who had risen to prominence in the curia as the chief fiscal officer of the papacy.[23] To subsidize the Albigensian Crusade, the pope simply robbed Jerusalem to pay Paris: he offered Philip a share of the monies that had been collected in France for the Fifth Crusade. That this had been his plan from the start is evident from a note appended to the Vatican register copy of the letter that promised the king a subsidy. According to this note, the bishops of Noyon and Meaux, together with the abbots of the Cistercian order in France, were commissioned to collect the twentieth and to distribute half of the proceeds for the Holy Land and the other half for the Albigensian Crusade. Moreover, copies of the grant to Philip were sent to all the clergy of France, so they would know that the pope had authorized the arrangement.[24]

At the same time somewhat different provisions were made for Occitania, where the clergy of the provinces of Narbonne, Auch, Vienne, Aix, Arles, and Embrun were directed to turn over to Bertrand, the papal legate, *all* the pro-

---

21. Pressutti, no. 1615 (5 Sept. 1218), and Potthast, no. 5904 (also a copy dated 7 Sept.). On the tax, see Strayer, *Albigensian Crusades*, pp. 116-117; R. Kay, "The Albigensian Twentieth of 1221-3," *Journal of Medieval History*, VI (1980), 307-315; J. M. Powell, *Anatomy of a Crusade, 1213–1221* (Philadelphia, 1986), p. 97.

22. Imposed by Innocent III's constitution *Ad liberandum terram sanctam* (14 Dec. 1215); Potthast, no. 5012; Latin text, appended to the canons of the Fourth Lateran Council as c.71, ed. A. García y García, *Constitutiones concilii quarti Lateranensis una cum commentariis glossatorum* (Vatican City, 1981), pp. 110-118. Cf. F. A. Cazel, Jr., "Financing the Crusades," in *A History of the Crusades*, ed. K. M. Setton, VI (Madison, 1989), 116-149, at pp. 136-137; Powell, *Anatomy of a Crusade*, pp. 44-47.

23. As Cardinal Cencius, he was, from 1188 to 1198, "the best known of all papal chamberlains," according to P. Partner, *The Lands of St Peter* (Berkeley and Los Angeles, 1972), pp. 224-225. His fame as *camerarius* rests on the *Liber censuum*, which he compiled (ed. Fabre-Duchesne, I, 1, n. 1); H. K. Mann, *Lives of the Popes in the Middle Ages*, XIII (London, 1925), pp. 7-8.

24. Pressutti, note after no. 1615, and Potthast, no. 5091.

ceeds of the twentieth that had been collected for the Holy Land; the whole amount was to be placed at the disposal of Amaury de Montfort,[25] and Bertrand was instructed to appoint agents for the collection and distribution of these funds.[26] Their work was not always easy, for some of the Provençal clergy insisted that the tax, which their representatives at the Fourth Lateran Council had approved to liberate the Holy Land,[27] could not be diverted to another use, even by the pope. A canon of Aix and his supporters stubbornly continued to maintain this position for over three years, even after they had been condemned as blasphemers and excommunicated. Eventually Honorius ordered that they be brought to Rome, and no more was heard of this first attempt by taxpayers to exercise the power of the purse within the Church.[28]

The subsidy itself brought few results. Although Philip Augustus could not resist the pope's tempting proposal, at fifty-four he was aging and loath to take to the field, so in May 1219 he once again sent his son, Prince Louis—this time with six hundred knights. After massacring the population of Marmande along the way, they arrived in mid-June 1219; but when their forty days of knight-service had expired, the French knights promptly departed for the north in August without having shaken Raymond's hold on his capital.[29] Nonetheless the subsidy had established a significant precedent. Honorius would not forget that he could secure the services of the French crown in return for a tax on the clergy of the kingdom. Indeed, to obtain another such tax was the principal purpose of the Council of Bourges seven years later.

After Louis' uneventful expedition, affairs languished in Occitania for several years, largely because until 1221 the energies of the papacy were devoted to the Fifth Crusade;[30] in fact, the papal contingent was en route to Egypt when Honorius had diverted its funds in September 1218.[31] What little Honorius did for

25. Pressutti, no. 1616; Potthast, no. 5902; Molinier, "Catalogue . . . Montfort," no. 165.

26. Pressutti, no. 1617, and Potthast, no. 5903.

27. Foreville, *Latran*, p. 272.

28. Pressutti, no. 3658 (23 Dec. 1221); Mann, *Lives*, XIII, 24.

29. Petit-Dutaillis, *Louis*, pp. 197–202; Belperron, *Croisade*, pp. 366–368; Madaule, *Albigensian Crusade*, p. 87; Wakefield, *Heresy*, p. 123; Sumption, *Albigensian Crusade*, pp. 204–205; Roquebert, *Epopée cathare*, III, 161–172. See also Doc. 9.1.

30. F. Rocquain, *La Cour de Rome et l'esprit de reforme avant Luther*, 3 vols. (Paris, 1893–1897), II, 9. On the papacy and the Fifth Crusade, see especially J. M. Powell, "Honorius III and the Leadership of the Crusade," *Catholic Historical Review*, LXIII (1977), 521–536, and his *Anatomy of a Crusade*, pp. 149–191; J. P. Donovan, *Pelagius and the Fifth Crusade* (Philadelphia, 1950), pp. 38–97; also S. Runciman, *A History of the Crusades*, III, 2nd ed. (Cambridge, Eng., 1955), 154–169; T. C. Van Cleve, "The Fifth Crusade," in *A History of the Crusades*, ed. K. M. Setton, II, 2nd ed. (Madison, 1969), 377–428.

31. Donovan, *Pelagius*, pp. 44–49.

the Albigensian Crusade during the years 1219-1221 can be seen from his commissions to the new papal legate, Conrad, cardinal-bishop of Porto, whom he
sent to Languedoc. The legate was instructed to impose a tax for the defense of
the faith, to discipline those bishops who were supporting Raymond VII, and
to threaten the cities of Toulouse, Nîmes, and Avignon with loss of their bishoprics if they were not obedient to Rome. Judging from the date of a grant of
special powers over disobedient monks, the legate left Viterbo about 13 December 1219.[32]

This new legate, Conrad von Urach, was new to the curia. Before he was
made cardinal in 1219, he had been the head of the Cistercian order, which had
long advocated extreme solutions to the perceived menace of the Albigensian
heresy, and these zealous prejudices account for Conrad's independent, not to
say insubordinate, behavior as legate.[33] Typical of Conrad's fruitless efforts to bol-
ster the sagging power of Amaury was the creation of the Militia of the Order
of the Faith of Jesus Christ, a military-religious order that was modeled on the
Templars, with the suppression of heresy as its primary mission. In the summer
of 1221 he collaborated with the Montfort family in establishing the order,
which secured the pope's approval but hardly lasted a decade.[34]

32. For the later commissions, see Pressutti, nos. 3452, 3451, 3486, 3431, 2511; Belperron,
Croisade, p. 371. The grant of special powers over disobedient monks is dated 13 Dec. 1219 by
Pressutti, no. 2301, and Potthast, no. 6183. Falko Neininger's now definitive account dates the
beginning of the legation from this letter: *Konrad von Urach* (Paderborn, 1994), p. 168. William
le Breton dates Conrad's legation from Lent 1220 (*Rec. hist. Gaules*, XVII, 774; XIX, 699 n.),
apparently reckoning from Conrad's arrival in Languedoc. A. Clément, following Vaissète, dates
the legation from Dec. 1219: "Conrad d'Urach, de l'ordre de Cîteaux, légat en France et en
Allemagne," *Revue bénédictine*, XXII (1905), 232-243, and XXIII (1906), 62-81, 373-391, at
p. 65. The letter was not entered in the Vatican register; the first enregistered correspondence
to Conrad is dated 21 Aug. 1220 (Pressutti, no. 2634); another earlier letter concerning him is
in the register but undated (Pressutti, no. 2511), which is dated 3 June 1221 in item 28 on the
Albigensian Roll: R. Kay, "Quelques ébauches des lettres papales conservées dans le *Rotulus
de negotio albigense* (1221-1225)," forthcoming in *Bibliothèque de l'Ecole des chartes*, CLX (2002).
33. For his biography, see Neininger, *Konrad*, and Clément, "Conrad d'Urach," and H. Zimmermann, *Die päpstliche Legation in der ersten Hälfte des 13. Jahrhunderts* (Paderborn, 1913), pp. 76-77.
34. Neininger, *Konrad*, pp. 188-189, and reg. nos. 79, 96, and 100. Pressutti, no. 3441 (7 June
1221), ed. *Rec. hist. Gaules*, XIX, 699; Pressutti, no. 3502 (16 July 1221), ed. Horoy, III, 865-866
(no. 444); Molinier, "Catalogue . . . Montfort," nos. 190-191; Kay, "Quelques ébauches," no.
24 on the Albigensian Roll. G. G. Meersseman, "Etudes sur les anciennes confréries dominicaines: IV. Les Milices de Jésus-Christ," *Archivum fratrum praedicatorum*, XXIII (1953), 275-308;
A. Forey, *The Military Orders from the Twelfth to the Early Fourteenth Centuries* (Toronto, 1992),
pp. 41-42; idem, "The Military Orders and Holy War against Christians in the Thirteenth
Century," *English Historical Review*, CIV (1989), 1-24, at p. 6; Sumption, *Albigensian Crusade*,
p. 206. In 1231, the order was absorbed by the Militia of St James of the Sword with Gregory
IX's approval (Meersseman, pp. 288-289).

In 1217 Raymond VII had styled himself simply as "Raymond, son of the lord Raymond, by the grace of God duke of Narbonne, count of Toulouse, marquis of Provence."[35] The next year his status changed, however, when he turned twenty-one during the siege of Toulouse. Raymond VI promptly ceded all his domains to his young son, who, having attained legal age, was now capable of possessing them in his own right. Thus, for four years before the death of the old count in August 1222, Raymond VII held his father's titles, headed the house of St-Gilles, and led the resistance against the intruders from the north.[36] The old count's retirement was a politic move because he was neither as popular nor as successful as his son, whose reputation had not been blemished by conciliar condemnation and suspicion of heresy.[37] Naturally, the papacy did not recognize Raymond's right to inherit those lands in Languedoc that Innocent III had transferred from the house of St-Gilles to the Montforts after the Lateran council; instead, the pope soon deprived the new count even of his title to those other lands, east of the Rhone, that had been sequestered and held in reserve for him by the Roman church after his father's condemnation. Honorius had already warned Raymond VII in December 1217 that the Roman church would not give him those lands unless he obeyed the pope and stopped attacking Simon.[38] The threat was repeated more strongly in June 1220, when Honorius plainly ordered him to obey or be disinherited.[39] Finally, on 25 October 1221, the pope confirmed the sentence of exheredation that the legate Bertrand had pronounced on Raymond VII, by which the count was deprived of any right that he might have to his father's lands.[40]

Cession and subsidy: the new papal plan, 1221–1222

Honorius had waited almost two years before at last confirming the exheredation of Raymond VII. By excluding the young count from his patrimony altogether, the Church was now committed to a radical solution in Occitania. Certainly Rome had little reason to hope that Amaury de Montfort could regain control

35. Devic-Vaissète, VIII, 695 (no. 192, ii, 11 May 1217). The formula varied, once mentioning only the county and several times adding that he was also "filius domine regine Johanne" (ibid., i, iii–iv).

36. Devic-Vaissète, VI, 548, 560; Strayer, *Albigensian Crusades*, p. 108 n.; Roquebert, *Epopée cathare*, III, 221-223.

37. Belperron, *Croisade*, pp. 368-369.

38. Devic-Vaissète, VI, 513; Pressutti, no. 945, and Potthast, no. 5645.

39. Pressutti, no. 2511, and Potthast, no. 6283; Roquebert, *Epopée cathare*, III, 188-190.

40. Pressutti, no. 3555; Devic-Vaissète, VI, 544; Roquebert, *Epopée cathare*, III, 205; Neininger, *Konrad*, p. 192.

of the lands he had lost to Raymond. His counteroffensive had lost all momentum when he failed to recapture Castelnaudary after an eight-month siege that ended in March 1221,[41] and the power of the Montforts was now confined to a few strongholds, such as Carcassonne, Béziers, and Narbonne. On 1 May, the legate Conrad, together with the bishops of Béziers, Nîmes, Agde, and Lodève, sent off an appeal to Philip. They wrote from Béziers, where they said they were living in constant fear of their enemies (although the city was not under attack). With many rhetorical colors and few facts, they begged Philip to intervene, most especially because the heretics were flourishing and multiplying.[42] In response, Philip sent a small force at his own expense that accomplished nothing.[43] By 1221 experience had proved that neither the sanctions of papal legates nor slight and intermittent assistance from the north was effectual. If Raymond was to be removed, it would have to be done by superior force. Since Amaury was incapable of defending the faith, the papacy could legally offer his lands to the first Christian crusader who was able to seize them, but it would have been unseemly to desert one who had been so loyal; and, moreover, such a plan no longer had much chance of success, both because Occitania was now united in its hatred of the invaders and because the French were not responding to the appeals for a new crusade that Honorius had been making since 1218.

Hence a new approach to the problem was needed. Since Philip Augustus' victories over the English, the French crown manifestly possessed the power to overwhelm Raymond. The papacy's problem was how to induce the king to intervene, not with token forces such as he had sent for brief periods in 1215, 1217, and 1219, but with the best army he could muster and for as long as it would take to conquer Occitania. This goal of massive royal intervention was first adopted by the curia in the spring of 1221, when Amaury's impotence was at last beyond doubt. To attract the French king, Honorius devised a plan that he gradually revealed in the course of the next twelve months. Again, as in 1219, the king was to receive a subsidy from the French church; but in addition, the Montforts were to cede their lordship in Occitania to the Capetians, thus giving the crown the strongest inducement to achieve and maintain control over the area. Honorius had hit on the right solution to the Church's problems in Languedoc, as subsequent events were to prove, but his new formula for subsidy and cession was only accepted in 1225 after much hesitation and negotiation, in which the Council of Bourges played a decisive role.

41. Strayer, *Albigensian Crusades*, pp. 119–120; Belperron, *Croisade*, pp. 370–371; Sumption, *Albigensian Crusade*, p. 205; Roquebert, *Epopée cathare*, III, 179–186, 199.

42. Neininger, *Konrad*, reg. no. 74 and pp. 189–190 (formerly dated 1223).

43. A. Cartellieri, *Philipp II. August, König von Frankreich*, 4 vols. (Leipzig, 1899–1922), IV, 556–557; Neininger, *Konrad*, p. 190.

The first element in the new plan was a subsidy from the French church.[44]
On 2 June 1221, the king was notified that Honorius had appointed three
French archbishops as his legates to promote the Albigensian Crusade, with
whom the king was exhorted, in the most general terms, to cooperate.[45] The
new legates were given plenary power (*plenaria potestas*) to grant indulgences and
to do whatever seemed might expedite the crusade.[46] Their powers were limited to the provinces that were assigned to them in the north of France; similar
instructions were sent to Cardinal Conrad, whose legation in the South was extended to include the province of Bordeaux, so that without offending the English
every province of the French church had its legate to promote the crusade.[47]

The principal function of these legates only became apparent in the fall, when
councils were held in every province, at which a twentieth of the annual income
of every cleric for a period of three years was granted to support the Albigensian Crusade.[48] The amount and term were identical with the tax for the recovery of the Holy Land that the clergy of Christendom had paid from 1216
to 1218; this time, however, the tax was imposed by legatine authority, and only
in one kingdom. The levy was by no means popular. Many clerical taxpayers
tried to evade payment by claiming exempt status; others made fraudulent returns or simply refused to pay.[49] Moreover, local rivalries also created resistance,
because the collection was administered by French archbishops who had their
own vested interests.[50] From this experience, the curia learned that its own personnel was more acceptable as tax collectors than were agents drawn from the
local hierarchy. The tax taught Honorius another lesson as well. The chapters
of the province of Reims protested that they had not been consulted in council,
as canon law required when bishops tax their subjects,[51] but Honorius disal-
lowed their complaint because "the burden of paying this twentieth was imposed
on you by the archbishop . . . [and his suffragans] not by ordinary power but by

44. Neininger, *Konrad*, pp. 189-190, 193-194.

45. Pressutti, no. 3423, ed. *Rec. hist. Gaules*, XIX, 696.

46. Pressutti, no. 3427, ed. Horoy, III, 835-840 (no. 419); cf. no. 3429.

47. Pressutti, nos. 3430 and 3451, ed. Horoy, III, 835 (no. 414) and 847 (no. 426); Neininger,
Konrad, reg. nos. 88 and 98.

48. Pressutti, nos. 3574, 3625, 3644, 3860, ed. Horoy, IV, 24 (no. 28), 51 (no. 62), 50 (no. 61),
117-118 (no. 142).

49. For details, see Kay, "Albigensian Twentieth," pp. 310-312. On the significance of the
tax, see also Strayer, *Albigensian Crusades*, pp. 116-117, and William E. Lunt, *Financial Relations
of the Papacy with England to 1327* (Cambridge, Mass., 1939), pp. 246-247. Neininger, *Konrad*,
pp. 194-195.

50. E.g. Pressutti, no. 3698.

51. The right of chapters to be represented in councils that discussed matters touching the
financial interests of the chapters was established by Honorius III himself in 1217 by the decretal *Etsi membra corporis* (Doc. 48).

apostolic authority." Still, he did concede that they had some cause for complaint, although he refused to reverse the legate's decision for fear that the crusade would suffer.[52] No doubt papal plenitude of power could set aside private rights when a case of pressing necessity arose, but it is noteworthy that Honorius was more observant of due process of law the next time he asked the French church for a subsidy, at Bourges in 1225.

At the same time that Honorius was arranging a massive subsidy for the crusade, he was also preparing to offer the Montfort lands to Philip Augustus. The first step was taken on 3 June 1221, when he confirmed Amaury's title to his father's lands in Occitania.[53] This was the same day that the legates were appointed to arrange for the twentieth, so we can be certain that from the start cession and subsidy formed two parts of a coordinated plan.[54] The next step, taken on 25 October, as we have already seen, was to declare that Raymond VII had forfeited all right to the lands his father had held.[55] With Amaury's rights confirmed and Raymond's set aside, the bait was ready. On 2 December 1221, an appeal to Philip was launched by the legate Conrad and the bishops of Lodève, Maguelonne, Agde, and Béziers. Amaury had informed them that he was prepared to cede his lordships in Occitania to the Capetians in perpetuity, and the legate and his associates strongly recommended the proposal and promised the cooperation of the Occitanian episcopate.[56] The pope himself did not immediately add his recommendation; instead, on 3 February 1222 he followed up his general appeal of the previous June with a brief reminder, which again was couched in very general terms, exhorting the king to help the crusade.[57]

The climax of the papal campaign to enlist Philip's support came in a third letter to the king, dated 14 May 1222.[58] Philip Augustus was first reminded that heresy was rampant in his kingdom, despite the Church's many efforts to suppress it. In principle, Honorius stated, the secular power was obligated to use the material sword against rebels when the spiritual sword was ineffectual; and, moreover, according to canon law, the Church could compel negligent princes to purge heresy from their lands. Having shown Philip the stick, Honorius pro-

---

52. Pressutti, no. 3959, ed. *Rec. hist. Gaules*, XIX, 721.

53. Pressutti, no. 3426, ed. *Rec. hist. Gaules*, XIX, 696; Molinier, "Catalogue . . . Montfort," no. 164a.

54. On or about 3 June 1221, the curia dispatched nine letters implementing the new Occitanian policy, and moreover sent copies of the drafts to an unidentified correspondent: R. Kay, "Quelques ébauches," Roll items 20–28.

55. Pressutti, no. 3555, ed. *Rec. hist. Gaules*, XIX, 715; see also n. 40 above.

56. *Rec. hist. Gaules*, XIX, 720–721; Petit-Dutaillis, *Louis*, p. 280; Neininger, *Konrad*, reg. no. 110 and p. 195. Amaury's letter is not calendared by Molinier because no copy survives.

57. Pressutti, no. 3774, ed. *Rec. hist. Gaules*, XIX, 718–719.

58. Pressutti, no. 3950, ed. *Rec. hist. Gaules*, XIX, 720–721.

duced the carrot: since Amaury had offered to cede his rights in Occitania to the king and his heirs in perpetuity, the pope now exhorted Philip to accept the offer, take the Cross, and perform his duty as king. In return, Honorius promised him the proceeds of the triennial twentieth, as well as the spiritual and temporal benefits of crusader status, especially stressing that the Church would protect his lands from rebels and invaders while he was crusading. In case the king supposed that Raymond had any right to the lands that Amaury was offering him, Honorius sent Philip a copy of the Lateran decree together with the explanation that Raymond had lost his rights because he had not kept the terms of that settlement.[59] The same explanation was sent to the archbishop of Reims as papal legate, with instructions to make the letter public if the king took the Cross.[60]

Honorius was apparently not counting on the king to campaign in the summer of 1222, for at the same time that he wrote to Philip in May, he also instructed his archbishop-legates in France to borrow against the anticipated receipts from the twentieth in order to have ready cash with which to pay mercenaries.[61] Moreover, he intensified the campaign to enlist new crusaders by appealing directly to the nobility and communes of France: they should arise and defend the honor of Christendom and France against the heretics.[62]

Attempts to reconcile Raymond with the Church, 1222–1223

Nothing came of these plans during the summer of 1222, for Raymond felt his position in Occitania was in no danger, and therefore he spent the season on the other side of the Rhone, seeking to regain control of his inheritance there.[63] Before he left for Provence, however, Raymond did what he could to disarm the threat of royal intervention. In June 1222, he appealed to King Philip "as his sole refuge." Professing his devotion to the crown, Raymond begged the king to help him effect a reconciliation with the Church, so that he could do homage to the king for his lands in France once his title to them had been recognized by the pope.[64]

Philip Augustus promptly acted on Raymond's request. He proposed to Ho-

59. Pressutti, no. 3977, ed. *Rec. hist. Gaules*, XIX, 722-723. Potthast (no. 7024) conjectured that the date should be 1223 because the edited text is dated from the Lateran, whereas on 20 May 1222 the curia was at Alatri. But the Vatican register for 1222, from which the edited copy was made, does in fact date the letter from Alatri, as Pressutti makes plain (but see his no. 4369).

60. Pressutti, no. 3977.

61. Pressutti, no. 3969, ed. *Rec. hist. Gaules*, XIX, 722.

62. Pressutti, no. 3948, ed. Horoy, IV, 142 (no. 168).

63. Belperron, *Croisade*, p. 374; Roquebert, *Epopée cathare*, III, 220-221; cf. Pressutti, no. 4061.

64. Devic-Vaissète, VIII, 759 (no. 220, dated 16 June); Cartellieri, *Philipp*, IV, 558 (22 June!); Belperron, *Croisade*, p. 374.

norius that Raymond and Amaury should divide between themselves the fiefs that they held from the king. Thus Amaury would get some land, Raymond could hold his legitimately, and peace would be restored to Occitania. The pope replied favorably on 12 October 1222, stipulating only that heresy must still be repressed, that restitution must be made for property taken from the Church, and that ecclesiastical liberties must be preserved. Conrad, his legate in Occitania, was instructed to implement the reconciliation with the counsel of the king, the three archbishop-legates in France, and any other French prelates he might care to consult.[65] Moreover, the pope made it clear that Conrad was authorized to make whatever arrangements he thought would expedite the settlement.[66]

The pope, at least, was expecting a peaceful solution, for in March or April 1223 he urged Philip Augustus to join Frederick II in the Sixth Crusade.[67] Of the negotiations during the winter of 1222-1223 we know little except that at one point the two counts supposedly met at Carcassonne to discuss the possibility of a marriage alliance.[68] When Honorius wrote to Conrad on 18 June 1223, he assumed that the two claimants were still negotiating with the legate, who was responsible for seeing that the Church's stipulations were met. Honorius wrote him to be sure that the counts did nothing to violate the property rights of the bishop of Viviers.[69]

Conrad attempts to revive the crusade, 1223

In accordance with his mandate to broker a settlement with Raymond, Conrad held a council at St-Flour in the Auvergne, at which Raymond reached an agreement with the bishop of Maguelonne concerning the castle of Melgueil (or Maugio).[70] On other issues there was apparently no agreement, so the legate

65. Pressutti, no. 4133, ed. Horoy, IV, 234 (no. 11); Neininger, *Konrad*, pp. 196-197, and reg. no. 136. Probably this commission authorized Conrad to summon French prelates from outside his legation (Doc. 49).

66. Pressutti, no. 4137 (29 Oct. 1222), ed. Horoy, IV, 235-236 (no. 14); Neininger, *Konrad*, reg. no. 139: "nos provide attendentes, quod ad hoc maxime legationis officium tibi commisimus generale, ut statuere valeas, quae negotio pacis et fidei videris expedire. . . ."

67. Pressutti, nos. 4262-4263, ed. *Rec. hist. Gaules*, XIX, 732-734.

68. This is doubtful because our source is an anecdote reported by William of Puylaurens that tells how the counts amused themselves at the expense of Raymond's guards, who were outside the castle, by pretending that Amaury had made him a prisoner. Raymond was allegedly prepared to put away his wife and marry Amaury's sister. *Chronica magistri Guillelmi de Podio Laurentii* 32, ed. and trans. J. Duvernoy (Paris, 1976), p. 115. Neininger, *Konrad*, p. 199.

69. Pressutti, no. 4395, ed. *Rec. hist. Gaules*, XIX, 732; Neininger, *Konrad*, reg. no. 154, and p. 199.

70. In June 1224, Raymond pledged to turn the castle over to the archbishop of Narbonne "ut compositio inter nos & ecclesiam Magalonensem tractata in concilio Sancti Flori perfi-

decided on his own initiative to revive the crusade. After the collapse of negotiations, Conrad headed north and a day or so later reached St-Pourçain, where
on 2 June he issued a summons to the prelates of northern France for a council to be held at Sens a month later, on 6 July (Doc. 49). From this letter it is
evident that Conrad had abandoned the current papal policy of reconciliation,
for the summons was loaded with alarmist propaganda designed to whip up new
fervor for a crusade. The Cathari are said to be thriving again in Occitania. Still
worse, they are now supposed to be part of an international conspiracy, for according to Conrad there was a Catharist pope in the Balkans, whose agent,
Bartholomew of Carcassonne, had been recognized by the "bishop of the
heretics" in Occitania, where the pseudopope's legate was now consecrating
bishops and establishing churches.[71] Consequently the French bishops are to
come to Sens "prepared to give counsel concerning the aforesaid business and
. . . to take steps to deal with the Albigensian business."[72]

What happened next is obscure. The council may have been held at Sens as
planned, or it may have been moved to Paris, perhaps for the convenience of
Philip Augustus, who was unable to attend because he was a sick and dying
man.[73] Wherever it met, Conrad's council was evidently persuaded by the
legate's supposed facts, which the northern bishops were in no position to re-
fute; they certainly recommended that the crusade be continued (Doc. 9.2).
Armed with this recommendation from the French church, Conrad and the
bishop of Toulouse seem to have approached Philip on his deathbed and found
him opposed to royal intervention.[74] But Conrad would soon have another

ciatur ad cognitionem domini pape" (Devic-Vaissète, VIII, 806). This positive result was
glossed over by William of Puylaurens, who wrote long after the event: "Et eiusdem legati
tempore, sumptis treugis sub spe pacis, fuere duo colloquia provisa ad tractandum, unum apud
Sanctum Florum, castrum Avernie, et aliud Senonis Burgundie metropolim civitatem. Tamen
pacis effectus in neutro est sequtus" (*Chronica* 33, ed. Duvernoy, p. 114).

71. Doc. 49, below. These stories of a Catharist pope seem to be based on a misunderstanding of the word "papa," which in the Greek East simply signified a parish priest. Actually there was no one leader of the Cathari but rather many. See S. Runciman, *The Medieval
Manichee* (Cambridge, Eng., 1947), p. 162. Garbled gossip from the Roman curia may well
have been Conrad's source of misinformation on Cathari in the Balkans, where Honorius
had sent a legate to fight the heresy: Pressutti, nos. 3594 and 3601 (3 and 5 Dec. 1221).

72. Doc. 49.4.

73. After reviewing the sources, Cartellieri decided that the place was uncertain (*Philipp*,
IV, 563).

74. William of Puylaurens learned this from an eyewitness, Fulk, bishop of Toulouse, who
accompanied Conrad to the Council of Sens/Paris: "'Scio, [rex] inquiebat, quod post mortem
meam insistent clerici quod filius meus Ludovicus assumat negocium Albigense . . .'": *Chronica* 32 (ed. Duvernoy, p. 116). The only southerners at Philip's funeral (15 July) were Fulk and
the bishop of Clermont-Ferrand: Neininger, *Konrad*, reg. no. 157.

opportunity, for on 14 July Philip died at Mantes, a day's journey west of Paris.[75]

Conrad persisted in his plan. Shortly after the legate had buried the old king,[76] he approached the new one, Louis VIII, and asked him to take counsel on the Albigensian issue, which is to say he wanted Louis to consider undertaking the royal crusade that his father had avoided. Louis replied that he himself would do nothing while he was uncertain of the state of his kingdom, but, since the French episcopate seemed eager to act, he gave them permission to do as they saw fit (Doc. 9.2). Somewhat later the legate approached Louis again, this time to urge that the king send reinforcements to Amaury, lest the count lose all his strongholds in Occitania. Louis obligingly sent ten thousand marks from the funds that his father's will had earmarked for defense or for a crusade.[77]

The legate realized that, for the moment, nothing more could be done at the French court, so he wrote Honorius a letter that the pope complained was impossibly vague. The legate claimed that "young Raymond" had refused to conclude the peace on the terms that the count himself had once proposed. Moreover, Conrad hinted that the heretics were worse than ever; therefore he had worked out a new plan with the advice of the prelates of his legation, and now requested permission to return to Rome and lay the proposal before the pope himself.[78] Evidently Conrad hoped to persuade the pope by the same arguments that he had already used in France.[79] On 10 September 1223, Honorius testily acknowledged his legate's request to be recalled, telling him to do what he thought best.[80]

Conrad came and laid his case before the pope and the cardinals, whom he persuaded to revert to the former plan of securing a massive royal intervention by offering the Montfort lands to the king, together with a substantial subsidy.

75. Cartellieri, *Philipp*, IV, 563-564.

76. Neininger, *Konrad*, reg. no. 157.

77. Doc. 9.3. On the will, see Cartellieri, *Phillip*, IV, 558-560, 566-570.

78. Pressutti, vol. I, p. lx, no. 64, ed. *Rec. hist. Gaules*, XIX, 736; Neininger, *Konrad*, reg. no. 167, and on Conrad's motives, pp. 202-204.

79. About this time, Conrad wrote an alarmist letter to the general chapter of his fellow Cistercians, telling how a Toulousan noble cut the arms off the crucifix on the high altar of the cathedral: Caesarius of Heisterbach, *Dialogus miraculorum*, book 5, chap. 22; *The Dialogue of Miracles*, trans. H. von E. Scott and C. C. Swinton Bland (New York, 1929), I, 346. I assign the letter to the 1223 chapter because its alarmist tactics resemble those of Doc. 49. The Cistercian chapter regularly met in mid-September: *Statuta capitulorum generalium ordinis Cisterciensis ab anno 1116 ad annum 1786*, ed. J. M. Canivez, II (Louvain, 1934), 49 (an. 1226, no. 6). J. Berlioz, *"Tuez-les tous, Deus reconnaîtra les siens"*: *Le Massacre de Béziers (22 juillet 1209) et la croisade contre les Albigeois vus par Césaire de Heisterbach* (Portet-sur-Garonne, 1994).

80. Pressutti, no. 4491, ed. *Rec. hist. Gaules*, XIX, 737; cf. Neininger, *Konrad*, reg. no. 167 and p. 202.

The decision was soon implemented by a series of letters that issued from the papal chancery during the last three weeks of December 1223. First the pope arranged to send Amaury ten thousand pounds so the count would not have to leave Occitania altogether.[81] Honorius, like Louis before him, was obviously convinced by the legate's argument that the future crusaders would need a military base. Next, Honorius wrote to Louis VIII on 13 and 14 December, first thanking him for the financial aid he had sent to Amaury and then urging him to take the Cross once more against the Albigensians.[82] The new king was offered the same incentives that Honorius had proposed to Philip in May 1222: Louis would receive both a clear title to the Montfort lands in the South and a substantial subsidy from the Church. The promise of a subsidy was reiterated by the three prelates who presented the pope's letters to the king, namely the archbishop of Bourges and the bishops of Langres and Senlis.[83] At about the same time, Honorius prodded his agents in France to complete the collection of the triennial twentieth so the war could continue.[84] Finally, Honorius informed Amaury of all these developments and urged him not to give up.[85]

Although the papacy was now clearly committed to war against Raymond if France would cooperate, still Honorius continued to press the count to comply with the Church's conditions for his reconciliation. For example, on 23 December the pope made sure that Raymond would not be reconciled until he had restored the castle of Melgueil to the bishop of Maguelonne, although agreement had already been reached on this issue.[86]

As it happens, the state of affairs in Occitania during the closing months of 1223 is known in unusual detail from a statement that the archbishop of Narbonne, together with the bishops of Nîmes, Uzès, Béziers, and Agde, sent to the king on 23 January 1224.[87] Amaury had unwisely used the money he received from Philip's legacy to hire a field army, which relieved the siege of Carcassonne; but, since Raymond refused to risk an open battle, little more could be done with the mercenaries. When the viscount of Narbonne went over to

81. Pressutti, no. 4606, ed. *Rec. hist. Gaules*, XIX, 739.

82. Pressutti, nos. 4615 and 4618, ed. *Rec. hist. Gaules*, XIX, 740-742; Neininger, *Konrad*, reg. no. 175.

83. Doc. 9.4. The embassy was commissioned in Pressutti, no. 4612, ed. *Rec. hist. Gaules*, XIX, 741.

84. Pressutti, nos. 4601, 4607, 4613, 4620, 4621.

85. Pressutti, no. 4614, ed. *Rec. hist. Gaules*, XIX, 740; Molinier, "Catalogue . . . Montfort," no. 202.

86. Pressutti, no. 4636 (cf. nos. 4630-4632, 4635), ed. *Rec. hist. Gaules*, XIX, 743; Roquebert, *Epopée cathare*, III, 243. For the compromise of St-Flour, see n. 70, above.

87. Devic-Vaissète, VIII, 782-786; Molinier, "Catalogue . . . Montfort," no. 203; Neininger, *Konrad*, p. 205.

Raymond, the archbishop was forced to leave the city because neither he nor Amaury could raise enough money to maintain a garrison there. They had hoped to be able to hold Carcassonne until Easter, but when the money ran out, the French mercenaries returned home, leaving the fortress virtually undefended. Amaury was forced to make a truce with Raymond on 14 January, after which he left for Paris and the archbishop for Montpellier. The archbishop's letter was meant to justify Amaury's actions to the king, but Louis' view of it was that "with the aid of said money [from Philip's legacy], said Amaury led back the knights and soldiers who were in said forts, and he surrendered the castles and fortifications that he held in that area" (Doc. 9.3).

What the archbishop did not explain was that the truce of 14 January 1224 was meant to hasten Raymond's reconciliation. According to the treaty between the rival counts, Raymond granted all his enemies a general truce for almost six months, until Pentecost (2 June), but allowed only two months' truce to Narbonne, Agde, and other lands held by Amaury, with the exception of Carcassonne and other castles then under siege, to which no truce was conceded. All this was granted on the understanding that Amaury was going "to consult his friends from France about what we [Raymond] have promised in order to have peace with the holy Roman church and Count Amaury, and to do what they counsel him to do; and in good faith he should try to obtain peace for us with the Church and himself." Finally, Raymond promised that if he and his supporters were fully reconciled with the Church by Pentecost, he would then give Amaury ten thousand marks of silver.[88] Shortly after the treaty was signed, Amaury set out for Paris, presumably to fulfill his part of the bargain, while Raymond sent a lawyer to Rome to secure papal recognition of the settlement,[89] and his efforts at the curia were supported by agents of the king of England.[90]

When Amaury arrived in Paris, he discovered that the situation had changed. Honorius' embassy had found the king agreeable to undertaking a crusade in the South under certain conditions, and Louis was sending a proposal to Rome for the pope's approval. Since Amaury found that his friends in France were

88. *Rec. hist. Gaules*, XIX, 215 n. and 732 n.; Belperron, *Croisade*, p. 377-378.

89. *Diplomatic Documents Preserved in the Public Record Office*, vol. I: *1101–1272*, ed. P. Chaplais (London, 1964), no. 136 = C. V. Langlois, "Notices et documents relatifs à l'histoire du XIIIᵉ et du XIVᵉ siècle," *Revue historique*, LXXXVII (1905), 55–79, at pp. 56–59: "Sciatis quod obtimos rumores audiveramus in curia quod dominus comes Tolosanus expulit jam omnes Gallicos de terra sua et vir providus et fidelis vester magister W[illelmus] de Avinion' est in curia pro absolutione ipsius comitis dante Domino impetranda" (dated early January by both editors).

90. Chaplais, *Diplomatic Documents*, no. 137: Henry III wrote the pope on Raymond's behalf and, probably in late January 1224, sent a copy to his agents in Rome with instructions to promote the count's reconciliation "with diligence."

counseling war, he did not scruple to join them, and in February he renewed his offer to cede the Montfort lands in Occitania to the king and his heirs in perpetuity. If the pope did not accept the king's conditions, however, the count reserved the right to withdraw his offer.[91]

The king's conditions were carefully drawn up with the counsel of his barons and bishops. In general, Louis insisted that he and legates of his choice have complete control over the operation, with all of the privileges and safeguards that the papacy could arrange, not to mention an immense subsidy. The terms may be summarized from Doc. 7 as follows: (1) The king and all who go with him shall enjoy all the privileges of crusader status. (2) The archbishops of Bourges, Reims, and Sens (who in 1221 had been made the pope's legates to promote the crusade in France) shall have powers of excommunication and interdict against anyone who persists in troubling the crusaders or their lands. (3) These legates shall have the same powers against those who refuse to pay what they pledge for the expedition. (4) The legates shall also have the same powers against royal vassals who refuse either to accompany the king or to pay him a subsidy instead. (5) The pope must arrange a ten-year truce with England. (6) Moreover, he must declare by his letters patent (a) that both Raymond VI and VII, together with the viscounts of Béziers and Carcassonne, have been lawfully deprived of every right to their French fiefs; (b) that those who challenge this decision are liable to excommunication by the archbishop-legates; and (c) that these fiefs are now Louis' to do with as he wishes. (7) The archbishop of Bourges is to have Conrad's legation, with full powers to reconcile all who make due satisfaction to the Church and to have the crusade preached throughout France. The papacy is to waive its right to hear appeals concerning any of the actions mentioned in the first seven articles. (8) Furthermore, the Church has to pay the king a subsidy of sixty thousand pounds *parisis* per annum for ten years for use in Occitania. (9) Also, the pope must secure the emperor's declaration that his subjects east of the Rhone will not hinder the king and his business in Occitania, and that the king can take punitive action against them if they do. (10) If the king goes in person under these conditions and carries out his obligations in good faith, the Roman curia from now on will leave him and his heirs free to delay the journey, to remain in Occitania, and to return back home again, all just as they please. (11) The petition closes with an ultimatum: if these articles, which are being transmitted to the Roman curia by the archbishop of Bourges and the

---

91. Teulet, no. 1631; Devic-Vaissète, VIII, 789; Molinier, "Catalogue . . . Montfort," no. 208; Roquebert, *Epopée cathare*, III, 254-255. By March or April, Henry III was trying to get "transcripta literarum domini pape, quas nuper impetravit per talem rex Francorum" and had heard that Louis might be making an expedition "ad partes Albigensium": Chaplais, *Diplomatic Documents*, no. 139.

bishops of Langres and Chartres, do not achieve their purpose, then the king shall henceforward not be held to go to Occitania, unless he wishes to.

Certainly the king was driving a hard bargain, but he did not think his terms were impossible. On the contrary, in February when he heard of the archbishop's exile from Narbonne, Louis wrote to the citizens, ordering them to hold the city for him, as he planned to march south in May.[92]

Honorius changes his mind, April 1224

Honorius' initial reaction to the petition was apparently favorable, for on 29 March he sent the king a privilege that enabled him to hear Mass in interdicted places, which would be appropriate if the expedition took place.[93] This letter most likely was brought back to the French court by two of the ambassadors, the bishops of Langres and Chartres, who left Rome about 2 April.[94] The archbishop of Bourges remained in Rome on business of his own, but the king's mission was accomplished, or seemed to be, for, after much deliberation with the cardinals, the pope had decided to accept the king's conditions. Conrad, who had come to Rome for the deliberations,[95] already had orders to convey Honorius' acceptance to the king and was receiving his final instructions on how to implement the decision—when the pope changed his mind.[96]

"A messenger arrived unexpectedly from the lord emperor, who promised and proposed so many things and so much to help the Holy Land that the lord pope and the Roman curia felt it was only proper to concentrate their efforts on the Holy Land and, for the moment, to postpone the Albigeois business" (Doc. 9.5; cf. Doc. 8.1). Frederick II had managed to escape service in the Fifth Crusade, for which he had volunteered, and ever since then Honorius had been urging him to fulfill that vow by leading the Sixth Crusade.[97] On 5 March 1224, the emperor had written a long letter to the pope, in which Frederick placed

---

92. Devic-Vaissète, VIII, 790.

93. Pressutti, no. 4900; Barbiche, no. 256; ed. Teulet, no. 1638. A typographical error misdates the letter "Mai." (for "Mart.") in Potthast, no. 7202, as is evident from its correct place in his series.

94. Doc. 8.1, dated 4 April, says they had already left; and a papal letter was addressed to the bishop of Chartres as late as 2 April (Pressutti, no. 4913), though it is possible that he left before receiving it.

95. His presence in mid-December is clearly attested in Pressutti, no. 4615, ed. *Rec. hist. Gaules*, XIX, 740–741. By 30 April 1224, Conrad was at Clairvaux on his way north to the royal court: Neininger, *Konrad*, reg. no. 191.

96. Doc. 8.1 and Doc. 9.5.

97. T. C. Van Cleve, "The Crusade of Frederick II," in *A History of the Crusades*, ed. K. M. Setton, II, 2nd ed. (Madison, 1969), 429–462, at pp. 430–439; Mann, *Lives*, XIII, 25–33, 57–77.

the blame for his delay on, among other things, the lack of response to the
preaching of the Sixth Crusade in Germany, England, and France. The emperor
maintained that the knights of England and France would not be free to take
the Cross for the Holy Land until a truce could be arranged between those kingdoms, and consequently he asked the pope to send a special legate to negotiate
such a truce.[98] The problem was a real one, for Frederick's complaint was based
on the experience of John de Brienne, the king of Jerusalem, who had been in
France the previous summer, and in England in the fall, preaching the crusade
without success.[99] Honorius clearly took the request seriously and responded
immediately, both in letters to Frederick[100] and to Louis. Conrad was sent back
to France with the king's letter and supplementary oral explanations, both of
which urged Louis to make a peace or truce with England for the sake of the
Holy Land, just as Frederick had requested.[101] Consequently, most modern writers have not doubted that Honorius' explanation of his sudden change of mind
was indeed the correct one. With good reason they discount the base motives
to which the contemporary chronicler, Philip Mousket, attributed the change:
he claimed that the Albigensians and the English bribed the curia to refuse the
king's petitions.[102] Nonetheless, Honorius may well have found on second
thought that a policy of postponement offered definite advantages. Belperron
and Strayer suggest that the pope hesitated to let Occitania become a royal domain because the king of France would be less easy to control than a mere
count.[103] No doubt this was taken into consideration at the curia, but I do not
think that it constituted a serious objection to the plan, since the king of France
could be trusted to maintain order and repress heresy in Languedoc just as he
did in his other domains. Roquebert argues, at much greater length, that the
Sixth Crusade was a diplomatic pretext, which enabled Honorius to avoid a royal
crusade under terms unacceptable to the papacy.[104] This view seems unlikely

98. *Historia diplomatica Friderici Secundi*, ed. J. L. A. Huillard-Bréholles, 6 vols. (Paris,
1852-1861), II, 412.

99. L. Bréhier, "Brienne (Jean de)," in *DHGE*, X, 704.

100. Pressutti, nos. 4903-4905.

101. Pressutti, no. 4919, ed. Neininger, *Konrad*, doc. 29; cf. idem, reg. no. 186.

102. Petit-Dutaillis, *Louis*, pp. 284-285, quoting Philip Mousket, *Chronique rimée*, vv.
24339-24344; Belperron, *Croisade*, p. 383. On the poet as a source, see Doc. 4.pr., below.

103. Belperron, *Croisade*, p. 383; Strayer, *Albigensian Crusades*, p. 125.

104. Roquebert, *Epopée cathare*, III, 263-276. Instead Neininger is inclined to accept Honorius' explanation for his about-face: *Konrad*, pp. 207-210. J. L. Pène proposes that the papacy feared losing the temporal possessions the Church had acquired as a result of the First
Albigensian Crusade (*La Conquête du Languedoc* [Nice, 1957], pp. 247-248); but they would
not have been—and in fact were not—affected by the transfer of Amaury's rights to the
French crown.

because, as it turned out in 1226, all of the conditions of 1224 were met—or, in the case of the subsidy, even exceeded—except for French control of the crusade (cf. Docs. 7 and 24-26). Instead, I would suggest that Honorius personally preferred to resolve the Occitanian problem by peaceful negotiation if possible, whereas the legate Conrad thought that a royal crusade was the only solution. The previous year Conrad had sabotaged the peace talks, while blaming the breakdown on Raymond, but now an embassy had recently given Honorius the count's solemn word that he was a truly devoted son of the Church who sincerely hoped for reconciliation.[105] Although the pope had let himself be persuaded by Conrad, he was by no means convinced; therefore, he welcomed the opportunity, provided by Frederick's appeal, to try once again to work out a peaceful solution. Honorius himself gave the best account of his personal priorities in a letter that he sent to the archbishop of Narbonne on the same day that he wrote to the king: "We may spare the material expenditures and personal perils that . . . are the expected cost of this venture, and which we would rather devote to helping the Holy Land."[106]

From whatever motives, Honorius wrote on 4 April 1224 to Louis VIII, explaining why at the last minute the king's petitions were not granted and urging him instead to promote the reconciliation of Raymond with the Church. He assured Louis that Raymond

> fears the power of your greatness so much that, if he knew you sincerely meant to use all your forces against him, he would not dare to wait very long for them but, in accordance with your wishes, would obey the orders of the Church, as he is offering to do out of hopefully true devotion. Therefore try your best to induce him by royal warnings and threats truly to make peace with God and his Church. Our conditions are: that the land be purged of heretics; that he make suitable reparation to churches and churchmen for the damages and injuries that have been inflicted on them up to now; that ecclesiastical liberty be provided for in the future; and that in the peace treaty everything possible be done to preserve the honor of . . . Amaury . . . [Doc. 8.2].

Early in May the legate Conrad arrived at the royal court with this letter that called on the king to change all his plans. Apparently the barons and prelates of France were already at the court, probably in readiness for the expedition, since Louis had planned to leave in May.[107] The king lost no time in consulting with

---

105. Pressutti, no. 4922, ed. *Rec. hist. Gaules*, XIX, 748; cf. Kay, "Quelques ébauches," item no. 1 on the Albigensian Roll.

106. Pressutti, no. 4922, ed. Devic-Vaissète, VIII, 777 (no. 228, v); Kay, "Quelques ébauches," no. 1 on the Albigensian Roll; Neininger, *Konrad*, pp. 207-208.

107. See above, n. 92.

them. On 5 May 1224 he delivered his formal response to the legate, the tone
of which is remarkably bitter and blunt. After reviewing the whole history of
Franco-papal negotiations over the Albigensian problem, with special emphasis
on Conrad's legation, the king concluded that, since the pope for the present
had not seen fit to grant the king's reasonable petitions, "we are freed from the
burden of this business, and we have declared this publicly in the presence of
all the prelates and barons of France" (Doc. 9.7). As for the pope's suggestion
that the king should use threats and warnings to terrify Raymond into submission, Louis told the legate that it was not the king's business to investigate the
religious beliefs of his subjects or to negotiate settlements in which faith is an
issue. "Since examination of the faith is the business of the Roman church, we
quite properly wish it to reach a settlement with the aforesaid Raymond just as
it sees fit, provided that our rights and our fiefs are in no way diminished, and
that no new or unusual burden is imposed on them" (Doc. 9.8). Frustrated and
indignant, the king had washed his hands of the whole affair. Apparently Conrad immediately began the process of Raymond's reconciliation by announcing that the pope had determined that the count's faith was indeed Catholic.[108]

Raymond is almost reconciled with the Church, 1224

When Honorius decided to attempt Raymond's reconciliation, the truce established for this purpose by the counts had less than two months to run until
its expiration on 2 June. Working against this deadline, the pope selected the
archbishop of Narbonne as his agent in Occitania and sent him instructions on
4 April, the same day that he wrote to the king. Conrad, the pope wrote, had
been sent to the French court with a list of the four conditions that Raymond
must satisfy: eliminate heresy, make restitution to the Church, guarantee ecclesiastical liberty, and make some provision for Amaury's honor. Honorius explained that he had decided to cancel the crusade because a recent embassy from
Raymond had assured him that the count was eager to cooperate and because
the resources required by the Albigensian Crusade could be put to better use
in the Holy Land. Therefore he ordered the archbishop of Narbonne to arrange
a conference with Raymond, to which the archbishop might, if he wished, invite the other bishops of Occitania. If Raymond was prepared to meet the four
conditions, the archbishop should hasten in person to Conrad and the king with
the news; in any event, he should keep the curia informed of the progress of the

108. William of Nangis (fl. 1300), *Chronique*, ed. H. Géraud (Paris, 1843), I, 171; Neininger,
Konrad, pp. 211 and 401 n.

negotiations.[109] The archbishops and bishops of Occitania were instructed on the same day to lend Narbonne whatever aid he required in these negotiations.[110]

The city of Montpellier was a papal protectorate,[111] and consequently the archbishop of Narbonne had taken refuge there when Amaury had gone north in January 1224.[112] Hence it was the most safe and convenient place for the elderly archbishop to confer with Raymond. Two talks, or *colloquia*, were held there during the summer of 1224.[113] The first one took place just as the truce was expiring at Pentecost (2 June 1224). What happened can be gathered from the many promises that Raymond and his associates made there in a lengthy document.[114] Raymond promised to satisfy all four conditions laid down by the pope, and to these were added a long list of restitutions to be made to prelates and churches in Occitania. Time was needed to work out the details, and therefore a second conference was scheduled for 22 August, the octave of the Assumption. Presumably the archbishop of Narbonne promptly went north to report the results to Conrad, as he had been instructed to do.

The archbishop of Narbonne also duly reported the proceedings at Montpellier to the pope and transmitted to him a sealed copy of the promises Raymond and his associates had made there; he explained that a second conference would take place on 22 August, after which Raymond would send an embassy to the curia with full power to conclude an agreement in his name. Honorius wrote back immediately, probably in early July, instructing the archbishop to do what he could to have Raymond implement his promises by the time of the August conference at Montpellier,[115] and (in a separate letter) he added that

109. Pressutti, no. 4922, ed. *Rec. hist. Gaules*, XIX, 748–749. Kay, "Quelques ébauches," no. 1 on the Albigensian Roll.

110. Pressutti, no. 4923, ed. Horoy, IV, 593 (no. 182). Kay, "Quelques ébauches," no. 2 on the Albigensian Roll, with *editio princeps* as Appendix B.2.

111. Pressutti, no. 4927 (8 April 1224), ed. Teulet, no. 16432 (II, 647).

112. See above, at n. 87.

113. *Colloquium* is the term used for the August session by both Raymond (Mansi, XXII, 1207) and Honorius (below, n. 115). Amaury, however, writing *in absentia* from the north, referred to the second meeting as a "concilium" (Mansi, XXII, 1208). I doubt that either session can be considered a church council because the archbishop's mandate was to *confer* with Raymond, and the other bishops were ordered to assist him if requested (see above, nn. 109 and 110).

114. This is the long, or June, version of Raymond's promises at Montpellier (*Cum sacrosancta ...—... ac valitorum*), ed. Molinier, "Catalogue ... Raimond," in Devic-Vaissète, VIII, 804–807 (no. 239) from the Albigensian Roll, item 3; cf. Kay, "Quelques ébauches," nos. 3 and 3a.

115. Pressutti, no. 5112, ed. Horoy, IV, 690 (no. 2); Kay, "Quelques ébauches," no. 4 on the Albigensian Roll.

Raymond's promises must be fulfilled before he could be reconciled;[116] moreover, the pope ordered the ecclesiastical authorities of Provence to give the archbishop of Narbonne whatever assistance he required to carry out his mandate.[117]

The second colloquium at Montpellier was attended by the archbishops of Narbonne, Arles, and Auch, together with their suffragans. Before it began on 22 August, Amaury wrote them from the north, begging that they conclude neither a peace nor a settlement with Raymond that would prejudice Montfort's rights. To forestall their action, he professed to believe that God would inspire the king to intervene decisively.[118] Since one of Honorius' conditions for Raymond's reconciliation was that Amaury's honor be provided for, this would evidently have to be done without his participation, but that was not impossible, as it would be up to Honorius to decide whether or not the settlement treated Amaury fairly. It was not in itself enough to suspend negotiations.

The immediate question was whether Raymond and the Occitanian bishops could come to terms. Raymond spent the first three days of the conference in satisfying the demands of the Provençal episcopate that had been specified in his promises made in June. What this entailed can be gathered from three surviving acts, issued on successive days, in which Raymond elaborately guaranteed the rights of the bishops of Nîmes, Carpentras, and Agde.[119] When the nobles

116. Pressutti, nos. 4066 and 4645, ed. Horoy, IV, 205-206 (no. 230) and 500 (no. 85)—both sub anno 1222; Kay, "Quelques ébauches," no. 5 on the Albigensian Roll.

117. *Recipimus quamdam scripturam* (Pressutti om.), ed. Kay, "Quelques ébauches," Appendix B.3, from item no. 6 on the Albigensian Roll.

118. Labbe-Cossart, XI.ii, 2335; Mansi, XXII, 1208-1210; *Rec. hist. Gaules*, XVII, 306-307 n.; Molinier, "Catalogue . . . Montfort," no. 209. The letter is undated; without explanation, Molinier dates it "Avant le 16 août 1224," i.e. ten days before the conclusion of the second colloquium.

119. Devic-Vaissète, VIII, 801-804 (no. 238): Nîmes on 24 Aug. (no. ii), Carpentras on 25 Aug. (no. iii), and Agde on 26 Aug. (no. iv); Molinier, "Catalogue . . . Raimond," in Devic-Vaissète, VIII, 1940-2008, nos. 85-87 (misdating the acts for Agde and Carpentras!). In August Raymond not only fulfilled the specific promises he had made in June concerning Agde but gave much more; none of the restitutions to the bishops of Nîmes and Carpentras, however, had been specifed in June. Evidently the June list was not definitive; the additions to Agde's restitutions confirm my redating of the long form of Raymond's promises to June.

In August, Raymond also issued a charter to the bishop of Agen: Mansi, XXII, 1209-1210 (23 Aug. 1224); Teulet, no. 1662 (24 Aug. 1224). In June Raymond simply undertook to restore to the bishop of Agen "ea que consueverat habere & tenere in civitate Agenensi & in episcopatu" (Devic-Vaissète, VIII, 806). The charter he gave in August, however, describes the restitutions in elaborate detail: "omnia ea quae in praesenti pagina inferius continentur: videlicet . . ." (Mansi, XXII, 1209C). This correspondence definitely establishes the date of the long version of the promises as June, not August. The restitutions to the bishop of Carpentras, on the other hand, were not specified in June, so the negotiations were evidently open-ended.

and the bishops had reached a mutually acceptable settlement, on 25 August Raymond repeated his earlier oath, from which the long list of required restitutions were now deleted because they had been satisfied; again, the count of Foix and the viscount of Béziers made the same promises. Raymond affirmed his unconditional adhesion to the faith of the Roman church; he promised to confiscate the property of heretics and to administer corporal punishment to them as well. Moreover, he would preserve the peace and would expel anyone who broke it. Churches and churchmen were to have all their rights fully restored, and their ecclesiastical privileges for the future were guaranteed by the individual charters that had already been granted. Beyond these promises, all of which had been made in June, Raymond offered to pay an indemnity of twenty thousand silver marks, from which sum Amaury could be paid whatever the pope thought right. Because Amaury had absented himself from both *colloquia*, Raymond explained that he was as yet unable to negotiate a settlement with Montfort, as Honorius had required him to do. If Honorius wished to amend any of these provisions, Raymond was willing to negotiate and promised to send his plenipotentiaries to Rome to conclude the peace.[120]

Peace now seemed all but certain. If the Occitanian episcopate was satisfied, would not the peace-loving pope confirm the treaty? Both sides sent off their delegations to Rome: the churchmen were led by the archbishop of Arles, Hugh Beroard, and Raymond's representatives included the viscount of Cavaillon and a professional lawyer.[121] They brought with them the new, short version of the promises Raymond and his associates made at Montpellier on 25 August. When the nuncios reached Rome, however, they found that in the meantime the pope had again lost faith in Raymond's good intentions. On 25 August, the very day that Raymond had made his peace at Montpellier, Honorius had written on behalf of the church of Viviers, in Provence. The town of Largentière with its silver mines was one of its most valuable properties, to which Raymond's father also had a claim; now the young count was asserting this right, and Honorius ordered neighboring canons to excommunicate Raymond unless he desisted.[122]

---

120. *Cum sacrosancta Romana ecclesia* ...—...*ad cognitionem domini papae*, ed. E. Baluze, *Concilia Galliae Narbonensis* (Paris, 1668), pp. 59–62, with the correct date, "viii. Kalend. Septembris" (25 Aug.); reprinted in Mansi, XXII, 1207–1208, with the faulty date "vii. Kal. Septembris" (26 Aug.).

121. Belperron, *Croisade*, p. 386. Raymond's delegation is listed in Doc. 10, below.

122. Pressutti, no. 5335, ed. Devic-Vaissète, VIII, 778–779; Neininger, *Konrad*, reg. no. 154. Vaissète's edition, based on notes taken by Baluze, is dated 25 Aug. 1224, whereas the Vatican register copy dates from 26 Feb. 1225; Baluze also had a copy of the latter. The earlier date at least indicates that the problem had come to the pope's attention in August; perhaps the bull was not delivered until after Honorius had decided against Raymond's reconciliation, or perhaps it was reissued just six months later because the mandate had not been carried out.

Honorius had reason to be upset, because he had stipulated in 1223 that these claims should be settled before Raymond was reconciled,[123] and Raymond's insistence on his right to the town caused the pope to doubt whether the count was negotiating in good faith. As Louis had shrewdly observed, all of Raymond's negotiations with the Church were in effect a test of his Christian faith: his compliance indicated orthodoxy, his independence the opposite. As a result, the curia could not decide whether or not to accept Raymond's proposed settlement of the Occitanian question. The indecision of the next few months is vividly reported on 22 December by two English agents at the curia, who were explaining to their principals back home why their business had been delayed:

> The nuncios of the count of Toulouse, together with bishops, knights, and clerics [from Occitania], have been staying at the curia ever since just after the feast of Saint Michael [29 September]. They have already deliberated with the pope and cardinals for many days over that business and are not done yet, so they are deferring the conclusion of our business until after Christmas. Hopefully the count will receive an agreeable response, although the king and the French are strongly opposing him.[124]

---

123. Pressutti, no. 4395, ed. Rec. hist. Gaules, XIX, 732: "in castro de Fanjau et Argentariae, cum pertinentiis ipsorum . . . " (see text above at n. 69). In 1207, Raymond VI had strengthened his position in the neighborhood of Largentière by building the castle of Fanjau to the east of the silver mine. Simon de Montfort received the castle as part of the Lateran settlement of 1215, but a few months before his death in 1218, the bishop convinced Pope Honorius that legally the castle belonged to the church of Viviers because it had been built on the church's land without its permission. Therefore, from the papacy's point of view, the count of Toulouse, whoever he might be, had no right to Fanjau. On the dispute over Fanjau and Largentière, see P. Babey, Le Pouvoir temporel de l'évêque de Viviers au Moyen Age, 815–1452, Annales de l'Université de Lyon, 3e sér. (droit), fasc. 14 (Paris, 1956), pp. 59–70, and J. Charay et al., Petite histoire de l'église diocésaine de Viviers (Aubenas-en-Vivarais, 1977), pp. 48–49; for the background of the dispute, see André Dupont, "Les Comtes de Toulouse et le Vivarais (Xme–fin XIIme siècle)," Bulletin annuel de l'Ecole antique de Nîmes, n. s., 5 (1970), 75–94, esp. pp. 87–89.

124. The agents were Geoffrey Craucumb and Stephen Lucy, representing the bishops of Bath, Lincoln, Salisbury, and Chichester. Chaplais, Diplomatic Documents, no. 153 = Shirley, Royal Letters, no. 209. A similar letter, with the same incipit but addressed to Henry III, is printed by Rymer, Foedera, I (1727), 273-274 = I.i (1739), 93; reprinted in Rec. hist. Gaules, XIX, 760-761 n. I have translated the one from Chaplais: "Verumptamen quia nuncii comitis Tholosani, episcopi, milites et clerici, qui post festum sancti Michaelis in curia uniformiter steterant, et papa cum fratribus jam per multos dies super facto illo licet nondum plene deliberaverant, distulerunt usque post natale de negociis nostris providere. Et sperabatur quod dictus comes competens responsum esset accepturus, licet rex et Gallici dicti sibi fortiter resisterent."

Honorius refuses to reconcile Raymond, January 1225

The decision that Honorius had to make was no easy one. When the English agents wrote their report in late December, the pope had already been lingering almost three months over the problem, and it is probable that he deliberated still another month. Even then Raymond's anxious ambassadors received an inconclusive answer. Although the pope did not accept the arrangements that Raymond had made with the local episcopate at Montpellier, still he did not repudiate them. Instead, on 31 January 1225 he wrote to Raymond (Doc. 10) that he had received his ambassadors, had heard them diligently, and had finally told them that he was sending the cardinal-deacon of Sant' Angelo, Romanus Bonaventura, as his new legate in France and Provence, with a mandate to reform whatever needed it. "When the legate arrives," Raymond was told, "attend to him so reverently and obediently, acquiesce to his wholesome admonitions and commands so humbly and effectually, that you may be worthy to deserve the favor of God and the apostolic see." Evidently Raymond was still out of favor, but what more Rome might want from him remained to be seen.

Within the month, the curia was more specific. On 26 February, Honorius issued (or reissued) his order of the previous August, by which Raymond was to be excommunicated unless he let the church of Viviers have the property it claimed from him. If the count does not comply, then "in vain is he deceiving himself that he can be reconciled, and in vain shall he carry on about the good faith with which he seeks after reconciliation."[125] Raymond was left to wonder whether this was the real problem or only a diversion. He might well recall with foreboding that the last time Honorius had raised such an objection, it was to keep Raymond busy while a crusade was being mounted against him.[126]

Now a royal crusade was in fact the pope's goal once again. After four months of hesitation, Honorius had decided to refuse the terms agreed on at Montpellier and instead to revive the project that had failed twice before. The Council of Bourges was one result of this decision, and consequently the reasons for this reversal are the crux of this survey chapter. Honorius' motives will always remain obscure, but much can be clarified by a critical review of the suggestions that other historians have made.

Because Honorius had postponed the king's crusade in favor of the Sixth Crusade, Petit–Dutaillis asserted with some plausibility that Frederick II:

was now disposed [in January 1225] to make the crusade in the Orient his own affair. These ideas were going to receive their consecration in the treaty of San

125. Pressutti, no. 5335, ed. *Rec. hist. Gaules*, XIX, 756 (see n. 123, above).
126. See text at n. 86, above.

Germano, concluded 25 July 1225. Instead of concerning all Christendom, as Honorius had formerly wished, the deliverance of the Holy Land would concern no more than Frederick II alone, vassal of the pope for Sicily. He no longer had any reason to reserve the French king's sword for combat overseas.[127]

It is true that, after the emperor had deferred his departure many times, Honorius demanded more concrete assurances, which he obtained in the treaty of San Germano.[128] As king of Sicily, Frederick pledged himself to go to the Holy Land in two years and in the meantime to provide stipulated quotas of knights and ships, but nothing in the treaty excluded the participation of crusaders from outside the Empire, much less from outside the Sicilian Regno.[129] Demonstrably, Honorius himself took no such exclusive view of the Sixth Crusade. When the departure date drew near in January 1227, the pope urged all the archbishops in Germany and northern Italy, as well as many bishops and abbots, to preach the crusade because the emperor would be sailing in August. Hence we may wholly discount Petit-Dutaillis's claim that from 1225 on the curia considered this to be a crusade of Frederick only as "vassal of the pope for Sicily." Instead, we may adopt the more moderate formulation proposed by James Powell, that in 1225 Honorius was planning a crusade "with Frederick as the central figure."[130] This wider view of the crusade is evident because Honorius sent the same letter to addressees outside of Frederick's domains: all of Hungary was canvassed, as well as a bishop in England and, most significantly, an abbot in Flanders, which of course was part of the kingdom of France.[131] Since the full list of addressees was only published from the Vatican register the year after Petit-Dutaillis's monograph appeared, his misinterpretation is excusable but no longer tenable. To be sure, in 1225 Honorius made little effort to attract the English and French to the crusade, but this was by necessity, not by policy. The two kingdoms were then at war and had been since Easter 1224; consequently, a crusade in the East would appeal to the French and English nobles even less than when John de Brienne had preached to them in 1223. Honorius' position in January

127. Petit-Dutaillis, *Louis*, p. 287. Strayer, *Albigensian Crusades*, p. 127, allows that this is "possible."

128. Pressutti, no. 5566; Huillard-Bréholles, *Historia diplomatica*, III, 42, and cf. II, 500; Van Cleve, "Crusade of Frederick," pp. 440-441; Mann, *Lives*, XIII, 77. Belperron, *Croisade*, p. 387, thought that the treaty had already been concluded before February 1225!

129. Huillard-Bréholles, *Historia diplomatica*, II, 501-503.

130. Powell, "Honorius III," p. 533.

131. Pressutti, nos. 6155-6157 and esp. 6160 (11 Jan. 1227). The Englishman was Peter des Roches, bishop of Winchester; the Fleming was the abbot of St-Pierre d'Audembourg, near Ostend. On the former, see N. Vincent, *Peter des Roches* (Cambridge, Eng., 1996), p. 233.

1225 was wholly consistent with his conviction, so dramatically announced in April 1224, that it was useless to preach the crusade in France and England when those countries were at war with one another.[132]

What diverted the French from the Sixth Crusade were greater opportunities and obligations at home. At the moment that Honorius decided against Raymond in January 1225, he had no idea when Frederick would finally leave or when the Anglo-French war would end. If both happened simultaneously, Frenchmen might indeed join the expedition to the Holy Land; but the chances were slender, especially in the near future, so the pope may well have thought that in the meantime the French could best serve the Church by crusading at home. In short, as of January 1225, the Sixth Crusade was no longer a relevant factor in the Occitanian problem, not for the reason that Petit-Dutaillis supposed, but simply because the crusade was dormant and the French at war.

This, however, was hardly reason enough to make the pope hesitate on the brink of peace. If we are to believe Honorius himself, the factors that weighed most heavily with him were the heresy and insubordination that infested Occitania. These were the themes that he stressed when he explained his decision to the French clergy on 15 February 1225 (Doc. 12.2). Moreover, it is noteworthy that heresy was not stressed as much as insubordination. Honorius did not claim, as Conrad had done in 1223, that the Albigensian heresy was flourishing worse than ever; instead, he complained that the Provençals had hardened their hearts, that they refused to receive discipline, and that they gloried in their military successes against the crusaders. It is impossible to know what, if anything, lay behind these vague complaints, but at the least they express a general mistrust of the good faith of Raymond and his supporters. According to Strayer, Honorius received this impression from "the bishops and abbots of Occitania [who] were almost unanimously opposed to Raymond VII. They had not trusted the father and they would not trust the son."[133] He thinks it "most likely" that the Occitanian episcopate convinced Honorius to change his mind at the last minute; Belperron had reached much the same conclusion,[134] and since the twentieth century's two leading scholars of the subject concur, theirs is certainly the prevailing opinion at present.

Nonetheless this explanation seems highly unlikely because, as we have seen, the Occitanian episcopate had made its peace with Raymond at Montpellier the preceding August. The bishops of Languedoc not only had declared that they were satisfied that Raymond was a good Christian but also had settled their differences with him. Moreover, Raymond had sworn that he would cooperate in

132. See n. 101, above.
133. Strayer, *Albigensian Crusades*, p. 127.
134. Belperron, *Croisade*, p. 387.

the repression of heresy and he had already made restitution to most churches and churchmen. This was the agreement that Honorius refused to confirm. It seems unlikely in the extreme that the bishops who made the agreement would have been its principal detractors, especially since nothing is known to have occurred that might have caused them to alter their opinion after the agreement was made. Raymond's dispute with his cousin, the bishop of Viviers, is the only possible exception, but this was evidently a side issue, because it was not raised by Honorius until after the settlement had been made at Montpellier, and then it did not prevent him from deliberating for five months, so the issue would not seem to have been a major point of difference.

The crusade becomes an instrument of French policy

If the temporal and spiritual lords of Languedoc had worked out a settlement in accordance with the guidelines laid down by the pope, who then had any interest in prolonging the dispute? Manifestly, only the king of France. Such was the conclusion of Dom Vaissète in the eighteenth century, and to me it still seems to provide the most satisfactory explanation. In favor of this view, above all there is the testimony of the English agents at Rome, whose diplomatic dispatches constitute the considered opinion of qualified observers. They not only state that the king of France and his agents opposed the reconciliation of Raymond, but they also identify one of the agents as Amaury's uncle, Guy de Montfort, an ardent crusader who had represented his brother Simon at the Fourth Lateran Council.[135] Obviously Louis was using all the influence he could muster in December 1224 to prevent Raymond from making his peace with the Church.

The problem, then, is why Louis had suddenly become interested in reviving the project of a royal crusade, which only the previous May he had never wanted to hear of again. Events of the intervening summer amply account for his change of heart. He had planned to campaign in Languedoc as a crusader, but when these plans were upset by Honorius in May 1224, Louis swiftly redirected his war effort against the English and their allies in Poitou. Ever since

135. Petit-Dutaillis claimed that "aucun texte précis ne permet de supposer que ces agents poursuivissent un autre but que d'intriguer contre les Anglais . . ." (*Louis*, p. 287). Belperron thought this judgment "peut-être un peu vite" and allowed, as does Strayer, that Guy was using his influence to rekindle the crusade (*Croisade*, p. 387; *Albigensian Crusades*, p. 127). There is in fact precise textual evidence that Guy acted as Louis' agent against Raymond, and moreover it occurs in the very letter that Petit-Dutaillis cited to document his sentence quoted above! The English agents report how they had encountered the French ambassadors at Viterbo, among whom they name Guy de Montfort; later in the same letter (n. 124, above), they state that Raymond's reconciliation is being opposed by Louis and "Gallici *dicti*," one of whom was obviously Guy.

John's condemnation by Philip Augustus in 1202, the French crown had been claiming Gascony by forfeiture and attempting to conquer it from the English. A four years' truce between the claimants had expired at Easter 1224, so Louis felt free to renew the war. His immediate objective, however, was the pacification of Poitou, where lords and towns took advantage of their position between Gascony and the French royal domain to shift their allegiance as often as seem expedient. The king's seneschal complained that he had no more authority over the barons of Poitou than a groom (*unum garciolum*),[136] and Louis was determined to bring the county under effective royal control as the first step in the reconquest of Aquitaine.

Accordingly, when the Albigensian Crusade failed to materialize in 1224, he rapidly changed his summer plans. Seven weeks later the army intended for Occitania was campaigning in Aquitaine. It was a remarkably large force in which the feudal host was heavily reinforced by mercenaries hired with the extensive contingency funds accumulated by Philip Augustus. Louis' unexpected change of plan caught the English by surprise, so the French offensive proved to be all but overwhelming. During July and August 1224, Louis not only reduced Poitou to obedience but also pushed south to the Garonne and into Gascony, occupying the fortress of La Réole only thirty miles from Bordeaux.[137]

When Louis returned from this unexpectedly successful summer campaign, most of his efforts were naturally directed towards defending and extending his conquests in Aquitaine. During the last quarter of 1224, he sought to consolidate his gains by making generous grants to key persons and places in the newly conquered areas.[138] At the same time, he was taking a variety of measures that were designed to isolate the English from any potential allies who might aid them in the counteroffensive that could be expected next spring. On 19 November his envoys were in Germany trying to prevent the marriage proposed between Frederick II's eldest son and the sister of Henry III; after much intrigue, they were successful, for on 7 November 1225 the king of the Romans married Margaret of Austria instead.[139]

Underlying the success of this mission was the work of another embassy that Louis had sent simultaneously to the Emperor Frederick II in Sicily. At Catania, on 24 November 1224, a treaty was signed between Louis and Frederick, the terms of which were to remain secret for over a year. One provision clearly served to isolate England, for the emperor promised that he would make no al-

---

136. Petit-Dutaillis, *Louis*, pp. 224–230.

137. Petit-Dutaillis, *Louis*, pp. 238–252; D. A. Carpenter, *The Minority of Henry III* (Berkeley and Los Angeles, 1990), pp. 370–375.

138. Petit-Dutaillis, *Louis*, pp. 252–256.

139. Petit-Dutaillis, *Louis*, pp. 263–265.

liance with either the king of England or his heirs. Moreover, both rulers agreed that each would not permit any of the other's rebellious, contumacious, or outlawed subjects to enter his lands.[140] Against whom was this latter provision directed? Not so much against the English and their supporters, I should think, as against French subjects whose lands lay adjacent to the Empire, and most notably against Raymond and his supporters in the event that they should oppose the king of France. Earlier in the year, Louis had foreseen difficulties with the Empire if he invaded Occitania and had asked Honorius to secure the emperor's permission for the king to fight against imperial subjects who sought to injure or impede the crusaders (Doc. 7.9). Since nothing came of that request, probably Louis attempted to make some such arrangement directly with Frederick, who would concede nothing more than the mutual exclusion of domestic enemies that was agreed on at Catania. Whatever the object of this provision may have been, at least one can be sure that in effect it would prevent Raymond from taking refuge in his lands east of the Rhone if Louis took the field against him.[141]

At the same time that Louis was isolating the English from the Empire, he was also trying to keep the papacy from condemning his aggression in Aquitaine. The pope was of course predisposed to defend his vassal, Henry III, who had been a ward of the papacy until the previous year, when Honorius had declared him to be of legal age at sixteen. As soon as Louis' summer campaign began, the English had sent a hasty appeal to Rome, and Honorius had reacted promptly but mildly with a letter to Louis.[142] Since the truce between the two kings had lapsed, Honorius could only complain that Louis' campaign was squandering resources that could better be used in the Holy Land. Louis effectively countered this argument by sending John de Brienne to Rome to plead the king's case against the English. As king of Jerusalem, John had been the principal pro-

140. Huillard-Bréholles, *Historia diplomatica*, II, 461–463; Petit-Dutaillis, *Louis*, p. 265.

141. Frederick later provided for a situation not covered by the Catania agreement. On 31 March 1225, when the emperor learned that Romanus had been sent to negotiate a settlement, he wrote to Raymond VII from Palermo forbidding him to alienate lands that he held as fiefs from the Empire: Teulet, no. 1700 (2:50); Molinier, "Catalogue . . . Raimond," no. 90 (Devic-Vaissète, VIII, 1955). In early February Frederick had already asked the pope to persuade Louis to do nothing that would affect Raymond's imperial fiefs: Chaplais, *Diplomatic Documents*, no. 162.

142. Pressutti, no. 5102, ed. *Rec. hist. Gaules*, XIX, 757–758 (3 Aug. 1224); Petit-Dutaillis, *Louis*, pp. 247–250. A few days later the English agents in Rome described the bull as "litteras ad regem Francie directas monitorias tantum et deprecatorias super treugis" and transmitted copies to England, noting that similar letters had been sent to the archbishop of Sens and the bishop of Senlis. The letter was not stronger, the agents explained, because all the pro-English cardinals were then on vacation: Chaplais, *Diplomatic Documents*, no. 144 ("1224, *c. August* 8") = Shirley, *Royal Letters*, no. 200.

pagandist for the Sixth Crusade, and now as Louis' spokesman he could argue more persuasively than anyone else that the two wars were in fact mutually compatible.[143]

Early in December 1224, the French diplomatic mission in Rome was reinforced by the arrival of Guy de Montfort and others, all of whom seem to have been intent on weakening and retarding Honorius' intervention on behalf of the English as much and as long as possible. For example, they spread a rumor around Rome that the English barons had invited Louis to invade England, as he had done in 1216-1217, and that "if the Roman curia tried to do anything contrary to the wishes of the king of France, the king would immediately set sail for England. . . . "[144] Whether taken seriously or not, this threat is our clearest indication that the French agents in Rome were striving above all to prevent the pope from taking any action that would weaken Louis' hold on his new conquests. Ultimately they achieved their goal, probably by suggesting that Louis was open to a negotiated settlement, since the legate Romanus was sent in February 1225 to conduct such negotiations. These then dragged on until Louis took the Cross against the Albigensians and in consequence gained the crusader's exemption from attack, especially from the English, to whom Honorius addressed a specific injunction to this effect in April 1226.[145] Thus there can be no doubt that the Second Albigensian Crusade eventually served to inhibit an English reconquest of Poitou.

The two issues were already intertwined in February 1225 when both matters were entrusted to Romanus, and indeed Honorius appears to have regarded them as interconnected as early as 18 December 1224, when he told the English agents that he would not give them an answer until after he had decided what was to be done about Raymond.[146] Hence it would seem that the king's message, which Guy de Montfort had presented to the pope a few days earlier, not only indicated Louis' revived interest in the crusade but also did so in a way that was calculated to restrain and retard Honorius' intervention in Aquitaine.

143. Chaplais, *Diplomatic Documents*, no. 153 = Shirley, *Royal Letters*, no. 209.

144. Chaplais, *Diplomatic Documents*, no. 153 = Shirley, *Royal Letters*, no. 209: "si aliquid in curia Romana contra voluntatem regis Francie fieret, incontinenti se transferret in Angliam . . . ." Cf. Petit-Dutaillis, *Louis*, p. 271; on Louis' previous invasion of England, see pp. 30-183.

145. Pressutti, no. 5904; Petit-Dutaillis, *Louis*, pp. 272-276.

146. The agents were representing not only certain bishops (see n. 124, above) but also the crown, since they reported Romanus' mission directly to the justiciar on 25 Feb. 1225: Chaplais, *Diplomatic Documents*, no. 162 = Shirley, *Royal Letters*, no. 215. The bishops evidently passed on the earlier letter to the crown, since the original was preserved in the royal archives; the news about Raymond's case was clearly what interested the crown, since the letter was endorsed "*Breve de Tholos'* . . . " (Chaplais, no. 153).

We can make a shrewd guess what that message was. Certainly Louis opposed the reconciliation of Raymond.[147] His grounds are suggested by his choice of messenger: Amaury de Montfort held his lands in Occitania from the crown, and therefore the king could protest against a settlement that deprived him of a blameless vassal. Earlier in the year, Louis had told the legate Conrad that it was Rome's business to work out a settlement with Raymond, but he had added significant qualifications: "provided that our rights and our fiefs are in no way diminished, and that no new or unusual burden is imposed on them" (Doc. 9.8). Now it would seem that he was asserting that right, probably maintaining that neither Amaury nor the king had consented to the settlement made at Montpellier. It was with good reason that Honorius had originally suggested that Amaury should participate in the deliberations, and it was by no means clear that the count had forfeited his rights by absenting himself, especially since he had vigorously urged the bishops to do nothing to prejudice those rights.

One way or another, then, it would seem that Louis was determined to add Occitania to the royal domain. Even if he did so without the pope's cooperation, the plan had definite advantages for France. Since Louis at this point was chiefly concerned with the recovery of Aquitaine from the English, his Occitanian policy probably was shaped to serve him against the English. And this it would do, for by gaining control of Languedoc, the French could both flank the English in Aquitaine and isolate them from Raymond VII, with whom they might be expected to ally.[148] But much more was to be gained by seeking the cooperation of the papacy. Above all, Louis would gain time to consolidate his gains from the English, because as long as Honorius was seriously considering Louis as his potential champion against the Albigensians, the pope would hesitate to alienate him by supporting the English wholeheartedly.[149] Moreover, once the king had taken the Cross, his status as a crusader would of course protect him and his lands from the English, so he could campaign in the south without overextending his forces. The net result promised to be an enormous addition to the French royal domain, amounting to all of modern France south of the Loire and west of the Rhone. Considering the stakes, the risks were few, and in

147. English agents at the curia reported: "Et sperabatur quod dictus comes [Raimundus] conpetens responsum esset accepturus, licet rex et Gallici dicti sibi fortiter resisterent": Chaplais, *Diplomatic Documents*, no. 153 (22 Dec. 1224) = Shirley, *Royal Letters*, no. 209.

148. The English did in fact seek an alliance with Raymond in 1225: Petit-Dutaillis, *Louis*, pp. 268–269.

149. As it turned out, the pope waited a year, until 8 Jan. 1226, before attempting to impose sanctions on Louis' supporters in Aquitaine, and then he was dissuaded at the last minute, probably because Louis was about to take the Cross: Petit-Dutaillis, *Louis*, pp. 274–275; Pressutti, no. 5775.

addition the crusade would veil Louis' opportunistic aggression with the virtue of piety.

Although there is no direct proof that Louis in December 1224 did threaten to wage a feudal war on Raymond, still no other explanation accounts so well for Honorius' mysterious change of policy. In this view, Honorius had a difficult choice thrust upon him. Assuming that the pope's goal was peace both in Aquitaine and in Occitania, he could achieve neither without Louis' cooperation. It would be useless for the Church to effect a reconciliation with Raymond if Louis was not prepared to accept the count as his vassal but was ready to wage war on him instead. Moreover, there could be no hope of peace in Aquitaine if Honorius not only supported the English but also gave them a new ally in Raymond, because Louis would in consequence be thoroughly alienated from the papacy and hardly disposed to accept papal mediation. The result would be war south of the Loire, a war which Honorius deplored in itself and regretted even more because it might undermine support for the Sixth Crusade. In order to avoid such a war, Honorius would have to sacrifice Raymond. Perhaps the pope reasoned that if Louis got what he wanted in Occitania, he would accept a compromise in Aquitaine. At any rate it must have been clear that nothing would be gained by reconciling Raymond if Louis would not recognize the settlement. That seems to have been the principal conclusion of three months of deliberation by Honorius with his cardinals. Hence the reconciliation was postponed indefinitely and the whole knotty problem of Louis' relations with Aquitaine and Occitania was left to the discretion of Romanus, the new legate who was sent to France in February 1225 to work out a solution. Apparently all that was decided at Rome was that a solution might better be found through direct negotiation with Louis.

CHAPTER 2

CARDINAL ROMANUS AND HIS
LEGATION TO FRANCE 1225

Who was this Cardinal Romanus in whom the curia placed such trust? We would like to know him better because for the next four years it was Romanus, not the pope, who gradually worked out a lasting solution in Occitania. That he succeeded where so many others had failed undoubtedly testifies to his extraordinary abilities as a diplomat; yet he remains a shadowy figure whom we know chiefly through his official acts. To be sure, we can trace the outlines of his career as a cardinal, but the character of the man himself can be glimpsed only at a few rare moments. Nonetheless, because the Council of Bourges was his council, which he summoned to implement his own policy and over which he presided, we must acquaint ourselves as far as is possible with his career and character, as well as with the authority that he possessed as papal legate.[1]

★ ★ ★

Like most cardinals at this period, Romanus was related to one of the noble families in the neighborhood of Rome. This much is declared in his letters of legation, where the pope describes him as a man "distinguished by noble birth," "outstanding for the nobility of his birth," and "conspicuous for his nobility of birth" (Docs. 10, 12.4, and 13.1). But which noble family that might be is not certain. The current consensus favors the Bonaventura family because in 1235 a certain Peter Bonaventura is identified as Romanus' nephew.[2] The Bonaventura family, however, were only a minor noble family;[3] the clan descended from one

---

1. Above all: Maleczek, *Kardinalskolleg*, pp. 189-195. Also A. Paravicini Bagliani, *Cardinali di curia e "familiae" cardinalizie dal 1227 al 1254* (Padua, 1972), I, 15. The following biographical sketch does not attempt to collect all the references to Romanus, which I am assembling in a chronological register that, though far from complete, already runs to over 200 items.

2. The evidence is marshalled by Maleczek, *Kardinalskolleg*, pp. 189-190, nn. 484 and 490. He concludes that it is not certain that Romanus' birth family was the Bonaventura. I suppose the difficulty is that Romanus may have been Peter's *maternal* uncle, and hence the cardinal would not himself be a Bonaventura by birth. Romanus' interest in Peter is the only indication of the cardinal's ties to the de Papa—Bonaventura clan: see below, nn. 28-30, 82-83.

3. In 1223, an English agent at the curia described one member, Nicholas, as "a noble Roman citizen": *Diplomatic Documents Preserved in the Public Record Office*, vol. I: *1101–1272*, ed. P. Chaplais (London, 1964), no. 121.

Cencius *de Papa*, who was dead in 1195,[4] and one of his sons was keeper of the wardrobe for the city of Rome.[5] Such an obscure noble family would hardly justify Honorius' assertions that Romanus was distinguished, outstanding, and conspicuous for the nobility of his birth.

An alternative is offered by Philip Mousket, the Flemish verse chronicler, who said of Romanus that "he was from the highest Romans, / From the Frangipani lineage; / Indeed he was a distant relative of the king" (Doc. 4, vss. 25377-79). Mousket was surely wrong about the Capetian connection, probably because he confused Romanus with his predecessor, Conrad von Urach, who through his mother was in fact distantly related to Louis VIII.[6] But the bourgeois poet could still be right about the Frangipani connection, which in 1225 would have conferred the high distinction Honorius claimed for Romanus' nobility. Throughout most of the twelfth century, the Frangipani had been one of the mainstays of the papacy in local politics, but in the decades around the turn of the century the family had first supported Emperor Henry VI and then had unsuccessfully opposed Pope Innocent III.[7] In Romanus' time, the Frangipani controlled the southern coast of the province of Campagna and Marittima for some thirty miles between Astura and Terracina,[8] and the strongest confirmation of Mousket's assertion is the fact that, as we shall see, it was precisely in this area that Romanus first proved himself useful to the papacy. Although the evidence for a Bonaventura connection remains more convincing, still the possibility of a link to the Frangipani should not be ignored, as it has been.[9]

---

4. Fabre-Duchesne, *Liber censuum*, I, 433-436 (nos. 180-181).

5. "Romanus Bonaventura vestararius Urbis": Auvray, no. 3035. This is not Cardinal Romanus; the *Liber censuum* identifies him as Cencius' son (ed. Fabre-Duchesne, I, 433, 435), and he himself had two sons; moreover, he obligingly conducted an English agent from Rome to the curia at Anagni (Chaplais, *Diplomatic Documents*, no. 121). The *vestiarius* was an officer of the papal curia since the late seventh century: Niermeyer, *Lexicon*, p. 1080, s.v.

6. F. Neininger, *Konrad von Urach* (Paderborn, 1994), p. 75 and Stammtafel I.

7. D. Waley, *The Papal State in the Thirteenth Century* (London, 1961), pp. 9, 11, 14-15, 46. The fortunes of the Frangipani can also be traced in P. Partner, *The Lands of St Peter* (Berkeley and Los Angeles, 1972), passim (Index, s.v. "Frangipani"); by contrast, he nowhere mentions the Bonaventura family. See also M. Ellis, "Landscape and Power: The Frangipani family and their clients in the twelfth-century Roman Forum," in *The Community, the Family and the Saint*, ed. Joyce Hill and M. Swan (Turnhout, 1998), pp. 61-76.

8. Waley, *Papal State*, p. 82.

9. Romanus' origins can perhaps be clarified by sifting through the mass of data collected by Giulio Savio, *Monumenta onomastica romana Medii Aevi (X–XII sec.)*, 4 vols. (Rome, 1999). There is much on the history of the de Papa—Bonaventura clan (e.g. nos. 22399-401 and 97448) but I find nothing new on Cardinal Romanus' putative connection to it.

The career of Romanus

Romanus' career as a cardinal spanned twenty-seven years, from 1216 to 1243.[10] He was one of the last cardinals to be promoted by Innocent III, who made him cardinal-deacon of Sant' Angelo *in foro piscium*. It was Popes Honorius III and Gregory IX, however, whom he chiefly served as cardinal; and it is in their registers that we catch glimpses of Romanus at work. From the beginning, he appears intermittently as a papal judge-delegate, which circumstance suggests that he had received legal training;[11] but his major work before 1225 had been as an administrator in the papal states. For at least two years, from March 1220 to March 1222, he was the rector, or governor, of the province of Campagna and Marittima—most southerly of the papal states, where the Frangipani family's interests lay—and it is possible that his term began as early as 1217 and ran as late as 1225.[12]

The high point of his career was undoubtedly his legation to France, which occupied him from 1225 until 1229. He not only made the arrangements for Louis' royal crusade and accompanied him on it in 1226, but also, after the king's death, he remained as the invaluable ally of Louis' widow, Blanche of Castille, who ruled as regent. Certainly his greatest achievement was the settlement with Raymond VII that he negotiated in 1229 at Meaux and concluded at Paris. Characteristically, it was a compromise, which left Raymond in possession of his lands but gave the crown a claim that eventually brought them into the royal domain. Having restored peace, Romanus completed his mission by reforming the Occitanian church, and the outstanding features of this reform are also characteristic. On the one hand, error was to be uprooted by regular inquisitions held by the local bishops; on the other, truth was to be implanted by education, for which purpose he founded the University of Toulouse. It was the solution of a cultured canonist.[13]

After this triumph, he retreated again into the obscurity of the Roman curia, where he served Gregory IX much as he had Honorius III. His services in France were suitably recognized by promotion: in 1231 he was designated cardinal-bishop elect of Porto and Santa Rufina, and he took office in 1235 after

10. Eubel, *Hierarchia*, I, 4, 35, and 47.

11. Pressutti, nos. 864 (1217), 3586, 3739, 4069, 5236 (1221–1222); Auvray, nos. 2319-2320 (4 Mar. 1227 n.s.).

12. In Waley's catalogue of the rectors of Campagna and Marittima, the last mention of Romanus' predecessor is on 5 Mar. 1217 and the first mention of his successor is on 16 Sept. 1225 (*Papal State*, p. 307). For Romanus as rector, see Pressutti, nos. 2350, 2691, 2855, 2857, 3470, 3888, and Maleczek, *Kardinalskolleg*, p. 189, n. 487.

13. P. Belperron, *La Croisade contre les Albigeois et l'union du Languedoc à la France (1209–1249)*, 2nd ed. (Paris, 1967), pp. 407-417.

Conrad's death.[14] The most important commission entrusted to him by Gregory IX was the negotiation of a peace between the city of Rome and the papacy in April and May 1235. Doubtless his local connections recommended him for this assignment, for the pope and most of the cardinals had withdrawn to Perugia while the Roman mob looted their palaces; only Romanus and the two other cardinals on the peace commission dared to remain in the city.[15]

Less certain but in the long run more significant is the part he played in the establishment of the papal inquisition. Its prototype would seem to be the inquest he mandated to discover suspect heretics in Languedoc during the last months of 1229. Although the work was done by the bishops, the undertaking was a legatine, and hence papal, inquisition, because the results were turned over to Romanus, who then decided the fate of the suspects, and moreover took the records back with him to Rome in early 1230.[16] A year later, as is well known, Gregory IX established the papal inquisition,[17] and one can safely assume that the pope was guided by Romanus' recent experience and unique precedent.

Other than this, most of his work was routine. For some months in 1234 he was simultaneously rector of two provinces of the papal patrimony—Tuscany and the duchy of Spoleto;[18] moreover, he appears to have been papal vicar for the twin province of Campagna and Marittima in 1236 and perhaps 1237.[19] Quite possibly he held other such offices of which no trace survives in the registers. At the same time he looked after the interests of the bishopric of Porto

14. Romanus is described as *episcopus electus Portuensis* for the first time in the papal registers on 18 April 1231 and for the last time on 11 Feb. 1235; as simply *episcopus Portuensis* he is first mentioned on 7 April 1235 (Auvray, nos. 622, 2424, and 3020).

15. Auvray, nos. 3020-3028, passim; Waley, *Papal State*, p. 143. The city officials swore a prescribed oath to keep the peace; the list is headed by one "dominus Romanus Bonaventure, vestararius Urbis" (Auvray, no. 3035), presumably the same man named in the *Liber censuum* (see above, nn. 4-5).

16. William of Puylaurens, *Chronica magistri Guillelmi de Podio Laurentii* 38, ed. and trans. J. Duvernoy (Paris, 1976), pp. 136-141.

17. *Excommunicamus et anathematizamus* (Feb. 1231); Potthast, post no. 9675; Auvray, no. 539; X 5.7.15, ed. Friedberg, II, 789; H. Maisonneuve, *Etudes sur les origines de l'Inquisition*, 2nd ed. (Paris, 1960), pp. 245-248. On antiheretic legislation in France during Romanus' legation, see Maisonneuve, *Etudes*, pp. 237-242.

18. Auvray, nos. 1716-1717 (12 Jan. 1234). His successors are first mentioned as being in office in April and August respectively: Waley, *Papal State*, pp. 309, 312.

19. On 26 June 1236 the pope directed Romanus, as "nostro vicario," to supervise the sale of some property in Anagni, which is in the province of Campagna and Marittima (cf. Auvray, no. 3208). Romanus' vicariate probably corresponds to the gap in the list of rectors of that province between Jan. 1236 and June 1237 (Waley, *Papal State*, p. 307). In all likelihood, he was not styled rector of the twin province because at this time it was under the control of the city of Rome, which had conquered it in 1235 (ibid., p. 142).

with the vigilance of a trained lawyer. Since its old papyrus charters dating from the tenth and eleventh centuries had deteriorated, he had them recopied and confirmed by the pope.[20] Furthermore, he vindicated the bishopric's right to certain vineyards and other properties that were in the hands of various Roman citizens.[21]

Romanus' French experience was not wasted at the curia, however, for Gregory IX commissioned him to hear five cases in 1238-1239 that involved French prelates.[22] Once, in making a policy decision concerning Raymond VII, Romanus was expressly named as the only cardinal whom the pope had consulted.[23] Again, when a case involving the Cistercian prior of Mazan, in the diocese of Viviers, needed special attention, Romanus was given legatine powers to settle it. [24] His final commission, issued on 12 February 1240, was to supervise the shaky finances of the canons of St Peter's in Rome.[25]

Towards the end of his career, in the conclave following the death of Gregory IX in August 1241, on the first ballot a minority of three cardinals voted for Romanus. The three included two future popes—Innocent IV and Alexander IV—and they represented the uncompromising, anti-imperial faction at the curia, which evidently felt Romanus could be relied on to continue Gregory IX's war on the Hohenstaufen. Since no candidate had the requisite two-thirds majority, Romanus voluntarily withdrew and his more conciliatory rival was eventually elected as Celestine IV, who died less than three weeks later.[26]

The character of Romanus

From these meager data gleaned from the papal registers, one gets the impression that Romanus was trained as a lawyer and was employed for most of his life as an administrator in the patrimony, but that in the crisis of December 1224 he proved to be the right man for the job. What qualities recommended him can be gathered from the occasional but illuminating references to him scattered in the sources.

Romanus' character is described for us twice, the two testimonials framing as it were his career as legate, for the earlier one introduced him to his new lega-

20. Auvray, nos. 3544-3564 (July–Sept. 1236).

21. Auvray, nos. 3955-3962 (25 Nov. 1237).

22. Auvray, nos. 4446, 4508, 4863, 4911, 4922.

23. Auvray, no. 4777.

24. Auvray, nos. 4924-4926 (Sept. 1239); cf. nos. 5076-5077.

25. Auvray, no. 5069.

26. T. C. Van Cleve, *The Emperor Frederick II of Hohenstaufen* (Oxford, 1972), pp. 456-458; cf. Matthew Paris, *Chronica majora*, ed. H. R. Luard, 7 vols., Rolls Series, no. 57 (London, 1872-1883), IV, 164-165.

tion in 1225, while the later one was a panegyric delivered at the reform Council of Toulouse, which he celebrated in 1229 at the end of his mission. In the first
instance, Pope Honorius described his legate in the letters of legation that Romanus carried with him as his credentials (Docs. 10, 12-13). The description was
varied slightly from letter to letter to make the most favorable impression on the
different recipients, so the three views lend a sort of stereoscopic depth to the
portrait. The longest of these sketches was sent by the pope to the ecclesiastical
authorities:

> Behold our beloved son Romanus, the cardinal-deacon of Sant' Angelo, a man
> outstanding for the nobility of his birth and manners, conspicuous for the dili-
> gence and persistence with which he pursues his goals, and the one among
> our brothers [the cardinals] whom we especially cherish and deservedly es-
> teem for his probity [Doc. 12.4].

Almost all these virtues also appeared in Honorius' letter to the civil authorities, the one exception being probity, for which the term "circumspection" was
used instead (Doc. 13.1). Although the two terms largely overlap, it was fitting
that his integrity be stressed to the clergy, who were all too conscious of the
venality of the Roman curia, whereas the lay nobility needed rather to be reassured that this was a man of the world whose counsel to the king would be wise
and cautious. Most likely the subtext was an implied contrast with his predecessor, the Cistercian fanatic Conrad von Urach. The rest of Romanus' virtues
would apparently be equally striking to both groups, and before all else his nobility.

   This prince of the Church was more than a noble by courtesy: he not only
was born into one of the great Roman families but also was every inch the nobleman in his behavior. His noble conduct, however, was not the intellectual and
moral perfection that Dante praised in Book 4 of the *Convivio*; by "nobility of
manners" Honorius simply meant that his legate was a paragon of the social
graces. This appears from a third letter, which the pope sent to Raymond VII,
in which Romanus is said to be "a man distinguished by noble birth, learning,
and charming manners" (Doc. 10). Thus we may conclude that one of Romanus'
greatest assets as a diplomat was an aristocratic set of good manners that would
do him credit in the highest circles of courtly society.

   The pope hastened to add that his legate had more solid virtues as well: especially persistence and industry, but knowledge also. They are the virtues of the
trained and disciplined administrator with years of experience at the Roman
curia. Again, perhaps they were meant to contrast with his predecessor, Conrad,
the abbot of Cîteaux who was made a cardinal expressly to represent the curia
as legate in Occitania.

Romanus did not disappoint the clergy of his legation. At his final legatine council at Toulouse in November 1229, Romanus' virtues were praised in a sermon by Hélinand, a reformed troubadour turned Cistercian:

> He goes without pomp, he does not pursue avarice, he does not run after presents, he does not seek our goods but ourselves. In a word—if I dare to say it— he is not a Roman, i.e. he does not go off after gold. He neither places his hopes in monetary treasures [Matt. 6.19] nor is he one of those legates we have sometimes known to have gone forth from the side of the lord pope as Satan went forth from the presence of the Lord [Job 1.21b]. Many of them, having been sent thus to the local churches, rage in the provinces as if Tisiphone, Magaera, or the other Fury had, in Claudian's phrase, emerged from hell to kindle evil deeds. Romanus loves righteousness, he is zealous for souls, he despises money.[27]

Evidently the preacher was particularly impressed with the legate's personal integrity, and this testimonial corroborates his reputation for *probitas* that Honorius had stressed in 1225. This quality is particularly worth remembering because the two major concerns of the Council of Bourges were both essentially financial questions. Because Romanus himself was an honest official, at least in financial matters, he could command the respect, and for the most part the co-

---

27. Sermon 26; Migne, *Pat. Lat.*, CCXII, 720B, emended from Paris, BnF, MS. lat. 14591, fol. 48v: "Nam ad exhibendam legato huic debitam reverentiam, et praeceptis ejus obedientiam, multum nos inter caetera inducere debet ipsius modestia praeceptoris. Non pompatice incedit, non sectatur avaritiam, non currit post munera, non nostra quaerit, sed nos. In summa <si auderem dicere, Romanus> non est, [ut multi]: id est non abit post aurum, nec sperat in thesauris pecuniae. <Non est de legatis illis quos aliquandos novimus sic egressos fuisse a latere domini papae, ac si ad ecclesiasm flagellandam egressus esset Sathan a facie Domini. Ita plerique versantur in ecclesiis, in provinciis debacchantur ac si ad tedas in facinus excitandam egressa sit ab inferis iuxta Claudianum, Thesiphone vel Megera.> Amator est justitiae, zelator animarum, pecuniae contemptor. . . . Nunc igitur hortor ut audiatis humiliter et devote, quae praecepta vobis transmisit in salutem animarum, et obedientes sitis secundum meum consilium" (720BC). In 1669 Dom Tissier, the original editor, omitted the text in <pointed brackets> and substituted "[ut multi]," doubtless to avoid scandal. The correct reading is supplied, albeit unwittingly, by Beverly M. Kienzle, "Deed and Word: Hélinand's Toulouse Sermons, I," in *Erudition at God's Service*, ed. J. R. Sommerfeldt (Kalamazoo, 1987), 267–276, p. 275, n. 31, from *Peter Abelard, Letters IX–XIV*, ed. E. R. Smits (Gronigen, 1983), pp. 109–110. See also M. J. J. Brial, "Hélinand," in *Hist. litt. Fr.*, XVIII (1835), 87–103, at pp. 97–98; A. F. Gatien-Arnould, "Hélinand," *Revue de Toulouse et du Midi de la France*, XX (1866), 287–302 and 345–356, at pp. 348–352; A. Lecoy de la Marche, *La Chaire française au Moyen Age*, 2nd ed. (Paris, 1886), p. 346; *Repertorium der lateinisches Sermones des Mittelalters für die Zeit von 1150–1350*, ed. J. B. Schneyer, 11 vols. (Munster i. W., 1969–1990), II, 617–622.

operation, of the clergy whom he had to tax. It is particularly noteworthy that the French clergy do not seem to have been at all upset that they had to pay an annual tax, called a "procuration," to support the legate, whereas in England at this time similar taxes elicited bitter complaints from the chroniclers. Indeed, our only indication that Romanus did collect procurations comes from an exemption that he granted to a Norman priory (Doc. 51). Like his nobility, Romanus' reputation for honesty must have been a major asset.

Since a major concern of the Council of Bourges was the practice of conferring French benefices on nonresident Roman curialists, it should be noted that Romanus, like other cardinals, was both a beneficiary and a patron. Before Romanus' legation, his nephew Peter had obtained a benefice at Laon.[28] His legatine commission empowered him "to confer dignities and benefices that have been vacant so long that giving them has devolved upon us" (Doc. 19). Accordingly, he provided his nephew, Peter Bonaventura, with benefices at Paris and Chartres, and after his legation both chapters protested that Peter was neither competent nor resident, but to no avail.[29] In 1225 the same Peter had received an annual pension from the king of England in lieu of an ecclesiastical benefice, which was granted as a favor to Romanus while he was mediating between France and England.[30] Moreover, Romanus' personal chaplain was made rector of a parish in the diocese of Rouen on the understanding that he would receive holy orders and reside there, as he swore to do; but Gregory IX nonetheless permitted him to serve through a vicar.[31] At his death, Romanus himself held a canonry at Senlis, though how long he had held it is unknown. Despite his reputation for honesty, Romanus died a rich man, for he provided Senlis with an endowment for an annual distribution in his memory of one hundred *solidi*.[32]

His generosity to Senlis was no doubt motivated in part by a sense of gratitude, but also in part by a desire to be well remembered, especially in the canons' prayers. Like other great churchmen of his day, Romanus sought the same favor on a more grandiose scale by securing a promise from the Cistercian general chapter that the entire order would pray for him on learning of his death, which

28. Maleczek, *Kardinalskolleg*, p. 189, n. 485, citing a letter of Romanus, dated Anagni, 22 May 1220, preserved in a Laon chartulary (Laon, Arch. dép. Aisne, G 1850, fol. 40v).

29. In 1231, Gregory IX tried to appease the chapters by arranging that the next incumbent would be both suitable and resident (Auvray, no. 1636); in 1233 he finally had to force compliance (Auvray, nos. 2085-2086).

30. See below, nn. 82-83.

31. Auvray, no. 5218. His name is given as "Rain.," standing for either Rainaldus or Rainerius.

32. In the Senlis necrology, Romanus is commemorated on 18 February as "quondam huius ecclesie canonicus": E. Müller, *Analyse du cartulaire, des statuts, etc. de Notre-Dame de Senlis, 1041–1395* (Senlis, 1904), p. 87, n. 4. This establishes his day of death as 18 Feb. 1243.

was duly done.[33] Pious provisions such as these, though conventional enough, were surely sincere, and they are the only traces we have of his personal spiritual life. No doubt the Christian faith was central to his life, but it was thoroughly intellectualized and institutionalized. Thus Hélinand's panegyric is remarkable for its stress on worldly rather than on spiritual virtues. To be sure, Romanus is said to be "zealous for souls," though even this may simply have been another way of praising his perseverance and industry.

His predominantly intellectual interests and attainments are especially evident in his one surviving sermon, *De poenitentia*, which enumerates the fifteen steps of confession by which the penitent ascends to Christ.[34] The manner closely resembles that of Innocent III,[35] to whose collected sermons this had been appended; thus, the theme is largely developed by the allegorical and typological exposition of biblical texts, with occasional references to Augustine and Gregory. Such a method required the sort of familiarity with biblical hermaneutics that Italians of Romanus' generation usually acquired at the University of Paris,[36] and this style of sermonizing, together with his lifelong affection for France, suggests that Romanus was one who did. But this sermon, like those of Innocent, also contains significant hints of nontheological interests as well. A distinction based on Aristotelian logic, distinguishing between lust *in genere* and its species, such as adultery or incest,[37] indicates a grounding in the liberal arts; but Romanus also shows that he had studied Gratian's *Decretum* in the schools by quoting a mnemonic verse from the Decretalist apparatus developed at Bologna.[38] Training as a canon lawyer is of course indicated by the curia's fre-

33. *Statuta capitulorum generalium ordinis Cisterciensis ab anno 1116 ad annum 1786*, ed. J. M. Canivez, II (Louvain, 1934), p. 65 (an. 1227, no. 47): "Item petitionem domini Romani cardinalis olim ex parte eius factam ad preces ipsius innovamus, ut videlicet audito eius obitu plenarium pro eo servitium per totum Ordinem persolvatur"; cf. p. 261 (an. 1243, no. 13). Similar petitions were granted, e.g., to Conrad von Urach, Simon Langton, and Richard Poore, bishop of Salisbury (p. 21, an. 1222, no. 41).

34. Migne, *Pat. Lat.*, CCXVII, 687–690, reprinted from *Spicilegium Romanum*, ed. A. Mai, VI (Rome, 1841), 578–582, from Vat. lat. 700 (saec. xiii 1/4). It is the only sermon recorded for Romanus in Schneyer's *Repertorium*, V, 345.

35. R. Kay, "Innocent III as Canonist and Theologian," in *Pope Innocent III and his World*, ed. J. C. Moore (Aldershot, Hants, 1999), pp. 35–49.

36. On Bible study at Paris in the late twelfth century, see J. W. Baldwin, *Masters, Princes and Merchants* (Princeton, 1970), I, 90–96.

37. Migne, *Pat. Lat.*, CCXVII, 690B.

38. The penitent ought to confess "omnes circumstantias; quae sunt: 'Quis, quid, ubi, quibus auxiliis, cur, quomodo, quando'" (ibid., 689D). Cf. the *casus*, probably by Benencasa (d. 1206), to Gratian, *Decretum*, D.5 de pen. c.1, "in qua notantur ea quae poenitentes debent considerare . . . et hoc etiam versu notantur: 'Quis, quid, ubi, quibus auxiliis, cur, quomodo, quando' . . . ." (my edition, Lyons, 1548).

quent employment of Romanus as a judge, but this display of school learning confirms it.

The sermon shows Romanus to have been a competent preacher, but one whose presentation was intellectual rather than affective. This is how he was remembered among the clergy of France, who circulated a tale about him that has been preserved by Etienne de Bourbon.[39] This *fabliau* relates an interview between Romanus and Robert, dauphin of Auvergne and count of Montferrand (1169-1234), who was a troubadour famous for his unlearned wisdom.[40] Romanus wanted to test this reputation for himself, so he asked the dauphin: "What is most useful to men in this world?" The troubadour replied, "Proportion, as the proverb says, *Mesure dure.*" "But how is proportion obtained?" persisted the cardinal; and he was told, "In moderation." Once again he pressed: "And how is it obtained in moderation?" Unerringly came the reply: "Between excess and deficiency." So Romanus departed, marveling at such good reasoning in a layman.

This anecdote reveals as much about Romanus as about Robert. Evidently the interview was not inquisitorial in purpose, because it was devoid of specifically Christian content. Although the cardinal's original question was susceptible of a pious response, he readily accepted Robert's secular approach. Evidently Romanus could recognize and appreciate Aristotelian ethics wherever he found them, and indeed he could use the techniques of a university examiner to sound the depths of another's understanding. Hence it appears that he had received scholastic training at one of the new universities, of which education he was sufficiently proud to make him amazed that anyone who was not a product of this Latin, clerical, university culture could view life in terms of Aristotle's ethics.

This impression is reinforced by Romanus' apparent interest in Maimonides' *Guide of the Perplexed*, the greatest philosophical treatise of the twelfth century. A certain Romanus had read the first, highly compressed Latin translation of that work and was puzzled by Maimonides' interpretation of Leviticus ii.11, so he requested someone conversant with Arabic—most likely Michael Scot, who had been in Italy since about 1220—to clarify the text. The result was an expanded translation of the *Guide*, accompanied by a summary of Maimonides' teachings, which was addressed simply to "Romanus" in the eighth year of Honorius III (24 July 1223-1224). The papal dating suggests that this all took place at the Roman curia, where papal patronage of Michael Scot significantly began in the same pontifical year.[41] Thus

39. Lecoy de la Marche, *La Chaire*, pp. 346-347.

40. T. B. Eméric-David, "Robert, dauphin d'Auvergne," *Histoire littéraire de la France*, XVIII (Paris, 1835), 607-615.

41. C. H. Haskins, *Studies in the History of Mediaeval Science* (Cambridge, Mass., 1924), p. 282; L. Thorndike, *Michael Scot* (London, 1965), p. 28; R. Kay, *Dante's Christian Astrology* (Philadelphia, 1994), pp. 275-279; Pressutti, no. 4682 (cf. 4871, 5025, 5470).

Romanus the patron has plausibly been identified as our cardinal, which is consistent with other indications of his scholastic bent.

* * *

Romanus, then, had been educated at one of the new universities, probably at Bologna, since his expertise lay in law. Certainly he shared the scholastic's confidence in the ability of human reason to discover truth through logical analysis, and accordingly he looked to the university rather than to the monastery as the institution that could preserve the faith in Occitania. Thus it was characteristic that he should include in the Church's 1229 settlement with Raymond provision for the foundation of a university at Toulouse. There can be no doubt that the plan was his, for the earliest extant recruiting announcement hoped that "the lord legate will summon other theologians and decretists here to enlarge the university . . . that they may magnify the place and people of Romanus."[42] Strange though it may seem, the inquisition into heresy that he also instituted at that time was part and parcel of the same scholastic mentality, which considered law to be the instrument by which human reason regulated society. Finally, his secular mentality is evinced in his choice of subordinates. Whereas Conrad, his predecessor, had insisted on having a Cistercian monk as his companion, Romanus had as his chaplain a man not sufficiently advanced in holy orders to serve as a parish priest. Presumably the latter was more of a clerk than a cleric, and that Romanus preferred him indicates a respect for worldly competence rather than for clerical status.[43] In sum, for better or for worse Romanus was an early example of the university-trained canon lawyer.

Something more of the man himself emerges from the reports of English agents at the curia. In September 1223, a royal clerk arrived in Rome to find only two cardinals there, since the curia was summering at Anagni; he reported that these two, one of whom was Romanus, "favored the French, which could work to our disadvantage."[44] Almost a year later, at the end of July 1224, two English abbots arrived and found that most of the cardinals were on vacation, scattered throughout the countryside; only Romanus and another cardinal had

42. Letter from the masters of Toulouse to other universities, written in 1229, perhaps by John of Garland. Latin text in Denifle-Châtelain, I, 129-131; trans. L. Thorndike, *University Records and Life in the Middle Ages* (New York, 1944), pp. 32-35.

43. On the chaplain ("Rain."), see n. 31, above. As cardinal, Conrad disciplined a Cistercian abbot who refused to provide him with a companion: Neininger, *Konrad*, reg. no. 59; A. Clément, "Conrad d'Urach, de l'ordre de Cîteaux, légat en France et en Allemagne," *Revue bénédictine*, XXII (1905), 232-243, and XXIII (1906), 62-81, 373-391, at p. 243, n. 3.

44. Chaplais, *Diplomatic Documents*, no. 121 = C. V. Langlois, "Le Fonds de l'*Ancient Corre-spondence* au *Public Record Office* de Londres," *Journal des savants*, n.s., II (1904), 380-393, 446-453, at pp. 388-389: "qui quasi in dampnum nostrum partem Francigenarum fovebant."

remained at the pope's side in Rome. Evidently in these years Romanus stayed
in Rome whether the pope was there or not; probably he had official duties
there, perhaps as the pope's *vicarius urbanus*. When the English approached the
two cardinals in 1224, urging that they should convince the pope to take immediate and drastic measures against the French invasion of Poitou, Romanus
responded cryptically that "they were not able to fulminate the Church."[45] The
envoys had no doubt that this proved he was pro-French, but it also shows him
to be a man of moderation, who did not want to cause an uproar in the Church
by having Rome commit herself to one side in a feudal war. Instead, he preferred
to have Rome stand available as a mediator between warring factions, and Romanus maintained this position so unswervingly that on the eve of his legation
he was able to convince another English embassy that as legate he would serve
the interests of England no less than those of France.[46] Nonetheless, his pro-
French sympathies were such that in February 1225 Honorius could assure Louis
VIII that Romanus "is directing his efforts to the honor and exaltation of you
and your kingdom, as we have long known for certain, and as your envoys have
come to know recently and frequently by many plain proofs" (Doc. 14.1).

Only one letter gives us an informal glimpse of Romanus the man. It was
written to a colleague in Rome, Master Thomas de Ebulo, to whom he sent a
frank censure of current thinking at the curia:

> We should avoid outrageous behavior towards kings and kingdoms these days
> because almost the whole world is more disposed to be hostile [to the papacy]
> than you and the others think. You are not aware of this when you are in your
> chambers [at Rome]; instead, you seem to be facilitating the downfall of God's
> Church by provoking kings and kingdoms to scandal and discord rather than
> to devotion to the Church [Doc. 22B.4].

The pope received a watered-down version of the same letter in which this vig-
orous passage does not appear (Doc. 22A). Thus we can be sure that here we have
penetrated Romanus' official persona and for once hear his own personal point
of view presented informally. That viewpoint proves to be consistent with the
experience of the English agents a year earlier, for in August 1225 his was still
the voice of moderation. Rome must not meddle in matters that do not concern her, he told Master Thomas; otherwise, she will alienate secular rulers on
whose devotion much of her power depends. This is the plea of a political realist whose earlier inclinations have been confirmed by experience in the field.
He recognized, as apparently many of the cardinals did not, that in the last analy-

45. Chaplais, *Diplomatic Documents*, no. 144 = Shirley, *Royal Letters*, no. 200: "dixit quod non
poterant ecclesiam fulminare."
46. Chaplais, *Diplomatic Documents*, no. 162 = Shirley, *Royal Letters*, no. 215.

sis the pope was powerless if men did not respect him. Romanus evidently had a reputation for practicing what he preached, for we have seen that he was especially recommended to the French clergy for his personal probity. Here we find him urging the Roman church to have the same sort of prudent regard for its public image. Respectability thus emerges as another of his characteristic concerns. It is also noteworthy that Romanus' remarkably good manners did not prevent him from speaking out strongly in favor of his convictions.

These qualities do much to explain Romanus' success as a diplomat, but one must add that he was particularly well suited for his mission because he was predisposed to favor France in general and Louis in particular. The English abbots who interviewed him in July 1224 had heard rumors to this effect, though they had also heard the same report about the other cardinal to whom they spoke, the future Pope Gregory IX: "It is said that both favor the king of France more than the king of England."[47] When Romanus was put in charge of the peace negotiations between France and England, however, the next English embassy examined his attitudes more carefully, "because many feel that there is some suspicion of familiarity (*familiaritas*) between him and the king of France."[48] They were using *familiaritas* in the loose, extended sense, since later in the same report the agents argued that if they were to travel back to France with the legate, they could operate "more familiarly and more usefully (*familiarius et uberius*)" because they would be in his retinue and thus close to his household, or *familia*. Consequently it is likely that on some occasion of which we have no record Romanus had been, as we would say, on familiar terms with Louis.[49] Whatever the bond may have been, it would seem that the king of France could not be expected to be particularly aware of it, for Honorius had to make the connection explicit in the legate's letter of introduction to Louis:

> Among our other beloved brothers [the cardinals], special affection (*speciali affectione*) makes our son Romanus, the cardinal-deacon of Sant' Angelo, zealous for your honor, as we have long known for certain and as your envoys have come to know recently and frequently by many plain proofs [Doc. 15.1].

Thus it appears that Romanus' special affection for Louis was something well known at the curia, and also that it was a prejudice that he made no effort to conceal. Moreover, Louis eventually acknowledged the closeness of the rela-

47. Chaplais, *Diplomatic Documents*, no. 144 = Shirley, *Royal Letters*, no. 200.

48. Chaplais, *Diplomatic Documents*, no. 162 = Shirley, *Royal Letters*, no. 215: "quia multi quandam familiaritatis suspicionem inter ipsum et regem Francie asserebant . . . ."

49. There is no reason to take *familiaritas* in the more specific sense of a relationship by blood or marriage, because, as we have seen, Philip Mousket was mistaken in believing the Frangipani were related to the Capetians (above, n. 6).

tionship by addressing Romanus as "his dearest and special friend" (Doc. 50). Most likely, in his youth Romanus had studied at the University of Paris and thereby had acquired a knowledge of French and an affection for France, which both would be valuable assets in his mission.

For whatever reason, at the time of his legatine appointment he was manifestly Louis' outstanding supporter in the college of cardinals. He himself did not deny his friendship for France when confronted by the two English embassies but adroitly side-stepped the question by insisting in all sincerity on his higher loyalty to the general welfare of the Church and to the cause of peace. From this and subsequent relations with the English we can conclude, therefore, that although he made no secret of his personal affection for France, still he was able to satisfy the English that this constituted no threat to their interests. Nonetheless his pro-French bias was a major qualification for his mission—indeed the only one that Honorius mentioned to Louis. Rome sent to France the cardinal who seemed the most likely to gain the confidence of the king.

The choice of Romanus, then, may be taken as an indication of Rome's new policy. Since Louis had created the current crisis, a cardinal was sent who could deal with him. As a known Capetian sympathizer, Romanus would certainly be well received. But because Honorius made no irreconcilable break with Raymond, it would seem that Romanus was given a free hand to work out what seemed to him to be the best solution under the circumstances. In other words, Honorius was placing his trust in just those qualities that he praised in Romanus. He was no enthusiast like Conrad; instead, he was a paragon of courtly and clerical culture who had the professional attitude of a canonist already tempered by years of administrative service at the curia. Above all, as a realist he wanted men to honor and respect the Roman church, and so to this end he could be counted on to deploy his talents for tactful courtesy and for dogged hard work. He was a man of moderation who could be expected to alienate as few as possible: thus he went as Honorius' bid for a moderate solution.

Romanus' commission and legatine powers

Compared with his predecessor, Conrad, the new legate referred back to Rome for instructions rarely. Presumably the pope trusted his judgment more and therefore gave him a freer hand. In theory the legal powers of both legates were approximately the same, but in practice Romanus was expected to act more independently. This expectation perhaps explains why the curia took such care in drawing up the credentials that authorized him to act as the pope's agent. Certainly Romanus was expected to make far-reaching commitments on the part of the papacy, and it was only prudent to keep a full record of the authority that permitted him to do so. Indeed, events proved the wisdom of such foresight, for his acts did not go unquestioned. Thus, to understand his mission we must review the powers that were entrusted to him in his letters of legation.

Romanus set out with perhaps as many as forty-five papal letters. This set is in fact one of the earliest to have been enregistered, and as such it has considerable interest in itself.[50] The complete contents of this diplomatic pouch are described below in the introduction to Documents 12-21; here we shall mainly be concerned with those letters that define his legatine commission proper.

A contemporary letter informs us that Romanus was "a legate sent from the pope's side (a latere)." In the terminology of that day, the expression legatus a latere was used to designate someone closely associated with the pope, normally but not necessarily a cardinal, who was sent from the curia with sufficient power to perform the mission entrusted to him independently.[51] Thus in the hierarchy of papal agents, the legate a latere ranked the highest and was the most powerful. In general, but with certain exceptions, he could do anything that the pope could do. This normal power of a legatus a latere was usually indicated in his letter of appointment by stating that he was to perform "the office of full legation (plene legationis officium)," and the dignity of his high office was stressed by a biblical allusion that echoed the Lord's appointment of the prophet Jeremiah: "Lo, I have set thee this day over the nations, and over kingdoms, to root up, and to pull down, and to waste, and to destroy, and to build, and to plant" (Jer. i.10). Both of these marks of a legatus a latere appear in Romanus' letters of legation:

> we have entrusted to the same cardinal the office of full legation . . . giving him free power to pull down and to uproot, to build and to plant, to appoint, to ordain, to enact, to define, and to do whatsoever he sees fit to do according to the prudence given to him by God [Doc. 12.5; cf. Doc. 13.1].

There were tacit qualifications, however, that defined these seemingly limitless powers. This is apparent because the general letters of legation were regularly supplemented by special letters that entrusted cases to a legate that were normally reserved for the pope's personal action. Although canon lawyers differed on precisely what cases were reserved to the pope, the principal ones that were not included in the office of full legation involved the right to alter diocesan boundaries, to transfer a bishop from one see to another, to summon a general council, and to grant exemptions.[52] Romanus' duties were in fact enlarged to include

50. Legatine commissions of this period are described by Karl Ruess, Die rechtliche Stellung der päpstlichen Legaten bis Bonifaz VIII (Paderborn, 1912), pp. 119-120.

51. Ruess, Legaten, pp. 108-112. For the quotation, see n. 59, below; cf. n. 27, above.

52. G. Paro, The Right of Papal Legation (Washington, DC, 1947), p. 94; Ruess, Legaten, pp. 124-125. R. C. Figueira, "Papal Reserved Powers and the Limitations on Legatine Authority," in Popes, Teachers, and Canon Law in the Middle Ages, ed. J. R. Sweeney and S. Chodorow (Ithaca, 1989), pp. 191-211.

two of these special faculties: one to hear the claims of the archbishop of Bourges
to primacy over Bordeaux, the other to be present at episcopal elections in
Provence and to direct the electors.[53] Moreover, he was also authorized to absolve
in a number of cases in which normally only the pope could give absolution.[54]

In addition to these reserved cases, there was one other important limitation
on the powers of "full legation": the legate's decisions were not final. Unless
the legate specified in an act that an appeal to the pope was precluded by the
phrase *appellatione remota* (or *postposita*), the way was open for recourse to Rome.
Even if the legate so stipulated, it was always possible that the pope might still
make an exception and hear an appeal regardless. In practice, of course, the pope
tended to uphold the acts of his legate, but the legate's acts were nonetheless
subject to review and were not absolutely binding on the papacy.[55] Thus we
must not be surprised to find the chapters of France appealing Romanus' decision at Bourges to tax the French clergy.

Among the ordinary powers of a legate *a latere*, we are particularly concerned
with those regarding councils. By Romanus' time these were well developed, for
legatine councils had been one of the most powerful instruments of the Gregorian reform movement. The office of full legation included the right to convoke a council from all or any part of the territory over which the legate had
been given authority. The legate presided over any council that he had summoned, and his authority was visibly expressed by the seating arrangements: his
seat was higher than any other, even though, like Romanus, he might be a deacon presiding over archbishops. Most important, the legate alone made the decisions; the others were present merely to give him counsel. Moreover, since the
middle of the twelfth century, these decisions were issued in the legate's own
name. Hence, like the legate's other acts, his conciliar decisions could be implemented immediately without papal confirmation, although by the same
token they could be appealed.[56]

★   ★   ★

Now that the general nature of Romanus' office is clear, let us consider its specific character. Among the several letters announcing his legation, the most important was the one that gave him authority over the clergy of his legation (Doc.
12). The ecclesiastical authorities to whom the letter was addressed are those
who were placed under his authority, so the epistolary address served to define
both the territorial extent of Romanus' legation and those persons subject to his

53. Pressutti, nos. 5328 and 5338 (cf. Doc. 20); Ruess, *Legaten*, pp. 153–155, 157.
54. Doc. 19; Ruess, *Legaten*, pp. 179–182.
55. Ruess, *Legaten*, pp. 172–173.
56. Ruess, *Legaten*, pp. 142–144.

jurisdiction within that area—in a word, borrowed by canonists from Roman public law, his "province." Honorius addressed Romanus' letter of legation to the following prelates:

> to his venerable brothers the archbishops and bishops, and to his beloved sons the abbots, priors, and other prelates of the churches located in the kingdom of France and in Provence; and to the archbishops of Tarentaise, Besançon, Embrun, Aix, Arles, and Vienne and their suffragans, and also to the abbots and other prelates of churches located in their dioceses.

Later in this study we shall have occasion to list all of the archbishoprics included in this description;[57] for the present, it is enough to state that Romanus' legation included not only the kingdom of France but also the kingdom of Burgundy, so he could operate freely on both banks of the Rhone.

In a long, florid prologue, Honorius laments the sorry state of affairs in the province of Narbonne and adjacent regions. Peter's ship, the Church, has been tossed by the tempests of the world so long that it seems that God himself is asleep (Doc. 12.1). More specifically, Honorius has been trying "to find the way and means by which we might be able to raise up the business of peace and the faith, which seemed to have gone under almost completely" in Occitania. His good efforts have been impeded, and indeed almost ruined, by the malice of the inhabitants, who do not receive his discipline with contrite hearts but instead glory in their old errors and in their recent successes (§ 2). Nonetheless, the pope reaffirms his faith in God, who shall soon favor his chosen people again (§3). Therefore, Honorius is sending Romanus, whom he characterizes briefly, to remedy the situation (§ 4). The new legate is also being sent to France and Burgundy because, to accomplish his mission in the Midi, it is "absolutely necessary to have the aid" of the king of France and his kingdom, and also because the legate has other, unspecified business in France. Therefore the pope has given Romanus the office of full legation with France, Provence, and Burgundy as his province (§ 5). Having explained the situation, Honorius concludes with his orders to the addressees:

> Therefore by apostolic writ we command and strictly enjoin all of you that you endeavor to receive him devoutly as legate of the apostolic see, or really to receive us in his person, and to treat him with honor; you are to assist him diligently and faithfully, and you must receive his wholesome recommendations and commands with humility and observe them without dispute. For we shall treat as valid the sentences that he inflicts with good reason on rebels, and (God willing) we shall cause them to be observed inviolably [§ 6].

57. See below, table 1 in chapter 3.

By contrast, the letter that Honorius wrote commending Romanus to the secular authorities is terse and without a hint of apology. It is addressed to all laymen holding positions of authority in the legate's province: "to the noblemen, dukes, counts, barons, and also the rectors and communities of cities and castles" (Doc. 13). Without preamble, they all are simply told that Romanus is being sent to deal with some unspecified but pressing business in France and Provence. The bulk of the brief letter paraphrases the tenor of the longer one to the clergy: Romanus' character is described and his commission stated (§ 1); then the same orders to receive him that were given to clergy are repeated to the laity (§ 2).

Two laymen received special letters introducing the legate. One, to King Louis, was a softened version of that sent to the secular authorities (Doc. 15). As we have already seen, it stressed the legate's personal affection for the king. The nature of his business, however, is masked in generality: he is being sent "because of the pressing necessity of dealing with complex affairs" (§ 1). Unlike the clergy and laity in general, the king is not commanded to obey the legate; instead, he is asked and exhorted to be reverently attentive to the legate's warnings and counsels, which he will find to his advantage. This evidently was more a letter of personal introduction than a formal diplomatic credential. The nature of the legate's business did not need to be explained to Louis, since the legation had been initiated at his request. The letter certainly suggests that Romanus was sent with the special purpose of serving as the king's adviser and helper.

The other letter (Doc. 10) had already been sent to Raymond VII of Toulouse weeks earlier, on 31 January 1225. The count is informed that Romanus is being sent as papal legate to the kingdom of France and to Provence for the purpose of reform. The count's cooperation is sought in a distinctive variation of the formula that Louis received. Raymond is not asked and exhorted; as an excommunicate, he is not even commanded; instead, he is told that if he wants to be reconciled, "you must be so reverently and obediently attentive to him [Romanus], and so humbly and effectually acquiesce to his wholesome warnings and commands that you may be able to deserve the favor of God and the apostolic see." The contrast with Louis' letter leaves no doubt that Romanus' mission was to help Louis in his plan to bring Occitania under royal control.

Taken together, these four letters of legation that we have just examined (Docs. 10, 12-13, 15) provide a rough outline of the approach that the new legate was to take. He was not coming to resume negotiations with Raymond, who was expected to obey or be damned. Romanus' diplomacy was directed instead towards Louis, with whom he came to collaborate in a royal crusade against Occitania. Louis would supply the men if the Church would finance the operation, and one of Romanus' principal tasks would be to arrange for a financial sub-

sidy from the French church. This explains why his letter of legation to the ecclesiastical authorities provided such an elaborate justification of his mission, and
why it plainly stated that the king's support was absolutely necessary. This letter
was designed to be read to the clergy assembled at the Council of Bourges as an
explicit assurance that the proposed royal crusade had the pope's approval. No
doubt the French clergy were all too well aware that in 1223 the legate Conrad
had, on his own initiative, secured their consent to a similar scheme that ultimately had proved unacceptable to Honorius. Now the pope was in effect assuring them that his new legate was implementing a policy that was Honorius'
own. Such an announcement would forestall objections, remove hesitations, and
generally strengthen support for the crusade. Since the secular authorities required no delicate handling of this sort, the letter to them was severely *pro forma*.

Romanus in France: minor acts of the legation

Armed with these commissions, Romanus left Rome on 3 March 1225; he
planned to spend Easter at Lyon, on the French border, and then to enter the
kingdom on Easter Monday, 31 March.[58] Apparently he kept to his timetable
fairly well, for by 14 April the king of England was expecting to hear at any moment that the legate had arrived in France,[59] and on 9 May Romanus dated a
letter from Paris.[60] Seven months later, Romanus held his legatine council at
Bourges as the first major step towards the royal crusade. The intervening
months were largely devoted to his two principal tasks—negotiating a truce and
promoting the crusade in Occitania—but at the same time he was also concerned with many lesser matters that we may note in passing to round out our
picture of the legate and his work.

★   ★   ★

Since most matters in canon law could be judged by a legate as well as by the
pope himself, Romanus naturally would receive many cases in which the litigants hoped to avoid a costly trip to Rome. Normally, he would act much as the

---

58. Chaplais, *Diplomatic Documents*, no. 162 = Shirley, *Royal Letters*, no. 215.

59. Henry III wrote to Llywelyn, prince of North Wales, that he was waiting "pro adventu
cuiusdam Legati, a latere Domini Papae ad Regem Franciae destinati, pro pace inter nos &
ipsum reformanda . . .": Rymer, *Foedera*, I (1727), 277, ad an. 1225. Day and month given by
Petit-Dutaillis, who concluded from this letter that Romanus arrived at the end of April
(*Louis*, p. 273), but obviously the legate could have been in France for several weeks before
the news reached England. Henry's source of information may have been no more than the
letter cited above in n. 48.

60. Chaplais, *Diplomatic Documents*, no. 167 = Shirley, *Royal Letters*, no. 237.

pope himself would have done: he would commission others to hear the case and report their findings back to him, whereupon he would pass sentence in his own name.[61] The loser, of course, could appeal to Rome, as we know happened in eight instances that are recorded in the papal registers.[62] We do not know precisely when Romanus dealt with any of these cases, but they are nonetheless noteworthy as an indication of his judicial modus operandi: he spent relatively little of his time on judicial matters, most of which he delegated to others.

One delegated case is especially noteworthy because it shows Romanus' skillful maneuvering in a difficult situation. His judges-delegate had upheld the decision of a lower court and thereby enabled debtors to evade their obligations; Louis VIII requested Romanus to provide a remedy, and although the legate could have done so, he was not about to alter canon law to accommodate the king; instead, he procrastinated by referring the matter to the pope, who apparently never replied, even after Louis repeated his request (Doc. 50).

We do not know how Romanus dealt with another thorny case, but it is worth mentioning because it shows the sort of problems that were referred to him. A former legate, Guala, had thoughtlessly required concubinary priests to go all the way to Rome to be reconciled, and although Honorius had recently permitted the bishops of Rouen province to deal with such matters locally, still the bishop of Coutances was uncertain what penance he should impose on a second offender, so he sent the case to Romanus (Doc. 52).

A few of the more important cases were heard by Romanus in person. For example, in October 1225 the bishop of Meaux and the abbey of Jouarre accepted him as arbitrator in a dispute, which he settled the next month in the abbey's favor.[63] Similarly, on 7 September he brokered a compromise between the Laon cathedral chapter and Enguerrand de Coucy.[64] He also gave personal attention to an attempt of some masters at the University of Paris to secede to Orléans and Angers.[65] Many of these cases had been assigned to him by the pope, for instance disputes over the seal of the University of Paris, over the election of a bishop of Carcassonne, and over the feudal status of the archbishop of Rouen.[66] One such case is relevant to the Council of Bourges. A dispute con-

61. E.g. the decision of Romanus' delegates in *Cartulaires de l'abbaye de Molesme*, ed. Jacques Laurent, II (Paris, 1911), 481 (no. 637); cited by Maleczek, *Kardinalskolleg*, p. 194, n. 509.

62. Auvray, nos. 409, 443, 622, 781, 1409, 1448, 1577, and 2841.

63. Auvray, no. 447. This is the only case that is dated in the registers; the others mentioned in this paragraph may have occurred at any time during the legation but are discussed here as being typical.

64. Maleczek, *Kardinalskolleg*, pp. 192-193, n. 502, citing Laon, Arch. dép. Aisne, G 1850, fol. 40v.

65. Auvray, no. 641; Potthast, no. 8735 (5 May 1231, inc. *Cum sicut nobis*).

66. See chapter 8, below, and Docs. 21 and 53.

cerning the claims of the archbishop of Bourges to primacy over Bordeaux had been in the courts for years, and Romanus was content to prolong it still further. The archbishop of Bordeaux had regularly refused to cooperate with the papal judges, and Romanus had the same experience with him; but the legate hesitated to impair his own effectiveness in France by pressing the matter. Instead, at the Council of Bourges he arranged the seating so as to avoid the issue, and at his suggestion both parties were summoned to Rome in 1227 to resolve it.[67]

He also seems to have taken personal cognizance of cases involving lapses of clerical discipline, especially the more delicate and scandalous ones.[68] For example, in the diocese of Thérouanne he deprived two Augustinian canons of their benefices, and at Reims he seems to have disciplined the provost of the cathedral chapter for dancing with an abbess and sending her a sexually suggestive gift.[69] Many of these irregularities turned up when the legate made a formal visitation, or inspection, of a religious house. A legate could visit any community, but usually he concentrated on those houses that were directly dependent on the pope and thus exempt from canonical visitation by their diocesan bishop. At St–Bertin, he cooperated with the abbot in suppressing a community of women associated with the monastery.[70] In another case, a personal visit to the monastery of St–Pierre at Uzerche, in the diocese of Limoges, convinced Romanus that the house was so corrupt it could not reform itself, so he put it temporarily under the control of the monastery of St–Michel at Cluse, in Savoy, and left the final decision to the pope himself. When the legate returned to Rome, he submitted a written report to Gregory IX, who made the arrangement permanent.[71] Early in his legation, Romanus had tried to visit the venerable monastery of Luxeuil, which refused to accept any visitor other than the pope himself, but Honorius rejected their appeal and directed Romanus to visit the house in person.[72] Although Romanus once did abuse his right of vis-

---

67. Auvray, no. 98 (30 May 1227). See intro. to Docs. 12–21, nn. 9–10.

68. An exception would seem to be the case of three canons who were accused of murdering their abbot; the Chronicle of Tours says that they were accused of this crime before Romanus' judges-delegate but fled rather than plead their case (*Rec. hist. Gaules*, XVIII, 308–309).

69. Auvray, nos. 2109 and 3782. On the latter, which is known only through a malicious rumor, see C. Cuissard, "Election de Guillaume de Bussi, évêque d'Orléans, et principaux actes de son épiscopat (1238–58)," *Mémoires de la Société archéologique et historique de l'Orléanais*, XXV (1894), 561–620, at pp. 577–581. The gift was the figure of a ram with gilded horns and genitals.

70. Doc. 38.1 and *Les Chartes de Saint-Bertin*, ed. D. Haigneré and O. Bled, 4 vols. (St–Omer, 1886–1899), including both Romanus' act (I, 337–338, no. 754) and its ratification by Gregory IX on 31 May 1230 (I, 344–345, no. 768).

71. Auvray, no. 459.

72. Pressutti, no. 5737 (29 Nov. 1225).

itation in order to pressure the cathedral chapter at Rouen to drop its appeal against the crusading tenth (Doc. 53), in general his record of visitation shows an extraordinary commitment to the curial program of monastic reform, which was to be an issue at the Council of Bourges (see chapter 8).

The record of the minor business of Romanus' legation is admittedly fragmentary, but it nonetheless conveys an overall impression of the legate's impact on the French church. Although he was not himself principally concerned with reform, still he made papal justice available through his judges-delegate. His decisions seem to have been wise ones, for on appeal Gregory IX rarely, if ever, reversed them. Thus with a minimum of personal attention Romanus was able to make his presence felt throughout his legation. Moreover, by intervening personally against moral delinquencies, he created for himself a reputation for integrity and rectitude that would gain the respect of the French clergy. The positive side of their experience of Romanus was eventually distilled in the eulogy by Hélinand. No doubt Romanus had earned their confidence.

Negotiations for an Anglo-French truce

Most of Romanus' energy was devoted to the major missions confided to him. Gaining the respect of the French clergy was itself a step towards the efficient organization of the crusade, but negotiations with Louis VIII claimed the greater part of his attention. The legate's position was a delicate one. On the one hand, he was supposed to arrange for a royal crusade, for which the good will of the king of France was all-important; on the other hand, he could not afford to alienate the king of England, who was one of the most important vassals of the papacy. Ever since the French invasion of Aquitaine, the English had been hoping that the pope would restore the status quo *ante bellum*, and to this end the English envoys were hoping in January 1225 to hasten Romanus' arrival in France.[73] At the same time, the English were preparing for a counteroffensive in Aquitaine, which began at Easter, just when the legate arrived in France, and which continued until November, when the French were finally forced out of Gascony, though not Poitou.[74] Even before Romanus had arrived in Paris, the tide of war had turned in favor of the English in Gascony, and consequently they were not inclined to compromise in the peace negotiations that he conducted before the crusade. The French, as we have seen, had been intriguing at Rome to prevent Honorius from condemning their invasion, and they had furthered

73. Chaplais, *Diplomatic Documents*, no. 162 = Shirley, *Royal Letters*, no. 215: "poterimus . . . adventum ejusdem [legati] in Franciam festinare. . . . "

74. K. Norgate, *The Minority of Henry the Third* (London, 1912), p. 252; N. Denholm-Young, *Richard of Cornwall* (New York, 1947), pp. 4–6.

that design by forcing him to return to the project of a royal crusade. As long as Honorius was relying on Louis' support in Occitania, the pope would not alienate him by giving the English the unqualified support they wanted in Aquitaine.

Romanus accordingly assumed the stance of a neutral intermediary between the two combatants. During the first year of his legation, he arranged for five English embassies to negotiate with Louis. In the end nothing came of these meetings, of which little more than the occasions and the participants are known with any certainty. Earlier investigators have made little attempt to penetrate the obscurity of these proceedings, but for us the effort is worthwhile because they were Romanus' principal preoccupation during the first months of his legation. Let us first review the established facts, and then make an excursus to determine Romanus' attitude towards the English during the negotiations. By this round-about route, we can arrive at a deeper understanding of the course of the negotiations and why they broke down.

★   ★   ★

Not long after the cardinal arrived in Paris, on 9 May 1225 he wrote a gracious note to the English justiciar, Hubert de Burgh, who in effect was ruling in the young king's name. Romanus praised the justiciar's devotion to the Roman church and urged him to show it now by procuring peace between France and England.[75] Hubert, however, had needed no invitation. The English had been expecting Romanus in April and had accordingly dispatched an embassy on 8 May to consult with him and treat with Louis. Two abbots were selected for the mission, from Westminster and Stratford,[76] and their relatively modest rank suggests that nothing conclusive was expected from the first contact. With the English spring offensive going well in Gascony, they were no longer as eager for the legate's good offices as they had been in February. The abbots were present at the royal great council that Louis held at Paris on 15 May. The occasion is known only from this notice in the Chronicle of Tours:

> On the octave of the Lord's Ascension, King Louis celebrated a council at Paris. There, with Romanus, cardinal of Sant' Angelo, the legate who had re-

75. Chaplais, *Diplomatic Documents*, no. 167 = Shirley, *Royal Letters*, no. 237, dated *sine anno*. Shirley placed the letter *sub anno* 1226, but Petit-Dutaillis correctly dated it 1225 (*Louis*, p. 273, n. 5).

76. *Rotuli litterarum clausarum in Turri Londinensi asservati*, ed. T. D. Hardy, 2 vols., Record Commissioners (London, 1833–1844), II, 72b (8 May 1225), with separate letters for Louis and the legate. For this and subsequent embassies, see Petit-Dutaillis, *Louis*, p. 273, and Norgate, *Minority*, p. 253.

cently come to France, the king carefully considered many things concerning the affairs of the kingdom, of the king of England, and of the land of the Albigensians [Doc. 3.1].

Evidently this preliminary discussion encouraged further negotiation, for as soon as news of the council reached England in late May, a second embassy was dispatched, this time composed of weightier lords, temporal as well as spiritual, for the bishops of London and Lincoln were accompanied by the earls of Pembroke and Essex.[77]

While waiting for the second English embassy, Romanus accompanied Louis into Flanders, where on 30 May at Péronne the king interviewed a hermit who was claiming with considerable success to be Baldwin IX, the lost count of Flanders.[78] The next episode we know from a rare surviving report made by Romanus to the pope. The new English envoys had arrived in Paris on 16 June demanding that Louis not only give up his recent conquests but also stop trying to win over the viscount of Thouars, one of the key lords of Poitou. Louis was of course not willing to accept these terms, and he almost broke off peace negotiations altogether, but Romanus persuaded him to send the English delegation back to Henry for better terms.[79] The English ambassadors were supposed to return with a new proposal by 29 July, but in the meantime Louis rendered their mission pointless by completely winning over the viscount. First he met with Aimeric de Thouars at Chinon on 2 July and extended the truce between them, which had just expired, for another twenty days.[80] This gave Louis the time he needed to persuade the viscount to change sides at the next royal council, which met at Paris on 21 July. The Chronicle of Tours summarized the result:

> King Louis convoked a council at Paris on the vigil of the feast of the Magdalene, and there in the presence of the legate and of the nuncios of the king of England, the viscount of Thouars did homage to the king.[81]

Although the English, who received their orders in London on 4 July, had had plenty of time to make a more attractive offer, and even to bribe the legate, the new alliance rendered their mission pointless, so on 24 July Romanus sent them home with polite assurances that he appreciated Henry's position and cooper-

---

77. *Patent Rolls of the Reign of Henry III, 1216–1225* (London, 1901), pp. 579-580, dated 30 May 1225.

78. Chronicle of Tours, in *Rec. hist. Gaules*, XVIII, 308; Petit-Dutaillis, *Louis*, pp. 396-398.

79. Chaplais, *Diplomatic Documents*, no. 171.

80. Chronicle of Tours, in *Rec. hist. Gaules*, XVIII, 308.

81. Chronicle of Tours, in *Rec. hist. Gaules*, XVIII, 308; Petit-Dutaillis, *Louis*, p. 263 (cf. p. 241) and reg. nos. 264-267 (p. 485).

ation.[82] Louis had won a great diplomatic victory because his hold on Poitou was now considerably strengthened by securing the loyalty of one of its greatest lords. To be sure, the viscount and his family were paid handsomely for their support, but the money was well spent, for they remained loyal to France thereafter. As we shall see, this victory probably had an adverse effect on the truce negotiations, however, because it deprived Louis of a negotiable issue. If the viscount had remained loyal to the English, Louis could have offered to include him in the proposed truce; but now the king had deprived the English of their last great foothold in Poitou and would hardly be inclined to relinquish his advantage.

After the submission of Thouars, both sides broke off peace negotiations for several months while Louis redoubled his efforts to retain La Réole, his last stronghold in Gascony and now his best bargaining point. Just before it fell on 13 November, a fourth peace conference took place at Melun on 8 November. In mid-October the bishops of Lincoln and Rochester had been sent with others to renew the negotiations;[83] once again they presented their proposals at a great royal council with the legate present, and we know a bit more about the proceedings:

> In this council [wrote the chronicler of Tours], there was a good deal of discussion about making a new truce between the king of France and the king of England, and also about the Albigensian business, but for the moment nothing could be decided about these matters [Doc. 3.2].

By this time a permanent peace was out of the question; only the possibility of a truce was discussed, and no agreement could be reached even on that. The reason for the deadlock is plain from another source: Louis was absolutely determined to retain what he held in Poitou. The Dunstable annalist gives Louis' reply to the English, which can be assigned to this occasion because he consulted Jean de Brienne, who in July had been absent in Italy.[84]

> Cardinal Romanus, legate of the apostolic see, was sent to France to warn King Louis that he should restore Normandy, Anjou, and Aquitaine to King Henry

---

82. Chaplais, *Diplomatic Documents*, no. 173 (24 July 1225). Romanus had personal reasons for gratitude, as Henry's agents came with promises "de promotione nepotum vestrorum et aliorum quorundam de vestris": *Patent Rolls, 1216–1225*, p. 580 (4 July 1225). Romanus evidently accepted the favor, for in October he was sent the first installment of his nephew's subsidy (see below, n. 83). On 2 July the English chancery had already placed Peter under royal protection (p. 537), and on 12 August he was granted a pension in lieu of a benefice (p. 543).

83. *Patent Rolls, 1216–1225*, pp. 552–553 (actually close letters); *Rotuli litterarum clausarum*, ed. Hardy, II, 64b and 83a. The bishop of Lincoln brought with him ten marks in cash, as the current year's half payment of the annual royal subsidy granted to Romanus' nephew, Peter *la Papa* (ed. Hardy, II, 64b and 65a).

84. L. Bréhier, "Brienne (Jean de)," *DHGE*, X, 698–709, at col. 704.

of England. After taking counsel with King John of Jerusalem and with his other barons, Louis replied that he would not return to the English one foot of the land that his father Philip had left to him when he died [Doc. 2.3].

The English annalist seems to have misapprehended the issue, which concerned not lands that Louis had inherited but the ones he had himself conquered the previous year. Still this confused account does suggest that the negotiations finally broke down because the king of France was not prepared to concede any part of Poitou, or even the besieged fortress of La Réole, which was all he really had to bargain with at that point.

Romanus and Fawkes de Bréauté

Our understanding of these rather obscure negotiations, and especially of Romanus' role in them, can be appreciably enlarged from a consideration of his involvement in a parallel series of events, namely the affair of Fawkes de Bréauté.[85] This Norman soldier of fortune had been one of King John's chief henchmen; during Henry's minority, he had remained a mainstay of the crown, but in 1224 the justiciar, Hubert de Burgh, had maneuvered Fawkes out of power. While Louis was invading Aquitaine in the summer of 1224, Henry and his vassals were besieging Fawkes' stronghold, Bedford castle. After its surrender, Fawkes was sent penniless into exile on 26 October. During the winter he was detained in France by Louis, but at Easter 1225 he set out for Rome to see if the pope would help him regain Henry's favor, or at least his own fortune. Honorius was sympathetic, both because he knew how loyal and useful Fawkes had been to the crown and because he already suspected him to be a victim of intriguing, jealous rivals at court. Therefore the pope agreed to intercede for him with Henry, and for this purpose he sent Otto, a subdeacon and papal chaplain, to England as his nuncio.[86] About the same time, on 4 June 1225, he instructed Romanus to get Louis to grant Fawkes asylum in France while he awaited reconciliation.[87]

85. D. A. Carpenter, *The Minority of Henry III* (Berkeley and Los Angeles, 1990), pp. 343-370; C. Ellis, *Hubert de Burgh* (London, 1952), pp. 67-86; N. Vincent, *Peter des Roches* (Cambridge, Eng., 1996), pp. 215- 222; Norgate, *Minority*, pp. 224-249; F. M. Powicke, *King Henry III and the Lord Edward* (Oxford, 1947), I, 61-66; K. O. Nowak, "Fawkes de Breauté" (Ph.D. diss., Stanford University, 1974), pp. 217-299.

86. Otto bore a letter on Fawkes' behalf from Honorius to Henry, inc. *Certum est fili* (unrecorded by Potthast and Pressutti!), which is known only from the Crowland annal for 1225: undated text in Walter of Coventry, *Memoriale*, ed. W. Stubbs, Rolls Series, no. 58, 2 vols. (London, 1872-1873), II, 272-274; cf. prolegomena to Doc. 44, below, and R. Kay, "Walter of Coventry and the Barnwell Chronicle," *Traditio*, LIV (1999), 141-167, at p. 155, n. 54.

87. Pressutti, no. 5519.

News of Otto's mission preceded him to England, however, and greatly disturbed the king, and more especially his counselors who had procured Fawkes' downfall, because in these machinations they had hoodwinked the pope and even ignored his orders.[88] They did not know precisely what Otto was empowered to do and feared the worst, so a trio of English agents was hurriedly dispatched to Rome with countercharges against Fawkes that would, it was hoped, turn the pope against him. In the meantime, Otto had to be neutralized, preferably by keeping him out of England, and by no means letting him bring Fawkes with him. Accordingly, the three agents were instructed to seek out Romanus on their way to Rome and enlist his aid. They found him at St-Omer during the third week of August 1225. After conferring with the legate for several days, the agents sent a detailed report back to London, which, with its postscript,[89] is our principal source for this curious episode that reveals better than any other the legate's talents in action.

The first of the English agents found Romanus on Monday, 18 August 1225. On the previous day, a messenger had brought Romanus the pope's letter instructing him to seek asylum for Fawkes, together with the news that Otto was on his way and that Fawkes had been captured by a personal enemy in Burgundy. Romanus had promptly written Louis to secure both release and asylum for Fawkes. The legate quickly changed his mind, however, when he read the letter from King Henry that the English agents brought for him. Honorius had angered the king by intervening in a matter that was none of his business, and unless Romanus could somehow restore the king's confidence, the English would no longer accept the papal legate as mediator in the peace talks. Accordingly, Romanus quickly counteracted his previous letter to Louis by having a royal clerk intimate to the king that Fawkes was an enemy of the French crown. At the same time Romanus also wrote to the pope and to certain cardinals, pointing out that by supporting Fawkes they were alienating the king of England and thereby making it impossible for the legate to negotiate the Anglo-French peace or truce without which Louis was unlikely to go crusading in the South (Docs. 22A and 22B).

Then Romanus worked out a plan that would delay matters for at least two months, so the English agents would have time to go to Rome, lay Henry's case before Honorius, and return. For our purposes, the details are less important than the fact that Romanus contrived them. First, Romanus would confer with Otto before the nuncio left France and would forewarn the English government of the nuncio's intentions to the extent that this could be done without a breach of confidence on Romanus' part. If Fawkes could be kept in captivity, probably

88. Pressutti, nos. 4566 and 5243; Powicke, *King Henry*, I, 56.

89. Chaplais, *Diplomatic Documents*, nos. 182–183 = Shirley, *Royal Letters*, nos. 221–222.

Romanus could persuade Otto to stay in France seeking his release; but if that failed, Romanus would try to keep Otto in France by showing him Henry's angry letter and by arguing that the nuncio should wait for further instructions from Rome. The English agents promised Romanus an immense bribe if Otto did stay in France, "although he refused to hear this." If, on the other hand, Otto went to England despite all the legate could do, then Romanus suggested other ways to deal with the situation:

> This is the advice of the legate [the agents reported] if Otto cannot be held back by any reason and should proceed to England. Let him be received with honor, but you should subtly contrive delays. First put off hearing how and why he has come and conferring with him about it. When this has finally happened, you should delay by deliberating about these matters. After consulting your ministers, you can tell him that you also wish to take counsel with your vassals because certain questions were raised that touch you and your kingdom, and you should set as distant a date for doing so as you can. As a last resort you should request that he do nothing about his business until you receive a papal mandate from Rome, and if necessary persuade him with a bribe.[90]

Here, more than anywhere else, we encounter Romanus the realist in diplomatic intrigue. Such Fabian tactics were certainly commonplace at the curia, and probably in London as well, but rarely do we find them expressly stated this way. Romanus went on to warn Henry not to let the nuncio communicate with Fawkes' supporters in England, lest the pope command a full-scale investigation in consequence of what Otto might learn. Finally, the legate gave the agents the letters he had written to Honorius and "to those cardinals in whom he placed special confidence" (Docs. 22A and 22B), and he explained to them that he had not elaborated his argument "lest he seem suspect or corrupt." The English took the letters and set off for Rome, while they sent a messenger back to London with their report and a copy of Romanus' complaints, together with a plea that his role in all this be kept absolutely secret (secretissima).

This episode is all the more tantalizing because we do not know in any detail how the plans worked out. Eventually Fawkes was liberated and Otto arrived in England, but whether Romanus succeeded in delaying these events is unknown. Probably the English had overreacted to the news of Otto's impending visit; certainly, he himself was surprised that Henry had been angered by his mission and protested, when he learned of it, that he had been sent only for "the advantage and honor of the realm."[91] Indeed, it is possible that the English agents en-

---

90. Chaplais, *Diplomatic Documents*, no. 182 = Shirley, *Royal Letters*, no. 221.
91. Chaplais, *Diplomatic Documents*, no. 190 = Shirley, *Royal Letters*, no. 223.

countered Otto on their way to Rome and found that their appeal was unnecessary. At least there is no record in the papal registers of any response to their appeal, probably because none was necessary. In fact, Henry had no trouble from Otto when the nuncio finally presented his message from Honorius. The pope asked that Fawkes' property and his wife be restored to him, and Henry replied that Fawkes had been justly condemned by due process of law and that anyway it was none of the pope's concern. "When Master Otto heard this, he stopped bothering the king any more about Fawkes" (Doc. 43.2). Fawkes reacted by returning to Rome, where he persuaded Honorius to send another nuncio to secure at least a reconciliation with his wife, who was independently wealthy; but Honorius prudently delayed this mission until July 1226, after the crusade was well under way.[92] Nothing came of the request, however, and Fawkes soon died at Troyes, burdened by poverty and debt.

Why no truce was made

This excursus on the affair of Fawkes provides an essential clue to the posture of Romanus in the negotiations for an Anglo-French truce. We must believe the legate when he writes both to the pope and to the cardinals about the consequences of alienating the English by supporting Fawkes:

> As a result, it seems that the negotiation of a peace or truce between the illustrious kings of England and France, for which God knows we have worked hard, cannot be brought to a successful conclusion. And thus in our opinion the Albigensian business may be as it were completely blown away [Doc. 22B.3; cf. 22A.4].

Thus it not only appears that Romanus was working zealously for peace, or at least a truce, but also that by late August 1225 his problems were with the English, who apparently were disinclined to accept any compromise solution. Moreover, these letters to the curia show us what Romanus' priorities were: his primary goal was the crusade, and he wanted to pacify the English because otherwise there might be no crusade. French policy was no doubt responsible for the connection. Early in 1224, Louis had insisted that he would not crusade for Honorius unless the pope arranged a truce with England (Doc. 7.5), and the need was now all the greater since the French had seized Poitou. Romanus' efforts for peace, then, were doubtless in earnest.

---

92. Pressutti, nos. 6016 (11 July 1226), ed. Horoy, V, 123–126 (no. 174), where the nuncio Otto's name (*Octo*) is mistakenly expanded to *Octavianus*; cf. nos. 6014 and 6017.

The surprising thing is that he failed to arrange a peace and yet the crusade did take place. This paradoxical turn of events strongly suggests that the situation changed at some time after the letter to Master Thomas (Doc. 22B) was written in late summer 1225. In the end Louis probably proved more flexible than he once had been. The reason was that by the end of the summer he had lost the means to conclude an acceptable truce.

In May 1225, when the negotiations began, Louis still had something to offer the English in Poitou, namely the viscounty of Thouars. As long as it remained loyal to the English, he would lose nothing by letting them keep it during a truce; but after the viscount's submission to Louis in July, this possibility was no longer a bargaining point. Poitou now formed a compact block that was at least nominally loyal to France, and Louis evidently felt that he could rely on the lords of Poitou, because during the crusade he left them behind to defend their lands against a possible English attack.[93] This hold on Poitou was an advantage that Louis was not about to surrender. Thus by mid-July the French had only one thing to offer the English in return for a truce—La Réole. As the English were then besieging it, Louis did what he could to hold on to his sole expendable advantage, but by November it was plain that this last outpost in Gascony would soon fall to the English. By gaining Thouars and losing La Réole, Louis found himself with nothing to offer the English that he was prepared to give. Accordingly he announced at the November conference that he would not consider ceding any land to the English. Presumably he would accept a truce on the basis of the status quo, but that proposal was disadvantageous to the English because they would gain nothing while Louis was consolidating his position in Poitou and extending his influence into Occitania.

Understandably the English broke off negotiations with Louis and turned again to Honorius. Two months later, on 8 January 1226, the papal chancery drew up a condemnation of those lords of Aquitaine, and especially the Poitivans, who had changed their allegiance from Henry to Louis.[94] This was the strong measure that the English had tried to secure in August 1224. The timing suggests that Honorius had put them off with hopes of a negotiated settlement, but when that failed, he felt obliged to condemn the turncoat barons. But according to the Chronicle of Tours, Honorius' condemnation was "immediately suspended because the king of France and the legate sent to Rome and also because money intervened."[95] No doubt Romanus did again insist that the crusade would be blown away; but it is hard to believe that the pope needed to be

93. Petit-Dutaillis, *Louis*, p. 276.
94. Pressutti, no. 5776.
95. *Rec. hist. Gaules*, XVIII, 313: "Sed Rege Franciae mittente ad curiam et legato, necnon et interveniente pecunia, literae illae statim positae sunt in suspenso."

reminded of this consequence, so it seems more likely that he had always intended to suspend his sentence.[96]

As the departure date for the crusade drew near, both sides made another effort to conclude a truce in March 1226. Although details are lacking, it would seem that at one point Romanus secured Louis' consent to terms that he thought were acceptable to the English, but at the last minute the negotiations failed for reasons unknown.[97] Accordingly, Louis' crusade took place while he was technically still at war with the English.

Romanus had prepared the pope for this eventuality. When Honorius received word that Louis had taken the Cross, the pope promptly instructed his legate, probably in mid-March 1226, not to let the crusading king molest the lands of Christian princes, especially those of Henry III. Further provisions for crusading without a truce came later that spring, for on 26 April, Henry was warned not to molest Louis during the crusade.[98] A state of war was no excuse, Honorius argued, since he had often urged the king of England to make a truce. According to canon law, Louis, as the temporal overlord of Occitania, was obliged to undertake the crusade, and hence he had no real choice in the matter. Therefore Henry must cooperate in three respects: first, he must not assist Raymond of Toulouse; second, if he wanted the papacy to force the barons of Aquitaine to honor their oaths of allegiance to Henry, then the king must not force the issue but wait patiently until the crusade is over; and third, he should not wage war on Louis, lest the French host assembled for the crusade be turned against the English, in which case Henry could expect no support from Honorius.[99] It was an appeal to political realism rather than to piety. Honorius offered Henry a carrot and a stick by promising the pope's support against the turncoat barons after the crusade and by threatening to withhold that and any other support if Henry prosecuted the war regardless.

96. According to the bishop of Coventry, writing apparently in 1227, the pope told him that cardinals had been opposed to the original condemnation but had advised the suspension, which he could not now revoke because they would not agree. Petit-Dutaillis, *Louis*, p. 274, citing Rymer, *Foedera*, I.i (London, 1816), 174 = I (London, 1727), 271, s.a. 1224. Undated letter to the bishop of Chichester, inc. *Dilectionem vestram latere*, primarily concerning a dispensation for Henry III to marry Yolande, daughter of the count of Brittany. Rymer found it in the Tower of London, but it does not appear with letters of like provenance in Chaplais, *Diplomatic Documents* (cf. no. 206).

97. Petit-Dutaillis, *Louis*, p. 275. Before making a truce or peace, Henry III sought the counsel of the count of La Marche, to whom he sent the abbot of Beaulieu on 21 March 1226: *Rotuli litterarum clausarum*, ed. Hardy, II, 149a. The letter was originally entered on the roll as being "*Legato Francie*," which was cancelled and "*Comiti Marche*" substituted.

98. Pressutti, no. 5904.

99. Pressutti, no. 5930 (13 May 1226).

Honorius did not want to alienate the English, and he feared that Romanus, in his zeal for the crusade, might overreact to some English border raid by excommunicating Henry III or his brother, Richard of Cornwall, count of Poitou and nominal commander of the English forces in Aquitaine. Therefore on 15 May, Honorius ordered Romanus not to excommunicate either of them except by the pope's express command; and both beneficiaries were so informed, with a warning that they do nothing to deserve such an order from Honorius.[100]

Thus the pope managed to maintain a delicate balance in his relations with both powers, and what is more, his efforts were for the most part successful. With the exception of one minor incident, the war in Aquitaine remained quiescent throughout the crusade of 1226. Although Romanus did not manage to secure a formal truce, nonetheless his yearlong efforts to retain the confidence of the English in the papacy made possible the informal armistice that Honorius imposed. Peace was preserved by giving the English good reason to prefer it to war and by balancing favors and threats to one side with similar ones to the other. Since the cardinals are said to have opposed the keystone of this plan—the condemnation of the forsworn barons of Aquitaine—Romanus may well have been its architect.

Romanus negotiates a Franco-papal crusade

At the same time that Romanus was trying to arrange an Anglo-French truce, he was also negotiating with Louis over the king's terms for undertaking a royal crusade in Occitania. From the Chronicle of Tours we know that both the truce and the crusade were on the agenda at the royal councils held at Paris on 15 May and at Melun on 8 November 1225. The two problems were interconnected, but at first the truce was more pressing because when Romanus arrived in April it was already too late in the season to arrange a crusade for the summer of 1225. The main issues were probably defined at Paris in May, and then during the summer the legate concentrated on the peace problem, which alone was considered at Paris on 21 July. If the crusade was to take place next summer, it would have to be planned before spring, so in the autumn of 1225 Romanus shifted his attention to this problem. It reappeared on the agenda of the royal council at Melun on 8 November, when king and cardinal probably arrived at a preliminary understanding; it was the main concern of the council of the clergy that the legate held at Bourges on 30 November, when Romanus began to implement his part of the bargain; and it was finally agreed upon at the great council held jointly by Romanus and Louis at Paris on 28–31 January 1226.

100. Pressutti, nos. 5938 and 5939.

Although no sources describe the issues that were involved, these can readily be inferred by comparing the terms on which Louis had proposed to undertake the crusade in 1224 (Doc. 7) with those that were finally agreed upon two years later in January 1226 (Doc. 26). The two documents are strikingly different. Indeed, only two minor points remained unchanged: those who took the Cross against the Albigensians were to receive the same indulgence that was granted to crusaders in the Holy Land (Doc. 7.1; Doc. 26.2), and the king was free to go to and return from the crusade as he pleased (Doc. 7.10; Doc. 24.1). All the other proposals that Louis had made in 1224 were altered, many of them drastically, and all but one in favor of the Church. This may seem strange in view of the fact that the proposals of 1224 had for a while been agreeable to Honorius, but the explanation is simply that the situation was different now. Then the initiative for a crusade had come from the Church; now it came from Louis. Although Honorius had been pressured by Louis into reopening negotiations for a crusade, the pope was no longer willing to concede as much as he once had been. The alarmist legate Conrad had been removed from the scene, and in the meantime it had become clear that a reconciliation with Raymond was a viable alternative. Therefore Romanus was in a position to drive a hard bargain with the king. The points of difference are worth considering in detail because they reflect and reveal the conflicting values of the two allies.

★　★　★

1. The most important question concerned the coordination of spiritual with temporal authority on the crusade. In 1224 Louis had wanted Conrad replaced as papal legate by the archbishop of Bourges, a French prelate over whom the crown could exert enough influence to virtually control the crusade. Moreover, he wanted the legate's decisions to be final and not subject to appeal to the pope (Doc. 7.7). Instead, in 1226 Louis accepted Romanus as legate with the tacit understanding that his acts, like those of most legates, were subject to papal review. It is more surprising that Honorius had once been prepared to grant Louis a Gallican *legatus natus* with absolute powers than it is that he eventually insisted that the crusade be a joint venture by France and the papacy, with the spiritual side under the control of a legate who was the pope's man.

2. Closely associated with this proposal had been another to grant special powers to three French archbishops—Bourges, Reims, and Sens—that in effect would put the spiritual powers of excommunication and interdict at the disposal of the crown to coerce those who hampered the crusade in various specified ways. In 1221 the papacy had given these same archbishops special powers to promote an Albigensian crusade, which in practice had largely been the power

to levy a tax on the clergy,[101] so the idea was not new, though the powers Louis proposed for them were. Probably Louis felt that closer control and more rapid action could be obtained by dividing France up into three legatine provinces, but Romanus had little difficulty in persuading him to drop the triumviral feature because it had not worked well in 1221-1224. Often papal power had not been respected then because it was wielded by local prelates who had their own well-established ambitions and enemies. More likely the problem in 1226 was whether the same result should be obtained by other means, for the king had had in mind some extraordinary applications of the Church's powers of coercion.

(a) First, an archbishop-legate should have the power to excommunicate, or interdict the lands of, all those, whether Frenchman or foreigner, "who disturb the peace of the kingdom of France or stir up the kingdom; and to do the same to all those who do so to the persons or lands of those who shall go with him" (Doc. 7.2). In 1226 Romanus and the prelates with him at Paris promised instead to excommunicate anyone "who invaded the kingdom or made war on it" (Doc. 26.4). Thus they not only eliminated the interdict but also defined the offenses more precisely. The king had probably objected that this alone was too mild, so as a compromise the 1226 version added that offenders would not be absolved until they had compensated their victims and, if they were aliens, until they had left the kingdom. We have already seen how Honorius III qualified the application of this clause to King Henry and his brother, Richard of Cornwall.[102]

(b) In 1224 both excommunication and interdict were requested for use against those Frenchmen who fought among themselves and would not make a peace or truce at the king's command (Doc. 7.2). Romanus would allow only excommunication but otherwise his grant repeated the original request almost word for word (Doc. 26.5), a circumstance which indicates clearly that the 1224 petition was the basis for the negotiations of 1225-1226.

(c) Louis had also wanted his archbishop-legates to be able to invoke spiritual sanctions against those who broke their oath to go into Albigensian country or to remain there (Doc. 7.3), but this provision was dropped altogether, probably because it lay within the legate's normal competence, and thus no special assurances were required for him to act in the interest of the crusade.

(d) Finally, in 1224 Louis had planned to levy a subsidy on those of his vassals who did not accompany him to Occitania, and he wanted both spiritual sanctions available to force them to pay (Doc. 7.4). This provision was also eliminated in 1226, perhaps because it would have created an alarming precedent for papal intervention in the collection of taxes that were essentially secular. The

101. Pressutti, no. 3427. See R. Kay, "The Albigensian Twentieth of 1221-3," *Journal of Medieval History*, VI (1980), 307-315.

102. See above at n. 100.

considerable increase that the legate arranged in the Church's subsidy for the crusade no doubt amply made up for whatever the crown lost by this change.

3. A ten-year truce with England had been another of Louis' demands in 1224 (Doc. 7.5). Doubtless the truce at first seemed even more important in 1225, since Romanus had made it his principal concern for months and as late as August 1225 still regarded it as the crusade's *sine qua non*; but, as we have seen, its importance dwindled by the end of the year, so much so that by January 1226 the king was prepared to take the Cross on the strength of the assurance that those who invaded his lands or made war on him would be excommunicated (Doc. 26.4). This change probably came about because Louis himself in the end proved the greatest obstacle to a truce when in November he refused to bargain away any part of his conquests. He would rather rely on only the protection afforded by his crusader status than make a disadvantageous truce. The original requirement for a truce was perhaps glossed over by assurances from the legate that he would continue to negotiate for a truce, as he was still doing in March, and that he would have Honorius reinforce the general protection for crusaders with a special warning to the English, which was sent in April.[103]

4. In 1224 Louis had also wanted Honorius to procure assurances from Frederick II that the emperor's subjects east of the Rhone would not impede the king's crusading, and that the king could attack them if they did, provided that the emperor's rights were not diminished (Doc. 7.9). This concern has disappeared from the agreement of 1226, though events were to prove the wisdom of it when Louis attacked the imperial city of Avignon and provoked a protest from Frederick. Louis' treaty with Frederick, signed at Catania on 24 November 1224, does not explain this omission, for it provided only that each ruler would not harbor rebels against the other.[104] The explanation appears, however, from Honorius' answer to Frederick when he complained about the siege of Avignon. On 22 November 1226, Honorius explained that Romanus had been instructed, both verbally before he left Rome and later by a letter, that it was the pope's will that heresy be purged from Provence and the kingdom of Arles in a manner such that the rights of the Empire would be preserved.[105] Evidently the pope thought that no further assurance was needed; indeed, he had not even informed Frederick of his good intentions. Most probably Romanus reassured Louis that the legate would assume full responsibility for any counterattacks against subjects of the Empire, as in fact he did.

5. To place the royal right to Raymond's French lands beyond doubt, in 1224 Louis requested a statement from Honorius to the effect that not only Raymond

103. Pressutti, no. 5904, ed. *Rec. hist. Gaules*, XIX, 772-773.
104. See above, chapter 1, n. 140.
105. Pressutti, no. 6058.

VI but also his son Raymond VII had been judicially deprived of any right to their French fiefs. Moreover, their supporters and all who fought against the king or opposed his crusade were to be similarly deprived. Finally, the pope was to confirm the right of the king and his heirs to lordship over these lands, and particularly the right to enfief them to whomever they wished (Doc. 7.6). In other words, what Louis wanted was a more sweeping version of the statement Honorius had sent to France on 20 May 1222.[106] The exheredation of Raymond VII had been confirmed by Honorius on 25 October 1221,[107] so the novelty of the proposal was that it would have the pope extend this penalty to others and acknowledge the crown's right to dispose of the vacant fiefs.

Yet Romanus did no such thing. All that he did in 1226 was to reaffirm the excommunication of Raymond and his supporters that had been in effect since 1217 (Doc. 26.3). This restraint could have proceeded from any one of a number of considerations, so it provides no certain clue as to the part this proposal played in the negotiations of 1225-1226. It seems likely to me, however, that it was not a major issue, since neither Raymond's exheredation nor Louis' lordship was in doubt. The aftermath of the First Albigensian Crusade had shown how difficult it would be to impose new, unpopular, northern lords on Occitania, so Romanus may well have had in mind the sort of solution that he effected in 1229, whereby Raymond and his supporters were retained but subjected to supervision from Rome and Paris. At least, for whatever reason, he left the door open for such a moderate compromise.

6. The last request, for a financial subsidy, is the key to all the others. In 1224 Louis had demanded an annual payment of 60,000 *livres* in money of Paris for ten years, to a total of 600,000 pounds (Doc. 7.8). Instead, in 1226 he was promised an annual tenth of all the ecclesiastical revenues of Romanus' legation for a period of up to five years, if the crusade lasted that long (Doc. 26.6), with certain exemptions (§7). No accounts of the collection survive, but one can nonetheless gain an approximate idea of the value of this grant from a similar one made to Louis IX for the Seventh Crusade in 1245, some twenty years later. Over a five-year period, a ten per cent tax on the revenues of the French church yielded a total of about 760,000 pounds paris, or an annual average of 152,000 pounds.[108] Louis VIII certainly received more than this, since Romanus' legation included not only the kingdom of France but also six other provinces that in political terms amounted to the kingdom of Burgundy. One can only guess

---

106. Pressutti, no. 3977; discussed above, chapter 1, at nn. 4 and 59.

107. Pressutti, no. 3555; cf. above, chapter 1, at n. 40.

108. W. C. Jordan, *Louis IX and the Challenge of the Crusade* (Princeton, 1979), pp. 79-80. To facilitate comparison, I have converted the figures that Jordan gives in *livres tournois* back into *livres parisis* (ibid., p. xiii).

what this additional area would have yielded, but if the amount was 50,000 pounds a year, then Romanus' total grant would have been in excess of 1,000,000 pounds paris. Thus Louis would have received two-thirds more than the total he originally asked for, and the annual amount, which he certainly received in 1226, would have been well over three times greater than what he had formerly requested.

The negotiators in 1226 must have had a good idea of what the yield would be for a tenth of the ecclesiastical revenues in France and Burgundy, because both kingdoms had contributed to pay a similar tax in 1216-1218 to support the Fifth Crusade, and France had more recently paid another in 1221-1223.[109] Thus Louis would have been well aware that he was getting more than he had asked for. This, indeed, must have been Romanus' strongest bargaining point: if the king would reduce his other demands, he would receive a much larger subsidy than he had originally suggested.

When Romanus and Louis concluded their bargain in January 1226, the legate could assure the king that the churches of his legation were committed to pay such a subsidy because he had already consulted them the previous November at the Council of Bourges. Thus it is now apparent that the council played a pivotal role in the negotiations, and we may turn at last to the proceedings of that assembly to see how Romanus committed the clergy of his legation to a tax on their income.

109. Kay, "Albigensian Twentieth."

CHAPTER 3

ORGANIZATION OF THE COUNCIL

The organization of a medieval council was determined by the letter of convocation that summoned the participants to assemble at a certain time and place for a stated purpose. Such a document reveals who summoned the council, why he convoked it, and whom he invited.[1] Unfortunately, the summons to the Council of Bourges does not survive, so our knowledge of the council's organization must be derived from other sources that, though abundant, are not always in agreement with one another on even the simplest matters, such as the time and place of the council. This chapter, therefore, will survey these sources systematically in order to determine the essential features of the conciliar organization at Bourges.

First we shall recover the basic elements of the summons: who called the council, when and where it was held, and for what purpose. Next we shall attempt to identify the participants, and finally we shall examine certain preliminaries to the session, namely the seating arrangements and the opening ceremonies.

Convocation of the council

Although Romanus' letter of convocation has been lost, we can gather what it must have been like from the one by which his predecessor, Cardinal Conrad, convoked the council of Sens in 1223, only two years earlier (Doc. 49.2–4). Conrad began by describing the alarming resurgence of heresy in Occitania; then, having established the need for a council, he issued his mandate to the convokees:

> ordering you by the lord pope's authority that we exercise in these parts, that you are to come to Sens on the octave of the apostles Peter and Paul next to come, where (God willing) the other prelates of France will be gathered together, and you should be prepared to give counsel concerning the aforesaid

1. A number of citation mandates to legatine councils prior to 1225 are printed by Mansi: Normandy 1070 (Mansi, XX, 8), Clermont 1077 (XX, 483), Autun 1077 (XX, 491), Poitiers 1100 (XX, 1125), Fleury 1100 (XXI, 11–12), Leon 1114 (XXI, 113), Angoulême 1117 (XXI, 185), London 1125 (XXI, 329). The organization and preliminaries to a council are treated systematically by Dominicus Jacobatius (d. 1527), *Tractatus de concilio*, printed in Mansi, vol. 0 (1903), pp. 1–88 (lib. 1–2).

business and, with the others there present, to take steps to deal with the Al-bigensian business. Otherwise we shall take care to report your disobedience to the lord pope [Doc. 49.4].

All the elements of a conciliar summons are present here. As the pope's agent in France, the legate requires that the convokees be present at the given time and place to advise him on stated business and to do what needs to be done about it. The convoker is careful both to state the authority by which he acts and to indicate that disobedience will be punished by the same authority. The summons was binding on all to whom it was addressed: "the archbishop of Rouen and his suffragans, and to the abbots, priors, deans, archdeacons, and chap-ters located in the province of Rouen" (Doc. 49.2). The summons was distrib-uted by sending a copy to each archbishop, who then distributed copies to his suffragans, each of whom in turn notified all the lesser addressees in his diocese.

Conrad's summons is comparable to those issued for English councils held in 1226 (Doc. 42.2-3, 8-9). *Mutatis mutandis*, the summons that Romanus issued in 1225 must have been much the same. Let us attempt, therefore, to reconstruct it by retrieving the relevant information from the surviving documents.

President

There can be no doubt that Romanus convoked the Council of Bourges and presided over it. All the Latin chroniclers say as much in one way or another,[2] but Romanus' relation to the council is described with even greater precision and authority by the pope, by the legate himself, and by the chapters that later appealed his decision. The chapters said that "the lord legate convoked a coun-cil of his whole legation at Bourges" (Doc. 32.2). Romanus himself stated that he had called the participants to meet at Bourges (Doc. 31.1), and particularly the chapters, whom he had instructed to send proctors to appear there "in our presence" (Doc. 29.1), where—according to the pope—"he received counsel" (Doc. 39.1). Thus it is firmly established that the Council of Bourges was in every sense Romanus' council: as papal legate, he convoked the churches within the jurisdiction of his legation to meet in a council over which he presided and which gave him counsel. Hence Bourges was a legatine council, which by def-inition is one over which a papal legate presides. In such a council, the legate "regulates the order of the questions to be discussed, directs the deliberations . . . ; he prolongs the debates beyond the set time and dissolves the council"; and,

2. Docs. 1.1, 2.3, 3.4, 5.2, 42.11 (Doc. 4.4 is vague on the point).

moreover, he can do all these things without taking counsel because they are done solely by reason of his authority as the pope's legate.[3]

Location of the council

According to almost all contemporary sources, Romanus held his council at Bourges. This is firmly attested by seven chronicles and five letters,[4] and contradicted only by Walter of Coventry (Doc. 1.1 c). The exception is readily explained by the nature of Coventry's ultimate source, the *Relatio*, in which the site of the council was not specified. In the other English sources that incorporated the *Relatio,* it was correctly connected with Bourges (Docs. 1.1W and 42.11), but the Fenland chronicler from whom Coventry was copying apparently knew less than his contemporaries about the circumstances, and so he guessed wrongly that the council was held in the cathedral city of the first bishop who was named in the *Relatio*—the archbishop of Lyon.

Why Bourges was chosen for the place of meeting we can only guess. Certainly it was the legate's prerogative to choose where he wished to meet with his counselors, and inasmuch as Conrad's council at Sens in 1223 was the only legatine council since the beginning of the century that had assembled prelates from all of France,[5] Romanus had no precedents to guide him, unless perhaps someone recalled that another legate, Robert of Courson, had chosen the city in 1214 for a legatine council that never took place.[6] Probably Romanus selected Bourges because its central location made it the most convenient rendezvous. In 1223, Conrad had preferred to remain in the neighborhood of Paris, close to the dying king; but Romanus, having already reached an agreement with the king, was less pressed for time and could afford to be considerate in his choice

3. N. Iung, "Concile," *Dictionnaire de droit canonique,* III, 1277. Because Romanus convoked more than one province to Bourges, the council can also be classified as a "plenary" one, although this distinction was not then current. In the twelfth and thirteenth centuries, a legatine council was subsumed under the larger category of a *concilium generale,* which "désignait tout concile présidé par le pape ou son légat, ou, du moins, réuni è son intervention (*alias ius habita auctoritate*)": G. Fransen, "L'Ecclésiologie des conciles médiévaux," in *Le Concile et les conciles* (Chevetogne, 1960), pp. 125-141, at 125-126. For qualifications, see H. J. Sieben, *Die Konzilsidee des lateinischen Mittelalters (847–1378)* (Paderborn, 1984), pp. 254, 263-264.

4. Docs. 1.2, 2.3, 3.4, 4.4, 5.2, 6, 42.11; 28.5, 29.1, 31.1, 32.2, 39.1.

5. Since 1200, legates had held over a dozen provincial or regional councils in France, some in the north and some in the South, chiefly in connection with the Albigensian problem, but only Sens 1223 included the whole of the kingdom.

6. Mansi, XXII, 953-954; C. J. Hefele and J. Leclercq, *Histoire des conciles d'après les documents originaux,* 11 vols. (Paris, 1907-1952), V.ii, 1316.

of venue.[7] Thus the convenience of the participants was the deciding factor, it would seem, if more urgent considerations did not intervene. Later in the century, the central location of Bourges continued to recommend the city as the site of legatine councils, which were celebrated there in 1240, 1268, and 1276.

Bourges had other advantages as well. The city and its banlieu, which had been purchased by the French crown around 1100, had long been part of the royal domain. Thus in 1225 it was the southernmost city in which royal power was firmly established. No doubt it was for this reason that Louis VIII made Bourges the rendezvous from which he finally launched his royal crusade in May 1226.[8] Moreover, its archbishop, Simon de Sully, had long been the leading French prelate to support the crusade in the South, and with good reason, since the Albigensian heresy flourished in the southern dioceses of his province— most notably in Albi. In 1221, Simon had been one of the three French archbishop-legates commissioned to promote the crusade in France.[9] More recently, he had been identified with the king's plans for a royal crusade, having traveled to Rome on Louis' behalf in 1223 and again in 1224;[10] and indeed, in the original proposal for a royal crusade, Simon had been the king's choice for a legate who would cooperate with the crown (Doc. 7.7). The position had gone to Romanus instead, but his disappointed rival continued to support the crusade.[11] If the council were held in Simon's cathedral city of Bourges, not only would that prelate's past services to the crusade be given some recognition, but he could also promote the cause in his capacity as host to the council. Thus Bourges was, to say the least, a city that would welcome all who supported the king's crusade.

Date of the council

The context of events, generally supplied by the chroniclers, leaves no doubt that the council took place in the year 1225. The principal exception is Roger Wendover, who put his account of the council under the year 1226 with the misleading statement that the Council of Bourges took place at "about this same time" (Doc. 43.11-12). This discrepancy is readily explained. Wendover inserted the *Relatio de concilio Bituricensi* (Doc. 1) between his accounts of the English councils of 13 January and 3 May 1226 because the latter council had modeled its response to *Super muros Jerusalem* (Doc. 41) on that described in the

---

7. Above, pp. 15 and 70.

8. Petit-Dutaillis, *Louis*, p. 276 (26 May 1226).

9. See above, pp. 12-15.

10. Petit-Dutaillis, *Louis*, pp. 282-283.

11. Simon not only helped to organize the crusade of 1226 (Docs. 24-27) but also accompanied the king: Petit-Dutaillis, *Louis*, p. 506, reg. no. 437.

Relatio—a connection that is made explicit in the Salisbury Register (Doc. 42.11-12). Another annalist who put the council under the year 1226 seems to have done so because he confused the meeting at Bourges with the royal council of January 1226 (Docs. 23-27). No explanation can be given for the same mistake in the Reginensis extract (Doc. 6) because its context is unknown; but, as shall be seen presently, numerical inaccuracy is characteristic of this source (see below, at nn. 25-26).

Strange to say, although more than a dozen sources attest the celebration of the council at Bourges, only two French chroniclers give any more precise indication of the date than simply the year. Both the Chronicle of Tours and Alberic of Trois-Fontaines agree that the council was held on the day of St Andrew the Apostle (Docs. 3.4 and 5.2), which normally is celebrated on 30 November. Most modern writers accordingly date the council 30 November 1225;[12] the exception was Dom Vaissète, who gave the date as 29 November but did not explain why he did so. Perhaps he noted that in 1225 St Andrew's day fell on the first Sunday in Advent, in which case, at least since the sixteenth century, St Andrew has been given his due by transferring his feast to another day;[13] but since such transfers are customarily made to a *later* day, it is hard to see why Vaissète moved the feast to an earlier one. (By the modern system, the feast of St Andrew would be transferred to the following Monday, 1 December.)[14]

At any rate, yet another source strongly suggests that the council was held on the traditional date for the feast of St Andrew. Louis VIII issued a safe-conduct for Raymond VII that, according to Petit-Dutaillis, was valid from 30 November until 25 December.[15] The former date would certainly have been the date of the council itself, since the safe-conduct would have to provide for the earliest possible date on which the count might begin his return trip, namely the first day on which the council was scheduled to meet. As the original safe-conduct mentioned the feast of St Andrew without stating the day on which that feast fell, I think we can assume that the council was celebrated on the saint's traditional day, 30 November, because otherwise the date to which the feast was transferred would have been stipulated for the sake of clarity. Thus it appears that the council took place on 30 November 1225, which was both the feast of St Andrew the Apostle and the first Sunday in Advent.

12. E.g. Petit-Dutaillis, *Louis*, p. 289.

13. The modern rules for such transfers can be found in the *Brevarium Romanum*, "Rubricae generales," 10: "De translatione festorum" (1914 revision of the 1568 edition).

14. Mas Latrie, *Trésor de chronologie*, cols. 327-328; but cf. 211-212, where the Maurist calendar treats St Andrew as a fixed feast.

15. Summary in Petit-Dutaillis, *Louis*, p. 488, reg. no. 285.

Purpose of the council

Of all the elements in a conciliar summons, the most important was the statement of purpose, because this determined the scope of the council's agenda. Knowledge of this was particularly crucial in the case of the representatives of cathedral chapters, who usually were given a mandate that legally empowered them to act only in the matters for which they had been summoned.[16] When a wide variety of concerns were to be treated, the summons could be cast in the most general terms, as for instance the Third Lateran Council, which was summoned in 1178 to reform the faith and morals of Christendom.[17] As we have seen, however, Conrad's legatine council of 1223 limited its agenda to the Albigensian affair (Doc. 49.4), but it is not altogether clear whether Romanus followed that precedent. Alberic of Trois-Fontaines, indeed, says that "In the city of Bourges a council was celebrated . . . ; it was about the state of the Church and of the Albigensians" (Doc. 5.2). This statement does correctly describe the range of topics that were actually discussed, for matters extraneous to the crusade were in fact raised, but most likely it is the chronicler's description of what occurred rather than of the purpose stated in the summons, because there is no reason to assume that the summons had stipulated any general business "de statu Ecclesiae."

On the contrary, there is every reason to believe that Pope Gregory IX accurately echoed the language of the summons when he stated that Romanus "convoked a council at Bourges for the business of peace and of the faith" (Doc. 39.1). Romanus himself described the purpose of his council in almost the same words: "we convoked [them] . . . for the aforesaid business," that is, "the business of the faith and of peace" (Doc. 31.1). This formula he evidently felt was the one that defined the mandate of the cathedral proctors who were present, for he goes on to say that he had them incorporate that phrase into the written counsels they gave him at Bourges. To have done so would have been pointless if the purpose of the council had not already been stated thus in the summons to the chapters, because only in that case would such a statemnt have served to define their proctorial mandate and hence make their counsels binding.

16. On the limitation of proctorial mandates, see G. Post, *Studies in Medieval Legal Thought* (Princeton, 1964), pp. 146–150.

17. *Quoniam in agro*, 21 Sept. 1178, ed. Mansi, XXI, 211B: "Quia in ecclesia Dei correctione videmus quamplurima indigere, tam ad emendanda, quae digna emendatione videntur, quam ad promulganda, quae saluti fidelium visa fuerint expedire: de diversis partibus personas ecclesiasticas decrevimus evocandas. . . . " Innocent III's summons to Lateran IV, however, gave a long and incomplete list of topics, most of them broad but a few specific, notably a financial subsidy to help the Holy Land: *Vineam Domini sabbaoth*, 19 April 1213 (Potthast, no. 4706), ed. Mansi, XXI, 961B.

Although the phrase "pro negotio pacis et fidei" surely expresses the essential purpose of the council, still this basic idea was probably elaborated somewhat in the citation mandate. Most likely Romanus was quoting this fuller form when he wrote that he had convoked the council *"To raise up again the business of peace and the faith, which had wholly collapsed,* and to uproot the heretical perversity of Albigeois and surrounding regions" (Doc. 29.1). Romanus chose these words carefully so there would be no doubt about his authority to levy a subsidy. The portion in italics above was quoted directly from his legatine commission that Honorius had sent to the ecclesiastical authorities (Doc. 12.2), and the rest is a paraphrase of the same document. In effect, then, the summons indicated by its language that the council was being summoned for a purpose that had been sufficiently justified to the recipients by the letter of legation that they had already received from the pope. Hence noncompliance was inexcusable.

Finally, it is noteworthy that the summons echoed the most specific statement of the legation's purpose, rather than the more generalized one expressed in the formal conferral of legatine powers (Doc. 12.5). Romanus thus indicated that this council had a special purpose for which the proctors should be sufficiently instructed to represent their chapters: they were to come prepared to counsel the legate concerning the *negotium pacis et fidei*. By so stipulating, Romanus was able to frustrate the chapters' objections to the tax he imposed as a result of the counsel he received at Bourges.

Composition

The churchmen who participated in the council included archbishops, bishops, abbots, archdeacons, deans, and also the proctors of the cathedral churches. Three chroniclers listed all these classes (Docs. 1.1, 3.2, and 6), and Romanus repeatedly gave a similar description (Docs. 29.1, 29.3, 31.1). Two sources that specify numbers, however, are in wide disagreement: the *Relatio* states that "about a hundred" bishops were present from nine provinces (Doc. 1.2), a statement opposed by the Reginensis extract's assertion that 113 bishops were present from sixteen provinces (Doc. 6). These discrepancies might be dismissed as another example of the numerical inexactitude of medieval chroniclers,[18] were not a more important question involved: was the council for all or only part of Romanus' legation? If only nine provinces were represented, then Bourges would seem to have been a national council of the French church; but if all fifteen of the provinces

18. E.g. there is drastic disagreement between the two extant lists of bishops who attended Lateran IV. Out of the fifteen provinces of Romanus' legation, only two (Aix and Embrun) are listed as having the same number of bishops in attendance. Both lists are reproduced by R. Foreville, *Latran I, II, III et Latran IV* (Paris, 1965), pp. 386–395.

of the legation were represented, the council would then have exceeded the political boundaries of the kingdom of France. Or, put in more practical terms, the problem is: were the ecclesiastical provinces that subsidized the king's crusade only those within his kingdom? Or did those from the kingdom of Burgundy contribute as well?

One cannot resolve the problem, as Petit-Dutaillis tried to do, by ignoring it. He accepted the indications that only French churchmen were consulted at Bourges about a subsidy for the crusade, but he saw no difficulty in asserting that the resultant tax was also paid by the six provinces of the legation that lay outside the kingdom.[19] If true, this would have been a flagrant violation of the newly established canonical principle that cathedral chapters must be consulted before they were taxed (Doc. 48). Since one cannot have it both ways, we must decide whether Bourges was a national council or not, and then account for the evidence to the contrary.

The definitive answer is found in the legate's own correspondence. In 1227, Romanus described the composition of the council in an open letter (Doc. 29.1):

> we formerly summoned these persons to Bourges: the venerable fathers the archbishops, bishops, and other prelates and men of religion, as well as the chapters of the cathedral churches *of our legation*, who were to appear in our presence by means of suitable proctors.

The crucial phrase "of our legation (*legationis nostre*)" at least implies that Romanus summoned capitular proctors from all of the churches to which his commission had been addressed (Doc. 12); presumably the phrase was also meant to apply as well to all of the "venerable fathers" previously mentioned. Either way, it seems to indicate that the council included representatives from the entire legation, and this impression is confirmed by the results of the council as Romanus described them in the same letter. On the written advice of all of the persons he consulted, Romanus granted the king "a tenth of *all* the ecclesiastical revenues *of our legation*" for the next five years (Doc. 29.5). This statement assures us not only that all of the churches of the legation were taxed, but also that they had all counseled it at Bourges. Hence there can be no doubt that all of the provinces of the legation were included in the council.

This interpretation is based on a single phrase—"decimam omnium proventuum ecclesiasticorum legationis nostre"—but we can be sure that it will bear the weight, for these were the exact words in which the grant had been made (Doc. 26.6), and they were subsequently used to describe it both by the legate

_____

19. Petit-Dutaillis, *Louis*, pp. 290 and 383.

(Doc. 31.1) and *mutatis mutandis* by the pope (Doc. 39.1). The phrase, then, was certainly worded with legal precision and must be taken literally: the grant was indeed for *all* the ecclesiastical revenues of the legation.

What provinces were included in Romanus' legation? His commission (Doc. 12) does not name them all explicitly; instead, it was addressed to the prelates of the churches "in the kingdom of France and in Provence" as well as to those of six provinces that were named: Tarentaise, Besançon, Embrun, Aix, Arles, and Vienne. The problem, then, is to determine what provinces the papal chancery understood to be included "in the kingdom of France and in Provence." The territory comprised by that phrase can readily be defined in negative terms (see map, figure 1). On the south, the Spanish province of Tarragona would not be included; on the east, the German provinces of Cologne and Trier also would not; and the remainder of the boundary would be defined by the six Burgundian provinces named in the letter of legation. Nine provinces fall within these limits, and there is good reason to believe that all of them were represented at Bourges because they all are named in the *Relatio* (Doc. 1.2): Lyon, Sens, Reims, Rouen, Tours, Bourges, Bordeaux, Auch, and Narbonne. Therefore we can conclude that Romanus' legation comprised fifteen ecclesiastical provinces, namely the six named in his commission plus the nine others named in the *Relatio*.

This conclusion can be confirmed by reference to the *Liber censuum* of the Roman church, a list of payments that the pope was entitled to receive from various churches. Of all the various inventories of the provinces of Christendom,[20] this source should reflect most closely the view of the papal chancery under Honorius III because he himself had compiled the book in the 1190s when he was the chamberlain of Pope Celestine III. With slight revisions, his list continued in use at the curia throughout the next century.[21] In the main part of the *Liber censuum*, the dioceses of Latin Christendom are grouped by province, and the provinces in turn are classified by geographical region. These data for the provinces of Romanus' legation are summarized in table 1.[22]

The significant fact for our purpose is that the suffragans of these fifteen provinces total 99. This corresponds well enough to the figure given in the

20. Notably (1) the *Provinciale*, probably written after 1187 by Boso, in the *Gesta pauperis scolaris Albini* (Vatican MS. Ottobon. 3057), ed. Fabre-Duchesne, *Liber censuum*, II, 96–104; cf. idem, Intro., pp. 55–56; and (2) the *Liber provincialis* appended to Matthew Paris, *Chronica majora*, ed. H. R. Luard, 7 vols., Rolls Series, no. 57 (London, 1872–1883), VI, 455–457.

21. Fabre-Duchesne, *Liber censuum*, Intro., 1, n. 1; H. K. Mann, *Lives of the Popes in the Middle Ages*, XII (London, 1925), 7–8.

22. Data summarized from Fabre-Duchesne, *Liber censuum*, I, 176–223. The diocese of Toulon was originally omitted from the list of Arles suffragans but was subsequently added (p. 183); I have included it in my total. It was also omitted from the *Liber provincialis* (above, n. 20); otherwise, the two lists agree for the provinces that concern us.

FIGURE 1. The legation of Cardinal Romanus 1225-1227

Relatio (Doc. 1.2), which reported that the suffragans at Bourges numbered "about a hundred (*circiter centum*)," and accordingly it confirms the conclusion reached above, that these fifteen provinces constituted Romanus' legation.

It is not clear why the curia described Romanus' legation so awkwardly (Doc. 12.5 and address). Perhaps the draft of his commission at first simply accredited him "in the kingdom of France and in Provence," to which the list of the six Burgundian bishops was subsequently added with a double purpose: to clarify what was meant by "Provence" and to enlarge the area of Romanus' legation

TABLE I   The provinces of Cardinal Romanus' legation

| | *Liber censuum* | | | Commission (Doc. 12) | *Relatio* Doc. 1.2) |
Province	Region	Rank	Number of suffragans	Rank	Rank
1. Tarentaise	Burgundy	1	2	1	–
2. Besançon	"	2	3	2	–
3. Embrun	"	3	6	3	–
4. Aix	"	4	5	4	–
5. Arles	"	5	8	5	–
6. Vienne	"	6	6	6	–
7. Lyon	France	1	4		1
8. Sens	"	2	7		2
9. Reims	"	3	11		3
10. Rouen	"	4	6	"in regno Franciae	4
11. Tours	"	5	11	ac in provinciae"	5
12. Bourges	"	6	7		6
13. Bordeaux	"	7	5		7
14. Auch	Gascony	1	9		8
15. Narbonne	"	2	9		9
			99		

to include the provinces of Besançon and Tarentaise, neither of which had ever been part of Provence.[23] Whatever the explanation for this peculiar formulation may be, the result, if not immediately clear, was at least sufficiently precise.

Since it is now established that the participants in the Council of Bourges were drawn from both the kingdom of France and from that of Burgundy, one may well wonder why the author of the *Relatio* omitted all mention of the Burgundians. How could this apparently eyewitness account have overlooked thirty bishops and six archbishops? The explanation is most probably to be found in the interests of the author. He was chiefly concerned with the bull *Super muros Jerusalem*, which was addressed to the prelates, not of Romanus' legation, but of the kingdom of France (Doc. 41). According to the *Relatio*, this bull was discussed at Bourges as an exclusively French affair. The proctors thought it might cause a scandal in "the Gallican church" (Doc. 1.7) and the legate replied that

23. In the *Liber censuum* (ed. Fabre-Duchesne, I, 176-188), Besançon and Tarentaise are grouped with Arles, Aix, Embrun, and Vienne under the heading "Burgundia." The *Liber provincialis* (above, n. 20) placed these two provinces in "Germania." They were not part of either the old Roman *Provincia Narbonensis* or of the medieval county, marquisate, or kingdom of Provence: see, e.g., map 31 in *The Cambridge Medieval History*, ed. J. B. Bury et al., III (Cambridge, Eng., 1922).

he had received the bull only after he had entered "Gaul" (Doc. 1.17).[24] Moreover, the *Relatio* tells us that only in connection with this matter did the proctors of different provinces deliberate together, and that they chose as their
spokesmen the proctors of the metropolitan chapters (Doc. 1.5-6). Since the author of the *Relatio* was presumably himself one of these proctors, it seems most
likely that his limited knowledge of the provinces represented at Bourges was
obtained by participation in the proctors' discussion of *Super muros*, which only
concerned the nine provinces that he names. The same explanation probably
also accounts for the statement in the Chronicle of Tours that Romanus assembled the prelates and chapters "of all of France" (Doc. 3.4).

To recapitulate our conclusions, it now appears that fifteen provinces were
represented at Bourges by thirteen archbishops and less than a hundred bishops.
These figures, however, are contradicted by another source, the brief notice that
Vaissète published from a Vatican Reginensis manuscript (Doc. 6):

> Chief among those present were 14 archbishops; two others were absent al-
> though bishops from their provinces were present. Altogether, however, there
> were 113 bishops present and 520 abbots, not counting the proctors.

Because the date, origin, and transmission of this source are unknown, one
cannot be sure whether the Reginensis account was garbled by one or more of
these factors. Nonetheless, in those cases where the correct figures are known,
we can at least suggest how errors may have crept into the Reginensis figures.
First, the statement that there were present "XIV. archiepiscopi." Let us assume
that the manuscript actually gave the correct number in Roman numerals—
XIII. This could easily have been misread as XIIII if, as in many Gothic cursive
hands, the upper right hand arm of the X were prolonged by a thick, downward
vertical stroke.[25] If so, "episcopi . . . CXIII." could also be explained as a similar
mistake for CXII—112 bishops. That figure would in fact be correct if the total
included all bishops, without distinguishing the thirteen metropolitans who were
present from the 99 suffragans. And the text, though admittedly ambiguous, does
seem to favor this interpretation:"Fuerunt autem omnes episcopi pariter CXIII"
(Doc. 6).[26]

24. Hence Wendover concluded from the *Relatio* that Bourges was a council of "the Gallican clergy" (Doc. 1.1W).

25. E.g. plate 50a in *Scriptura Latina libraria*, ed. J. Kirchner (Munich, 1955).

26. Another possibility is that the Reginensis chronicler, like the author of the *Relatio*, took
Bourges to be a council of the Gallican church, and, to discover how many provinces were
included therein, consulted a list of provinces that reckoned those of Gaul to be sixteen in
number: e.g. that of Albinus in *Liber censuum*, ed. Fabre-Duchesne, II, 96 (no. 68) headed:"Galliarum provincie sunt numero XVI." This hypothesis, however, would not explain how Reginensis arrived at the total of 113 bishops present.

The figures of the *Relatio* and the Reginensis extract can be controlled by a third source, a contemporary chronicle from St-Martial of Limoges, in the province of Bourges. According to this account, among those present were "xiij. archbishops and xviij. bishops."[27] Most important, the chronicle confirms our emendation of Reginensis' number of archbishops to thirteen. But it solves one problem only to create another: how do we explain the ridiculously low number of bishops—eighteen instead of something like a hundred? Again, an emendation is in order. The most likely explanation is that the text should read not "xviij." but "xcviij. episcopi," giving a plausible number very close to a hundred, as the *Relatio* reported, though probably a bit too high, as it seems unlikely that all but one of the 99 possible bishops would have been present.

★ ★ ★

Now that the discrepancies in our sources have been accounted for, the general composition of the council seems firmly established. Next let us consider the participating classes one by one, and discuss the specific features of each.

Archbishops

Each of the thirteen archbishops present at Bourges can be identified from contemporary records. Their names and the years they held office can be gleaned from standard reference works;[28] but, having done this, it seems pointless to present the reader with a list of names and dates. It should suffice to note the few details that concern the presence of these archbishops at the council. In fact, the prosopographical data present only one potential conflict with the account of the *Relatio*. According to that source, the archbishop of Auch was present at the council (Doc. 1.2), but it is not certain that the office was filled on 30 November 1225. The old archbishop, Garsias de l'Ort (*de Horto*), had died on 12 May 1225, and it is over a year before Amanianus (or Amanevius) de Grisinhac is attested as his successor by a papal letter dated 23 May 1226.[29] Episcopal records

27. Continuation by Stephan de Salvaniec of the *Chronicon Bernardi Iterii, armarii monasterii S. Marcialis*, ed. H. Duplès-Agier, *Chroniques de Saint-Martial de Limoges* (Paris, 1874), p. 120: "Anno ab incarnatione Domini Mº. CCº. XXVº, in festivitate sancti Andree apostoli, fuit consilium quod Romanus cardinalis tenuit apud Bituricas de negocio quod cristiani habebant contra Arrianos de Toloza, et fuit ibi comes Tolozanus et comes *de Fois*, et xiij. archiepiscopi et xviij. episcopi, et multi abbates et priores et prepositi, et tractaverunt de pace." On the author, see Duplès-Agier, pp. xlviii–xlix.

28. I have consulted both *Gallia Christiana* and Eubel, *Hierarchia*.

29. Pressutti, no. 5952. The letter concerned an inquest at the monastery of Condom that he conducted while bishop of Tarbes-Bigorre; cf. Pressutti, nos. 3548 and 3553, addressed to his predecessor at Tarbes and dated 18 and 22 Oct. 1221.

from the province of Auch are less complete than most, so it is hardly surprising that there is no record of when Amanianus was installed as archbishop.[30] Under the circumstances, it is probably best to accept the *Relatio*'s evidence as the earliest attestation of Amanianus as archbishop. Certainly the six months between the death of his predecessor and the council allowed enough time for the new archbishop's election and Rome's confirmation of it. At any rate, he was in all likelihood present at Bourges, if not as archbishop or archbishop-elect, then at least as bishop of Tarbes-Bigorre, from which see he was translated to Auch.[31]

According to the *Relatio*, only one archiepiscopal see in France was unfilled at the time of Bourges: "the church of Narbonne was vacant" (Doc. 1.2). This vacancy can be verified. It was caused by the death of Arnaud Amaury, the abbot of Cîteaux who came to Languedoc as a missionary against the Albigensians and remained, first as papal legate and then as archbishop of Narbonne. Although at first he had been an implacable enemy of Raymond VI, since 1215 disputes with Simon de Montfort had led him to favor the restoration of Raymond VI and later of Raymond VII. It was through his efforts that Raymond VII had made his peace with the Occitanian episcopate at Montpellier in the summer of 1224 (above, pp. 24-27), and his death a month before the Council of Bourges deprived Raymond of the old prelate's support.[32] As in the case of Auch, we do not know when the new archbishop of Narbonne, Peter Ameil (*Amelii*), assumed office, but it was not later than 16 March 1226.[33] Probably he had not yet been elected at the time of the council, at least if we are to take the *Relatio* literally, because strictly speaking a church could no longer be said to be vacant after the election had taken place.[34]

The author of the *Relatio* proves to be equally well informed about the other archiepiscopal absentee: "the archbishop of Bordeaux was at Rome" (Doc. 1.2). This was William Amanieu (1207-1227), who had gone to the curia to complain that, because of his loyalty to the English, he was being molested by the king of France. The affair is documented both by the archbishop's own account

30. *Gallia Christiana*, I, 1232 (last attested at Tarbes on 20 Sept. 1225), I, 991-992 (first attested at Auch in 1226); cf. Eubel, *Hierarchia*, I, 123.

31. Eubel, *Hierarchia*, I, 474; see also n. 30, above.

32. J. R. Strayer uses the career of Arnaud (or Arnaldus) Amaury as an amusing leitmotif in *The Albigensian Crusades* (New York, 1971), pp. 89-126 passim. The significance of his death is remarked by Devic-Vaissète, VI, 596. In general, see *Dictionnaire de biographie française*, II, 390-393, s.v. "Amalric (Arnaud)."

33. *Gallia Christiana*, VI, 65; Eubel, *Hierarchia*, I, 373. A papal bull was addressed to him on 19 May 1226: Pressutti, no. 5944.

34. This follows from the principle, well established in canon law before 1225, that election confers on the electee a right to his office: see R. L. Benson, *The Bishop-elect* (Princeton, 1968), pp. 139-144.

of it, which he sent to Henry III of England,[35] and by the letters that Honorius issued to remedy the situation.[36] Although sickness was a canonically acceptable excuse for absence from a council,[37] there seems to be no evidence to support Vaissète's assertion that the archbishop of Bordeaux excused his absence from Bourges on this ground.[38]

The six other French archbishops whom the *Relatio* lists as present at Bourges could all have been there, since each of their sees was occupied at the time of the council, and the same is true of the six Burgundian archbishops.[39]

Bishops

According to the *Relatio*, there were "about a hundred" suffragan bishops present at Bourges (Doc. 1.2). As we have seen, there were in fact 99 suffragans all told in the provinces that were represented at Bourges, but it is impossible to discover how closely attendance at Bourges approximated this number. Episcopal records at this period are so few and so scattered that most pontificates are attested by only a few documents and some by none at all. Only rarely can the absence of a bishop from Bourges be established, as may be in the case of the bishop of Avignon, who perhaps witnessed a document at Cremona on 25 November 1225, just five days before the council.[40]

More often the data are insufficient to indicate whether the see had a bishop at the time of the council. Frequently the latest known date for one pontificate falls before 30 November 1225, while the earliest date for the next incumbent comes after the council.[41] In a few cases, the new bishop is first attested as being in possession of the see in 1225 or 1226, so that the see may have been vacant

35. *Diplomatic Documents Preserved in the Public Record Office*, vol. I: *1101–1272*, ed. P. Chaplais (London, 1964), no. 146 = Shirley, *Royal Letters*, no. 208; cf. Petit-Dutaillis, *Louis*, p. 275.

36. Pressutti, nos. 5943 and 5951 (19 and 22 May 1226).

37. Gratian, *Decretum* D.18 c.10, ed. Friedberg, I, 56; cf. D. B. Weske, *Convocation of the Clergy* (London, 1937), pp. 82–86.

38. Devic-Vaissète, VI, 594.

39. Eubel, *Hierarchia*, I: Lyon (p. 330), Sens (471), Reims (440), Rouen (447), Tours (531), Bourges (142); Tarentaise (498), Besançon (140), Embrun (242), Aix (96), Arles (104), Vienne (559). I list them in the order of Docs. 1.2 and 12.

40. *Gallia Christiana*, I, 816 (25 Nov. 1225); but another copy, from a Carpentras MS, is dated 14 Nov. 1224: *Historia diplomatica Friderici secundi*, ed. J. L. A. Huillard-Bréholles, 6 vols. (Paris, 1852–1861), II.i, 464–466. At neither date was Frederick anywhere near Cremona, however, so Huillard-Bréholles had doubts about the authenticity of this charter. Another witness was John Halgrin, who was consecrated archbishop of Besançon on 19 Oct. 1225 and appears to have been at Bourges.

41. Eubel, *Hierarchia*, I: Cavaillon (p. 178), Angoulême (240), Lescar (295), Lectoure (298), St-Pol-de-Leon (302), Oloron (376).

on the day of the council.[42] In other cases, the interval between the two testi-
monia is so great that one can suspect that a whole pontificate is missing from
the series.[43] One diocese had two new bishops between 1218 and 1232 for
whom no date at all has been recorded,[44] while it is not clear whether or not
another diocese changed bishops at all between 1221 and 1237.[45]

In all, there are fourteen sees out of 99 for which we have insufficient data to
tell whether they were vacant or not at the time of Bourges. No doubt some
of these obscurities might be clarified by further investigation,[46] but from the
present state of the evidence it would not seem unreasonable to set the number of vacant sees at three or more. Probably other bishops, like Bordeaux and
Avignon, were out of the country at the time, while yet others were unable to
travel by reason of age or sickness. If some nine or ten suffragan sees had no
bishop at Bourges, the author of the *Relatio* would still not have been too far off
in setting the number at "about a hundred suffragans."

We can accept the *Relatio's* rough estimate on other grounds as well. Since
the author was unaware that the six Burgundian provinces were included in the
council, he could not have derived his number of suffragan bishops from some
inventory of dioceses arranged by provinces. In the nine French provinces he
names, the suffragan bishops total 69,[47] a number which could hardly be described as "about a hundred." Furthermore, it could not have been based on his
experience with the proctors of cathedral chapters, since, as we have seen, he
seems to have worked with only the ones from France. Therefore, the number
of suffragans reported by the *Relatio* was in all likelihood based on actual observation. True, we cannot be sure whether his observation was a more or less
careful count of miters at the council's celebration or merely an impression, but
the former method seems to be the more likely one because the estimate does
in fact correspond closely to the total possible number of suffragans. Since the
author of the *Relatio* had misapprehended the number of provinces present, he

42. Eubel, *Hierarchia*, I: Carcassonne (p. 166), Conserans (203), Elne (238), Poitiers (399).

43. Eubel, *Hierarchia*, I: Glandèves (p. 264) and Mâcon (330).

44. Belley: Eubel, *Hierarchia*, I, 131. The reliability of the Belley *fasti* for this period is disputed; hence both pontificates are considered doubtful by L. Alloing, "Belley (diocèse de),"
DHGE, VII (1933), 886–902, at col. 890.

45. Aire: Eubel, *Hierarchia*, I, 72. A(rnaldus) and Augerus may be the same person: see *Gallia Christiana*, I, 1155–1156.

46. In all doubtful cases, I have verified Eubel's data in *Gallia Christiana*; in only two cases
was the doubt removed: Eubel, *Hierarchia*, I, 123 (Avignon) and 516 (Bazas), respectively clarified by *Gallia Christiana*, I, 816 and 1199.

47. *Liber censuum*, ed. Fabre-Duchesne, I, 188–211, and Matthew Paris, *Chronica majora*, ed.
Luard, VI, 455–457. With the *Liber censuum*, I count Narbonne as a province of Gaul; the *Liber
provincialis* (above, n. 20), regards it as a Spanish province.

would not have been able to approximate the correct number of suffragans except by counting them. Hence his report of "about a hundred suffragans" is probably not too far off; my guess would be closer to ninety.

"Other prelates and men of religion"

Thus far the statements of Romanus have been our most reliable guide in reconstructing the composition of the council, but his list of the participants is not without difficulties. In his letter of 17 May 1227, the legate recalled that he had summoned "archbishops, bishops, and other prelates and men of religion" (Doc. 29.1). A little later in the same letter, when the last two groups are mentioned again in reverse order, he clearly distinguished "men of religion" from "other prelates of churches" (Doc. 29.3). A few days later, however, he listed the participants again in another letter, and this time the religious men were omitted from the list: he had received "the counsel of the venerable fathers the archbishops, the bishops and other prelates of churches, and also of the proctors of the cathedral churches" (Doc. 31.1). Since that letter concerned only the obligation of the secular clergy, the consent of the regular clergy was irrelevant; hence the latter may have been dropped from the list because they were not relevant to the context of Document 31. Nonetheless the omission does bring out an important fact: the "other prelates of churches" were not monks but members of the secular clergy. In using the term "alii ecclesiarum prelati" here, Romanus was again echoing his letter of legation, which was addressed *inter alia* to these prelates (Doc. 12.pr.). Although the Bourges dossier says nothing more specific about these secular prelates,[48] they can be identified more precisely in two other contemporary councils. The summons to the council of Sens in 1223 was addressed not only to bishops and chapters but also to "abbots, priors, deans, [and] archdeacons," all of whom were mandated to come (Doc. 49.2, 4). Since both the abbots and priors were monastic officials, only the deans and archdeacons would be members of the secular clergy. Moreover, the phrase "prelates of churches" accurately describes them: deans and archdeacons both typify those prelates "who have offices in the administration of dioceses, and enjoy an independent and proper jurisdiction. . . ."[49] This usage is confirmed by Roger Wendover's account of the council of London that was held on 13 January 1226. The

---

48. William of Andres said that the clergy at Bourges included both "bishops and other prelates" (Doc. 37.2), but he may well have had regular as well as secular prelates in mind, especially since he himself was a monk.

49. *The Catholic Encyclopedia*, XII, 386. For a contemporary discussion of this kind of prelacy, see Hostiensis (Henricus de Segusio), *In primum Decretalium librum commentaria* (Venice, 1581; reprint, Turin, 1965), fol. 159rv, ad X 1.31.3, v. *Ecclesiastica sententia*.

chronicler records that "many bishops accordingly assembled there together with other prelates" (Doc. 43.4). Actually, the summons to the same council had called more specifically for the bishops to summon "the deans of their cathedral churches and their archdeacons, as well as the abbots and conventual priors" (Doc. 42.2). Indeed, Wendover himself records the presence of Archdeacon John of Bedford, who was the spokesman for "the bishops and ecclesiastical prelates" (Doc. 43.6). Thus it seems clear that in the early thirteenth century, deans and archdeacons were commonly described as "prelates of churches," and hence we must understand that these were the secular prelates who, other than the bishops, were present at Bourges.

Monastic superiors also were summoned. Romanus avoided using their various proper titles and instead classed them together as "men of religion (*viri religiosi*)" (Doc. 29.1, 3); the *Relatio*, however, specified that they were "abbots and priors" (Doc. 1.2). Since the letter of legation, which seems to have been otherwise echoed in the summons, was specifically addressed *inter alia* to abbots and priors[50] (Doc. 12.pr.), these no doubt are the ones that Romanus intended by his general term "men of religion."

Strictly speaking, the priors at Bourges should be termed "conventual priors," as they were in the summons to the council of London in January 1226 (Doc. 42.2). "The *conventual prior* is the independent superior of a monastery that has no abbot; he rules in temporals and spirituals just like an abbot."[51] Most chroniclers were content simply to record the presence of "abbots" (Docs. 3.4 and 4.4). The Reginensis extract gave their number as 520 (Doc. 6); probably that total should be understood to include conventual priors as well. Although that number is not improbable, the other numerical inaccuracies in this source do render it suspect.

Proctors of the cathedral chapters

The prelates whom Romanus summoned to Bourges were the ones to whom his commission had been addressed. He went beyond this model, however, by also especially including in his call "the chapters of the cathedral churches of our legation, who were to appear in our presence by means of suitable proctors (*per procuratores idoneos*)" (Doc. 29.1). Elsewhere he simply referred to this group as "the proctors of the cathedral churches" (Doc. 31.1). Our other sources are less precise: the *Relatio* says there was "a proctor from each chapter" (Doc. 1.2); the

50. Priors, however, are not mentioned in the address to the provinces that were neither French nor Provençal (Doc. 12.pr.). Evidently this was nothing more than a slip of the pen, because there were many Cluniac priories in the area: see *Atlas zur Kirchengeschichte*, ed. J. Martin (Freiburg i. B., 1970), map 47.

51. *Catholic Encyclopedia*, XII, 428.

Chronicle of Tours says that the summons included "chapters of all of France" (Doc. 3.4); and the Reginensis memorandum simply notes that "proctors" are not included in the headcount (Doc. 6).

Once again, Romanus appears to have echoed most accurately the tenor of his summons, while the other sources used the term "chapter" more loosely. It was in fact important to stipulate that the chapters were those of the cathedral clergy, because there were other kinds of chapters as well, which, moreover, were sometimes cited to send proctors to ecclesiastical councils. In general, a chapter is "any corporate body responsible for an ecclesiastical institution";[52] its many varieties at this period can be seen in the summons to the council held at London in May 1226, which called for "proctors, namely both from cathedral churches and from prebendal ones, and from monasteries and other monastic and collegiate houses" (Doc. 42.3). Therefore, when Romanus specified only proctors from the cathedral churches, he excluded many other kinds. Our French sources assumed that no other kind would be called.

These proctors made the Council of Bourges a landmark in the history of representation. It was not quite the first council at which cathedral chapters were represented, but it was the first known occasion on which their presence was more than a formality. The *Relatio* celebrates the success of the proctors at Bourges. For the first time, the chapters' right to be heard in the councils of the Church had saved them from unwanted taxation. Moreover, the chapters used this council as a test of whether a chapter must pay a tax to which it had not given its voluntary consent. Thus the Council of Bourges provides our earliest case history of how capitular proctors gave both counsel and consent in ecclesiastical assemblies. In other words, this is our earliest record of representative government in action.[53] The presence of these proctors accordingly deserves special attention, and in particular we must ask why they were summoned to Bourges and what powers they had as members of the council.

Representation

Before 1217, cathedral chapters had no legal right to be represented at church councils.[54] To be sure, from time to time individual members of the chapters are

---

52. The *Oxford Dictionary of the Christian Church*, ed. F. L. Cross, 3rd ed. by E. A. Livingstone (Oxford, 1997), p. 320.

53. The significance of the proctors at Bourges was first appreciated by E. Barker, *The Dominican Order and Convocation* (Oxford, 1913), p. 35.

54. By "representation" here, I mean participation through an authorized delegate, "as when a community confers on an individual the right to act in its name by a specific act of election." Other forms of medieval representation were by personification or mimesis: see B. Tierney, "The Idea of Representation in the Medieval Councils of the West," in his *Rights,*

mentioned in conciliar acta, but there is no reason to suppose, as some have
done, that they were there by right, much less as representatives of their chapters.[55] All members of the chapter were of course personally present at a bishop's
diocesan synod because all the clergy of the diocese were obliged to participate.
As late as the twelfth century, however, members of the cathedral chapters had
no right to participate in the deliberations of the councils of their province.
These, according to Gratian, were "councils of bishops," the purpose of which
was "correction," that is, the enforcement of existing ecclesiastical laws,[56] which
properly was the concern of the prelates and not of their subjects, among whom
were the chapters.

This situation altered at the end of the twelfth century, when the clergy began
to be taxed. According to canon law, a bishop could not make major commitments concerning the property of his church without consulting his clergy, and
consequently they came to be admitted to the deliberations of councils that were
considering matters with fiscal implications for the clergy. The early canons of
the Church had recognized the right of all the diocesan clergy to advise their
bishop concerning ordinations, to witness his judicial proceedings, and to consent to any major alienation of church property.[57] By the end of the twelfth century, however, these rights, and more especially the ones concerning property, were
understood to belong, not to the diocesan clergy at large, but to the chapter of
the bishop's cathedral.[58] Thus it was that, when church property came to be taxed,
the canonists were in agreement that the cathedral chapters should be consulted.[59]

Laws and Infallibility in Medieval Thought (Aldershot, Hants.: Variorum, 1997), item XI, pp. 25
(quotation) and 27 (chapters).

55. E. W. Kemp, "The Origins of the Canterbury Convocation," *Journal of Ecclesiastical History*, III (1952), 132-143, at p. 135, cites the council of Narbonne 1212 (Devic-Vaissète, VIII,
619) to "show that the presence of abbots and representatives of the cathedral chapters was
normal at that time. At Narbonne in 1212 there were five abbots, an archdeacon, a sacrist, a
precentor, a dean, and a canon of various churches in the province." In Visigothic Spain, the
bishop was supposed to bring his clergy, as well as some laymen, with him to the provincial
council: council of Tarragona 516, c.12, ed. T. Bruns, *Canones apostolorum et conciliorum saeculorum IV. V. VI. VII.*, ed. A. Neander (Berlin, 1839), II, 18.

56. Gratian, *Decretum*, D.18, dict. ante c.1, ed. Friedberg, I, 53.

57. Gratian, *Decretum*, D.24 c.6, C.10 q.2 c.1, C.12 q.2 c.53, C.15 q.7 c.6, and *Decretales*
3.10.1, ed. Friedberg, I, 89, 617, 704, 758, and II, 501.

58. *Decretales Gregorii IX* (= X) 3.10.3-6, ed. Friedberg, II, 502-504. F. Lot and R. Fawtier,
Histoire des institutions françaises au Moyen Age, 3 vols. (Paris, 1957-1962), III, 179-180, 188-192.
Although E. U. Crosby stresses diversity and complexity in the chapters' exercise of propri-
etary rights, he allows that in effect they did possess them by 1200: *Bishop and Chapter in
Twelfth-Century England* (Cambridge, Eng., 1994), pp. 13, 381-385, 391-395.

59. On the relation between bishop and chapter in canon law, see B. Tierney, *Foundations
of the Conciliar Theory* (Cambridge, Eng., 1955), pp. 106-131, esp. pp. 108-109.

The method of consultation was another question. In the twelfth century, it was the bishop who consulted his chapter, a group of anywhere from a dozen to, in exceptionally rich churches, a hundred persons, who could feasibly meet together and all participate in a discussion. But in the thirteenth century, when all the chapters of a province, or of a kingdom, or even of all Christendom, were to be consulted, it obviously would be impracticable for the chapter to attend distant councils as a body. The lawyers, however, were ready with a solution. With the growth of papal monarchy in the twelfth century, cathedral chapters by 1200 were accustomed to carry their lawsuits to the Roman curia, where the litigants were represented by proctors. Sometimes these proctors were sent with specific instructions that limited their actions; sometimes they were given a general, unlimited mandate with "full power (*plena potestas*)," which was in effect a power of attorney that conferred on the proctor the power to do whatever the one who sent him could do.[60] Either way, the proctor represented his principal, and therefore provided a familiar legal means by which any corporate community, such as a cathedral chapter, could be consulted *in absentia*.

Although the justification for, and the means of, capitular representation at the greater councils of the Church were already present in canon law by the close of the twelfth century, the two elements were not combined until, at the end of his pontificate, Innocent III, that great innovator among popes, ordered chapters to send representatives to the Fourth Lateran Council. His summons was sent on 19 April 1213 to the bishops, who were instructed to pass it on to "the chapters of all the churches, not only of cathedrals, but also of others, so they may send the provost or dean or other suitable men to the council as their representatives (*pro se*), because several matters will be treated there that especially concern the chapters of churches."[61] Their presence was justified, since the council did indeed discuss matters that touched the property rights of the chapters: a subsidy was voted to support the Fifth Crusade and capitular resources were further taxed by a plan whereby a prebend in every cathedral chapter, as well as in other chapters that could bear the expense, was to be reserved for a grammarian who would provide free instruction, while metropolitan

60. See esp. G. Post, "*Plena potestas* and Consent in Medieval Assemblies: A Study in Romano-canonical Procedure and the Rise of Representation, 1150-1325," in his *Studies*, pp. 91-162, esp. 103-108, for the application of the concept to representative assemblies. Although primarily concerned with diplomatic applications, D. E. Queller offers a clear account of the development of procuration in general: *The Office of Ambassador in the Middle Ages* (Princeton, 1967), pp. 26-59.

61. Mansi, XXII, 961E: "Injungatis autem vos, fratres archiepiscopi & episcopi, ex parte nostra universis ecclesiarum capitulis, non solum cathedralium, sed etiam aliarum, ut praepositum, vel decanum, aut alios viros idoneos, ad concilium pro se mittant, cum nonnulla sint in ipso tractanda, quae specialiter ad ecclesiarum capitula pertinebunt."

churches were also obliged to support a theologian.[62] But, beyond the fact that
the capitular proctors were summoned, we know nothing more about their participation in Innocent's great council. Nonetheless, the Fourth Lateran Council marks the beginning of capitular representation at ecclesiastical councils.

Innocent had provided the chapters with a precedent that they soon claimed
as their right. The next year, in 1216, the cathedral chapters of the province of
Sens sent proctors to a provincial council held at Melun,[63] who insisted that,
since they had been invited, they should be permitted to participate in the deliberations, which in such councils in the past had often affected their interests.
When the archbishop and his suffragans refused to let these proctors participate, the
chapters appealed to Pope Honorius III, who decided in favor of the chapters on
25 February 1217. "Those chapters," he wrote, "ought to be invited to such councils and their nuncios (*nuntii*) admitted to the deliberations (*tractatus*), especially
those about matters that evidently concern the chapters themselves" (Doc. 48.3).

This decretal, *Etsi membra corporis*, firmly established the chapters' right to be
heard through their representatives at ecclesiastical assemblies. The decision has
great significance in the growth of western parliamentary institutions because it
fostered the development of the theory, as well as the practice, of political representation. In the long run, its role in the development of representational theories was undoubtedly more important, for this text provided the canonists with
the opportunity to extend the application of the Roman-law maxim "What
touches all should be approved by all (*Quod omnes tangit, ab omnibus debet comprobari*)."[64] Honorius had declared that the chapters should especially be consulted in matters that touched them; the *Glossa ordinaria* commented that this
had been said with good reason because of the principle *Quod omnes tangit,*

62. *Constitutiones concilii quarti Lateranensis una cum commentariis glossatorum*, ed. A. García y
García (Vatican City, 1981), pp. 59–60 (c.11 on *magistri*) and p. 113 (c.71 on the crusade). *Quia
nonnullis* (c.11) extended the scope of Lateran III (1179), c.18 = X. 5.5.1. Lateran IV did not,
as has often been supposed, provide for the presence of persons other than the metropolitan
and his suffragans at the annual provincial councils mandated by c.6 (*Sicut olim*). The misapprehension is based on an addition to the original text: "ad metropolitanum et suffraganeos
[et alios] in concilio subsequenti . . ." (ed. cit., p. 53). M. V. Clarke thought that the reference
to "others" opened the way for a broadened base of representation: *Medieval Representation and
Consent* (London, 1936), p. 297; Barker, *Dominican Order*, p. 33, used italics to stress the interpolated phrase but did not comment on it. Friedberg's apparatus (II, 747, n. 9) indicates that
the phrase appeared in the *Decretales* (1234) but not in the manuscript texts of the council's
constitutions. The phrase was introduced into the text of the conciliar collections by the *editio Romana* of 1612: see García's edition, pp. 34 and 53; cf. Mansi, XXII, 991–992.

63. Mansi, XXII, 1087–1090; Hefele-Leclercq, *Histoire des conciles*, V.ii, 1399.

64. The broadest survey of this maxim is by Y. M. J. Congar, "Quod omnes tangit, ab omnibus tractari et approbari debet," *Revue historique de droit français et étranger*, 4th ser., XXXVI
(1958), 210–259; but G. Post's earlier essay remains fundamental: "A Romano-canonical
Maxim, *Quod omnes tangit*, in Bracton and in Early Parliaments," in his *Studies*, pp. 163–238.

which the glossator proceeded to trace through Roman and canon law with a long series of allegations.[65] By stressing the principle on which Honorius had based his decision, the canonists opened the way for its extension to analogous situations. Thus, although the decretal expressly provided only for capitular representation at provincial councils, by the principle of *Quod omnes tangit* its application could be extended to include groups other than chapters and provincial councils. This process of extension is evident in the *Glossa ordinaria*, which goes on to explain how even laymen ought to be present when matters touching them, such as matrimony, are being discussed.[66] The decretal *Etsi membra corporis*, therefore, became the *locus classicus* for the application of the *Quod omnes tangit* principle to representative assemblies.

The theoretical implications of the decretal only began to emerge a generation after it was issued in 1217;[67] its impact on practice was more immediate, though slower and more sporadic than one might expect. As far as we know, capitular proctors were first summoned to a *provincial* council in 1226, some nine years after the practice had been mandated. This occurred in England, and recurred there later that same year. The second summons exceeded the minimum requirements of the decretal by also inviting noncathedral chapters to send their representatives (Doc. 42.3). Both councils were called to respond to *Super muros Jerusalem* (Doc. 41) and, consequently, had capitular property as their principal concern. During the next twenty years, the presence of capitular proctors is not recorded at any English provincial councils; however, they were called to councils of the papal legate Otto there in 1237 and 1240 and to a special clerical assembly in 1246, all of which were principally concerned with granting papal subsidies.[68] In the second half of the thirteenth century, however, proctorial representation became increasingly common in English councils and gradually gave rise to a separate assembly of the clergy, which in the next century came to be known as the convocation of clergy.[69]

65. Glossa ordinaria ad X 3.10.10, v. *contingere* (ed. Lyon, 1548, p. 609): "Et merito: quia quod omnes tangit, ab omnibus debet comprobari. . . . " The glossator, Bernard of Parma, also lists *Quod omnes tangit* as a noteworthy feature (*notandum*) of this decretal.

66. Ibid.: "Laici vero huiusmodi conciliis interesse non debent, nisi specialiter invitenter. . . . Vel etiam nisi specialiter tractaretur causa fidei. . . . Vel nisi tractaretur de matrimonio: quia cum tales causae eos tangant, possunt interesse. . . . "

67. The *Glossa ordinaria* to the *Decretals* was compiled by Bernard of Parma, with four successive recensions between 1241 and 1266: S. Kuttner and B. Smalley, "The 'Glossa Ordinaria' to the Gregorian Decretals," *English Historical Review*, LX (1945), 97–105, at p. 100.

68. Powicke-Cheney, *Councils & Synods*, II.i, 241, 185–293, and 389–390.

69. A conspectus, now to be used with caution, was provided by Weske, *Convocation* (1937). The principal documents are now conveniently available with critical commentary in Powicke-Cheney, *Councils & Synods*, I.ii (1964). Many particular points are clarified by Kemp in *Journal of Ecclesiastical History*, III (1952), 132–143.

Much the same pattern is found in France, where there is no evidence that capitular proctors participated in provincial councils until 1235, some eighteen years after Honorius had ordered the archbishop of Sens to admit the chapters' agents to his councils.[70] Indeed, the presence of proctors at French provincial councils only comes to be normal in the last quarter of the century.[71] As in England, proctors first appear in French councils that were considering papal mandates for a subsidy. Since the Fourth Lateran Council, the papacy had reserved to itself the right to approve any tax on the clergy,[72] and in fact the taxes levied on the French clergy in the decade after 1215 were all imposed by the papacy to support one crusade or another. The first levy had been decreed in the Fourth Lateran Council (c.71), at which proctors had been present; but strange to say, the chapters were not consulted when the next crusading tax was granted by a series of legatine councils held in the northern French provinces in 1221.[73] The chapters of Reims province objected to the tax because they had not been consulted, and although Honorius III conceded that they had some reason to complain, yet he insisted that they pay. Strictly speaking, he explained, their presence had not been necessary because the grant was not made by a provincial council—to which *Etsi membra corporis* would have entitled them to be invited— but instead by the authority of a papal legate.[74] This decision was dated 17 May 1222, and it is probably no coincidence that hardly a year later Legate Conrad took care to include capitular proctors in his summons to his council at Sens on 6 July 1223 (Doc. 49). As we have seen, this council, like Bourges, was called to secure the French church's support for the Albigensian crusade (above, pp. 16–17), and it is memorable as the first legatine council that included capitular proctors.

The next time chapters were invited to a council was in 1225, when Romanus summoned them to Bourges. Thus the Council of Bourges is the third recorded

70. Proctors appear in two Reims provincial councils in 1235, held at St-Quentin and Compiègne: Mansi, XXIII, 365–370.

71. Evidence summarized by R. Kay, "The Making of Statutes in French Provincial Councils, 1049–1305," Ph.D. diss., University of Wisconsin (Madison, 1959), p. 130.

72. Lateran IV c.46, ed. García, *Constitutiones*, pp. 85–86 (X 3.49.7, ed. Friedberg, II, 656), renewing Lateran III (1179) c.19 (X 3.49.3), which had required that the bishops and clergy consent to a tax.

73. In the provinces of Reims and Sens, the archbishop-legate consulted only his suffragans: Pressutti, nos. 3574 and 3625, ed. *Rec. hist. Gaules*, XIX, 715–717. In the provinces of Rouen and Tours, where the legate was an archbishop from another province, the legate is said to have made the decision after having taken counsel ("provida deliberatione statueris"): Pressutti, nos. 3644 and 3860, ed. Horoy, IV, 50, and *Rec. hist. Gaules*, XIX, 719. In all likelihood only the bishops were consulted in these provinces as well. See also R. Kay, "The Albigensian Twentieth of 1221–3: An Early Chapter in the History of Papal Taxation," *Journal of Medieval History*, VI (1980), 307–315, at pp. 310–311.

74. Pressutti, no. 3959, ed. *Rec. hist. Gaules*, XIX, 721.

case of proctorial representation in an ecclesiastical assembly, and it is the first occasion for which any record survives of what part the proctors played at the council. From the foregoing sketch, it is evident that Bourges was typical of the occasions on which proctors were summoned in the first half of the thirteenth century. The chapters' right to attend councils that concerned them had been created by the papacy, and papal legates both in France and in England were more ready to recognize and extend that right than were the bishops. In 1225, however, it remained to be seen whether the inclusion of the chapters was anything more than a legal formality. For the first time on record, the advantages and limitations of capitular representation were to be tested in practice at Bourges.

★　★　★

The reason why Romanus summoned the cathedral chapters to his council should now be clear. Canon law gave them a claim to participate in the discussion of affairs that affected their interests. This claim could be ignored, as it was in 1221, but to do so provided the chapters with an excuse for not paying any tax that might be levied without their participation and also with cause for an appeal to Rome if they were forced to pay. Obviously, delay was undesirable when ready money was needed, as it was for the crusade, so the prudent course was to include them in the decision-making process.

According to the Romano-canonical theories of procedure that were current in the thirteenth century, the consent of these representatives was involuntary. By the fact that they had participated they were bound to accept the outcome of the proceedings, just as litigants who appear before a court are bound to accept its decision. To put it simply, they had a voice in the proceedings but not a vote. In distinction to "sovereign" consent, this kind has been termed "procedural" or "judicial-conciliar" consent.[75] A person who represented himself before a council or court would express such consent by presenting himself before the assembly, but a corporate community that was represented by a proctor would express its collective consent in the mandate by which its proctor was constituted. The essential requirement was that the proctor should be given full powers to act for his constituents, without the right to refer back to them for further instructions. Unless the summons to a council was carefully worded to specify that agents be sent with full powers, they might be sent only as messengers or observers without the requisite power to commit their constituents.

Just such an evasion was practiced by the chapters that were summoned to Bourges. After the council, they claimed in 1227 that "the nuncios of the chapters assembled there so that they might bring back to their chapters those things

75. The elaboration of these distinctions was one of Post's principal contributions: see his *Studies*, chaps. 3-4, and esp. pp. 161, 163, 170, and 213-237 passim.

that were discussed or enacted in that council, in order that the chapters might deliberate about them. Absolutely no power of consenting was granted to the nuncios" (Doc. 32.2). No doubt *Etsi membra corporis* lent color to their argument, for
Honorius had in fact stated that the chapters should send nuncios (*nuntii*), that is
to say "spokesmen," to the provincial council (Doc. 48). But was this consistent
with the citation mandate they had received from Romanus? From a legal point
of view, everything hinges on that, and, as we know, the summons has been lost.

For the present purpose, however, this loss is not hopeless, because a reconstruction can be guided by the citation mandates that survive for similar councils called in 1223 and 1226, just before and after Bourges. The extant copy of
Conrad's summons of 1223 is addressed to "the archbishop of Rouen and his
suffragans, and to the abbots, priors, deans, archdeacons, and chapters located in
the province of Rouen" (Doc. 49.2). All of them are ordered to come ready to
counsel the legate what should be done about the resurgence of heresy and "to
take steps to deal with the Albigensian business" (Doc. 49.4). Conrad had been
abbot of Cîteaux and certainly was no canon lawyer. He carefully described the
desired effect without specifying the legal means: the chapters, like the rest, were
to come prepared to advise and to take decisive action. It seems likely that Romanus retained something of this rough and ready formula in his summons, since
the appellant chapters in 1227 were careful to develop a loophole: whatever
things might be established (*statuerentur*) in the council, the chapters claimed the
right to reconsider, and in effect to ratify, such decisions (Doc. 32.2).

By 1226, however, this loophole had been quite precisely plugged by a citation formula modeled on Romano-canonical judicial procedure. In February
1226, the bishop of Salisbury was instructed by his metropolitan to "indicate to
all the chapters that they are to send proctors," to a council at London in May.
"And indicate to all the aforesaid [chapters] that they are to deliberate in the
meantime and come fully instructed to reply to the lord pope's nuncio concerning the petition that he has made on the part of the lord pope . . . " (Doc.
42.3). Not only were proctors now specified, but the nature of their mandate
was signified by the stipulation that they come "fully instructed (*plene instructi*)."
The phrase echoes, and indeed attempts to improve upon, the more usual requirement that a proctor be "sufficiently instructed (*sufficienter instructus*)," which
implied that he must come equipped with full powers to act for his constituents.[76]

There is some reason to believe that Romanus had already tried, with less
success, to draft a summons that similarly implied that a general, unlimited proctorial mandate was required. Again our source is his own review of the events
that led him to authorize the crown to sequester the chapters' goods until they

76. Post, *Studies*, pp. 131–138.

paid their taxes (Doc. 29). His method, wherever it can be verified, was to sub-stantiate his case by quoting or closely paraphrasing the documents in the case.[77] Thus I think we can safely assume that the tenor of his summons is preserved in his later statement that he had called "the chapters of the cathedral churches of our legation, who were to appear in our presence by means of suitable proc-tors (*per procuratores idoneos*)" (Doc. 29.1).

Whereas Conrad had stated only the desired result and had left the chapter to devise the legal means to effect it, Romanus took a more legalistic approach by specifying that the chapters should be represented by "suitable proctors." Each word had a precise legal significance. A *procurator* was one who was legally au-thorized to act as another's agent; he was rendered *idoneus* by his personal qual-ifications, including his character and legal status, but most especially by his knowledge, both of the law and of the facts of the case.[78] Thus an agent who was a "suitable proctor" would be both personally and legally qualified to act without reference back to his constituents. Evidently, when the chapters sent nuncios instead of proctors to Bourges, they deliberately ignored the precise specifications of the citation mandate.[79] Indeed, it is quite possible that the sum-mons was even more explicit, since we know it only from Romanus' later de-scription, which may well have abridged a more extensive formulation into the concise phrase *procuratores idoneos*. If so, the summons probably called for proc-tors who were *sufficienter* (or *pleni*) *instructi*, which implied that they should be invested with *plena potestas*.[80] But since the text of the summons to Bourges has been lost, it is better to assume that this refinement first was introduced in the Canterbury summons of 1226, which stipulated proctors *pleni instructi* (Doc. 42.3). Nonetheless, we know enough about Romanus' summons to recognize that it was a landmark in the development of conciliar citation mandates. For the first time, a conciliar summons had used the technical terminology of Romano-canonical judicial procedure to describe the chapters' representatives. Conciliar representation *per procuratores idoneos* could proceed by rules already well established as part of court procedure. This analogy to private law was to provide the model for subsequent development of representative assemblies dur-ing their formative years in the thirteenth century. As the first conciliar sum-

---

77. Doc. 29.1 echoes the letter of legation (Doc. 12.pr. and § 5; Doc. 29.5 repeats the prom-ise of Doc. 26.6, and Doc. 29.6 paraphrases the mandate to pay (Doc. 28.5-7). Moreover, Doc. 29.3-4 appears to quote his charge to the council and the tenor of the *consilia* he received.

78. Post, *Studies*, pp. 137-138.

79. The distinction between *nuntius* and *procurator* is thoroughly discussed by Queller, *Of-fice of Ambassador*, pp. 3-59, esp. pp. 41 and 57-59.

80. As, for example, in the phrase of Innocent III: "per procuratores idoneos, ad omnia suf-ficienter instructos" (X 1.5.5, ed. Friedberg, II, 48).

mons to employ the terminology of the Roman law of representation, the summons to Bourges instituted this development.

Other persons present

The prelates and proctors were Romanus' counselors; together with him they constituted the council proper. But, as was usual at purely ecclesiastical councils, other persons, even laymen, might attend, either as invited observers or as interested parties. Since the council was the legate's highest court, persons might appear before it to seek justice, to defend themselves, or simply to petition the legate with the greatest possible publicity.[81] Thus eighty excommunicated masters of the University of Paris appeared before the council begging the legate's forgiveness for their assault on him (Doc. 3.6).

The two claimants to the county of Toulouse were of course both present, since the ostensible purpose of the council was to find a solution to the problem created by their conflicting claims. Two sources note only the presence of Raymond VII (Docs. 2.3 and 4.4.), but the more detailed narratives also mention Amaury de Montfort (Docs. 1.3 and 3.4), as does our most reliable source, Romanus himself (Doc. 29.1).

The different titles that are accorded to each of the rival claimants in the sources epitomize the situation on the eve of the council. Only Romanus styled Raymond "the former count of Toulouse" (Doc. 29.1), as the curia had been doing since 1221 (above, p. 10); most other sources simply called him "the count of Toulouse" (Docs. 1.3, 2.3, and 3.4), the exception being Philip Mousket, who for the sake of a malicious rhyme used an even more neutral style—"the count of St-Gilles" (Doc. 4.4), which appears also in the Reginensis extract (Doc. 6). On the other hand, although Amaury still was officially styling himself "duke of Narbonne, count of Toulouse, and lord of Montfort,"[82] no one else took the first two titles seriously any more. In the *Relatio* he appears as "the lord of Montfort," while both Romanus and the Chronicle of Tours style him "the count of Montfort" (Docs. 1.3, 3.4, and 29.1).

Both claimants no doubt appeared accompanied by their supporters. The Limoges chronicle states—so ungrammatically that it appears to have been an afterthought if not a later addition—that the "comes de Fois" was there (see above, n. 27). Since Roger-Bernard, the count of Foix, had been a party to both Montpellier conferences in the summer of 1224, it is not surprising that he would

81. Iung, "Concile," *Dictionnaire de droit canonique*, III, 1271; Glossa ord. ad X 3.10.10, v. *contingere*, quoted above, n. 66.

82. Teulet, no. 1675, dated Nov. 1224.

have come to Bourges as well, perhaps with the viscount of Béziers, Raymond-Roger Trencavel the younger, who also signed the Montpellier promises.[83]

Neither Raymond nor Amaury—not to mention any of their supporters—was a member of the council. They all appeared before the legate, who, with the assistance of his chosen counselors, was sitting in judgment on their claims.

Raymond came to the council with a safe-conduct from the king. It was issued less than three weeks before the council, at Melun when Louis was there for the royal council on 8 November (Doc. 3.2).[84] Count Thibault of Champagne was instructed to meet Raymond on 25 November at La Souterraine, on the frontier between the counties of Berry and La Marche about fifty kilometers southwest of Bourges,[85] and to conduct him, together with his followers and his goods, in safety to Bourges and back again before the safe-conduct expired at Christmas.[86] Of Raymond's movements before the council we know only that he had been at Cahors, the northernmost of his cities, on 10 October, so he may have already been expecting an invitation to the council, as Vaissète suggested.[87]

Was Louis VIII also at the council? Wendover, in his preface to the *Relatio*, says that he was invited (Doc. 1.1). Moreover, William of Andres, after describing the council in a sentence, added this last entry for 1226: "Exhorted by the lord legate and accompanied by him, King Louis and many nobles, both bishops and lay magnates, prepared and organized themselves to fulfil their vow as crusaders against the Albigensians" (Doc. 37.2). Although William most probably meant this sentence to describe the situation at the end of January 1226 (Docs. 23–27), the transition was not evident to his successor, John Le Long (*Longus*), who in 1375 revised the sentence to read: "In this council [at Bourges] the king of France and many nobles, together with the legate himself, took the Cross" (Doc. 38.2).

Beyond doubt the king was not there. Wendover, and Matthew Paris who revised his work, could have gathered this from their source, the *Relatio*, which reported that Romanus insisted that the written opinions he had received at the

83. Mentioned above as Raymond's associates (pp. 25–27).

84. In the style of the royal chancery, the document is dated only by month and year, but it would have been no later than 8 Nov. 1225, for the king returned to Paris on the day of the council: Petit-Dutaillis, *Louis*, p. 440.

85. L. S. Le Nain de Tillemont, *Vie de Saint Louis, roi de France*, ed. J. de Gaulle, I (Paris, 1847), p. 380. Tillemont apparently thought that Raymond was at Melun and was given safe conduct through the lands of Thibault: see Devic-Vaissète, VI, 593, n. 3 by Molinier. La Souterraine (*apud Subterraneum*) is on the Creuse in the modern arrondissement of Guéret.

86. Petit-Dutaillis, *Louis*, p. 488, reg. no. 285.

87. Devic-Vaissète, VI, 593.

council be kept secret because "he wished to show them to the king and to notify the pope" (Doc. 1.5). Had the king been present, such a precaution would
scarcely have been plausible. Furthermore, the king had an alibi, which is established from a list of the sums he collected in lieu of lodging from his vassals
when he stayed with them. By this right of gist (*gîte*) he received 155 *livres* on 29
November 1229 when he was staying "in the house of the bishop of Arras."[88]

★ ★ ★

Finally, this discussion of the council's composition may be summarized by
adding together our results:

Archbishops	13
Suffragan bishops	99
Abbots	520
Archdeacons	114
Deans	114
Proctors	114
	974

This total would be the *maximum* number of regular members, allowance having been made for the two absent archbishops; attendance in the other categories
was undoubtedly less than perfect, though how much less is difficult to estimate.
The number of suffragans given above is the total number of bishoprics in the
fifteen participating provinces (99), of whom I would guess that perhaps ten percent were absent. The figure for abbots comes from the unreliable Reginensis
extract, and although the basis for this number is unknown, I suspect that it, too,
is a maximum that should be reduced—again by at least ten percent—to no
more than 470 abbots. The last three groups are computed on the assumption
that each diocese sent an archdeacon, a dean, and a capitular proctor to the council. Since fifteen archdioceses and 99 dioceses were represented at Bourges, 114
would be the maximum size for each group. The deans and archdeacons, who
like the bishops and abbots were summoned personally, would be subject to
the same assumed attrition rate of perhaps ten percent. Death or sickness would
not thin the rank of the proctors to the same extent, however, because in most
cases a substitute could be appointed. Thus probably less than five percent of the
chapters were not represented by a proctor. All this, of course, is very rough

---

88. N. Brussel, *Nouvel examen de l'usage général des fiefs de France*, 2 vols. (Paris, 1727), II, 547:
"Sabbato ante festum sancti Nicholai, in domo Episcopi Attrebatensis. Gistum VII^{xx}XV. l."
This is from the list entitled "Gista Domini Regis (Gîtes de Louis VIII)" in the Register *Qui
es in coelis*, fol. 31, which was in the archives of the Chambre des comptes when Brussel examined it. See also Petit-Dutaillis, *Louis*, p. 440, based on Brussel's transcript.

guesswork, and the discounts that I have suggested are perhaps too modest, but I think it safe to say that the clerical members of the council are not likely to have exceeded 880 in number.

Seating

Bringing thirteen archbishops together inevitably raised the problem of precedence. The relative ranks of bishops within each province was not in question because they frequently met together in provincial councils, but the thirteen archbishops who assembled at Bourges hardly ever appeared at the same council, and when they did, some always took the occasion to assert their claims to primacy over others. The last time a council comparable to Bourges had been held in France, at Tours in 1163, the preliminary bickering over the seating arrangements had led the pope to declare that "anyone could take and hold any place."[89] At the Fourth Lateran Council, the metropolitans all seem to have been seated together, but there is no indication that the seating arrangements took precedence into account.[90] Indeed, that would seem unlikely, since a major question of precedence still remained undecided on the third day of the council.[91] Romanus, too, was confronted with the problem of precedence at Bourges, and neither the nature of the primatial claims nor his solution is entirely clear. Let us first attempt to clarify the problem and then consider what remedy the legate may have devised for it.

The *Relatio* is our only source for the dispute over primacy at Bourges (Doc. 1.2), but the surviving versions do not agree as to what claims were being made. Since Walter of Coventry omitted the relevant passage altogether, there is no easy way to resolve the differences between the other two versions, given by Roger Wendover and the Salisbury Register. Since each version will have to be judged on its own merits, let us consider each in turn, weighing its strengths and weaknesses.

According to Wendover's version, two metropolitans at the council claimed primacy: Lyon over Sens, and Rouen over Bourges, Auch, and Narbonne:[92]

89. R. Somerville, *Pope Alexander III and the Council of Tours (1163)* (Berkeley and Los Angeles, 1977), pp. 26–27.

90. S. Kuttner and A. García y García, "A New Eyewitness Account of the Fourth Lateran Council," *Traditio*, XX (1964), 115–178, at p. 124, lines 16–19. Cf. Somerville, *Council of Tours*, pp. 25 and esp. n. 62, p. 89.

91. Kuttner-García, "Fourth Lateran Council," p. 124, lines 41–43.

92. See Doc. 1.2; cf. Doc. 43. Text, including punctuation, as in Oxford, Bodleian Library, MS. Douce 207, fol. 189rb. Except for orthographic variants and punctuation, the text is identical with Matthew Paris' *Chronica majora* (Cambridge, Corpus Christi College, MS. 16, fol. 62va).

Set quoniam Lugdunensis archiepiscopus vendicabat sibi primaciam super archiepiscopum Senonensem & Rothomagensis super Byturicensem, Auxianensem, Narbonensem, & eorum suffraganeos timebatur de discordia & ideo non fuit sessum quasi in concilio set ut in consilio.

The claims of Lyon are altogether plausible, as we shall see, but those of Rouen are not. In the seventeenth century, Le Nain de Tillemont already suspected that the passage according primatial claims to Rouen might be corrupt,[93] and in the eighteenth century, Dom Vaissète soberly declared that he could discover no foundation for Rouen's alleged pretensions.[94] These doubts are firmly grounded in both geography and history. None of the three provinces are adjacent to Rouen, and what is more, there is no record, either before or since, that Rouen ever claimed to be their primate. Far from seeking primacy over others, Rouen had been subject to the primacy of Lyon since 1085.[95] Thus, since the pretensions attributed to Rouen in Wendover's version of the *Relatio* seem to be extremely unlikely, that text can be dismissed as corrupt.

The Salisbury Register attributes all the pretensions to Lyon alone: that archbishop is said to have claimed primacy over Sens, Rouen, Bourges, Bordeaux, Auch, and Narbonne:[96]

Set quia Lugdun' vendicavit sibi primatiam super Senon', Rothom', Bitur', Burdeg', & Axitanum & Narbon', et eorum suffraganeos timebatur discordia, & ideo non fuit sessum ut in concilio sed velud in consilio.

This claim, though not completely likely, is far more plausible. In the second century, Lyon had been not only the primatial church of Gaul but also, with one exception, the only bishopric.[97] Naturally, when other archbishoprics appeared in Gaul, Lyon could claim primacy over them, and it was still doing so in the thirteenth century. Thus Matthew Paris, annotating his copy of the *Liber provin-*

93. Tillemont, *Saint Louis*, I, 375: "L'archevesque de Rouen prétendoit la primatie et le rang sur ceaux de Bourges, Auch et Narbonne (*s'il n'y a faute dans l'auteur*). Celuy de Lyon la prétendoit sur Sens et sur Rouen, et apparemment sur les autres, puisqu'on tenoit qu'il avoit autrefois esté primate de toutes les Gaules."

94. Devic-Vaissète, VI, 594: "On ne comprend pas sur quel fondement les archevêques de Rouen pouvoient prétendre la primatie dans les trois provinces dont on vient de parler."

95. E. Caillemer, "Des Conflits entre l'église de Lyon et l'église de Rouen relativement à la primatie," *Mémoires de l'Académie des sciences, belles-lettres et arts de Lyon, Sciences et lettres,* 3rd ser., XIII (1913), 353–387, at p. 353.

96. Doc. 1.2; cf. Doc. 42. Text and punctuation from Trowbridge, Wiltshire County Record Office, D 1/1/1, p. 140.

97. L. Duchesne, *Fastes épiscopaux de l'ancienne Gaul*, 2nd ed., 3 vols. (Paris, 1907–1915), I, 40, gives Narbonne as the exception; but Lyon and Vienne are the only Christian communities in second-century Gaul noted in the *Atlas zur Kirchengeschichte*, map 2.

cialis, noted that "the archbishop of Lyon . . . is primate of all the Gauls."[98] However much Lyon might claim, the papacy only recognized Lyon's primacy over the three provinces of Rouen, Tours, and Sens, which at the time of Augustus had all been included in the Roman province of Lyon and which later had been distinguished in the *Notitia dignitatum* as Lugdunensis II, III, and IV. In 1079, two bulls of Pope Gregory VII had recognized Lyon's primacy over all three; Paschal II had confirmed this in 1116, and there the matter stood in 1225.[99] Thus the Salisbury version is not impossible; Lyon may have been pressing its claims to primacy over the other provinces of Gaul.

Yet inconsistencies in the Salisbury version keep it from being convincing. In the first place, it is unlikely that Lyon would be claiming precedence over the two archbishops who were absent—Bordeaux and Narbonne. Comparison with Wendover's version permits us to eliminate Bordeaux, for the name seems to have been thoughtlessly interpolated into the Salisbury version. Narbonne, too, would seem to have been an addition, but one that was found in the exemplar common to all English versions of the *Relatio*. Nonetheless, an earlier interpolation is suggested by the triple conjunction that concludes the Salibury list of provinces claimed:"et Axitanum et Narbonensem et eorum suffraganeos." Since Narbonne, because absent, does not fit the sense of the passage, we must conclude that the series originally ended with Auch and that Narbonne was subsequently added.

Even thus improved, the Salisbury text is still suspect. If Lyon was, as this version suggests, trying to assert its primacy over all the Gauls, then why was the province of Reims not included? The omission of Tours might be explained by the fact that Lyon's primacy over that province had been officially established since 1079. But the same was true of Rouen and Sens; why, then, were they included? Evidently the Salisbury version, though more satisfactory than Wendover's, still poses so many problems that it also must be considered corrupt.

The situation invites some emendation of the text. Let us assume, as we did above, that Bordeaux and Narbonne were not part of the seating problem because they were absent. That leaves us to account for five metropolitan sees that are mentioned in both versions of the passage: Lyon, Sens, Rouen, Bourges, and Auch. Lyons, as we have seen, was officially recognized as the primate of Sens and Rouen, so only Bourges and Auch really are in need of an explanation, and that is readily supplied. At the time of the council, the archbishop of Bourges

98. Matthew Paris, *Chronica majora*, ed. Luard, VI, 457, n. 3: "Archiepiscopus Lugdunensis . . . primas est omnium Galliarum. . . . "

99. *Gallia Christiana*, IV.i, 3–4, IV.ii, 8–9; A. Luchaire, *Manuel des institutions françaises* (Paris, 1892), p. 27; A. Rony, "Saint Jubin, archevêque de Lyon, et la primatie lyonnaise," *Revue d'histoire de l'église de France*, XV (1929), 409–430.

was actively pressing his claim to be recognized as primate of Aquitaine, which included not only Bordeaux but Auch as well.[100] Indeed, there is every reason to believe that the precedence problem at the council was raised by the archbishop of Bourges. The primatial rights of Lyon had been recognized by the papacy since 1079, whereas those of Bourges were currently being adjudicated before a papal judge-delegate, who in fact was Romanus himself.[101] Bourges thus would have been seeking any opportunity to strengthen his claim. As host to the council, and most probably in consequence its master of ceremonies as well, the archbishop of Bourges would have been in a position to propose seating arrangements that favored his pretensions. If the legate had accepted such a proposal, Bourges could then claim something close to papal approval for his primacy. Under these circumstances, it would be truly surprising if the archbishop of Bourges had not insisted on his pretended rights at the council. This reconstruction of the passage in Doc. 1.2 is therefore sufficiently justified:

> Sed quia Lugdunensis vendicavit sibi primatiam super Senonensem et Rothomagensem, Bituricensis super Burdegalensem et Auxitanum [et Narbonensem] et eorum suffraganeos. . . .

Translated into the provincial nomenclature of the *Notitia dignitatum*, Lugdunensis I would accordingly be claiming primacy over Lugdunensis II and IV, and Aquitania I over Aquitania III. Considered in these terms, since Narbonensis was always a province distinct from the Aquitaines, "et Narbonensem" must be regarded as an ignorant interpolation, as the superfluous *et* suggests; and moreover it is easy to see why Lyon made no claim over Reims (Belgica II). The only difficulty unresolved is why the *Relatio* did not also include Tours (Lugdunensis III), which since 1079 was no less subject to Lyon than were Rouen and Sens.

Since neither version of the *Relatio*'s primacy passage mentions Tours, the likelihood is that it did not appear in the exemplar. The erroneous addition of Narbonne to the exemplar assures us that the passage had been reviewed and revised, however uncritically, so we must assume that the omission of Tours was not an oversight. Why, then, would Tours be omitted intentionally? Most likely because the author of the *Relatio* did not care to acknowledge that Tours might be subject to the primacy of Lyon. If the *Relatio* was written by one of the proctors of a cathedral chapter, as seems most probable, then the author would have had a financial interest in denying the primacy of Lyon over his province, be-

---

100. L. de Lacger, "La Primatie et le pouvoir métropolitain de l'archevêque de Bourges au XIIIᵉ siècle," *Revue d'histoire ecclésiastique*, XXVI (1930), 45-60, 268-330, esp. pp. 53-61.

101. Pressutti, no. 5328.

cause the cathedral chapters of a province that was being visited by its primate were liable to pay him a fee (*procuratio*).[102] As long as this possibility cannot be excluded, I do not think Tours can be restored to the text as a probable conjecture of the author's intention. On the other hand, we have at least a plausible explanation for the omission of Tours from the text, and what is more, a possible indication that the author of the *Relatio* came from one of the dozen cathedral chapters in the province of Tours.

To summarize: the question of primatial precedence would seem to have been raised before the council convened. Almost certainly the archbishop of Bourges, probably under the pretext of making the local arrangements, proposed a seating order based on his primacy and that of Lyon. No doubt it was the legate who vetoed this proposal and in its place substituted another manner of seating the archbishops that was not based on precedence. But what that alternative arrangement might have been we can only guess. According to the *Relatio*, "it was feared there would be discord; and for that reason they did not sit as in a council but as if in consultation (*in consilio*)" (Doc. 1.2). What does that mean? It is easier to say how they were *not* seated than how they were. What was being avoided was the sort of arrangement that was used in 1237 at the legatine council of London, where the legate sat on a dais with the archbishop of Canterbury in the place of honor on his right and York in second place on his left.[103] Probably the archbishops at Bourges sat together, facing the platform occupied by the president, as at the Lateran in 1215 and as Matthew Paris depicted the legatine council held at London in 1237.[104] Possibly they sat with the legate on the platform, facing the rest of the council, as in 1237, but either way, the guiding principle would have been that within the archbishops' section, "anyone could take and hold any seat."[105] All that can be said for certain is that each archbishop was not sitting with the bishops of his province, because in the course of the proceedings it was necessary for each metropolitan to collect his suffragans before deliberating with them (Doc. 1.5).

★ ★ ★

One is tempted to imagine the council taking place in the huge interior of the cathedral of St-Etienne as it exists today, but such was not the case, for in 1225

---

102. X 1.33.17 *Humilis*, ed. Friedberg, II, 202–203; cf. Post, *Studies*, p. 174, and Lacger, "La Primatie," p. 296.

103. Powicke-Cheney, *Councils & Synods*, II.i, 241. Matthew Paris ignored this arrangement in his illustration of the council (see frontispiece).

104. *The Illustrated Chronicles of Matthew Paris*, ed. R. Vaughan (Cambridge, Eng., 1993), p. 124, from Cambridge, Corpus Christi College, MS. 16, fol. 109r (see frontispiece).

105. Above, nn. 89–90.

the present structure was only half complete. Work on the new Gothic cathedral had begun in 1195, and by 1214 the eastern half had been completed, including the immense hemispherical chevet, which could hold two hundred persons—the entire clergy of the archdiocese—and the first straight bay. By careful planning, this had been achieved without disturbing the old nave, which for over a decade after 1214 was linked to the new choir and sanctuary in the chevet. This was the configuration that obtained in 1225 and until construction resumed sometime before 1230.[106] Consequently we can picture the Council of Bourges as taking place with the soaring chevet as its backdrop. No doubt the legate himself was centrally seated in front of the main altar, while the choir could accommodate the archbishops and probably the bishops as well; but the rest of the participants would have been crowded into the old nave, which was less than half the size of the present one.[107]

Ceremonial

Medieval councils ordinarily were celebrated with a more or less elaborate liturgical ritual. At Bourges a shorter form was probably used because the agenda was too crowded to indulge in the leisurely rituals commonly provided for councils that were spread over three days or more. Although our sources are silent about the liturgical aspect of the Council of Bourges, enough is known about similar occasions to justify some suggestions as to how the council was celebrated.

In the first place, there was no set form for a legatine council such as Bourges. Appropriate forms for diocesan and provincial councils are provided in the medieval collections of liturgical *ordines*, or orders; but no *ordo* survives that was expressly intended for a legatine council. No doubt the legate adapted one of the existing forms for his purpose. Consequently, the problem is to identify the sources on which Romanus would most likely have drawn. Since he was a cardinal-deacon, not a bishop, he is unlikely to have possessed his own *Pontificale*, or book of episcopal ceremonies. Even if he had a *Pontificale*, it would have offered him no explicit guidance for this occasion, as there are no conciliar *ordines* specifically designed for a legatine council.

Most likely, he adopted the simple ceremony used for the opening session of the Fourth Lateran Council: after Mass, everyone was seated; the hymn *Veni creator* was sung, followed by the collect *Actiones nostras, quaesumus, Domine*, and finally by a sermon.[108] The Mass might have been that of the Holy Spirit, which

106. R. Branner, *The Cathedral of Bourges and Its Place in Gothic Architecture*, 2nd ed. (New York, 1989), pp. 14, 19, 55–56, and figs. 10–11 for the state of construction in 1214 and 1232.
107. Branner, *Cathedral of Bourges*, p. 19 and fig. 4.
108. Kuttner-García, "Fourth Lateran Council," p. 124, lines 25–32.

was commonly used at councils in England, and though rarely associated with councils in France, may have been suggested to Romanus by its use in the law faculty at Bologna.[109] All of these elements were readily and commonly available—the Mass and collect in the *Missale Romanum*[110] and the hymn in the *Brevarium Romanum*[111]—so Romanus could easily have appropriated them for a service modeled on the Fourth Lateran Council.

On the other hand, Romanus may have left the ceremonial arrangements up to his host, the archbishop of Bourges. If this were the case, the archbishop might well be guided by his *Pontificale*, but unfortunately no pontifical of Bourges provenance has survived for the period before 1225; indeed, the only pre-1225 conciliar order used in that province is based on one used at the Council of Limoges in 1031, known through its tendentious adaptation by Adhemar of Chabannes, which was never widely distributed.[112] This provincial *ordo* does, however, include the prayer *Actiones nostras*,[113] which otherwise was rarely put to conciliar use before the Fourth Lateran Council.[114] Thus it is just possible that *Actiones nostras* was still being used at Bourges councils and would have been the archbishop's conciliar collect of choice.

Of course it is also always possible that the brief ceremony at Bourges was based neither on the precedent of the Fourth Lateran Council nor on local practice at Bourges: there was an abundance of conciliar *ordines* to draw on. For example, the collect may have been *Adsumus, sancte Spiritus, adsumus*, a Visigothic

109. Weske, *Convocation*, pp. 140-141; the Mass is specified in a thirteenth-century order from the diocese of Meaux (Sens province): Martène-Durand, *Thesaurus*, IV, 891. Cf. R. J. Schoeck, "Medieval Lawyers and the Red Mass: Towards a History of the Mass of the Holy Ghost," *Saint Louis University Law Journal*, V (1958), 274-279, ascribing the Mass to Alcuin.

110. In the 1920 edition of the *Missale Romanum*, the Mass of the Holy Spirit is one of the "Missae votivae"; *Actiones nostras* forms part of the "Gratiarum actio post missam."

111. In the *Brevarium Romanum*, the hymn *Veni creator spiritus* has been used at Pentecost since the tenth century for Vespers, and since the twelfth century for Terce: *New Catholic Encyclopedia*, XIV, 600.

112. *Die Konzilsordines des Früh- und Hochmittelalters*, ed. Herbert Schneider, MGH, Ordines de celebrando concilo (Hanover, 1996), p. 577 (ordo 27.10). On Adhemar's confections, see idem, pp. 111-117.

113. "Actiones nostras, quesumus, domine, et aspirando preveni et adiuvando prosequere: ut cuncta nostra operatio et a te semper incipiat, et per te cepta finiatur. Per." Text from Paris, BnF, MS. lat. 934, fol. 10v–11r. The prayer was doubled in length by the addition of another clause ("ut . . . gaudeamus") in a Catalan conciliar order ca. 1000 (Schneider's ordo 27.3, p. 587).

114. An exception is Schneider's ordo 29.3 (p. 587; Catalonia, ca. 1000). *Actiones nostra, quaesumus, Domine* goes back to the Gregorian Sacramentary (early seventh century?); it was suitable for many occasions—e.g. in late twelfth-century French pontificals, it appears in orders for dedicating or consecrating churches: Sens, Bibl. mun., MS. 9, fol. 68r, and Paris, BnF, MS. lat. 934, fol. 10v–11r (cf. n. 113, above). After 1225, the prayer is found in a number of French synodal *ordines* (Lodève, Meaux, Sens).

composition, often attributed to Isidore of Seville, that was widely diffused in France.[115] This prayer invokes the Holy Spirit to guide the participants in their judgments and to prevent the miscarriage of justice "so that we are neither led astray by ignorance, nor swayed by favoritism, nor corrupted by the acceptance of a gift or regard for a person."[116] Whether Romanus was guided by the Lateran precedent or by French *ordines*, the result was probably much the same. The conciliar ceremony proper probably took up less than fifteen minutes between an early morning Mass and a sermon that served to introduce the business of the day. When, at the end of the first session, the council was—unexpectedly, it would seem—adjourned overnight (Doc. 2.3), an even shorter variation of the same service would have been used to open the second session. Judging from other multiday conciliar *ordines*, probably the sermon was omitted and a different collect was used.[117]

★　★　★

As the first order of business, the legate had his letter of legation (Doc. 12) read aloud before the assembly (Doc. 1.3). This was the usual procedure at legatine councils,[118] since they existed only in virtue of this document that gave the legate his authority to convoke and preside over the prelates of his legation. Those who heard Romanus' letter would have had no doubt that, as the pope's accredited agent, he had full authority to do whatever seemed best to him. He had gathered together the prelates and proctors of his legation—over eight hundred of them—for one purpose: in order to commit them and their churches to finance a royal crusade against the Albigensians.

---

115. On the origin, see Schneider, *Konzilsordines*, pp. 142 and 177, n. 26; on the diffusion, see his list (p. 599, no. 19). The incipit varies, the modern form being *Adsumus, Domine, adsumus*; cf. the mixed form *Assumus, domine sancte spiritus, assumus* (Schneider, p. 356, ordo 9.3, saec. xi).

116. "Adsumus, sancte spiritus, adsumus peccati quidem inmanitate detenti, sed in nomine tuo specialiter adgregati. Veni ad nos, adesto nobis, et dignare inlabi cordibus nostris. Doce nos, quid agamus; quo gradiamur, ostende; quid efficiamus, operare. Esto solus et sugges<t>or et effector iudiciorum nostrorum, qui solus cum deo patre et eius filio nomen possides gloriosum. Non nos patiaris perturbatores esse iustitiae, qui summe diligis aequitatem, ut in sinistrum nos non ignorantia trahat, non favor inflectat, non acceptio muneris vel persone corrumpat; sed iunge nos tibi efficaciter solius tuae gratiae dono, ut sic in cunctis teneamus cum moderamine pietatis iustitiam, ut et hic a te in nullo dissentiat sententia nostra et in futuro pro bene gestis consequamur premia sempiterna." From Schneider's ordo 2.3 (p. 177).

117. See, e.g., Schneider's ordo 2B (pp. 190-192).

118. Weske, *Convocation*, p. 126; e.g. Powicke-Cheney, *Councils & Synods*, II.i, 238.

CHAPTER 4

GRANTING THE ALBIGENSIAN TENTH

The prelates and proctors who assembled at Bourges knew from their summons that they had come to help the legate devise a solution to the Occitanian problem. Conrad's council two years earlier must have made most of them aware that royal intervention was one of the possibilities, but before and during his council Romanus took care not to make this appear to be the goal. Instead, he directed the council's attention to the possibility of a peaceful solution, which indeed was the only topic that was thoroughly discussed at Bourges. As Romanus later explained, "it seemed expedient to us that we first diligently consider whether peace could be made between those nobles [Raymond and Amaury]" (Doc. 29.2). His plan, quite simply, was to convince his counselors that they could not in good conscience advise him to make peace with Raymond; if he succeeded, then they would be forced to accept royal intervention as the alternative. Perhaps the legate made this dilemma clear from the beginning; certainly, his final charge to his counselors was posed in terms of either peace or war. Probably during the proceedings he concentrated on making peace seem impossible, so that his council would accept war as the inevitable alternative.

The entire proceedings can be reconstructed to a degree that is remarkable for councils of this period. Partly this is because the Council of Bourges provided most churchmen with their first opportunity to learn Raymond's position, since up to then negotiations had been shrouded in secrecy. Thus chroniclers were moved to record what seemed to them both notable and novel. Partly, too, clerical chroniclers sympathized with Raymond because his loss was also theirs; writing about the injustice done to him at Bourges was for them another way of complaining about papal taxation. Thus clerical chroniclers have left four independent accounts of the peace negotiations: the *Relatio* (Doc. 1.3–5), the Dunstable Annals (Doc. 2.3), the Chronicle of Tours (Doc. 3.4), and Roger Wendover's annal (Doc. 43.16). In varying degrees, all these accounts by clerics seem well disposed towards Raymond; their good will contrasts sharply with the uninformed hostility of the bourgeois chronicler, Philip Mousket, who neither knew nor cared what the issues were (Doc. 4.4). Finally, these sources can all be controlled by Romanus' own version of the deliberations (Doc. 29.2–4). Each of these accounts is selective, but their fragments record precise and seldom contradictory facts that, taken together, permit us to reconstruct at least the general tenor of the proceedings.

The problem of Raymond's reconciliation

The first phase of the council was structured by Romanus as an adversary proceeding between Raymond and Amaury. "Publicly in the presence of all those named above [the prelates and proctors]," the legate recalled, "we heard and understood both what Raymond chose to propose for his side and the count of Montfort for his" (Doc. 29.2). But the chroniclers do not agree about the precise order in which the arguments were advanced. One eyewitness account presents Amaury's arguments first (Doc. 1.3) and another begins with a full statement of Raymond's appeal (Doc. 3.4). Who spoke first is of little importance, however, because both eyewitnesses make it clear that the parties engaged in a running debate. One reports a second speech by Amaury (Doc. 1.4), while the other simply says that there was "much argument back and forth" (Doc. 3.4). Each chronicler tried to summarize the long debate in a few sentences, so it is not surprising to find that the literary presentation varies. What is important is that there is substantial agreement on the arguments that were advanced; the order of presentation, though it could afford some insight into forensic tactics, is relatively unimportant and cannot be reconstructed from our sources. Accordingly, we are left to impose our own order on these materials, and this can best be done by viewing them as a resumption of the negotiations that had been suspended ten months ago when Romanus was sent to France (above, p. 29).

The issues had been clearly defined by Honorius in April 1224, when the pope laid down four conditions for Raymond's reconciliation: the count would have to eliminate heresy from his land; he should make restitution to the Church; he had to guarantee ecclesiastical liberty; and, finally, he ought to make some provision for Amaury's honor (above, p. 24). By the end of August 1224, the Provençal prelates with whom Raymond had twice conferred at Montpellier were satisfied that Raymond could and would fulfill the pope's conditions (above, p. 26). True, some of the details remained undecided, but these were left for the pope to settle; and for good measure, Raymond had sworn an oath that, if the pope demanded more of him, he would do his best to obey, provided only that he was not obliged to violate the rights of his feudal overlords, the emperor and the king of France.

At this point in the negotiations, the only major point that remained unresolved was a settlement with Amaury, who had refused to participate in the Montpellier conferences. Raymond had hoped to circumvent the problem by paying a huge indemnity of twenty thousand marks to the papacy, which the pope could divide between Amaury and the injured churches of Occitania as he saw fit.[1] But the pope, most probably under pressure from King Louis (above, pp. 32-37), had refused to penalize Amaury for absenting himself from Montpellier and had even declined the responsibility of placating his unsuccessful champion. This punctilious concern for Amaury's rights was, of course, a delaying tactic. As long as Amaury refused to accept any offer that Raymond proposed, the reconciliation could be postponed indefinitely—and certainly would be, inasmuch as Amaury was not free to dispose of his rights since he had given Louis an option on them in February 1224 (above, pp. 19-20).

Negotiations were thus suspended in January 1225, and Romanus was sent with power to resume and conclude them as he chose. He kept Raymond waiting for ten months and then reopened the case by bringing together the two claimants at Bourges. Thus the proceedings there had every appearance of being a continuation of the negotiations at Montpellier fifteen months earlier. Since Raymond had already come to terms with the Occitanian church, peace between Raymond and Amaury was the only unsettled issue. Hence Romanus put that issue in first place on the agenda: if they could reach an agreement, Raymond could be reconciled. It was, as the legate said, what "seemed expedient to us" (Doc. 29.2).

Raymond presents his case

Yet this was no mere peace conference between the two rival claimants. Above all, the Council of Bourges was a trial of Raymond. The fundamental fact was that he was an excommunicate, and probably had been since he had attacked Beaucaire in May 1216 (above, p. 4).[2] This fact was so obvious to our clerical sources that none of them bothered to mention it, though it is clearly implicit in the Chronicle of Tours, which tells us that when Raymond came to Bourges "begging that the bosom of holy mother Church be opened to him, he humbly requested absolution" (Doc. 3.4). It is our bourgeois source, Philip Mousket, that puts the matter plainly: Raymond left the council as excommunicated as when he came, or more so if that were possible (Doc. 4.4).

The decision whether Raymond was to be reconciled or not lay entirely with Romanus. He could have conducted negotiations privately if he chose, but in-

1. Raymond's oath, correctly dated Montpellier, 25 Aug. 1224, ed. Mansi, XXII, 1207-1208 (misdated 26 Aug.).

2. Raymond's excommunication was attested long after the event by Honorius, who on 29 June 1220 and again on 3 June 1221 reminded Raymond that he had been excommunicated for invading both the lands reserved for him (May 1216) and his father's former lands (Sept. 1217): "excommunicationis sententia propter hoc in te latam a multis jam annis . . ." (Pressutti, nos. 2412 and 3434, ed. Horoy, III, 457 and 832).

stead he wished to involve the churches of his legation in the decision because their participation would commit them to war, and to war taxes, if they could not counsel Romanus to make peace with Raymond. Thus Bourges took the form of the legate's high court, over which he presided as judge, assisted by the other members, who sat as his counselors. After Raymond had had his hearing, the question they would have to answer was this: Was Raymond "to be absolved on the basis of what he had offered" (Doc. 29.4)?

Thus neither Romanus nor Raymond took the agreement at Montpellier as granted. Instead, Raymond repeated all the offers he had already made at Montpellier and Rome. This was necessary, of course, partly because most of the prelates and proctors did not know what his earlier offers had been, and partly because certain points doubtless required clarification. Hence Raymond did not limit himself to the issue of peace with Amaury, which Honorius had left unresolved, but carefully repeated his former offers for the benefit of a new audience that would have to decide whether he was offering enough to justify his reconciliation. Accordingly, in reconstructing the case that Raymond presented at Bourges, we shall have to take his earlier offers at Montpellier into account. Since the order of presentation at Bourges is unknown, let us adopt the one used at Montpellier, which begins with the least controversial matters, proceeds through the agreements reached at Montpellier, and concludes with the difficult problem posed by Amaury's claims.

★ ★ ★

1. *Raymond's faith.* At Montpellier, Raymond had promised first that "we shall observe the Catholic faith just as the holy Roman church preaches and teaches it."[3] Since his personal faith had never been in question, this assurance was easily given and readily accepted. The matter was so unimportant that only one chronicle troubled to note Raymond's profession at Bourges, where he assured the legate that "we hold the Catholic faith" (Doc. 2.3). More striking were his various proposals to demonstrate his faith. According to one source, "he offered to purge himself" (Doc. 3.4), and according to another, the count also offered "to undergo an examination of his faith if the legate wished" (Doc. 43.16). The same sources also agree that he was prepared to "mend his ways" as a repentant sinner was expected to do (Doc. 3.4). More specifically, "Raymond offered to give full satisfaction to God and holy Church as a faithful Christian if he had failed to do his duty in any way, which he did not recall having done" (Doc. 43.16).

2. *Heretics.* It was harder to guarantee the faith of his subjects, but Raymond had sworn nonetheless at Montpellier that "we shall equally and faithfully cause the Catholic faith to be observed throughout our land just as the holy Roman

3. Mansi, XXII, 1207C.

church preaches and teaches it. Moreover, we shall faithfully purge our land of heretics in this manner: we shall confiscate the goods and punish corporally the persons of those whom the Church judges to be heretics."[4] In effect, he was acknowledging his willingness to assume the responsibility that the Fourth Lateran Council had imposed on temporal lords to repress heresy in their lands.[5] The issue was a crucial one, for it had been the downfall of Raymond's father, who had never been able to deal with heretics as the Church wished. Therefore the solutions that the son proposed at Bourges were particularly noted. The chronicler of Tours remembered that Raymond offered "to the best of his ability to do justice to all convicted or confessed heretics in his land without delay, and from now on to expedite their eradication" (Doc. 3.4). Moreover, Raymond backed up this general statement with a specific plan by which his subjects would have to pass the same examination of their faith that he had offered to undergo himself. "There [at Bourges], with many pleas, Raymond had tried to persuade the legate to come to each of the cities of his land to inquire into the articles of their faith. And if the legate should find anyone who held opinions contrary to the Catholic faith, the count promised that he himself would exact full justice from them according to the judgment of holy Church" (Doc. 43.16).

Before the papacy established the Inquisition in 1231 as an organized, permanent, and ongoing inquiry into the faith of Christians, such an inquest as Raymond proposed was the most methodical and efficient means available for uprooting heresy. Striking though this offer doubtless was, the means were relatively unimportant, since it was the Church's business, not Raymond's, to identify heretics. The important point for Raymond's reconciliation was that he agreed to impose and inflict civil penalties on those whom the Church judged to be heretical. He must acknowledge that the Church alone was competent to judge matters that concerned the Christian faith, and, what is more, that the temporal ruler who wished to remain in good standing with the Church was obliged to penalize the person and property of anyone whom the Church had condemned as a heretic.

The statements quoted above suggest that Raymond agreed to comply without reservation, even though he added the qualification that the heretics should be destroyed "in such a way that the righteous may not perish by mistake instead of the impious" (Doc. 2.3). Yet under the circumstances it seems most unlikely that he would have shown himself in any way hesitant to accept the judgments of the Church. Instead, I think this remark must be regarded as a plea that heretics be condemned by due process of law, as they would be if his proposal

---

4. Mansi, XXII, 1207C.

5. *Constitutiones concilii quarti Lateranensis una cum commentariis glossatorum*, ed. A. García y García (Vatican City, 1981), pp. 47-51 (Lateran IV, c.3 = X 5.7.13).

for an inquest were adopted. What it rejects is the indiscriminate slaughter of whole populations on the principle that "God will know his own."[6]

3. *Rebels*. Although civil order was not on the pope's list of essential issues, it evidently was seen as a problem by the Provençal churchmen who negotiated the Montpellier settlement. There Raymond swore that "we shall keep full and unbroken peace in our entire land, and we shall cause it to be kept most fully by expelling from our boundaries those who break the peace."[7] Raymond made the same offer at Bourges but with a new variation: "He also promised that he would make his land obedient to the Roman church in every other way (*de cetero*), and would make it peaceful and secure as well" (Doc. 3.4). Obedience to Rome would have become an issue in the event that the legate undertook a general inquest, for Wendover explains that "if the legate found any city to be rebellious" on the tour that Raymond was proposing, the count also promised that "if any city refused to obey, he would do all that he could to compel that city and its inhabitants to give satisfaction" (Doc. 43.16).

4. *Restitution*. Honorius was more concerned that Raymond make restitution to the Church and had made this one of his essential conditions. Accordingly, at Montpellier Raymond had given his word in June that "we shall restore the rights of churches and churchmen to them in full," and by the end of August he had satisfied most of the bishops. Moreover, he had offered to pay Honorius twenty thousand silver marks, which the pope could use to indemnify Amaury and injured clerics as he saw fit.[8] This method of compensation was abandoned at Bourges, and instead Raymond acknowledged his unlimited liability to repay the churches directly: he promised "that he would restore to clerics their revenues in full and would suitably make good their losses" (Doc. 3.4).

5. *Ecclesiastical liberty*. Honorius had been equally insistent that Raymond should guarantee ecclesiastical liberty, and the count's response at Montpellier seems to have been entirely satisfactory. "We shall observe the liberties of churches and other religious places," he promised, "and we shall cause them to be observed most fully in future and forever."[9] Our sources, however, are silent

6. Although the remark may be apocryphal, the indiscriminate slaughters are not: e.g. Béziers 1209, Toulouse 1212, Marmande 1219. The remark was attributed to Arnaud Amaury, the papal legate with Simon de Montfort at the capture of Béziers in 1209, by Caesarius of Heisterbach, *Dialogus miraculorum* 5.21 (composed 1219-1223), ed. J. Strange, 2 vols. (Cologne, 1851), I, 301-302. English trans. in R. Kay, *The Broadview Book of Medieval Anecdotes* (Peterborough, Can., 1988), pp. 227-228. For an extended discussion, see J. Berlioz, *"Tuez-les tous, Dieu reconnaîtra les siens"* (Portet-sur-Garonne, 1994). It is noteworthy that Honorius III shared Raymond's concern that the innocent might suffer (see n. 36, below).

7. Mansi, XXII, 1207C.

8. Mansi, XXII, 1207C.

9. Mansi, XXII, 1207C.

about this matter at Bourges. Probably Raymond routinely repeated his assurances, which seemed unremarkable and hence went unreported. Otherwise, if he had failed to respond to a question on which the pope had laid particular stress, surely he would have been so pressed to comply that the chroniclers would have taken notice.

Thus it appears that at Bourges Raymond renewed the offers he had made at Montpellier to maintain his own orthodoxy, to repress heretics and rebels, to make restitution to the clergy, and to preserve ecclesiastical liberties. He certainly touched on four of the five issues, and probably the fifth as well; in each case his position seems to have remained substantially the same; and none of these old issues seems to have stirred up any controversy at Bourges. Judging from the reaction of the chroniclers, we can see that Raymond's new audience was indeed impressed by his offers. The legate, however, did not care how far Raymond was prepared to cooperate, just so long as there was one last step that the count would *not* take. Therefore the critical issue at Bourges was, as Romanus stated, the question of peace between Raymond and Amaury.

6. *Amaury.* Raymond's stumbling block was to be the final condition for his reconciliation, namely that he provide for Amaury's honor. The state of the problem in November 1225 can best be seen from Raymond's previous offer, made fifteen months earlier at Montpellier:

> Furthermore, we shall give twenty thousand marks of silver to the Church, to be paid in suitable installments, for the losses and injuries suffered by churches and churchmen, and so that the honor of the count of Montfort can be provided for, which we do out of reverence because the honor of the Roman church and of the lord pope requires it. This payment shall be made provided that the lord pope absolve us from the claim that the count of Montfort is making against our land and our assets and provided that the lord pope cause the pertinent instruments to be returned to us that the same count of Montfort or his father is said to have received from the same lord pope or from the lord king of France or his father.[10]

Raymond was evidently careful not to acknowledge under oath that Amaury had any right to the lands he claimed in Occitania. Moreover, Raymond was not at all certain what royal or papal charters Amaury could produce to substantiate his claims. He did, however, want to establish clear title to his lands, which he proposed to accomplish both by having Amaury surrender his muniments and by having the highest court in Christendom declare that Montfort had no claim to the lands of St-Gilles. Raymond would not allow that his rival had any right to compensation, but he did acknowledge that the papacy

10. Mansi, XXII, 1207C.

was honorbound to make some provision for Amaury. Thus, out of reverence for the papacy rather than in recognition of Amaury's claims, he would provide it with the means to settle its account with Amaury as it saw fit. By lumping the money for Amaury together with the ecclesiastical reparations, Raymond even avoided placing a cash value on the Montfort claims. Assuming that Honorius was indeed eager to negotiate a peaceful settlement, as he had been in 1224, the proposal was a tactful compromise that should have satisfied all parties.

Amaury asserts his rights

But at Bourges there was to be no compromise. Both our eyewitness accounts provide virtually identical versions of Amaury's appearance before the council. According to the *Relatio*, he "requested the restitution of the land that the lord pope and King Philip of France had conferred on his father, Simon, and in proof of the gift he produced documents from both the pope and the king" (Doc. 1.3). The Chronicle of Tours is more specific about the documents that Amaury exhibited in opposition to Raymond: he "displayed letters of Pope Innocent and also of King Philip of France that contained both the condemnation of the said count of Toulouse and the donation of the land of the Albigensians made to his father Simon de Montfort" (Doc. 3.4). Both documents can be identified from this description: the one from Innocent III was *Quantum ecclesia laboravit*, the ordinance of the Fourth Lateran Council that distributed the lands of Raymond VI, a copy of which was sent to Simon de Montfort on the day it was issued, 14 December 1215;[11] the one from Philip Augustus was the charter that recorded the king's reception of Simon as his vassal at Melun on 10 April 1216.[12]

Amaury also strengthened his case by defaming Raymond's character without justification. According to Wendover, who interpolated the remark in his version of the *Relatio*, Amaury "added that, by judgment in the general council at Rome, Count Raymond had been deprived because of heresy from at least the greater part of the land that he now held" (Doc. 1.3, app. crit.). Although, as Kuttner and García have shown, a careless reading of *Quantum ecclesia laboravit* could lead even a Vatican clerk to think that Raymond VI had been deprived "propter heresim," in fact he had only been vaguely declared "negligent (*cupabilis*)," and no judgment whatsoever had been passed on his son.[13]

Amaury's case was simplicity itself: having asserted his rights and demonstrated them by producing unquestionable documentary evidence, he had done everything necessary to establish those rights before a medieval court of law;

11. Potthast, no. 5011, ed. *Rec. hist. Gaules*, XIX, 606. See also chap. 1, n. 4.

12. *Rec. hist. Gaules*, XIX, 646 n.; see above, p. 0.

13. S. Kuttner and A. García y García, "A New Eyewitness Account of the Fourth Lateran Council," *Traditio*, XX (1964), 115-178, at pp. 141-142, esp. n. 73.

now he was demanding that the legate and his council should recognize Montfort's title and make Raymond surrender Occitania to him.

The legate then asked Raymond whether he was prepared to comply, and the reply was: "I indeed shall not give my inheritance to another. I lost it because of a military defeat, and when that proved to be only temporary, I regained it justly. Nevertheless, for the sake of peace I shall pay him three thousand marks" (Doc. 2.3). This response was only to be expected: after all, Raymond had come to Bourges to bargain, not to capitulate. And why should he surrender? The people of Occitania clearly preferred his rule to that of Amaury or any northerner, and his recent successes suggested that his troops could more than hold their own against an unwanted invader. Moreover, he knew that he was already acceptable to the Occitanian church, and given Rome's vacillating attitude towards him in recent years, it was reasonable to suppose that in time the pope, too, would reach an accommodation with him. The greatest risk he ran was a royal crusade, but if he could weather that storm, eventually either Rome or Paris would recognize him; if not, he would at least maintain his honor by defending his heritage. Therefore he pursued the course he had already set at Montpellier and attempted to compensate Amaury for his losses, changing only the pretext, which now became "the sake of peace" rather than reverence for the papacy. In retrospect, of course, he was right, for in spite of everything he was reconciled in 1229; but even at Bourges his decision to defend his patrimony must have seemed prudent and honorable.

Proposed trial by the twelve peers of France

For the most part, the chronicles attempt only to indicate the basic position that each claimant defended without reporting the ensuing debate in detail, except to note that there was "much dispute on both sides" (Doc. 1.5). One fragment of the exchange has been preserved, however, which suggests that Raymond had been countering Amaury's claims by arguing that in feudal law neither pope nor king was competent to deprive a vassal of his fief without a judgment against him by his peers. It was probably in response to some such contention as this that Amaury asked Raymond "to submit himself to the judgment of the twelve peers of France" (Doc. 1.4).

He was referring to an institution that has intrigued French historians because it flits like a will-o'-the-wisp across the first half of the thirteenth century, mentioned too often to ignore but never clearly enough for us to be sure that it was something that was done rather than merely talked about.[14] Judgment

14. The state of the question is summarized, with references, in *Histoire des institutions françaises au Moyen Age*, ed. F. Lot and R. Fawtier, II (Paris, 1958), 297 n., to which may be added the older view in Devic-Vaissète, VII, 74-81, with comments by Molinier.

by peers was, of course, an established principle of feudal society; all free men claimed the right to be judged, not by their lord, but by their equals, and the highest nobles were especially insistent.[15] With the rapid growth of royal justice in the reign of Philip Augustus, the great nobles of France who sought justice in the king's court found themselves being judged there not only by their peers but also by royal officials trained in law but drawn from the lesser nobility. Not wishing to become *déclassés*, the higher nobles resisted this innovation by claiming that the greatest vassals of the crown could be judged only by one another. Scholars cannot agree whether the twelve peers of France were a recognized judicial body before this crisis arose, or even whether they ever exercised the exclusive jurisdiction that they claimed, but there is no doubt that some such claims were being made at the time of the Council of Bourges. In 1224, when the royal court was about to hear a case involving the countess of Flanders, who was one of the twelve peers, it was argued that only the "peers of France" should sit in judgment on her, but this plea was rejected on the ground that it was already the customary practice for a peer to be judged by royal officials as well as by the peers.[16] This decision did not discourage peers, and especially Flanders, from continuing to claim the right for at least another twelve years.[17]

Thus Amaury's suggestion was consistent with the contemporary ambitions of the great vassals to be judged only by one another. Nonetheless, historians have been hesitant to accept the report of Amaury's proposal as authentic because it limits the number of peers to *twelve*, which no French source before this time does. To be sure, that number of peers was specified as early as 1211 by an English author, Gervase of Tilbury, but it has been suspected that he may have derived it from the legends of Charlemagne rather than from contemporary practice.[18] Since the earliest list of the twelve peers likewise comes from an English author, Matthew Paris,[19] Petit-Dutaillis was inclined to believe that Amaury's appeal, which he knew only from Wendover's version, was fabricated by the chronicler from a quite possibly mythical English tradition then unknown in France.[20] These doubts have now been dispelled by the discovery that in fact

15. M. Bloch, *Feudal Society* (London, 1961), pp. 368-370.

16. Petit-Dutaillis, *Louis*, pp. 350-351 and 479 (reg. no. 218).

17. C. Petit-Dutaillis, *The Feudal Monarchy in France and England from the Tenth to the Thirteenth Century* (London, 1936), pp. 240-241.

18. Petit-Dutaillis, *Louis*, p. 351, citing Molinier in Devic-Vaissète, VII, 78 n. Nonetheless Gervase may have been reliably informed, since he had been employed as a clerk by one of the peers—the archbishop of Reims—in the 1180s: *Dictionary of National Biography*, VII, 1120.

19. *Chronica majora,* ed. H. R. Luard, Rolls Series, no. 57, V, 606-607.

20. Petit-Dutaillis, *Louis*, p. 350.

Wendover was at this point copying a genuinely French source, namely the *Relatio* (Doc. 1). Hence Amaury's proposal emerges as the earliest authenticated indication that the peers of France were twelve in number.

Moreover, we can be sure that Raymond could claim to be one of the twelve, though whether as count of Toulouse or as duke of Narbonne is not clear.[21] Later in the century, when Matthew Paris gave the first full list of the twelve peers, the count of Toulouse was counted as one of six lay peers, along with the counts of Flanders and Champagne and with the dukes of Burgundy, Normandy, and Aquitaine; the six ecclesiastical peers were the archbishop of Reims and the bishops of Laon, Langres, Beauvais, Châlons-sur-Marne, and Noyon.[22]

Viewed in the light of these facts, Amaury's suggestion appears to have been a possible solution to the deadlock they had reached. If Raymond complained that his patrimony had been given to the Montforts without due process of feudal law, then by all means let the claimants submit their dispute to a tribunal on whose competence both rivals could agree. By the standards of their class, it would have been the optimal solution, but nonetheless Raymond declined. Perhaps the preponderance of ecclesiastical peers and of northerners held little hope for him, but in his reply Raymond found a better reason not to submit himself to the judgment of the other eleven peers. "Let the king receive my homage," he told Amaury, "and then I shall be ready to submit, because otherwise some would perhaps not accept me as their peer" (Doc. 1.4). The point was well taken, because a peer was by definition one of the king's great vassals. Thus Raymond would put himself at a grave disadvantage by accepting judgment by peers without first doing homage to the king, for if he recognized the jurisdiction of the court but it did not consider him to be a peer, then he would have weakened his case and strengthened Amaury's position.

Thus it appears that it was a skillful legal maneuver on Amaury's part to invoke the privilege of the twelve peers, and Raymond with equal finesse rejected it. Probably each side advanced many other proposals, but only this one seemed worth recording because of its romantic association with the legends of Charlemagne and his twelve peers. For the rest, we know only that there was "much dispute on both sides" (Doc. 1.5); so much, indeed, that "with the hope of peace as his pretext, the legate took another day to discuss these things more fully with the parties" (Doc. 2.3). Romanus himself says that the council heard whatever both parties cared to propose (Doc. 29.2), which suggests that as president he

21. Vaissète argued that the count of Toulouse became a peer only in 1229, when the duchy of Narbonne was ceded to the crown: Devic-Vaissète, VII, 80; cf. their n. 26 on the question (1st ed., III, 575-580).

22. Matthew Paris, *Chronica majora*, ed. Luard, V, 606-607. The same list is printed from a manuscript dated 1331 in Devic-Vaissète, VII, 79.

made no attempt to limit the exchange but rather showed himself willing to prolong it until a deadlock had been clearly reached.

Romanus' ultimatum to Raymond

Although he gave Raymond and Amaury free rein, Romanus was not an impassive observer. Both Wendover and the Dunstable annalist tell us that the legate presented Raymond with an ultimatum that the count refused to meet. At what point in the proceedings this occurred is not clear. In the Dunstable Annals, the count is warned towards the close of the first session, which is adjourned when his response is conciliatory but not entirely satisfactory (Doc. 2.3); in Wendover's account, the legate apparently delivers his ultimatum after Raymond has made his last plea (Doc. 43.16). It is possible that both accounts may be describing the same confrontation, for the council may have reassembled for a second session only to find that nothing had changed overnight, so that the discussion was not resumed. But even if the count was given an opportunity to reconsider this refusal, the reiteration would only have made the point more impressively. The important thing is that both sources agree that the legate brought the entire proceeding to a point by demanding that Raymond surrender his inheritance. This, as Wendover recognized, was the crux of the council:

> with many pleas, Raymond had tried to persuade the legate.... But the legate had no use for all these offers, nor was this Catholic count able to gain favor unless he would take an oath for himself and his heirs forsaking his inheritance [Doc. 43.16].

The oath it would seem was conceived as a supplement to the one that Raymond had previously taken at Montpellier. The chief item left unsettled there could now be concluded—if Raymond met Amaury's terms. The Dunstable account has Romanus confronting Raymond with a wider range of demands:

> he warned the count of Toulouse that he should return to the Catholic faith with all his people, and that he should restore to Amaury de Montfort the land of the Albigensians, which the Roman church had granted to Amaury and which had been taken away from the count without due process of law [Doc. 2.3].

Here it is assumed that Amaury had already presented his case and had proved to the legate's satisfaction that Montfort was the legal titleholder who had been illegally dispossessed by Raymond. Presumably, then, the legate had already stated an opinion on that, and having given his judgment, was now asking Raymond whether he was prepared to comply. In Dunstable's account, Raymond is also asked to reaffirm the offers that he had made earlier at Montpellier, but this would seem to have been a formality, since we have seen that these issues were reviewed at Bourges, not because they were unsettled, but only to familiarize the council with what had already been worked out.

The critical issue, both chroniclers agree, was whether Raymond was prepared to surrender his inheritance. Moreover, the legate was responsible for making this question the crux of Raymond's case. If Romanus had left his counselors free to decide whether Raymond deserved reconciliation on the basis of what the two claimants had said, support for Raymond might have been widespread. Certainly it was among the chroniclers, on whom Raymond made a generally favorable impression, which is perhaps best summed up by the *Relatio*: "Raymond offered to do for the Church and the king whatever he ought to do for his inheritance" (Doc. 1.4). But Romanus did not ask his counselors for their general impression; instead, he posed specific questions that he had carefully structured to insure the answer that he wanted to hear.

The structuring process began when Romanus ruled that Amaury's demand for the return of Occitania not only was his legitimate right but also was acceptable to the Roman church. The next step, as we have seen, was to demand that Raymond accept these impossible terms. Evidently the legate declared that to be reconciled, Raymond must take an oath to turn his inheritance over to Amaury. The moment of Raymond's refusal must have been the dramatic climax of the council, as the legate meant it to be. Everyone saw that Raymond was not prepared to obey the legate. In consequence, Romanus could summarize the impasse thus:

> But neither peace nor any kind of agreement between them could be made with honor for the Church, and Raymond did not indicate that he was ready and willing to obey the commands of the Church, as he should have done [Doc. 29.2].

In other matters Romanus has proved to be our most reliable source for the council, and his description of the position into which he had maneuvered Raymond, if read with care, is no exception. The legate's tactics are accurately described, but in veiled terms that require explanation. For instance, he indicates that "the honor of the Church" was the criterion for an acceptable agreement between the parties. As Raymond had acknowledged at Montpellier, "the honor of the Roman church" was involved in any settlement with Amaury because the Montforts owed their position in Occitania to the papacy. At Bourges it was the legate, and the legate alone, who decided whether a given proposal satisfied the honor of the papacy. This appears from his account, which states that the failure to find an honorable settlement occurred *before* he called for counsel; since a value judgment clearly is implied, Romanus himself must have made it. Evidently he precluded any hope of peace by declaring that Rome's honor required nothing less than complete satisfaction for Amaury.

Even more enigmatic is the legate's assertion that "Raymond did not indicate that he was ready and willing to carry out the commands of the Church, as he should have done." Other accounts of Raymond at Bourges convey quite the opposite impression. The justification for this surprising statement lies in the instructions that Honorius sent to Raymond the preceding January, when the count was told that "you must be so reverently and obediently attentive to him [Romanus], and so humbly and effectually acquiesce to his wholesome warnings and commands (*monitis et mandatis*) that you may be able to deserve the favor of God and the apostolic see" (Doc. 10). Thus Honorius had made blind obedience to his legate a new condition for Raymond's reconciliation. But this was precisely what Raymond failed to do at Bourges, where the legate "warned (*monuit*)" him to restore the Montfort lands (Doc. 2.3). Since Romanus explicitly states that Raymond was unwilling to carry out the "commands (*mandatis*) of the Church," it seems likely that the legate went a step further and commanded him to take "an oath for himself and his heirs forsaking his inheritance" (Doc. 43.16). Either way or both, by refusing to comply with the legate's demands, Raymond made his reconciliation impossible *ipso facto*. This explains why Romanus laid particular stress on Raymond's obligation to obey: *any* disobedience on Raymond's part provided a sufficient reason not to reconcile him.

Once we have penetrated the legate's obscure account of the proceedings at Bourges, his strategy there becomes manifest. He set up a situation in which his counselors had no choice but to declare that Raymond should not be reconciled. All that was needed on Raymond's part was a dramatic refusal to obey the legate, and that was provided by requiring him to surrender his inheritance to Amaury. The whole affair was truly a travesty of justice, staged by the legate in order to obligate his counselors to pay willy-nilly for the war that was the only alternative to Raymond's reconciliation.

Romanus takes counsel

The critical maneuver in the legate's plan came after the facts had been laid before his counselors: now he had to elicit from them the opinion he wanted to receive, which would bind them to pay a war tax. For this purpose, the council went into secret session, as the Chronicle of Tours records: "After much argument back and forth, the legate and the bishops finally took secret counsel on the matter, and thus they sent the count back home with the business unfinished" (Doc. 3.4). For most medieval church councils, this would be the end of the story, since confidential proceedings usually passed unrecorded; but the case of Bourges is fortunately an exception because a dispute subsequently arose over what had occurred, and both the legate and his opponents, the cathedral chapters, put their versions of the meeting on record. As usual, the legate provided the fullest and most accurate account (Doc. 29.3-4):

> Then [after Raymond and Amaury had presented their cases] the aforesaid archbishops, bishops, men of religion, other prelates of churches, and proctors of cathedral churches gave us counsel separately. We charged them to do so in virtue of obedience, and warned them that if they did not give us salutary counsel on this according to their consciences, they would answer on Judgment Day in the presence of the judge of all. Their counsel was that Raymond was by no means to be absolved on the basis of what he had offered (*secundum oblata*). Instead, they counseled that by every means we were to induce the late Louis, illustrious former king of France, to undertake that business, and to beg him to do so on the part of the Church, since no one else could raise up that business and purge that land from heretical perversity. And if he assumed that business, a tenth was to be given to him of all ecclesiastical revenues for as long as five years, if the aforesaid business lasted so long.

Like a judge charging a jury, Romanus carefully made his counselors aware of their duty. They had been ordered by the pope to assist and obey the legate (Doc. 12.6), and now Romanus commanded them to do so by giving him counsel: abstention would be insubordination. Moreover, he charged them to give him "salutary counsel according to their consciences." The choice that was presented to them, then, was above all a moral choice. They were obliged to give him a *consilium salutare*, that is, advice that would lead to a satisfactory outcome of the Albigensian affair. Thus the legate posed the question in a way that left them little choice. Their moral obligation, imposed by the legate's command, was to indicate what, in their opinion, would best serve the cause of peace and Catholicism in Occitania. If they failed to do so, Romanus warned them, they would not be doing their duty to God and would pay the penalty at the Last Judgment. In other words, they were strictly bound to answer the questions that he put them without taking extraneous considerations into account.

After these preliminaries, Romanus must have reviewed the case, pointing up the crucial issues and then formulating the questions that he wanted answered. These questions were probably phrased in the same terms as the responses that he later reported, so the critical question was: should Raymond be absolved on the basis of what he had offered? Most likely the legate instructed his counselors to consider especially Raymond's refusal to offer acceptable restitution to Amaury, taking into account that Amaury's claims had already been declared just, that the honor of the Roman church precluded any compromise, and that Raymond had ignored the legate's monition and/or mandate, even though the count knew he could not be reconciled unless he obeyed. These considerations being given, the conclusion followed inevitably—Raymond could not be reconciled.

If the council agreed—and it could hardly do otherwise—then it was its duty to advise Romanus what was the best way to restore faith and order in Languedoc. It was not the council's business to devise a plan, but only to react to one that was presented to it, most probably by the legate himself. Again, the answer he received is the mirror image of the question that was asked, and its terms indicate that the proposal was accompanied by an argument to the effect that any other solution would be unsatisfactory. Probably past experience was recalled to convince the council that "there was no way in which the business could be carried out effectively without his [the king's] presence." No one seems to have disputed this conclusion; instead, the discussion focused on "the kind of aid to be given to the Albigensian business" (Doc. 32.2).

The legate's role at this point is not in doubt, for he appears as the chief advocate of the proposed tax in the account given eighteen months later by the dean of the Paris chapter:

> when the legate consulted [the proctors] concerning the kind of aid to be given to the Albigensian business, and when he tried to convince them that for this purpose a tenth of the goods of the Church should be paid for five years if the late King Louis undertook the business and participated in person, the nuncios replied that they had no power of consenting about this, and that they were not able to exceed the powers that had been set as their limits. Hence they would be speaking for themselves, not for the chapters; and it seemed clear to them that the practical plan was to pay the aforesaid tenth only if otherwise the king would not wish to undertake that business and participate in person, because they thought there was no way in which the business could be carried out effectively without his presence [Doc. 32.2].

This testimony must be used with care. The dean was trying to justify the chapters' refusal to pay the tax after the king had died, and consequently he mentioned only what suited his case and neglected to report the legate's reaction. No doubt, as he said, the chapters' agents claimed that they were sent, not as procurators empowered to act for their chapters, but as nuncios only capable of conveying messages to and from the legate. But Romanus must have been unimpressed by this ploy, for the citation mandate had ordered the chapters to send *procuratores*, and if they failed to do so, then they were contumacious and as such were bound to accept the judgment of the court to which they had been sum-

moned.[23] On learning that some capitular representatives were not duly qualified proctors, the legate could have excluded them from the proceedings forthwith and declared that their consent had been given by default; instead, he
tactfully permitted them to have their say. Whether Romanus pointed out the
flaw in their argument or not, the dean does not say; but it seems likely that he
did, because the chapters paid the tax without protest as long as Louis VIII lived
(Doc. 32.3). It was the king's death, not some defect in capitular consent, that
offered an excuse not to pay.

Thus the crucial point in the dean's account is the chapters' insistence that
the grant not be made unless the king was willing to participate in person. It is
doubtful, however, that they made an issue of this at Bourges, because the king
had been planning to take part in person all along (Doc. 7.10). Ultimately that
was provided for in the agreement (Docs. 26.1 and 28.1), but nothing suggests
that the alleged concern of the chapters' representatives had any effect on the
terms. Although the king was assured that if he died his vow would not place
his heirs under any obligation (Doc. 24), no comparable provision was made
for the tenth, which could—and in fact did—continue to be paid to his heirs.
Probably the proctors at Bourges only approved the proposal laid before them
by the legate, perhaps expressing particular approval of one feature of the plan.

The dean's account is nonetheless valuable for the glimpse it gives of the procedure that was followed in the secret session. The legate appears as the strenu-
ous advocate of a plan that he has proposed: in particular, he attempts to justify
the rate and term of the income tax that his plan requires. But there are responses
from the members as well, even from the humblest ranks.

Given the size of the assembly, however, these interventions at the general
session were probably few. Had the council been smaller, extended discussion
would have been practicable; but the legate had a solution. According to the *Relatio*, he "ordered each of the archbishops then present to take his suffragans aside,
discuss the matter with them, and deliver an opinion in writing" (Doc. 1.5). This
explains what Romanus meant when he wrote that the prelates and proctors
"gave us counsel separately" (Doc. 29.3). In 1227 he still had these sealed *consilia* on file and cited them as proof of the counsel he had received (Doc. 29.4).
The language of the *Relatio* indicates that each archbishop submitted the *consilium* as "his opinion," and this accords with the practice of French provincial
councils, whose acts usually were issued in the name of the metropolitan alone.[24]
Probably each group followed the customary procedure of provincial councils,

23. G. Post, *Studies in Medieval Legal Thought* (Princeton, 1964), pp. 136-137.
24. R. Kay, "The Making of Statutes in French Provincial Councils, 1049-1305," Ph.D.
diss., University of Wisconsin (Madison, 1959), pp. 88-93.

in which the suffragans as well as the metropolitan each had a decisive vote, whereas the other members merely had the right to be consulted.[25]

This did not preclude the possibility that the participants in the provincial decision all indicated their counsel in some fashion. Such indeed must have been the case, since in 1227 Romanus claimed that he had promised the king a subsidy "on the advice of their [the chapters'] proctors and of almost the entire council [at Bourges]" (Doc. 29.8). Evidently he had some means of determining whether his proposition was approved unanimously or not. That information was apparently expressed as the counsel of all the participants. Romanus stated that his grant to the king was done on the counsel of the prelates and proctors at Bourges, "just as is more fully contained in *their* counsels that were drawn up in writing and sealed" (Doc. 31.1). While it is not impossible that the provincial *consilia* were sealed by all of the participants, that seems unlikely. In a province made up of twelve dioceses, such as Reims or Tours, the resultant document would have to bear the forty-eight seals of the secular prelates and proctors, not counting those of abbots and other monastic prelates, which seems improbable, though not quite impossible.[26] The more usual practice would have been for the counsel to be drawn up in the name of the archbishop, with a statement that the bishops indicated their consent by sealing the document, and also with some indication that the lesser prelates and the capitular proctors had been consulted.[27] At this period, however, conciliar diplomatic practice was not uniform, even within a single province, so the likelihood is that the legate prescribed the form of the document he wished to receive. All that can be inferred from the existing evidence is that, although the counsel ran in the archbishop's name, nonetheless it did indicate that the other prelates and proctors of his province were parties to that counsel. Moreover, we can be sure that the counsel that the legate received was not unanimous, but whether that was expressed as the decision of a whole province or whether only particular counselors dissented, we do not know.

In all likelihood, however, the opposition came from the province of Bordeaux, which at this time was not only under English control but was also being actively harassed by the French crown and was resisting the primatial claims of the crusading, royalist archbishop of Bourges. Bordeaux would hardly have fa-

25. Ibid., pp. 182–187.

26. Cf. Doc. 23, which was written on a long strip so that twenty-nine seals might be appended.

27. E.g. the Council of Saumur 1276, for the province of Tours (Mansi, XXIV, 159–166), where the consent of proctors was purely procedural, being sufficiently expressed in the statement that they had been summoned. See Kay, "Making of Statutes," for a detailed analysis of capitular counsel (pp. 134–140) and consent (pp. 171–177).

vored a crusade that would aggrandize its enemies. Given this hostility, the system of deliberation by provinces would have served to contain Bordeaux's opposition and prevent it from persuading other provinces to resist. This advantage, however, was probably not the principal reason why Romanus had the provinces give him separate counsel.

The written *consilia* submitted to the legate were a novelty in the procedure of church councils. Far from being "a method often employed," as Belperron thought,[28] the device hardly ever occurs in thirteenth-century ecclesiastical councils. To be sure, in the fourteenth century the components of English provincial councils increasingly deliberated apart from one another and reported the results in writing,[29] but the only other instance of written *consilia* that I have encountered in thirteenth-century church councils is another, later application by Romanus. At the council of Toulouse in 1229, Romanus held an inquest into heresy, and the assembled bishops heard the testimony and submitted their written opinions to him separately, "and thus they were able to expedite many things in a short time."[30]

Efficiency would likewise have recommended the procedure adopted at Bourges, where the unusually large assembly was too unwieldy to function well as a deliberative body, but the dispute over precedence (above, pp. 107-111) may also have recommended the innovation. Little is known about the voting procedure normally employed by medieval councils, but most likely the practice of the early Church was still observed, which was modeled on that of the Roman senate, where each senator voted in turn, beginning with the most senior and ending with the most junior.[31] According to Gratian's *Decretum*, bishops should sit in council and sign conciliar decrees in the order of their seniority, which was determined by date of consecration to the episcopate; but this rule did not apply to the archbishop, whose precedence was determined by the dignity of his church.[32] Hence it could have been argued that, if the archbishops at Bourges were to deliver their *consilia* to the legate verbally, they should observe the order of precedence. Since Romanus had already avoided the problem of precedence by having participants "not sit as in a council but as if in consultation (*in consilio*)" (Doc. 1.2), he probably adopted the device of written counsels in order to eliminate the possibility of a dispute over which metropolitan should have the

28. P. Belperron, *La Croisade contre les Albigeois et l'union du Languedoc à la France (1209–1249)*, 2nd ed. (Paris, 1967), p. 389. He also imagines that each member of the council submitted his opinion separately.

29. D. B. Weske, *Convocation of the Clergy* (London, 1937), pp. 126-142.

30. William of Puylaurens, *Chronica*, ed. and trans. J. Duvernoy (Paris, 1976), p. 139.

31. E. W. Kemp, *Counsel and Consent* (London, 1961), p. 16.

32. Gratian, *Decretum*, D.17 c.7 and D.18 c.1, ed. Friedberg, I, 53.

honor of publicly announcing his opinion first. Very likely the procedure was
the legate's own invention, since Romanus on another occasion impressed a contemporary chronicler with the cleverness, efficiency, and novelty of his administrative solutions.[33]

Later the chapters were to complain that Romanus made no ordinance concerning the tenth in their presence at Bourges (Doc. 32.5), but obviously such
an announcement would have been premature. Until Louis was committed to
the crusade, the legate wisely chose to keep his options open; his decision was
announced subsequently (Doc. 28). Instead, when the archbishops had submitted their written *consilia*, the legate "excommunicated all those who should disclose their counsels concerning this matter to anyone, saying that he wished to
show them to the king and to notify the pope" (Doc. 1.5).[34] Taken at face value,
this precaution would seem to have been designed to facilitate negotiations with
the crown. This way he could reveal his plan (*consilium*) when and to whom he
pleased; it left him room to maneuver. The unusual feature was not secrecy, for
conciliar business was normally confidential, but rather that the legate did not
conclude the council formally by announcing his decision either to Raymond
or even to his counselors.

Indeed, Romanus avoided the usual formality of a closing general session at
which the results of a council were announced; in fact, the monastic members
of the council do not seem to have participated at all in the second day's session,
for a chronicler from Cluny was under the impression that the secular clergy,
who gave the legate counsel and accordingly were charged by him beforehand
and afterwards were warned not to disclose their counsels, were better informed
as to the legate's intentions than were most of the participants. That at least is
how I interpret the monk's cryptic remark: "since many people were there [at
Bourges], not all of them were aware of the aforesaid cardinal's secret."[35]

One suspects, however, that only the marginal participants were left in doubt
as to the outcome, for Raymond must have realized that his refusal to surrender his lands was sufficient cause for nonreconciliation, and those present at the
second session must have perceived what Romanus was proposing to do. It seems

33. William of Puylaurens, *Chronica*, ed. Duvernoy, p. 139.

34. This prohibition suggests a legal question of some nicety that I can raise but not resolve: was a procurator accordingly forbidden from reporting his action to his principal?

35. *Chronicon Cluniacense* (last entry in 1237): "MCCXXV, mandatum fuit concilium ecclesiasticis personis à quodam cardinali commoranti in urbe Bituricarum; sed, cùm multae
personae ibi interessent, de secreto supradicti cardinalis non omnes conscii fuerunt." Paris,
BnF, MS. lat. 12768, fol. 227, a copy by Dom Claude Estiennot (fl. 1673–1684), ed. *Rec. hist.
Gaules*, XVIII (1822), 743. For details, see *Repertorium fontium historiae Medii Aevi*, III (Rome,
1970), 312.

unlikely that secrecy was enjoined in order to prevent the counselors from discussing the proceedings among themselves, since the members from each
province already knew one another's views and perhaps the collective result of
their deliberations as well.

★ ★ ★

The council broke up, then, without hearing the legate's decision. This situation, perhaps better than anything else, demonstrates the legal status of the council: it was not for the council to decide—that was the legate's prerogative. The
proper function of the council was to give him counsel, which he was not bound
to follow, though, like any prudent administrator, he would be wise to do so.
Romanus in fact did not need the council to help him make up his mind; instead, it was a propaganda device that served to build a consensus in favor of
the heavy tax he meant to impose on the churches of his legation. Above all,
he wanted the churches to pay promptly, without dilatory appeals to Rome;
moreover, with an astute eye to long-range effects, he did not want to make
the papacy unpopular. The best way to achieve these goals was to obtain the
prior consent of the clergy who were to be taxed, and this alone was his reason
for calling the Council of Bourges.

Romanus carefully orchestrated the proceedings so as to lead his counselors
to the conclusion that a tax would be necessary. The first step was to have
Amaury insist that Raymond return Occitania to him. Romanus backed him up
by declaring that the claim was legitimate and that the honor of the Roman
church demanded that Amaury be satisfied. Next, Romanus commanded Raymond to comply, with the predictable result that Raymond refused and thus gave
the legate a pretext for not reconciling him. Romanus then ordered his counselors to advise him what was the best way to establish peace and the Catholic
faith in the South. Specifically, he asked their opinion on each of two alternative questions: should Raymond be reconciled on the basis of the offers he had
made at the council, and, if not, then should the legate induce Louis VIII to undertake a crusade against the heretics by offering him ten percent of the clerical incomes in the legation for the next five years? Since the answer to the first
question was a foregone conclusion, in view of the conditions laid down by
the papacy for Raymond's reconciliation, the only real question was whether
the plan that Romanus proposed was the best alternative. The legate set forth
his reasons for believing that a royal crusade was now the only solution and that
it would not be possible without the subsidy he suggested. Finally, each of the
fifteen provinces retired to discuss his propositions and to decide on its responses.
Obviously Romanus was successful, for almost all of them agreed that the crusade was the only way, and moreover they promptly paid the first installment

of the resultant tax. Thus, from Romanus' point of view, the council was a success because it committed the churches of his legation to the king's crusade, not only by legal obligation but also by moral conviction.

The temptation is strong to deplore Romanus' conduct. Under the pretext of seeking peace, defending the faith, and doing justice, he shepherded his flock in the opposite direction and fleeced it to boot. It must be remembered, however, that he did these things as the executor of a policy for which he was not responsible, and even Honorius can be excused for choosing to cooperate with Louis rather than leave him to wage a purely feudal war on Raymond over which the Church would have no control. When the situation changed after Louis' death, Romanus was to work even more successfully for the compromise that eventually brought about Raymond's reconciliation and a lasting peace in Occitania. So far as we can discern his personal inclination, he seem to have usually avoided making enemies for himself and for the Roman church, to whose interests he was devoted. Therefore, even when entrusted with an unpleasant and perhaps distasteful mission, he strove to minimize discord, conscious perhaps that a less skillful and diplomatic agent would only make things worse. If his manipulations at Bourges seem cynical, the blame must rest on Rome rather than on Romanus. He was above all an able exponent of the then dominant tradition of curial policy that relied on legal and diplomatic skill to maintain the papal leadership of Christendom.

The council at Paris, 28–31 January 1226

For Romanus, the Council of Bourges was a necessary preliminary to the main objective of his diplomatic mission, which was to arrange a second Albigensian Crusade that would be conducted by Louis VIII. Two years ago Louis had proposed the terms under which he would undertake the enterprise (Doc. 7), and Romanus was now in a position to grant them, albeit with important modifications that would enable Rome to exercise greater control over the crusade.

Between Bourges and Paris

What was his next step? Philip Mousket, the bourgeois chronicler in verse, imagines that the clergy at Bourges decided "that the Albigensians should be destroyed" and sent their sealed decision to the pope, who confirmed it. The embassy returned to France with a papal letter urging the king to conquer the heretics and kill them all, which, having been read at a royal council at Melun (Mousket says), persuaded the king and his barons to take the Cross (Doc. 4.5–8). Surely Mousket was mistaken about the place of the council, since Paris is specified by the Chronicle of Tours (Doc. 3.7), not to mention the three original surviving charters dated *Parisius* (Docs. 23, 24, and 27). Very likely he confused the Paris meeting with an earlier royal council held at Melun on 8 November 1225, where the Albigensian crusade was discussed inconclusively (Doc. 3.2).

But was Mousket right in asserting, with much detail, that the decision taken at Bourges against Raymond was subsequently referred to the pope, who not only confirmed it but replied with a rousing exhortation to undertake the crusade? It is not impossible, since the two months between the meetings at Bourges and Paris was just enough time for a round trip to Rome; moreover, Romanus did announce at Bourges that he planned "to show them [the sealed counsels he had received] to the king and to notify the pope" (Doc. 1.5). But Mousket's account is suspect because we have no other indication that Honorius wrote such a letter: the chroniclers do not mention it, no copy survives, and most especially it was not enregistered, as such an important communication surely would have been. Most likely Romanus did just what he promised to do, *and in that order*: first he showed the king the sealed counsels he had received at Bourges, and then, after the king had taken the Cross, Romanus notified the pope. We know that Honorius responded about a month later; he was delighted to hear that the king had undertaken the crusade, although he was concerned lest good Catholics in Occitania might suffer from it.[36] While it is not improbable that Romanus submitted an interim report after Bourges, it is unlikely that it elicited a letter in reply such as Mousket described, for legally there was no need for the pope to review the counsels received by his *legatus a latere*, much less to confirm Romanus' judgment at Bourges. Evidently Mousket did not understand that Romanus was empowered to act for the pope without reference back to his master, so in order to justify the crusade according to the chronicler's limited understanding, he invented an embassy that never took place.

Thanks to an English spy, we are better informed than Mousket as to what the king and legate were doing between the councils of Bourges and Paris. On an original parchment sheet, preserved today in the English royal archives, is a summary of the agreements that were about to be concluded at Paris (Doc. 25). It was probably included in a letter now lost, so we have no definite indication of how the information was obtained, but we can be sure that the author was summarizing a draft of the promises that Romanus and the French prelates were going to make a few days later (Doc. 26), because almost half of the report reproduces the text of the promises verbatim. The events it describes in the future

---

36. Pressutti, no. 5848, ed. *Rec. hist. Gaules*, XIX, 771. Pressutti is probably right in dating this "28 Febr.–March," i.e. a month after the Paris council, even though the letter was enregistered with no. 5939, dated 15 May.

tense are expected to take place momentarily ("in presenti"), so it must have been dispatched just before the conference began on 28 January.

Presumably the exemplar was a draft intended for discussion and revision at the Paris conference because there are extensive differences between this version and the final one, which cannot be ascribed to a hasty or careless summary, since they occur in precisely those clauses that most interested the king of England and therefore would have been reported to him without alteration. These provisions, corresponding to those of Doc. 26.3–5, regulate the excommunication of those who make war in France or against it, and it seems most likely that some of the differences between the two versions are due to revisions made in the draft as the result of discussion with the king's vassals at the Paris conference. Although they preserve precious indications of the process of royal decision making, we need not examine them in detail because none of them concern the tenth. Indeed, it is most significant that the terms of the tenth had already been settled on well before the council, and whatever advice Romanus received from the prelates at Paris made no difference in the outcome. For the rest, the changes in the draft version show that Romanus was flexible where feudal matters were concerned and also was helpful in improving the awkward drafting of the royal chancery.[37]

An overview of the Paris assembly

What is certain is the outcome of the negotiations, so let us concentrate on what was done publicly at Paris in an assembly that lasted for four days, from Wednesday 28 January through Saturday 31 January 1226. Our sources are excellent: the narrative of the Chronicle of Tours (Doc. 3.7–8) and the legal record, consisting of four charters, three of them sealed originals (Docs. 23, 24, and 27). From these sources, we can reconstruct the course of events, which it may be useful to summarize at the outset.[38]

On the opening day, Romanus publicly excommunicated Raymond and his supporters; moreover, he publicly acknowledged that the lands of these heretics now belonged to Louis and his heirs. Amaury de Montfort, whose claims the Council of Bourges had judged to be better than Raymond's, together with his uncle Guy, now surrendered their rights to Louis, including the title deeds.[39] Accordingly, the way was open for a royal crusade. Probably the way was then paved by an inflammatory sermon; certainly the king took counsel with all those

37. For further details, see Doc. 25.pr.

38. For the dating of the charters, see the prolegomena to Docs. 23–27.

39. Doc. 3.7. Amaury mentions his act in an extant letter dated 1229: Martène-Durand, *Vet. script. coll.*, I (1724), 1225. Cf. Petit-Dutaillis, *Louis,* pp. 291 and 491 (reg. nos. 313–314).

present, both laymen and clerics, about the advisibility of the undertaking; and the legate took separate counsel with the bishops and archbishops on whether to grant the king a clerical subsidy.

The result of these deliberations was solemnized on the third day, 30 January.[40] First the lay barons formally acknowledged that they had advised the king to undertake the Albigensian affair, and they promised to support him in it as long as he was involved (Doc. 23). Next came the most dramatic moment of the proceedings: Louis received the Cross from the legate and took his vow as a crusader, "and many knights and great men of the kingdom of France were signed with the Cross along with the king" (Doc. 42.10 c). Afterwards, the legate, seconded by the prelates, attested that the king's vow was taken subject to certain reservations: he could return from Albigeois whenever he wished, and the vow was a personal one that did not bind his heirs (Doc. 24). The king's promises were paralleled by those made by the legate, again in association with the bishops (Doc. 26). Briefly, crusader status was granted to all who had just taken vows; Raymond and his supporters were excommunicated again, and so were all who invaded the kingdom of France or made war there; and most important, for five years the king was to receive a tenth of the net annual revenues of all churches in Romanus' legation. Finally, the bishops remained for a day longer in Paris to seal a certified copy of Romanus' letters of legation (Doc. 27).

Nature of the assembly

Before examining some of these documents in greater detail, let us inquire what the nature of this assembly was. In its composition, it most closely resembled a royal council, with lesser lords from the royal desmesne heavily represented. Bishops are the only kind of churchmen present, and they were few in number: the five archbishops of Reims, Bourges, Sens, Rouen, and Tours, with ten of their suffragans plus the bishop of Langres, a suffragan of Lyon. Romanus could have summoned many more from the fifteen provinces of his legation, as he did to Bourges, where thirteen archbishops and perhaps ninety bishops appeared (see chapter 3, above). The chronicler of Tours qualifies the bishops who took the Cross at Paris as being from Louis' kingdom (Doc. 3.8), and that would seem to have been the principle of selection: they were Louis' lords spiritual, who could be expected to accompany him on the projected crusade. But at the Paris assembly, they gave counsel not only to the king but also to the legate (Docs. 3.10, 29.5, and 32.3) and were associated with him in his acts (Docs. 24 and 26), so

---

40. The Salisbury Register's chronicle says that Louis took the Cross on 29 January (Doc. 42.10c), but the chronicler of Tours is to be preferred because he not only was better placed to be well informed but also displays a more extensive knowledge of the proceedings.

to some extent it was the legate's council as well. Therefore it was a council of the so-called "mixed" type, which the chronicler of Tours termed a *generale concilium* because it embraced two specific kinds of council—the royal and the legatine—and he made this twofold character clear by stating that it was celebrated by the king *and* by the legate (Doc. 3.7).

A conditional crusade

In early 1224 Louis had petitioned the pope to grant some ten conditions without which he was not prepared to undertake an Albigensian crusade (Doc. 7). As we saw in chapter 1, Honorius eventually decided to meet the king's demands and dispatched Romanus to make the arrangements. The results of his negotiations are embodied in the charters issued at Paris in January 1226, and by comparing these with the conditions laid down two years earlier, several things will become apparent: on the one hand, that the king's basic requirements were not negotiable, and on the other, that Romanus succeeded in simplifying and qualifying the means of attaining these goals. Although we are chiefly interested in how he contrived to finance the crusade, his handling of the other royal conditions also deserves our attention because it reveals how he operated as a diplomat and lawyer.

The principal difference between the two arrangements was that in 1224 the king wanted his own archbishops, of Reims, Sens, and especially of Bourges, to be invested with legatine powers, which they would exercise at the king's command rather than the pope's (Doc. 7.7). For these native legates (*legati nati*), Honorius substituted Romanus, a legate veritably sent from the pope's side (*legatus a latere*), who would represent the pope as co-director of the crusade. Most of the powers that Louis had asked to be granted explicitly to his native legates were implicit in Romanus' legatine commission (Docs. 12-13), though this may not have been generally recognized. Accordingly, a number of the 1224 conditions were rendered unnecessary because Romanus would accompany the crusade and use his comprehensive powers, not at the king's discretion but at his own, thus enabling the papacy to retain a measure of control rather than ceding it to the French. Hence the 1226 agreement contains no provision for the excommunication of those who refuse to pay what they have pledged for the crusade, or of royal vassals who neither accompany the king nor pay scutage in compensation (Doc. 7.3-4). The latter case was dealt with rather differently in 1226. Since royal vassals might argue that they were not obliged to accompany their lord on a crusade that was his personal undertaking, in 1226 they were expressly obligated, both by having counseled him to take up the Albigensian business and by having promised to assist him in it, and they formally certified their obligation in Document 23. Similarly, article 7 of the 1224 petition was rendered unnecessary, since Romanus was Conrad's counterpart and his legatine jurisdiction included France together with Occitania and its circumadjacent provinces (Doc. 12); when he had the crusade preached (Docs. 3.9 and 43.16), he needed no special authorization, and likewise he could reconcile the penitent.

For the most part the king got what he had requested in 1224, though not always in the way he had proposed. The title to Raymond's lands is a case in point. In 1224 Louis had requested papal letters patent depriving Raymond and his supporters of their French lands and confirming that these now belonged to the king (Doc. 7.6). Romanus fulfilled this demand without issuing the explicit documentation Louis had required; it was enough that the papacy had already conferred these lands on the Montforts, as Romanus had ruled at the Council of Bourges. Since Amaury's title was now secure, Louis' requirement could be satisfied simply by transferring the title to him, which the Montforts did at Paris (n. 39, above). In this case, Romanus evidently found a simpler means than the involved one the king's lawyers had proposed.

In other cases, the changes were few, but they exhibit the finesse of an experienced canon lawyer. For instance, in 1224 Louis had insisted that he would not obligate himself for any extended service as a crusader, and his heirs for none at all; he would agree to a single, token personal appearance in Albigeois, but nothing more unless he saw fit (Doc. 7.10); and this unusual, limited, and conditional crusader's vow was not only acknowledged by Romanus but also casuistically justified (Doc. 24). Nonetheless, Louis wanted all the perquisites of a crusader for himself and all who joined his crusade, especially the indulgence and remission of sins already given to those who vowed to go to Jerusalem (Doc. 7.1).[41] Romanus granted the standard indulgence explicitly (Doc. 26.2), which he defined in accordance with current canonistic practice as that granted by the constitution *Ad liberandum*;[42] among other things, it conferred the remission of sins Louis had stipulated, and accordingly that redundant reference was deleted, although that benefit was the principal advantage to be stressed when Romanus had the crusade preached (Doc. 3.9; cf. Doc. 26.7). The Chronicle of Tours adds that the preachers offered remission of all vows, as well as of sins, except the vow to crusade in the Holy Land (Doc. 3.9).

In 1224, Louis had asked for elaborate safeguards to insure the peace and security of his kingdom; in 1226, he got more and less than he had hoped for. It had not occurred to him to invoke the protection of the Church, but in 1226

41. On the spiritual privileges of a crusader, see J. A. Brundage, *Medieval Canon Law and the Crusader* (Madison, 1969), pp. 144–153.

42. Lateran IV, c.71, ed. García, *Constitutiones*, pp. 110–118. Brundage, *Canon Law and the Crusader*, pp. 82–83.

this was expressly granted to the king, his family, *his kingdom*, and indeed to all participants (Doc. 26.1), even though such protection was a traditional privilege accorded to crusaders.[43] Moreover, Romanus excommunicated invaders, rebels, and those who engage in private warfare, and interdicted their lands as well (Doc. 26.4-5; cf. 3.10), just as Louis had requested (Doc. 7.2). This provision was particularly directed against the English and their allies, who were seeking to regain Poitou,[44] as became evident in May when Honorius was persuaded to make an exception for Henry III and his brother, Richard of Cornwall.[45] But Romanus was not able to comply with Louis' desire for a truce with the English (Doc. 7.5), though not for want of trying, as both he and the pope had been seeking to broker one for months, and would continue to do so.[46] Eventually, in place of a truce Honorius formally warned Henry III not to support Raymond or make war on Louis,[47] and when the English prepared an invasion nonetheless, the pope succeeded in preventing it.[48]

Louis had also asked the pope to obtain assurances from Emperor Frederick II that his subjects east of the Rhone would not impede the crusade, and if they did, that Louis had the emperor's permission to fight them (Doc. 7.9). By 1226 the pope's intervention was no longer necessary, since Louis himself had negotiated such an agreement with the emperor directly, in the treaty of Catania (November 1224), which Frederick's son Henry, king of the Romans, had reaffirmed at Trent in June 1226, just as Louis was preparing to besiege the imperial city of Avignon.[49]

The terms of the subsidy

Our principal concern is with the financial subsidy that Romanus promised Louis. Originally, in 1224 Louis had asked the Roman church for 60,000 pounds *parisis* per annum for ten years (Doc. 7.8); what he got in 1226 was a tenth of net clerical revenues for five years (Doc. 26.6). Clearly the term had been reduced by half, but it is harder to ascertain the amount of the clergy's annual con-

---

43. Protection was provided by Lateran I (1123), c.10, and reaffirmed in *Ad liberandum*: Brundage, *Canon Law and the Crusader*, p. 166.

44. Petit-Dutaillis, *Louis*, pp. 270-275.

45. Pressutti, nos. 5938-5939 (15 May 1226), ed. Horoy, V, 83-84 (nos. 143-144).

46. See above, chap. 2, pp. 67-70. Petit-Dutaillis, *Louis*, pp. 268-278. Cf. Doc. 15. Negotiations continued into the next reign, resulting in several brief truces and a yearlong one beginning in July 1227: E. Berger, *Histoire de Blanche de Castille, reine de France* (Paris, 1895), pp. 90-91.

47. Pressutti, no. 5904 (27 April 1226); cf. Doc. 43.17.

48. Petit-Dutaillis, *Louis*, p. 277.

49. Petit-Dutaillis, *Louis*, pp. 265-266.

tribution. The chronicler of Tours stated that it was 100,000 pounds (Doc. 3.10), but he did not specify whether these were pounds in the money of Paris or Tours; if, as seems reasonable, he was reckoning by his local standard, then the sum would be only 80,000 pounds *parisis*. Either way, however, the tenth would evidently yield more per annum than had originally been asked for.

In 1226 probably no one had any means of arriving at a reasonable estimate of the costs of the crusade. Whether the Fifth Crusade (1213-1221) was under-funded is an open question, but James Powell thinks it was.[50] Certainly the twen-tieth imposed on the clergy to support that crusade was increased for the next one, both in the 1224 plan and in the 1226 grant, to a tenth. Moreover, when Louis IX sought a clerical subsidy for the Seventh Crusade (1248-1254), he man-aged to have the twentieth that was originally proposed for it increased to a tenth.[51] Although the accounts for St Louis' crusade are fragmentary today, enough survives to indicate that his tenth yielded much more than was expected of a clerical tenth in 1226. St Louis' tenth was for an extended France, termed "Gaul," that was roughly comparable to Romanus' legation; it was levied first for three years, then renewed for another two. Altogether, it yielded, according to Jordan's "very rough best estimate," 750,000 pounds *parisis,* or an average of 150,000 per annum.[52]

Did the chronicler of Tours underestimate the annual value of a clerical tenth by nearly half? Possibly, but there are reasons to suppose that his estimate may have been realistic. The papacy had experimented with a variety of ways to collect crusading subsidies before Gregory IX finally centralized the process by entrusting it to papal collectors in 1228.[53] Sometimes the papacy had commis-sioned four local clerics; sometimes papal nuncios or legates were in charge, supervising local agents; once, in 1221-1223, Honorius put the process in local hands by making three French archbishops (Sens, Reims, Bourges) papal legates *ad hoc*.[54] The last experiment had been a fiasco, and these same archbishops were among Romanus' counselors at Paris; presumably it was on their advice that an-other system was tried instead: the collection of the tenth was put in the hands of the crown (Doc. 26.9). As we shall see, this also created a variety of difficul-

---

50. J. Powell, *Anatomy of a Crusade, 1213–1221* (Philadelphia, 1986), p. 102.

51. W. C. Jordan, *Louis IX and the Challenge of the Crusade* (Princeton, 1979), p. 79; J. R. Strayer, *Medieval Statecraft and the Perspective of History* (Princeton, 1971), p. 162, n. 3.

52. Jordan, *Louis IX*, p. 80. His figure is 950,000 pounds in money of Tours, which I have converted to money of Paris (factor of 0.8).

53. See W. E. Lunt, *Financial Relations of the Papacy with England to 1327* (Cambridge, Mass., 1939), p. 247, and his "List of Collectors" (pp. 610-624).

54. R. Kay, "The Albigensian Twentieth of 1221-3," *Journal of Medieval History*, VI (1980), 307-315.

ties, but only one is important for our present purpose: the tax could only be collected effectively from those areas in which royal authority was strong. Hence, out of the fifteen provinces of Romanus' legation that were taxed, only four complained of the collection—Sens, Reims, Rouen, and Tours, which were precisely the four in which royal power was strongest. In other words, returns from the other eleven provinces might reasonably be expected to be spotty, and the chronicler of Tours may well have taken this into account in his estimate of the annual amount of the subsidy, which would explain why roughly the same area could yield twice as much twenty-odd years later when the papacy collected the money directly.

Be that as it may, in 1226 the tenth for five years probably seemed like a reasonable exchange for 60,000 pounds *parisis* for ten years. If the former was thought to be worth 100,000 pounds Tours money (or 80,000 Paris), the expectation would seem to have been that a shorter but more intensive campaign would achieve sufficient results. The reasons for the tradeoff are obscure, but the papacy may well have hesitated at imposing a tax for a term as long as ten years, which was of unprecedented length.[55]

Who was eligible for tax-exempt status must have been worked out piecemeal (Doc. 26.7). Although later in the century the four orders exempted by Romanus regularly received this privilege, it was not firmly established in 1226. Thus in 1221-1222, when the northern French provinces determined the details of a similar tax, the province of Sens provided no exemptions at all, while three other provinces opted to exempt the Hospitallers, Templars, Cistercians, and Premonstratensians.[56] Although none of these four orders were formally consulted by Romanus at Paris, very likely their interests were represented by lobbyists, since Romanus later stated that he went to Paris accompanied not only by bishops and archbishops but also by "prelates of other churches," who he did not include among his counselors (Doc. 29.5). To this conventional list of exemptions were added the prelates who went on the crusade, which included most of the bishops and archbishops whom Romanus consulted (Doc. 3.8); they were no doubt all the more willing to approve of a tax that need not affect them personally, and from Romanus' point of view it would be an advantage to have the most prominent churchmen participating in the campaign.[57] The final cat-

---

55. The rate also was unprecedented. Previous clerical income taxes had been a fortieth for a year (1199) and a twentieth for three years (1215, 1221): Lunt, *Financial Relations*, pp. 240-247; Kay, "Albigensian Twentieth," p. 310.

56. Kay, "Albigensian Twentieth," pp. 309-310. The Cistercians and Premonstratensians were exempt from earlier taxes, but not apparently the military orders: Lunt, *Financial Relations*, pp. 240-244. All but the Premonstratensians were exempt in 1244 (p. 208); all four in 1272 (p. 231).

57. For the bishops who went on the crusade, see below, chap. 5, n. 2.

egory is the most interesting: any clerical participant designated by either king or legate. The principal beneficiaries would be members of the royal and legatine entourages, but because *familia* was not specified, as it was for the prelatial exemptions, both leaders were empowered to dispense valuable patronage as they saw fit. Significantly, this provision, which was not made in the draft version, was added at the last minute.

Who granted the tenth?

In the history of medieval representative institutions, the crucial question was: who has the power to decide? And more often than not the issue was joined over the imposition of taxes. In England, parliament eventually won the all-important "power of the purse"; in the Church, the conciliarists of the fifteenth century similarly sought to limit the sovereign power of the papacy. The tenth of 1226 was the first in France to provoke taxpayers to question the legality of a grant on the grounds that they had not been consulted, and consequently we must examine the evidence with some care.

The grant of 1226 itself is ambiguous, because Document 26 runs in the name of the legate, the archbishops, and the bishops. Did they all make the grant? If so, why could only a small group of bishops commit the whole of Romanus' legation? The answer is that, according to the conventions of thirteenth-century conciliar diplomatic, the acts of a council ran only in the name of its head, even though the members, his counselors, might also be named. Such was normally the case with the statutes of French provincial councils, which often named both the metropolitan and his suffragan bishops;[58] all ambiguity was removed from the decrees of general councils, which were issued in the pope's name alone, and only after the council had been dissolved.

The Chronicle of Tours represented the grant of 1226 as having been made by the legate "with the assent of some of the bishops" (Doc. 3.10). But *assensus* itself is an ambiguous term that does not necessarily imply a correlative power of dissent that can prevent a proposed action. In this case, however, we can be sure the bishops raised no objection at Paris, for Romanus later reminded them that none of them had opposed the grant in any way (Doc. 30.2).

But Romanus was aware that, according to canon law, the head of an ecclesiastical body was obliged to consult its members, according to the Romano-canonical principle of *quod omnes tangit*: "What concerns all must be discussed by all in common—*Quod omnes similiter tangit, ab omnibus comprobetur.*"[59] In ac-

58. Kay, "Making of Statutes," pp. 88-93.
59. *Codex Justinianus* 5.59.5.2, ed. P. Krueger (Berlin, 1880), p. 231. Post, *Studies*, chap. 4. Cf. J. Gaudemet, "Unanimité et majorité," *Etudes historiques à la mémoire de Noël Didier* (Paris, 1960), pp. 149-162, at 159-161.

cordance with this principle, Romanus had consulted the clergy of his legation about the subsidy at the Council of Bourges, and when he informed them of the grant made at Paris, he expressly stated that it was done "with the approbation of the holy council assembled at Bourges" (Doc. 28.5). What is more, he had the provinces represented at Bourges give him written, sealed counsel that he should offer Louis a tenth of their income for five years (Doc. 29.4), so his grant was demonstrably made on their advice. In the same document he also clarified the role of his cosigners at Paris: the legate himself made the grant "on the advice of those archbishops and bishops who were present with us" (Doc. 29.5).

Some sixteen months later, however, the cathedral chapters of four provinces were to object that they had not been called upon to participate in the Paris negotiations, and that in their absence Romanus had made the grant "after having conferred (*tractatu habito*) with some bishops" (Doc. 32.3). Thus both sides in the subsequent dispute did agree that the bishops at Paris did not actually make the grant; they only discussed it with Romanus and gave him advice. We have already seen how their advice probably is reflected in the provisions concerning the collection of the subsidy and exemptions from it.

Who, then, made the grant? When Pope Gregory IX had to decide whether the subsidy was granted with due process, he declared that it was made by Romanus alone, and the pope justified his decision by citing the letters of legation (Doc. 12.5) that authorized Romanus to enact or ordain whatever he thought would expedite the Albigensian business (Doc. 39.4). In other words, although Romanus was legally obliged to be prudent and take counsel, he was not obligated to follow the advice he received. In the end, the decision was his alone.

This explains the otherwise mysterious *vidimus* of Romanus' letters of legation, which the bishops certified at Paris (Doc. 27). It was dated the day after the documents they issued jointly with Romanus (Docs. 24 and 26) and differs from them both diplomatically and paleographically. Nonetheless, it was not an afterthought, for the precouncil agenda had stipulated that Romanus should deliver to the king a *transcriptum* of his letters of legation sealed by the archbishops and bishops who were present (Doc. 25.4). Certainly the point of the *vidimus* is that someone wanted it placed beyond a doubt that the engagements of the previous day derived their legal validity from Romanus' legatine authority. Although we can only guess who suggested this precaution, its purpose was clearly to give the king written proof of the legate's authority to act, because the transcript was to be delivered to the king, and moreover it was carefully preserved in the royal archives. Probably while negotiating the subsidy, Romanus had explained that legally the grant was authorized by the legate, and since the proof of his legatine authority was a document that the king had never received, Louis naturally insisted on having a certified copy for his records.

CHAPTER 5

COLLECTING THE ALBIGENSIAN TENTH

Once France and the papacy had agreed on the terms for a royal crusade, the partners lost no time in implementing it. The one campaign to which the king was personally committed was to begin in the spring of 1226; the army was to assemble at Bourges in the middle of May. That schedule presented no special difficulties for Louis, since the crown routinely organized summer campaigns a few months in advance; in this case, the leaders met at Paris on 29 March to work out the details (Doc. 3.11). The same month, probably at that royal council, the bishop of Auxerre compounded his obligations to the king on the plea of ill health; he acknowledged that in return for six hundred pounds paris, the king had remitted the bishop's obligations to serve personally in the host and to send knights on the Albigensian crusade, as well as "the tenth that we are likewise held to pay to the same [king] from our revenues for the aforesaid business of Albigeois."[1] This demonstrates not only that the tenth was being collected by the crown, as provided at Paris (Doc. 26.9), but also that it was being treated as a debt owed to the king. Many bishops were to discharge all these obligations by participating in the expedition.[2]

Unlike the king, Romanus was pressed for time, because he had to publicize the crusade, so after the Paris assembly broke up, he remained at Paris and spent the next week notifying the fifteen archbishops of his legation of the recent agreement. No doubt he wrote to the more distant recipients first; the notification to the nearby archbishop of Rouen was not dispatched until 5 February (Doc. 28.10). The archbishop was less prompt in transmitting the message down the hierarchy, for he must have had it for a week before passing it on to the bishop of Avranches on 16 February (Doc. 28.11), and the bishop was positively dilatory in not notifying the abbot of Mont-St-Michel until 12 March. By then there was barely time for the crusade to be preached and for those who joined it to get to their rendezvous at Bourges on 17 May.

1. Petit-Dutaillis, *Louis*, p. 493, reg. no. 328; ed. Teulet, no. 1751: "pro decima quam similiter de proventibus nostrorum redditium tenemur solvere eidem pro negocio Albigensi supradicti. . . ." This bishop, Henry of Villeneuve, was present at Paris in January 1226 (Docs. 24, 26–27).
2. Petit-Dutaillis reckoned two archbishops, of Sens and Reims, and a dozen bishops, including Arras, Beauvais, Cambrai, Chartres, Laon, Langres, Limoges, Noyon, and Tréguier (*Louis*, p. 295; cf. Teulet, II, 86, 97).

Although the chief purpose of Romanus' mandate was to have the crusade preached, the recipients were provided with the necessary background information. Romanus recited the principal provisions of his recent acts at Paris: Louis had taken the Cross and had been placed under the Church's protection; Raymond and his supporters were excommunicated, as were those who waged war in France; and the crown had been granted a ten percent tax on the ecclesiastical income of fifteen provinces. All this was repeated almost verbatim from the promises made to the king at Paris (Doc. 26.1–8 = Doc. 28.1–7), with one significant addition: the tenth was granted, the legate added, "with the approbation of the holy council assembled at Bourges" (Doc. 28.5). At this point, however, collection of the tenth was not an issue, for the first installment was not due until November, and Romanus neglected to mention that the crown would collect it (Doc. 26.9).

Nonetheless the letter shows that Romanus was anxious to raise as much money for the crusade as possible. The preachers were instructed to offer the crusading indulgence not only to those who accompanied the king but also to those who instead provided "an appropriate amount of their goods to assist the aforesaid business"; the reward of the latter was to be proportionate to the amount of their contribution (Doc. 28.8).

The crusade of Louis VIII

Four weeks after Easter 1226, on 17 May, in response to the king's summons, the crusaders converged on Bourges, the designated rendezvous. Our only source is the chronicler of Tours, a canon whose chapter objected to the legate's highhanded grant of the tenth, so his account stresses the fund-raising aspects of the occasion (Doc. 3.12–14). Apparently the preaching of the crusade, though done on short notice, had been effective. Everyone who had taken the Cross showed up, including those who were "old men, boys, women, poor, or infirm," all of whom fulfilled their vow by paying some portion of their net worth, which the legate had each person state under oath. The legate's instructions on preaching the crusade had, of course, provided for contributions of this kind (Doc. 28.8), but the chronicle somewhat clarifies how his vague criteria were applied in practice.

From the Chronicle of Tours we also learn that Louis did not rely entirely on volunteer crusaders; instead, he summoned the entire feudal host, that is, everyone who owed military service to the crown, who all presented themselves at Bourges ready to perform their obligatory forty days of service. Some were permitted to commute their service into a money payment (scutage), but apparently the decision was up to the king, for many of them were forced to accompany him unwillingly. Although all this was standard practice, the chronicler presented it as an instance of the king's avarice.

For maximum rhetorical effect, the chronicler made his own complaints the climax of his account, and these deserve special attention because they are the first evidence of opposition to the tenth (Doc. 3.14). It appears that many recipients of the legate's mandate to pay the tenth did not agree that it had been granted, as he claimed, with the approbation of the Council of Bourges in which they had participated. The chronicle simply states that many abbots came unbidden to the rendezvous, together with the representatives of cathedral chapters, in order to protest against the way in which the tenth had been granted. While they did not mind paying a subsidy for the crusade, they protested that they did want to preserve their right of consent, which they were prepared to argue had not been exercised, though it is not clear whether they had in mind the proceedings at Bourges or at Paris, or both. Their complaints went unheard, for both king and legate refused to give them an audience, "and so they departed, silently cursing the business of the Cross and of the king." Both on this occasion and subsequently, Romanus showed himself secure in the legality of his actions and not disposed to justify them, though his motives for ignoring complaints remain obscure.

The campaign of 1226

For the next twelve months, no one seems to have made an issue of the tenth. Loyally, though not without misgivings, the chapters paid the first installment in November 1226 (Doc. 32.3), but by Easter 1227 they were emboldened to refuse further payment because events had taken a new turn. The canon of Tours, armed with hindsight, declared that the disasters of the intervening year were foreshadowed at Tours on the eve of the rendezvous by a thunderstruck cross and some violent deaths, which "openly proclaimed both an impediment to the business of the Cross and some future damage to the king and kingdom of France" (Doc. 3.12). In order to understand why the chapters dared to challenge the tax, we must see what happened during this eventful year. This can better be accomplished by a brief, interpretative sketch than by a detailed account.[3]

The force that Louis led south in May 1226 was the largest ever deployed against the heretics and their supporters. It was not enough, however, to cause Raymond to capitulate without a fight, as the pope had once predicted he would (Doc. 8.2); instead, the count retreated to Toulouse and prepared for the worst. Most of the lords and cities of Languedoc were not so brave and honorable; many, but not all, formally submitted to Louis, acknowledging him as liege lord

---

3. On the crusade, see esp. Devic-Vaissète, VI, 599-620; Petit-Dutaillis, *Louis*, pp. 297-328; P. Belperron, *La Croisade contre les Albigeois et l'union du Languedoc à la France (1209–1249)*, 2nd ed. (Paris, 1967), pp. 390-400; J. R. Strayer, *The Albigensian Crusades* (New York, 1971), pp. 130-136.

and begging for mercy. The submissions began in March and grew in number and importance as the royal army advanced, until, by the end of the campaign in October, Louis controlled Languedoc north of a line joining Agen, Albi, Carcassonne, and Narbonne. He established administrative districts (*sénéchausées*) that remained the units of royal government until the French Revolution, and he left behind about five hundred knights to garrison the key strongholds.

All this was achieved almost without a fight. The only major opposition that Louis encountered was the city of Avignon, which was situated east of the Rhone in Provence, and thus was in the Empire. Like earlier crusaders, Louis' army chose to cross the Rhone at Lyon and follow the east bank down to Avignon, where it could use the famous bridge to enter Languedoc. At first the Avignonese were willing to cooperate if Romanus would lift the long-standing interdict from their city, but the agreement broke down when the French arrived. Each side naturally blamed the other, and historians have followed suit. My impression is that Louis and the legate were determined to make an example of Avignon, which they certainly did; it was besieged for three months (June–August), and when it surrendered it was to the legate rather than the king, who was paid damages for his efforts and garrisoned the city for the papacy. Indeed, the French then occupied the whole marquisate of Provence, which also lay east of the Rhone, again in the name of the Roman church. Thus Romanus had much to gain by diverting the crusade against subjects of the Empire; Louis, too, profited because the siege enabled him to display his power without alienating Languedoc, the region he would have to govern if his crusade were successful.

For whatever reason, the royal army devoted its best campaigning weather to the siege; afterwards it moved unopposed in a triumphant progress towards Toulouse but stopped four miles short of the city and started home in October. On the return trip, Louis unexpectedly fell ill, probably of dysentery, and died within a week, on 8 November in the small town of Montpensier in Auvergne.

The first six months of Queen Blanche's regency

Louis IX, the heir to the throne, was only twelve, so by the terms of his father's will, the regent was his widow, Queen Blanche of Castille.[4] "To all intents and purposes," wrote Robert Fawtier, "she may be counted among the kings of France,"[5] for she alone ruled the kingdom for the next ten years or so. It was no easy task, as she not only had to maintain and conclude the ambitious royal initiative in Languedoc but also had to prevent Henry III from regaining the

4. The following paragraphs are primarily based on E. Berger, *Histoire de Blanche de Castille, reine de France* (Paris, 1895), pp. 46-95.

5. R. Fawtier, *The Capetian Kings of France* (London, 1960), p. 28.

continental lands that England had lost to France since 1204. Six weeks after Louis VIII's death, the English began preparations for a major campaign in the spring by providing themselves with money, transportation, and especially allies. Raymond VII was ready enough to ally with Henry against their common enemy, but neither could offer the other anything but moral support. In the west of France, however, during the month of December Henry was able to secure the defection of some of the greatest vassals of the French crown, notably the count of Brittany, Peter de Dreux "Mauclerc," and the count of La Marche, Hugh IX of Lusignan; the next month two great lords from eastern France, the counts of Champagne and of Bar, marched to join the coalition.

Such shifts in allegiance had been the rule in France before the military successes of Philip Augustus had established Capetian hegemony over the barons. His son and successor, Louis VIII, had been able to maintain and extend royal power, but now it appeared that the Capetian *imperium* might dissolve, as had the Plantagenet "empire" before it. It was the most critical moment for the French monarchy, and under the leadership of Queen Blanche the crown proved equal to the challenge. Much of the credit, of course, belongs to the corps of administrators that had made royal governance an efficient reality during the past two reigns, but Romanus and the papacy deserve their fair share as well. The papacy as overlord of England had played an active and decisive role in the equally critical minority of Henry III, but its only authority in France was the protection of the kingdom and the royal family for the duration of the Albigensian crusade (Doc. 26.1).[6] This was enough to keep Romanus at the queen's side at the major moments of the crisis, beginning with the young king's coronation at Reims on 29 November. Indeed, during the next four years Romanus and the queen were so often together that it was commonly said they were lovers.[7]

As the coalition was concentrating its forces at Thouars, Blanche promptly assembled the French host and marched to nearby Chinon, arriving on 21 Feb-

6. The new pope, Gregory IX, eventually renewed this in May: Potthast, no. 7897–98 (10 May) and 7920 (27 May). Berger, *Blanche*, pp. 89–90.

7. In 1241, the rumor was alleged by Emperor Frederick II as one reason why Romanus should not be pope: "cui [Romano] electioni opposuit se imperator; habuit enim ipsum infamem . . . propter persecutionem universitatis Parisiacae, quinetiam dicebatur corrupisse reginam Franciae B[lanchiam]. . . . " Matthew Paris, *Chronica majora*, ed. H. R. Luard, Rolls Series, no. 57, 7 vols. (London, 1872–1883), IV, 165. Paris preserves (and improves) a goliardic epigram directed against Romanus by the Paris students in May 1229, when they dispersed because the legate failed to protect them from being brutalized by Blanche's police: "*Heu, morimur strati, / caesi, vincti, spoliati; / mentula legati / nos facit ista pati*—Alas, we die, knocked down, / beaten, conquered, stripped; / the legate's dork / makes us suffer these things" (original form in Matthew Paris, *Historia Anglorum*, ed. F. Madden, Rolls Series, no. 44, II [London, 1866], 309, n.).

ruary. By this show of force, which was followed by a series of generous concessions, she was able to detach the leading rebels from the English coalition: the
counts of Champagne and Bar decided at the last minute not to join (2 March)
and the counts of Brittany and La Marche soon both submitted to Louis IX at
Vendôme (16 March). Romanus was with the queen on this expedition; apparently he did what he could to help her by threatening the English and their allies with excommunication and interdict, so that Gregory IX subsequently had
to restrain him.[8] Throughout the crisis, the French clergy maintained their traditional loyalty to the crown, no doubt strongly encouraged by Romanus.

Meanwhile in Occitania, the war against Raymond VII and his allies continued on a small scale. In December 1226, as the coalition was forming in the
north, the crown reassured its troops and supporters in Béziers that money and
supplies were on the way to Albigeois.[9] In January the French were able to take
Varilhes, while during the same winter Raymond took Auterive and his allies
recaptured Limoux. Clearly the French were maintaining their presence in
Languedoc with difficulty, and the effort was not self supporting.

The taxpayers' revolt of 1227

At this juncture the second installment of the tenth came due at Easter 1227,
and when the cathedral chapters of four provinces refused to pay it, Romanus
resorted to extreme measures to force their compliance; in response they appealed to the pope, who eventually decided against them. The controversy deserves our close examination because one of the key questions was whether the
chapters' proctors at Bourges had consented to the tenth; it has a more general
interest as well because the unusually extensive documentation shows that at this
early stage in the history of clerical taxation, the law was not clear as to what
constituted consent. These matters can best be treated by analyzing each document in turn, but because the history of the controversy must be reconstructed
from scattered clues, it will be convenient to bring these together at the outset
in a chronological summary that will be subsequently justified.

Overview of the controversy

When the first installment came due on 1 November 1226, the taxpayers began
paying without protest, but as soon as they heard of the king's death on 8 November, some cathedral chapters refused to pay any more of that installment.
The legate warned them to pay in full, but he did not make an issue of it be-

8. Berger, *Blanche*, pp. 89–90.
9. Berger, *Blanche*, p. 94.

cause the kingdom was then in a state of crisis. However, by Easter (11 April 1227), when the second installment was due, the chapters again made only a partial payment (Doc. 29.7), and again Romanus warned them to pay in full. But since the political crisis had been resolved in March, the government was better able to deal with recalcitrant taxpayers, so on 17 May the legate authorized the crown to sequester the delinquent chapters' goods, which were to be held until they paid the first year's tenth in full (Doc. 29). Moreover, he disabled the Church's normal defenses against the seizure of ecclesiastical property by laymen, though only when they did so to force payment of the tenth (Doc. 30).

These provisions were not put into effect immediately, for ten days later, on 27 May, the chapters of four provinces—Reims, Sens, Tours, and Rouen—jointly appealed against the tenth to the new pope, Gregory IX, and asked for his protection against possible secular coercion (Doc. 32.5). Romanus ignored the appeal, which should have forestalled sequestration, for nine days later, on 5 June, he ordered that a version of his letter of 17 May (Doc. 30) be read aloud to the chapters and then returned to him (Doc. 31). At Paris this was done within the next week by two officials, whereupon the chapter's assets were confiscated, as the dean of Paris soon complained to the pope (Doc. 32).

When Gregory received the Paris complaint a month later, on 18 July 1227 he promptly ordered Romanus to revoke his authorization of 17 May (Doc. 33); at the same time the pope commissioned three French prelates to do so if the legate himself did not within three days (Doc. 34), and Gregory also notified the complainant chapters of his action (Doc. 35). In effect, the chapters had secured a court injunction that restored their property until the pope could hear both sides of the case and decide whether they were obliged to pay the tenth.

While the case was pending, Romanus improvised other ways to secure payment. Presumably he obeyed the injunction when he received it in mid–August 1227; but about the same time he persuaded two royalist prelates—the archbishop of Sens and the bishop of Chartres—to assume the payments for all of the cathedral chapters in Sens province, which was agreed to be fifteen hundred pounds paris per annum (Doc. 36). Consequently the Sens chapters withdrew their appeal to Rome, thus weakening the case of the remaining three provinces, especially since the appeal had been initiated by one of them—Paris, which because of its association with the university was the chapter with the most clout at the curia. Not much later, around 1 September, Romanus attempted to intimidate another ringleader, the cathedral chapter of Rouen, by making an official visitation, or tour of inspection, there; but his conduct was so obviously prejudiced that he only provoked the chapter to complain to the pope (Doc. 53).

In September Romanus set out for Rome, accompanied by the compliant archbishop of Sens and several tax-exempt Cistercian abbots. We do not know

how he defended himself against the chapters' complaints; certainly in his earlier accounts of the case he had constructed an elaborate rationale for the chapters' consent, which he claimed was given both by their counsels at Bourges and
by their partial payment of the tax, and he may well have repeated these arguments before the curia. Be that as it may, when Gregory handed down his decision on 13 November, it was based on only one consideration: the legate had
been fully empowered to do whatever he thought would expedite the Albigensian business (Doc. 39), so the issue of consent was bypassed. In the end the
chapters were obliged to pay simply because the pope, through his legate, had
commanded them to do so.

The decision to sequester

As seen from the documents, the dispute over the Albigensian tenth begins *in
medias res* with the legate's decision, dated 17 May 1227, to let the crown sequester the goods of the delinquent chapters (Docs. 29 and 30). This came just
a year (to the day) after the rendezvous at Bourges, which the chapters' representatives left "silently cursing the business of the Cross and of the king" because
their protest went unheard (Doc. 3.14). Our best source for the controversy during the intervening year is the legate's review of the considerations that justified
his decision, which are set forth at length in Document 29 and summarized in
Document 30. Let us examine each document in turn, paying special attention
not only to the notable features of its contents but also to its function.

Document 29 is an open letter addressed to no one in particular, and most
likely it was never circulated; certainly it was not the letter that was later read
to the Paris chapter on 5 June (Doc. 32.7). Instead, it seems to have been immediately deposited in the royal archives as a memorandum of the legate's motives for permitting the crown to sequester the chapters' goods. It does not in
itself grant that permission, for it has no dispository clause but only records in
a past tense that such a concession was made ("concessimus," 11). Its apparent
purpose was to provide an authenticated record of the reasons for and the terms
of that concession. As a convenient summary of the case against the chapters,
the royal chancery repeatedly copied it into its chartularies for ready reference,
while carefully preserving the original.

The first and most important step in Romanus' argument is that the chapters
consented to the tenth. He establishes that they did this in two ways: first, by
sealing their *consilia* to him at the Council of Bourges, and secondly, by voluntarily paying some part of both the first and second installments of the tenth
(Doc. 29.8). These arguments reveal what Romanus' strategy had been at
Bourges, and we have already made use of them (above, pp. 128-132); what is

noteworthy here is how heavily Romanus' argument rests on those *consilia*, and consequently on the decision he forced on the chapters at Bourges. Also notable is the admission, made as an apparently irrelevant afterthought, that the tenth was approved by "almost (*fere*) the entire council" (§ 8), which suggests that Romanus prudently adopted the opinion of the majority of his advisers.

Romanus had an answer to the chapters' contention that they had not consented to the grant made at Paris in January 1226 because they were not represented there. Their *consilia* at Bourges approved Romanus' course of action: he was to urge Louis to undertake the crusade and to grant him a tenth if he did (Doc. 29.4). But in his memorandum, Romanus carefully avoids the suggestion that any further consent to the grant was given at Paris. Accompanied there by various prelates, he presented the case for a crusade to the king as he had been counseled to do at Bourges; then, as Romanus had elaborately interpreted the event elsewhere (Doc. 28.1), by divine intervention the king was inspired to take the Cross; finally, the legate granted the tenth, since the prelates with him advised that it was necessary in order to implement the will of God (Doc. 29.5).

Romanus also contends that the chapters consented to the tax by paying it. An argument to that effect could be made if the chapters had not done so under protest, which is probably why, according to the Chronicle of Tours, Romanus had refused to hear their delegation in May 1226 (Doc. 3.14). From the two versions of Romanus' account, it is clear that the chapters paid both installments in part (Docs. 29.7 and 30.2). Although it is easy to guess why they stopped paying the first installment after hearing of the king's death, since the kingdom was in turmoil and it was doubtful whether the crusade would be continued, yet it is difficult to understand why they paid any part of the second installment. Probably the legate's statement conceals a more complicated state of affairs: for instance, perhaps some of the chapters that were protesting in May had paid in April before joining the taxpayers' coalition. It is distinctly suspicious when one of Romanus' training omits such logical quantifiers as "some" or "all." A further, unexplained complication appears in Document 31, where Romanus distinguished between those in arrears and those in contempt (§ 1).

Having shown how the chapters had consented to the tenth, Romanus next establishes their guilt. By not paying the royal tax collectors, the chapters have broken the promise to which they consented; moreover, they have compounded their offense by ignoring the legate's frequent mandates to comply (Doc. 29.8), and for this contempt of Romanus' authority they must make separate amends (§ 11). Nothing more is known about these legal proceedings, but it is a reasonable guess that most recently a single mandate was issued that gave the chapters thirty days to comply, since the sequestration order came a little more than a month after Easter. But Romanus says that they had been "warned many times *(pluries admoniti),*" so it would seem likely that multiple mandates were issued in connection with the first installment (Doc. 29.8).[10]

Finally, to justify the extreme measures he is about to take, Romanus shows that otherwise the crusade is bound to fail. The crown had notified the legate that it would have to withdraw its troops in Occitania if the tenth was not paid. The crown's position was realistic, for the recalcitrant chapters were major contributors to the tenth. As has been previously observed, their provinces were the part of Romanus' legation that contained the royal demesne and hence was subject to effective tax collection; to be sure, many monasteries also contributed (and followed the chapters' appeal with sympathetic interest, for example in Doc. 37), as did some bishops, though many had avoided the tax by going on the crusade (Doc. 26.7).

These, then, are the considerations with which Romanus justified his decision to let the crown sequester ecclesiastical goods, even though in principle the Church strongly opposed lay seizures of its property. No doubt each of his arguments could be supported by citations of Roman and canon law, and, although such refinements might clarify his reasons, the thrust of his thought is evident enough without them. Perhaps the most remarkable feature of this document is that, more than any other, it represents Romanus' own view of the matter, for it is a memorandum designed to record his rationale for the sequestration. While this *aide-mémoire* is admittedly an *ex parte* statement, it presents his side of the case as he conceived it.

How Romanus proceeded against the rebels

Document 30 is the mandate that transmitted Romanus' decision down the ecclesiastical hierarchy and provided for its implementation. The considerations rehearsed at length in Document 29 are compressed here into a brief summary (§ 1-3), after which the recipients are forbidden to use the usual canonical sanctions against anyone involved in sequestering the goods of delinquent chapters (§ 4), and for good measure they are deprived of the power to do so in this case (§ 5). In consequence, the chapters were stripped of their normal defenses against laymen who seize church property. The letter was addressed to a wide range of persons beginning with the archbishops and bishops, including abbots and prelates, and concluding with the clergy and laity of Romanus' legation. Significantly, the cathedral chapters were not expressly named as addressees, perhaps so that they would have no express right to receive a copy of the letter.

---

10. Strictly speaking Doc. 28 cannot be counted as a warning to pay the tenth, since the grant is announced but not included in the disposition clauses.

Romanus was evidently uneasy about the measures he was taking, for he took elaborate precautions to prevent the chapters from obtaining a copy of his orders against them. The suppression of evidence makes it difficult to determine just how the sequestration was implemented, but the process can nonetheless be reconstructed by reading Documents 31 and 32 in conjunction.

Let us begin with Document 31, which was addressed to the archbishop of Tours on 5 June. The legate orders the archbishop to have read to the chapters of his province "the penalties (*penas*) that we formerly established against those guilty of such contempt, which you can plainly see in the letter issued concerning this." The letter referred to is not the one sent on 5 June but another that had been sent earlier to the archbishop; he is required to return *both* letters to the legate (§ 2).

The letter that the archbishop was directed to have read cannot be Document 30, which suspended the sanctions provided by canon law against the seizure of church property, because it does not "plainly" impose any "penalties" on the chapters. Instead, it was an expanded version of Document 30, as is evident from the summary of that letter as the Paris chapter remembered it (Doc. 32.7). The Paris précis summarizes Doc. 30.4-5, but between these paragraphs it inserts a list of penalties: those who refuse to pay the tenth cannot be promoted to major orders and cannot participate in elections. Consequently it would seem that Document 30 was a version prepared for the king, who wanted to be sure that the secular authorities were exempt from ecclesiastical sanctions against sequestration but to whom these clerical penalties were of no concern.

The version with penalties was sent to Tours and the other archbishops sometime after 17 May, when the sequestration order was issued (Doc. 29), but apparently with instructions to postpone publication until that was authorized by the legate. Why the postponement? Again, the sequestration proceedings at Paris provide the answer. Two letters were read to the Paris chapter: one, as we have just seen, was from the legate; the other was from the king, which specified what kinds of chapter properties were subject to sequestration (Doc. 32.8). Most likely the legate delayed publication of his order until he and the government could work out the details of the operation, after which still more time would have been required for the royal chancery to draw up the necessary documents and distribute them to the crown's local agents—no small task, since thirty-nine cathedral chapters were involved. Probably Romanus' order suspending sanctions and imposing penalties was distributed to the archbishops soon after 17 May in order to prevent them and their subordinates from invoking sanctions in anticipation of the confiscations (Doc. 30.5).

But why did Romanus not want the chapters to have a copy of his letter? After the other obscurities about the sequestration have been cleared up, this one remains something of a mystery. Evidently his reason concerned the letter's content rather than the original, authentic document itself, since they were not to be given even a transcript (Doc. 31.2 and 32.6). We shall see that as late as 5 June Romanus was probably still not aware that the chapters had appealed to the pope; but undoubtedly he would have foreseen this as a possibility that he might have to face, and perhaps he was simply making their appeal as difficult as possible, for they would have to prove their case without documentary evidence. In other words, perhaps he was playing for time, hoping to prolong the appeal; such a delaying tactic was a commonplace of canonistic procedure, and it would make sense under the circumstances, since the crusade, which still had four years to run, might well be over before the case was decided, given the usual snail's pace of litigation at the curia. In the event, of course, the chapters received abnormally prompt justice, but the legate seems to have done what he could to impede it. In addition, Romanus may also have worried that his actions might be illegal, since he had abrogated the clerical immunity that was one of the most cherished principles of canon law. Although he was confident that his legatine commission permitted him to override the usual course of canon law, still as a canonist he might well be uneasy about acting *supra jus*, and at any rate professional prudence would prompt him to cover his tracks.

The dean of Paris complains to the pope

The taxpayers' side of the story is known chiefly from a long complaint that the dean of Paris addressed to Pope Gregory IX some time around the middle of June 1227. This letter was not an appeal in the strict legal sense; instead, its principal purpose was to inform the pope of the sequestration in the well-founded hope that he would consider it an outrage and intervene (Doc. 32.6-8). The letter's persuasive intent is especially evident in its opening and closing sections, which seem overwrought to modern sensibilities but to contemporaries were a *captatio benevolentiae* that flattered by assuming Gregory's mastery of the Bible and persuaded by showing how he was destined to help appellants by virtue of his names as cardinal and pope (§ 1, 9). This display of erudition, elegance, and ingenuity also advanced the writer's purpose more subtly by indirectly reminding the pope that he was being addressed by the chapter of Notre-Dame de Paris, arguably the most learned in Europe, and also mother of the university of which Gregory himself was an alumnus.[11]

Before announcing his distressing news, however, the dean prepared the way at length, first by reviewing the reasons why the chapters took exception to the

---

11. Maleczek, *Kardinalskolleg*, p. 128, n. 18.

tenth (Doc. 32.2-4), then by quoting the dispositive section of the chapters' appeal of 27 May (§ 5), of which only this fragment has survived. Some of the reasons the dean advanced must have been borrowed from the appeal's now lost *narratio*, but he may well have elaborated those or added other arguments of his own. It would be a waste of ingenuity to attempt to distinguish the appellant chapters' rationale from that of the dean, since the pope was not moved by either of them. Initially, Gregory responded to the outrageous sequestration (Docs. 33-35), that is to Doc. 32.6-7, and his final decision (Doc. 39) dealt exclusively with the allegations of the dispositive clause, that is, to Doc. 32.5. In short, the dean was presenting the pope with the chapters' partial point of view, which they took seriously even though canonists at the curia might not agree. As a rare witness to the taxpayers' point of view, these arguments deserve our consideration, however brief.

The issue of consent. According to the dean of Paris, the chapters never consented to the tenth, and to establish this, he offers the chapters' interpretation of the events of the last six months. First of all he claims that, because the chapters' proctors came to Bourges with a limited mandate, they could not consent (Doc. 32.2); but he ignores the fact that this was contrary to Romanus' summons, which required the chapters to be represented "by means of suitable proctors (*per procuratores idoneos*)."[12] Next, the dean alleges that the proctors, speaking for themselves, advised a grant limited to the king's lifetime (§ 2); this, as we have seen, may have been presented as an oral argument during the discussion, but it most likely was not reflected in the sealed *consilia* on which Romanus based his case.[13] Finally, the dean repeatedly insists that the chapters were never consulted subsequent to the Council of Bourges (§ 3-4).

Presumably the full text of the chapters' appeal of 27 May rehearsed some such arguments, which the extant dispositive clause simply sums up by stating that the legate imposed the tax "without our consent" in virtue of "a certain ordinance made, it is said, at Bourges, to which we never consented and which was never made known to us by public proclamation." Moreover, although the chapters admit that the legate could have imposed the tax arbitrarily if expressly authorized by papal mandate to do so, they argue that this would require a special mandate rather than a general one (Doc. 32.5). For Gregory, this was the nub of the matter, and he disagreed (Doc. 39).

Romanus, it will be remembered, had argued that the chapters had consented to the tenth by the fact that they had paid the first installment (Docs. 29.7 and 30.2). The dean counters this argument by declaring that "they paid not because

12. Doc. 29.1. See the discussion of the proctorial mandates above, pp. 94-104.
13. On the *consilia* at Bourges, see above, p. 131.

they had in mind some promise, which in fact had never been made previously, but rather they did so with joyful hearts, out of pure generosity, lest they might seem to be not supporting so great a business" (Doc. 32.3). This statement most likely does report their motives for paying, because, according to the Chronicle of Tours, the chapters had been ready to contribute an uncompelled gift as early as the Bourges rendezvous in May 1226. What they feared, both then and thereafter, was that a precedent might be established by which they could be taxed without their consent; what they had expected, and still wanted, was a papal exhortation to contribute voluntarily, which had been the approach Honorius III had taken in 1221 for the previous Albigensian tenth.[14] Their fears were justified, for Romanus' procedure at Bourges set a new precedent, of nonvoluntary clerical taxation by papal mandate. It had already been followed in England in October 1226, though less offensively than in France, for the English crown had tactfully declared that the grant was a gracious aid prompted by generosity.[15]

The dean and the legate seem to disagree on how much of the tenth the appellant chapters actually paid. The legate's story is that the first installment was paid, "although not fully after the king's death" (Doc. 29.7; cf. 30.2) and that the appellant chapters had "refused to pay that tenth in full at the said two terms now past" (§ 8). The dean says "they fully paid half" and adds, oddly, that "they would have freely and liberally paid the other part of the tenth, which if it had been paid would have been the greater part, if God had kept the said king unharmed and persistent in that business" (Doc. 32.3). These statements can be reconciled, I think, by taking the dean to mean that they were in the *process* of paying fully when news of the king's death arrived; they then stopped paying, so that the *greater* part of the first year was not paid, that is, the unpaid balance from the first term plus all due at the second term. These statements are most significant for the point on which they are in agreement: the chapters stopped paying when the king died, which bears out the dean's contention that from the start the chapters were prepared only to support a crusade led by Louis VIII.

What happened in the matter during the six months after the king's death is largely unknown. The chapters evidently expected the legate to follow up his repeated orders that they should pay, but neither the chapters nor the dean mention these orders to the pope; instead, the dean only exemplifies their suspicions with a rumor that the legate promised the queen that "he would even give her

14. Honorius urged all Christians in Conrad's legation to grant a *collecta* for the war against the heretics: *Rec. hist. Gaules*, XIX, 699, misdated 1220 (probably June 1221); Pressutti, no. 3486. In a companion letter, the legate was instructed to induce all in his legation to pay the tax: ed. F. Neininger, *Konrad von Urach (+1227)* (Paderborn, 1994), p. 535, no. 16.

15. E.g. the grant of the English clergy to the king on 13 October 1226 was said "ex sola gratia et liberalitate processisse": Powicke-Cheney, *Councils & Synods*, II.i, 159.

our capes" (Doc. 32.4), referring to the hooded cloaks that were the canons' distinctive dress. No doubt the chapters justified their appeal more substantially, but all we know is that they *did* appeal on 27 May 1227. In general, they hoped that the pope would agree that they were not obliged to pay the tenth; but more particularly, they planned to forestall the legate's impending sanctions by placing "our persons and property and benefices and our clerical status under the protection of the apostolic see" (§ 5), which they would receive *ipso facto* by making an appeal.

The organization of this appeal was no small task, as it involved the thirty-nine cathedral chapters in the four ecclesiastical provinces of Reims, Sens, Tours, and Rouen. One can only speculate on how it was done. All that can be said with certainty is that the Paris chapter seems to have played the leading role, since the letter of appeal was delivered to the curia by a priest who represented only the diocese of Paris (Doc. 32.5); similarly, it was the dean of Paris who in Document 32 reported the sequestration. We can be sure, however, that the other chapters were committed to the appeal, because when the Sens chapters, including Paris, withdrew from the appeal (Doc. 36), the other three provinces continued to press the case at great expense (Doc. 37.5), and Gregory's decision was addressed only to them (Doc. 39). I think it unlikely that representatives of the thirty-nine chapters ever assembled and worked out a common course of action; instead, I would guess that the Paris chapter drew up a proposal and circulated it. Perhaps the chapters assembled and deliberated by province, as they had at Bourges, but it seems more likely that all the arrangements were made by correspondence borne by envoys.

How the sequestration was implemented

About two weeks after the appeal of 27 May, in the second week of June or so, the property of the Paris chapter was sequestered. All we know about the implementation of Romanus' mandate of 17 May (Doc. 29) comes from the dean's letter (Doc. 32.8). Two officials appeared before the chapter to notify it of the action. One was the unnamed *prévôt* of Paris, the royal officer in charge of the city, who represented the crown; the other official, "Magister P. Carnifex," probably was an agent of the bishop of Paris, since Romanus had instructed the archbishops to have his mandate executed by the bishops (Doc. 31.2). The title of *magister* indicates that the bishop's agent held the highest university degree, most likely in canon law; his ominous surname was probably noted because in Latin *carnifex* signifies not only a butcher—the man probably belonged to the Bouchier family, which held small fiefs in the royal demesne[16]—but also an execu-

16. See Doc. 32, n. 12.

tioner, torturer, or simply a villain. Being proficient in Latin, Master P. must have
been the one who read the mandates aloud, and as a canonist he was the one
most likely to have responded to questions.

Two letters were read to the assembled canons of Notre-Dame, one from the
legate, the other from the king. We are already familiar with most of the legate's
letter, the operative parts of which were reconstructed from memory by the dean
with remarkable accuracy (Doc. 32.7 = 30.4). To the general sanctions that Romanus had mandated on 17 May, he now added two more that suspended several of the canons' most cherished rights. First he deprived them of all hope of
ecclesiastical advancement; specifically, they were declared *inelegibiles*, that is, incapable of being elected, particularly to the office of bishop (as in fact the dean
was in the following year).[17] By papal dispensation, some canons held their
prebends before becoming priests, usually for a set period of time, and they were
now prohibited from advancing to major orders, so that they were in danger of
losing their benefices when the grace period expired. Finally, Romanus excluded
the rebel canons from participating in the election of a new bishop, and moreover he attempted to divide the chapter by placing such an election in the hands
of those canons who did not oppose the tenth.

The king's letter announced the details of the sequestration (Doc. 32.8). The
goods of each chapter were to be taken over by one of the crown's local fiscal
agents, the *prévôts*, each of whom was responsible for administering royal finances
in one of the forty-odd districts into which the demesne was divided.[18] This
provision clearly indicates that the sequestration could only be implemented
within the royal demesne. With the exception of Paris, each church was assigned
a custodian, whose function is not made clear: most probably he assumed complete control of the church's property and business affairs, just as royal agents did
when exercising the crown's regalian rights after the death of a bishop or abbot.[19]
Since the purpose of the sequestration was punitive, it is understandable that the
chapters were deprived of every possible source of income. The dean stressed
that the crown took control of even "patrimonial" property, which had been donated for a specific pious purpose, such as poor relief, that would not be served
while it was in royal hands. Similarly, benefices that were being treated as the
chapter's common property were not only confiscated but were in danger of
being alienated to the crown.[20] In Paris, the chapter's cloister was exempted, but
not the houses of canons outside the compound—such as the house in which

17. See Doc. 32, n. 1.

18. J. W. Baldwin, *The Government of Philip Augustus* (Berkeley and Los Angeles, 1986),
pp. 43–44.

19. Baldwin, *Government*, pp. 48–50.

20. See Doc. 32, nn. 15–16.

Abelard wooed Heloise—with the result that the evicted canons had to live in the cloister, where they were "packed in together so tightly" that they were tempted to relieve the pressure by leaving Paris and thus deserting their official duties in the cathedral, which were their *raison d'être*. We are left to guess just what was done elsewhere, but probably cathedral canons throughout northern France dispersed, seeking refuge with family or friends, as their crowded Parisian counterparts were preparing to do. Even cemeteries, which were holy ground usually exempt from lay invasions, were occupied by the crown's agents. Consecrated edifices, that is, the church buildings themselves, were probably not occupied, but the sequestration deprived them of their infrastructure, namely the patrimonial revenues set aside for maintenance and the benefices that paid the salaries of the staff. The canons did not lose their capes and other personal property, but without their regular sources of income, they were poor as the proverbial church mice.

The scope of the royal confiscations indicates that the cathedral chapters were not the only groups involved in the tax revolt. The original appeal was in the name of the chapters "and all from these provinces who support us" (Doc. 32.5). From the royal order it appears that these supporters included at least monasteries and noncathedral collegiate churches, as well as "other places" that were not ecclesiastical corporations. For the purposes of the appeal it was not necessary to list them all, but the *prévôts*, who collected the tenth, knew precisely who was in arrears, and evidently sequestered their goods accordingly.

Gregory IX intervenes

The formal appeal of 27 May had been addressed to the pope and to the cardinals (Doc. 33.3) and seems to have been treated according to curial routine, which would be to assign the case to a panel of auditors who would eventually make a recommendation to the pope. The dean's letter of mid-June, on the contrary, was directed to Gregory personally, and it elicited an immediate and characteristic response.

Gregory, as has been remarked above, was a Paris alumnus and consequently well disposed to the Paris chapter. Indeed, he is likely to have viewed Paris, and France in general, in the roseate light of school-day memories, since in his long career as a cardinal (1198-1227) he traveled in Germany and more extensively in Italy, but never went back to France. In his letter this affection for the idealized France of his youth combined with other aspects of his paradoxical personality. Above all he was a canon lawyer,[21] who was consequently appalled at

---

21. Maleczek, *Kardinalskolleg*, p. 129, n. 26; for Gregory as cardinal, pp. 126-134.

Romanus' subversion of due process and ecclesiastical liberty. This theoretical knowledge was reinforced by thirty years of practical experience at the papal curia, where as cardinal-bishop of Ostia he had been head of the college of cardinals and the pope's principal adviser, first under his cousin Innocent III and afterward under Honorius III. These impressive qualifications were often offset, however, by an impatient, impulsive, and headstrong temperament that often led him to make ill-considered judgments, the most famous of which was his hasty excommunication of Frederick II when the emperor was forced by illness to return from the Sixth Crusade.[22] Moral rectitude, not to say asceticism, was a stern keynote of his character; he was a long-time admirer and personal friend of both St Dominic and St Francis, especially the latter, to whom he acted as legal adviser in the drafting of the definitive Franciscan Rule of 1223.[23]

Gregory's response to the dean of Paris reflects these diverse qualities. First of all, it was immediate; his three letters dated 18 July (Docs. 33–35) must have been composed just a few days after he received the dean's letter. The action was wholly Gregory's own, for there is no mention of his having taken counsel with the cardinals, which is so often specified in papal letters. Since Gregory eventually decided that Romanus had been authorized to act as he did (Doc. 39), the pope evidently overreacted. What particularly troubled him? The best indications, because not for public consumption, are the reasons given in Romanus' reprimand: first, because the decision to permit sequestration was deliberate; Gregory was less inclined to blame precipitate actions, to which he himself was prone (Doc. 33.4). Secondly, with characteristic concern for legality and especially for due process, he was outraged by Romanus' disregard of the rules of canonistic procedure, since the chapters' appeal should have forestalled the implementation of the legate's plan (§ 5). In short, Gregory did not actually condemn the sequestration in itself but rather he faulted the legate's actions on technical, procedural grounds. He did not explicitly censure placing the collection in the hands of laymen, which consequently remained a viable option, but his institution in 1228 of a new system of papal tax collectors[24] strongly suggests that, like most canonists, he preferred to minimize lay interference in clerical affairs.

What Gregory did in July 1227 was simply to nullify the sequestration order of 17 May and its consequences; in effect, he issued an injunction to suspend collection until the chapters' appeal could be judged on its merits. The principal provisions were his instructions to Romanus (Doc. 33.6): (1) Romanus was

22. Potthast, post no. 8043 (29 Sept. 1227) and 8049 (late Oct.).

23. *St. Francis of Assisi: Writings and Early Biographies*, ed. M. A. Habig, 4th ed. (Quincy, Ill., 1991), pp. 54–55.

24. W. E. Lunt, *Financial Relations of the Papacy with England to 1327* (Cambridge, Mass., 1939), p. 247.

given three days to revoke his sequestration order (Doc. 29) as well as its *seque-lae*; (2) furthermore, he was to make it clear that anyone who, on the basis of that order, did violence to the appellants or their goods would be excommunicated; and finally (3) he was to see that the sequestered goods were restored to their owners.

To insure that these instructions were carried out, Gregory commissioned three French prelates—the bishops of Le Mans and Orléans and the abbot of Bourgmoyen at Blois—to execute his commands if Romanus was unwilling, unable, or slow to do so (Doc. 34). Although it would be extremely unlikely that a legate would disregard the pope's express instructions, he could nonetheless avoid compliance by traveling beyond the boundaries of his legation, where he had no authority. This was a real possibility, for sooner or later Romanus was bound to go back to the curia to justify his actions, as in fact he did a few weeks after receiving Gregory's reprimand, and to forestall this excuse for noncompliance Gregory provided the commission as a backup.

In several respects, the commissioners' instructions expanded on those given to Romanus. Presumably he did not need to be told that, before those who violated ecclesiastical goods were excommunicated, they were first to be duly warned, as this was standard practice; moreover, an appeal to Rome would not postpone their excommunication (Doc. 34.4). More important was a new charge for the commissioners alone: they were given the power to protect the persons and property of all who traveled to Rome in connection with this case (§ 5). This charge was obviously not one that Romanus could be expected to execute, since it required continuous residence in France, while the likelihood was that he would be going to Rome to present his side of the case.

These instructions to Romanus and the commissioners took care of the practical, legal aspects of the crisis; it remained for Gregory to placate the French taxpayers. He returned the dean's compliments in kind, with an extravagant display of sympathy couched in the elegant, intricate Latin for which Gregory is famous (Doc. 35.1). Perhaps it was not all mere rhetoric, for Gregory was indeed capable of shedding tears in public, as he did at the canonization of Francis of Assisi.[25] The pope had a more concrete message for the French, however: he did not wish the Albigensian crusade to fail because Louis VIII had died, and he indicated, most tactfully, that its continued success depended on the uninterrupted payment of the clerical tenth (§ 2–3). He did not want Romanus' mishandling of the situation to alienate the taxpayers, whom he praised for their willingness to support the crusade (§ 3), and he concluded with a promise "to do everything

25. Gregory's official biographer says that the pope read the canonization decree with "his eyes bathed in tears": *Vitae Pontificum Romanorum*, quoted in Habig's Franciscan omnibus (n. 23, above), p. 1603.

that seems to us ought to be done according to God and decent conduct in order to preserve your honor and status" (§ 6). In plain words, the pope shared the chapters' concern to preserve what they called "ecclesiastical liberty," but a case of necessity, such as the need to defend the faith against the heretics, might nonetheless override their legal rights (as indeed it did). In short, although Gregory removed the immediate cause of the chapters' complaint, he did not commit himself on the legitimacy of the tenth but left their appeal *sub judice*.

Romanus undermines the coalition

Gregory's interlocutory letters probably arrived in Paris about 20 August, and Romanus no doubt obeyed the pope's instructions; if he had not, it is unlikely that he would have been entrusted with a second legation to France, as he was in 1228. There is, however, no documentary or chronicle evidence that the pope's commands were carried out; none of the letters were even preserved in the royal archives. The only possible indication of compliance is that the chapters' representatives were able to travel unhindered to Rome (Doc. 37.5; cf. 34.5).

We do have abundant evidence, however, that Romanus was busy in August undermining the coalition of chapters. "He kept threatening bad things indeed against all persons of the Gallican church who opposed him, and against them he was contriving worse things" (Doc. 37.4). This vignette by William of Andres, though placed in the context of events a few weeks later, probably characterizes the legate's tactics throughout the controversy, and it is best exemplified in two incidents that date from August.

Sens pays the tenth. At an unknown date in August 1227, Romanus succeeded in detaching the whole province of Sens from the alliance of appellant chapters. He did this, perhaps without their consent, by having someone else assume responsibility for their share of the tenth (Doc. 36). The key figure in this unusual transaction was Walter Cornut, archbishop of Sens (1222-1241), a *magister* who owed everything to royal patronage. His family was allied by marriage to the powerful Clément clan, from which came Philip Augustus' tutor, several marshals of France, a leading royal counselor, and another bishop.[26] Walter, whose mother was a Clément, first appears as a *magister* and royal clerk in 1206; subsequently at Paris he rose to be first canon, next dean, and almost bishop, until the king finally secured him the archbishopric of Sens.[27] Such a man would do whatever he could to support the crown. His associate in the transaction was another Walter, bishop of Chartres (1219-1234) and former abbot of the Bene-

26. Baldwin, *Government*, pp. 33-34, 66, 113, and index s.v. "Alberic," "Eudes," "Giles," "Henri," and "Robert."

27. Baldwin, *Government*, pp. 121, 307, 441.

dictine monastery of Pontigny in the diocese of Auxerre, who was less obviously
a royalist. Although his motives are not apparent, still there can be no doubt that
the crown trusted him to represent its interests, for in 1224 he had been one of
the three bishops selected by Louis VIII to negotiate a crusade on his terms at
the curia (Docs. 7.11 and 8.1). Moreover, as a monk he may have had little sympathy for his own cathedral canons, and no doubt he was also moved by a genuine desire for peace as well as zeal for the crusade. Both men had accompanied
Louis VIII on the crusade, thus demonstrating their loyalty to the crown and
their zeal for the crusade, as well as exempting themselves from paying the tenth
(n. 2, above).

Whatever their motivations, the two bishops struck a remarkable bargain.
"For the chapters of the cathedral churches of the province of Sens," they agreed
to pay 1500 pounds paris per annum for five years. Presumably this discharged
the obligation of those chapters, because they dropped out of the coalition: "Sens
quickly withdrew its appeal" (Doc. 38.3) and the pope's subsequent decision accordingly omitted Sens from the list of appellant provinces (Doc. 39.3). The
amazing thing about the deal is the amount that was paid, which was roughly
ninety percent less than the Sens chapters' share of the tenth. The Chronicle of
Tours (Doc. 3.10) reported the annual yield of the tenth as 100,000 pounds in
money of Tours (80,000 *parisis*).[28] Perhaps the chronicler wrote after Gregory
IX accepted that figure as a compromise proposed by the appellant chapters
(Docs. 37.5 and 38.5), which accordingly would most probably be somewhat less
than the ten percent of the ecclesiastical revenues that the crown could have collected. But either way, 80,000 pounds *parisis* per annum is a fair, though rough,
approximation of what the Albigensian tenth was worth to the crown.[29] Sens
was neither the richest nor the poorest of the four provinces; it cannot be too
far off to estimate its share as a quarter of the total, or 20,000 pounds *parisis* per
annum. And yet, since the two bishops agreed to assume the obligation at the
rate of 1500 pounds *parisis* per annum,[30] the crown was apparently willing to
give the Sens chapters a discount of more than ninety percent!

The reason, of course, was that Romanus and Blanche were desperate to
break up the coalition of chapters from the four provinces. If the appeal were
successful, the crown stood to lose at least 320,000 pounds *parisis*. To detach the
most prestigious province, including the Paris chapter that had organized the
appeal, they were prepared to sacrifice nearly a quarter of this sum—about
74,000 pounds. Accordingly, the two cooperative bishops were not only induced

28. See text after n. 49, chap. 4, above.
29. See the text at nn. 50–55, chap. 4, above.
30. There can be no doubt about the accuracy of this figure, since the original instrument survives in the royal archives.

to settle for a modest amount but were also authorized by the legate to obligate their churches and successors to pay if they could not do so (Doc. 36.2), so the crown would certainly get its money.

Romanus at Rouen. As William of Andres observed, the legate kept on threatening his opponents and plotting against them until the case was settled (Doc. 37.5). By late August, the pope's injunction was implemented in France, and the legate was preparing to go to Rome to answer the allegations of the appellant chapters; but before he left he did what he could to intimidate the Rouen chapter. The evidence for this rather obscure episode is presented in the prolegomena to Document 53; here I shall assume that the interpretation argued there is correct.

Late in August, it seems, Romanus hastened to Rouen to deal with the archbishop's quarrel with the crown over timber rights. While in the city, he took the opportunity to apply pressure to the cathedral chapter. As legate he had the right of visitation, which is to say the right to conduct a judicial inquiry—an inquest, or inquisition—concerning the morals and competence of any clergy in his legation. He began the proceedings by assembling the canons, together with some of the local laity, and preaching a public sermon in which "he threatened and defamed" the canons even before he had begun to collect evidence against them (Doc. 53.3). Then he conducted his inquest, and the canons maintained that "he was excessive in inquiring" (§ 1). Moreover, after collecting evidence that the canons required correction, he postponed doing anything about it (§ 2), perhaps to gain leverage in his negotiations with the archbishop, but more probably to induce the canons to withdraw their appeal against the Albigensian tenth. In reaction to these tactics, the canons of Rouen drew up a protest to the pope in which they recused Romanus as a prejudiced judge who should be disqualified from pronouncing judgment on them. We do not know what came of this appeal, but we may guess that it formed part of the dossier against Romanus that the chapters' proctors took with them to Rome in September.

Apart from this inquest concerning only the Rouen cathedral chapter, the canons also alleged that Romanus "has oppressed many spiritual persons in this church and very many in other churches by defamation, suspension, excommunication, and appropriation of benefices" (§ 5). Except for the defamation, these actions are all penalties that could be imposed on French clerics for concubinage according to the controversial constitution made by the legate Guala in 1208, and there is other evidence that Romanus had been enforcing that law. Under the year 1226, William of Andres reports: "Among other things that he [Romanus] corrected in the diocese of Thérouanne, he punished many priests with a heavy punishment on account of the sin of incontinence" (Doc. 37.1); probably they include the two Augustinian canons of that diocese whom he deprived of their benefices.[31] In the same province, Romanus supposedly disciplined the provost of the cathedral chapter at Reims for having an affair with an abbess.[32] That Romanus was intent on enforcing Guala's constitution in Rouen province appears from the delicate case of a concubinary priest that the bishop of Coutances referred to Romanus (Doc. 52), probably in 1226 when the legate was in Avranches (Doc. 51). Since these incidents seem to have taken place in 1226, and thus antedate the taxpayers' coalition of 1227, they may reflect nothing more than a conscientious effort to reform the clergy. Certainly the reforms that he instituted at the monastery of St-Bertin were received as made in good faith and reported at length, though well over a century later, by John Longus (Doc. 38.1).[33] Similarly, Romanus was determined to do his duty and inspect the exempt monastery of Luxeuil, even though the monks objected that the pope could only do that in person.[34] But none the less certainly, the Rouen canons regarded Romanus' inquisitions as oppressive and William of Andres characterized the penalties he imposed as harsh ("gravi"). One recalls the way in which he grossly overreacted to the Paris university riot in 1225 (Doc. 2.1) by destroying the careers of at least eighty masters, a penalty that was so extreme and unwise that he eventually had to moderate it somewhat (Doc. 3.6).

Romanus goes to Rome

Shortly after his visit to Rouen, Romanus set out for Rome to defend his handling of the Albigensian tenth. William of Andres tells us all that is known about the trip:

> the legate returned to Rome like a victor with his accomplices and the enemies of our coalition. Along the way he stopped at the Cistercian general chapter and added the abbots of Cîteaux and Clairvaux to his retinue, which included certain bishops and abbots whom he had created and the archbishop of Sens; they all followed him to support the queen [Doc. 37.4].

Since the Cistercians customarily held their general chapter in mid-September, Romanus' journey must have taken place then.[35] It was a clever tactic on his part

31. Auvray, no. 2109.

32. Auvray, no. 3782. See n. 69, chap. 2, above.

33. He was summarizing documents from the St-Bertin archives. For two examples, see above, chap. 2, n. 70.

34. Pressutti, no. 5737.

35. Berger, *Blanche*, p. 98. Since 1210, the Cistercian general chapter began on 13 Sept., the eve of the feast of the Holy Cross: J. B. Mahn, *L'Ordre cistercien et son gouvernement des origines au milieu du XIII* siècle (1098–1265), 2nd ed. (Paris, 1982), p. 174.

to enlist the support of the two leading abbots of the Cistercian order, which
at that time was still the most prestigious in Latin Christendom. Their cooperation was a foregone conclusion because the Cistercians, having been exempted
from the Albigensian tenth (Doc. 26.7), had no financial interest in the outcome,
and moreover they had long made it their mission to destroy the Albigensian
heresy, as we know best from the career of Conrad of Urach, the abbot of
Cîteaux who resigned in order to fight Albigensians full time as papal legate.[36]
Not surprisingly, Romanus was also accompanied by Archbishop Walter of Sens,
who, because he owed his whole career to Capetian patronage, could always be
counted on to support the queen.

The rest of the legate's entourage are less easily explained. The Andres chronicler evidently thought it noteworthy that Romanus included in his retinue "certain bishops and abbots whom he had created" (Doc. 37.4), as well he might, for
it was not within the ordinary powers of even a cardinal-legate to create
prelates.[37] Indeed, so unusual was it that John Longus mistook the passage to
mean that Romanus had created the abbots of Cîteaux and Clairvaux, which is
demonstrably false.[38] Romanus, however, had special powers that enabled him
to do what most legates could not. Among other things, Honorius had empowered him to fill benefices and other ecclesiastical dignities that had been vacant so long that the choice devolved on the papacy (Doc. 19). Furthermore,
Romanus was authorized to be present at all elections of prelates that took place
in Provence when the legate happened to be there, and the electors were always
obliged to hear his advice (Doc. 20). Finally, he was directed to settle a disputed
election to the bishopric of Carcassonne (Doc. 21). Thanks to these extraordinary powers he could be said to have "created" a number of prelates, although
in most known cases he simply exercised an overwhelming influence on the
lawful electors. During his first legation, between April 1225 and September
1227, seven Provençal bishoprics were filled: Auch, Avignon, Carcassonne, Narbonne, Perpignon, Tarbes, and Valence,[39] as well as the Burgundian archbishopric of Besançon (Doc. 5.1). Romanus certainly decided who was to be the
bishop of Carcassonne, for he had a papal mandate to do so; he probably gave
advance approval to most, if not all, of the others. No doubt he also influenced
the choice of many monastic prelates as well in Provence, though it would be ex-

36. See chap. 1, pp. 9-24, above. Before the erstwhile troubadour Folco of Marseille became the bloodthirsty bishop of Toulouse (1205-1231), he had been abbot of the Cistercian
house at Torronet (1201-1205): *Enciclopedia dantesca*, II (1970), 955.

37. H. Zimmermann, *Die päpstliche Legation in der ersten Hälfte des 13. Jahrhunderts* (Paderborn, 1913), pp. 273-274.

38. Neither house had a new abbot since 1225: *Gallia Christiana*, IV, 804-805 and 992.

39. See the episcopal *fasti* in Mas Latrie, *Trésor de chronologie*, cols. 1362-1520.

tremely difficult to determine which ones, and the same is true of long-standing vacancies throughout his legation. But enough can be determined to justify the chronicler's assertion that Romanus had "created" prelates, some of whom accompanied him to Rome, where they could be expected to work for their benefactor's cause.

Close on Romanus' heels followed proctors from the three remaining appellant provinces—Reims, Tours, and Rouen (Doc. 37.5). They can hardly have spent more than a month in Rome before the pope's decision was handed down on 13 November, so they received speedy justice, at least by the ponderous standards of the curia. The case was treated with such dispatch because the fate of the Albigensian crusade, which was one of the pope's cherished projects, depended on whether or not the French crown continued to receive the promised subsidy. Even when prodded into action, the *curiales* operated in an atmosphere of bureaucratic complexity and intrigue, to negotiate which required patience and the payment of innumerable customary gratuities. Later the capitular proctors were to complain of the "rebuffs and injuries" they had suffered from the curia (§ 5), but many of these were probably nothing out of the ordinary, although Romanus undoubtedly had his supporters in the curia (Doc. 22B) who could, and most likely did, make things even more difficult for his opponents. The proctors also had to contend with their own "neighbors" in Romanus' entourage, who commanded far greater prestige and influence than did the proctors, not to mention greater financial resources, for the queen was prepared to spend lavishly to retain the tenth (cf. Doc. 36). Of course the representatives of the taxpayers' alliance also "spent a great deal" (Doc. 37.5), and in the end, given the legal ethics of the day, neither the maneuvers nor the expenditures of the two parties is likely to have influenced the outcome materially.

Gregory IX confirms the tenth

The pope's decision, at least as he reported it to Louis IX, was remarkable for its concision (Doc. 39). It contains no trace of the concerns that so agitated him in July; indeed, the bull ignores almost completely the complexities that have prolonged our story. This economy of detail is significant in itself, because papal judgments of this sort often go on for pages narrating the facts of the case; but in this instance they were evidently considered to be irrelevant. Instead, the bull begins with a brief summary that for the most part follows the legate's own account (Doc. 29.1–5): the Council of Bourges had advised him to offer the king a quinquennial tenth, which he did (Doc. 39.1–2). Gregory also notes an important provision that had never been made public: the money was the king's to spend as he wished provided that he or his men were actively pursuing "the business of peace and of the faith" (§ 2 = Doc. 25.6). This presumably answered the chapters' argument that their obligation had ceased with the death of Louis VIII.

For Gregory, the only relevant question was whether Romanus was authorized to make the promises he did. The affirmative answer is supported by two citations: first, legates in general were commissioned to do what seemed expedient to them; and second, Romanus had been specifically empowered to do "whatever seemed to him, according to the prudence given to him by God, might expedite the [Albigensian] business" (Doc. 39.4; cf. Doc. 12.5). In other words, the granting of an Albigensian tenth was ultimately Romanus' prerogative, which is doubtless why he had his letters of legation certified by the bishops at the Paris assembly where the grant was made (Doc. 27). Consequently, Gregory confirmed the grant of the Albigensian tenth and assured the king that it would be paid in full (Doc. 39.5).

Thus the pope mostly avoided the issue of consent, but not entirely. In his narration, Gregory stated that at Bourges Romanus had "received the counsel (*consilium accepisset*)" that he should offer the subsidy to the king (Doc. 39.1). But later the bull acknowledges that this was done "on the advice of almost the whole (*pene totius*) Council of Bourges" (§ 5), just as Romanus himself had admitted earlier (Doc. 29.8: "fere totius concilii"). Even though Romanus alone made the decision, canon law required that before reaching a conclusion, he should observe due process by taking counsel with all concerned, in accordance with the principle of *quod omnes tangit*. Similarly, it may be noted, this time Gregory himself acted on the advice of the cardinals (§ 5), as he had not done in July.

Romanus' disregard for the rights of the chapters, which had caused Gregory to reprimand his legate in July, was passed over in silence. The legate evidently had convinced the pope that he had acted "for evident necessity and for business serving the interests of God's Church" (Doc. 39.4), both of which took precedence over the rights of the Church's constituent parts. And of course it was the pope, or his legate, who decided what was in the interest of the whole Church and whether a case of "evident necessity" existed. Hence this decision drew the Latin church yet another step down the road to absolute papal monarchy.

Yet the taxpayers' protest was not entirely in vain. According to the Andres chronicle, they successfully petitioned the pope to convert their obligation from a percentage of their net annual income to a lump sum, which was "to be assessed at the agreed [annual] sum of one hundred thousand pounds tours for four years" (Doc. 37.5). This account is confirmed by the Chronicle of Tours, which valued the Albigensian tenth at just this amount, though for the full five years rather than just four (Doc. 3.10). The conversion was advantageous to the taxpayers because it simplified their relations with the royal tax collectors, and especially the bookkeeping, as it was no longer necessary to calculate the gross and net annual income of each church. Instead, the share of each church could be prorated, probably on the basis of valuations that had been compiled for earlier taxes.

Gregory, too, learned an important lesson from the Albigensian tenth. The next year, in 1228, he instituted a new system of papal tax collectors,[40] which became the usual way of administering taxes imposed by the papacy. Thus the scandal of laymen seizing ecclesiastical property, which had so outraged Gregory in July, was permanently avoided in the future.

★ ★ ★

The story of the Albigensian tenth ends with Gregory's decision. Presumably the tax was duly paid, although it ceased to be a matter of record one way or the other. It must have been paid for only three of the five possible years because the Second Albigensian Crusade ended at Easter 1229. Early in 1228 Romanus had returned to France, where he continued to act as Blanche's chief adviser for the next two years, but by the end of 1228 it was evident that a stalemate had been reached in Occitania, so a lasting peace with Raymond was negotiated at Meaux and ratified at Paris on 12 April 1229, the week after Easter. Two provisions of this treaty especially reflect Romanus' concerns. One was the need to root out heresy: Raymond was obliged to offer a substantial reward to anyone who denounced a heretic; later that year, in November, Romanus held a council at Toulouse in which he organized a systematic heretic-hunt parish by parish under the direction of the local bishops. It was a prototype for the papal inquisition that was instituted in 1231, of which Romanus himself may well have been one of the architects.[41] His other contribution to the 1229 treaty of Paris was the foundation of a university at Toulouse as a bulwark of orthodoxy in the heartland of heresy. Raymond was obliged to contribute four thousand marks to pay the salaries of professors in the faculties of arts, theology, and canon law. Here again Romanus took a personal interest, supervising the selection of the first masters.[42] With the implementation of the treaty of Paris, Romanus' work in France was accomplished; by Easter 1230 he was back in Rome, where he was rewarded by promotion to cardinal-bishop of Porto (succeeding Conrad of Urach!) and his talents were utilized in various sensitive positions, such as the administration of the papal patrimony.[43]

40. Lunt, *Financial Relations*, p. 247.

41. See above, chap. 2, text after n. 15.

42. C. E. Smith, *The University of Toulouse in the Middle Ages* (Milwaukee, 1958), pp. 35-36, 47-49.

43. Maleczek, *Kardinalskolleg*, pp. 193-194; Strayer, *Albigensian Crusades*, pp. 136-137, 144-147.

In retrospect, Romanus seems to have exercised a moderating, if not positively benign, influence on the course of events. The overall plan under which
he operated must be credited to Honorius III, who emerges from the story as
more wise than vacillating, while Romanus appears as his able and devoted instrument. I am led to these paradoxical conclusions by a consideration of the
1229 treaty of Paris, which appears to be an elaborated version of the Montpellier accords of 1224. When Honorius was confronted by Louis VIII's refusal
to accept Raymond as his vassal, with the consequent prospect of a feudal war
in Languedoc, he realized that Raymond's reconciliation with the Church would
not in itself bring peace to Languedoc. The immediate problem, then, was to
find a way to prevent, or at least control, the impending French conquest of the
South, and the pope's answer was to revive and restructure Louis' discarded proposal for a royal crusade, but with the all-important difference that the king
would now have to cooperate with a papal legate *a latere*, who could guide and
perhaps control the operation. The papacy's long-range goal was to stabilize the
religious and political situation in Languedoc, which it was now obvious could
only be done with the assistance of a popular local leader such as Raymond, but
the cooperation of the king of France was also necessary to make sure Raymond
kept his promises.

In my view, Romanus was sent to France with a brief to achieve these goals.
The first step, which we have watched him pursue single-mindedly, was to
arrange the royal crusade; when it took place, the operation was a model of
church–state cooperation, headed jointly by king and legate. I suspect that the
siege of Avignon was Romanus' idea; it demonstrated royal power without alienating the people of Languedoc, and incidentally it brought Provence under papal
overlordship. If Louis' death had not intervened, Raymond would probably have
sued for peace before the next season's campaign, but he had two years' respite
while Blanche put her son's house in order. Meanwhile, Romanus cultivated the
confidence of the queen-regent, and when France and Toulouse were ready to
come to the conference table, Romanus was virtually in a position to dictate the
terms.

The interpretation I have sketched deserves to be substantiated in detail elsewhere; here it is mentioned only by way of epilogue in order to suggest that
we have not been seeing the better side of Romanus. All his cunning maneuvers were but the means to a worthy end—a workable, durable peace in Languedoc—and he achieved what seems to me to be the best solution possible under
the circumstances. He was not a zealot but a diplomat.

CHAPTER 6

A PROPOSAL FOR FINANCING
PAPAL GOVERNMENT

Bourges was the first recorded council attended by proctors since Honorius III had declared that they must be consulted when their interests were involved (Doc. 48).[1] Romanus had duly summoned them because canon law required their presence, but he had structured the proceedings so that opposition to the crusade and the tenth was strongly discouraged and moreover could not be expressed openly. Having collected their written and sealed counsels, the legate dismissed the proctors, and if they had complied, this early experiment in representative government would have offered little hope to the governed that it was worth their while to participate in conciliar deliberations. But the proctors were determined to make the most of their presence at the council, for they had heard of a still greater threat to their financial interests that they felt should be considered by the council. In the bull *Super muros Jerusalem* (Doc. 41), the pope had proposed a new way of financing papal government by appropriating a fixed part of the revenues of ecclesiastical corporations for the benefit of the Roman curia. At the proctors' request, Romanus expounded the plan to the council and then let them voice their objections at great length; in view of the overwhelmingly negative response, he postponed the question to see how the English reacted to the proposal. One of the participants—almost certainly a proctor—did what he could to show his English counterparts how to resist the proposal, so it would never become an issue in France again. Ignoring the customary confidentiality of conciliar proceedings, he wrote a detailed account of the Council of Bourges (Doc. 1), which did indeed provide the English with the model for their response. From the point of view of the governed, this episode must be accounted the first success of representative government; for the ecclesiastical historian, however, the rejection of Honorius' proposal was an ungenerous mistake, since the reforms he sought might have reduced the curia's corruption and avarice, which eventually contributed to the Protestant Reformation. The next

1. Proctors of cathedral chapters had been summoned by Innocent III to the Fourth Lateran Council in 1215, but this established no right or precedent, because a pope could summon anyone he wished to consult. See my article "'Ad nostram praesentiam evocamus': Boniface VIII and the Roman Convocation of 1302," *Proceedings of the Third International Congress of Medieval Canon Law, Strasbourg, 3–6 September 1968* (Vatican City, 1971), pp. 165–189.

two chapters will trace in detail the whole remarkable history of *Super muros Jerusalem*, with special emphasis on its consideration at the Council of Bourges.

The problem of financing papal government

The problem that Honorius addressed in *Super muros* was caused by the twelfth-century growth of papal government without any regular income adequate to support it. Around the year 1000, both ecclesiastical and royal governments in the Latin West had modest resources and their governmental functions were few, but in the course of the eleventh century, the West began to experience economic growth and prosperity, which made strong central government possible whenever a ruler could somehow get his subjects to pay for it. The Normans in the Italian Regno and in England were most successful at doing this, and their governments were accordingly the strongest and most sophisticated in Western Europe in the twelfth century. Their affluence and consequent power were the envy of less fortunate secular princes, who would have eagerly imitated these innovations if they had had the resources to do so.

As a result of the Gregorian reform movement of the later eleventh century, the pope became the monarch of the Church and modeled the institutions of his central government on those of the secular monarchies. Beginning in 1049, the papacy attempted to reform the western church by insisting on the strict observance of the legal norms established by church councils, papal decretals, and the Fathers of the Church, which collectively constituted an inchoate body of canon law. The key to this ambitious program was the pope's position as the ultimate interpreter and enforcer of canon law, which no one then realized had been conferred on him by decretals forged in the ninth century. By 1122, the reforming popes had attained their proximate goals, most important of which was the general acknowledgment of the pope's authority to act as "the omnicompetent court of appeal" for all Christendom.[2] As a result, the papal curia was flooded with an unprecedented number of appeals from every ecclesiastical court. By mid-century, Bernard of Clairvaux was denouncing the abuse of appeals,[3] but neither he nor anyone else found a way to discourage frivolous appeals.[4] Two generations later, on the eve of the Council of Bourges, the situa-

2. The apt phrase is F. W. Maitland's, *Roman Canon Law in the Church of England* (London, 1898), p. 103.

3. Bernard of Clairvaux, *De consideratione ad Eugenium papam tertiam libri quinque*, III.ii.6-12, trans. J. D. Anderson and E. T. Kennan, *Five Books on Consideration* (Kalamazoo, 1976), pp. 85-93. Cf. J. Benzinger, *Invectiva in Romam* (Lubeck and Hamburg, 1968), pp. 83-91.

4. On frivolous appeals, see C. R. Cheney, *From Becket to Langton* (Manchester, 1956), pp. 63-64, 70.

tion was, if anything, worse, for according to the chronicle written by Burchard, the provost of Ursberg:

> There remained hardly any bishopric, ecclesiastical dignity, or even a parochial church that was not made the subject of litigation, and the case would be brought to Rome itself, but not with empty hands.[5]

It was the cost of making appeals to Rome, not their number, that troubled Burchard. Simply put, the reason for the high cost of justice at the curia was that the papal bureaucracy had expanded to handle the influx of appeals, but the papacy lacked the resources to compensate its new officials adequately. The traditional way, of course, had been patronage; the pope appointed the leading clergy of Rome and its vicinity, namely the cardinal-bishops, priests, and deacons, who received an income, or "living," from their respective churches. Thus Romanus was the cardinal-deacon of Sant' Angelo, and moreover, to provide for his expenses as legate he was also given the income from the church of St Stephen on the Caelian Hill (Doc. 18). We are less well informed about the means of compensating lesser officials of the curia. Some, no doubt, had more modest livings provided by the churches of Rome, for example as canons of such collegiate churches as St John Lateran, but the number of Roman churches was fixed and the places in them often went to the sons of local nobles.

Consequently, as the curia's workforce expanded to cope with the rising volume of business, the pope simply had to pay the added officials out of his own resources.[6] Easier said than done, however, for although papal government had greatly increased in the twelfth century, yet there was no corresponding increase in revenue, because most of the pope's income was fixed by tradition. Like other lords great and small in Europe at this time, he derived most of his wealth from his landed estates; in the pope's case, these were collectively known as "the patrimony of St Peter" and yielded domanial income in such diverse forms as rents, tolls, services, and payments in kind.[7] In addition to his seigneurial revenues, the pope also was entitled to a variety of traditional payments in virtue of being pope, which are recorded in the *Liber censuum* that was compiled in 1192 by the papal chamberlain Cencius Savelli, who later became Pope Honorius III.[8] One

---

5. *Burchardi praepositi Urspergensis chronicon*, MGH, Script. rer. Germ., 16, 2nd ed. by O. Holder-Egger and B. von Simson (Hanover, 1916), p. 82 (ad an. 1198, but written before Burchard's death in 1231): "Vix enim remansit aliquis episcopatus sive dignitas ecclesiastica vel etiam parochialis ecclesia, que non fieret litigiosa et Romam deduceretur ipsa causa, sed non manu vacua." The rest of the passage is given below in n. 32.

6. I. S. Robinson, *The Papacy 1073–1198* (Cambridge, Eng., 1990), p. 247.

7. W. E. Lunt, *Papal Revenues in the Middle Ages*, 2 vols. (New York, 1934), I, 58.

8. Ed. Fabre-Duchesne, *Liber censuum*.

kind of *cens* was a small annual fee paid by monasteries that had been taken under papal protection and hence freed from the local bishop's control.[9] Another was an annual "tribute" paid by lay lords who were vassals of the Holy See, as was the case with the king of England since 1213;[10] yet another was "Peter's pence," a penny contributed by each household with a certain income in England and some Baltic kingdoms.[11] Payment of all these papal perquisites was intermittent and irregular, and although the yield was small in comparison with that of the crusading subsidies collected from the clergy in the thirteenth century, still in 1225 the census in its various forms was a major component in the papal budget.

As a result, salaries at the papal curia were necessarily modest in the extreme, and in the course of the twelfth century they came to be supplemented by a variety of expedients, most of which were widely resented. These deserve our special attention because the proposal of *Super muros* was designed to eliminate them and to provide instead a regular, adequate income for the personnel of the papal court.[12] First there were a variety of fees for drafting, sealing, and otherwise processing paperwork. Already in 1105, Ivo of Chartres was told they were a necessary cost of doing business at the curia, since "neither pen nor parchment is to be had there free of charge."[13] Until the time of Innocent III, however, there was no fixed scale of fees,[14] which invited payments far out of proportion to the services rendered, especially if one wished expeditious action. Moreover, those seeking favors from the curia, including a favorable judgment, were well advised to come bearing gifts.[15] An English litigant in 1163 reckoned that gifts were about twenty percent of his costs in securing a judgment from the curia,[16] which as tips go today is generous though not extravagant. These gifts, not to say bribes, were euphemistically known as "offerings" or "blessings";[17] usually they were

9. Lunt, *Papal Revenues*, I, 61–63; Robinson, *Papacy*, pp. 269–273.

10. Lunt, *Papal Revenues*, I, 63–64; Robinson, *Papacy*, pp. 273–274.

11. Lunt, *Papal Revenues*, I, 65–71; Robinson, *Papacy*, pp. 274–281.

12. Argued with thirteenth-century examples by G. Barraclough, "The Making of a Bishop in the Middle Ages," *Catholic Historical Review*, XIX (1933), 275–319, at pp. 302–306.

13. Ivo of Chartres, *Epistola* 133 (see n. 17, below).

14. This reform is known only from the *Gesta Innocentii III*, an anonymous biography written ca. 1208: Migne, *Pat. Lat.*, CCXIV, col. lxxxB (c. 41). On the reform, see J. E. Sayers, *Papal Government and England during the Pontificate of Honorius III (1216–1227)* (Cambridge, Eng., 1984), p. 17. On the *Gesta* and its author, see most recently J. M. Powell, "Innocent III and Petrus Beneventanus: Reconstructing a career at the papal curia," in *Pope Innocent III and his World*, ed. J. C. Moore (Aldershot, Hants., 1999), pp. 51–62.

15. W. E. Lunt, *Financial Relations of the Papacy with England to 1327* (Cambridge, Mass., 1939), pp. 179–180.

16. Cheney, *Becket to Langton*, pp. 57 and 67.

17. Ivo of Chartres, *Epistola* 133: "dicunt cubicularios et ministros sacri palatii multa exigere . . . quae oblationis vel benedictionis nomine palliantur, cum nec calamus nec charta gratis ibi (ut aiunt) habeatur . . . " (Migne, *Pat. Lat.*, CLXII, 142C).

made to influential individuals, both great and small, but sometimes a lump sum was presented as a *benedictio*, which was then distributed, apparently by curial custom. Thus in 1126 the Spanish archbishop of Santiago de Compostela sent 300 pieces of gold, of which 220 went to the pope and 80 to the curia.[18] Thus, when Hélinand praised Romanus because "he does not run after presents," it was high praise indeed, because the expectation was that *curiales*, and especially cardinals, eagerly did seek after gifts.[19]

Rome's reputation for avarice

These financial expedients quickly tarnished the reputation of the Roman curia, so much so that by the end of the twelfth century the very name ROMA was said to be an acronym for the biblical tag *Radix Omnium Malorum Avaritia* (I Tim. vi. 10).[20] Though the earliest satire on Rome's avarice appeared at the outbreak of the Investiture Contest in 1076,[21] the principal themes were developed in the twelfth century and then elaborated and repeated until the Reformation.[22] In an age when reality often fell far short of professed ideals, hypocrisy was a favorite target for indignant moralists, whose anger could most safely and effectively be vented in ridicule.[23] Sober-minded modern historians repeatedly caution us not to take these jokes too seriously,[24] but there can be no doubt that they troubled Honorius III, who, while attempting to discredit them with an *argumentum ad hominem*, still put forth his proposal of *Super muros* in an attempt to remove their cause. Thus we must sample a few of these jibes in order to appreciate what the pope had in mind when he complained of "many who grumble about the expenses incurred by those who come to the apostolic see" (Doc. 41.2).

18. Robinson, *Papacy*, p. 265, citing the *Historia Compostellana* III.10 (Migne, *Pat. Lat.*, CLXX, 1173B). See R. A. Fletcher, *Saint James's Catapult: The life and times of Diego Gelmírez of Santiago de Compostela* (Oxford, 1984), pp. 205, 214.

19. Hélinand, sermon 26 (Migne, *Pat. Lat.*, CCXII, 720B; see n. 27, chap. 2, above): "non currit post munera." The greed of many identifiable cardinals is satirized in the *Tractatus Garsiae* (n. 26, below).

20. Walter Map, *De nugis curialium*, ed. M. R. James in *Anecdota Oxoniensia*, Mediaeval and Modern Series, pt. XIV (Oxford, 1914), p. 82: "nomen Roma ex avaricie sueque diffinicionis formatur principiis; fit enim ex R et O et M et A et diffinicio cum ipsa 'Radix Omnium Malorum Avaricia.'" Cf. P. Lehmann, *Die Parodie im Mittelalter*, 2nd ed. (Stuttgart, 1963), p. 41.

21. Lehmann, *Parodie*, pp. 25-26.

22. Lehmann, *Parodie*, pp. 25-57.

23. Best analysis by J. A. Yunck, "Economic Conservatism, Papal Finance, and the Medieval Satires on Rome," *Mediaeval Studies*, XXIII (1961), 334-351. Cf. Benzinger, *Invectiva in Romam*, pp. 74-115; and R. M. Thomson, "The Origins of Latin Satire in Twelfth Century Europe," *Mittellateinisches Jahrbuch*, XIII (1978), 73-83.

24. R. W. Southern, *The Making of the Middle Ages* (New Haven, 1953), p. 154; Cheney, *Becket to Langton*, pp. 67-68.

The oldest joke, dating back at least to 1076, was that the Roman church was devoted to the cult of red gold and pale silver, represented by means of etymological allegory as St Rufinus and St Albinus.[25] By 1099 the conceit had expanded into an account of the translation of their precious relics to the shrine of St Cupidity and St Avidity near the Roman basilica of Holy Avarice.[26] A similar play on words suggested the parody *Gospel according to Marks of Silver*, which first appears among the *Carmina Burana* (1230), although Paul Lehmann thought it had originated in the second half of the twelfth century.[27] In the earliest extant version, the doorkeepers, chamberlains, and cardinals scorn the meager gifts of a poor cleric but not those of a rich one, and in the end even the pope gets his share.[28]

Clever parodies like these probably troubled Pope Honorius less than what was being commonly said concerning the curia. Our most reliable report of public opinion on the subject comes from John of Salisbury, who in 1156 informed Pope Adrian IV that, among other things, men were saying that

> the Roman church, which is the mother of all churches, treats the other churches more like a stepmother than a mother. In it sit Scribes and Pharisees, placing on men's shoulders unbearable burdens, to carry which they themselves would not lift a finger. They lord it over the clergy and set no example to the flock that is proceeding by the straight and narrow path to eternal life. They amass precious furnishings; they load their tables with gold and silver. They never, or rarely, admit a poor man, and then not for the sake of Christ but for vainglory. They make trouble for the churches, stir up lawsuits, set clergy and people at odds, and have no compassion at all for the misery of the afflicted. They rejoice in stripping the churches bare, and whatever profits themselves they regard as a pious act. They do justice not for the sake of truth but for a price, since you can get everything for a price today—even though you will have to pay for it again tomorrow.[29]

A few years later, in 1161/1162, Gerhoch of Reichersberg, a German theologian, summed it up with a tag from Virgil: "The 'sacred hunger for gold'[30] and silver

---

25. Lehmann, *Parodie*, pp. 25-26.

26. *Tractatus Garsiae*, ed. and trans. R. M. Thomson (Leiden, 1973), p. 31. Cf. Lehmann, *Parodie*, pp. 26-30; Southern, *Making*, p. 153; Robinson, *Papacy*, 198.

27. Lehmann, *Parodie*, pp. 40-41.

28. *Carmina Burana* 44 (21), ed. Lehmann, *Parodie*, pp. 183-184; also ed. K. Langosch, *Vagantes Dichtung* (Bremen and Leipzig, 1968), pp. 280-283. Cf. Southern, *Making*, pp. 152-153; Robinson, *Papacy*, 198-199.

29. John of Salisbury, *Policraticus* VI.24, ed. Migne, *Pat. Lat.*, CXCIX, 623CD (my trans.). Cf. Benzinger, *Invectiva in Romam*, pp. 81-82.

30. *Aeneid* III.56-57: "quid non mortalia pectora cogis, / auri sacra fames?" Dante has Statius echo the passage while accusing himself of avarice: "per che non reggi tu, o sacra fame / dell'oro, l'appetito de' mortali?" (*Purg.* XXII.40-41).

in the [papal] curia has grown so great that the whole world cannot satisfy it, even though [the members of the curia] are prepared to drain it dry."[31] Unlike most of his contemporaries, Gerhoch pointed out that there were mitigating circumstances, for Rome's avaricious appetite, he explained, was due to *necessitas*. Less judicious was his compatriot, the chronicler Burchard of Ursberg (d. ca. 1231), who after describing the increase of appeals to Rome added this invective:

> Rejoice, our mother Rome, since the flood-gates of the earth's treasures are opened unto you, so that streams and mounds of money flow to you in great quantities. Be happy over the iniquity of the sons of men, since in recompense of such great evils, reward is given unto you. Be merry over your handmaid Discord, for she springs from the pit of the infernal abyss, that much loot in money may be accumulated by you. You have that you have always thirsted for! Sing a song! for you conquer the world through the malice of men, not through your religion. Their devotion or pure conscience does not bring men to you, but the perpetration of many a wicked deed and the decision of lawsuits purchased for a price.[32]

Papal provisions

By the time of Honorius III, most complaints about curial avarice were directed against bribery, since the sliding scale of fees for producing documents had been eliminated by Innocent III.[33] There was, however, another expedient for supporting the personnel of papal government, by providing members of the curia with benefices in faraway churches, from which they would derive an income without being resident. This arrangement was a natural extension of the usual way of providing a living for *curiales*, which, as we have seen, was to assign them an office in some Roman church with its attendant income. The difference, of

---

31. Gerhoch of Reichersberg, *De investigatione antichristi* 19, ed. E. Sakur, MGH, Libelli de lite, III (Hanover, 1897), 329: "Cuius necessitatis occasione auri et argenti sacra fames adeo eidem curiae aucta est, ut a toto orbe tantum nequeat inferri, quantum illi exhaurire parati sunt." Trans. Robinson, *Papacy*, pp. 267–268. Cf. Benzinger, *Invectiva in Romam*, pp. 91–95.

32. Burchard, *Chronicon* (n. 5, above), p. 82: "Gaude, mater nostra Roma, quoniam aperiuntur kataracte thesaurorum in terra, ut ad te confluant rivi et aggeres nummorum in magna copia. Letare super iniquitate filiorum hominum, quoniam in recompensationem tantorum malorum datur ibi precium. Iocundare super adiutrice tua Discordia, quia erupit de puteo infernalis abyssi, ut accumulentur tibi multa pecuniarum premia. Habes quod semper sitisti, decanta canticum, quia per malitiam hominum, non per tuam religionem orbem vicisti. Ad te trahit homines non ipsorum devotio aut pura conscientia, sed scelerum multiplicium perpetratio et litium decisio precio comparata."

33. See n. 14, above.

course, was that there could be no pretense of their performing the duties of the office in person; at best the office holder could appoint a vicar to do the job for him for a modest stipend. In an age when few rulers had a cash income from which to pay their clerical staff, such an arrangement was the usual way to provide support for royal and episcopal officials; it presupposed that the provider had the right to fill the position with a qualified person of his choice, and lords great and small, lay and ecclesiastical, commonly enjoyed this right of patronage over one or more churches, as the pope did in the vicinity of Rome.[34]

There was nothing unusual, therefore, in having a patron provide a benefice for one of his clients; moreover, he might do so for someone else's client, as a favor. Papal provisions began as requests for such favors, the earliest known one being a request by Innocent II to the archbishop of Compostela.[35] Similar requests became increasingly common in the course of the twelfth century, and under Alexander III they came to be used to provide livings for clerks of the papal court.[36] Sometimes, if the patron was not a layman, the request took the form of a command—a mandate *de providendo*—that had to be obeyed in virtue of the pope's *plenitudo potestatis*, although direct provisions of this kind were still rare, in England at least, as late as the pontificate of Innocent III.[37] Although the pope could and did provide to major benefices, such as bishoprics and abbeys, these do not concern us, as it was by provision to minor benefices that the papal bureaucracy was supported.[38]

To establish the context of *Super muros*, we chiefly need to know the extent of papal provisions under Honorius III. Fortunately the evidence for this pontificate is more abundant than for the preceding ones. The register of Honorius' letters, which Pressutti compiled from the Vatican registers and the extant originals known to him, contains 6288 items.[39] According to the educated guess of Jane Sayers, these represent slightly more than thirty per cent of the 20,574 letters that she reckons Honorius sent during his eleven-year pontificate.[40] In 1911, Hermann Baier published a statistical analysis of the provisions to minor

34. G. Barraclough, *Papal Provisions* (Oxford, 1935), pp. 50–65; G. Mollat, "Bénéfices ecclésiastiques en Occident," *Dictionnaire de droit canonique*, II (Paris, 1937), 407–449, at cols. 418–420.

35. Robinson, *Papacy*, p. 289.

36. Robinson, *Papacy*, p. 290. Examples of early requests for papal provisions are collected in L. Thomassin, *Vetus et nova ecclesiae disciplina circa beneficia et beneficiarios*, 3rd ed. (1st Latin), 3 vols. (Paris, 1691), II, 121–122 (II.i.43).

37. Cheney, *Becket to Langton*, p. 80. The variety of forms in use before 1216 is discussed by H. Baier, *Päpstliche Provisionen für niedere Pfründen bis zum Jahre 1304* (Munster i. W., 1911), pp. 205–218.

38. Barraclough, *Papal Provisions*, p. 8, n. 1.

39. *Regesta Honorii Papae III*, ed. P. Pressutti, 2 vols. (Rome, 1888–1895).

40. Sayers, *Papal Government*, p. 56.

benefices in this and subsequent thirteenth-century papal registers,[41] and although his attempt to compare the practice of successive popes no longer seems methodologically sound, because the principles on which letters were registered varied from one pontificate to another,[42] still the evidence from Pressutti's register considered in itself is sufficiently homogeneous to indicate the sort of persons Honorius was providing to benefices and where these were located, which is all we need to know for our present purpose.

According to Baier's count, over eleven years (1216-1227) Honorius made 229 provisions to minor benefices, of which 94 were to *curiales*; many of the others were intended to support study at a university. The geographical distribution of the 229 is relevant to our inquiry, since *Super muros* was thought to have been sent to Spain[43] and the Empire, as well as to France and England, where it became an issue (Doc. 1.17). Baier's analysis[44] found that France provided Honorius with the greatest number of benefices (100), followed in declining order by Italy (45), Germany (38), England (16), Spain (15), the Orient (11), with one each for Hungary and Scandinavia, and two for unspecified places. These figures certainly demonstrate that the practice was widespread and in this pontificate France carried the heaviest burden, but it would be extremely difficult to say to what extent they correspond to the resources of the respective areas, though it may be noted that neither the numbers nor the proportions remained constant in subsequent pontificates. For example, over fourteen years (1227-1241), the next pope, Gregory IX, provided to only 105 benefices, in this order: France (35), England (21), Germany (18), Italy (17), Spain and the Orient (6 each), and one each in Hungary and some unspecified place.

"It would be unsafe to infer that these papal nominees were the cause of widespread resentment," Cheney warned; that was to come later, in the 1240s, as is well known from the bitter protests of Robert Grosseteste and Matthew Paris.[45] Therefore it would seem that Honorius was seeking to substitute a variation on the relatively acceptable practice of papal provisions for the widely unpopular one of bribing curial officials.

41. As appendices to Baier, *Päpstliche Provisionen*, pp. 227-295.

42. Barraclough, *Papal Provisions*, pp. 26-29. Factors influencing the selection of letters for registration are discussed by Sayers, *Papal Government*, pp. 65-75.

43. Although Spain was not a political entity at this time, *Hispania* was a collective term in current use at the curia: e.g. Honorius addressed a letter to "Universis prioribus, et fratribus Hospitalis Ierosolimitani per Yspaniam constitutis" (Pressutti, no. 5485; cf. no. 5559, to the church "in Ispania"). Similarly, the provinces "in Ispania" are grouped together in the *Liber provincialis* given by Matthew Paris, *Chronica majora*, ed. Luard, Rolls Series, no. 57, 7 vols. (London, 1872-1883), VI, 457.

44. Baier, *Päpstliche Provisionen*, pp. 227-228, Appendix 1: "Verzeichnis der Provisionen."

45. Cheney, *Becket to Langton*, p. 82; Barraclough, *Papal Provisions*, p. 11.

Baier also classified Honorius' provisions according to recipient, and the result shows clearly how they were being used to support *curiales*. Of his 229 provisions, some 94 (41%) were made to members of the papal court, who included: the pope's relatives (2), chancery officials (17), papal chaplains (18), papal subdeacons (30), a papal acolyte, the papal chamberlain, and the papal penitentiary (1 each), plus 24 clerks belonging to the households of 14 cardinals.[46] Since the cardinals, each assisted by his own household staff, did curial service as legates, administrators, and especially as judges, the last category represents at best indirect service to the curia,[47] while the other 70 appointments provided support for the pope's own officials.

It is difficult, but not impossible, to specify what the duties of many of these curial officials were under Honorius' regime; at the least, the titles are not always self explanatory. For example, in a document of 28 February 1225, Master Otto of Tonengo was entitled *both* subdeacon and papal chaplain, as well as *auditor litterarum contradictarum*, a major judicial office.[48] Furthermore, the six notaries, who were the senior chancery officials, "usually had the rank of papal subdeacon."[49] Sayers has assembled a mass of detail on the lesser men who held the rank of scribe (*scriptor*) in the papal chancery; she estimates that at one time or another some sixty or seventy of them served under Honorius.[50] Usually they were provided with a canonry, since a higher office, such as archdeacon, would have required residence.[51]

Finally, it is likely, though by no means certain, that Honorius used provisions to support the papal household more extensively than his predecessor, Innocent III, had done. Although the evidence Baier assembled for the latter pontificate[52] does not readily lend itself to comparison in this regard, the list of "Providees and Italians in English Benefices" 1170-1213 compiled by Cheney is nonetheless suggestive.[53] Innocent provided English benefices for ten persons, of whom

46. Baier, *Päpstliche Provisionen*, pp. 244-246, Appendix 2: "Verzeichnis der Kurialen und Ausländer."

47. J. E. Sayers, "Centre and Locality: Aspects of Papal Administration in England in the Later Thirteenth Century," in *Authority and Power: Studies . . . Presented to Walter Ullmann*, ed. B. Tierney and P. Linehan (Cambridge, Eng., 1980), pp. 115-126, at p. 118. Romanus himself held a canonry at Senlis (n. 32, chap. 2, above). The fundamental study of the *familia cardinalis* is by A. Paravicini Bagliani, *Cardinali di curia e "familiae" cardinalizie dal 1227 al 1254* (Padua, 1972), esp. pp. 445-506.

48. Sayers, *Papal Government*, p. 39.

49. Sayers, *Papal Government*, p. 30.

50. Sayers, *Papal Government*, p. 42. About seventy *sigla* of Honorius' scribes are listed in her Appendix 1, often with biographical details (pp. 197-207).

51. Sayers, *Papal Government*, pp. 44-45.

52. Baier, *Päpstliche Provisionen*, pp. 12-25.

53. Cheney, *Becket to Langton*, pp. 178-181. Of the twenty persons listed, the last five do not concern us, being royal providees; also excluded are five others before 1198.

four were curial officials. The clearest instances are Cardinal John, the papal chancellor, and Master Britius, a papal notary; moreover, in two other cases curial service seems indicated by the title *magister*, which in curial usage "was probably a 'courtesy' title, not an academic one."[54] In one of these cases, Master John *le Romeyn*, a Roman nobleman, appears to have been in papal service under Innocent and Honorius, after which he emigrated to England; in the other, Master John de Colonna may have received his benefice as a favor to his uncle, who was a cardinal. Nepotism was certainly a major motive for Innocent's papal provisions: he provided an English benefice for one of his own nephews and five for those of his cardinals, including the one just mentioned. (The tenth Innocentian provision in Cheney's list went to Huguicio Lombardus, with no apparent connection with the curia; he may well have been a poor and deserving student.[55]) Thus it appears from this admittedly small sample that Innocent's provisions were used somewhat more for nepotism than in direct support of curial officials. If so, comparison with Baier's figures suggests that under Honorius the expedient of provisions to maintain the papal household was on the increase. This tendency would help to explain why Honorius sought to regularize the situation by the proposal of *Super muros*.

★ ★ ★

Honorius also had strong personal motives for his proposal. No one in the curia was better acquainted both with the needs of the chancery and with the inadequacy of existing financial resources, for in the 1190s he had been not only acting chancellor but also the chief financial officer (*camerarius*).[56] As cardinal, Cencius Savelli had held the latter position for a decade (1188-1198), and by his compilation of the *Liber censuum*[57] showed that he was particularly concerned to maximize papal revenue; he knew through intimate personal experience that the traditional sources of papal income were inadequate to support the growth of papal government in the late twelfth century. In particular he was in touch with the requirements of the chancery, which he had headed as acting chancellor for over three years (Fall 1194 to January 1198). For reasons unknown, Innocent III removed him from both offices, promoted him from cardinal-deacon to cardinal-priest, and made little discernible use of his services. But

---

54. Sayers, *Papal Government*, p. 31. The academic title *magister*, indicating one who was trained in law, was also in use at the curia (Robinson, *Papacy*, p. 106).

55. The name is of no help, since it was extremely common. For instance, Wolfgang Müller found 93 distinct individuals named "Uguccio" in published twelfth-century charters from Pisa alone: *Huguccio* (Washington, D.C., 1994), p. 26, n. 14.

56. The most detailed biography of Honorius is Sayers, *Papal Government*, pp. 1-12; see pp. 15-16 for his "unrivalled knowledge" of both the chancery and the camera. Further details in the briefer account by Maleczek, *Kardinalskolleg*, pp. 111-113.

57. See n. 8, above.

when Cencius became pope himself, he seems to have been more concerned
with the material support of the papal household than Innocent had been, and
especially by means of papal provisions. Of all his early experiences, however,
the most significant for *Super muros* was certainly his personal involvement in
the negotiations during 1196 with Emperor Henry VI, who was the first to propose that the curia be supported by a permanent allocation of prebends.[58]

Speculation aside, it is abundantly clear that Honorius did provide benefices
throughout Europe to support his *curiales*, and this practice, together with the
widespread complaints about curial venality, supplies much of the institutional
context needed to understand *Super muros*.

One feature of Honorius' plan, however, was suggested by a constitution of the
Third Lateran Council (1179) that decreed that "in each cathedral church there
should be provided a suitable benefice for a master who shall instruct without
charge the clerics of the cathedral church and other poor scholars. . . . "[59] The
intention was to insure the maintenance of cathedral schools by reserving a
benefice in each chapter for a qualified elementary school teacher, but, since
canons were typically drawn from the social and intellectual elite, they resisted
the intrusion of a mere schoolmaster into their select group. Consequently in
1215 the Fourth Lateran Council renewed this decree but altered its terms—
significantly, for our purpose—by stipulating that "The income of one prebend
shall be assigned by the chapter to each master. . . . The incumbent does not
by this become a canon but he receives the income of one as long as he continues to teach."[60] The earlier decree had in effect reserved a benefice for a
resident teacher, but for this arrangement Innocent III substituted a less controversial means of support, by having the chapter simply pay the schoolmaster
the cash equivalent of one prebend. As we shall see, proposals to provide a regular income for *curiales* underwent a similar transformation: first, following the
lead of Lateran III, proposing the reservation of a prebend, and later altering this
to a cash equivalent.

Two proposals reported by Gerald of Wales

Honorius' proposal was not a new idea. This is certain because in *Super muros*
he says that at the time of the Fourth Lateran Council (1215), the plan had been

---

58. G. Baaken, "Die Verhandlungen zwischen Kaiser Heinrich VI. und Papst Coelestin III.
in den Jahren 1195-1197," *Deutsches Archiv für Erforschung des Mittelalters*, XXVII (1971),
457-513, at pp. 503-505.

59. Lateran III, c. 18 (= X 5.5.1, ed. Friedberg, II, 768-769), trans. in *Decrees of the Ecumenical Councils*, ed. N. P. Tanner (London, 1990), p. *220.

60. Lateran IV, c. 11 (= X 5.5.4, ed. Friedberg, II, 770), trans. in *Decrees of the Ecumenical
Councils*, ed. Tanner, p. *240.

favored by "a great many ecclesiastical prelates and men of great reputation," but nonetheless Innocent III had decided not to put it on the agenda (Doc. 41.6). This trustworthy testimony is corroborated and elaborated by a less reliable source, Gerald of Wales, who first relates at length how Emperor Henry VI had proposed such a plan shortly before his death in 1197, and to this account he then adds a note stating that Innocent III had proposed a modified version of that plan in 1215 but did not press the issue when it became apparent to him that the council would not approve it (Doc. 40). Elsewhere I have argued that, despite Gerald's reputation for fabulation and rhetorical elaboration, his account is basically correct,[61] so here I shall consider him to be a reliable witness and accordingly will summarize his report and place it in its historical context.

The proposal of Emperor Henry VI

According to Gerald, Henry VI proposed a two-step procedure for endowing the Roman church (Doc. 40.3): in the first stage, the emperor would implement the plan in the Empire, in the second, the rest of Christendom would formally adopt the same arrangement in a council convoked for the purpose. Henry proposed support at two distinct levels—a greater one for the pope and a lesser one for the rest of the curia. As the lion's share, the pope was to receive perpetual title to "the best canonry" in the richest churches, which Gerald defines as not only archiepiscopal, or "metropolitan," churches, but also "other pontifical churches, namely the greater and wealthier ones." The "plain and simple episcopal churches" were to supply the rest of the *curiales* with "prebends and annual incomes" appropriate to the rank of each: Gerald specifies that these would be assigned to the cardinals "according to their grade and order, and also to the chaplains and clerics who serve in the chapel of the lord pope and constantly assist in his services." Although Gerald does not explain, these "services" included not only liturgical ones but also the work of the papal chancery, since at this time the personnel of the chapel and chancery were closely interconnected.[62] In addition to the pope and the curia, Henry's plan also provided similar support for the maintenance of the Roman basilica of St Peter.

In his diffuse way, Gerald explains why Henry's plan failed: the emperor was travelling in haste to Rome "in order to bring it to a conclusion through his own intervention," when suddenly he died (Doc. 40.5). Gerald has surely telescoped events here, for Henry was last in the vicinity of Rome in November 1196, on his way south to his Italian Regno, where he died the following year at Messina

---

61. R. Kay, "Gerald of Wales and the Fourth Lateran Council," *Viator*, XXIX (1998), 79–93, summarized in Doc. 40.pr.

62. Sayers, *Papal Government*, pp. 16–17.

on 28 September 1197.[63] Gerald's mistake is not surprising, inasmuch as he is re-peating a story that he probably heard a decade earlier, which probably stressed the proposal rather than the reason it was not adopted.

In a general way, however, Gerald's story seems plausible. There is no doubt that during the last thirty months of his reign, from April 1195 onwards, Henry was negotiating with Pope Celestine III; we have a series of letters borne by the negotiators as they shuttled back and forth between the two courts,[64] but his-torians can only guess the content of their negotiations. In 1927, Volkert Pfaff argued that the proposal reported by Gerald was Henry VI's "highest offer";[65] he identified it with an offer Henry had referred to ("talia obtulimus") in a let-ter to Celestine that he wrote on 17 November 1196, when the imperial court was in or near Tivoli, about thirty kilometers west of Rome.[66] The offer, Henry stressed, was a novel one that had never been made to the papacy before, either by his father, Frederick Barbarossa, or by any other emperor. In response to this offer, Henry relates, the pope sent a delegation of three cardinals, including the papal chamberlain, Cencius Savelli, which was the only time during these papal–imperial negotiations that he appears as an emissary.[67] This delegation, Henry continues, informed him that peace could not be concluded on the basis of his most recent offer, and that the pope wished to suspend negotiations until after Epiphany (6 January 1197).

Henry's letter of 17 November 1196 corresponds to Gerald's account for at least three reasons: (1) Henry's plan was a novel one; (2) it was presented while he was in the vicinity of Rome; and (3) the pope included his chief financial of-ficer, Cencius, in the delegation. To these points may be added a fourth, less se-cure one: (4) In 1182/1183, Frederick Barbarossa had made an offer that would have provided the papacy with a regular income. As recompense for the loss of the lands that Matilda, countess of Tuscany (d. 1115), had willed first to the pa-pacy and then to Emperor Henry V, Frederick proposed to pay a tenth of the

63. *Regesta Imperii*, ed. J. F. Böhmer, Bd. IV, Abt. iii: *Die Regesten des Kaiserreiches unter Hein-rich VI.*, 2nd ed. by G. Baaken (Cologne, 1972), pp. 231-233, 249 (nos. 571-574, 614a).

64. Baaken has reviewed the circumstances in detail: "Verhandlungen" (n. 58, above), pp. 479-509.

65. V. Pfaff, *Kaiser Heinrichs VI. höchstes Angebot an die römische Kurie (1196)* (Heidelberg, 1927), esp. pp. 40-44.

66. Inc. *Cum in tractatu pacis*, ed. MGH, Const., I (1893), pp. 524-525, no. 376 = *Regesta Im-perii* (n. 63, above), IV.iii, pp. 531-532 (no. 572). Baaken has corrected the mistaken date (idem and "Verhandlungen," pp. 467-470) and has plausibly emended the impossible place ("Capue") from Capua to Capannace, halfway between Tivoli and Rome ("Verhandlungen," pp. 471-473), although the latter correction is not mentioned in his edition of the register.

67. Baaken, "Verhandlungen," pp. 469-470.

Empire's annual Italian revenue to the pope and a ninth to the cardinals.[68] Henry's reference to the offers of his predecessors is too vague for us to be certain, but if the offer of 1196 was one that provided the papacy with an assured annual income, then the likelihood is that Henry had Barbarossa's earlier offer in mind.

In 1971 Gerhard Baaken subjected Pfaff's thesis to a searching critique. By establishing new dates and places of issue for the documents, he radically revised Pfaff's account of the negotiations, but this revision only served to strengthen the argument given above, since on 17 November Henry's letter would have been written in the vicinity of Rome, not at Capua, as previously supposed.[69] The thrust of Baaken's critique was to challenge Pfaff's thesis that the proposal to provide prebends for the pope and his court was Henry's "highest" offer. Baaken concedes that it may have been discussed at any stage of the negotiations from October 1196 onwards, but he argues persuasively that it was at no time the main issue, and it certainly was not Henry's "höchste Angebot."[70] Since the negotiations of 1195-1197 are a crux in the history of papal–imperial relations,[71] Baaken's qualifications are by no means trivial; nonetheless, they are largely irrelevant to our present purpose and indeed serve to corroborate Gerald's account (see text after n. 67, above).

Consequently, we can place Gerald's account in its historical context. In the autumn of 1196, in the course of long negotiations with the papacy, Henry VI proposed that the curia's financial problems could be resolved if every cathedral in Latin Christendom set aside one prebend (or its equivalent) for the benefit of the Roman church. As far as we know, this idea originated in Henry's court.

The Fourth Lateran Council

"At the time of the general council did not a great many ecclesiastical prelates and men of great reputation favor this plan?" Honorius asked in *Super muros* (Doc. 41.6). Very likely he had in mind the campaign that Gerald of Wales had mounted in favor of the proposal, for the only one whom we know favored the proposal was Gerald himself. Apparently he restructured his work in progress,

68. P. Munz, *Frederick Barbarossa* (Ithaca, 1969), pp. 364-365 (cf. pp. 326-329); B. Gebhardt, *Handbuch der deutschen Geschichte*, 9th ed. by H. Grundmann, I (Stuttgart, 1970), p. 410; Pfaff, *Höchstes Angebot*, pp. 8-9. According to Peter Partner, the proposal included not just the Matildan lands but more generally "the ownership of imperial and papal lands in Italy": *The Lands of St Peter* (Berkeley and Los Angeles, 1972), pp. 216-217.

69. See n. 66, above.

70. Baaken, "Verhandlungen," pp. 510-511.

71. The historiographic context is reviewed by Baaken, "Verhandlungen," pp. 457-460.

the *Speculum Ecclesiae*, to recommend the revival of Henry's plan, and he made sure that Stephen Langton, the archbishop of Canterbury, had a copy before he left to attend the Lateran council; a second copy went to the cathedral chapter of Hereford, which was also represented there. But in addition to these few known proponents, Honorius' recollection suggests that there were many more.

Gerald only reported Henry's plan without proposing an alternative version of his own. After the council was over, he added a note to his *Speculum* stating that Innocent III had elaborated a new plan, "namely that the Roman church would collect and irrevocably appropriate to itself for the future a tenth part of the revenues of each and every cathedral church throughout the world" (Doc. 40.7). Apparently Innocent removed the subsidy from the context of papal provisions, and instead of seeking prebends he substituted the biblical concept of the tithe (*decima*; cf. Leviticus xxvii.30–32, Deuteronomy xiv.22–24). Once before, in 1199, the papacy had imposed a tax based on a percentage of clerical income, though only a fortieth, and the device was used again in the triennial twentieth of 1215, as a result of the Fourth Lateran Council;[72] thereafter, papal taxes were normally and frequently based on a percentage of clerical income. But a trace of Henry's proposal remained in that Innocent limited his tax to cathedral churches' endowments, "which had come from the abundant donations of the faithful" (Doc. 40.7). Perhaps Innocent, always a theologian first, thought that a biblical precedent would recommend his plan; but he probably gained little, if anything, by distancing his plan from the system of papal provisions, for percentage-based income taxes were by no means popular.

Honorius and Gerald have different explanations of why the plan was not adopted by the council. According to Gerald: "But because all the clergy and the part of the council that was larger and of greater authority were by no means willing to consent to these things, he [Innocent] made little progress in the matter and was not able to carry into effect his plan as he had conceived and proposed it" (Doc. 40.7). Honorius simply says that "the apostolic see deferred the proposal lest it seem that the council had been called for that purpose" (Doc. 41.6). The latter reason seems plausible, since Innocent had, contrary to previous practice, summoned the proctors of cathedral chapters, most likely because, according to the principle of *quod omnes tangit*,[73] current canonistic thought required their participation in matters affecting their rights, as the tax imposed by the council for the crusade certainly did.[74] Honorius' account suggests that Innocent's proposal was discussed and then withdrawn in the face of an objec-

72. Lunt, *Financial Relations*, pp. 240–246.

73. See Doc. 48.pr.

74. Lateran IV, c.71, ed. A. García y García, *Constitutiones concilii quarti Lateranensis una cum commentariis glossatorum* (Vatican City, 1981), p. 113 (inc. *Ad liberandum*). See also n. 72, above.

tion that was raised. Unfortunately, almost nothing is known of the process by which the canons of the Fourth Lateran Council were prepared; our sources only record their presentation to the whole council for formal approval,[75] but most likely this was preceded by a good deal of less formal consultation during which advocates and opponents of the proposal could voice their opinions. Such an arrangement would explain how Honorius could be sure of both the pros and cons that were raised "at the time of the great council" even though they were not expressed in a formal session.

Gerald's account is consistent with this reconstruction. He says that Innocent *proposed* the plan, but this need not mean it was laid before the whole council. And he gave up the plan when it became evident that "the clergy"—by which he means the proctors of the chapters, the interest group most affected by the proposal—and the *maior et sanior pars* of the council, that is, the prelates, "were by no means willing to consent to these things" (Doc. 40.7). Gerald, who was an archdeacon learned in canon law, picked his words carefully; he does not say that a vote was taken but only that Innocent discovered that if a vote had been taken, the preponderant part of the council would not have agreed. Thus both our sources suggest that Innocent's plan never was submitted for formal approbation by the council; instead, it was proposed informally and quietly dropped.

Honorius III's proposal: The bull *Super muros Jerusalem*

Ten years passed before Honorius III revived the proposal by sending the letter *Super muros Jerusalem* (Doc. 41) to the prelates of at least France and England, and perhaps those of other countries as well. Romanus, who probably was not in Rome when the letter was dispatched,[76] thought that copies had been sent to the Empire and Spain as well (Doc. 1.17),[77] but if so, no trace of their reception has been preserved.[78] Because the letter is the subject of the present chapter, the

75. S. Kuttner and A. García y García, "A New Eyewitness Account of the Fourth Lateran Council," *Traditio*, XX (1964), pp. 163–164.

76. See p. 203, below.

77. The Fenland Continuator declared that "the same or a very similar letter was being promulgated in all the lands subject to the pope" (Doc. 44.3), but this statement was most likely derived from the *Relatio*, which was the next item in his continuation (Doc.44.4 = Doc. 1).

78. Friedrich Bock identifies over 450 originals of Honorius III's letters, and none of them bear the date 28 January 1225, which was that of the French and English copies of *Super muros Jerusalem*; moreover, none of the Potthast and Pressutti numbers he gives is that of our bull: "Originale und Registereinträge zur Zeit Honorius III," *Archivio paleografico italiano*, II–III (1956–1957), no. 1, pp. 101–116. Thus it would seem rash of Albert Hauck to have assumed that the bull was sent everywhere: "Die Bestimmung war aber ohne Zweifel allgemein": *Kirchengeschichte Deutschlands*, 5th ed., 5 vols. (Leipzig, 1904–1920), at IV, 784, n. 2.

reader may at this point wish to consult the full text (Doc. 41), though to repeat it here would be superfluous; instead, in the next few pages I will introduce
it by a combination of paraphrase and commentary.

To begin, it is perhaps curious that the letter is addressed only to ecclesiastical *prelates*, that is, to the heads of ecclesiastical corporations—including not only
bishops and archbishops but also abbots, priors, and similar heads of religious
houses—since the proposal affected the property rights of the *members* of these
corporations no less than of their heads. Although canonists generally understood that the head represented the whole corporation,[79] still in a case touching their rights, he had to consult the members, as Honorius himself had
insisted.[80] Hence it was enough to address the prelates because it could be
presumed that they would not act unilaterally in such a matter. Yet from the outset there was an undeniable vagueness about how and by whom the proposal
was to be approved, which was to be reflected in the distinctly different ways
that the matter was handled in France and England.

The preamble sets the tone of Honorius' proposal. In elegant generalities, the
pope explains to the prelates that he is concerned about what men think of him;
he wants to have a good reputation, to provide for his honor. But this can be
difficult because he must also satisfy God by acting according to his conscience.
He wants to "satisfy both God and man, and if not as we wish and ought, at least
as we are permitted and are able" (Doc. 41.1). This introspective tone is far removed from the pronouncements of a triumphalist papal monarch, confident in
his plenitude of power; it is deliberative, even tentative, and thus appropriate to
a proposal that requires the consent of the governed. By example, the pope is
asking the prelates to search their souls diligently while considering his proposal.

When Honorius finally approaches his point, it at first appears that what is
worrying him is that "many grumble about the expenses incurred by those who
come to the apostolic see" (Doc. 41.2). Evidently he assumes that everyone will
know what he is talking about, because instead of detailing the complaints, he
surprisingly attempts to minimize them. The grumblers ("mumurantes") complain in private while publicly accepting the status quo. Defensively, the pope
rejects the notion that judgments at the curia can be influenced by bribery, even
when, in the name of mercy or equity, an exception is made to the requirements
of strict justice. Moreover, he suggests that the high cost of litigation at Rome
is due, not to gifts to the *curiales*, but to the padded expense accounts of dishonest

---

79. B. Tierney, *Foundations of the Conciliar Theory* (Cambridge, Eng., 1955), pp. 117–127;
idem, "The Idea of Representation in the Medieval Councils of the West," item XI in his
Rights, Laws and Infallibility in Medieval Thought (Aldershot, Hants.: Variorum, 1997), pp. 25–26.
Cf. Doc. 53.4.

80. See Doc. 48.pr.

lawyers. In short, Honorius can hardly acknowledge the existence of the problem he is proposing to solve.

The pope next explains his motives (Doc. 41.3). Even though the grumbling was often unjustified, it should be stopped by removing the occasion; moreover, he felt pressed to initiate such a reform before it was formally demanded by his subjects.[81] Therefore Honorius conferred with the cardinals, and together they unanimously agreed to revive a plan worked out by "our predecessors." Later he will make it plain that he is referring here to the plan that Innocent III prepared for the Fourth Lateran Council (§ 6), but for the moment it is enough to assure the prelates that the proposal is not a new idea:

The plan is this: In each and every cathedral church, and in any other church that has prebends, one prebend is to be set aside for the use of the apostolic see. And in the meantime, until this arrangement can be implemented, the income from these prebends is to be assigned to duly qualified persons. However, [in cases where there are no prebends, namely] in monasteries and other houses living under a rule, and in collegiate churches, and also from the goods of bishops, instead of a prebend a given part of the income is to be set aside for this purpose, the amount of which is to be determined by the resources available [Doc. 41.4].

The proposal provides for taxation of two distinct kinds of income—one "prebendal" and the other not. The prelates Honorius was addressing certainly knew the difference, but for the modern reader it may be helpful to provide some definitions and draw some distinctions. A chapter or college of priests, secular or regular—called "canons" in either case—might be established in any church for the purpose of saying the Mass and the daily offices, as well as performing all the duties relative to the maintenance of that church and its congregation. This was the usual means at this time of staffing a cathedral, but the arrangement might also be employed by any church sufficiently well endowed to support a chapter, which would then be a "collegiate" church, that is, one having a college of canons.[82]

---

81. E.g. the most famous such complaint was that of Robert Grosseteste, bishop of Lincoln, now elucidated by two contributions in *A Distinct Voice: Medieval Studies in Honor of Leonard E. Boyle, O. P.*, ed. J. Brown and W. P. Stoneman (Notre Dame, 1997), one by J. Goering, "Robert Grosseteste at the Papal Curia" (pp. 253-276), and the other by F. A. C. Mantello, "'Optima Epistola': A Critical Edition and Translation of Letter 128 of Bishop Robert Grosseteste" (pp. 277-301).

82. A collegiate chapter has been defined as a noncathedral church that has a chapter: J. Gaudemet in *Histoire des institutions françaises au Moyen Age*, ed. F. Lot and R. Fawtier, III (Paris, 1962), p. 192. Cf. the less succinct definition by A. Luchaire, *Manuel des institutions françaises* (Paris, 1892), p. 51; for their types by origin, see ibid., p. 62. For background, see also C. Dereine, "Chanoines (dès origines au XIIIe s.)," *DHGE*, XII, 353-405.

Prebends were found only in those churches served by the secular clergy, who were permitted to possess private property and who were not required to live in common. The chapter, or college, was the legal owner of the endowment provided to support the canons; this capitular property was divided into a certain number of parts called "prebends." Although some were better than others, even within a given church, each prebend was supposed to yield enough annual revenue to support one canon.[83] When a canon was granted such a portion, he was said to have received a *beneficium*, a "benefice," the benefit he gained by performing his official duty (*officium*).[84] A church that utilized prebends to recompense its secular canons was known as a "prebendal" church. Frequently, however, dissatisfaction with the chapter of secular canons caused their replacement by a chapter of canons regular, such as the Augustinian canons, the canons of St-Victor, or the Premonstratensians.[85] Canons regular lived in common without possessing private property, so the chapter's revenues, instead of being divided into prebends for *beneficia*, were dispersed from a common treasury. A church that replaced secular with regular canons was still a collegiate church but no longer a prebendal one.

These distinctions make plain the tenor of Honorius' request. From such churches as employed the convenient system of prebends—cathedral and collegiate churches with chapters of secular canons—he desired the annual income of one prebend. But in other cases, where the shares were not established by custom, the percentage of the annual payment would have "to be determined by the resources available" (Doc. 41.4). The proposed formula was relatively simple for a community that held property in common: to determine the value of one portion, the community's total net income[86] was to be divided by the number of its members. This rule would apply to "monasteries and other houses living under a rule, and in collegiate churches," that is, in those staffed by regular rather than by secular canons. The formula was not applicable, however, to one category of nonprebendal contributors, namely the bishops, whose resources varied greatly. Presumably some fraction of the bishop's income would be assigned to the pope,

---

83. Gaudemet in Lot-Fawtier, *Histoire des institutions*, III, 191; Luchaire, *Manuel*, p. 59.

84. G. Mollat, "Bénéfices ecclésiastiques," *DHGE*, VII, 1237-1270, at col. 1237: "le bénéfice ecclésiastique est le droit de jouissance que détient un fonctionnaire ecclésiastique sur les revenus de la dotation d'une fonction qu'il remplit en vertu de l'autorité ecclésiastique, à titre viager et inamovible." The classic monograph on benefices is the monumental treatise by Thomassin, cited above (n. 36), first published in 1678-1679 in three folio volumes.

85. For the Gregorian reforms and the canons regular, see Dereine, "Chanoines," *DHGE*, XII, 401-404.

86. I assume the tax would be on *net* income, which was certainly the case with the Albigensian tenth (Doc. 26.6); similarly, the yield from a prebend would be only a fixed portion of the net income of the property that formed its endowment.

the amount of the fraction varying according to the extent of his income, but we have no clue as to how, and by whom, the determination would be made. Evidently the proposal had not been thought out in detail, for, as we shall see, it did not provide for all the possible cases, since Romanus had to devise solutions to some problem cases presented to him at Reims.[87] Details aside, it is clear that the tax was to be paid by those who would chiefly benefit from it, for the burden was to be borne by the ecclesiastical corporations and persons who, rather than the lower clergy, frequently brought litigation to the Roman curia.

After having outlined the nature of his proposed tax, Honorius goes on to explain its purpose (Doc. 41.5). The proceeds were "to be paid into a common fund" that would be used to provide "the necessities of life" for all members of the papal court, from the pope down to the humblest doorkeeper. To make it clear that there would be no one unprovided for, Honorius provides a comprehensive list: to the pope and the cardinals, he adds "chaplains, chancery officials, doorkeepers, and other officials of the apostolic see." He does not say how, or by whom, the stipends are to be allotted, probably because the curia's previous guidelines were to be followed,[88] by which the pope himself received the lion's share and the cardinals the bulk of the remainder, on the supposition that their "necessary expenses" were greater than those of functionaries who did not have to maintain extensive households.

Finally, Honorius tells the taxpayers what benefits they can expect from the proposed innovation. From now on, he promises, it will be illegal for any curial official to receive gifts. With lawyerlike precision, he left no loopholes: gifts are not to be solicited in any way, and unsolicited gifts cannot be accepted. Offenders will receive "harsh punishments" and "public humiliation," which in effect leaves the penalties up to the pope's discretion. Since no law is effective unless it provides penalties that are sufficient to deter the offender, Honorius' proposition would have been more convincing had he specified the punishments, for example dismissal from papal service, or loss of all benefices, as was the case for concubinary priests.[89]

Honorius was not proposing to offer free justice, however, for he distinguished between legitimate court costs and illegitimate gratuities. "All services would be performed gratis for everyone coming on any kind of business" to the curia, he declared, "*except* for the customary payment for the bull." He was referring to the tax paid at the time a bull was sealed; it covered "the cost of the parchment, ink, lead, silk and hemp."[90] Thus, as Ivo of Chartres had observed

87. Doc. 1.9 and after n. 9, chap. 7, below.
88. On division of gifts at the curia, see above, at n. 18.
89. See Doc. 52.pr.
90. Sayers, *Papal Government*, p. 47; Lunt, *Financial Relations*, p. 522.

more than a century before, at Rome "neither pen nor parchment is to be had free of charge."[91] This was fair enough and corresponded to the usual practice of other chanceries at the time. In short, Honorius' tax would pay for the services of his officials but not for the materials expended.

Now that Honorius' plan is clear, we can compare it with its predecessors.[92] Curiously, it resembles Henry's plan rather than Innocent's. The latter, at least as reported to Gerald of Wales, was simply a ten percent tax on the revenues of cathedral chapters. The plan of 1225, however, was much broader in scope, embracing secular and regular communities of every sort, not just cathedral chapters; moreover, with the probable exception of episcopal income, the contributions were not calculated on a percentage basis. Instead, like Henry VI, Honorius intended to tax all prebendal churches by permanently appropriating one prebend for the curia; but the emperor's plan, at least as we know it, was altered and elaborated in the 1225 proposal. Most notably, the distinction between rich and poor churches was sensibly replaced by the creation of a common fund from which curial stipends were to be paid. Otherwise, the plans may have been roughly similar, though it is hard to be sure since we only have a sketch of Henry's plan; still, like Honorius', it certainly contemplated non-prebendal revenue, as is clear from the specification that "prebends and annual incomes" were to be distributed (Doc. 40.3). Thus it would appear that *Super muros* was essentially a revised version of Henry's proposal, even though the bull cited the plan of 1215 as its precedent.

After proposing his plan, Honorius goes on in *Super muros* to urge its adoption (Doc. 41.6). He appeals for the "counsel and aid" of the prelates in this matter, which implies that both their moral and material support is required, and furthermore *consilium* suggests support in a deliberative setting, whether conferring with their respective communities or debating and voting in a church council. Like Gerald (Doc. 40.2, 5), but with admirable economy, Honorius reminds the prelates of a daughter's moral obligation to support her mother, and he invokes the precedent of Innocent III to assure them that the plan was no novelty but a sound idea whose time had now come.

But the addressees were no doubt impatiently reading on in the letter to discover in the dispository clause (Doc. 41.7) what the pope meant them to do about his proposal. Was adoption of the plan compulsory or voluntary? It could be either, since the pope at his discretion could exercise his *plenitudo potestatis* to impose this or any other proposal short of heresy. Without doubt the letter was, formally speaking, a papal *mandate*, as contemporaries recognized, for two chroniclers and the archbishop of Canterbury all expressly refer to it as "the lord

91. Quoted above, nn. 13 and 17.
92. See above at nn. 61–75.

pope's mandate."[93] But contemporaries also realized that in its effect, the letter was a request. Thus the archbishop of Canterbury convoked a council "to reply to the lord pope's nuncio concerning the petition (*super petitione*) that he has made on the part of the lord pope" (Doc. 42.3; cf. 42.11).[94] Roger Wendover likewise understood that the pope was asking for, rather than commanding, acceptance of his proposal, for in paraphrasing the tenor of *Super muros*, the chronicler has Honorius say that his plan requires consent:"*si volueritis consentire*"— literally, "if you should wish to consent" (Doc. 43.5). As Lunt perceived,[95] the apparent contradiction can be resolved by a close reading of the text (Doc. 41.7):

> Therefore we advise, ask, and exhort all of you in the Lord by apostolic writ ordering that you devote such influence and effective effort to carrying out this program, both in cathedral churches and in the others mentioned above, *that it will be evident from the result* how much you care for the decorum of the Lord's house, how much the love of the Bridegroom and bride excites you, how much the prospect of lifting of many burdens motivates you, and how much the common welfare persuades you.

The prelates are ordered, to be sure, but only to show *how much* these lofty considerations move them. If they don't much care for the common welfare and the rest, then they can refuse the pope's petition and still be in compliance with his command. Thus, as Lunt put it, "the letter had the technical form of a mandate and the practical effect of a request."

To sweeten what otherwise would have been an impossibly bitter pill, Honorius concludes with a promise to moderate his use of papal provisions (Doc. 41.8). As soon as the proposal of *Super muros* has been adopted, the pope promises that when "prebends granted to Roman clerics or by the apostolic see . . . happen to become vacant, they shall revert to their own churches." He does not, however, promise to end the practice of papal provisions, as a superficial reading might suggest. Instead, his intention was to prevent a prebend from being conferred on alien clergy "successively—*successive*." In other words, a given prebend is not to be held by the pope's appointee twice in a row; however, it could still conceivably be held *alternately* by a local appointee and by a papal one.

Honorius had already addressed this problem in 1221, when he received a complaint from York that a living was being passed on from one papal providee to another without the patron's knowledge. On 18 February, he notified the archbishop, dean, and chapter of York that he had decided that from now on

93. Wendover in Doc. 43.4; the Salisbury Register in Doc. 42.2, 5.

94. According to Lunt, "A chronicler of Abingdon also spoke of the 'petitions' of the lord pope," citing Cambridge, Trinity College, MS. 993, ad an. 1226: *Financial Relations*, p. 185, n. 1.

95. Lunt, *Financial Relations*, p. 185.

when a benefice of any kind was vacated, only the patron was to confer it on a suitable person.[96] The same day he generalized this decision by instructing the archbishop of York to publish it throughout England,[97] and eight days later he had the archbishop of Canterbury do the same.[98] But the new rule by no means prevented Honorius from subsequently providing benefices in England—for example at Lincoln for a papal scribe[99]—so it would appear that in 1221 he was only seeking to prevent *successive* papal appointments to the same benefice. The language of *Super muros* indicates that in 1225 he was proposing to extend this policy, which previously had applied only to England, to include all of Latin Christendom. It was a concession, but neither as generous nor as extensive as an inattentive reading might suggest.

★   ★   ★

Before going on in the next chapter to see how Honorius' proposal was received, let us pause briefly to consider its intrinsic merits. As we have just seen, it is doubtful that adoption of the scheme would have significantly inhibited the use of papal provisions.[100] But they were peripheral to his plan, the thrust of which was to prohibit curial officials from accepting gifts. Certainly a simple prohibition would not suffice, since that had already been tried to no effect, even though the penalties were formidable.[101] If gratuities were to have been elimi-

96. Inc. *Ne liberalis devotio*, ed. J. Raine, *The Register, or Rolls, of Walter Gray, Lord Archbishop of York* (London, 1872), pp. 138-139; Pressutti, no. 3106, and *Calendar of Entries in the Papal Registers relating to Great Britain and Ireland*, ed. W. H. Bliss, 11 vols. (London, 1893-1921), I, 79.

97. Inc. *Cum hii qui*, ed. Raine in *Reg. W. Gray*, pp. 137-138, and again in *The Historians of the Church of York and its Archbishops*, Rolls Series, no. 71, III (London, 1894), 113-114; Pressutti, no. 3107, and Bliss, *Calendar*, I, 79.

98. Inc. *Cum hii qui* (26 Feb. 1221), not in the Vatican Register (Pressutti, no. 3122) but ed. Powicke-Cheney, *Councils & Synods*, II.i (Oxford, 1964), 96-98; Potthast, no. 6569.

99. Pressutti, no. 4145 (9 Nov. 1222). For other correspondence concerning English benefices after *Cum hii qui* (Feb. 1221), see Pressutti, nos. 4342, 4682, 5985, 5986, 6103, 6191, 6210.

100. In this regard Jane Sayers seems unduly optimistic: "Had Honorius's scheme for the central revenue been accepted by the provincial churches, the development of provisions—which so affected the fourteenth-century Church—would have been nipped in the bud with consequences that can only be surmised": *Papal Government*, p. 191. The plan "would surely have changed the course of later history" (p. 193).

101. "*Institutio cancellarie super petitionibus dandis et recipiendis* . . . [10] Ad hec si pro justitia vel spirituali negotio promovendis fiat pactio vel certa promissio, et dans et recipiens ab officio et beneficio suspendatur, si clericus fuerit, et offerens insuper careat inpetratis; laicus vero excommunicetur et de curia litteris impetratis privatus nichilominus repellatur": Fabre-Duchesne, *Liber censuum*, II, 461-462 (no. 209). Although entered in the *Liber censuum* along with documents dating from the 1220s, as Muratori observed, this set of in-house regulations was apparently in effect before 1206: Sayers, *Papal Government*, pp. 19-21, citing R. von Heckel, "Studien über die Kanzleiordnung Innocenz' III," *Historisches Jahrbuch*, LVII (1937), 258-289, at p. 259. A longer, later version is given by M. Tangl, *Die päpstlichen Kanzleiordnungen von 1200–1500* (Innsbruck, 1894), pp. 53-55.

nated at the curia, the next step surely would have been to provide the *curiales* with an adequate regular income, so Honorius' plan was well conceived. How effective it would have been is quite a different question, since the honesty and integrity even of modern civil-service bureaucracies are too often marred by scandal. Moreover, it would have been especially difficult to eliminate gift-giving in a society where that was the custom—as is still notoriously the case in contemporary Italy. Consequently, I think it doubtful that even at best Honorius' plan could have enjoyed more than moderate success.

Still, from an administrative point of view, it would have been a step in the right direction, if only because it would have insured the papacy of a regular source of income, and historians who view the growth of central government as an admirable success story would laud this as progress. Taxpayers, on the other hand, are never apt to consider bigger government as a desirable end in itself; they may want better government, to be sure, but they must be convinced of the need before they are prepared to pay for it. Such was not the case with *Super muros*, as the next chapter will show.

CHAPTER 7

THE REJECTION OF FISCAL REFORM

Super muros Jerusalem was, as we have seen, a request rather than a command; its adoption required consent, but *whose* consent was not clear. Since the bull was addressed only to the prelates of churches, it would appear *prima facie* that Honorius was indicating that only their consent was required. This interpretation was in fact the one assumed by papal agents in both France and England when the bull first arrived there, probably in the fall of 1225; both the legate Romanus and the nuncio Otto proceeded to secure the prelates' consent to the proposal without reference to the various chapters whose property rights were affected. But as an afterthought in both countries it was recognized that in such a case the consent of the chapters was required as well, and moreover that, according to Honorius' own pronouncement in *Etsi membra corporis* (Doc. 48), the decision had to be arrived at in common, that is to say, at a meeting in which all the interested parties could participate. The result was that the chapters had their day in court, first at Bourges in November 1225 and later at London in May 1226. Together, these councils constitute a landmark in the development of clerical representation because of their novel composition, which included representatives of ecclesiastical corporations;[1] but the one at Bourges is the more remarkable, because there the proctors intervened effectively to block a proposal to which the prelates might otherwise have consented. For the first time the voice of representatives carried weight in an assembly, at least as far as we know, since the *Relatio* (Doc. 1) is the only detailed account of conciliar deliberations that has survived from these earliest days of representative government. The present chapter will follow the fortunes of *Super muros* first in France, and then in England.

Super Muros in France

The first occasion on which Honorius' request was discussed in France was at an assembly held, not at Bourges, but at Reims. The only source for this fact is

---

1. On the novelty of proctors at Bourges, see pp. 94-101, chap. 3, above; on London 1226, see text before n. 53, below.

the *Relatio*, and there it was long obscured by textual corruptions,[2] which a critical edition has now removed. Our information comes from the proctors of the
metropolitan chapters, who were afraid that they would not have an opportunity to present their arguments against *Super muros*. "The reason for our fear,"
they said, "is that when you were at Reims, you spoke with certain persons there
and ordered some bishops to reserve prebends for the use of the lord pope when
they become vacant" (Doc. 1.7).

The conference at Reims on 19 October 1225

To what occasion were they referring? We have few indications of Romanus'
itinerary in 1225. If, as may be supposed, he often accompanied the king's peri-
patetic court, then the royal itinerary offers four occasions on which the king
moved north and east of Paris, though never approaching the vicinity of Reims.[3]
But the most likely opportunity for Romanus to meet with "some bishops" at
Reims was the consecration of a new archbishop of Besançon,[4] which, according to Alberic of Trois-Fontaines, took place at Reims on Sunday, 19 October
1225 (Doc. 5.1), when the royal court was far to the south, on the other side of
Paris.[5] Alberic says that the archbishop was consecrated by Romanus' authority
("huius auctoritate"), which might mean that he settled a disputed election, but
more probably indicates that he presided at the ceremony, even though as a mere
deacon he could not actually participate in the act of consecration, which can
be done only by bishops.[6] Either way, Romanus was certainly present at the
event, which naturally would be attended by a number of bishops as well. No
doubt the ceremony was held at Reims rather than Besançon partly because the

2. The correct reading is preserved by the Crowland-Fenland tradition (ACM, lines 44
and 58 in Doc. 1.7 and 9), but this was long obscured by Wendover's better known version
(W), which altered "essetis Remis" to "ceteris regnis" in the first passage and omitted the second one. The Salisbury Register (S) added further confusion by reading "Rome" for "Remis"
in the second instance and by omitting the first. Evidently the references to Reims perplexed
English readers.

3. Petit-Dutaillis, *Louis*, pp. 439-440.

4. Jean of Abbeville, mistakenly surnamed (H)Alegrin, was a Paris master of theology;
within a year of his consecration at Besançon he was promoted to be cardinal-bishop of
Sabina: A. Paravicini Bagliani, *Cardinali di curia e "familiae" cardinalizie dal 1227 al 1254* (Padua,
1972), pp. 21-28.

5. Petit-Dutaillis, *Louis*, p. 440. During October, the king, progressing southward, made the
following stops, identified here in present-day usage: 6 Oct., Andrésy (dép. Yvelines); 22 Oct.,
Boisville-le-St-Père, and 23 Oct., Santilly-la-Vieux (both Eure-et-Loire); 24 Oct., Blandy
(Essonne), in the Beauce.

6. Paravicini Bagliani simply states that "Giovanni fu consacrato archivescovo di Besançon
da Romano Bonaventura cardinale legato" (*Cardinali di curia*, p. 26).

consecrand was the dean of Amiens, his native diocese and a suffragan of Reims, but probably the weightier reason was that this venue would spare the legate a long trip into Burgundy.

Events that brought bishops together, such as the consecration at Reims, but also dedications of churches and royal councils, afforded the participants an opportunity to conduct business unrelated to the main event. Thus it is virtually certain that the occasion of the conference that the proctors at Bourges alluded to was the consecration that took place six weeks earlier at Reims. This conclusion is confirmed by the likelihood that *Super muros* had only arrived in France a short time before the Reims consecration on 19 October.

The publication of *Super muros*

The bull is securely dated: all the copies, both the English and the French, have a *datum*-clause stating that it was issued on 28 January 1225 (Doc. 41.8). Roger Wendover reliably informs us, however, that the letter was brought to England by the papal nuncio, Master Otto (Doc. 43.1), who arrived in September 1225,[7] at least seven months after the formal date of the letter. Moreover, it appears that the letter came to France after Romanus' arrival there on Easter Monday, 31 March 1225,[8] for he told the proctors at Bourges that "when he was at the curia he had never consented to this exaction, and he had received the letter after he had come to Gaul, and then he had been very distressed about the matter" (Doc. 1.17). If the purported date of the letter were correct, then Romanus' first assertion would be extremely dubious, since he certainly must have been at the curia at that time preparing for his legation, which was first announced on 31 January (Doc. 10); but his excuse must have been plausible to the proctors, for they certainly did know when the letter came to France, or (to be more precise) when copies of it were distributed to the addressees. Consequently I think we must accept Romanus' statement as accurate and conclude that *Super muros* came to France after he did; furthermore, given that the bull reached England in September, the same date would seem the most likely one for its distribution in France as well. Hence the consecration at Reims in mid-October would have provided the earliest occasion for perplexed prelates to seek Romanus' interpretation of the request. Why the letter was antedated is a mystery about which I can only speculate.[9]

7. Powicke-Cheney, *Councils & Synods*, II.i, 155.

8. See n. 58, chap. 2, above.

9. A parallel, and probably interrelated, case of antedating is Honorius' mandate *Cum ecclesia secularium*, addressed to the English prelates, who were ordered to pay Henry III a subsidy, presumably to support his campaigns in France. Although dated 3 Feb. 1225, it appar-

The interpretation of *Super muros*

The discovery that Honorius' request arrived in France only weeks before the Reims consecration helps us to understand the exchange there between Romanus and the bishops. The letter required interpretation because what was being asked for was not clear. First Honorius had asked that in every prebendal church one prebend be set aside for his use; but then he went on to explain that when income was not divided into prebends, "instead of a prebend, a given part of the income is to be set aside for this purpose, the amount of which is to be determined by the resources available" (Doc. 41.4). Since "the goods of bishops" fell into the latter category, they of course wanted to know more precisely how their share was to be determined and what its amount would be. Romanus obliged by laying down a clear set of rules, which the *Relatio* states:

> In view of the legate's own interpretation of the bull at Reims, the loss would be even greater than at first seemed apparent, because in fact *two* prebends were demanded from each cathedral, one from the chapter and the other from the bishop's share. The same rule would apply to monasteries that distinguish between the shares of the abbot and the community, but only one monk's share would be required from monasteries that share their goods in common [Doc. 1.9].

Thus Romanus ruled that a bishop would owe the equivalent of a prebend in his own cathedral; this was a simple, practical formula that avoided the necessity of some sort of complex assessment of relative ability to pay, which Honorius' vague formulation seemed to imply. Since Romanus went on to provide a similar rule for monasteries, it would seem that the "certain persons" seeking his interpretation at Reims included monastic prelates as well as bishops.

Consent and implemention

After interpreting *Super muros*, Romanus also provided for the implementation of its provisions: the *Relatio* states that at Reims he "ordered some bishops to reserve prebends for the use of the lord pope when they become vacant" (Doc. 1.7). On the face of it, such a provision appears to regard the grant as a *fait accompli*; but, while it is not impossible that Romanus secured piecemeal consent from some prelates at Reims, or at least sounded them out, still it seems far more

ently did not arrive in England until July, and then the crown postponed its implementation until May 1226, just after the *Super muros* crisis had been dealt with. Perhaps the curia wished to make it appear that the *Super muros* proposal, which was optional, antedated that of *Cum ecclesia secularium*, which was not. Documents in Powicke-Cheney, *Councils & Synods*, II.i, 158-163; commentary in W. E. Lunt, *Financial Relations of the Papacy with England to 1327* (Cambridge, Mass., 1939), p. 188.

likely that he meant to present the proposal formally at Bourges to all those to whom it was addressed, for only there could they approve it in common, as the canonistic principle of *quod omnes tangit* required.

What then is to be made of Romanus' order that some bishops should reserve vacant prebends for the pope's use? Since the relevant document does not survive, no certain answer can be given; the likelihood is that it was analogous to similar reservations that had been made in the past,[10] if not to general provisions concerning the filling of vacancies that were occasionally addressed to bishops even when the benefices were not in their gift.[11] If *Super muros* was approved, the reserved prebends could be used in accordance with the new system; otherwise, they could be filled at the pope's discretion. The principal divergence from customary practice would seem to be that no particular beneficiary was named when the reservation was made. In sum, it was probably an act of prudence on the legate's part, intended to provide for a future contingency.

Super muros at Bourges

Although contemporary French chroniclers rightly stressed the trial of Raymond VII as the main event of the Council of Bourges, for the author of the *Relatio* and his English audience, not to mention modern historians,[12] the most noteworthy feature of the proceedings was the discussion of *Super muros*. About a third of the *Relatio* is devoted to Raymond's case, and the rest relates in great detail the proctors' arguments against Honorius' proposal; moreover, the partiality of the account appears even greater when one discovers that it fails to mention two other important incidents at Bourges: the bishops' resistance to monastic visitation and the reconciliation of the Paris masters (see chapter 8).[13] Such was not the perspective of most of our other sources, for only one of the seven other independent accounts of the council bothers even to mention the discussion of *Super muros* (Doc. 3.5).[14] In other words, the *Relatio* was composed

10. Innocent III had declared that a papal legate could reserve the right to collate to a benefice not yet vacant and exercise that right if the benefice fell vacant during his term of office: X 3.38.28 (*Cum dilectus filius*, 1206). Cf. G. Mollat, "Bénéfices ecclésiastiques en Occident," *Dictionnaire de droit canonique*, II (Paris, 1937), 407-449, at col. 419.

11. E.g. the letters Honorius III addressed to the archbishops of Canterbury and York in 1221: Powicke-Cheney, *Councils & Synods*, II.i, 96-99. See at nn. 96-98, chap. 6, above.

12. See n. 28, below.

13. It is possible that the *Relatio* originally concluded with a brief account of the other acta, since the text that has come down to us is manifestly truncated at the beginning (see Doc. 1, n. 4); but even so, *Super muros* was clearly the preponderant interest of the author.

14. The other seven independent accounts are Docs. 2-6 plus the chronicles of Cluny (*Rec. hist. Gaules*, XVIII, 743) and Limoges (n. 27, chap. 3, above).

for a particular purpose: to preserve a record of the proctors' resistance to Honorius' scheme, probably for immediate use in England, and perhaps for posterity as well.

In his preoccupation with the substance of the arguments *e contra*, the *Relatio*'s author neglected to specify the context in which they were delivered. Consequently, before addressing the arguments themselves, we must attempt to determine just how they were delivered. The reconstruction can be readily accomplished by harmonizing the *Relatio*'s account (Doc. 1) with that of the Chronicle of Tours (Doc. 3). Raymond's case ends with the division of the council into provincial discussion groups and the excommunication of all who reveal their secret counsels (Doc. 1.5): "After this, he [the legate] gave the chapters' proctors leave to return home but retained the archbishops, bishops, and abbots" (§ 6). These appear to be three announcements that Romanus made *in pleno concilio* before the group broke up for the provincial sessions. During the recess, the provinces presumably deliberated as instructed, though the *Relatio* does not say so; instead, it focuses on another meeting during the recess, in which the capitular proctors decided to protest their exclusion from the next session of the council. In the reported discussion, *Super muros* is not mentioned; what is stressed instead is the chapters' right to participate in conciliar deliberations that affect their interests, which was recognized in the decretal *Etsi membra corporis* (Doc. 48). "After long deliberation, these proctors therefore sent to the legate the proctors of the metropolitan churches . . . " (Doc. 1.6).

The *Relatio* does not state when the delegation approached the legate, whether during recess or at the opening of the next session; indeed, the rest of the account could be read as a discussion *in camera* between Romanus and the metropolitan proctors, which concluded with the legate's assurance that he would postpone action on *Super muros* indefinitely, so the proctors' further presence at the council was unnecessary. But the Chronicle of Tours permits us to locate the *Relatio*'s amorphous string of arguments more precisely in the sequence of events. In the Tours version, Raymond's case ends when "the legate and the bishops finally took secret counsel on the matter" (Doc. 3.4), which corresponds to the provincial deliberations specified by the *Relatio*.[15] The chronicler then passes directly to the next item of business: "After this, on the pope's behalf the legate requested" the grant proposed in *Super muros*. Thus it is certain that the matter was not settled *in camera* but in council.

Having sketched the proposal of *Super muros*, the Chronicle of Tours then summarizes the ensuing discussion succinctly (Doc. 3.5):

> Some of the bishops had already consented to this when the nuncios of the chapters objected to all of this in the presence of the legate and everyone else.

15. For the end of Raymond's case, see p. 134, chap. 4, above.

> The nuncios asserted that the chapters they represented were in no way about
> to do this and were at no time about to allow it. . . . And thus the apostolic
> precepts . . . about prebends . . . remained pending.

From this it appears that the proctors addressed the legate on two occasions. The first time was surely before the council reconvened, because the delegates declare that "we are amazed that in this council you did not bring the matter up while we whom it specially concerns were listening" (Doc. 1.7). This, then, was an appeal made *in camera* to the legate during the recess; there the proctors of the metropolitan chapters urged the legate to include *Super muros* in the council's agenda and to admit the capitular proctors to the discussion. From the Tours account it is evident that Romanus agreed to both requests.

One can only speculate whether he would have raised the question in the proctors' absence: on the one hand, *Super muros* was not addressed to them, and he had discussed it without them at Reims; on the other, as they were quick to point out, they had a legal right to be consulted. There was no established due process for such a request, as is evident from the improvised arrangements made to answer it in England,[16] and consequently one can only guess how Romanus meant to proceed in the matter. I think it most likely that he did intend to present the proposal only to those to whom it was addressed, after the proctors had left. Whatever he planned to do about *Super muros*, my impression is that he was determined not to let it interfere with his crusading mission.

The proceedings *in pleno concilio* concerning *Super muros* are evident in outline, principally from the Chronicle of Tours quoted above, with a little help from the *Relatio*. First the legate made Honorius' request known, probably by having the bull read aloud; then he himself acted as advocate for the proposal and, by presenting the arguments in its favor, "was trying to persuade them to consent" (Doc. 1.8). It was at Bourges, then, not at Reims, that consent was sought; the legate's presentation was not just a public announcement but was intended to elicit consent, so that if Romanus' appeal had succeeded, the churches of his legation (or at least the ones addressed in the French version of *Super muros*) would have accepted Honorius' plan.

After the legate had presented the pope's request, by both reading the text and extolling its advantages, the time had come for the members of the council to respond. Apparently the proctors had to wait their turn, for the bishops spoke before they did, and at least some "had consented" (Doc. 3.5), presumably by speaking in favor of the plan. We are not told how the other prelates responded, if at all; perhaps they chose not to speak, but more likely the author of the *Relatio* did not report their reactions in order to magnify the achievement of the proctors, which he was celebrating.

16. See Doc. 43.1, 4, and pp. 220–225, below.

The high point of the proceedings, both for the *Relatio* and the chronicler of Tours, came when it was the proctors' turn to declare their views. The Tours account, quoted above, simply states that the proctors said they would never consent to the pope's proposal; the *Relatio*, by contrast, gives a great many arguments against the plan without raising the issue of consent. Presently we shall examine these arguments in detail, but for the moment it is sufficient to note that they are cast in the form of counsels or opinions. Except for the proctor from Lyon, whose *bon mot* was most likely not uttered until after the prelates had spoken (Doc. 1.8), the proctorial spokesmen are not identified. It is possible that only one person spoke on behalf of all, as was the case at London in January 1226 (Doc. 43.6-7), but the accumulation of a wide variety of reasons suggests instead that these observations were made by a succession of speakers, who exhibit the variety of experience that the proctors saw as their special strength (Doc. 1.6). This impression is borne out by the narrator's consistent attribution of the arguments to the proctors collectively,[17] possibly because, being himself a member of the delegation, he could recall the gist of the speeches without being able to identify many of the speakers, who would have been strangers to him.

The final moment in the drama comes when the legate responds after listening to all the pros and cons. The canon of Tours, after recording the nuncios' assertion that their chapters would never grant Honorius' request, simply concludes his account by stating that this apostolic precept "remained pending" (Doc. 3.5). The *Relatio*, however, elaborated. First, Romanus secured the goodwill of the irate representatives by assuring them that he was on their side: "he replied that when he was at the curia he had never consented to this exaction, and he had received the letter after he had come to Gaul, and then he had been very distressed about the matter" (Doc. 1.17). Given his devious dealings elsewhere, these assurances are subject to some legitimate doubt; but now that we know that *Super muros* came to France some six months after Romanus, it seems that he was telling the truth. The sorrow he professed, however, proceeded, not from any sympathy with the chapters, but was, I think, of a piece with his exasperation with curial meddling in national affairs, which he expressed so bluntly to his fellow cardinals in the case of Fawkes de Bréauté: "We should avoid outrageous behavior towards kings and kingdoms these days because almost the whole world is more disposed to be hostile [to the papacy] than you and the others think" (Doc. 22B.4). Most likely he regarded Honorius' proposed financial reform as just one more threat to the success of the Albigensian Crusade, which was his principal concern.

17. "Et contra, ipsi procuratores allegabant [Doc. 1.9] . . . Item addiderunt [§ 10] . . . dixerent [§ 11] . . . addiderunt [§ 12] . . . non tacuerunt [§ 14] . . . dixerunt [§ 15, 16]."

Postponement was his solution in this and an equally sensitive case that will be discussed in the next chapter. Like the clever lawyer he was, Romanus explained away the provisions he made at Reims by finding a loophole: they were not to be implemented until everyone had consented to the proposal (Doc. 1.17). Furthermore, he shifted the burden of consent from the French church to the others whom he supposed had received *Super muros*—the churches of England, the Empire, and the Spanish kingdoms. "He also added that he would proceed no further in the matter until [the others] . . . should consent, which he hardly believed could happen." One French proctor would not let the matter rest there but did what he could to forestall English consent to the measure by composing the *Relatio* and quickly sending it to England.

Counsel and consent

One might hope that this episode, about which so much is known, would enable us to see how conciliar decisions were arrived at; but inasmuch as no decision was made, it only shows one phase of the decision-making process, namely that of *tractatus*, or deliberation. To be sure, this could be an expression of consent if the proposal received nothing but approval; otherwise, there would have to be a second phase in which the decision was made. Romanus recognized the existence of this decisive phase when "he also added that he would proceed no further in the matter" (Doc. 1.17). Had he wished to force the issue, he could have proceeded as he did in the case of Raymond, or he might have side-stepped it by referring the decision to individual diocesan synods or provincial councils to be held at some later time; but evidently he chose to avoid the issue by postponing it indefinitely. No doubt the proposal could have been rejected outright at Bourges, as it was at London in May 1226, but evidently Romanus preferred to evade the issue rather than to settle it.

The proctors' arguments

In the *Relatio* the proctors' objections are marshaled in an order that is at once rhetorically artful and forensically effective. While it is always possible that the *Relatio*'s author imposed this arrangement on his material, still it seems more likely that the proctors themselves coordinated their presentation in advance, since we know that they deliberated together before making it (Doc. 1.6). Accordingly, in reviewing these arguments, as we now shall do, I will assume that the *Relatio* preserves the original order of presentation (Doc. 1.9-16). Since the reader can readily consult both text and translation, it will not be necessary to repeat the arguments verbatim; instead a paraphrase with commentary will more usefully serve to interpret the text.

The most forceful argument is placed prominently at the beginning: Honorius' plan would diminish a chapter's resources to accomplish its mission. Each chapter would lose at least one member, together with his liturgical assistance, counsel, and contribution to the local economy (for the lost income would be spent in Rome). No doubt the impact of each kind of loss was developed in oral presentation, probably with particular stress on the loss of "aid in performing divine service," which was the chapters' *raison d'être*. Perhaps it was a second speaker who enlarged on the enormity of the loss by pointing out that, by the legate's interpretation at Reims, each chapter would in fact lose two prebends (Doc. 1.9).

After this objection, which anyone in Latin Christendom would find persuasive, the point of view becomes that of the governed, and consequently the appeal is now directed to the legate's sense of justice. Since Honorius' scheme would require an annual collection of revenues, the proctors suppose that this would entail a resident papal agent in every province, if not every diocese (Doc. 1.10). This requirement was a reasonable inference from contemporary governmental practice, for manorial lords regularly employed bailiffs to manage their fiscal affairs, while greater lords often had an agent who supervised the management of their more scattered holdings,[18] and similarly the king of France had his.[19] What the proctors found objectionable was not so much the proliferation of papal government as the cost of it, which they surmised they would have to bear. They assumed that the new papal agents would be supported in the same way that present ones were, namely by procurations. Originally *procuratio*, as the ecclesiastical counterpart of the French royal *gîte*, was the right of a papal agent and his retinue to be lodged and entertained at a cathedral or monastery; but by 1225 legates, nuncios, and other envoys were routinely demanding that houses in their jurisdiction should make an annual payment that was the cash equivalent of the cost of such a visit, even though none was made.[20] Such was certainly the practice of Romanus, as the exemption he granted to an obscure Norman priory attests (Doc. 51). The proctors' guess was quite correct, for in 1228 when Gregory IX initiated a system of papal tax collectors, they were indeed sup-

18. E.g. Ralph Neville employed Simon de Senlis as overseer for his various estates: J. Boussard, "Ralph Neville, évêque de Chichester et chancelier d'Angleterre (+ 1244) d'après sa correspondance," *Revue historique*, CLXXVI (1935), 217-233, at pp. 226-227.

19. Both the *prévôts* and the *baillis*, who by this time were gradually replacing them, were fiscal agents for the royal domain: Petit-Dutaillis, *Louis*, pp. 363-368; J. W. Baldwin, *The Government of Philip Augustus* (Berkeley and Los Angeles, 1986), pp. 35-36, 43-50, 125-128.

20. W. E. Lunt, *Papal Revenues in the Middle Ages*, 2 vols. (New York, 1934), I, 107-111; Lunt, *Financial Relations*, pp. 532-534, 539-540. For France, *Histoire des institutions françaises au Moyen Age*, ed. F. Lot and R. Fawtier, III (Paris, 1962), pp. 213, 375.

ported by procurations.[21] The proctors at Bourges, then, had rightly perceived that there were additional, hidden costs to Honorius' proposal. It is less clear why they further objected that such a collector, being the pope's agent, "might perform the duties proper to a legate." What they most likely feared was closer supervision from Rome, and especially legatine visitations, such as Romanus was making in his legation.[22]

The third objection (Doc. 1.11) was even less calculated to persuade the legate, since it argues that the proposed system will enable the pope to pack the prelacies of France with foreigners loyal to him. It begins with the supposition that when a chapter is electing a bishop, the pope might disrupt the process by ordering some outsider to be present on his behalf. Although generally speaking this was not a common occurrence in then current practice, still the assumption was not as farfetched as might at first appear, because Honorius had in fact given Romanus a special mandate to be present at the election of prelates in Provence (Doc. 20), and some Provençal proctor at Bourges may well have suggested that such intervention set an ominous precedent. The argument next supposes that, in some unspecified way, the pope's man would so divide the electors that they could not reach a decision within the six-month time limit imposed by canon law.[23] In that case, the election would devolve on a superior, but in 1225 canonistic opinion was divided as to whether that would be the bishop's metropolitan or the pope himself.[24] The proctors at Bourges assumed, no doubt for the sake of argument, that the election would devolve on the curia, and then concluded that the result would be the appointment of "Romans, or those most devoted to them, in all or most of the churches." Consequently, they observed, these pro-Roman prelates "would care more for the Roman curia than for the king or the kingdom." Tenuous though the argument may be, it clearly reflects the French chapters' apprehension at the ever-increasing extension of papal power over the Gallican church. Ironically, Honorius' proposed remedy for the unpopular papal provisions to *minor* benefices is here opposed by arguing that it would lead to an analogous Romanization of *major* benefices.

Having discussed how the plan would affect the French church, the proctors go on to consider its effects on the Roman curia (Doc. 1.12). It would not

21. Lunt, *Papal Revenues*, I, 11, 40; idem, *Financial Relations*, pp. 247-249, 541-542.

22. See Docs. 51-53 and R. Kay, "Romanus and Rouen: A Papal Legate's Tainted Visitation in 1227," *Annales de Normandie*, LI, no. 2 (2001), 111-119.

23. Provided by the constitution *Nulla* of the Third Lateran Council (c. 2 = X 3.8.2, ed. Friedberg, II, 488).

24. G. Barraclough, "The Making of a Bishop in the Middle Ages," *Catholic Historical Review*, XIX (1933), 275-319, at pp. 290-291. In dispute was Innocent III's decretal *Bone memorie* of 1202 (X 1.6.23, ed. Friedberg, II, 66-68).

be to their advantage, the proctors argue, to provide a regular income to curial officials, because without gifts or bribes they would have no incentive to perform their duties expeditiously, so that business at the curia would be prolonged indefinitely. The objection is enlivened by touches of cynical, anticurial satire of the sort that by now was the commonplace refuge of frustrated and disillusioned litigants at Rome; its deployment here indicates how deep-seated and widely accepted this negative stereotype had become.[25]

The Roman theme is developed, probably by another speaker, on the assumption that the promised reforms could be circumvented (Doc. 1.13). Even though *curiales* were restrained from accepting gifts directly, they would find ways to receive them through intermediaries; moreover, the gifts would have to be larger, "for small gifts mean nothing to the rich." It is curious that this argument, which completely undercuts Honorius' proposal, should not have been given more prominence. No doubt it would have been difficult to elaborate further how such illicit bribery might be contrived; probably elaboration would have been unnecessary, for all concerned surely recognized that there was no limit to the inventiveness of devious courtiers, lawyers, and bureaucrats.

At this point another speaker should have chimed in to suggest a second way in which the proposal could be circumvented, but apparently he missed his turn (Doc. 1.15). His objection assumed that enforcement would be based on a promise not to receive gifts, which would be required of the first beneficiary but might not bind his successors. Of course this objection could have been readily met by requiring an oath of office from each successive incumbent, just as had long been the custom for bishops and many secular rulers; but the point was irrelevant because it incorrectly assumed that each benefice that was reserved for the pope's use would be assigned to an individual, whereas the plan advanced in *Super muros* was to use the income from the reserved benefices to create a common fund out of which salaries were to be paid (Doc. 41.5). No mention was made there of an oath; instead the punishments Honorius promised for gift-takers would presumably have been established by papal decree. The very irrelevancy of this objection assures us of the accuracy of the *Relatio's* report, which uncritically preserved a bad argument based on imperfect understanding of the proposal. For those familiar with the deliberations of modern political assemblies, or even academic ones, this misapprehension has the ring of authenticity.

Had our mistaken speaker not broken in with his irrelevant objection, the proctors' presentation would have ended with two strong appeals to the legate's

25. For anticurial satire, see pp. 179-181, chap. 6, above. The proctors' use of satire at Bourges is illuminated by J. A. Yunck, "Economic Conservatism, Papal Finance, and the Medieval Satires on Rome," in *Change in Medieval Society*, ed. by S. L. Thrupp (New York, 1964), pp. 72-85.

sensibilities. The first (Doc. 1.14) concluded the series of Rome-related arguments with a warning that the enrichment of the curia could only exacerbate the factional conflicts that were endemic between the city's noble families, presumably by raising the stakes, since the ecclesiastical offices for which they were in constant competition would now confer not only power but also wealth. Evidently some of the French proctors, while doing business at the curia, had observed Roman politics at first hand, and what impressed them was not so much the conflict of ambitious families, which was to be expected throughout Europe, as their capacity to coalesce into irreconcilable factions whose mutual hostility could readily be kindled into insane violence. All this Romanus knew far better than the proctors could have; most of his career was spent in this explosive atmosphere, and indeed some ten years later he was to prove to be one of the three cardinals who could deal with the Roman nobles on a rampage.[26]

The final objection is surely the most dramatic and unexpected of all. "My lord," the last speaker said to Romanus, "may zeal for the Church universal and the holy Roman see move you, because we fear that the result of universal oppression would be general schism, which God avert!" (Doc. 1.16). One would hardly expect anyone in the Latin West, and especially the clergy, to be anticipating schism in 1225. To be sure, emperors had had their antipopes, but the most recent papal-imperial schism had ended in 1177, and the Third Lateran Council (1179), by revising the procedure for electing a pope, had precluded the emperor's claim to settle a divided election. For the next hundred and fifty years, no schism split the Latin Church, and the next recurrence was but a feeble gesture by Louis the Bavarian in 1328; the Great Schism of 1378 came some fifty years later still. It is surprising, therefore, that the proctors at Bourges raised the specter of schism in 1225, when the prestige of the papacy was at its height, and even more significant that they contemplated a *general* schism, not just an imperial one. Evidently the extension of papal power under Innocent III had provoked more resentment among the middle-level clergy, whom the Bourges proctors represented, than has been commonly recognized. Their concerns were distinctly middle class, for what moved them deeply enough to consider schism was not a matter of high politics, protonationalism, or even ecclesiastical discipline; instead, the threat that stirred them up was a loss of property. No wonder that they so readily imputed greed and avarice to the Roman curia, for these were their own underlying values, or if you will, besetting sins.[27]

Is this talk of schism to be discounted as an isolated incident? Although such

26. See at n. 15, chap. 2, above.

27. Psychoanalysts might well regard the proctors' satiric treatment of curial avarice as an instance of "reaction formation": cf. S. Sutherland, *The International Dictionary of Psychology*, 2nd ed. (New York, 1996), p. 385.

talk is rarely documented for this period, there is nonetheless evidence that it was current. Cardinal Romanus himself seems to have encountered similar subversive grumbling earlier that year, when he warned his colleagues in Rome that they were provoking "the downfall of God's Church by provoking kings and kingdoms to scandal and discord rather than to devotion to the Church" (Doc. 22B). Consequently it would appear that such disgruntled sentiments were commonplace enough but rarely expressed, as least in writing. It is significant that they surface here at Bourges, which provided the earliest institutional opportunity for such grievances to be aired, and in the first recorded speech on behalf of the disgruntled clerical middle class.

★ ★ ★

Taken one by one, the proctors' objections are comprehensible enough, but their overall purpose remains obscure. We have noted in passing that many of the arguments, although addressed to Romanus, cannot have been intended to persuade him. It is likely, for example, that he would consider it an advantage to have French bishoprics filled with papal appointees; similarly, in view of the taxes he imposed on the French clergy, as well as the procurations he exacted from them, it is unlikely that Romanus would have found it objectionable that the chapters might have to pay the expenses of papal agents. The proctors were all surely well versed in rhetoric, the third liberal art, and many of them were most probably experienced lawyers as well, so the unpersuasive character of their arguments cannot be attributed to ineptitude or naïveté. Hence it seems more likely that their arguments were not designed to secure the legate's sympathy but were intended to serve another purpose, which simply was to demonstrate that the chapters would never consent to Honorius' proposal. Thus the objections were framed to present the chapters' point of view, and collectively they certainly conveyed the message that, for a variety of reasons, the chapters opposed the plan. As the chronicler of Tours put it, through their representatives the chapters declared that they "were in no way about to do this and were at no time about to allow it" (Doc. 3.5).

SUPER MUROS IN ENGLAND

Strange to say, the Council of Bourges has been remembered more in England than France, because the growth of representative government has been a favorite theme of English historians. Indeed, the studies of Bourges and its aftermath in England are so numerous and distinguished[28] that one hesitates to

28. E. Barker, *The Dominican Order and Convocation* (Oxford, 1913), pp. 34–36, 45–47; J. A. Robinson, "Convocation of Canterbury: Its Early History," *Church Quarterly Review*, LXXXI (1915), 81–137, at pp. 86–88; H. K. Mann, *Lives of the Popes in the Middle Ages*, XIII (London,

attempt yet another retelling of the story; but we must at least complete our history of the reception of *Super muros Jerusalem*, and the effort will not be wholly redundant, because the standard account has difficulties and uncertainties that require critical discussion. Since the narrative thread must repeatedly be broken to examine matters of detail, it will again be convenient to provide a summary of undisputed events before fleshing out this skeleton.

Overview

The bull *Super muros* was brought to England in September 1225 by Master Otto, a papal nuncio. When he laid the proposal before Henry III, Otto was told that before responding the king would have to consult the clergy and laity of the whole kingdom. Accordingly, the prelates (but not representative proctors) were summoned to London for a conference to be held on 7 January 1226. When the assembly finally convened on 13 January, however, the clergy refused to answer the pope's petition because of the absence of the king, who was bedridden at Marlborough, and of a number of bishops, who were attending him. Accordingly it was necessary to reschedule the meeting for 3 May, by which time Otto had left England, so the archbishop of Canterbury presided, again at London. On this occasion the corporate ecclesiastical bodies were represented by proctors for the first time in England. Our sources agree that this second London council unanimously advised the king to reject the *Super muros* proposal, though each chronicle gives a different rationale for the decision.

Otto's mission

When the archbishop of Canterbury, Stephen Langton, returned from Rome in 1221, according to the reliable Dunstable annalist he brought with him a promise that in his lifetime the pope would never send a legate to England.[29] Since Langton died in 1228, the indult was still in force when *Super muros* was dis-

---

1925), 143-144; F. M. Powicke, *Stephen Langton* (Oxford, 1928), pp. 158-159; W. E. Lunt, "The Consent of the English Lower Clergy to Taxation during the Reign of Henry III," in *Persecution and Liberty: Essays in Honor of George Lincoln Burr* (New York, 1931), pp. 117-169, at 126-132; D. B. Weske, *Convocation of the Clergy* (London, 1937), pp. 42-43; Lunt, *Financial Relations* (1939), pp. 178-186; F. M. Powicke, *King Henry III and the Lord Edward*, 2 vols. (Oxford, 1947), I, 346-348; E. W. Kemp, *Counsel and Consent* (London, 1961), p. 68; Powicke-Cheney, *Councils & Synods*, II.i (1964), 155-158; G. Post, *Studies in Medieval Legal Thought* (Princeton, 1964), pp. 124-125; J. E. Sayers, *Papal Government and England during the Pontificate of Honorius III (1216–1227)* (Cambridge, Eng., 1984), p. 191.

29. *Annales prioratus de Dunstaplia*, ed. H. R. Luard in *Annales monastici*, Rolls Series, no. 36, III (London, 1866), p. 74: "quod legatus in vita ipsius nequaquam in Anglia mitteretur"; Powicke-Cheney, *Councils & Synods*, II.i, 52. On the annalist, see Doc. 2.pr.

tributed; consequently its introduction in England was entrusted, not to a legate, but to a nuncio, who was neither as powerful nor as prestigious an agent, being in effect "a living letter," who could communicate his master's message but lacked the authority to do anything except what he was explicitly instructed to perform.[30] For this delicate mission, Honorius chose a rising member of his household, Otto of Tonengo, whose home was in the Piedmont, near Asti. In 1225 Otto was not a cardinal but only a subdeacon and chaplain in the papal household, and this was his first recorded independent mission, although subsequently, as a cardinal from 1227 to 1251, he had a long and successful career in diplomacy.[31]

When Otto arrived in England in September 1225,[32] he bore several messages to King Henry III: Wendover says he came "pro magnis ecclesie negotiis Romane" (Doc. 43.1). All the English chroniclers, who are our only source for Otto's nunciature, agree that the adoption of *Super muros* was not his only objective. Both Roger Wendover and the Fenland annalist record Otto's unsuccessful attempt to reconcile Henry with Fawkes de Bréauté, which was made soon after the nuncio's arrival and was promptly abandoned when rebuffed by the king (Docs. 43.2, 10, and 44.1).[33] Probably Otto was also involved in the papal efforts to broker a truce between France and England, which continued throughout his mission;[34] this supposition best explains the trip he took to France in early 1226.[35] But the chroniclers all give the impression that *Super muros* was the principal purpose of Otto's mission, because they agree that at the time he was dispatched Honorius also "sent nuncios throughout the whole world" with the same proposal (Doc. 43.2; cf. Docs. 2.2 and 44.3 = 1.1ACM). While this assertion may be based on Romanus' surmise reported in the *Relatio* (Doc. 1.17), we can at least be certain that Honorius himself considered *Super*

---

30. D. E. Queller, *The Office of Ambassador in the Middle Ages* (Princeton, 1967), pp. 5–8, 66.

31. Paravicini Bagliani, *Cardinali di curia*, pp. 77–97, esp. pp. 81–82 for Otto's first mission to England; Sayers, *Papal Government*, pp. 39–40. Powicke-Cheney thought the nuncio Otto and the cardinal Otto were "probably" the same person (*Councils & Synods*, II.i, 155), but Paravicini Bagliani does not hesitate to consider them identical (p. 81). From the pen of Matthew Paris we have a conventional representation—hardly a portrait—of an older Otto, mitered and clean-shaven, presiding over the legatine council of London in November 1237, which is reproduced in *The Illustrated Chronicles of Matthew Paris*, trans. and ed. by R. Vaughan (Cambridge, Eng., 1993), p. 124, and as the frontispiece to the present study.

32. Lunt, *Financial Relations*, p. 185; Powicke-Cheney, *Councils & Synods*, II.i, 155.

33. On the Fawkes affair, see n. 85, chap. 2, above; N. Vincent, *Peter des Roches* (Cambridge, Eng., 1996), p. 224.

34. For the truce negotiations, see pp. 60–70, chap. 2, above.

35. He was back in England by 13 March 1226: *Rotuli litterarum clausarum in Turri Londinensi asservati*, ed. T. D. Hardy, 2 vols. (London, 1833–1844), II, 102a. Cf. Lunt, *Financial Relations*, p. 186, n. 2.

muros to be his nuncio's major unfinished business when he finally recalled him and provided for its conclusion by the archbishop of Canterbury (Doc. 43.13).

The council at London on 13–14 January 1226

The English version of *Super muros* was addressed to the prelates of the kingdom of England—"prelatis per regnum Anglie constitutis" (Doc. 41). Otto could have sent copies to the archbishops of Canterbury and York to be transmitted down the hierarchy, just as Romanus probably distributed *Super muros* in France, and as he certainly did another mandate (Doc. 28). The evidence that Otto did so too is slight but persuasive: a copy of *Super muros* (Sa) was apparently entered in the Salisbury Register *before* the summons to consider the proposal in January was received (Doc. 42.1-2).[36]

Otto then proceeded to pave the way for the proposal's acceptance in England by seeking the king's approval. Wendover says the nuncio delivered a letter to Henry III, presumably an *in eodem modo* copy of *Super muros* addressed to the king. "But when the king learned the gist of the letter, he replied that he alone neither could nor should decide a matter that touched all the clergy and laity of the whole kingdom in general" (Doc. 43.1). He accordingly consulted the archbishop of Canterbury, and on his advice the king decided to assemble "all the clergy and laity" at London in January to discuss the matter, "after which he [the king] would do there what seemed just to everyone." According to Wendover, then, the assembly was to be, not a church council, but a royal one.

The crown no doubt did issue a summons for this event to the lay magnates, but it was up to the archbishops to summon the clergy. The summons sent out by Canterbury survives in the Salisbury Register (Doc. 42.2, 8), where it is noted that it was received about 30 November 1225. The mandate was transmitted, as was the custom in the province of Canterbury,[37] by the archbishop to the dean of his suffragans, the bishop of London, who in turn sent a copy to each bishop. Judging from the somewhat similar distribution of Romanus' mandate, which took over five weeks (Doc. 28.10-12), Langton probably issued his summons in late October, about a month after Otto arrived in England.

Since the occasion was a royal council to consider a request addressed to all the prelates of the kingdom, the archbishop of York must have issued a summons to his suffragans as well, of which no trace survives. Powicke and Cheney

36. On the placement of the relevant entries and the change of scribal hands, see Doc. 42.pr.

37. E. W. Kemp, "The Canterbury Provincial Chapter and the Collegiality of Bishops in the Middle Ages," in *Etudes d'histoire du droit canonique dédiées à Gabriel Le Bras*, 2 vols. (Paris, 1965), I, 184-201. Powicke-Cheney, *Councils & Synods*, II.i, 155, n. 2.

were reluctant to assume that the northern province was involved, but there can be no doubt that both archbishops were supposed to be present, because Wendover notes the absence of the two "archiepiscopi" (Doc. 43.7).[38]

Langton's mandate instructs his suffragans to summon "the deans of their cathedral churches and their archdeacons, as well as the abbots and conventual priors" (Doc. 42.2). In other words, the members of various ecclesiastical bodies were to be "represented" by their heads, according to a common if undemocratic medieval concept of representation.[39] Thus the archdeacons represented the interests of the secular parish clergy in their archdeaconries, as indeed they were to do even when the other, corporate bodies were represented by proctors (Doc. 42.3). Evidently Langton, in framing the summons, did not think it necessary to include capitular proctors in accordance with *Etsi membra corporis* (Doc. 48), which he perhaps may have interpreted narrowly as applicable only to provincial, or at least exclusively ecclesiastical, councils. More likely, however, he simply summoned all the parties to whom *Super muros* was addressed.

Indeed, the character of the January assembly was from the outset, perhaps intentionally, indeterminate. Without naming the event, the archbishop simply required that all those summoned should "come to London in order to hear the lord pope's mandate" (Doc. 42.2), and the Salisbury Register describes the assembly in precisely the same vague terms (Doc. 42.5), as does Wendover, who is the only one to suggest it was some sort of council or counselling ("terminus consilii," Doc. 43.4). From Wendover's account, discussed above, it would seem that the original plan was to convene the interested parties, both lay and clerical, to hear Otto's presentation of *Super muros* and to advise the king how he should respond to it. It was an *ad hoc* response to an unusual request, and most likely did not quite fit into conventional categories.

Time and place

Langton's mandate instructs all those he summons "to come to London on the morrow of the Lord's Epiphany" (Doc. 42.2), that is, the day after 6 January, so

38. Powicke-Cheney, *Councils & Synods*, II.i, 155: "Whether prelates of the northern province were summoned and, if so, by what means, we do not know." In his list of councils of the church of England, C. R. Cheney was inclined to consider it a national council ("English?"): *Handbook of British Chronology*, 2nd ed. by F. M. Powicke and E. B. Fryde (London, 1961), p. 551. But in her revision of the list, D. E. Greenway had no doubt about the nature of the council ("English"): idem, 3rd ed. by E. B. Fryde et al. (1986), p. 594.

39. Thomas Aquinas, *Summa theologiae* II–II q.57 a.2 and esp. q.63 a.3 resp.: "Sicut principes et praelati honorantur etiam si sint mali, inquantum gerunt personam Dei et communitatis cui praeficiuntur" (ed. P. Caramello [Turin: Marietti, 1952], II, 311); Brian Tierney, *Foundations of the Conciliar Theory* (Cambridge, Eng., 1955), pp. 4–5, 125–127; G. Post, *Studies*, pp. 112, 150, 319.

the assembly was originally scheduled for 7 January 1226. This date, however, conflicts with all our other sources, which also differ on the place. The various reports can be conveniently summarized:

Doc.	Source	Date	Place
42.2	Summons	7 January	London
42.5	Salisbury	13 January	London
42.7	Salisbury	"same day"	St Paul's
43.1	Wendover	13 January	Westminster
43.4	Wendover	13 January	Westminster

The differing dates can readily be explained in view of the attendant circumstances. When the participants assembled on Wednesday, 7 January, it would seem they discovered that the meeting had been postponed for six days, until Tuesday, 13 January, because the king had been taken ill after Christmas and presently was at Marlborough in critical condition,[40] attended by both archbishops and many bishops (Doc. 43.3). The chroniclers, writing about a past event, quite naturally reported the day on which it eventually took place. The other differences can most readily be accounted for by assuming that the deliberations took place over several days and in several places. This assumption finds support in Wendover's statement that after the nuncio made his presentation, the prelates "went off by themselves to discuss the matter privately, and after they had deliberated on the proposal for a long time," they replied to Otto through a spokesman (Doc. 43.6). Although Wendover does not say so, these events may well have taken place on two successive days and at two different places.

The proceedings of the January council

We have two accounts of the council, written from different perspectives. The first, by a canon of Salisbury, was written two or three months after the event[41] and is a brief summary primarily intended to provide the context of the documents he was copying (Doc. 42.7). For the Salisbury canon, the council was an exclusively ecclesiastical, and indeed provincial, event: "a great crowd of clergy convened at London in St Paul's church" but "nothing was done at that time"

40. The Salisbury Register records the king's itinerary: Christmas at Winchester, then at Clarendon near Salisbury on 28 Dec. 1225, then thence to Marlborough, "ubi per aliquot septimanas aegrotabat": *Vetus registrum Sarisberiense*, ed. W. H. Rich Jones, Rolls Series, no. 78, I (London, 1883), pp. 44–45.

41. In the Salisbury Register, the same hand goes on to record the arrival on 1 March of the summons to the council of 3 May, but not the acta of that council, which are a later addition (see Doc. 42.pr.).

because of the archbishop of Canterbury's absence. He simply ignored the absence of the archbishop of York and the presence of many laymen, and he saw no need for the presence of either the king or of bishops and prelates other than from his own province of Canterbury. Indeed, the canon's informant may not have realized that the crowd of unfamiliar faces contained prelates from the northern province.

Roger Wendover, on the other hand, provides considerably more detail, which may have been given its present form five to ten years after the event, although of course the monk of St Albans probably was working from notes made earlier. According to Wendover, the participants included "many bishops . . . together with other prelates and crowds of laymen" (Doc. 43.4), which included John Marshal and other royal *nuntii* (Doc. 43.8). Moreover, he makes it clear that the archbishop of York was expected to attend but was, like Canterbury, prevented by the king's illness (Doc. 43.7), so the participants apparently included the clergy of both provinces.

The original intention was doubtless to have the proceedings conducted "in the presence of the king," as was the case in May when he could attend (Doc. 43.14-15), but who was supposed to preside is not clear. In May the archbishop of Canterbury certainly did, but this duty was enjoined on him by the pope when he recalled Otto. What seems to have happened is that the papal nuncio took charge and attempted to accomplish his mission despite the absence of the principal participants. As long as he confined himself to his role as the pope's spokesman, no one objected, since after all it was evident from the summons that the purpose of the assembly was to hear him deliver the pope's proposal (Doc. 42.2); but the English prelates did object when he exceeded his authority by adjourning the council to a day of his choice (Doc. 43.9).

According to plan, the nuncio "publicly read the letter [*Super muros*] aloud in the presence of all" (Doc. 43.4). "After making this proposal, Master Otto, speaking on the lord pope's behalf, urged the prelates to consent, and he stressed the advantages that were noted in the letter cited above" (Doc. 43.6). Wendover emphasizes Otto's official function as the pope's mouthpiece; the nuncio first delivered his message in writing and then explicated and advocated it, as was customary for nuncios in diplomatic practice.[42] It is significant that, although Wendover has assured us that there were "crowds of laymen" present (Doc. 43.4), he expressly states that Otto's appeal was directed exclusively to the prelates; he "urged the prelates to consent" (Doc. 43.6), because the bull had been addressed to them, and they were assembled before him to hear and answer it.

Thus far, Otto proceeded much as Romanus had done at Bourges (Doc. 1.8), and now that the proposal had been fully presented, the next step in conciliar

42. Queller, *Office of Ambassador*, pp. 6-8.

procedure would have been to discuss it. At Bourges, discussion directly followed presentation, but at London that was not done, probably to avoid discussing ecclesiastical matters in the presence of laymen.[43] After Otto's presentation, "the bishops and ecclesiastical prelates who were present in person went off by themselves to discuss the matter privately" (Doc. 43.6). Where they went is not stated, but St Paul's seems the most likely venue, since it is mentioned solely by the Salisbury canon, who reported only the exclusively ecclesiastical aspects of the proceedings at London (Doc. 42.7). If so, we must infer that the proceedings began and ended at Westminster Abbey, about two miles from the cathedral, and hence that, because of the time-consuming relocation, the proceedings most likely extended over two short January days.

At St Paul's, the prelates "deliberated on the proposal for a long time," and finally "they designated Master John, archdeacon of Bedford, as their spokesman (Doc. 43.6).[44] His title of *magister*, taken together with his office of archdeacon, surely indicates a man trained and experienced in canon law, and his subsequent speech, which relies heavily on contemporary legal thought, bears out this supposition.

Back at Westminster, probably the next day (14 January, the feast of St Hilary), the prelates' spokesman gave their response to the nuncio, evidently in a second session of the mixed council, because both prelates and laymen were present (Doc. 43.8). Master John's reply was based on the Romano-canonical maxim, "What touches all (*quod omnes tangit*) must be approved by all in com-

43. Although canon law did not explicitly exclude laymen from church councils, by 1226 the tendency was to do so; the decision was usually regarded as the president's prerogative. In France, a synodal *ordo* (1209~1213) appended to the statutes of Paris stipulated that, after the opening prayers, lection, and sermon, "licentiabit episcopus laicos et scholares et alios clericos qui non debent synodo interesse": *Les Statuts synodaux français du XIIIᵉ siècle*, ed. O. Pontal, I (Paris, 1971), p. 92 (p. 44 for date). C. R. Cheney notes that Sinibaldo dei Fieschi (Pope Innocent IV) in his *Apparatus* to the *Liber extra* (ad X 3.5.29 *Grave nimis*, ed. Friedberg, II, 478) omitted laymen from the list of those to be admitted to a provincial council, even though they were included in the authority he cited (Gratian, *Decretum* D.18 c.17 *Decernimus*, ed. Friedberg, I, 58): *English Synodalia of the Thirteenth Century* (Oxford, 1941), p. 13; cf. p. 33. The rules confidently laid down by F. L. Ferraris (d. 1760) are weakly supported by his citations: "Laici autem non permittuntur interesse Conciliis Provincialibus, nisi ad Justitiam petendam, vel defendendam [X 3.10.4 and 4.1.1]; in Ecclesiasticis enim negotiis, et ubi tractatur de Clericorum correctionibus, non sunt vocandi Laici, immo omnino sunt excludendi [X 1.6.56]": *Prompta biblioteca canonica*, 8 vols. (Paris, 1852–1857), II, 827, s. v. "Concilium," art. 2, no. 27. For a more nuanced and flexible treatment, see Prospero Lambertini (Pope Benedict XIV, d. 1758), *De synodo dioecesano*, 2 vols. (Ferrara, 1760), I, 117-118 (3.9.8).

44. Master John of Houton, archdeacon of Bedford 1218-1231, then of Northampton 1231-1246 (both in the diocese of Lincoln): J. Le Neve, *Fasti Ecclesiae Anglicanae, 1066–1300*, rev. ed. by D. E. Greenway, III (London, 1977), pp. 42, 31-32.

mon."[45] He argued (Doc. 43.7) that Honorius' proposal concerned the interests of not only the English prelates, to whom *Super muros* was addressed, but
also those of laymen whose property rights would be affected by the proposed
gift. Much of the wealth of many bishops consisted of fiefs that they held from
the crown, and these could not be assigned to the pope without the permission of the king, who as feudal lord had granted them. Similarly endangered
were the property rights of the patron of an alienated benefice, who would lose
his right of advowson, the English practice that entitled him to present, or nom-
inate, a candidate to fill a vacant benefice of which he was patron.[46] The prelates,
speaking through John of Houton, reminded the nuncio that all these interests
had to be consulted—and the allusion to *quod omnes tangit* implied that they must
be consulted not separately but in common. But such was not presently the case,
since the king was ill at Marlborough and "the archbishops, some bishops, and
other prelates of churches are also absent." Consequently, the response concluded, the prelates assembled in London "ought not and cannot" reply to the
nuncio "because if we were to presume to do so, it would be prejudicial to all
of the absent prelates."

After invoking the rights of the crown and the patrons at length, this conclusion comes as something of a surprise, since only the rights of the absent
prelates are specified as being the decisive factor. The explanation would seem
to be that the prelates who had deliberated at St Paul's were responding only for
the clergy; if their response had been favorable, the laymen would have had their
day in court at Westminster, and, as we shall see, the crown's agents were prepared for this eventuality. Furthermore, since the original purpose of the whole
assembly was to advise the king (Doc. 43.1), if both laymen and clergy at Westminster had concurred in approving the pope's plan, they could have delivered
their counsel to the king at another time for his action, just as the prelates at St
Paul's delivered theirs to the nuncio; so the king's absence in itself did not in-
validate the proceedings. Moreover, canon law would not support the contention that the prelates at St Paul's were unable to reach a decision without the
consent of the absent prelates, since they had been duly summoned and consequently were bound by law to consent to decisions made in their absence.[47]

Why did the prelates convened at St Paul's not simply reject the papal proposal? It is unlikely that the presence of the king and the missing prelates would

45. On *quod omnes tangit*, see at nn. 64-65, chap. 3, above.

46. *The Oxford Dictionary of the Christian Church*, 3rd ed. by F. L. Cross and E. A. Livingstone (Oxford, 1997), pp. 21-22, s. v. "advowson," with bibliography.

47. Post, *Studies*, pp. 176-228. Absence due to a royal command, however, was a legitimate excuse for not attending a provincial council: Gratian, *Decretum* D.18, c.13, ed. Friedberg, I, 57. Whether the prelates who attended the sick king had this excuse is unknown.

have altered their view of the matter, and the prospect of a second convocation can hardly have been appealing. Although there is no obvious explanation for their position, one may nonetheless speculate: perhaps out of respect or fear they hesitated to act contrary to the wishes of their leaders, which were as yet unknown to them; perhaps, regardless of the niceties of canon law, they really did feel strongly that all concerned should be present; or perhaps they were playing for time, in the knowledge that Langton had already requested Otto's recall, and, given the subsequent dispute over when to reconvene, this reason seems most likely to me.

After Master John had delivered the prelates' opinion to Otto, there was an opportunity for the king's agents, led by John Marshal,[48] to canvas the bishops who held fiefs directly from the crown; they were strictly forbidden "to assign their lay fiefs to the Roman church" (Doc. 43.8). Since the bishops seem to have been lobbied individually, it would appear that Otto called a recess while he considered what to do next. The royal agents were not sure what his next step would be, and lest he insist that a decision be made on the spot, they were preparing for the worst. As it turned out, their precautions were unnecessary.

In a church council, a duly constituted presiding officer, such as a legate or an archbishop, would have had the authority to reject his counselors' excuse and insist that they answer the question; but Otto was only a nuncio and the nature of this assembly and his authority over it as president were doubtful. As a qualified canonist, *Magister* Otto must have perceived the flaws in the prelates' excuse, but he was above all a diplomat charged with securing consent to a sensitive proposal, so he wisely did not force the issue.

The nuncio's solution to the impasse was to dissolve the present council and hold another one when the king and the absent prelates could attend (Doc. 43.9). He attempted to fix the day for the next meeting, suggesting "a day in the middle of Lent" (Doc. 43.9), which in medieval usage would have been the fourth Sunday in Lent (29 March 1226).[49] Perhaps unsure of his authority to dictate the day, he apparently asked if his decision were agreeable. "But those present refused to agree to the proposed date without the assent of the king and the others who were absent." Their objection was firmly grounded in law, for the day of a council was set by the one who summoned it, and in the case of a provincial council this was the prerogative of the archbishop,[50] and of the king

48. John Marshal (1170?–1235), first baron Marshal of Hingham and grand-nephew of William Marshal I, earl of Pembroke; for a summary of his long career in royal service, see *Dictionary of National Biography*, XII (1917), 1106-1108. For many further details, see S. Painter, *William Marshal* (Baltimore, 1933), passim.

49. Mas Latrie, *Trésor de chronologie*, col. 649, s.v. "Media Quadragesima."

50. Gratian, *Decretum* D.18 c.13-15; X 1.6.28 and 5.1.25, ed. Friedberg, I, 97, and II, 71-74, 747.

in the case of a royal council. This seemingly minor confrontation is significant because it shows not only the assembly's reluctance to accept the authority of its *ad hoc* presider but also the importance of the proposed date. As I have already suggested, the assembly members wanted to allow enough time to have Otto recalled, and as it turned out they were right, for the nuncio was about to leave England on the eve of the May council. It is worth noting that Otto accepted the objection and accordingly adjourned the session *sine die*, leaving it to the king and the archbishops to set a new date.

The council at London on 3 May 1226

By late January,[51] the date for the resumption of the business was set for the second Sunday after Easter (3 May), and Archbishop Langton accordingly sent out a new summons (Doc. 42.3 = 42.9), which, after passing through the usual channels, arrived at Salisbury on Quinquagesima Sunday (1 March). As before, the stated purpose of the meeting was "to reply to the lord pope's nuncio concerning the petition that he has made on the part of the lord pope." The second citation mandate differed from the first in several respects, some more important than others. This time the event was explicitly called a *concilium*, both in the summons itself and in the bishop of Salisbury's letter of transmittal (Doc. 42.3), and since the summons was directed to Canterbury's suffragans, a council of the province of Canterbury is indicated. This specification does not, however, exclude the possibility that the provincial council was held in conjunction with a royal council, which I shall presently argue was the case.

Another, minor variation was the express recognition that four abbots in the province were exempt from attendance, namely those of St Albans, Westminster, St Edmond's, and St Augustine's Canterbury. These abbeys were immediately subject to the Holy See, and consequently the pope would have to deal with them directly.[52] Evidently they had objected to the inclusive language of the earlier summons, which was now refined to take their special status into account.

By far the most important change was the inclusion of proctors for the ecclesiastical corporations affected by the proposal. In addition to citing the prelates who had been called to the January council, Langton instructed the bishop of London to "indicate to all the chapters that they are to send proctors, namely both from cathedral churches and from prebendal ones, and from monasteries

51. Since the Salisbury copies are undated, I have calculated the date of issue on the same assumption used for the previous summons (see after n. 37, above), namely that distribution required five weeks, as was the case with Doc. 28.

52. Lunt, *Financial Relations*, pp. 220-223, 463; I. S. Robinson, *The Papacy 1073–1198* (Cambridge, Eng., 1990), pp. 226-235.

and other monastic and collegiate houses" (Doc. 42.3).[53] Moreover, all the representatives "are to deliberate in the meantime and come fully instructed (*plene instructi*) to reply" to the proposal.[54] As the first surviving summons of such proctors, this is generally recognized to be a landmark in the history of clerical representation,[55] although of course proctors are known to have participated in earlier councils, most prominently in the Council of Bourges. Indeed, I would suggest that it was the presence of proctors at Bourges that prompted Langton to include them in his second summons. We have noted above that his first citation mandate was probably issued in late October 1225 and certainly was received in Salisbury on 30 November, the very date of the Council of Bourges (see before n. 37, above); it is not unreasonable to suppose that by the time the second summons was issued, probably in late January, the *Relatio*, which was well known in England by May (Doc. 42.11), had already arrived in England. Most likely the report was sent as soon as possible, since it was in the author's interest to forestall the adoption of *Super muros* in England. Hence it appears that, although the proctors at Bourges had been summoned to approve the Albigensian tenth, their unexpected protest against *Super muros* provided a precedent for the English consideration of, and resistance to, Honorius' proposal.

To determine the scope of the May council, we must go beyond the evidence of the surviving summons. The Dunstable annalist, who is an unusually reliable source, calls it a "comprovincial council" and then goes on to report the reply of the Canterbury province, adding that "other provinces gave much the same response" (Doc. 2.2).[56] Now the adjective *comprovincialis* has two senses: either "the bishops having their sees in one and the same church province" or "comprising more than one church province."[57] In the first sense, the phrase *concilium comprovinciale* would be an awkward, ambiguous redundancy for *concilium provinciale*; in the second, however, it would signify precisely that more than one province was involved. The likelihood, therefore, is that the Dunstable annalist used the term to indicate that York as well as Canterbury participated in the May council; that he reported only Canterbury's reply suggests that the provinces

---

53. In fact the bishop of London did not follow his instructions to the letter but simply passed the citation mandate on to his fellow suffragans and let them in turn summon all the concerned parties in their respective dioceses, as the letters of transmittal make plain (Doc. 42.3).

54. See Post, *Studies*, pp. 63–109, on the legal background of "full instructions," and pp. 127–160 on the place of *plena potestas* in the development of representative institutions.

55. Barker, *Dominican Order*, pp. 46–47; Robinson, "Convocation," p. 88; Weske, *Convocation*, p. 43; Lunt, *Financial Relations*, pp. 185–186; Powicke-Cheney, *Councils & Synods*, II.i, 155.

56. Lunt understood York to have been one of the "other provinces": *Financial Relations*, p. 186, at n. 6.

57. Niermeyer, *Lexicon*, p. 232.

deliberated separately in London, and he recorded only the response of his own province, lumping York's together with that of Bourges, which was cited at the council (Doc. 42.11). This interpretation is borne out by the statement of the Salisbury Register that a suffragan of York province, the bishop of Durham, died at Peterborough "while travelling in great haste to that council in London" (Doc. 42.13).[58] These indications are confirmed by Wendover's plain statement that "the prelates of England" were present at the council (Doc. 43.14).

Otto's recall

On 1 March the Salisbury chapter received its summons to the May council, and with it came a request from the nuncio Otto for his procuration (cf. Doc. 42.4a).[59] Like all papal agents, he was entitled each year to collect the cash equivalent of one night's lodging and entertainment from cathedral chapters and the wealthier conventual churches, even though he did not visit them in person. Otto devised a new method of collecting his procuration money, by asking each bishop to collect what was customarily due from the cathedral chapter and religious houses in his diocese; but, significantly, this was a request rather than a command, which a nuncio had no power to impose. The nuncio's request was moderate and set by English custom: from each church he required no more than two marks of silver, which was half the amount due to a papal legate.[60] No doubt he was aware that earlier procurations had been unpopular and were commonly regarded as yet another way in which the Roman curia enriched

58. Wendover, who gives a more extensive account of the bishop of Durham's death, says that "for a most disgraceful lawsuit that he was prosecuting against his monks, he was hastening to the day set at London (*ad diem Londoniis constitutum*) with a mighty commotion of repetitious lawyers": Roger Wendover, *Chronica, sive Flores historiarum,* ed. H. O. Coxe, 4 vols. (London, 1842), IV, 126; cf. Matthew Paris, *Chronica majora,* ed. H. R. Luard, III (London, 1876), 111. Because this passage "gives another reason for the bishop's last journey," Powicke and Cheney are not convinced that he was going to participate in the council (*Councils & Synods,* II.i, 156); but the day he meant to arrive in London was certainly that set for the council, since Wendover gives 1 May as the day of his death ("Obiit autem primo die mensis Maii," p. 127). If he had to be in London for the council, it would not be unusual for him to take the opportunity to transact other business there as well.

59. Text in *Vetus registrum Sarisberiense,* ed. Rich Jones, I, 371-372: "procurationes pro me exigi faciatis, michi London. quam citius poteritis transmissuri; ita tamen quod unaquaeque procuratio summam duarum marcarum ullatenus non excedat." On procurations in general, see n. 20, above; on Otto's, see Lunt, *Financial Relations,* pp. 539-540.

60. The mark was two-thirds of a pound sterling (13$s.$ 4$d.$). Wendover gives two figures: two marks (Doc. 43.2), which agrees with the nuncio's letter (n. 59, above), and "with the proviso that no procuration should exceed the amount of forty shillings" (Doc. 43.10), i.e. two pounds. I follow Lunt's interpretation, *Financial Relations,* p. 540.

itself, so in his letter Otto justified his request by explaining that this procuration would be used to defray the expenses of his stay in London, which was protracted by the delay in securing a reply to *Super muros*. Clearly he was doing his best to dispel the greedy image of the curia from the minds of those who would be participating in the upcoming council.

When the bishop of Salisbury received Otto's request on 1 March, he supposed that the nuncio would be remaining in London at least until early April, since he set 29 March as the deadline for payment of the procurations, which he would then send to Otto.[61] In fact, Otto did travel extensively, including a trip to France, where he still was in the early weeks of March,[62] possibly helping to patch up a last-minute truce between Henry and Louis before the new Albigensian Crusade was launched in May. He returned to England some time before Easter (19 April) and was traveling north to Northumberland, collecting procurations along the way, possibly from places that did not adopt his scheme for voluntary collection *in absentia*. He had only reached Northampton, however, when he received an unwelcome letter from the pope "that entirely revoked his power as nuncio and expressly stated that as soon as he saw the letter he should return to Rome" (Doc. 43.13). Honorius' letter may well have contained a reprimand, since reportedly Otto could hardly bear to read it and, when he was finished, "with a depressed look . . . threw it into the fire." He seems to have been about to leave England when the May council took place, since on 2 May the king arranged for Otto to receive one thousand marks "ad opus suum."[63]

Proceedings of the May council

Wendover assures us that the nuncio's recall was "issued at the request of the archbishop of Canterbury," who could well object that Otto's mission violated the spirit, though not the letter, of the pope's promise that he would send no more legates to England during Langton's lifetime.[64] At any rate, Otto's unfinished business was entrusted to Langton: "In accordance with express instruc-

61. *Vetus registrum Sarisberiense*, ed. Rich Jones, I, 372–373.

62. *Rotuli litterarum clausarum*, ed. Hardy, II, 102a. Otto was back in England by 13 March, when his return trip "usque in Angliam" had already been paid for in Dover; however, three days later, on 16 March, the crown was arranging cross-Channel transport for him "versus partes suas eunti" (ibid., p. 102b).

63. *Patent Rolls of the Reign of Henry III preserved in the Public Record Office*, II (London, 1903), 27–28. The money had been set aside by the crown to pay its annual tribute to the papacy. On 21 March, Otto had received two lesser installments (ibid., p. 24). Cf. Lunt, *Financial Relations*, p. 145.

64. See n. 29, above.

tions in the lord pope's letter, Otto ordered Stephen archbishop of Canterbury to convoke the king and all the prelates of England and without fail to inform the lord pope of their response concerning the business on which Otto had been sent" (Doc. 43.13). Of course Wendover did not have it quite right here, since the summons had already been issued about two months earlier,[65] but when the council did convene, Langton surely presided (Docs. 42.11 and 43.14).[66]

What sort of a council he presided over is not clear. The report in the Salisbury Register is of no help, for it is cast in vague and indefinite terms that could apply to any kind of council (Doc. 42.11). The Fenland account is definite enough but unfortunately is also not trustworthy:[67] *Super muros* "was read aloud in the presence of king Henry and the counts and barons, and in the presence of the archbishop and his suffragans and clergy. The response [was] given for the king and the clergy . . . " (Doc. 44.5). The Dunstable annalist, as we have seen, calls the assembly a "comprovincial council" but says that it replied for the province of Canterbury (Doc. 2.2). These accounts all simplify what from Wendover's more detailed description appears to have been a complex and perhaps anomalous event (Doc. 43.14).

According to Wendover, a council summoned by Langton met at Westminster. Acting as president, the archbishop had *Super muros* "read aloud in the presence of the king and the prelates of England" (Doc. 43.14). Not surprisingly, the request was promptly discounted: the prelates "were provoked to laugh among themselves at the greed of the Romans." Probably, as at Bourges, there was next an opportunity for at least the proctors to express their opinions in this general session; but sooner or later the king "conferred privately with the prelates and some of the magnates" (Doc. 43.15). Thus the king made his decision with the counsel of the same mix of prelates and lay lords that he had intended to consult in January. It is unclear whether laymen other than the king were admitted to the general session; if not, as seems likely, it would be considered an ecclesiastical council of the English church.[68]

After the king had taken counsel, the general session reconvened to hear his decision and probably to approve it as well, since the Salisbury Register states

65. Wendover was ill-informed because St Albans did not receive a summons (before n. 52, above).

66. Although written ca. 1226, and thus not long after the May council, the Gamma recension of the Fenland chronicle supposed that Otto himself presided (Doc. 44.5). The continuator responsible for §5 thus reveals that, although his account is nearly contemporaneous with the event, he himself was not an eyewitness and hardly knew what happened.

67. See preceding note.

68. Cheney, in the *Handbook of British Chronology*, 2nd ed., citing the Salisbury Register and Wendover, listed it as probably a provincial council (p. 551: "Canterbury?"); but D. E. Greenway decided that it was indeed a national council (idem, 3rd ed., p. 594: "English").

that the response was given by "everyone unanimously" (Doc. 42.11). Wendover says the king "gave this response to the archbishop" and "after this speech, everyone was granted leave to depart" (Doc. 43.15). Thus it is evident that the general session was regarded as the formal occasion on which the pope's agent received the English response to *Super muros*. Originally it was to have been given to the papal nuncio, but on his departure, Langton had been instructed to receive it instead. This circumstance reinforces our view that, ecclesiastically speaking, the council was a "comprovincial" one for all England.

Reasons for the rejection

All our sources agree that the king declined to grant the pope's request, but each of the four accounts offers a different rationale. The most likely explanation for this variety is that the king's speech advanced a number of reasons for his decision. Almost certainly the speech was not delivered by the king himself but by an accomplished orator acting as the royal spokesman, or *prolocutor*, and his performance would have been suitably elaborate and eloquent; the content was most likely based on the more persuasive counsels that had been voiced in the private session. Consequently, rather than seeking to identify the "right" reason, one should suppose that each chronicler recorded what impressed him the most about the response. Let us accordingly describe the four reasons for the rejection of *Super muros*.

1. The Fenland continuator claims that England already supported the papacy sufficiently by reason of the one thousand marks that the crown paid annually as tribute, in accordance with the agreement King John made with Innocent III in 1213 (Doc. 44.5).[69] This argument, if it was ever made, represents the king's point of view, since the tribute was paid out of the royal treasury and cost the English churches nothing. While it is not impossible that the royal spokesman remarked that the papacy was already getting quite enough support from England, still the assertion is doubtful, coming as it does from a manifestly ill-informed source (see at nn. 66–67, above).

2. The Dunstable annal (Doc. 2.2), written under the supervision of a competent canonist if not by his hand, has the king putting off the pope with good legal arguments. Tacitly invoking the principle of *quod omnes tangit*, the response argues that a proposal that affects Latin Christendom as a whole cannot be approved country by country, or province by province, but must have the consent of a general council of the entire Church. Moreover, the property rights of the patrons of the benefices involved must be considered, as the archdeacon of Bedford had told Otto at the January council (Doc. 43.7), and even if some mag-

69. On the tribute, see Lunt, *Financial Relations*, pp. 135–136.

nates were present at the May meeting, they could not speak for the hundreds of absent patrons.

3. Wendover records a tactful but evasive speech, the nub of which was simply: "we shall wait to see how the other kingdoms respond to these demands" (Doc. 43.15). This, of course, was just the way Romanus dealt with the matter at Bourges, and if every kingdom similarly passed the buck, the only solution would be to bring the proposal before a general council.

4. The Salisbury Register simply states that the "response was modeled on the one given to the legate of France in the council that he celebrated at Bourges," after which the entire *Relatio* is inserted into the record (Doc. 42.11-12). While it is not impossible that some of the proctors' objections made at Bourges may have been repeated at the English council, I think it far more likely that the London response was modeled not on theirs but on Romanus' postponement of the matter, which would agree with Wendover's account.

* * *

Honorius took no for the answer to *Super muros*. We know his proposal was abandoned with no intention of renewing it, because *Super muros* and any correspondence concerning it were all omitted from the register for Honorius' tenth year, which came to an end in July 1226, since the chancery apparently felt they were of no further use.[70] Nonetheless, there were several later, interrelated attempts to secure a permanent donation of benefices, but only from England. (1) In 1241, Gregory IX requested that some of the richer English Benedictine houses each assign the patronage of a church to St Peter's Rome, but the king forbade them to do so.[71] (2) In 1244, Innocent IV's nuncio, Master Martin, brought a number of proposals to England, the substance of which is now known only indirectly and vaguely. In a council at London (Lent? 1245), the English prelates rejected Martin's proposals, invoking *quod omnes tangit* to refer certain (unspecified) ones to the upcoming Council of Lyon. After quoting their response *in extenso*, Matthew Paris says it was directed against "an exaction of *churches and prebends* and of a pecuniary aid."[72] With some ingenuity, Lunt reconstructed the package deal Martin tried to negotiate; in Lunt's opinion, it included an extension of the request Gregory IX had made to certain monasteries in 1241.[73] (3) According to the Dunstable annalist, Innocent IV at the

70. Sayers, *Papal Government*, p. 72.

71. Lunt, *Financial Relations*, pp. 205-206; J. E. Sayers, "Centre and Locality," in her *Law and Records in Medieval England* (London: Variorum, 1988), item I, p. 124.

72. Matthew Paris, *Chronica majora*, ed. Luard, IV, 375-376 = Powicke-Cheney, *Councils & Synods*, II.i, 391-392.

73. Lunt, *Financial Relations*, pp. 208-209.

Council of Lyon did ask the English to make a permanent donation to the papacy of the best prebend in every cathedral and, from every abbey and priory, the patronage of a church worth at least forty marks; but "proctors of the king and kingdom" effectively objected.[74] More cautious than Lunt, Powicke and Cheney simply printed the various complaints occasioned by Master Martin's mission without attempting to determine precisely what he was after.[75] All in all, it seems likely that Innocent devised his own variation on the schemes suggested in 1196, 1215, and 1225, but this time the justification was not fiscal reform of the curia, about which nothing was said in 1244-1245, but instead simply the papacy's desperate need for money to pay for its war with Frederick II. Therefore we may conclude that Honorius' vision of fiscal reform died with *Super muros.*

Whatever happened later, the English refusal in 1226 was crucial in killing Honorius' version of the plan, not only because the English were his last hope, but also because from the start the chances for success were greater in England, as Innocent evidently reckoned they still were in 1244-1245. In France, the Albigensian Crusade had first priority, as Honorius himself recognized by entrusting *Super muros* to Romanus, whose crusading agenda was already firmly established. In England, however, the proposal had no rival; it was delivered by a nuncio sent primarily for that purpose, and when he was recalled, Honorius took care to provide an alternate means of securing a response. Perhaps he was relying on the good will of Henry III, but if so he failed to reckon with the hostility of the king's advisers, led by Stephen Langton, and even more so with the widespread unpopularity of the proposal. At St Albans, Wendover, like his successor Matthew Paris, never missed an opportunity to express resentment at papal exactions and provisions for Italians, so the grass-roots reaction is best gauged by the Salisbury Register, in which the *Super muros* affair marks the beginning of a continuing interest in fiscal politics. The Salisbury canons quickly grasped the advantage of participating through procuratorial representatives in deliberations that affected the chapter: hardly four months after the May council, they were resisting the next subsidy by calling for a provincial council at which they would be represented.[76] Thus the London council of May 1226 was, as has often been observed, the beginning of an English tradition of representative government. Surely this was the most significant and enduring consequence of the Council of Bourges, for the *Relatio* not only provided the English with the model for their response but also suggested to them that their resistance would be strengthened by including in the second London council the representatives of the affected corporations.

74. *Annales monastici,* ed. Luard, III, 167-168.
75. Powicke-Cheney, *Councils & Synods,* II.i, 388-401.
76. Powicke-Cheney, *Councils & Synods,* II.i, 163 (August 1226).

CHAPTER 8

MONASTIC REFORM AND REPENTANT MASTERS

The Council of Bourges was the largest ecclesiastical assembly held in France up to that time, and in Latin Christendom only the Fourth Lateran Council had been larger. The unprecedented size of both councils was of course due to the new practice of summoning representatives of monastic and secular chapters, which continued to enlarge attendance at subsequent general councils. Events of such size provided a rare occasion for impressing and informing a wide clerical audience, and Romanus accordingly took the opportunity at Bourges to include two other matters in his agenda. In the last closed session, he attempted to secure support for the pope's most recent efforts to promote the reform of Benedictine monasteries; then, in the final, public session he staged a dramatic reconciliation of the eighty Paris masters who had been excommunicated for assaulting him earlier that year. Although both events are recorded only by the chronicler of Tours, who rightly regarded them as minor incidents, still they deserve our attention, if only to complete the record of conciliar activity at Bourges.

MONASTIC GENERAL CHAPTERS AND VISITORS

After Romanus had presented Honorius' request in *Super muros Jerusalem* and the various reactions to it had been heard, he had another piece of papal business to be laid before the council. According to the Chronicle of Tours (Doc. 3.5):

> The legate also announced that the lord pope had commanded two bishops to depose any abbot whatsoever at the dictum of the four abbots whom he had designated to visit all of the abbeys in France and to correct their excesses. On hearing this, the archbishops and bishops saw that by this they would lose all jurisdiction whatsoever over abbeys, so they unanimously replied that as long as they lived they were not about to permit this. And thus the apostolic precepts, both about prebends [*Super muros*] and about the deposition of abbots, remained pending.

Unlike the council's previous agenda items concerning the crusade and *Super muros*, on both of which scholars have often commented, this one has never been explicated before. Consequently we shall have to reconstruct the immediate context of Honorius' mandate, but because this was only one small part of a larger papal program to reform the religious orders, we must first sketch the broader context, which is already well known.

The development of monastic general chapters and visitors

Honorius III, like Innocent III before him, and Gregory IX and Innocent IV after him, attempted to reform almost every monastic order in Christendom except the Cistercians and their imitators, which these popes regarded as having an adequate mechanism for self renewal. But because the mandate read at Bourges concerned only the Benedictines, the following account will focus on them to the exclusion of the Augustinian canons regular and other orders affected by the statute *In singulis* of the Fourth Lateran Council.

These reforming popes were dismayed by the variety of practices that had grown up in houses supposedly living under the Rule of St Benedict, and they were determined to eradicate not only the most blatant departures from it—such as luxurious meals and dress, personal possessions, and liturgical laxity—but also latter-day abuses undreamed of by Benedict, among which were absentee and self-indulgent abbots, fiscal irresponsibility, and favoritism. Although this program of reform was pertinent and proper, it was not imposed upon the whole Benedictine order until after 1563, when the Council of Trent insisted that all of the Black Monks must form themselves into congregations that would set and maintain standards. This ultimate solution, however, was the outgrowth of a policy initiated by Innocent III, which in the Middle Ages was successful only in some places and rarely for very long.

The principal obstacle to reform that frustrated Innocent and his successors was the fact that the Benedictines were united only by a common rule. Originally, each abbey was an independent entity, subject only to the bishop of the diocese in which it was situated; and by the thirteenth century, many abbeys had become "exempt" from the local bishop's jurisdiction by subjecting themselves directly to the pope.[1] Such an exemption could be enjoyed by other monasteries that subjected themselves to an exempt one, as was famously the case with the network of houses associated with Cluny (founded 909), although the degree of control exercised by the mother house varied widely. Cluny, for example, regularly assembled the priors subject to its abbot in a "general chapter," but the abbots attached to Cluny did not attend, so the meeting was in effect a "general chapter of one abbey."[2]

The next step was to assemble the heads of all houses living under a given

1. J. Vendeuvre, *L'Exemption du visite monastique* (Paris, 1907), chap. 3; J. Hourlier, *Le Chapitre général jusqu'au moment du Grand Schisme* (Paris, 1936), pp. 10–11.

2. Hourlier, *Chapitre général*, pp. 37, 72; J. B. Mahn, *L'Ordre cistercien et son gouvernement dès origines au milieu du XIIIe siècle (1098–1265)*, 2nd ed. (Paris, 1982), pp. 245–246.

rule in a so-called "general chapter." The Cistercians were the first to do so, as early as 1117, and two years later the institution was incorporated in their by-laws, the *Charta caritatis*.[3] Every year all the abbots of the order met together at Cîteaux under the presidency of its abbot; collectively they agreed on new statutes for the order and served as its high court.[4] The system was rapidly adopted by other young monastic orders, including the Carthusians, the Premonstratensians, the Gilbertines, the Grandmontines, and the Canons-Regular of St-Victor; eventually in 1200 even the Cluniacs followed suit.[5] The chapter-general served not only to unite preexisting orders but also to create new associations, notably an annual assembly of Benedictine abbots in the province of Reims, which is particularly relevant to our inquiry.[6] This association was formed in 1131, met again the next year, and received Innocent II's approval despite the opposition of his legate, Matthew of Albano.[7] Although documentation is sparse, four meetings of the chapter are attested between 1139 and 1170;[8] when the chapter reappears fifty years later, in 1220, it is making a fresh start in conformity with the requirements of the Fourth Lateran Council, so its continual existence seems extremely improbable.[9]

3. Mahn, *Ordre cistercian*, p. 61; Hourlier, *Chapitre général*, pp. 41-48. For a summary of the ongoing controversy over the development of the Cistercian constitution, see J. E. Sayers, "The Judicial Activities of the General Chapters," *Journal of Ecclesiastical History*, XV (1964), 18-32 and 168-185, at pp. 18-22.

4. Mahn, *Ordre cistercien*, pp. 173-216.

5. Hourlier, *Chapitre général*, p. 73 (Cluny dated 1202, citing Migne, *Pat. Lat.*, CCIX, 882-883); Mahn, *Ordre cistercien*, pp. 243-246; G. Schreiber, *Kurie und Kloster im 12. Jahrhundert*, 2 vols. (Stuttgart, 1910), II, 324-334. Sayers surveys the spread of the general chapters: "Judicial Activities," pp. 22-29.

6. The only recorded twelfth-century attempt to form a chapter-general of Benedictine abbots, other than the one in Reims province, occurred in Saxony in 1140; twenty years later the chapter was not functioning: U. Berlière, "Les Chapitres généraux de l'ordre de S. Benoît," *Revue bénédictine*, XVIII (1901), 364-398, and XIX (1902), 38-75, 268-278, 374-411, at pp. 40-41. Dom Berlière's preliminary surveys of medieval Benedictine chapters-general remain useful, both for a lucid overview and for data not repeated in his later studies: "Les Chapitres généraux de l'ordre de S. Benoît avant le IVe concile de Latran (1215)," *Revue bénédictine*, VIII (1891), 255-264, and "Les Chapitres généraux de l'ordre de Saint Benoît du XIIIe au XVe siècle," *Revue bénédictine*, IX (1892), 545-557.

7. U. Berlière, *Documents inédits pour servir à l'histoire ecclésiastique de la Belgique*, I (Maredsous, 1894), 93-102; idem, "Le Cardinal Mathieu d'Albano," *Revue bénédictine*, XVIII (1901), 113-140, 280-303, at pp. 285-287; idem, "Chapitres généraux," *Revue bénédictine*, XIX, 385-386; Hourlier, *Chapitre général*, pp. 69-72; P. Schmitz, *Histoire de l'ordre de Saint-Benoît*, III (Maredsous, 1948), 43-44.

8. Berlière, *Revue bénédictine*, XIX (1902), 387; Schmitz, *Histoire*, III, 45. In 1170 one abbot presided with the title of "prior" and the assembly was referred to as a *capitulum*.

9. The fresh start is indicated by the presence of two Cistercian abbots (see at n. 31, below). Berlière seems to have assumed that the tradition was unbroken: see n. 36, below.

In the twelfth century, the initiative to assemble in chapters-general came from the participating abbots; in the thirteenth century, however, the papacy attempted to impose the institution from above as an instrument of monastic reform. Throughout his innovative pontificate, Innocent III displayed remarkable concern for the spiritual and temporal welfare of the monastic orders.[10] His most pressing problem was how to monitor the numerous exempt monasteries for which he was directly responsible. A few, such as Farfa, Subiaco, and Montecassino, he visited personally; many others were visited by his legates or *ad hoc* commissioners, but he realized that this piecemeal, occasional approach was largely ineffective and needed to be replaced by systematic and regular inspections. In 1203 he hit on the expedient of mandating general chapters of exempt monasteries in several regions—Lombardy; Tuscany, Spoleto, and the Marches; England; and parts of France.[11] The experiment failed—perhaps it was not even implemented outside of Italy—but Innocent retained its basic concept, of papally mandated monastic general chapters, and around it built a better system, which he introduced at the Fourth Lateran Council. In the meantime, two local initiatives suggested to him that it would be simpler to organize monks in units that corresponded to existing, familiar boundaries: either in a kingdom, as the Benedictines of Denmark proposed in 1206, or in an ecclesiastical province, as those of Rouen suggested in 1210.[12] On the eve of the Lateran council, Gerald of Wales circulated his own proposal for a system of chapters and visitors for all the Benedictines, which though not novel in itself may well have influenced Innocent's revised scheme.[13]

Monastic visitation

The most innovative aspect of Innocent's 1203 experiment had been to link the chapter-general with another well established institution, the visitation of religious houses.[14] Since at least the sixth century, each bishop had the acknowl-

10. U. Berlière collects instances, mostly unrelated to chapters-general, in "Innocent III et la réorganisation des monastères bénédictins," *Revue bénédictine*, XXXII (1920), 22-42, 145-159.

11. *Tacti sumus dolore*, 27 February 1203 (Potthast 1843), ed. O. Hageneder et al., *Die Register Innocenz' III.*, VI (Vienna, 1995), pp. 68-69 (an. 6, ep. 46). On the assemblies of 1203, see M. Maccarrone, "Riforme e innovazioni di Innocenzo III nella vita religiosa," in his *Studi su Innocenzo III* (Padua, 1972), pp. 223-337, at pp. 228-246. Maccarrone prints the text of *Tacti sumus dolore* from the original received by the prior of Camadoli, together with the acta (Appendices 1-2, pp. 328-334).

12. Maccarrone, "Riforme e innovazioni," pp. 243-245.

13. R. Kay, "Gerald of Wales and the Fourth Lateran Council," *Viator*, XXIX (1998), 79-93, at pp. 83, 88-89; cf. Doc. 40.pr., below.

14. The essential guide to the institution of visitation and its records is N. Coulet, *Les Visites pastorales*, Typologie des sources du Moyen Age occidental, ed. L. Genicot, fasc. 23 (Turn-

edged right and duty to visit and correct the religious houses within his diocese; because the practice was authorized by canon law,[15] it came to be termed "canonical visitation." Religious houses that were exempt from episcopal jurisdiction were subject to visitation by the pope or his delegate. But an alternative system of visitation was developed in the twelfth century by the Cistercians, whereby each monastery was visited by the abbot of the house that had founded it;[16] the task of visitation was thus decentralized, and consequently these visitations played no part in the work of the general chapter of the whole Cistercian order, although both institutions contributed to the maintenance of monastic discipline—the chapter by making rules and the visitations by enforcing them. When Innocent attempted a regional reform of exempt monasteries in 1203, he recognized that both functions were necessary, and he adapted them to the circumstances of the Benedictines by making the general chapter responsible for the visitation of its members. Since all the houses involved were exempt from episcopal jurisdiction, Innocent's original plan of 1203 did not threaten the bishops' rights of canonical visitation, as his later version of 1215 certainly did.

In singulis regnis: A monastic reform by the Fourth Lateran Council

In 1215 Innocent expanded and refined his earlier experiments in the constitution *In singulis regnis* (Doc. 45), which was his attempt at the Fourth Lateran Council to reform the monastic orders.[17] As we shall see, some provisions of the statute were unclear and others inadequate, so I shall first describe those aspects that concern us and then discuss their ambiguities and shortcomings.

The intent of the statute was to insure that all the regular clergy in Latin Christendom would be periodically reformed by chapters and visitors. Those who, like the Cistercians, already held chapters were excluded; the others were to celebrate a chapter every three years. The directive named no particular order but instead specified that the general chapters were to be attended by "abbots and those priors who do not have their own abbot," which would chiefly embrace Benedictines; almost as an afterthought canons regular were included as well within the scope of the statute (Doc. 45.1, 9). The determination to extend the benefits of the general-chapter system to every male religious community

hout, 1977). J. Gilchrist gives a good brief summary in the *New Catholic Encyclopedia*, XIV (1967), 718–719, s.v. "Visitation, canonical, history of."

15. Gratian, *Decretum* C.18 q.2 cc.16–17 (ed. Friedberg, I, 833–834), both from the Council of Orléans 511.

16. Mahn, *Ordre cistercien*, pp. 217–228.

17. The most extensive examination of *In singulis* and its reception is M. Maccarrone, "Le costituzioni del IV concilio Lateranense sui religiosi," *Dizionario degli istituti di perfezione*, V (Rome, 1975), 474–495; I cite the reprint in his *Nuovi studi su Innocenzo III*, ed. R. Lambertini, (Rome, 1995), pp. 1–45, esp. pp. 19–36 for *In singulis*. Hourlier, *Chapitre général*, pp. 87–93.

was certainly the most prominent, if not the most novel, feature of the new plan. The territorial universality of its scope, in contrast to the earlier piecemeal, regional plan of 1203, was stressed by the opening words, which prescribed that such general chapters should be held "in every kingdom or province."

A few organizational guidelines were also provided. Two local Cistercian abbots were to be invited, and they would choose two members of the chapter to join them as co-presidents, the four having a veto power over the decisions of the chapter (Doc. 45.3, 5). The lifestyle and expenses of the participants were also provided for in detail (§ 2, 7), but how the plan was to be implemented was hardly addressed.

The most controversial feature of *In singulis* was a new system of monastic visitation. At each general chapter, an unstated number of visitors were to be appointed, who would visit all the member monasteries on the pope's behalf (*vice nostra*) "to correct and reform those things that seem to require correction and reform" (Doc. 45.8). This provision was controversial because, in the case of nonexempt houses, it seemed to usurp the bishop's prerogative of canonical visitation, even though the preface to the canon declared that its provisions were made "saving the right of diocesan bishops" (§ 1). The only guidance given for coordination between the bishop and the visitors was in the case of a superior whom the visitors decided should be deposed; if his house was not exempt, they were to notify his bishop, and should he prove uncooperative, they were then to refer the matter to the pope. What was to be done in the case of exempt houses was not stated, but presumably the visitors could act immediately, since they were authorized to act on the pope's behalf (*vice nostra*, 8). Moreover, how the visitors were to implement their other reforms was also unstated and hence open to interpretation and dispute. The situation was further complicated by an express declaration that the bishops were expected to continue visiting monasteries under their jurisdiction (§ 11), preferably before the chapter's inspection.

Finally, neither the chapters nor the visitors were granted any power to enforce their decisions, except against laymen "or anyone else" who harmed monastic persons or property (§ 12). In other cases, such as an abbot who refused to attend the chapter or to implement the visitors' recommendations, apparently the only recourse was to refer the problem to the pope (§ 10).

Even from this selective description, it should be evident that as a piece of legislation, *In singulis* was not well thought out.[18] The most glaring omission was any indication of how the new system was to be initiated. Who was to convoke the first chapter? Who decided whether the chapter was to include a whole kingdom, such as France, or just an ecclesiastical province, such as Reims? Who

18. Cf. the faults listed by Hourlier, *Chapitre général*, p. 93; Berlière, *Revue bénédictine*, IX (1892), 547–548.

selected and invited the Cistercian abbots? The failure to address these basic questions handicapped the implementation from the start, and in practice most often nothing happened unless the pope provided the initiative. The statute exhibits certain signs of being the product of a committee whose members amended the proposal in petty details, such as regulating the size of a participant's retinue, without considering just how the whole program was to be implemented and enforced. At a guess, *In singulis* was framed in consultation with abbots rather than canonists.[19]

The statute offers little direction on the organization of the second and subsequent chapters-general. The first one was to be presided over by two Cistercians and two chapter members of their choice, but were the Cistercians to be invited only to the startup session? And if not, how many co-presidents were later chapters to have? As we shall see, Honorius III repeatedly mandated chapters at Reims that included the Cistercians, but this seems to have been an anomaly, for in the province of Canterbury the Cistercians were present only at the first general chapter, which thereafter had only two co-presidents.[20]

Canonistic commentaries

In singulis and the other Lateran statutes were commented on by canonists even before they were incorporated in the *Decretals of Gregory IX* (1234): Johannes Teutonicus, Vincentius Hispanus, and Damasus all wrote commentaries before 1220,[21] which accordingly reflect canonistic opinion before the Council of

19. The shortcomings of *In singulis* are an important indication of how the statutes of the Fourth Lateran Council were framed, about which nothing much is known for certain. The *communis opinio* is that the drafting was done at the curia under Innocent's supervision, guided at times by the preconciliar suggestions he had solicited in the summons, but without public discussion or debate at the council, except for cc. 1-3 and 71. E. g., M. Maccarrone, "Il IV Concilio Lateranense," *Divinitas*, V (1961), 270-298, at p. 284; idem, "Costituzioni," pp. 2-3; C. R. Cheney, "A Letter of Pope Innocent III and the Lateran Decree on Cistercian Tithe-paying," reprinted in his *Medieval Texts and Studies* (Oxford, 1973), pp. 277-284; and S. Kuttner and A. García y García, "A New Eyewitness Account of the Fourth Lateran Council," *Traditio*, XX (1964), 115-178, at p. 164. In his edition, however, García cautiously prefers to attribute the canons solely to Innocent's own hand, since he alone is mentioned as author by contemporary sources (n. 21, below, ed. cit., pp. 5-11).

20. *Documents Illustrating the Activities of the General and Provincial Chapters of the English Black Monks, 1215–1540*, ed. W. A. Pantin (London, 1931), Appendix V (p. 293). Cf. Hourlier, *Chapitre général*, pp. 100-104.

21. *Constitutiones concilii quarti Lateranensis una cum commentariis glossatorum*, ed. A. García y García (Vatican City, 1981): Johannes Teutonicus (written 1216~1220, p. 180), ad c.12, pp. 204-206; Vincentius Hispanus (second half of 1217, p. 278), ad c.12, pp. 306-308; Damasus (1215~1220, p. 411), ad c.12, pp. 424-425. Johannes' views were later incorporated into his *glossa ordinaria* to the *Liber extra*.

Bourges.[22] All three commentators attempted to flesh out the deficiencies of the statute and illuminate its obscurities by drawing analogies to established canonistic practice. Although it would be tedious and here unnecessary to present their arguments in detail, a summary of some of their elucidations will show to what extent existing law could explicate the obscurities of this statute. Both Johannes and Vincentius thought it necessary to explain that the statute applied to exempt houses ("privilegiati") as well as nonexempt ones. The mechanics of decision making also needed clarification: Vincentius pointed out that the visitors were to be appointed with the consent of the chapter; Damasus argued that capitular decisions were valid if approved by three of the four presidents; if two of the four dissented, the matter would have to be referred to the pope. Contumacious absentees were to be punished in some unspecified way and suspended from office until the next chapter, according to Vincentius, who added that this was to be done by the chapter and its presidents; Damasus agreed but specified only that they should be punished, not suspended.

Problems of jurisdiction particularly challenged the three commentators. Vincentius noted that *In singulis* established three jurisdictions: the chapter had a right to the services of two Cistercian abbots; the presidents and the visitors each also had certain (unstated) powers; and all three jurisdictions, in his opinion, were held as powers delegated by the pope.[23] Vincentius did not attempt to define the powers of the visitors, but both Johannes and Damasus discussed at length whether the visitors could correct abuses without usurping the bishop's right of canonical visitation. Damasus maintained that because the statute expressly reserved the bishops' rights, "therefore if they [the visitors] attempt anything in prejudice of the bishops, they would exceed the limits of their mandate; hence they can do nothing."[24] Johannes, however, while agreeing in principle, pointed out a loophole: the visitors could correct abuses in nonexempt houses if the bishop of the place was *negligent*, and moreover they could correct them immediately in exempt houses.[25] He is quick to close the loophole, however, for

22. Less relevant are the later canonists cited by Hourlier, *Chapitre général*, pp. 256-259, and Maccarrone, "Costituzioni," pp. 23-24, 32-33.

23. *Vincentii Hispani Apparatus*, ed. García, *Constitutiones*, p. 307, lines 20-24: "et omnes credo habere delegatam a summo pontifice."

24. *Damasi Apparatus*, ed. García, *Constitutiones*, p. 425, lines 16-19: "quia data est eis potestas saluo iure diocesanorum episcoporum, ut in principio huius constitutionis dicitur. Vnde si in preiudicium episcoporum aliquid attemptarent, fines mandati transgrederentur, unde nichil agerent . . ."

25. *Joannis Teutonicus Apparatus*, ed. García, *Constitutiones*, p. 205, lines 30-33: "Numquid ergo fit preiudicium episcopo loci? Cum tamen in principio capituli dixerit 'Saluo iure diocesani' [Doc. 45.1], ideo dici potest quod tunc demum corrigent, cum episcopus fuerit negligens, et in exemptis statim corrigent."

he goes on to argue a sample case pro and con. Johannes insists that episcopal jurisdiction should not be impaired: "If he [the bishop] were not negligent, by what right would those visitors therefore usurp his right by correcting abuses themselves? Because [according to canon law] if the jurisdiction of every bishop is not preserved intact, what else is it than a confounding of ecclesiastical order?"[26] In the end, Johannes concludes that, even if the bishop has been negligent, the most that the visitors can do is to report the matter to him and admonish him to do his duty, because otherwise "what the visitors enact in his diocese contrary to his wishes is to his detriment and prejudice."[27]

Implementation of *In singulis* in the province of Reims, 1215–1225

Because the Lateran decree failed to indicate who was to take the initiative in calling the first general chapters, it is no surprise that implementation was slow and spotty. How Honorius III attempted to remedy the deficiencies of the new canon is a long and complex story that we need not follow in detail, since the uproar at Bourges was the outcome of his efforts to implement *In singulis regnis* in the province of Reims. In order to understand the brief entry in the Chronicle of Tours (Doc. 3.5), we must accordingly reconstruct the progress of the pope's efforts in only this one province.

The Benedictine abbots of Reims province had celebrated general chapters between 1131 and 1170 (see above at notes 7–9), but it is doubtful that the tradition was still operative fifty years later. Almost certainly the new system had not yet been adopted in 1219, when Honorius commissioned the archbishop of Reims to reform the exempt monastery of St-Remi without mentioning any previous inspection by the chapter's appointed visitors but citing as his reason "frequent complaints that have come to us."[28] Later that year, in November, Honorius began a campaign to implement *In singulis* by directing the archbishops, bishops, and other prelates of certain kingdoms and provinces to convoke general chapters of Black Monks within the year. Although the Vatican register noted only a copy sent to Antioch, the bull was evidently widely distributed, because originals issued in the same month have been reported from Ireland and

26. Ibid., lines 34–44: "Si non fuit negligens, quare ergo usurpant illi uisitatores ius suum in corrigendo? Quia si cuilibet episcopo sua iurisdictio non seruatur, quid aliud est quam quod ecclesiasticus ordo confunditur, ut [Gratian, *Decretum* C.11 q.1 c.39, ed. Friedberg, I, 638]."

27. Ibid., p. 206, lines 42–44: "Vel ideo defertur hic episcopo negligenti quia in alio detrahitur ei et preiudicatur quod constituuntur uisitatores in sua diocesi eo inuito."

28. *Officii nostri debitum* (16 July 1219), Pressutti, no. 2148, ed. Horoy, III, 268. The pope had received complaints: "frequentes ad nos clamores peruenerint."

Sweden, as well as from two French provinces, namely Bourges[29] and Rouen;[30] consequently it is most likely that a copy was also sent to Reims.

That assumption is borne out by the fact that the Benedictines of Reims province did celebrate a general chapter at St-Quentin under the new system soon thereafter, probably in 1220. With the Cistercian abbots of Foigny[31] and Vaucelles as co-presidents (and hence in conformity with *In singulis*), the chapter drew up a series of twelve statutes, which were submitted to the pope for his approval by the abbot of Andres in person.[32] Honorius approved the legislation on 20 May 1221, with the express reservation that his confirmation should in no way prejudice the rights of either churches or their prelates.[33] The statutes cast no light on the conduct of the general chapter, but they do prescribe a system of visitation, which is more fully elaborated than any other surviving from the decade 1215-1225. The chapter appoints six abbots to serve as visitors in the twelve dioceses of the province; annually a team of two is to visit the monasteries and nunneries assigned to it "and whatever they find needs correction, whether in the head or in the members, they are to report concerning nonexempt houses in writing to the general chapter."[34] Nothing is said about how the chapter was to deal with such visitation reports, but given the express reservation of the bishop's rights, probably the chapter was obliged to refer each report concerning a nonexempt house to its ordinary for action.

The new Reims system did not work well in practice. The first indication of its inadequacy comes from the diocese of Cambrai, where in 1223 the bishop supported the Benedictine abbot of Honnecourt in disciplining two monks for reporting the abbot's fiscal irregularities to the pope; Honorius appointed two canons of Arras to look into the matter.[35] There is no suggestion that the sys-

29. *Expectavimus hactenus spectantes* (19, 22, 23 Nov. 1219), Pressutti, no. 2268, ed. Horoy, III, 352-355.

30. *Expectavimus hactenus expectantes* [sic] (20 Nov. 1219), ed. J. F. Pommeraye, *Sanctae Rotomagensis ecclesiae concilia* (Rouen, 1677), pp. 203-205, "Ex Archivo Cathedralis Ecclesiae."

31. In Horoy's edition (see n. 33), the name is "de Jumien." but Dom Berlière conjectured that this was a copyist's error for "de Fusnien.": "Notes pour servir à l'histoire des monastères bénédictins de la province de Reims," *Revue bénédictine*, XI (1894), 36-38, 136-138, at p. 138, n. 1. Hourlier, *Chapitre général*, p. 91.

32. Abbot William of Andres (see Doc. 37) noted this mission in his chronicle: MGH, SS, XXIV, 761.

33. *Benedicti vos* (20 May 1221), Pressutti, no. 3391, ed. Horoy, III, 815-818: "ita tamen quod exinde nec ecclesiis, nec aliquibus ecclesiarum praelatis, praejudicium generetur" (col. 817).

34. Ibid.: "et quicquid invenirent corrigendum tam in capite quam in membris scriptum referant ad capitulum generale."

35. *Ex parte conventus* (4 Nov. 1223), Pressutti, no. 4557, ed. Horoy, IV, 453-454. An earlier letter concerning the case has not survived. Judging by the *Liber censuum* (ed. Fabre-Duchesne, I, 195), Honnecourt does not seem to have been an exempt house.

tem of capitular visitors approved in 1221 had played any part in the affair, perhaps because, even if they had visited Honnecourt, their report would not have
been submitted to the chapter until its next triennial meeting, which was presumably scheduled for some time in 1223.

Sapientia que ex ore

A second and much stronger indication that the system was not working came
a year later, in December 1224. Honorius had come to recognize that *In singulis* could not be implemented in Reims province without some drastic
changes. In the bull *Sapientia que ex ore*, addressed to the abbots of St-Remi
Reims and of Marchiennes, he declared that "up to now little or nothing useful has resulted" from *In singulis*, for two reasons: first, because the intended participants "have failed to assemble at such a chapter," and second, because "those
who are supposed to preside there do not seem to have any power to compel
rebels to obey" (Doc. 46.3). Therefore he ordered the recipients of his bull to repeat the process of organizing a general chapter for their province, to be held
at St-Remi within a year; that he considered the former startup session at St-
Quentin in 1220 to have been inadequate is indicated by his injunction to again
include two Cistercian abbots.[36]

In order to make *In singulis* effective, Honorius introduced a number of significant changes. First, the chapter was to be held annually, not every three years
·(Doc. 46.6).[37] Honorius says this is so that the chapter's statutes "shall be remembered better and observed more," but it would also greatly expedite action on the visitors' recommendations, which according to the statutes of 1220
were to be submitted to the next chapter. Next, *Sapientia* explicitly stated that
the heads of "both exempt and nonexempt" houses must participate (§ 4), as
the commentators had argued was the intent of the Lateran canon, though
apparently many exempt abbots had disagreed and refused to participate. Furthermore, the addressees are empowered to excommunicate those who contu-

---

36. The English records show that the Cistercian abbots were present only at a province's
first general chapter (see at n. 20, below). Ignoring Honorius' assertion that the system had
not been a success (Doc. 46.3), Berlière cited *Sapientia que ex ore* as proof that Reims province
"resta fidèle à cette tradition" of celebrating general chapters since 1131: "Honorius III et les
monastères bénédictins, 1216-1227," *Revue belge de philologie et d'histoire*, II (1923), 237-265,
461-484, at p. 251.

37. Henceforth, this departure from *In singulis* became standard curial policy: thus on 14
June 1225 Honorius empowered the abbot of Tournus (dioc. Châlons-sur-Marne, prov.
Reims) to celebrate an *annual* general chapter with the abbots and priors subject to him: *Cum
a nobis petitur*, Pressutti, no. 5536 (not enregistered). *Sapientia* evidently prompted the abbot
to petition for authorization to hold general chapters under the new terms.

maciously failed to attend the first chapter without a valid excuse, and (significantly) this could be done as soon as the absentees had been warned once, "since the obstacle of any kind of contradiction or appeal has been removed" (§ 4). What is more, the presidents of future chapters are granted the same power (§ 7). Similarly, excommunication is authorized as the penalty for not observing decisions made in the first and subsequent chapters (§ 4, 7). Obviously, these provisions were important improvements, since the principal reason that *In singulis* had proved ineffective was that it had provided neither penalties nor the coercive power to enforce them. Finally, the visitors are told what to do in case the superior of an exempt house needed to be deposed, which was not specified in the Lateran canon: they are to notify the pope immediately (§ 8), as Johannes Teutonicus had suggested.

What concerned the bishops at Bourges was Honorius' attempt to force them to act on the visitors' recommendations. In the copy of *Sapientia* that he sent to the Reims Benedictines, he hardly touches on the deposition of nonexempt superiors: "in other cases," he declared, the visitors "are to proceed in the manner prescribed by the aforesaid [Lateran] council" (Doc. 46.8). The procedure provided by *In singulis* is simply that the visitors should notify the bishop who has ordinary jurisdiction over the house, "so he can attend to the matter himself; if he does not, then the visitors are to refer the case to the apostolic see for review" (Doc. 45.8). But Honorius was now determined to force the bishops into compliance; accordingly, he addressed a second version of *Sapientia* to the archbishop of Reims and his suffragans, which concluded with a distinct threat (Doc. 46.9b):

> Wherefore we command all of you by apostolic writ, enjoining that you do not delay in removing the heads of monasteries whom the aforesaid visitors shall have informed any one of you are to be removed from their places in your diocese, since the obstacle of any kind of contradiction of appeal has been removed.[38] *Otherwise you have good reason to dread that less jurisdiction over them may be relinquished to you than you have had up to now and still have.*

In other words, a bishop might lose some or all of his rights of canonical visitation if he refused to depose a superior denounced to him by the chapter visitors. Honorius was no doubt relying on his *plenitudo potestatis*, the plenitude of power that enabled him to override any canon of human origin, but to do so

---

38. The phrase "sublato cujuslibet contradictionis et appellationis obstaculo" is that used concerning members who contumaciously absent themselves from a general chapter (Doc. 46.4; cf. 7, "appellatione postposita"); *In singulis* specified that decisions of a general chapter were not subject to these impediments (Doc. 45.5).

in this case would be, in the phrase quoted by Johannes Teutonicus, "a confounding of ecclesiastical order" (at note 26, above), for the pope would be unilaterally altering a bishop's traditional canonical authority. This, I believe, was what the bishops at Bourges were protesting.

Cum ex officio vestro

When the Council of Bourges met on 30 November 1225, nearly eleven months after the threat of *Sapientia* was issued, the bishops were certainly not yet in compliance with its demands, for on 3 November Honorius renewed his warning in harsher terms (Doc. 47). Evidently the complaints had multiplied, for the bishops now were ordered to "in no way oppose those who wish to celebrate a chapter and to correct delinquents" (§ 3) as well as to "see to the removal of the abbots subject to your control whom the chapter or visitors instructed you to remove" (§ 4). Most important, the threat was repeated, this time in no uncertain terms: *"you should fear lest we concede to the general chapter and visitors the jurisdiction that you have over the abbots subject to you"* (§ 5).

If this were the letter that Romanus told the council about, its strong and unveiled threat would doubtless have justified the bishops' outraged reaction. But while it is just possible that a fast courier could have carried the letter from Rieti, where the curia was, to Bourges in just twenty-eight days, still we cannot be sure that this happened. It is also possible that Romanus had advance notice of the impending action and made his announcement on the basis of inside information. But *Sapientia* itself, with its distinct though veiled threat, would have been enough to provoke the bishops, and Romanus may simply have taken the occasion to apprise all the bishops in his legation of the new hard line that Honorius was taking.

Either way, there are other signs that *Sapientia* had disturbed the French episcopate. The bishop of Arras, who was a suffragan of Reims, seems to have been worried that he might lose his right of canonical visitation, perhaps because some of his fellow bishops had misused theirs, and accordingly he asked Honorius to take the extraordinary step of confirming in writing that the bishop of Arras could indeed visit and correct the nonexempt regular houses subject to him; his request was granted in August 1225.[39] A few months later, in November, the pope issued a similar declaration to the bishop of Troyes, a suffragan of Sens, because the Benedictines and canons regular of his diocese "considered your jurisdiction to be diminished" by *In singulis* "and consequently they boldly

---

39. *Quoniam amplius consuevit* (9 Aug. 1225), Pressutti, no. 5590, ed. Horoy, IV, 909.

acted towards you contrary to custom." Honorius reassured the bishop "that no prejudice to your right is generated by that statute."[40]

By September 1225, Honorius realized that more specific guidelines were needed to coordinate relations between the bishops on the one hand and the chapter presidents and visitors on the other. The pope accordingly issued a decretal, *Ea que pro religionis*, which eventually found its place in the *Decretals of Gregory IX* just after *In singulis*, which it supplemented.[41] Although the bull was issued on 13 September, well before the Council of Bourges, it is by no means clear that it was known in France less than three months later, since the recipients were Italian, namely "the abbots and monks in Lombardy and the march of Treviso." At any rate, it did not occasion the uproar at Bourges, which was caused by letters sent to French bishops (Doc. 3.5); nor was it apt to do so: although, following *In singulis*, it provided that negligent bishops be reported to the pope, still it neither threatened them with loss of jurisdiction nor hinted at any other sanctions.

What happened at Bourges

We are now in a position to interpret the brief report of the Chronicle of Tours, which was quoted at the beginning of this chapter (Doc. 3.5). The chronicler is manifestly confused in supposing that there were "four abbots whom he [the pope] had designated to visit all of the abbeys in France and to correct their excesses." Although the canon *In singulis regnis sive provinciis* did offer the option of a chapter-general for a whole kingdom, as its *incipit* reminds us, the regnal alternative was never contemplated, much less mandated, for France, where the general chapters were organized by ecclesiastical province. Evidently our chronicler, who most likely attended the council as a proctor, had imperfectly grasped the details of the matter. While it is possible that the proctors withdrew from the session after *Super muros* had been discussed because the other business did not concern them, this seems unlikely, because all Romanus planned to do was make an announcement that, though controversial, was not confidential. Therefore, I suppose that when the proctors had had their say, they returned to their place behind perhaps as many as eight hundred other participants, where it would have

40. *Tua nobis fraternitas* (28 Nov. 1225), Pressutti, no. 5735, ed. Horoy, IV, 957-958. Bishop Robert of Troyes, probably a canonist himself (cf. Pressutti, nos. 2000 and 5787), was often commissioned by Honorius to deal with monastic problems (Pressutti, nos. 4247, 4675, 5474, 5738). The circumstances cited by Honorius indicate that chapters-general had been organized in Sens province, although they are otherwise unrecorded (and unlisted by Berlière). Cf. Maccarrone, "Costituzioni," p. 36.

41. *Ea que pro religionis* (13 Sept. 1225), Pressutti, no. 5643, ed. Friedberg, II, 601-602 (X 3.35.8); Potthast no. 7817 (no date). It is known only from the Vatican register and canonistic collections.

been difficult to hear what the legate was saying. And because our canon of Tours was not affected by *In singulis*, he probably lacked the background that would have enabled him to make sense of what he could hear; moreover, being uninterested, he was perhaps inattentive as well. Furthermore, to the uninformed it might have seemed that all of France was involved, since protests could have come not just from the bishops of Reims province but also from those of Tours and Sens, which certainly had Benedictine general chapters, and possibly from those of Bourges and Rouen as well.[42]

The chronicler's unfamiliarity with *In singulis* is also evident in his confusion of the "four abbots" with the visitors. The Lateran canon, of course, never specified a given number of visitors, leaving each chapter free to appoint as many as were necessary. The Reims chapter of 1220, as we have seen, set the number of visitors at six (at note 34, above). The chronicler's "four abbots" are surely the four presidents that *In singulis* prescribed for the initial, organizational meeting of each chapter; thereafter the number was reduced to two, the services of the Cistercians being no longer required, unless a second startup chapter was deemed necessary, as in *Sapientia*.

Despite these misapprehensions, the chronicling canon of Tours can hardly have been mistaken about the general character of the proceedings. He reports that, after dealing with *Super muros*, Romanus "added (*adiecit*)" that the pope had ordered two bishops to depose abbots who had been denounced to them by chapter visitors. This sounds like an announcement rather than a reading of one or more papal letters. The substance of the announcement, when purged of its misunderstandings, is precisely what Honorius had mandated in *Sapientia* and again in *Cum ex officio vestro* (Docs. 46.8 and 47.4), with a threatened loss of jurisdiction in both cases. Since the latter bull was Honorius' latest pronouncement on the matter—so recent that it may not have been known in France at the time the council met—we can be sure that the pope had not carried out his threats; he was still making them. Hence Romanus' announcement must have been based on *Sapientia* and perhaps its follow-up. What then are we to make of the "two bishops" who are said to have received these letters, which were addressed to the archbishop of Reims and his suffragans? Most likely they were the principal offenders whose intransigence occasioned the warning letters, one of whom may have been the bishop of Cambrai (see at note 35, above). Since Honorius would surely have informed Romanus of the complaints he had received, it was probably on the basis of some such private communication that Romanus could tell the council that the behavior of two bishops was the cause of the pope's letters to Reims.

42. Berlière, *Revue bénédictine*, XIX (1902), 393 (Tours), 376 (Bourges), and 393 (Rouen). On Sens, see n. 40, above.

The purpose of Romanus' announcement must have been to let all the bishops of his legation know to what lengths Honorius was prepared to go to enforce *In singulis*. Although the chronicle states that the "apostolic precepts, both about prebends [*Super muros*] and about the deposition of abbots [*Sapientia*], remained pending" (Doc. 3.5), it seems unlikely that the bishops were being asked to consent to the latter one; they were simply being informed. Still the outcome remained to be seen, for Honorius had yet to carry out his threats, and the outraged reaction of the bishops, which Romanus surely reported, conveyed a message that Rome could not wisely ignore. In fact, the threats were never carried out.

Consequences

Moreover, Honorius had second thoughts about the bull *Sapientia*, which had appeared in the first recension of his decretal collection, the *Compilatio quinta*, complete with the offensive threat to diminish the jurisdiction of noncompliant bishops.[43] By May 1226, however, *Sapientia* had been deleted from the definitive version of Honorius' compilation that was transmitted to Bologna.[44] Indeed, the whole attempt to reform the Benedictines in the province of Reims seems to have been put on some shelf in the curia for the next ten years. In 1235, Pope Gregory IX started all over again in the bull *In medio ecclesie*, which, in terms reminiscent of *Sapientia*, recommenced the process of organizing a general chapter for Reims, again under the guidance of two Cistercian abbots, because the Black Monks had not complied with "our oft-repeated mandate," so that "all the results were useless."[45] Like Honorius, Gregory mandated annual meetings, and moreover he demanded that the next chapter send him a writ-

43. The portion of *Sapientia* that was included in the *Compilatio quinta* is printed by L. E. Boyle, "The Compilatio quinta and the Registers of Honorius III," *Bulletin of Medieval Canon Law*, n.s., VIII (1978), 9–19, at pp. 15–16.

44. For details, see Doc. 46.pr. I assume, with Stephan Kuttner, that the *Compilatio quinta* was officially promulgated on 2 May 1226, the date of the colophon in a London manuscript: *Repertorium der Kanonistik (1140–1234)* (Vatican City, 1937), p. 382, n. 2. The first recension, which included *Sapientia*, apparently represents the state of the work in January 1226, when Tancred, the compiler, left Rome to become archdeacon of Bologna, just at the time that news of the bishops' reaction at Bourges would have reached Rome. Evidently Tancred's work was reviewed and revised before it was officially sent to Bologna in May. Cf. Boyle, "Compilatio quinta," pp. 9–10.

45. *In medio ecclesie* (4 May 1235), ed. Auvray, no. 2548 (III, 51–53): "isti [monachi] non sciderunt hactenus corda sua, nec mandatum nostrum, sepius repetitum, a viis suis pessimis recesserunt, sed, prevaricationes prevaricationibus apponentes, omnes, tam prelati quam subditi, a disciplinis regularibus declinarunt, omnesque inutiles sunt effecti, et vix invenitur in eis qui bonum faciat . . . " (col. 52). Schmitz, *Histoire*, III, 55–59.

ten report. Finally, he provided his own set of statutes to be observed by all Benedictines, which among other things specified that the visitors appointed by the chapter should make annual inspections and report back to the chapter.[46]

The bishops' protest at Bourges therefore seems to have been effective in persuading Honorius and his successor that it would be imprudent to transfer the episcopal right of canonical visitation to the general chapter or its visitors. This lack of coercive power doubtless contributed to the ineffectiveness of *In singulis*, but it was only one of many factors. Gregory certainly put the blame on the Benedictines themselves, because many houses were unwilling to alter their established, comfortable customs, and they resisted the attempt to curtail the long-standing autonomy of their abbeys. Even in England, where Benedictine general chapters met quite regularly, the system instituted by *In singulis* seems to have borne little fruit;[47] on the Continent, it is doubtful that the system was ever implemented everywhere and certain that it had still less effect.[48] In 1336, Pope Benedict XII attempted to overhaul the chapter system by dividing Christendom into thirty-six Benedictine provinces—Reims and Sens together constituted one—but again the Black Monks resisted a reform imposed from above.[49] Only in the fifteenth century did the Benedictines themselves take the initiative to reorganize the order into congregations, which was made the norm by the Council of Trent and remains the principle of Benedictine organization today.[50] Those who remember Innocent III as an innovative reformer are apt to forget the comparative failure of *In singulis*,[51] but he deserves credit nonetheless for a good idea that was several centuries before its time.

In the meantime, bishops were prompted to use their right of canonical visitation rather than lose it. *In singulis* had indeed instructed them to forestall the capitular visitations with episcopal ones (Doc. 45.11), and the latter often proved to be more strict and formidable than the former.[52] The visitations of Arch-

46. *Statuta ordinis nigri*, ed. Auvray, no. 3045 (II, 319-332); cf. Auvray, no. 2549. *The Register of Eudes of Rouen*, trans. S. M. Brown (New York, 1964), pp. 737-746. Statute 52, concerning visitors, appears virtually unaltered in both recensions of Gregory's statutes (ed. cit., col. 331).

47. M. Gibbs and J. Lang, *Bishops and Reform, 1215–1272* (Oxford, 1934), p. 153; Sayers, "Judicial Activities," p. 31. Maccarrone, however, stresses the positive, benign effects of the system: "Costituzioni," p. 36.

48. Given the sparse documentation, "il y a beaucoup de chances que le décret 'In singulis regnis' ait été en général mal observé": Hourlier, *Chapitre général*, p. 91.

49. Schmitz, *Histoire*, III, 66-72.

50. V. Dammertz, *Der Verfassungsrecht der benediktinischen Mönchskongregationen in Geschichte und Gegenwart* (St Ottilien, 1963), pp. 46-85.

51. E.g. *In singulis* is ignored by J. Sayers, *Innocent III* (London, 1994); H. Tillmann describes it in half a paragraph: *Papst Innocenz III*. (Bonn, 1954), p. 157.

52. *Chapters of the Augustinian Canons*, ed. H. E. Salter (Oxford, 1922), p. xliii.

bishop Odo Rigaldus of Rouen (1248-1269) are the best known because the most completely recorded,[53] but traces of many more have been collected by Christopher Cheney,[54] and their efficacy is attested by the considerable number of abbots and priors whom bishops deposed or forced to resign.[55]

Finally, if the bishops' outrage at Bourges was, as I have argued, in reaction to a threatened exercise of the papal plenitude of power, then the incident reflects the tension between Innocent III's new style of papal government and the older tradition based on Gratian's *Decretum*.[56] As such, the episode is of special interest because it not only shows the episcopate's unwillingness to accept any unilateral abridgement of its canonical rights but also reveals the papacy's prudence in not pursuing a controversial and unpopular solution. Though not a major landmark in the constitutional history of the Church, the bishops' resistance to Honorius' threats was nonetheless a decisive skirmish, won by the entrenched episcopacy.

THE REPENTANT MASTERS OF PARIS

The Chronicle of Tours concludes its account of the Council of Bourges with a brief note, as a follow-up to an episode it had reported earlier the same year (Doc. 3.6):

> Then about eighty masters of Paris who had participated in the assault against the legate mentioned above and who found themselves bound by the legate's sentence, in this council begged absolution from the legate, and their petition was immediately granted.

The assault on the legate was a famous incident, which three chronicles describe in long, breathless sentences and colorful detail (Docs. 2.1, 3.3, and 4.1-2), but some background is required to appreciate these accounts. The pope had assigned Romanus to judge a long-standing dispute between the university and the bishop of Paris, which among other things concerned the university's right to have its own seal. The long struggle of the Paris masters to establish themselves as a legal corporation independent of the authority of the local bishop and

53. *Regestrum visitationum archiepiscopi Rothomagensis*, ed. T. Bonnin (Rouen, 1852); *The Register of Eudes of Rouen*, trans. S. M. Brown (New York, 1964).

54. C. R. Cheney, *Episcopal Visitation of Monasteries in the Thirteenth Century*, 2nd ed. (Manchester, 1983).

55. From thirteenth-century English episcopal registers, Gibbs and Lang compiled a list ("by no means exhaustive") of twenty-one depositions and four resignations: *Bishops and Reform*, p. 151. For France, see Berlière, "Honorius III," pp. 259-260.

56. R. Kay, *Dante's Swift and Strong* (Lawrence, Kans., 1978), pp. 117-118, 124-141.

his chancellor is a story that has often been told,[57] from which we need to extract only the details concerning the episode of the seal. By 1215 the papacy had recognized that the masters of Paris constituted a corporation that could regulate its internal affairs.[58] In 1221, however, the bishop of Paris complained to the pope that the new *universitas magistrorum et scolarium* had exceeded the limits set by the statutes of 1215 and was usurping jurisdiction over its external affairs from the bishop; he particularly cited the recent fabrication of a seal, which would enable the *universitas* to make contracts and to delegate powers of attorney to its proctors.[59] Honorius III obliged the bishop by appointing three judges-delegate, including Stephen Langton, to break the new seal and to settle the dispute,[60] but they accomplished nothing, so the matter was returned to the curia. While the case was pending, Honorius authorized the use of the seal to authenticate the credentials of the university's proctors in the lawsuit.[61] Eventually the case was referred to Romanus, who effected a permanent compromise on most points at issue[62] but had the seal broken. The legal consequences of having no seal were not as great as the disappointed rioters had imagined, for as Gaines Post has shown, the university was able to function as a corporation for the next twenty years by using someone else's seal when necessary.[63] This was an awkward, makeshift solution, however, and in 1246 the Paris masters successfully petitioned Innocent IV to grant the university a seal of its own.[64]

Against this background, the assault itself may be conveniently summarized, though the three chroniclers' accounts deserve to be read *in extenso* for their immediacy and flavor (Docs. 2.1, 3.3, and 4.1-2). According to the Chronicle of Tours, the legate made up his mind altogether too quickly, without due deliberation, and having determined that the university had no right to possess its own seal, he had it broken on the spot (Doc. 3.3).[65] The disappointed litigants hurled

---

57. For a convenient summary, see G. Leff, *Paris and Oxford Universities in the Thirteenth and Fourteenth Centuries* (New York, 1968), pp. 23-34.

58. G. Post, "Parisian Masters as a Corporation, 1200-1246," *Speculum*, IX (1934), pp. 421-445; reprinted in his *Studies in Medieval Legal Thought* (Princeton, 1964), pp. 27-60, to which my citations refer: pp. 37, 60.

59. Denifle-Châtelain, I, 102 (no. 45; cf. no. 41); Post, *Studies*, pp. 49, 56, 58.

60. *Venerabilis frater* (2 April 1221), Pressutti, no. 3222, ed. Denifle-Châtelain, I, 98-99 (no. 41).

61. *Inimico homine* (31 May 1222), Pressutti, no. 4012, ed. Denifle-Châtelain, I, 102-104 (no. 45); Post, *Studies*, pp. 49-50.

62. Denifle-Châtelain, I, 113-114 (no. 58); Post, *Studies*, p. 50, n. 130.

63. Post, *Studies*, pp. 53-57.

64. Post, *Studies*, p. 57; Denifle-Châtelain, I, 194-195 (no. 165); P. Kibre, *Scholarly Privileges in the Middle Ages* (Cambridge, Mass., 1962), p. 99, and see also p. 91.

65. The Chronicle of Tours says that Romanus broke the seal himself (Doc. 3.3), but the Dunstable annalist reports with greater likelihood that he simply had it broken (Doc. 2.1).

insults at the legate, and when his servants tried to clear the court, they were attacked and wounded. The legate fled to the bishop's palace for safety, but an armed crowd of masters and students broke down the main gate, and while they were trying to force the doors to the chapel and the great hall, Romanus retreated to the last available refuge, in the tower. He was opportunely rescued by the king's men, who arrested a hundred and forty *scolares* and put them in chains and in prison. The legate himself promptly left town, but not before imposing harsh penalties on his attackers: not only were they and those who supported them excommunicated, but he also promulgated a sentence against the supporters to this effect (Doc. 2.1):

> that guilty masters were never to lecture again, either there [in Paris] or anywhere else; that those among the guilty who held benefices were to lose the ones they held as well as any hope of holding others in the future; and that those who were in holy orders were forever suspended from exercising their functions. And on some who transgressed more seriously, he imposed heavier punishments.

Given the legal expertise informing the Dunstable Annals, this report is most likely accurate. Presumably the stringent penalties just described were directed against the eighty masters who had supported the rioters but were not themselves among the hundred and forty students apprehended within the bishop's palace compound. What happened to the students is unknown, but the masters were evidently forgiven.

The Dunstable account of the penalties contains no suggestion that they could ever be commuted, but from the Chronicle of Tours we discover that the masters were forgiven. Probably that possibility would have been evident from Romanus' sentence, but the full text has not survived. We do have the next best thing, however, for on 20 November 1225 Honorius published a decree that appears to have been inspired by the assault on Romanus, his cardinal-legate.[66] Those who are in any way involved in an assault on a cardinal, or even defend it after the fact, are guilty of sacrilege and *lèse-majesté*; they become infamous and outlaws with no recourse to the courts; they lose the right to make or benefit from wills; they and their descendants cannot hold ecclesiastical offices; they are deprived of all fiefs, benefices, and offices; their goods are confiscated, their buildings destroyed, and their creditors released. But there is an alternative to these devastating disabilities—they may be "absolved sufficiently and suitably."[67]

66. *Summa providentia principis* (20 Nov. 1225), Pressutti, no. 5726, ed. Horoy, IV, 950 (no. 55). Although not included with Honorius' decretals in the *Compilatio quinta* or the *Liber extra*, it does appear in the *Bullarium magnum Romanum*, 26 vols. (Turin, 1857-1885), III, 410 (no. 76).

67. Pressutti's summary (no. 5726): "cum autem fuerint absolvendi primo sufficienter et idonee caveant quod inferendae poenae parebunt."

Accordingly, it seems most likely that Romanus' sanctions were subject to a similar opportunity for absolution.

But how was he induced to grant absolution? No doubt he had acted rashly, as he often did, and perhaps he simply thought better of his decree when his temper had cooled, but surely the penalized masters also had powerful intercessors who urged him to be merciful. Although the Chronicle of Tours, by inserting its account of the Paris riot between two events in the month of November (Doc. 3.1-3), suggests that the riot also took place in that month, still an earlier date would be indicated if Honorius' decree of 20 November was prompted by the assault on Romanus. If so, the pope would have had time to instruct his legate on how to deal with the offending rioters. No doubt the king of France, traditionally a protector of the university of Paris as the chief adornment of his capital, would also have intervened on behalf of the eighty masters, who must have constituted the greater part of the university's teachers, and whose loss would consequently cripple the institution. For whatever reason, Romanus relented and was content to have the masters humiliated publicly.

Under what terms the masters were reconciled is unknown. What is clear is that Romanus chose to humiliate them in the most public way possible, at the largest clerical assembly France had yet known. Although the chronicler simply states that the reconciliation was the last event of the council (Doc. 3.6), it seems unlikely that it took place in the closed session where *Super muros* and *Sapientia* were discussed, for traditionally the reconciliation of penitents was a public event.[68] Accordingly, Romanus surely made this unprecedented reconciliation part of the final, closing ceremonies that would be open to the general public,[69] so that the masters' humiliation received the greatest possible publicity.

68. *Pontificales*—the collections of liturgical services used by bishops—usually contained special *ordines* for penitents. Romanus most likely used the *Pontificale secundum consuetudinem et usum Romanae curiae* (saec. xiii in.), in which the penitential orders directly follow the one for celebrating a church council: *Le Pontifical romain au Moyen-Age*, II: *Le Pontifical de la curie romaine au XIIIe siècle*, ed. M. Andrieu (Vatican City, 1940), pp. 479-486. It provides an *Ordo ad dandam penitentiam* (cap. 46) in which a penance is imposed (§ 14) before absolution is given (18). Since Doc. 3.6 states that the Paris masters petitioned for "absolutionem," this would seem to have been the appropriate form, though the *Pont. Rom. cur.* also adds a generalized *Ordo ad reconciliandum penitentem* (cap. 47). The *Pontificale Guillielmi Durandi* (1293-1296) provides an order for altering the status of clerics, including "in reconciliatione seu restitutione," which would have been appropriate for the masters; it also specified that "non iniungitur eis sollempnis penitentia sicut laicis": *Le Pontifical romain au Moyen-Age*, III: *Le Pontifical de Guillaume Durand*, ed. M. Andrieu (Vatican City, 1940), pp. 606-607 (III, vii, 18).

69. Although excommunications were often pronounced at the end of ecclesiastical councils, reconciliations were an occasional rather than a regular feature of the closing ceremonies. Two *ordines* for diocesan synods (saec. xi et xii) do provide for them, however: *Die Konzilsordines des Früh- und Hochmittelalters*, MGH, Ordines de celebrando concilio, ed. H. Schneider (Hanover, 1996), pp. 464 and 488. See the preceding note for the close association of councils and reconciliation in *Pont. Rom. cur.*

AFTERWORD

The Foreword to these chapters stressed three reasons for studying the Council of Bourges: as the earliest record of representative government in action; as an extended example of counsel and consent in medieval assemblies; and as an episode in the Second Albigensian Crusade. It would be redundant, and hence tiresome, to recast these anticipatory explanations as conclusions, since these have already been amply provided in the course of this study. Instead, in this Afterword I want to view the council and its associated events as typical of the pontificate of Honorius III.

Historians have usually found it easy to pass lightly over Honorius' decade (1216-1227), coming as it does between two flamboyant and combative popes— Innocent III and Gregory IX—but the age of Honorius is deserving of attention because then, perhaps more than at any other time, the papalist vision of Christian society was realized, for better or for worse. True, the same is often said of the reign of Innocent III (1198-1216), but probably that pontificate would more accurately be characterized as an age of innovation, in which Catholic Christendom was renewed by a sweeping wave of reforms that culminated in the Fourth Lateran Council. When Innocent died within a year of his great council, it was up to his successor to consolidate the gains, to implement the policies, and to perpetuate the vision of the great reformer.

Honorius has often been perceived as an indecisive ruler, but this was in no small measure the result of the position in which he was placed by his predecessor. Although Innocent laid the foundations of the papal monarchy by enunciating doctrines such as the pope's plenitude of power, held in virtue of his position as Christ's vicar on earth, with the related claim to judge all human actions in terms of Christian morality (*ratione peccati*), still, as students of ecclesiology have recognized, the great innovator often formulated these revolutionary doctrines vaguely and hesitated to apply them in practice; instead, he proceeded with a circumspect regard for the rights of his subjects that were already established in canon law. It was a delicate balance that Honorius continued to maintain, with the result that because he was not arbitrary, he often appears indecisive.

Innocent's pattern of governance might have persisted for decades, but in fact a less sensitive balance was soon dictated by a new political crisis. Honorius' successor, Gregory IX (1227-1241), though disposed to continue the Innocentian program of reform, involved the Church in an expensive and desperate struggle with the Hohenstaufen, which provided the "case of necessity" that justified frequent extraordinary measures, such as arbitrary taxation. *Necessitas* then

pressed Innocent IV (1243-1254) even further towards absolutism, which the
great lawyer-pope justified by making explicit the hierocratic tendencies that
were indefinite in his namesake's ecclesiology. Consequently, in retrospect the
reign of Honorius appears as a brief decade during which Innocent III's style of
papal leadership continued to govern the Church.

Viewed from this perspective, the stories that intersected at the Council of
Bourges appear in a distinctive light, as the characteristic product of their age.
This is evident most obviously in Honorius' attempts to implement the Benedictine chapters-general mandated by the Fourth Lateran Council. Relying with
undue optimism on the good will of all concerned, Innocent III had left local
abbots to take the initiative in organizing themselves but had provided the chapters with no authority to compel either participation in their meetings or obedience to their visitors' decisions. Even worse, he glossed over the inevitable conflict
of jurisdiction between bishops and chapters, leaving Honorius to sort it all out.
Theoretically, the papal plenitude of power should have sufficed to set things
right, but in practice neither Honorius nor his successors dared go so far, at least
not in the face of the outraged protest expressed by the bishops at Bourges.
Honorius was obliged to implement the Lateran decree piecemeal because there
was no consensus that the system of monastic general chapters was necessary.

Plenitudo potestatis was his trump card, which could not be wasted rashly; he
could play it effectively only when there was an undeniable, unquestionable need
to override established rights, such as the eradication of heresy. Thus the Albigensian tenth was in the end justified by Romanus' legatine mandate to do whatever seemed prudent to him in order to resolve the Albigensian crisis. What is
more, early on he was well aware that this delegated power was sufficient to
authorize the imposition of a tax no matter what the taxpayers counseled, as is
evident from the precautionary *vidimus* of his letters of legation (Doc. 27).

Nonetheless, it is significant that Romanus did not tip his hand to the chapters, who protested the tax under the impression that they were only liable to
pay taxes to which they had consented. To be sure, canon law required Romanus
to consult the taxpayers, and hence the Council of Bourges was an obligatory
step in the decision-making process. But Romanus did not flaunt his arbitrary
power; instead he structured the proceedings of the council not only to minimize the impact of any opposition but also to elicit the counsels he desired to
hear, thus disposing his subjects to accept the tenth as the necessary means to attain an end that was undeniably good, namely the suppression of heresy. In doing
so, Romanus was a realist who recognized that to be effective, a ruler's arbitrary
act must be acceptable to his subjects.

Legalism was the foundation on which such clerical consent was based—or
rather a particular kind of legalism, which now can only be understood by an

act of historical reconstruction. The renaissance of the twelfth century had fostered the revival of Roman law and the birth of canon law. Consequently, Romanus' generation cherished the vision of a Christian society regulated by law, and it was all too aware that for fifty years canon law had been in a state of flux, being modified by a seemingly endless stream of papal decretals that only began to abate with the publication of the Gregorian decretal collection in 1234. In the meantime, churchmen were optimistic that the new science of jurisprudence could revolutionize public morality, just as theologians of the age were confident that Aristotelian logic could discover hidden truths in Scripture. Hence in the dispute over the Albigensian tenth, both sides by tacit agreement operated within the established but flexible framework of canon law, which each interpreted in its own favor, hoping to secure the desired result by learned and skillful advocacy. Specifically, no one in 1225 was sure to what extent canon law protected the property rights of clerical corporations or how far a pope dared go in overriding them.

The same tensions are evident in Honorius' attempt to reform the finances of the papal curia. Popes had long used their plenitude of power to provide benefices for *curiales*, but this affected only the use of property, not its ownership. The various schemes to cede benefices to the papacy in perpetuity, however, all involved a transfer of ownership, and no pope from Celestine III to Innocent IV was prepared to use his *plenitudo potestatis* to confiscate property without regard for the rights of its lawful owners. Accordingly, neither Honorius nor any other pope attempted to implement the proposal of Emperor Henry VI without securing the owners' consent. And every consultation, from the Fourth Lateran Council to the First Council of Lyon—but most notably at Bourges—elicited responses so strongly negative that nothing was done. Things might have been different if Honorius had been able to argue that the welfare of the Church was threatened by the current system of doing business at the curia; but there was no case of evident, unobjectionable necessity, such as heresy, so in *Super muros* he could only plead for a permanent subsidy on the weaker grounds of convenience and propriety. Thus the pope no less than his subjects was constrained by regard for the law.

The legalistic context was not, however, divorced from social and political reality. The curia realized that however great papal power might be in theory, still it had practical limitations. When Romanus warned his master and colleagues not to alienate whole kingdoms and their kings (Doc. 22), he was speaking as one curialist to another, doubtless voicing a common concern. Similarly, when the proctors at Bourges warned that *Super muros* could lead to schism (Doc. 1.16), they recognized that a law-abiding society was ultimately based on consent of the governed. Innocent III's recent conflicts with the kings of England

and Germany were a constant reminder that the fabric of Christendom was a fragile construct.

Honorius was the executor of Innocent's legacy not only in law but also in diplomacy. However much Innocent had been determined to rule the Papal States directly, beyond the boundaries of the Patrimony he was content to let others rule, although he was remarkably keen to supervise their exercise of temporal power. Notoriously, Innocent multiplied the grounds on which the pope could intervene in the affairs of Christian rulers: most evidently as feudal overlord of England, the Regno, and a few lesser states; more occasionally, as the arbiter of disputed elections in the Holy Roman Empire; and above all as the supreme judge of Christian morality, whenever a ruler's misconduct of government involved sin (*ratione peccati*). Honorius inherited this policy and pursued it with more success, or at least greater acceptance, than either his predecessor or his successors. Whereas Innocent had abused his guardianship of Frederick II, Honorius did all he could to promote the emperor's interests; moreover, he displayed all the virtues of a good feudal lord in preserving the patrimony of the young Henry III, so that the prestige of the papacy as the disinterested arbiter of Christendom never stood higher than in his pontificate.

France presented the greatest challenge to Honorius' good intentions, for over this kingdom his power was in no way temporal, only spiritual. When faced with the political fact of Raymond VII's restoration, Honorius could not control events but nevertheless could influence them by astute diplomacy. During the summer of 1224 Honorius had secured by negotiation everything he required for a peaceful settlement in Languedoc, except for an honorable settlement with Amaury de Montfort, but that was blocked by Louis VIII, who had secretly arranged to acquire Montfort's lordship in the South for himself. Rather than let Louis wage a unilateral, feudal war against Raymond, Honorius decided that another crusade was the lesser of two evils, because in a joint Franco-papal operation Rome would at least be a moderating influence.

Romanus was the pope's instrument in implementing this policy. His first objective was to organize the crusade, and especially to secure a clerical subsidy for the king; as we have seen, he attained this goal with single-minded, unrelenting efficiency. But once the crusade got under way, it proved to be more a demonstration in force than an attempt to overwhelm Raymond, and if Romanus did not actually devise this prudent plan, he at least influenced its course, especially in diverting the crusade to the siege of Avignon, in which he undoubtedly played the leading role. His finest hour, however, came with Louis' untimely death, when Romanus made himself the mainstay of Queen Blanche's regency, providing both counsel and financial support that proved crucial to the survival of the Augustan monarchy. This service surpassed Honorius' previous succor of royal widows and orphans because in this case the papacy's only obligation was a moral one; by this disinterested act of mercy, papal prestige and credibility were raised to new heights.

The immediate consequence, of course, was that in 1229 Romanus had secured the queen's confidence and deserved her gratitude, so he had a free hand to negotiate the Peace of Paris, which was the compromise solution that should have followed the Montpellier accords of 1224. Although Honorius did not live to see the culmination of Romanus' legation, he was surely its architect, and the result embodied his preference for moderate, peaceful solutions. Viewed in this papal perspective, the Second Albigensian Crusade was a necessary evil, a means justified by the end, and the outstanding example of a pope exerting what influence he could muster to direct world affairs on a better course in an imperfect world. Rarely if ever again was the papacy able to guide Christian princes in the manner of Innocent III.

DOCUMENTS

LIST OF DOCUMENTS

Section one: Narrative accounts of the council

Dec. 1225	1	*Relatio de concilio Bituricensi*	270
	2	Annals of Dunstable	290
	3	Chronicle of Tours	294
	4	*Chronique rimée* of Philip Mousket	304
	5	Chronicle of Alberic of Trois-Fontaines	316
	6	Chronicle of MS. Reginensis 171	318

Section two: Franco-papal negotiations preliminary to the crusade

Jan./Feb. 1224	7	Louis petitions Honorius to grant his conditions	326
4 April 1224	8	Honorius urges Louis to reconcile Raymond	332
5 May 1224	9	Memorial of Louis VIII, reviewing and ending negotiations	336
31 Jan. 1225	10	The pope announces Romanus' legation to Raymond	340
[31 Jan.] 1225	11	Prolongation of the truce in Provence	344
		Preparations for Romanus' legation: Docs. 12–21	346
15 Feb. 1225	12	Letter of legation for Romanus to the ecclesiastical authorities	348
13 Feb. 1225	13	Letter of legation for Romanus to the civil authorities	356
[Feb.] 1225	14	Advance notice of the legation to Louis VIII	358
15 Feb. 1225	15	Letter of legation to Louis VIII	360
[12] Feb. 1225	16	Safe-conduct for Romanus to a secular lord	362
12 Feb. 1225	17	Safe-conduct for Romanus to ecclesiastical authorities	362
20 Feb. 1225	18	A Roman church is given to Romanus	364
15 Feb. 1225	19	Various special powers for Romanus	366
13 Feb. 1225	20	Elections of prelates in Provence	368
[13] Feb. 1225	21	The disputed election of a bishop of Carcassonne	370
20 Aug. 1225	22	Romanus' remonstrances on defending Fawkes	370
[29] Jan. 1226	23	The French barons counsel Louis to crusade	376
[30] Jan. 1226	24	Certification of Louis' intention	380
late Jan. 1226	25	Draft version of the Paris promises	382
[30] Jan. 1226	26	The Paris promises to the king	386
31 Jan. 1226	27	*Vidimus* of Romanus' letters of legation	392

Section three: Collection of the tenth for the crusade

5 Feb. 1226	28	The legate's mandate to pay the tenth	400
17 May 1227	29	Romanus authorizes sequestration	406
17 May 1227	30	Romanus prohibits sanctions against the crown	414
5 June 1227	31	Romanus notifies the chapters	416
mid-June 1227	32	The Paris chapter appeals to the pope	418
18 July 1227	33	The pope's injunction to Romanus	430
18 July 1227	34	The pope commissions three prelates as judges	434
[18] July 1227	35	The pope notifies the chapters of his injunction	438
Aug. 1227	36	Two bishops engage to pay the tenth for the Sens chapters	442
Aug.–Nov. 1227	37	William of Andres: How the pope approved the tenth	444
Aug.–Nov. 1227	38	John Longus: How the pope approved the tenth	446
13 Nov. 1227	39	Gregory IX informs the king that the chapters must pay the tenth	452

Section four: Proposals for financing papal government

1196	40	Gerald of Wales on Henry VI's proposal	458
28 Jan. 1225	41	The proposal of Honorius III: *Super muros Jerusalem*	468
1226 & 1229	42	The Salisbury Register	478
1226~1232	43	The annals of Roger Wendover	490
1226	44	The Fenland continuation of the Crowland annal for 1225	510

Section five: Monastic provincial chapters

1215	45	Innocent III establishes monastic chapters-general	520
20 Dec. 1224	46	Honorius III implements a general chapter	526
3 Nov. 1225	47	Honorius III reiterates his order to bishops	532

Section six: Miscellaneous

25 Feb. 1217	48	Honorius III mandates capitular representation	538
[2] June 1223	49	Summons to a legatine council at Sens	544
[1226]	50	Louis VIII asks Romanus to enforce debtors' oaths	550
1226	51	Romanus exempts a priory from legatine procurations	554
[1226]	52	A concubinary priest is sent to Romanus	556
[Sept.] 1227	53	The Rouen chapter recuses Romanus	560

INTRODUCTION TO THE DOCUMENTS

Before the footnote, historians often included whole documents in their narratives. Herodotus, for example, quoted inscriptions, oracles, and prophecies (VIII.20, 22, 77). Monastic chroniclers were particularly given to reproducing documents *in extenso*, and some, like Matthew Paris, adopted the practice of relegating them to an appendix. By the seventeenth century, historians commonly supplemented a narrative history with a section of documentary "proofs" (*preuves*), which often was as long as the preceding narrative; the examples best known today are such great Maurist projects as *Gallia Christiana* and the *Histoire générale de Languedoc*. Since the nineteenth century, however, historians have usually been content to cite earlier collections of printed documents in a more or less economical footnote, with perhaps a few unpublished texts added in a brief appendix. To be sure, some vestige of the older system survives in the French *thèse d'état*, in which the candidate demonstrates competence by producing both a polished exposition and a detailed examination of the sources used; but for the most part modern historical works rest on the documentary base laid down in the golden age of erudition without either examining or discussing it.

For a variety of reasons, the present work returns to the former practice of providing the reader with all the relevant documents. As explained in the Foreword, the purpose of this monograph is to present a complete picture of a single council, as a model for the renovation of the conciliar corpus. Terse footnotes citing the old source collections will not serve most readers, since these works are to be found only in great research libraries, and even there they often cannot be consulted readily, so in the first place it is simply convenient to bring the sources together in a documentary appendix. Rather than just reprinting the old editions, however, in almost every case I have prepared a new edition of the text from the extant manuscripts, a task which, though laborious, has proved worthwhile, since even respected editors such as Martène and Vaissète occasionally misread the text, skipped lines, and in one case even omitted the date. Moreover, by systematically collecting all of the documents relevant to my theme, I have discovered not a few hitherto unpublished ones, the first edition of which requires no apology.

Unlike the Maurists, who barely indicated the source of their documents, I have provided all but the most self-evident ones with prolegomena that seek to place the document in context, so the reader will be in a position to evaluate the source without recourse to reference works and specialist literature. These prolegomena also provide the opportunity to discuss technical problems of dating, provenance, authorship, and the like, both more extensively and systematically than would be desirable in a footnote. Finally, by resolutely exploring even the most commonplace sources, such as Gerald of Wales and Walter of Coventry, I have been led to make new discoveries that enhance their value as witnesses.

Finally, I have provided English translations of my documents, in order to make these documents accessible to a wider readership. Since any translation is necessarily an interpretation, mine will be useful even to seasoned scholars as an indication of my understanding of the text. The translations are intended, above all else, to convey the sense of the original to a modern reader, while retaining technical and historical terms. Consequently, when necessary I have not hesitated to break up long Latin sentences into shorter English ones, to rephrase nontechnical expressions, or even occasionally to paraphrase obscure passages. Nonetheless, for the most part the translations do follow the Latin closely, departing from it only in the interest of clarity.

★　★　★

The following remarks will elucidate the bibliographical indications that accompany each document. In addition to these standard rubrics, many documents are introduced by further comments that should be self explanatory.

Manuscripts. Under this rubric are listed all the medieval manuscript witnesses to the text, usually in declining order of authority. An alphabetic siglum (A, B, C . . .) is assigned to each, by which the manuscript is designated in the critical apparatus. The present location of each manuscript text is given in full— repository, shelfmark, and folios—and sometimes alternative designations are provided as well, such as former locations (for example *olim* Colbert MS. 2669) or nicknames (for instance Delisle's "Register F"). The paleographic date is regularly given in this form: saec. xiii 1/4 = first quarter of the thirteenth century.

References to printed catalogues of manuscript collections are generally not given, as these can be readily ascertained from P. O. Kristeller, *Latin Manuscript Books Before 1600: A List of the Printed Catalogues and Unpublished Inventories of Extant Collections*, 4th ed. by S. Kramer, MGH Hilfsmittel no. 13 (Munich, 1993).

Post-medieval manuscript copies are cited selectively. Before the Vatican Archives were opened in 1881, several copies of the papal registers for our period were made: today one is in the Biblioteca Vallicelliana (Rome) and another, made for La Porte du Theil, is in the Bibliothèque nationale de France (Paris) as part of the Collection Moreau. Because these copies have no independent value, they have usually not been cited in the list of manuscripts; reference is occasionally made to them, however, to explain how errors crept into the *textus receptus*. Selective reference is likewise made to the transcripts in the Collection Baluze, also in the Bibliothèque nationale de France.

Editions. In this category are listed all the printed editions known to me, arranged by date of publication and numbered with arabic numerals (1, 2, 3 . . .). Whenever possible, I also indicate the manuscript source(s) on which a given edition was based. For the full titles of source collections cited, see the List of Abbreviations (pp. xv–xviii, above), which usually employs the forms recommended by the *Repertorium fontium historiae Medii Aevi.*

References. Works that mention the document or provide its context are cited here in full, in alphabetical order. When these references are specific to a given document, *they are not repeated in the general Bibliography.* Moreover, coverage is selective, not exhaustive. Under this rubric will be found the full citation for works that are cited in abbreviated form in the introduction to the document.

Text. Here I identify the manuscript on which the edition is based and indicate which other ones have been collated. I also note the extent of my acquaintance with these manuscripts; usually the transcript has been made from a photocopy and, when possible, verified by collation with the original.

Editorial Principles

Since the acts of church councils form part of canon law, I have been guided in my edition by the principles laid down by Stephan Kuttner: "Notes on the Presentation of Text and Apparatus in Editing Works of the Decretists and Decretalists," *Traditio*, XV (1959), 452-464. The details need not be reiterated here, but the reader should be aware of the conventions governing the use of critical signs in the text:

<pointed brackets> enclose words not in any manuscript; the editor has supplied them as an emendation to the text.

[square brackets] enclose words (a) that occur in the base manuscript but should be suppressed, or (b) that are supplied from another manuscript: the *apparatus criticus* indicates which is the case. Either way, square brackets are used when the editor wishes to bring important differences to the reader's attention; minor alterations of both kinds are noted only in the *apparatus criticus.*

(parentheses) enclose remarks provided by the editor that are not and never were part of the text. Accordingly they are used to insert cross-references, supply dates and place names, and expand personal names.

In several small ways I have departed from Kuttner's precepts. The most evident is in my preference for distinguishing *v* and *j* from *u* and *i* respectively. To be sure, editing is easier when consonantal forms are represented by *u* and *i*, but reading the resultant text is more difficult, so for the reader's convenience I have opted for the less esoteric convention. In the orthography of proper names, I reproduce the form found in the base manuscript, including the truncated forms of place names—except when the sense of the passage depends on case endings, as in Doc. 1.2. Also, as a matter of convenience, I have supplied section numbers (in **bold face** type), both to facilitate comparison of texts and to simplify documentation. Like Kuttner, for proper names I follow the spelling of the base manuscript; unlike Kuttner, however, I capitalize all proper names and expand personal ones, though not those of places. Finally, Kuttner's preferred system of keying notes to the text by line numbers is ill suited to word processors and has, moreover, no great advantage when only a few notes are required; therefore, I have adopted the less elegant system of keying the *apparatus criticus* by literals (a, b, c . . .) and the *apparatus fontium* by numerals (1, 2, 3 . . .).

The principles above apply to texts that I myself have edited. When I reprint a published text, as in Docs. 4-6 and 38-39, I have respected the orthography and punctuation of the edition, as I would in quoting any printed text, but I do translate the editor's critical signs and conventions into my own system.

SECTION ONE

NARRATIVE ACCOUNTS OF THE COUNCIL

Document I
RELATIO DE CONCILIO BITURICENSI

The historian always hopes to find new evidence, and even well-worked fields do not disappoint him. Often the advance is made by turning from chronicles, letters, and legal documents to new kinds of sources. The account books of government and business, the service books of the Church, the armorials and genealogies of heraldry, scholastic learning in all its forms, and inscriptions on coins, seals, and monuments all supply new types of written evidence. Moreover, the work of art historians, numismatists, archeologists, and topographers provides the historian with the mute testimony of material objects. Nonetheless, chronicles and documents remain the core around which the historian weaves these new strands, and this core itself is never complete. The editions of known sources are improved and, better yet, new sources are discovered. Many remain in archives and manuscript collections, while others have been published in obscure or rare works. Paradoxically, new documents can also turn up in the most obvious places. The present one has been recovered from the pages of the best-known chronicles of its age, where it has gone unrecognized for centuries. Although this case is probably exceptional, the process of reconstruction has an interest of its own as yet another means of discovering and improving our medieval documentation.

★　★　★

The most detailed and reliable source for the history of the Council of Bourges is a lengthy eyewitness account that survives in three independent versions, all of English provenance.[1] One version has been familiar to scholars since the sixteenth century, the other two were first printed in the nineteenth. The account was long thought to be the work of an English chronicler, either Matthew Paris or Roger Wendover, who was suspected of inventing much of the detail, but this charge was dispelled by Professor Lunt, who argued that all three versions are derived from a French original, the *Relatio de concilio Bituricensi,* which is no longer extant.[2] The text presented below attempts to reconstruct the lost French original from the three extant English versions. In this prolegomenon I shall jus-

---

1. A preliminary version of Doc. 1 was published as R. Kay, "An Eyewitness Account of the 1225 Council of Bourges," *Studia Gratiana,* XII (1967), 61-80. The edition presented there was based on a collation of *printed* texts, whereas the one below is based on the *manuscripts,* which are discussed in detail in the prolegomena to Docs. 42-44.

2. W. E. Lunt, *Financial Relations of the Papacy with England to 1327* (Cambridge, Mass., 1939), p. 186. The title is mine, the words Wendover's: Doc. 1.1 W: "sicut sequens relatio declarabit."

tify my reconstruction of the *Relatio* and establish its authority as the principal source for the Council of Bourges.

Until 1842 the *Relatio* was available to scholars only in the version included by the famous historian Matthew Paris in his *Chronica majora,* an annalistic history of the world from the Creation to 1259, the year of Matthew's death.[3] The *Relatio* is inserted in the annal for 1226 between the accounts of two English councils held in that year (Doc. 43) in response to the bull *Super muros* (Doc. 41). It gives a brief summary of Raymond VII's trial at Bourges (Doc. 1.2-5), followed by a lengthy résumé of the discussion of *Super muros,* in which the proctors of cathedral chapters played the leading role (Doc. 1.6-17).

This annal for 1226 was not, however, originally compiled by Matthew Paris. Like most of the *Chronica majora* prior to 1236, it was the work of Roger Wendover, Matthew's predecessor as historiographer at St Albans monastery. Wendover had himself compiled a chronicle, the *Flores historiarum,*[4] which Paris revised and incorporated into his own. The portion of the annal for 1226 with which we are concerned was taken over virtually unchanged, as is shown by a comparison of the *Chronica majora* with the surviving copies of the *Flores.* Although there is some dispute over the authorship of the earlier portions of the *Flores,* there is no doubt that Wendover himself wrote at least the last twenty annals (1215-1234), including that for 1226.[5] Because he died in 1236, we can be sure that he copied the *Relatio* into the *Flores* within ten years of the events it records.

Historians who knew the *Relatio* only in the Wendover-Paris version did not realize that it was an authentic document inserted into a chronicle. Rather it was thought to be an untrustworthy account composed by a distant and prejudiced chronicler. In the eighteenth century, the Italian conciliar collector G. D. Mansi took Paris to be the author. Noting an apparent conflict between the account

---

3. *Matthaei Parisiensis, monachi Sancti Albani Chronica majora,* ed. H. R. Luard, Rolls Series, no. 57, 7 vols. (London, 1872-1883); *Relatio* in III (1876), 105-109. The *Chronica majora* was edited by Matthew Parker in 1571 and again by William Wats in 1640. The latter was the source for the conciliar collectors: Labbe-Cossart, XI (1671), 292-294; reprinted *inter alia* by Mansi, XXII (1778), 1215-1218. On the chronicler and his work, see Doc. 43.pr., below.

4. First ed. by H. O. Coxe, *Rogeri de Wendover Chronica, sive Flores historiarum,* English Historical Society, 4 vols. (London, 1841-1842) and *Appendix* (1844); *Relatio* in IV (1842), 118-123. Luard's edition of the *Chronica majora* distinguishes Wendover's text from Paris' additions by printing it in smaller type, but not reliably: see R. Vaughan, *Matthew Paris* (Cambridge, Eng., 1958), p. 31. Second ed. by H. G. Hewlett, *Rogeri de Wendover liber qui dicitur Flores historiarum,* Rolls Series, no. 84, 3 vols. (London, 1886-1889); *Relatio* in II (1887), 299-304. On the complete unreliability of both Coxe and Hewlett's editions, see the review by W. H. Stevenson, *English Historical Review,* X (1888), 355-360. For further details, see Doc. 43, below.

5. Vaughan, *Matthew Paris,* pp. 22-28.

of the *Relatio* and certain documents, he immediately concluded that Paris was a malicious liar. Evidently Mansi did not attempt to reconcile the discrepancy because he believed that any document is more reliable than the account of a chronicler, and he assumed that the *Relatio* was merely the latter.[6] At the end of the nineteenth century, a far better historian than Mansi was hardly less skeptical. Petit-Dutaillis knew that Wendover was responsible for the 1226 annal, but he characterized the *Relatio's* account of the trial of Raymond VII as "témoignage douteux." He was especially suspicious that the appeal to judgment by the twelve peers for France (Doc. 1.4) was Wendover's invention.[7] The failure to recognize the documentary nature of the *Relatio* as it stands in Wendover's version is somewhat understandable, because it is a unique document for its period. Conciliar proceedings were conducted under the seal of secrecy and normally no record of the discussion was kept. Since historians knew no comparable documents and had every reason to think them nonexistent, they concluded that this exception was the rhetorical fabrication of an English chronicler.

With the discovery of a second version of the *Relatio,* yet another English chronicler was suggested as its author. This version occurs in the *Memoriale* of Walter of Coventry, a chronicle that was compiled about 1293 or slightly thereafter.[8] Coventry's version of the *Relatio* (C) also survives in two earlier manuscripts, A and M; all three of them are derived from a common ancestor, Beta (see Doc. 44). The unknown author of the Beta annal for 1225 apparently completed his work before the Council of London met in May 1226, because an account of it was added in C and M, whereas A had a different continuation. Stubbs collated all three manuscripts in his edition of the *Memoriale,* though he had a less complex view of their interrelationship, for he believed that C and M were simply derived from A (College of Arms, MS. Arundel 10), which is commonly called "the Barnwell Chronicle." The Barnwell book certainly is the oldest of the three, having been written about 1232, which makes it contemporary with Wendover.

Stubbs was aware that Barnwell's account of Bourges closely resembled Wendover's, but the similarity only suggested to him that one chronicler had copied from the other. He did not consider the possibility that both were independent versions of a lost original. "In the details of the last year [1225]," he wrote of the *Memoriale,* "it has some sentences in common with Matthew Paris and Roger of Wendover. These, I am inclined on examination to think, are more probably drawn by those writers from this work than *vice versâ.*" His comparison was

6. In Baronio-Theiner, XX, 502, ad an. 1225, no. 34, n. 1.

7. Petit-Dutaillis, *Louis,* pp. 290, 350.

8. *Memoriale fratris Walteri de Coventria,* ed. W. Stubbs, Rolls Series, no. 58, 2 vols. (London, 1872–1873), I, xxii; *Relatio* in II, 276–279.

specifically based on the *Relatio,* for he stated that "the similarity comes out most strongly in the account of the mission of the legate Otho in 1225," in which the *Relatio* is included.[9]

Stubbs' attribution of the account to the Barnwell anonymous, although long current because enshrined in his preface to the Rolls edition, was soon recognized to be untenable. In 1885, Felix Liebermann printed extracts from the Barnwell chronicle, which he reconstructed from Stubbs' edition, and in passing he correctly pointed out that Wendover and "Barnwell" must both have drawn the Bourges account from a common source, because the better reading was preserved sometimes by one, sometimes by the other.[10]

Just at the time that Liebermann was writing, a third English version of the *Relatio* was published, which, although not itself that common source he postulated, did reveal both the true origin of the account of the Council of Bourges and its connection with the English councils held to discuss the demand for a papal subsidy. It survives in the Salisbury cathedral chapter's *Vetus registrum,* sometimes called "the register of St Osmund" (Doc. 42, below).[11] About 1229, its compilers arranged and annotated the liturgical and legal documents which the chapter had accumulated, including several relating to the bull *Super muros* (Doc. 41, below). Evidently they were particularly anxious to record that recent threat to their community, for they transcribed the bull twice into the register. Moreover, they not only likewise duplicated the citation mandates to the English councils that considered *Super muros* at London in January and May 1226 but also summarized the proceedings. From this Salisbury summary we learn that the French document had a special relevance to the English council that the chroniclers had not noted. At London in May 1226, "everyone unanimously gave him [the archbishop] a negative response to what had been previously requested by the lord pope, and this response was modeled on the one given to the legate of France in the council that he celebrated at Bourges, which reads as follows: . . ." (Doc. 42.11), and the text of the *Relatio* is then given (§ 12).

This passage supplies the clue to the *Relatio*'s true identity, but historians have been slow to realize its full implications. First came the recognition by Barker that "the proceedings of the French assembly formed the model for those of the English," but he made no mention of how the French council came to be known in England.[12] Lunt was more precise when he stated that the English

9. Ibid., I, xlii.

10. MGH, SS, XXVII (1885), 184, n. 16.

11. *Vetus registrum Sarisberiense alias dictum Registrum S. Osmundi episcopi: The Register of St. Osmund,* ed. W. H. Rich Jones, Rolls Series, no. 78, 2 vols. (London, 1883-1884), I, ix–xi, and II, vii–x, on the MS; *Relatio* in II, 51-54.

12. E. Barker, *The Dominican Order and Convocation* (Oxford, 1913), p. 35.

clergy at London "had before them a detailed account of the proceedings of a French clerical council held at Bourges. . . . The form of the account, evidently written, . . . was read at the council."[13] He did not make clear that the Salisbury register not only preserves this account but also explicitly presents it as the one used at London.

These facts place the *Relatio* in a new light. It is not the composition of an English chronicler, as those who knew it only in the Wendover-Paris and Barnwell-Coventry versions had supposed. Rather, it is the document read at London, of which three contemporary versions survive—Salisbury, Wendover, and Barnwell-Coventry. Moreover, by comparison of the three versions it can be demonstrated that each is independent of the other. No one version reproduces the original text faithfully, but if each has independent authority, the original can be reconstructed definitively whenever two of the versions agree. Of the three, Barnwell-Coventry deviated the least from the original *Relatio.* By a rough approximation, Coventry (C) dissents from the combined reading of Salisbury (S) and Wendover (W) in only about 25 instances. Salisbury is twice as bad (50 times against CW) and Wendover strays the farthest (80 readings against CS). Wendover frequently retouched his text, chiefly in the interests of clarity and style, often adding a phrase or altering the wording. Not all of his revisions were innocent, however; a few are tendentious distortions of his source, for instance the addition of "in dolo" (§ 6) to impugn the legate's intentions.

Although Wendover altered the text in many small details, he omitted no passage of any length, except for a section that he deleted only to rephrase it and work it in at another point (*apparatus fontium,* n. 7). By comparison, the other versions both do suppress passages: Salisbury omits about a dozen lines (for example in § 6, 7, and 17) and Barnwell-Coventry twice as many (§ 2–6). Each version, then, omits at least one substantial passage found in the other two. Consequently, none could be the exemplar of the others: each is an independent version. Detailed study of the lesser differences confirms this independence. The stemmatic relationship of the *texts* (not manuscripts) is represented in figure 2.[14]

Presumably all three versions derive from the London exemplar that was brought back by delegates to the council at London; certainly this was the case with the Salisbury version. What we are able to reconstruct is this common exemplar, the copy used at London. Because it included the report of Raymond's trial, which was utterly irrelevant to the problems of the English clergy, we may be reasonably certain that the London exemplar contained the complete text without abridgement, just as it had been received from France.

13. Lunt, *Financial Relations,* p. 186.

14. The diagram includes only the manuscripts used in establishing the present text. The tradition of each text is treated more fully in the introductions to Docs. 42–44.

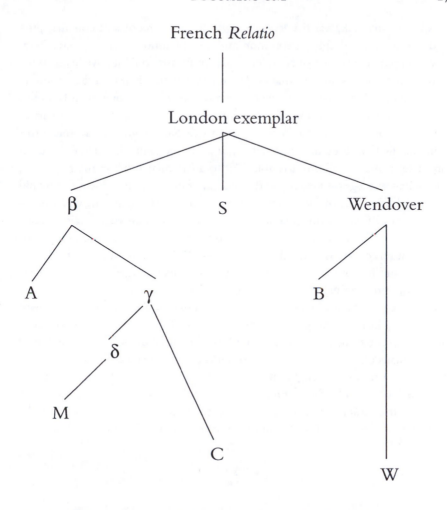

French *Relatio*

London exemplar

β   S   Wendover

A   γ   B

δ

M

C

W

A = London College of Arms, MS. Arundel 10 ("Barnwell" chronicle)
B = Cambridge, Corpus Christi College, MS. 16 (Mathew Paris' *Chronica majora*)
C = Cambridge, Corpus Christi College MS. 175 ("Walter of Coventry")
L = London, BL, MS. Add. 35,168 (Crowland annals)
M = Magdalene College, Oxford, MS. lat. 36
N = Society of Antiquaries MS. 60 (Black Book of Peterborough)
S = Cotton Claudius A. v. (Spalding annals)
V = Cotton Vitellius E. xiii

FIGURE 2.   Stemma of *Relatio de concilio Bituricensi*

Why, we may ask, was the *Relatio* drawn up? Such reports of conciliar proceedings are exceedingly uncommon and would almost certainly have been frowned upon as a breach of confidence. By no means could it have been an official document. Instead, internal evidence suggests that it was in fact an unofficial memorandum written by one of the proctors who was present at Bourges. Certainly the narrator's point of view is that of a proctor, for the greater part of the report concerns the proctors' objections to *Super muros*. To a prelate this would hardly have been the outstanding feature of the council, and in the French chronicles it plays a subordinate role. But to a capitular proctor, the request of *Super muros* was a grave matter and the success of the proctors' objections would seem the high point of the meeting. If we assume that the author was a proctor, it is not difficult to imagine how such an account came to be written contrary to conciliar custom. Proctors had only recently acquired the right to attend church councils.[15] Unlike the prelates, they were responsible to a constituency, and not unnaturally one of them might feel obliged to draw up a report of the proceedings to present on his return home.[16] One of the proctors, flushed with the victory over the dreaded proposal of *Super muros* and perhaps more than a little impressed by the effectiveness of the new privilege of proctorial representation, must have hastened to write it all down for the benefit of his capitular colleagues while the arguments *pro et contra* were still fresh in his mind. Someone then thoughtfully sent off a copy to his English counterparts, who used it to good effect.[17] From internal evidence, it would appear that the author of the *Relatio* was from the ecclesiastical province of Tours, because he omitted that province from the list of those over which Lyon claimed primacy (Doc. 1.2).[18]

★   ★   ★

15. See above, chap. 3, pp. 95-101.

16. A decade earlier, a participant in the Fourth Lateran Council ("the Giessen Anonymous") drew up a similar report. His editors opined, without explanation, "that he was reporting back to a prelate, or prelates, in Germany" (p. 120), but I think it more likely that he was a proctor reporting back to his chapter: S. Kuttner and A. García y García, "A New Eyewitness Account of the Fourth Lateran Council," *Traditio*, XX (1964), 115-178.

17. One evidence of such cross-Channel exchanges is the rapid migration of a routine English letter to Normandy, where it was copied into Avranches, Bibl. mun., MS. 149, fol. 109va (on the manuscript, see Doc. 28, below). In this letter, Thomas of Chopham, bishop's official at Salisbury, notified his counterpart at Winchester of his decision in a marriage case and bade him enforce it. The undated letter could not have been written more than a few years before it was copied circa 1226 (see Doc. 41, below), since Thomas was subdean of Salisbury from 1214 to 1233: *Fasti Ecclesiae Anglicanae, 1066–1300,* IV: *Salisbury,* ed. D. E. Greenway (London, 1991), pp. 38-39, 60.

18. For detailed discussion, see above, chap. 3, at n. 99.

The text presented below is a reconstruction of the London exemplar of the *Relatio,* which can be made with sufficient accuracy for the historian's purposes because most of the text survives in three independent versions. The provisional reconstruction that I published in 1967 was prepared by collating printed texts of the three versions; for the present edition, I have gone back to the manuscripts, which has enabled me to improve the text considerably, chiefly because the transcription of the Salisbury Register in the Rolls edition is often faulty. Each of the three traditions is treated at greater length later in this study in connection with other documents, but for the sake of convenience the witnesses to each tradition are identified below and characterized briefly.

Salisbury Register

S = Trowbridge, Wiltshire County Record Office, D 1/1/1, pp. 140-141 (fols. 70v–71r); entry made in 1229. For details, see Doc. 42, below. I have taken this as my base text against which the other witnesses were collated. S was preferred here to the Barnwell-Coventry version, which was my base in Doc. 41, because the Salisbury scribe, though occasionally misreading his text, was not improving it by frequent verbal transpositions, as were the other witnesses whose alterations of word order are usually not recorded in the *apparatus criticus.*

Barnwell-Coventry

This tradition is discussed in the introduction to Doc. 44. Three witnesses to it were consulted for this edition, all of which ultimately derive from a common ancestor, Beta (see stemma for Doc. 44). When they disagree, the better reading is usually indicated by S and/or W, but no one is markedly more accurate than the others. All significant variants are reported in the apparatus, but not transpositions and most orthographical peculiarities. Each was collated from a photocopy.

A = London, College of Arms, MS. Arundel 10, fols. 105ra–105vb (saec. xiii 2/4), the so-called "Barnwell Chronicle."

C = Cambridge, Corpus Christi College, MS. 175 (ca. 1300), fols. 175rb–176ra, the *Memoriale* of Walter of Coventry; cf. ed. W. Stubbs, Rolls Series, no. 58, II (1873), pp. 276-279. As Stubbs' apparatus indicates, A mostly agrees with C; both are close and careful copies from Beta. Several times the word order of C agrees with SW against A (not recorded), and once, with MW, it preserves the better reading against A (*dominantium,* var. r in § 12).

M = Oxford, Magdalen College, MS. lat. 36, fols. 196v–197v. Like C, a witness to the Gamma branch (see stemma in Doc. 44), but without the minor improvements introduced by C (mainly unreported transpositions).

Wendover

As the prolegomena to Doc. 43 explains, there are two extant witnesses to Roger Wendover's lost autograph (designated *b* in the stemma for Doc. 43), but we cannot always be sure that either of them contains the text as Wendover first wrote it; some revisions by his successor, Matthew Paris, are evident in the margins of B and others—by Paris or Wendover himself or some third person—may have been tacitly incorporated in B and/or W. The *Relatio,* however, is a notable exception to this general rule, because when either W or B agrees with the other witnesses to the *Relatio,* that almost certainly must have been the reading of the *b*-text too. Actually, as Luard's apparatus shows, there are few significant differences between B and W. But generally they also agree in their frequent, though usually insignificant, transposition of words or phrases (rarely recorded in my apparatus), which indicates that these revisions of the *Relatio* were present in the *b*-text and consequently were the work of Wendover rather than Paris. Consequently, I attribute the 1226 annal to Wendover alone.

W = Oxford, Bodleian Library, MS. Douce 207, fols. 189rb–189vb, a late copy (ca. 1300) of Roger Wendover's *Flores historiarum*. Except for transpositions and orthographic peculiarities, the readings of this manuscript are fully reported in my *apparatus criticus*.

B = Cambridge, Corpus Christi College, MS. 16, fols. 62va–63ra (1240s), the earliest copy of Matthew Paris' *Chronica majora*. I have collated a photocopy of the manuscript against Luard's edition, which proves to be admirably accurate. In my *apparatus criticus,* I record variants from this manuscript only when they clarify W's place in the transmission of the text.

Text

When three independent witnesses (for example ASW) agree, the text is clearly that of the original. When one such reads against the other two, the majority reading has been accepted. When all three traditions disagree, the choice has been up to the editor. About a third of the text is attested by only two of the three traditions; here again the text cannot be firmly established and the editor has had to choose the better reading. Fortunately, these decisions seldom alter the sense, so the reconstructed text of the *Relatio* is adequate for the historian's needs. From the apparatus, it will be apparent that I have been reluctant to adopt Wendover's readings, even (or especially) when they improve the Latinity or clarity of a passage, because he freely made stylistic alterations in the documents that he included in his chronicle.

Those portions of the text that are enclosed in [square brackets] are later additions to the original text of the London exemplar. Otherwise, the editorial conventions are those described above in the general introduction to these documents.

The *apparatus criticus* records all the variant readings with these exceptions: orthographic differences, transpositions which do not affect the meaning, and the variant readings within the Wendover-Paris tradition given by Luard, which have been eliminated because they have no value for establishing this text. The apparatus does not report the errors of previous editors. In this document, word order presented a special problem because the copyists freely altered it; to record these variations would have cluttered the apparatus needlessly, so I have tacitly restored the word order of the original when ACMW agree against the base S. In general, however, ACMS agree in word order, while stylistic transpositions are characteristic of W.

The translation by J. A. Giles of Wendover's version of the *Relatio* is a literal rendition into Latinate Victorian English.[19] Although adequate for the general reader, it often glosses over the details of conciliar procedure with which this study is so often concerned, so while often following Giles, I have not hesitated to paraphrase when a literal translation would not convey the technical sense of the passage. Only the established text of the original *Relatio* has been translated here. Except for the first section and the titles, the additions in the Latin text [indicated there by square brackets] have in principle been omitted from the translation, although in practice they occasionally have crept back into a paraphrase.

---

19. *Roger of Wendover's Flowers of History,* trans. J. A. Giles, Bohn's Antiquarian Library (London, 1849), II, 469–473.

ACM[1]

W[1]

[DE CONCILIO BITURICENSI CUI PRESEDIT ROMANUS FRANCORUM LEGATUS.

Cum autem talia vel prossus si-milia[2] per universarum terrarum spatia pontifici summo subjecta prius essent promulgata—et quicunque ea audierunt, tinnierunt ambe aures eorum[3]—legatus quidam, Romanus nomine, a Roma directus in Galliam, concilium celebravit apud Lugdunum Gallie.]

Hoc eodem tempore venit magis-ter Romanus ad partes Gallicanas a domino papa missus ut ibi legationis officio fungeretur. Quo cum pervenis-set, fecit convocare regem Francorum cum archiepiscopis, episcopis et clero Gallicano ad concilium cum comite Tholosano, pro quo principaliter ad partes illas idem legatus missus fuerat, sicut sequens relatio declarabit.]

<RELATIO DE CONCILIO BITURICENSI>[a]

2 Convenerunt igitur[b][4] ad concilium[c] Lugdunensis, Senon',[d] Remens', Rothomag', Turon', Bituric',[e] Axitanus[f] archiepiscopi; Burdeg'[g] Rome fuit, Narbon' ecclesia vacabat. Convenerunt etiam[h] ix.[i] provinciarum suffraganei circiter centum cum abbatibus et[j] prioribus et singulorum[k] capitulorum procuratoribus.[l] Sed quia[m] Lugdunensis[n] vendicavit[o] sibi primatiam super Senononensem et[p] Rothomagensem, Bituricensis super[q] Burdegalensem et[r] Axitanum[s] et[t] Narbonensem[5] et eorum suffraganeos, timebatur[u] discordia, et ideo non fuit sessum ut in concilio[v] sed velut[w] in consilio.

3 Quibus sedentibus et lectis[x] tunc primo[y] litteris legationis in publico, comparuerunt[z] comes Tholosanus ex una parte et dominus Montisfort'[a] ex altera, qui[b] petiit restitui terram[c] quam dominus papa et Philippus rex Francie[d] contulerunt S.[e] patri suo, exhibens super donatione facta utriusque munimenta pape scilicet et regis.[f]

[a] *titulum scripsi*   [b] igitur *om.* S   [c] concilium] capitulum ACM, apud Bituricam civitatem *add.* W   [d] Senon' *om.* W   [e] Bituric'] et *add.* S   [f] Auxianensis W   [g] Burdeg'] vero ... et *add.* W   [h] etiam] igitur W   [i] novem CM   [j] et *om.* S   [k] et singulorum] singulorumque S   [l] procuratoribus] mandatum summi pontificis audituri *add.* W   [m] quia] quoniam W   [n] Lugdunensis] archiepiscopus *add.* W   [o] vendicabat W   [p] et] *om.* S, archiepiscopum *add.* W   [q] Bituricensis super: *tr.* W, super *om.* S   [r] Burdegalensem et *om.* W   [s] Auxianensem W   [t] et] *om.* W   [u] timebatur] de *add.* W   [v] Sed quia—consilio SW: *om.* ACM   [w] ut ... velut] quasi ... ut W   [x] et lectis] lectisque ACM   [y] tunc primo *om.* W   [z] comparuerunt—6 Post hoc SW: *om.* ACM; comparuerunt] apparuerunt W   [a] dominus Montisfort'] Symon de Montis fortis W   [b] qui] sibi *add.* W   [c] terram] Reimundi comitis Tholosani *add.* W   [d] Francorum W   [e] S.] sibi et W   [f] regis] Addiditque comitem Reimundum abjudicatum fuisse Rome in concilio generali propter heresim ad minus a parte majori terre quam nunc tenet. E contra comes *add.* W

ACM[1]   W[1]

[CONCERNING THE COUNCIL OF
BOURGES, AT WHICH ROMANUS, LEGATE
OF THE FRENCH, PRESIDED.

Because the same or a very similar letter[2] had previously been promulgated throughout all the lands subject to the pope—and both of the ears of everyone that heard it tingled[3]—a certain legate, Romanus by name, who had been sent into Gaul from Rome, celebrated a council at Lyon.]

At this same time Master Romanus came to Gaul, having been sent by the lord pope to act as his legate there. On his arrival, he summoned the king of the French, together with the archbishops, bishops, and Gallican clergy, to a council with the count of Toulouse, which was the main reason that the legate had been sent there, as the following account will show.]

<ACCOUNT OF THE COUNCIL OF BOURGES>

2 Consequently[4] the archbishops of Lyon, Sens, Reims, Rouen, Tours, Bourges, and Auch assembled at the council. The archbishop of Bordeaux was at Rome, the church of Narbonne was vacant. There also assembled about a hundred suffragans from nine provinces, together with abbots and priors and a proctor from each chapter. But because the archbishop of Lyon claimed primacy for himself over the archbishops of Sens and Rouen, [and] Bourges over Bordeaux and Auch, and Narbonne,[5] and their suffragans, it was feared there would be discord; and for that reason they did not sit as in a council but as if in consultation.

3 When all were seated, then first of all the letters of legation were read publicly. Next, the count of Toulouse appeared before them to present his side of a dispute and the lord of Montfort the other. The latter requested the restitution of the land that the lord pope and King Philip of France had conferred on his

1. Each English chronicler composed his own introductory remarks to the French *Relatio*. For the context in the Salisbury Register, see Doc. 42.11.

2. Doc. 41, *Super muros Jerusalem*.

3. I Samuel iii.11.

4. *Igitur* ("consequently") implies an introductory statement, which apparently has been lost, since neither of the prefaces printed above seems to fit: W treats the *Relatio* as a self-contained document ("as the following account will show"), while A takes a distant view of the legation ("a certain legate, Romanus by name").

5. The phrase "and Narbonne" appears in all the MSS but seems to have been a misinformed afterthought, as the extra *et* suggests, because no archbishop ever claimed primacy over Narbonne (see chap. 3).

4 Reimundus vero[g] optulit se satisfacturum[h] erga ecclesiam[i] et regem[j] quicquid debebat[k] facere pro hereditate sua. Et[l] cum peteret ab eo pars adversa ut ipse[m] subiret judicium xii. parium Francie,[n] respondit Reimundus: "Recipiat rex homagium meum et paratus ero[o] subire, quia forte aliqui[p] non haberent me pro pari."

5 Cumque utrimque[q] plurimum fuisset altercatum, precepit legatus[r] tunc ibi[s] presentibus archiepiscopis ut unusquisque, vocatis[t] seorsum suis suffraganeis cum illis,[u] deliberarent[v] super illo[w] negotio et consilium suum traderent[x] in scriptis.[y] Quo facto[z] excommunicavit omnes qui sua consilia super hoc alicui[a] revelarent, dicens se velle ea regi[b] ostendere et domino pape significare.

6 Post[c] hoc[z] dedit[d] licentiam procuratoribus capitulorum redeundi[e] ad propria, retentis tamen archiepiscopis, episcopis et[f] abbatibus,[g] unde non immerito timuerunt ne procurata eorum absentia, qui majoris erant[h] prudentie et experientie, et pre multitudine potentiores contradicere,[i] maxime cum <experimenta> multorum sint[j] multa, habito tractatu cum singulis et non[k] in communi[l] aliquid statueretur[m] in prejudicium omnium.[n6] [o]Dicti[p] ergo[q] procuratores post diutinam deliberationem miserunt ad legatum procuratores metropolitanarum ecclesiarum qui[o] dixerunt:[r]

7 "Domine, audivimus quod habetis litteras speciales a curia[s] de exigendis prebendis in omnibus ecclesiis[t] conventualibus[u] et[v] miramur quod[w] in hoc concilio,[x] nobis audientibus, nichil proposuistis[y] quos specialiter tangit.[a] Rogamus[b] in Domino[c] ne istud[d] scandalum oriatur per vos in ecclesia Gallicana, scientes[e]

---

[g] vero *om.* W   [h] satisfacturum] facturum W   [i] ecclesiam] Romanam *add.* W [j] regem] Francorum *add.* W   [k] deberet W (*et* B)   [l] Et] Tunc W   [m] ipse *om.* W [n] Francie] Gallie W   [o] ero] sum W   [p] aliqui] aliter W (*et om.* B)   [q] Cumque utrimque S: Cumque hinc inde W   [r] legatus] singulis *add.* W   [s] ibi *om.* W   [t] vocatis] convocatis W   [u] illis] eis W   [v] deliberet S   [w] illo] prefato W   [x] traderent W: traderet S, legato *add.* W   [y] in scriptis] redactum in scripto W   [z] Quo facto] legatus *add.* W [a] alicui *om.* W   [b] regi] Francorum regi W   [c] Post] *rubr.* "Quod legatus dedit procuratoribus in dolo licentiam recedendi" *praem.* W   [d] dedit] legatus dedit in dolo W   [e] redeundi] revertendi W   [f] et *om.* ACM   [g] abbatibus] et simplicibus prelatis *add.* W [h] qui majoris erant] cum majoris essent S   [i] contradicere] ad contradicendum W   [j] experimenta multorum sint] etiam peccata (*emendavi; forte* experi[ta] *male legitur*) multorum sint ACM, peccata malorum sunt S   [k] non] ne S   [l] maxime cum—in communi ACMS: *om.* W   [m] statueret ACM   [n] omnium] absentium prelatorum W   [o] Dicti—ecclesiarum qui ACMW: *om.* S   [p] Dicti] *praem.* Quo circa W   [q] ergo *om.* W   [r] dixerunt ACM: dixerunt legato S, coram eo hujusmodi allegarunt W   [s] curia] Romana *add.* W   [t] in—ecclesiis *om.* S   [u] conventualibus] sive cathedralibus *add.* W   [v] et S: quapropter plurimum ACM, quo circa multum W   [w] quod] non *add.* W, nichil *add.* CM   [x] in hoc concilio] de hoc in concilio A, in concilio de hoc CM   [y] nichil proposuistis] proposuistis eas W, proposuistis CM   [a] tangunt W   [b] Rogamus] Unde *praem.* W, Et rogamus et obsecramus ACM   [c] in Domino *om.* S   [d] istud] hoc S   [e] scientes *om.* M

father, Simon, and in proof of the gift he produced documents from both the pope and the king.

4 Raymond offered to do for the Church and the king whatever he ought to do for his inheritance. And when the opposing party asked him to submit himself to the judgment of the twelve peers of France, Raymond replied: "Let the king receive my homage and then I shall be ready to submit, because otherwise some would perhaps not accept me as their peer."

5 After much dispute on both sides, the legate ordered each of the archbishops then present to take his suffragans aside, discuss the matter with them, and deliver an opinion in writing. When this had been done, he excommunicated all those who should disclose their counsels concerning this matter to anyone, saying that he wished to show them to the king and to notify the pope.

6 After this, he gave the chapters' proctors leave to return home but retained the archbishops, bishops, and abbots. This gave the proctors good reason to fear. They thought themselves to be more experienced and prudent than the prelates, and better able to contradict [the legate] because of their numbers, especially since the experience of many is more varied. If they departed, something might be enacted that would affect the interests of all adversely as the result of a discussion held, not in common, but only with individual members of the whole group.[6] After long deliberation, these proctors therefore sent to the legate the proctors of the metropolitan churches, who said to him:

7 "My lord, we have heard that you have special letters from the curia that demand prebends in all conventual churches, and we are amazed that in this council you did not bring the matter up while we whom it specially concerns were listening. We beg you in the name of the Lord not to be the cause of scandal in the Gallican church, for we are certain that such a plan could not be put

---

6. Wendover apparently believed that a chapter could be represented by its prelate—such as a dean or prior—and he altered his text accordingly (see vars. g and l in § 6).

quod sine magno[f] scandalo et dampno inestimabili[g] non[h] posset[i] cum effectu attemptari;[j] quia, esto quod aliqui consentirent,[k] nullus esset consensus[l] de re[m] que omnes tangit,[n] cum fere omnes majores[o] et generaliter[p] omnes subditi, necnon[q] rex et omnes principes,[r] parati sunt[s] contradicere et resistere[t] usque ad capitis[u] expositionem et omnis honoris privationem, presertim[v] cum videatur[w] imminere per hoc subversio[x] ecclesie[y] et regni. Ratio[z] nostri timoris est quod cum essetis Remis, ibi[a] habuistis sermonem cum[b] quibusdam, et aliquibus[c] episcopis precepistis[d] ut cum vacaverint prebende, reservent eas[e] ad opus domini pape."[f]

8 Cum[g] autem[h] niteretur legatus persuadere ut[i] consentirent,[j][7] allegavit commoda que[k] inde provenire possent,[l] videlicet[m] quod amoveretur infamia[n] ab ecclesia Romana[o] que est caput[p] ecclesiarum,[q] cum nullus de curia[r] etiam oblata[s] reciperet.[t] Ad hoc[u] respondit[v] procurator[w] Lugdunensis:"Domine,[x] nullo modo volumus esse sine amicis in curia."[y]

9 Et contra, ipsi[z] procuratores allegabant incommoda sua, scilicet dampna rerum consiliorum et[a] auxiliorum divinorum[b] obsequiorum, que in ecclesiis

[f] magno] maximo W   [g] scientes—inestimabili ACMW: quia hoc S   [h] non] ne CM [i] posset: *add.* istud ACM, *add.* hoc W, potest S   [j] cum effectu attemptari] ad effectum perduci W   [k] aliqui consentirent] aliquis assentiret W   [l] consensus] ejus assensus W [m] de re] de rebus W   [n] quia—tangit ACMW: *om.* S; quia—tangunt W   [o] majores] necnon *add.* S   [p] generaliter *om.* S   [q] necnon] *om.* S, et *add.* W   [r] principes *om.* S [s] sint S (*et* B)   [t] et resistere *om.* S   [u] capitum S   [v] presertim *om.* S   [w] videatur] eis *add.* ACM   [x] per hoc subversio] propter hoc scandalum subveriosque W (*et sic sed om.* que B)   [y] ecclesie] generalis *add.* W   [z] Ratio] autem *add.* W   [a] essetis Remis ibi] ceteris regnis non W   [b] cum *om.* W   [c] et aliquibus *om.* W   [d] precepistis] et abbatibus *add.* W   [e] eas *om.* W   [f] Ratio—pape ACMW: *om.* S   [g] Cum] *rubr.* "Quod legatus a prelatis exegit duas prebendas dari ecclesie Romane" *et* His auditis *praem.* W; Cum—consentirent ACMW: Cumque S   [h] autem *om.* W   [i] ut] omnes *add.* W   [j] consentirent] ostendit tunc primo domini pape autenticum in quod "exegit a singulis ecclesiis cathedralibus duas prebendas, unam a capitulo et alteram ab episcopo. Et in cenobiis similiter, ubi sunt (nisi sint B) diverse portiones, abbatis" scilicet "et conventus," duas exegit ecclesias, unum ab abbate et aliam a conventu;"equali facta distributione bonorum suorum, a conventibus quantum pertinet ad unum monachum, sicut ipse interpretatus fuerit" legatus, et ab abbate tantundem tunc *add.* W (*vide notam 7 in app. font.*)   [k] allegavit commoda que] allegatum esset commodum quod S   [l] posset S   [m] videlicet] scilicet S   [n] infamia] illud ... scandalum W   [o] ab ecclesia Romana M (Rome AC): a Romana ecclesia W, a curia Romana S [p] caput] mater omnium W   [q] ecclesiarum] precipue *add.* ACM, concupiscentia scilicet (que *add.* B) radix est omnium malorum *add.* W; que—ecclesiarum *om.* S   [r] de curia ACMS: pro aliquo negotio in curia Romana faciendo aliquid offeret vel aliquis W   [s] etiam oblata S: sponte *inser.* ACM, oblata W   [t] reciperet ACM (*et* B): recipiet W, susciperet S   [u] Ad hoc W: Tunc ACM, *om.* S; *rubr.* "Objectiones procuratorum contra exactiones predictas" *praem.* W   [v] respondit] responsum est S   [w] procurator] archiepiscopi *add.* W [x] procurator—domine *om.* S   [y] curia] et largitate donorum *add.* W   [z] Et contra ipsi ACM: Et S, Alii eque W   [a] et *om.* W   [b] divinorum S: dominorum et ACM, *om.* W

into effect without great scandal and incalculable harm, because if only some were to consent, there would be no consensus in a matter which concerns everyone. As a matter of fact, almost all prelates and all subjects in general, as well as the king and all the nobles, are ready to oppose and resist, even to the danger of their lives and the loss of all their dignities, especially since this scheme seems to threaten the ruin of the church and the kingdom. The reason for our fear is that when you were at Reims, you spoke with certain persons there and ordered some bishops to reserve prebends for the use of the lord pope when they become vacant."

8 When the legate was trying to persuade them to consent,[7] he alleged the advantages which might ensue, namely that the plan could put an end to the bad reputation of the Roman church, which is chief of the churches, since no one in the curia would receive even gifts. To this, the proctor for Lyon replied, "My lord, by no means do we wish to be without friends in the curia."

9 Against the legate's arguments, the proctors alleged the disadvantages of the proposal. First they maintained that the plan would deprive them of the property, counsel, and aid in performing divine service that [resident] canons, their friends, and their servants provide in the churches. In view of the legate's own

---

7. At this point, Wendover inserted a passage (given in the *apparatus criticus*, var. j in § 8), based on a later passage in *Relatio* 9 that he had suppressed; the portions he borrowed are indicated by quotation marks in the *apparatus criticus*.

possent fieri per canonicos et suos amicos et suam[c] sequelaiu, maxime cum ex-
igantur a singulis cathedralibus ecclesiis due prebende, una a capitulo et altera[d] a
portione episcopi, et similiter in cenobiis ubi divise sunt portiones abbatis et conventus, et a conventibus tantum quantum pertinet ad unum monachum, equali
facta distributione bonorum suorum, sic enim ipsemet interpretatus fuit Remis.[e]

10 Item addiderunt oppressiones que fierent,[f] esset[g] enim in qualibet diocesi[h] vel ad minus in provincia necessarius[i] unus continuus procurator Romanus,
qui non vivere[j] de proprio sed procurationes et graves exactiones exigeret[k] ab
ecclesiis majoribus et forte minoribus, ut[l] nullus remaneret[n] impunitus;
nomenque procuratoris habens fungeretur[n] vice[o] legati.

11 Item dixerunt[p] imminere turbationes capitulorum, forte enim[q] demandaret[r] papa cui[s] vellet, procuratori suo[t] vel alii, ut vice sua interesset electionibus,
qui eas turbaret. Et sic lapso tempore devolveretur ordinatio[u] ad curiam,[v] que in
omnibus vel pluribus ecclesiis Romanos poneret, vel tales qui[w] plurimum essent
devoti.[x] Et sic nulle essent partes indigenarum prelatorum vel principum, cum
multi[y] principes[z] sint viri ecclesiastici, qui potius curie Romane quam regi vel
regno providerent.[a]

12 Insuper[b] addiderunt quod si proportionaliter fieret distributio[c] in curia,
omnes fierent[d] divites, cum multo plus essent recepturi de quolibet regno[e] quam
rex proprius, et sic majores non solum divites sed[f] ditissimi fierent.[g] Cum igitur
vermis divitum sit superbia, majores vix causas audirent sed in immensum eas
protelarent;[h] minores inviti scriberent cum scirent se nichil recepturos.[i] Cujus
rei signum[j] in evidenti est, quia et modo protrahunt negotia[k] post[l] obsequia[m]
percepta[n] et securitatem de percipiendis,[o] et sic periclitaretur justitia et oporteret
conquerentes mori[p] in januis Romanorum[q] tunc plenissime dominantium.[r]

---

[c] suam] domesticam ACM   [d] et altera ACM: alia S (*cf.* et alteram W, *supra in app. crit.,*
var. j intra § 8)   [e] que in ecclesiis—Remis ACMS: *om.* W; ipsemet interpretatus fuit Remis
ACM (*et* V): interpretatum fuit Rome S (*cf.* ipse interpretatus fuerit legatus W, *supra in app.*
crit., var. j intra 8)   [f] Item—fierunt ACMS: in hunc modum W   [g] esset] erit W
[h] quibuslibet diocesibus AC, quibusdam diocesibus M   [i] necessarius] nuntius W   [j] vivet
W   [k] exiget W   [l] ut] et S   [m] remaneat W   [n] fungetur W   [o] vice] officio W
[p] dixerent S   [q] enim *om.* A   [r] demandaret W] domum daret AM (*tr.* C), mandaret S
[s] cui] cum W   [t] suo *om.* S   [u] ordinatio] electio W   [v] curiam] Romanam *add.* W
[w] qui] eis *add.* W   [x] devoti] ignoti S   [y] multi] plurimi S   [z] principes *om.* W
[a] providerent] vellent providere S   [b] Insuper] Item W   [c] distributio] bonorum *praem.*
W   [d] fierent] essent S   [e] de quolibet regno *om.* W, *ante* essent CM   [f] sed] et *add.* W
[g] et sic—fierent *om.* S   [h] protelarent] different et W   [i] cum scirent—recepturos *om.*
W; recepturos S: perceptturos ACM   [j] signum] experimentum W   [k] protrahunt nego-
tia] protrahuntur A, protrahimur CM   [l] post] etiam post W   [m] obsequia] beneficia S
[n] percepta W: precepta ACM, accepta S   [o] securitatem de percipiendis ACM: securitatem
de perciendis non prestarent S, securitatem percipiendi W   [p] mori] morari *forte*   [q] Ro-
manorum] Romanarum A, *om.* CM   [r] tunc—dominantium *om.* S; dominantium CMW:
dominationum A

interpretation of the bull at Reims, the loss would be even greater than at first seemed apparent, because in fact *two* prebends were demanded from each cathedral, one from the chapter and the other from the bishop's share. The same rule would apply to monasteries that distinguish between the shares of the abbot and the community, but only one monk's share would be required from monasteries that share their goods in common.

10 Next they spoke of the oppression that the plan would entail, since it would be necessary for Rome to have a resident administrative agent in every diocese or at least in every province. He would not live at his own expense but theirs, for he would demand procurations and heavy exactions from the greater churches and perhaps from the smaller ones, so everyone would suffer. Moreover, since he would be the pope's proctor, he might perform the duties proper to a legate.

11 Furthermore they said that the chapters would be in danger of falling into discord, for the pope would perhaps order anyone he chose—his proctor or somebody else—to be present on his behalf at their elections, and this agent might disrupt them. And thus when the legal time limit for them to agree on a candidate had expired, the election would devolve on the curia, which would place Romans, or those most devoted to them, in all or most of the churches. As a result, there would be no indigenous elements among the prelates, or princes—since many of the princes are ecclesiastics—who then would care more for the Roman curia than for the king or the kingdom.

12 They added moreover that if the income from the prebends were to be distributed among the members of the curia in proportion to their rank, they all would become rich, since collectively they would be likely to receive much more from each kingdom than the king himself. Under this system, the higher officials would not only become rich but would be the richest men in the world. As a result, since arrogance is the besetting sin of the rich, the higher officials would scarcely hear cases but would put them off indefinitely; the lesser officials would draw up documents unwillingly when they could expect nothing in return. The proof of this is evident, because now they prolong a matter after having received presents before the trial and being assured that more will follow afterwards. Thus it is clear that under the new plan, justice would be endangered and complainants would spend the rest of their lives waiting outside the doors of Romans, who would then lord it over them absolutely.

13 Item cum vix possibile sit fontem cupiditatis desiccari, quod[s] nunc faciunt per se tunc facerent per alios, et suis procurarent dari munera multo[t] majora quam nunc; modica enim in conspectu divitum cupidorum nulla sunt.[u]

14 Post omnia pericula ipsius[v] civitatis Romane non tacuerunt,[w] facerent enim[x] multe divitie cives[y] insanire, et sic inter diversas parentelas tante[z] orirentur seditiones quod posset timeri[a] de ruina[b] totius civitatis, cujus nec etiam modo est omnino expers.[c]

15 Item dixerunt quod licet[d] qui modo possiderent[e] se obligarent[f] ad non recipiendum,[g] forte successores eorum[h] ratam non haberent illam obligationem.[i]

16 Ultimo dixerunt:[j] "Domine,[k] moveat vos zelus universalis ecclesie et sancte sedis Romane, quia si omnium esset universalis oppressio, posset timeri ne immineret generalis discessio, quod Deus avertat."

17 His auditis respondit legatus, ut videbatur, plurimum motus[l] in bono,[m] se cum esset in curia numquam huic exactioni consensisse, et ipsum litteras[n] accepisse postquam[o] ingressus fuerat[p] Galliam, et tunc eum super hoc plurimum[q] doluisse. Addidit etiam quod quicquid precepit super hoc, se tali conditione licet tacita intellexisse, si imperium et alia regna consentirent, que omnia consimiles habuerunt litteras, ut putabat. Addidit etiam[r] se nichil amplius super[s] hoc attemptaturum donec imperium et regna[t] Anglie et Hispanie[u] consenserint,[v] quod minime creditur[w] posse provenire.

---

[s] quod] qui W (et quod B)   [t] multa C   [u] modica—sunt om. M   [v] ipsius om. S
[w] Post—tacuerunt ACMS: Item W   [x] enim om. W   [y] cives] Romanos add. W
[z] tante om. S   [a] possent timere ACM   [b] de ruina] excidium W   [c] nec—expers
ACMW: modo omnino expers non est S   [d] quod licet] si S   [e] possiderent ACM: possident S, presentes sunt W   [f] obligassent S   [g] ad non recipiendum] id non susciperent
W   [h] eorum om. ACM   [i] ratam—obligationem ACM: non habebunt ratam hujusmodi
obligationem S, nec illam obligationem ratam haberent W   [j] Ultimo dixerunt ACMS: Novissime autem sic negotium concluserunt W   [k] Domine om. ACM   [l] motus] commotus W   [m] ut—bono ACMW: om. S   [n] litteras] super hoc add. S   [o] postquam]
priusquam ACM   [p] fuerat AMW: fueram C, fuit S   [q] tunc eum super hoc plurimum
S: tunc plurimum super hoc ACM (hoc om. A et corr. marg. A[1]), se multum super hoc W
[r] quod quicquid—Addidit etiam ACMW: om. S (homoioteleuton); Addidit etiam] Adjunxit insuper W   [s] super] de ACM   [t] regnum S   [u] imperium—Hispanie] per regna alia W
[v] consentirent S   [w] minime creditur] credidit non W

13 Also, since it is hardly possible for the fountain of avarice to be dried up, what they now do in person they would then do through intermediaries. And they would see to it that their agents received much larger gifts than are now given, for small gifts mean nothing to the rich.

14 After citing all these disadvantages, they did not omit the dangers to the city of Rome itself, for great wealth would turn the citizens into madmen. In consequence, such great quarrels would arise between the various factions that the whole city might be destroyed by this strife, which indeed already threatens it.

15 Also they said that although the officials who now occupy the benefices might promise to receive nothing else, perhaps their successors would not be bound by that promise.

16 Lastly they said, "My lord, may zeal for the Church universal and the holy Roman see move you, because we fear that the result of universal oppression would be general schism, which God avert!"

17 The legate seemed to be favorably impressed by their arguments, for when he had heard them out, he replied that when he was at the curia he had never consented to this exaction, and he had received the letter after he had come to Gaul, and then he had been very distressed about the matter. And he added that any provisions he made to implement the scheme he regarded as being subject to the tacit condition that the Empire and the other kingdoms would consent, which he thought all had similar letters. He also added that he would proceed no further in the matter until the Empire and the kingdoms of England and Spain should consent, which he hardly believed could happen.

Document 2
ANNALS OF DUNSTABLE

Two aspects of the Council of Bourges are reported in the annals of the Augustinian priory at Dunstable, about thirty-five miles north of London. Under the year 1225, the annalist recounts the student riot in Paris; his next year's entry describes the trial of Raymond. In neither case can we identify the chronicler's source, but both accounts were probably drafted only a few months after the events they describe.

The author of the Dunstable annals for 1225 and 1226 has usually been taken to be Richard de Mores (or Morins), prior of Dunstable from 1202 to 1242 and a canonist trained at Paris and Bologna, who was the originator of the annals kept by his house in the thirteenth century. The project began when he compiled a summary of events in chronological order from the Incarnation to 1210, but his subsequent role in the continuation of the annals down to his death in 1242 is uncertain. Luard supposed that Richard himself wrote the annals 1210–1242 and that others continued his work annually until 1297 (Luard, pp. ix–xi). But in 1969 C. R. Cheney argued persuasively that the annals after 1210 were mainly the work of one of Richard's subordinates, although after 1220 the prior himself probably supervised the work and perhaps occasionally "lent a hand" (Cheney, p. 229).

In the 1220s the compiler combined contemporary reports with documents and with information derived from written sources. His method, it would seem, was to note down reports as he received them and then to improve their literary form months, or even years, later. Thus our extracts are most likely based on near-contemporary reports that were elaborated somewhat later for literary effect.

The earliest account is not necessarily the most accurate, however. When writing of matters known to him personally, the Dunstable annalist was remarkably reliable, as his editor affirms (p. xxxii), but when writing of French affairs, he could be no more trustworthy than his informants, of whom we know nothing for certain. For the Paris riots, we may guess that his source was some English student who had returned home when the legate closed the university. In the earnest assurance that the English at Paris took no part in the disturbance,

---

Eodem anno (1225), coram Romano legato Francie de mandato Honorii pape, orta contentione inter episcopum Parisiensem[a] et cancellarium suum

[a] *pariensem* A

we may be hearing the echo of that informant's alibi, which the chronicler, who had himself studied and taught at Paris almost forty years earlier, would have willingly repeated with the double pride of patriot and alumnus.

Even less can be inferred about his source for the events at Bourges. We can be sure that the prior's account is not copied from the other chroniclers because it contains a unique detail: Raymond's offer to make a financial settlement with Amaury. This is probably not his invention, for it is consistent with Raymond's readiness to make whatever concessions were necessary to retain his inheritance. The Dunstable account must nonetheless be used with caution, for we cannot be sure that it represents anything more than the report of the council current in England. As such it is to be compared with Wendover's treatment of the same material (Doc. 43.16).

MS.—(A) London, BL, MS. Cotton Tiberius A. x, fols. 25ra–26rb; damaged by water.

Ed.—H. R. Luard, *Annales prioratus de Dunstaplia (A. D. 1–1297)* in *Annales monastici,* Rolls Series, no. 36, vol. III (London, 1866), pp. 97–98, 100–101.

Text transcribed from photographs of A; subsequently verified from the original.

Author.—C. L. Kingsford in *Dictionary of National Biography,* s.v. "Morins, Richard de" (1895). For the identification of the canonist Ricardus Anglicus with the prior of Dunstable, see S. Kuttner and E. Rathbone, "Anglo-Norman Canonists of the Twelfth Century: An Introductory Study," *Traditio,* VII (1949–1951), 327–339. Robert C. Figueira, "Ricardus de Mores and His *Casus decretalium:* The Birth of a Canonistic Genre," in *Proceedings of the Eighth International Congress of Medieval Canon Law, San Diego, University of California at La Jolla, 21–27 August 1988,* ed. S. Chodorow, Monumenta iuris canonici, series C: Subsidia, Vol. 9 (Vatican City, 1992), pp. 169–187, esp. n. 3 for bibliography. Idem, "Ricardus de Mores at Common Law—The Second Career of an Anglo-Norman Canonist," in *Regensburg, Bayern und Europa: Festschrift für Kurt Reindel zu seinem 70. Geburtstag,* ed. Lothar Kolmer and Peter Segl (Regensburg, 1995), pp. 281–299.

Chronicle.—C. R. Cheney, "The Making of the Dunstable Annals, A.D. 33 to 1242," reprinted in his *Medieval Texts and Studies* (Oxford, 1973), pp. 209–230.

A quarrel had arisen between the bishop of Paris and his chancellor on the one hand and the university of students on the other. In the same year [1225], by command of Pope Honorius, the parties appeared in the presence of Romanus, the legate to France, and by the legate's final judgment the seal of

ex una parte et universitatem scolarium ex altera, per difinitivam sententiam legati dampnatum et fractum est sigillum universitatis, et similiter ipsius privilegia condempnata. Unde scolares moti excanduerunt in legatum et opprobria ei intulerunt, quos dum famuli legati repellere vellent, percutere famulos ceperunt, ita quod plerique hinc inde erant vulnerati, quidam etiam interfecti. Interim etiam legatus recepit[b] se in palatium episcopi et misit ad regem, qui tunc presens fuerat in urbe, pro auxilio. Sed scolares interim hostia palatii confregerunt, et dum irruentes in palatium, hostium camere et capelle frangere niterentur, in turrim palatii legatus ascendit: et ecce, familia regis superveniens, et legatum a manibus eorum liberavit, et centum quadraginta scolares infra januam episcopi inventos, vinculis et carceribus mancipavit. Hiis autem omnibus magistri et scolares Anglie nec interfuerunt nec tante presumptioni consenserunt. Legatus autem in huius sceleris fautores huiusmodi sententiam promulgavit: quod magistri nec ibi nec alibi de cetero legerent, beneficiati beneficia habita et spem habendi alia perderent, ordinati perpetuo suspenderentur. Et quibusdam qui gravius excesserant, penas intulit graviores.

. . . .

2 Anno ab incarnatione Domini millesimo cc° vicesimo vi°, missus est a sede Romana magister Otto in Angliam, qui petiit a singulis cathedralibus ecclesiis unam prebendam meliorem post primam, et ab abbatiis et prioratibus beneficium competens—et donec illud vacaret, beneficium competens de cameris—, ad sustentationem ministrantium summo pontifici. Et similes nuntii missi sunt in Franciam et alias provincias. Et responsum est concilio comprovinciali Lond' convocato quod tales redditus non conferet Cantuariensis provincia sine concilio generali et assensu patrinorum[c] suorum; alie vero provincie non dissimiliter responderunt.

. . . .

3 Eodem anno (1226), Romanus cardinalis, apostolice sedis legatus in Franciam missus ut moneret Lodovicum regem ut restitueret Henrico regi Anglie, Normanniam, Andegaviam, et Equitaniam, qui habito consilio cum Iohanne rege Ierosolomitano et cum aliis baronibus suis, respondit quod non redderet Anglis unum pedem terre quem Philippus pater suus ei in morte dimisit. Legatus vero, hoc negotio sic intermisso, transtulit se totum ad causam Albigensium; et Bituris celebrato consilio, monuit comitem Tholosanum ut cum omnibus suis rediret ad fidem catholicam, et terram Albigensium restitueret Amarico de Monte forti quam Romana ecclesia ei contulerat, et de qua terra[d] fuerat preter-

___

[b] ricipit A
[c] = patronorum *sicut leg. Luard (cf. Latham, p. 336)*
[d] terra *scripsi; litterae tres illegibiles (forte* t²a*) A*

the university was condemned and broken, and likewise the privileges of the university were condemned. Provoked by this, the students were consequently inflamed with anger against the legate and hurled insults at him; when the legate's servants wanted to drive them away, the students started striking the servants, with the result that most of them were wounded and one was even killed. Meanwhile the legate retreated into the bishop's palace and sent to the king, who was then present in the city, for help. But meanwhile the students broke down the palace door; they rushed into the palace, and while they were trying to break the doors of the chamber and chapel, the legate climbed up into the palace tower. But behold! the king's men appeared on the scene and freed the legate from the students' hands. A hundred and forty students were found inside the bishop's gate, and the king's men put them in chains and in prison. The English masters and students did not participate in any of these things, and they did not approve of such great presumption. Against those who supported this crime, however, the legate promulgated a sentence, the gist of which was that guilty masters were never to lecture again, either there or anywhere else; that those among the guilty who held benefices were to lose the ones they held as well as any hope of holding others in the future; and that those who were in holy orders were forever suspended from exercising their functions. And on some who transgressed more seriously, he imposed heavier punishments.

. . . .

2 In A. D. 1226, Master Otto was sent from the Roman see into England. For the support of the servants of the pope, he requested from each of the cathedral churches one of the better prebends (but not the best), and from abbeys and priories a suitable benefice; and until such a benefice became available, its equivalent was to be provided from the common funds. And similar nuncios were sent into France and the other provinces. A comprovincial council was convoked at London, which replied that the province of Canterbury would not contribute such gifts without a general council and the approval of the benefices' patrons; other provinces gave much the same response.

. . . .

3 In the same year [1226], Cardinal Romanus, legate of the apostolic see, was sent to France to warn King Louis that he should restore Normandy, Anjou, and Aquitaine to King Henry of England. After taking counsel with King John of Jerusalem and with his other barons, Louis replied that he would not return to the English one foot of the land that his father Philip had left to him when he died. Thus the negotiations were broken off, and instead the legate concentrated his efforts wholly on the case of the Albigensians. He celebrated a council at Bourges, in which he warned the count of Toulouse that he should return to the Catholic faith with all his people, and that he should restore to Amaury de

misso iuris ordine spoliatus. Comes vero respondit: "Nos fidem catholicam te-
nemus; si quis vero hereticus in terra nostra inventus fuerit, volumus ut confun-
datur, ita tamen ut iustus pro impio non pereat. Ego vero hereditatem meam
alteri non dabo, quam bellica clade perddidi, et ea cessante iuste recuperavi.
Verumtamen pro bono pacis tria milia marcarum ei numerabo." Legatus itaque
cepit alium diem inter partes sub spe pacis ad plenius deliberandum super hiis.
Interim autem rex, de consilio legati, data pecunia Almarico, emit ab eo totum
ius et cartas quas habebat de terra Albigensium. Quo facto, motus spiritu cupiditatis sive spiritu pietatis, Deus scit, sanctificavit super eos prelium quasi contra hereticos. Ita quod tum metu regio tum predicatione legati, profecti sunt de
corona Francie in partes illas circa c. milia virorum, cum thesauro et machinis
infinitis.

Document 3
CHRONICLE OF TOURS

The most detailed narrative source for the French crown's intervention in the
Albigensian Crusade is the *Chronicon Sancti Martini Turonensis auctore anonymo
canonico eiusdem monasterii*. As this modern title indicates, the chronicle was prepared for the church of St-Martin in Tours by one of its canons during the
1220s. For the annals before 1220, he refashioned an older universal chronicle
written at Auxerre, substituting the local history of Tours for that of Auxerre.
Then he continued the chronicle with his own account of the years 1220-1227,
for which his history is a contemporary source of exceptional value. The last
recorded event is the death of Honorius III on 18 March 1227.

Molinier, in his historiography of medieval France, judged the Chronicle of
Tours to be "de première importance pour l'histoire de Philippe Auguste et de
Louis VIII; c'est la meilleure chronique du règne de ce dernier" (III, 88). Petit-
Dutaillis, the standard authority on Louis VIII, esteemed it as "une chronique
entièrement originale et du plus haut intérêt . . . bien supérieure aux autres

Montfort the land of the Albigensians, which the Roman church had granted to Amaury and which had been taken away from the count without due process of law. The count replied: "We hold the Catholic faith. If any heretic shall be found in our land, we wish that he may be destroyed—but in such a way that the righteous may not perish by mistake instead of the impious. But I indeed shall not give my inheritance to another. I lost it because of a military defeat, and when that proved to be only temporary, I regained it justly. Nevertheless, for the sake of peace I shall pay him three thousand marks." And so, with the hope of peace as his pretext, the legate took another day to discuss these things more fully with the parties. Meanwhile, however, on the legate's advice the king gave money to Amaury and bought from him all the rights and charters that he had concerning the land of the Albigensians. After this had been done, the legate preached a holy war against them as if against heretics, and God knows whether he was moved by the spirit of piety or of avarice. Accordingly, because they were both in awe of royalty and moved by the legate's preaching, about a hundred thousand men from the crown of France set out for those parts, taking with them treasure and engines of war beyond measure.

---

chroniques françaises de la même époque." The canon of Tours he characterized as "un homme intelligent et consciencieux; il a vu Louis VIII de très près à plusieurs reprises, et était parfaitement au courant des affaires monarchiques."

A canonry at St-Martin afforded excellent opportunities to learn of royal affairs from eyewitnesses, since that church was a royal monastery, of which the king himself was abbot. Moreover, some of the canons were always clergymen in government service who held their benefices as profitable sinecures and lived at court. The chronicler was not one of these, for his fund of provincial anecdote places his residence at Tours beyond doubt, but his absentee colleagues were the best of informants for events at court.

Internal evidence provides what little we know of the author. The connection with Tours is demonstrated on every page (for example § 12), but only close reading revealed that his house was St-Martin rather than Marmoutier, as was once believed. For his name, we have only the conjecture of Salmon (p. xviii), who attributed the anonymous chronicle to Péan Gâtineau because he is the only author of the period who is known to have been a canon of St-Martin, whose patron saint's *vita* he versified into 10,316 lines of indifferent French. The identification remains a possibility that cannot be proven.

In the conciliar collections, the *Chronicon Turonense* and the *Relatio* (Doc. 1) are the only sources for the Council of Bourges. As Labbe and Cossart suggested when they introduced the pair into the conciliar corpus, the concise summary of the Tours annalist complements the more diffuse *Relatio,* providing a reliable check on the longer account as well as many details unique to itself.

MSS.—Five manuscripts of the chronicle have survived, but only one contains the account of our council. Three of the manuscripts are the canon's first redaction of his work, in which the continuation was carried down to August 1225 (including only § 1 below). The other two are his second redaction, which continued on to 1227, but one of these manuscripts has lost its last pages that contained the annals for 1219-1227. Thus a single manuscript contains the text of our § 2-14 (fols. 255rb–260va). This belonged successively to the Jesuit Collège de Clermont in Paris (MS. 645), the Meermans (MS. 745), Sir Thomas Phillipps (MS. 1852), and the Deutsche Staatsbibliothek in Berlin (MS. Phillipps lat. 145).

Ed.—No edition of the chronicle is at once complete and critical. (1) The annals before 1219 were published by Martène-Durand, *Vet. script. coll.*, V (1729), 917-1072, from Paris, BnF, MS. lat 4991—the truncated copy of the second redaction. (2) Martène's edition was reprinted in the appropriate volumes of the *Rec. hist. Gaules;* lacunae were filled from the Clermont MS, which Careau transcribed (pp. xi–xii): our passages in XVIII (1879), 308-314. (3) The portions concerning Touraine were printed from the Clermont MS by A. Salmon, *Recueil des chroniques de Touraine = Bulletin trimestriel de la Société archéologique de Touraine,* no. 1 (Tours, 1854), pp. 64-161. (4) Parts of German interest were critically ed-

---

In octabis vero ascensionis Domini (15 May 1225) Ludovicus rex concilium Parisius celebravit, ubi cum Romano sancti Angeli[a] cardinali, qui de novo in Franciam legatus advenerat, multa de negotiis regni,[b] regisque Anglie et terre Albigensium pertractavit.

· ·

2 Postea in octabis omnium sanctorum (8 November 1225) Ludovicus rex Francie concilium convocat Meleduno, ibique archiepiscopi et episcopi Francie, presente legato, petebant instanter a rege[c] et a suis baronibus iurisdictionem omnium hominum super mobilibus de quibus homines ecclesiarum eos in

[a] Angeli] diaco<no> *in mg. add.* A, *om.* B
[b] regni] sui *in mg. add.* A, *om.* B
[c] rege] Francie *add. et del.* A

ited by O. Holder-Egger, MGH, SS, XXVI (1882), 458-476, including § 1 and
11-13 (pp. 470 and 472-473). (5) To Potthast's list of edited fragments should be
added the *editio princeps* of § 2-6 in Labbe-Cossart, XI.i (1671), 290-292;
reprinted in Mansi, XXII (1778), 1213-1215. Labbe, who had previously edited
other fragments of this chronicle, was probably the contributor.

Text.—Rather than attempt to resolve the discrepancies between the various
transcripts of the Clermont MS (cf. 2-5, above), I print the text from a microfilm of the Clermont MS (siglum A), with the kind permission of the Deutsche
Staatsbibliothek; variants for § 1 are given from Holder-Egger's edition of Bern,
Bürgerbibliothek, MS. 22 (siglum B).

Refs.—For discussion and bibliography, see first the introduction to Holder-
Egger's edition (pp. 458-459). For L. Delisle's description of the MSS, see *Hist.
litt. France*, XXXII (1898), 537-546; also the general account by Victor Le Clerc
in XXI (1895), 676-679. Molinier, *Sources*, no. 2515 and Introd., § 167. Potthast,
Wegweiser, I (1896), 275. Petit-Dutaillis, *Louis*, p. xviii. For Péan Gâtineau (= Païen
Gastineau, Paganus Gatinelli), see Bossuat, *Manuel* (1951), nos. 3335-3337; Moli-
nier, *Sources*, no. 1323. The Clermont MS is superbly described in *Verzeichniss der
von der Königlichen Bibliothek zu Berlin erworbenen Meerman-Handschriften des Sir
Thomas Phillipps*, II: *Der lateinischen Meerman-Handschriften*, by Valentin Rose
(Berlin, 1892). Also issued as *Verzeichniss der lateinischen Handschriften*, Bd. I
(Berlin, 1893) in the series Handschriften-Verzeichnisse der Königlichen Bib-
liothek zu Berlin, Bd. XII.

O n the octave of the Lord's Ascension [15 May 1225], King Louis celebrated
a council at Paris. There, with Romanus, cardinal of Sant' Angelo, the
legate who had recently come to France, the king carefully considered many
things concerning the affairs of the kingdom, of the king of England, and of the
land of the Albigensians.

. . . .

2 Afterwards, on the octave of All Saints [8 November 1225], King Louis of
France convoked a council at Melun. There, in the presence of the legate, the
archbishops and bishops of France urgently asked the king and his barons for jurisdiction over all men who might be sued by churchmen in a bishop's court regarding movable property; and they maintained that the Gallican church was
vested with this jurisdiction. The king opposed them and asserted with the clear-

causam traherent coram ipsis, et iurisdictione ista dicebant investitam esse ecclesiam Gallicanam. Quibus rex se opponens, argumentis evidentissimis asserebat hoc esse dissonum rationi. . . . Tandem interveniente Dei gratia et legato,
causa ista ab utraque parte posita est in suspenso. In eodem nempe concilio satis
tractatum est de treuga inter regem Francie et regem Anglie reformanda necnon et de negotio Albigensi, sed ad presens nichil super hiis potuit reformari.

   3 <Q>UALITER UNIVERSITAS PARISIORUM <FA>CIT FIERI SIGILLUM PRO UNI-
VERSI<TA>TE QUOD PROPTEREA FUIT FRACTUM <PER> LEGATUM PAPE.[d] Tunc
cum universitas scolarium Parisiensium in preiudicium Parisiensis ecclesie sigillum proprium confecisset dictoque sigillo universitatis negotia sigillarent,[e]
Parisienses canonici coram legato, qui Parisius venerat, super sigillo scolares conveniunt, et multum ab utraque parte super hoc allegantes quid sit iuris, in legatum protinus compromittunt, illudque sigillum proprium ei reddunt. Qui habito
super hoc admodum festinato consilio, prefatum sigillum coram omnibus ibi fre-
git, omnesque qui deinceps Parisius sigillum universitatis facerent vinculo ana-
thematis[f] innodavit. Quo audito, clamor in celum attollitur, rumor per urbem
ingreditur, scolares conveniunt, et ad domum legati cum gladiis et fustibus conveniunt tamquam ad latronem; quorum adventum legati homines cognoscentes,
portas obstruunt, arma rapiunt, se dominumque suum a furibundis scolaribus
defendentes. Tandem post urgentes assultus scolarium, post portarum fractionem,
post lapidum fulminationem, cum fere legatus suique homines caperentur,
Ludovicus rex, qui paulo ante a Meleduno venerat et infortunium legati
audierat, servientes et milites ibi misit qui scolares nimis[g] et alios[h] repulserunt,
et legatum et gentem suam[i] indempnem, non tamen sine effusione sanguinis,
servaverunt. Quo facto, legatus ab urbe egreditur cum conductu, excommunicans generaliter scolares qui hunc assultum fecerant et alios qui ex parte eorum
interfuerant in assultu.

. . . .

   4 In sequenti vero festo sancti Andree apostoli (30 November 1225), dictus
legatus convocatis archiepiscopis, episcopis, abbatibus, et capitulis totius Francie,
Byturis concilium celebravit, ubi Raimundus comes Tolosanus veniens et
gremium sancte matris ecclesie sibi apperiri petens, absolutionem humiliter pos-
tulavit, sui purgationem offerens et emendam, et pro posse suo de omnibus terre

---

   [d] Qualiter—pape] *tit. in mg. truncato* A; *duas litt. quae ab initio quatuor linearum desunt, sup-*
plevi
   [e] sigillarent] -ret *et litt.* n *supra lineam inser.* A
   [f] anathematis] anathmatis *scr. et corr.* A
   [g] nimis] minis *leg. in edd.*
   [h] alios] aliis AB, alios *recte emend. Holder-Egger*
   [i] suam *supra lin. add.* A

est possible arguments that this was not in accord with reason. . . . Finally, by the intervention of God's grace and the legate, both parties agreed to postpone the case. In this council there was a good deal of discussion about making a new truce between the king of France and the king of England, and also about the Albigensian business, but for the moment nothing could be decided about these matters.

3 HOW THE UNIVERSITY OF PARIS HAD A SEAL MADE FOR THE UNIVERSITY THAT WAS CONSEQUENTLY BROKEN BY THE POPE'S LEGATE. The Paris university of scholars had had its own seal made, which was detrimental to the rights of the church of Paris, and they sealed the documents of the university with that seal. Because of this, the Paris canons summoned the scholars to appear before the legate, who had come to Paris. After each party had cited many texts to prove the law was on its side, they eventually agreed to let the legate decide which one was right, and they gave him the seal itself. After taking counsel on the matter altogether too hastily, then and there the legate broke that seal in the presence of all. And all who henceforth should make a seal of the university at Paris, he bound with the penalty of anathema. When the sentence was heard, a cry went up to the heavens; the news went throughout the city; the scholars assembled and together they went to the legate's house with swords and cudgels as if they were after a thief. When the legate's men became aware of their arrival, they blocked the gates and seized arms in order to defend themselves and their lord from the infuriated scholars. The scholars pressed forward in one assault after the other; the gates were broken and stones were thrown; the legate and his men were almost taken—when at last King Louis, who had come from Melun not long ago and had heard of the legate's troubles, sent foot soldiers and knights there, who drove back the scholars and others with great violence and saved the legate and his people unharmed, though not without bloodshed. After this the legate left the city under escort, and he excommunicated in general all scholars who had made this assault and any others who were present at the assault and supported them.

. . . .

4 On the following feast of St Andrew the Apostle [30 November 1225], the said legate convoked a council at Bourges to which he summoned the arch-bishops, bishops, abbots, and chapters of all of France. Count Raymond of Toulouse came; begging that the bosom of holy mother Church be opened to him, he humbly requested absolution. He offered to purge himself and mend his ways, and to the best of his ability to do justice to all convicted or confessed heretics in his land without delay, and from now on to expedite their eradica-tion. He also promised that he would make his land obedient to the Roman church in every other way, and would make it peaceful and secure as well; and

sue hereticis convictis vel confessis iustitiam indilatam, et ad eos deinceps exstyr-
pandos operam efficacem; promittens etiam quod terram suam obedientem de
cetero Romane ecclesie redderet et pacificam et securam, et quod clericis suos
redditus in integrum restitueret, et dampna eis congrue resarciret. Quibus Amorricus comes de Monte forti obvians, litteras pape Innocentii necnon et Philippi
regis Francie ostendebat in quibus continebatur et dicti comitis Tolosani dampn-
natio et terre Albigensium Symoni de Monte forti,[j] patri suo, facta donatio,
sic-uti asserebat. Tandem post multas altercationes legatus et episcopi super hoc
secretum consilium habuerunt, et sic negotio infecto comitem ad propria
remiserunt.

5 Preterea cum legatus ex parte domini pape per totum Francie regnum
peteret fructum duarum prebendarum in unaquaque abbatia et in qualibet
ecclesia cathedrali, et in aliis ecclesiis conventualibus fructus unius prebende tantummodo, ad summi pontificis usus in perpetuum retinendos, et iam ad hoc
episcoporum aliqui consensissent, capitulorum nuntii hiis omnibus coram legato
et coram omnibus obviarunt, asserentes capitula pro quibus venerant hoc nullo
modo factura nulloque tempore concessura. Adiecit etiam legatus quod dominus papa duobus episcopis dederat in mandatis quod ad dictum quatuor abbatum quos ad visitandas abbatias totius Francie et ad corrigendos excessus earum
destinaverat, abbates deponerent universos. Quo audito, archiepiscopi et episcopi, videntes se per hoc in abbatiis iurisdictionem omnimodam perdidisse, se
hoc nunquam quamdiu viverent concessuros, unanimiter responderunt. Et sic
precepta apostolica tam de prebendis quam de depositione abbatum in pendulo
remanserunt.

6 Tunc fere octoginta magistrorum Parisius qui contra legatum in supradicto
assultu fuerant et ligatos legati sententia se videbant, absolutionem a legato in
dicto concilio petierunt petitamque protinus receperunt.

. . . .

7 QUALITER REX FRANCIE FUIT DOMINUS COMITATUS THOLOSANI.[k] Tertia
autem die post conversionem sancti Pauli apostoli (28 January 1226), scilicet feria
quarta, Ludovicus rex Francie et legatus generale concilium Parisius celebrarunt,
in quo idem legatus auctoritate domini pape Raimundum comitem Tolosanum
suosque complices excommunicavit et terram illius tanquam dampnati heretici
Ludovico regi Francie et heredibus eius in perpetuum confirmavit. Amorricus
etiam[l] comes de Monte forti et Guido patruus eius quicquid iuris habebant in
predicta terra regi Francie et illius heredibus quitaverunt, et litteras inde con-
fectas eidem regi protinus reddiderunt.

[j] dampnatio *add. et canc.* A
[k] Qualiter—Tholosani] *tit. in mg.* A
[l] etiam] autem *male leg. Careau*

that he would restore to clerics their revenues in full and would suitably make good their losses. In opposition to these proposals, to substantiate his claims Count Amaury de Montfort displayed letters of Pope Innocent and also of King Philip of France that contained both the condemnation of the said count of Toulouse and the donation of the land of the Albigensians made to his father Simon de Montfort. After much argument back and forth, the legate and the bishops finally took secret counsel on the matter, and thus they sent the count back home with the business unfinished.

5 After this, on the pope's behalf the legate requested the income of two prebends in each abbey and in every cathedral church, and in other conventual churches the income of only one prebend, all of which were to be kept in perpetuity for the pope's use. Some of the bishops had already consented to this when the nuncios of the chapters objected to all of this in the presence of the legate and everyone else. The nuncios asserted that the chapters they represented were in no way about to do this and were at no time about to allow it. The legate also added that the lord pope had commanded two bishops to depose any abbot whatsoever at the dictum of the four abbots whom he had designated to visit all of the abbeys in France and to correct their excesses. On hearing this, the archbishops and bishops saw that by this they would lose all jurisdiction whatsoever over abbeys, so they unanimously replied that as long as they lived they were not about to permit this. And thus the apostolic precepts, both about prebends and about the deposition of abbots, remained pending.

6 Then about eighty masters of Paris who had participated in the assault against the legate mentioned above [§ 3] and who found themselves bound by the legate's sentence, in this council begged absolution from the legate, and their petition was immediately granted.

. . . .

7 HOW THE KING OF FRANCE BECAME LORD OF THE COUNTY OF TOULOUSE. On the third day after the conversion of St Paul the Apostle [28 January 1226], which was a Wednesday, King Louis of France and the legate celebrated a general council at Paris, in which the legate, by the authority of the lord pope, excommunicated Count Raymond of Toulouse and his accomplices and bestowed his land, as that of a condemned heretic, on King Louis of France and his heirs in perpetuity. In addition, Count Amaury de Montfort and his uncle Guy renounced whatever rights they had in the aforesaid land in favor of the king of France and his heirs, and then they immediately gave the king a written statement to that effect.

8 Quo facto, rex habito diligenti consilio sequenti feria sexta (30 January) cum omnibus fere episcopis et baronibus regni sui signo crucis dominice insignitur, ut a vinea domini Dei Sabbaoth, quam iam diu aper ille Tolosanus exterminaverat, inutilia eradicaret et utilia propagaret.

9 Sicque legatus, super fide regis et principum commotus nimia pietate, per regni provincias delegat viros probabiles qui in remissionem omnium peccatorum crucem assumendam contra Albigenses hereticos predicarent, et cruce signatos et res eorum sub ecclesie tutela reciperent, et excepto voto peregrinationis Jerosolimitane, eos ab omnibus aliis votis necnon et delictis absolverent et quitarent.

10 Cum assensu etiam quorumdam episcoporum addidit legatus in hoc gratiam pietati quod quolibet anno usque ad quinquennium centum millia librarum super decimam reddituum et proventuum clericorum promisit regi coram omnibus se daturum; et si ad hoc decima non posset sufficere, thesauros sancte ecclesie traditurum; excommunicans generaliter omnes illos qui terram regis quamdiu esset in partibus Tolosanis invaderent et alios qui regi super hoc obviarent vel regis propositum impedirent.

· ·

11 Postea in dominica qua cantatur "Letare Ierusalem" scilicet iiii. kalendas Aprilis (29 March 1226), Ludovicus rex apud Parisius [concilium]^m convocavit, ibique multa cum legato, episcopis, et baronibus tractans de negotio^n Albigensi, universis et singulis regni sui qui ei debebant exercitum mandavit per litteras et precepit ut quarta dominica post resurrectionem dominicam (17 May) in occursum eius cum armis debitis apud Byturicas convenirent; sic tractantes negotia, sic parati quod possent cum eo in partibus^o Tholosanis quamdiu ibi moram faceret demorari.

· ·

12 Per idem tempus, xvii. kalendas Iunii (16 May 1226) apud Turon' circa vesperum duo homines in Ligeris fluvio perierunt, statimque venti turbine et tonithruo subito movente in ecclesia beati Martini, in qua usque ad hec tempora sicut dicebatur fulgur nunquam ceciderat, fulgur corruit, crucem magnam ferream frangens et eradicans que sita erat super turris sancti Nicholai pinnaculum: per hoc aperte denuntians et crucis negotium impeditum et venturum regis et regni Francie detrimentum.

13 Tunc comes Marchie a rege monitus et legato, filiam comitis Tholosani quam filio suo desponsaverat, reddidit comiti Tholosano. Quo facto, rex, legatus, universique et singuli^p qui cruce signati erant xvi. kalendas Iunii (17 May)

---

^m concilium] *manus recentior in mg. suppl.* A

^n negotio] negoti *scr. et litt.* o *supra lineam inser.* A

^o transmarinis] *add. et canc.* A

^p singuli] singul' *scr. et litt.* i *add.* A

8 After this was done, the king diligently consulted almost all the bishops and barons of his kingdom, and on the following Friday [30 January] he was marked with the sign of the Lord's Cross, so that he might uproot useless things and propagate useful ones in the vineyard of the Lord God of Sabaoth, which that wild boar of Toulouse had devastated for a long time.

9 The legate was moved by the great piety of the king and the magnates concerning the Christian faith, and consequently he assigned competent men to preach throughout the provinces of the kingdom. To those who assumed the Cross against the Albigensian heretics they were to promise remission of all sins, and they were to take those signed with the Cross and their goods under the protection of the Church, and they were to absolve and dispense them from all sins and vows, except the vow to make a pilgrimage to Jerusalem.

10 With the assent of some of the bishops, the legate out of piety also added this favor to the king: in the presence of all he promised the king that every year for up to five years he would be given a hundred thousand pounds to be derived from a tenth of the income and revenues of clerics; and if the tenth failed to produce that sum, the difference would be made up from the treasures of holy Church. He also excommunicated in general all those who might invade the king's land while he was in the area of Toulouse, and also others who might oppose the king in this regard or impede the king's purpose.

. . . .

11 Next King Louis convoked a council at Paris on the Sunday when "Laetare Jerusalem" is sung, namely on the fourth day before the kalends of April [29 March 1226]. And there, after discussing many things about the Albigensian business with the legate, the bishops, and the barons, he sent letters to everyone in his kingdom who owed him military service ordering and instructing them to assemble fully equipped at his rendezvous at Bourges on the fourth Sunday after Easter [17 May]; they should put off other affairs and come prepared to remain with him in the Toulouse area as long as he might stay there.

. . . .

12 At the same time, on the seventeenth day before the kalends of June [16 May 1226], about the time of vespers, two men drowned in the Loire river at Tours. And immediately after this came whirlwinds and sudden thunder, and a lightning bolt fell on the church of St-Martin, which they say had never been struck by lightning before, and it broke and destroyed the great iron cross that was on the pinnacle of St Nicholas' tower. This event openly proclaimed both an impediment to the business of the Cross and some future damage to the king and kingdom of France.

13 Then the count of La Marche [Hugh X de Lusignan], having been warned by the king and legate, returned his son's fiancée [Joan] to her father, the count

apud Bytur' ex omni parte conveniunt; ibique rex et legatus super negotio Albigensi multa consilio episcoporum et principum ordinant et discernunt. Nam legatus a senibus, pueris, feminis, et pauperibus, et infirmis cruce signatis maiorem partem nummorum quos iuramento prestito se habere dicebant, ad crucis negotium retinebat; et eos sic absolutos ad partes suas protinus remittebat. Rex vero a multis qui ei debebant exercitum recepit pecuniam infinitam, alios secum duxit renitentes admodum et invitos, exceptis Turonicis, Lemovicensibus, et Pictavinis, quos cum comite Marchie ad tuendam Pictaviam dereliquit.[q]

14 Aderant ibi abbates clericique innumeri a capitulis suis missi regi et legato humiliter supplicantes ne liberam ecclesiam Gallicanam petendo decimam ecclesiasticorum proventuum et reddituum subicerent servituti, cum non ad hoc conventus et capitula consensissent, et parati essent et crucis et regis et regni negotio auxilium competens impertiri. Sed rex et legatus eos audire super hoc noluerunt, sicque illi clam maledicentes crucis et regis negotio recesserunt.

[q] dereliquid A

Document 4
CHRONIQUE RIMEE OF PHILIP MOUSKET

All but one of the accounts of the Council of Bourges are narrated by clerics in Latin. The exception is a verse chronicle of the kings of France that Philip Mousket (Mouskes), a rich burger of Tournai, wrote in French for middle-class laymen like himself. For the reign of Louis VIII, it is an independent account, written perhaps fifteen years later, by an honest and uninventive contemporary who had hardly more than a general knowledge of royal affairs. In the passages given below, the facts are much the same as in the Latin chronicles, but the story is told from quite another point of view. Mousket's outlook is bourgeois rather than clerical, which opens for us a new perspective on familiar events. Because the author's intentions and attitudes give this work its peculiar value, I shall introduce him at greater length than the impersonal monastic chroniclers.

The poet tells us little of himself explicitly except his name and an early date in his life—he was present at the sack of Tournai in 1213. From internal evi-

of Toulouse. When this had been done, the king, the legate, and everyone who had taken the Cross came from every part of the kingdom and assembled at Bourges on the sixteenth day before the kalends of June [17 May]. There the king and legate decided and ordered many things with the counsel of the bishops and leading men. Now the legate had those crusaders who were old men, boys, women, poor, or infirm swear under oath how much money they had; then he kept most of it for the business of the Cross and sent them home forthwith, their vows having been thus fulfilled. Moreover the king received immense sums of money from many who owed him military service, while others he took with him although they were altogether opposed and unwilling. The men of Tours, Limoges, and Poitou, however, he left behind with the count of La Marche to guard Poitou.

14 Also present there were abbots and innumerable clerics who had been sent by their chapters to the king and legate humbly begging them not to reduce the free Gallican church to servitude by demanding a tenth of ecclesiastical proceeds and revenues, since the monasteries and chapters had not consented to this, even though they were ready to present an aid suitable for the business of the Cross and the king and the kingdom. But the king and the legate refused to hear them about this, and so they departed, silently cursing the business of the Cross and of the king.

---

dence, however, it appears that he began writing his poem about 1240 and died about five years later. Local records attest that members of Mousket's family were prominent in Tournai during the thirteenth century as rich merchants and local magistrates (*échevins*). Philip's name appears only once (1236/1237), so it would be rash to maintain that he himself was either a businessman or a politician; with even less justification he has been called a gentleman or a knight (Walpole, Le Clerc). What is certain is that he was of the *haute bourgeoisie,* with the means and leisure to write for his own amusement (Walpole, p. 395).

By the standards of his day, his tastes were middle class rather than aristocratic, for he seems oblivious to current courtly and clerical fashions in poetry or history. With the complacency of a provincial middlebrow, he ignored the trend to vernacular prose histories that produced Villehardouin and Robert of Clari, but instead he cultivated the *declassé* tradition of versified history, which had been high literary fashion in the previous century.

The result was an immense, rambling poem of 31,286 rhymed octosyllabic verses, which takes its manner from the *chansons de gestes* and its form from the courtly romances. In the prologue, the poet announces his intention "Des Rois de Franche en rime mettre / Toute l'estorie" (vss. 4–5), but he soon convinces us that before his own lifetime *estoire* for him means legend. Beginning with the Trojan founders of the Gaulish monarchy, he jingles along, drawing his tales from a variety of sources, all in French as far as we can tell, with a marked taste for historical fiction. A full third of the poem celebrates the reign of Charlemagne, who loomed largest of all kings in the popular imagination. Save for his own times, then, Mousket's chronicle is worthless as factual history. With the reign of Philip Augustus, however, the fables begin to give way to facts. From 1210 on, the *Chronique* is a reliable source for the history of Flanders, and after 1225 for France as well (Holder-Egger). The narrative continues down to 1243, within a year or so of the author's death.

Artistically, the work was a failure. The poem survived Mousket in a single copy, which accumulated dust until exhumed by the erudition of the seventeenth century. If the snub was intentional, it speaks well for medieval taste, since the bourgeois of Tournai was a mediocre poet by any standard. That, at least, is the unanimous verdict of his modern critics, who deplore both his technique and imagination. Undismayed by want of talent, he rhymed falsely, padded lines profusely, and rambled on at his own tedious pace. The reader, both lost among vague generalities obscuring the matter and dulled by monotony of manner, finds himself twice bored. The poet, to his credit, strove to versify his sources as literally as possible, but to fit them to the mold of meter and rhyme, he interlarded innocuous verbiage. Had Mousket been a poet of imaginative force and polished artistry, he might have breathed such life into his inventions that they would be indistinguishable from fact, but the very mediocrity of his mind prevented him from eking out his facts persuasively.

When the contemporary part of the chronicle was published in 1838, its reliability was somewhat suspect, but within fifty years Mousket had earned a reputation no worse than most monastic chroniclers. Holder-Egger assured the readers of the MGH that if the verbiage were but cleared away and due allowance made for poetic license, much would be found that was trustworthy. The principle is clear enough, but in practice it is not so easy to discern fact from fancy. Take, for example, the account of the Paris riot (§ 1–2). The sense of Mousket's 136 words can easily be compressed into 53: "Five months later, Romanus came to Paris, where he ordered the masters who claimed certain privileges to produce their charter, which two popes and some archbishops had allegedly approved. When he tore it up, they attacked him and killed one of his men. But King Louis sent his troops, who saved the legate."

To tighten loose constructions, remove repetitions, and omit value judgments presents no difficulty. The problem is rather which details to retain as genuine and which to discard as embellishment. The two popes sound circumstantial enough to stay, but the archbishops were clearly dragged in by their stoles for a rhyme. For the same reason the crossbowmen must be excluded from the catalogue of royal troops. Once this most circumstantial element has been rejected, the others are easily dismissed as a pallid formula akin to "all the king's horses and all the king's men." These are judgments with which not everyone may agree, but they illustrate how the historical critic must guard against pseudofacts introduced by the poet. To complicate matters, some details, which such arguments might explain away, are in fact authentic. Thus, the internal critic must spare the legate's one man killed, whom the Dunstable annalist also mentions (vs. 25368 and Doc. 2.1).

When the poet uses his license to elaborate facts, he is easily detected, or at any rate suspected. More difficult to perceive are his simplifications, which the final negotiations on the crusade (§ 6-8) illustrate better than the riot scene. After a patently fictional recitation of the pope's appeal that Louis received at Melun, we are simply told that the king took the cross, but not that this took place at Paris after several days of deliberation.

Enough has been said to show the characteristic difficulties that attend this versified history. Had Mousket been a greater poet, he would have been a worthless chronicler. But at heart he was an historian, so much so that we may believe he hobbled his poetry to preserve the sense of his sources. If he had written the history of his age in prose, surely he would have achieved more.

The abortive union of poetry with history has raised special questions of evaluation; two general ones remain: how reliable were his sources? how was he biased? For the contemporary annals 1210-1243, we can discover few if any written sources. Some detect the influence of Alberic of Trois-Fontaines (Doc. 5), but none is evident in the passages given below. Indeed, for the events with which we are concerned, I doubt that Mousket consulted written sources at all. Except for the few episodes which he witnessed himself—and hastens to tell us so—he must have relied on word of mouth. Evidently his informants were adequate, for generally he has the facts straight. They must have been the ordinary bearers of news to one who lacked friends at court, council, and university. Wherever fellow Walloons played no part, he can give no more than a bare epitome. Occasionally he found an eyewitness, as for the siege of Avignon, which he describes at length in circumstantial detail. This exception to his customary brevity and generality suggests that Mousket conscientiously proportioned his narrative to his knowledge: apparently he put into verse just what he had heard at Tournai as the news of the day.

A few strokes suffice to delineate his prejudices and predilections. By culture he was French, and indeed may have known no other tongue. Living as he did just within the frontier may perhaps have sharpened his sense of cultural identity, of which the phrase *nos François* is a constant reminder. In politics, Philip was so much the royalist that his ambition was to raise a poetic monument to the French crown. The *esprit laïque* tinged his piety, inasmuch as clerical avarice is a favorite theme (§ 10), but for the most part he respected the hierarchy as thoroughly as he loathed the heretic. These attitudes are typical rather than personal; they mark him as a spokesman for his class—the emergent bourgoisie, newly rich and already possessed of a distinctive style in religion, politics, and culture. Only his cultural enthusiasms and limitations set him apart from his class as an individual. No intellectual, as Walpole justly writes, "he was master of few arts. . . . But he must have had an immense interest in history, and gratified it by drinking in the national story from every popular source" (p. 407). Other would-be gentlemen of his generation shared his taste for the legendary past, but Mousket alone let this fascination lead him to the lengths of the *Chronique rimée*.

MS.—Unique copy in Paris, BnF, MS. franç. 4963.

Ed.—(1) Complete edition by Baron F. de Reiffenberg, *Chronique rimée de Philippe Mouskès,* Collection de chroniques belges inédites, 2 vols. (Brussels, 1836-1838), with a biographical *Supplément* (1845). (2) Conclusion (vss. 27137-31286) edited by J. N. de Wailly and L. Delisle, *Rec. hist. Gaules,* XXII (1865), 34-81. (3) Portions of German interest edited by A. Tobler, MGH, SS, XXVI (1882), 718-821, with an historiographic preface by O. Holder-Egger. (4) New edition in preparation by R. Mantou.

25351   Apriés V mois, ne plus ne mains,
            I kardenaus, mestre Roumains,
            Qui déuist iestre sages pestres,
            Vint à Paris, manda les mestres,
25355   Qui d'une francise parloient,
            Dont privilège bon avoient,
            Confermé de II apostoles
            Et d'arcevesques à estoles.
            Mestre Roumains lor commanda
25360   A aporter et demanda.
            Et li mestre li aportèrent,

Text.—Selections below (vss. 25351-25484) are included only in Reiffenberg's edition (II, 486-491), from which they are printed here. His transcription is often said to be faulty (Molinier, Bossuat), but Tobler's collation of ca. 10,000 verses discovered on the average only one error per sixty lines, which is tolerable if not exemplary.

Translation.—I gratefully acknowledge the help I have received, first from Norris J. Lacy, who encouraged my first efforts, and then from Caroline A. Jewers, whose vigilance has greatly improved the final version.

Refs.—The editors' introductions are recommended; also Petit-Dutaillis, *Louis,* pp. xxi–xxii. For the vernacular quasi-historical sources and a general appreciation, R. N. Walpole, *Philip Mouskés and the Pseudo-Turpin Chronicle,* University of California Publications in Modern Philology, vol. XXVI, no. 4 (Berkeley and Los Angeles, 1947), 327-440, esp. § 4. Still of value is V. Le Clerc, *Hist. litt. France,* XXI (1847), 698-702; but not A. Duval in XIX (1838), 861-872. For editions, Potthast, *Wegweiser,* I (1896), 797. For older literature, Molinier, *Sources,* no. 2522 and Introd., § 174; for more recent titles, Bossuat, *Manuel* (1951), nos. 3770-3779, and *Supplément,* nos. 6198-6199, and esp. R. Mantou, "Phillipe Mousquet," in *Dictionnaire des lettres françaises:* [Vol. 1] *Le Moyen Age,* ed. R. Bossuat et al., 2nd ed. by G. Hasenohr and M. Zink (Paris, 1992), pp. 1146-1147.

25351   After five months, neither more nor less,
       A cardinal, Master Romanus,
       Who was said to be a discreet priest,
       Came to Paris [where] he summoned the masters
25355   Who claimed to have a franchise
       That gave them a fine privilege,
       Confirmed by two popes
       And by archbishops in stoles.
       Master Romanus ordered them to come
25360   And asked that they bring it.[1]
       And the masters brought it

    1. Mousquet leaves the matrix of the university's seal out of his story; instead, he has the legate destroy a document (*francise,* vs. 25355; cf. 25364). The same is true of Alberic of Trois-Fontaines (Doc. 5.2).

Tout ensanble si li mostrèrent.
Li cardenaus, en leur despi,
Devant leur ious lor dérompi,
25365 Par son orguel et par folage;
    2 Et li mestre furent volage,
Armé se sont, si l'asalirent,
Et I sien home li ocisent.
Mais li rois Loéis le sot;
25370 Si tramist al plus tos k'il pot
Ses siergans et ses cevaliers,
Et avoec ses arbalestriers.
A force les ont départis.
Ensi demora li estris,
25375 Et se ne fust blous pour le roi,
Ocis l'éuissent à desroi.
    3 Mais il iert des plus haus Romains,
Del linage des Froiepains;
S'iert parens le roi d'auques loing.
25380 Or il aida à son besoing,
Quar petit li valust sa gille.
    4 Droit à Béorges al concille
S'en ala, et li arcevesque
I furent, abbé et évesque.
25385 Et s'i vint li quens de St.-Gille,
Ki n'i fist vallant une tille
De sa besougne, quant vint là,
Qu'escuméniiés s'en r'ala,
Ausi com il i fu venus,
25390 Voire plus, s'il pot estre plus.
Quar il ot tantes fois menti,
Que nus à lui ne s'asenti:
Par trives fu aconduis là,
Et par trives lues s'en r'ala.
25395   5 Et I et autre et li clergiés,
Ki là furent aparilliés,
Se traisent tot à une corde,
Pour Dieu et pour miséricorde,
Que les Aubugois destruiroient.

As a group so they might show it to him.
The cardinal, holding them in contempt,
Tore it apart before their eyes

25365 Because he was proud and foolish.
　　2 And the masters overreacted;
They had armed themselves, so they assaulted him,
And they killed one of his men.
But King Louis learned of it;

25370 So as soon as he could, he sent
His footmen and his horsemen,
And with them his crossbowmen.
They [the masters] were dispersed by force.
Thus the strife abated,

25375 And if it were not for the king,
They would have killed him [Romanus] outrageously.
　　3 But he was from the highest Romans,
From the Frangipani lineage;
Indeed he was a distant relative of the king.

25380 Now he helped him when he needed it,
Because he [the king] was not good at subterfuge.
　　4 Straight to Bourges to the council
He went, and archbishops
Were there, and abbots and bishops.

25385 And the count of St–Gilles came there,
Who wasn't worth a piece of string
When he went there, because of his insufficiency;[2]
He went back again excommunicated
Just as he had come,

25390 Or more so if he could be more.
For he had lied so many times
That no one believed him.
He was conducted there thanks to a truce,
And by the truce he went straight back again.

25395 　　5 One and all and the clergy
Who were assembled there
Unanimously decided
For God's sake and for mercy
That the Albigensians should be destroyed.

2. Mousket is not sure what Raymond's fault was, but the poet cloaks his ignorance in generality: the count was *lacking* something—perhaps faith, favor, humility, luck, or just a good case.

25400 Et grant pardon sour sus feroient.
I escrit fisent lues entr'aus,
Et s'i pendirent leur saiiaus;
A l'apostolie l'ont tramis,
Que li siens saiiaus i fust mis.
25405 Et l'apostolies otroïa
Quan que li clergiés li proïa.
    6 Quant on ot le brief despondu,
Si a lues son saiiel pendu
Li pappe, et tantos li mesages
25410 S'en vint arière, comme sages,
A Meléun, ù li baron
Furent od le roi d'environ;
Et s'i furent li arcevesque
Abbé, prélat et li évesque.
25415   7 Si ont tuit de leur volenté
Au roi Loéys créanté
Que d'Aubugois la crois presist,
Et sien fust quan qu'il conquesist,
Tout quitement lui et son oir,
25420 Cités et castiel et avoir,
Fors çou que sainte glise monte;
Et n'i tenist-on plait ne conte
Des Aubugois à espargner,
Clerc ne vilain ne chevalier,
25425 Ne feme ne petit enfant,
Mais tout tuast-on maintenant:
S'iroient li boin devant Dieu,
Et li mauvais en mauvès lieu.
Et ki sour le roi mesferoit,
25430 Entretant com il là seroit,
N'i auroit nul si haut de lui
Qu'autel pardon n'éuist sor lui,
Com d'en Aubugois à aler,
Et c'iert autant com d'outre mer.
25435 Et dut tenir li rois sans gierre
Tot en pais deçà mer la tière.

25400 And they would grant great indulgences for doing so.
 And they set things down in writing immediately
 And then affixed their seals to it.
 It was transmitted to the pope,
 So that his seal might be placed on it.
25405 And the pope granted
 What the clergy requested.
 6 When the letter was presented,
 The pope put his seal on it immediately,
 And the sagacious messengers
25410 Came back right away
 To Melun,[3] where the barons
 Were in the king's presence;
 And archbishops were there,
 And abbots, prelates, and bishops.
25415 7 Completely of their own will
 They have promised to King Louis
 That the Cross would prevail in Albigeois,
 And when he had conquered it, it would be his
 In full title for him and his heirs,
25420 Cities and castles and possessions,
 Except for holy Church's share.
 And no one considered pleas or plans
 To spare the Albigensians,
 Neither clerics nor peasants nor knights,
25425 Nor women nor small children,
 But now they should all be killed:
 The good ones would go into God's presence
 And the bad ones would go to the bad place.
 And whoever wronged the king
25430 During his stay there [in Albigeois],
 There would be none so high-born
 Who would not have such a pardon imposed on him
 As to go to Albigeois,
 And this was just like going [crusading] overseas.
25435 And without war the king was to hold
 The land on this side of the sea in peace.

3. The conference was in fact held at Paris (see chap. 4, after n. 37).

8 Ensi l'apostoles manda,
Et li rois ki s'en amenda,
Prist la crois et tout si haut conte.
25440 Et si, com la vérités conte,
A tout le clergiet dut avoir
Li rois le disme de l'avoir,
Tant com il i seroit en tasque.
Et diut mouvoir apriés la Pasque,
25445 Et jusqu'à VII ans là manoir,
Il u ses gens, par estavoir;
Et gens mener tout à son coust,
Ançois que venist à l'aoust,
Pour la tière faire pupler
25450 De gent crestiène, pour capler.
Madame Blance l'otroïa,
La roïne, c'on moult proisa.

                . . . .

25467   9 Ceste nouviele fu séue
En Aubugois et connéue,
Qu'il ièrent pris en tel haor,
25470 Si se croissièrent de paour,
Comme pour aler outre mer,
C'on n'es péust de rien blasmer.
Mais cele crois k'il orent prise
Fu fause et de tous maus esprise,
25475 Car il doutèrent les François,
Ki grévés les orent ançois.
        10 Toutes voies fist-on le don,
Par la contrée, del pardon,
Tel com li pape l'avoit dit,
25480 Mais il i ot I contredit
Des kapiteles pour le disime
Que refusoient il méisme,
Et non pourquant s'aparilloient
D'aler, cil qui croissiet estoient.

8 Thus the pope ordered
And the king, who complied,
Took the cross and all of the highest nobles.

25440   And consequently, as truth tells,
The king was to have from all the clergy
A tenth of their wealth
As a tax as it were.
And he should set out after Easter,

25445   And remain there up to seven years,
He and his people, by necessity;
And everyone was to go at his own expense,
Just as he does in the host,
In order to people the land

25450   With Christian folk to do battle.
Madame Blanche, the queen, authorized it,
An action of which many approved.

. . . .

25467   9 When this news was known
And understood in Albigeois,
Because they [the French] were held in such hatred,

25470   They [the Southerners] took the cross out of fear,
Just as if they were going overseas.
For doing this one cannot blame them in any way.
But this cross that they had taken
Was false and considered to be completely bad,

25475   Because they feared the French
Who previously had done them great harm.
    10 Everywhere throughout the country
The gift of the indulgence was made
Just as the pope had declared it.

25480   But there was opposition
From the chapters concerning the tenth,
Which they themselves refused [to pay].
Nonetheless those who had taken the cross
Prepared themselves to go.

Document 5
CHRONICLE OF ALBERIC OF TROIS-FONTAINES

All too rarely does the character of a monastic chronicler shine through in his work, but the Cistercian monk Alberic of Trois-Fontaines is a memorable exception. Of the man himself we know only his name, *Albericus* (Aubri) and his community—Trois-Fontaines, in the diocese of Châlons-sur-Marne—but his character permeates his work. Like many another religious, he compiled a universal chronicle, from Creation to 1241, which was begun no later than 1227 and finished before 1251. The conventional procedure would have been to appropriate an earlier chronicle, add elements of local history, and then continue it (for example Doc. 3); but Alberic adopted a distinctly different course. Curious by nature, he accumulated thousands of scraps of information, which he literally compiled into a chronological series. The result was hardly a polished narrative, but rather a transcript of his notes, one for each paragraph, often complete with citation. Like a magpie, he gathered the bad with the good from an extraordinary range of sources. Not only dozens of earlier writers about history and travel, but also epitaphs, genealogies, charters, correspondence, law books, and (to our scandal or delight) vernacular legends and romances—all were grist to his industrious mill. For us his most grateful trait is the relish with which he garnered small, precise details, especially for the local history of his native Champagne. The history of Trois-Fontaines itself he excluded in principle, perhaps to be reserved for a separate history.

From about 1215 on, Alberic's storehouse is a contemporary record, often of unique value. Obviously, a compilation is no better than its sources, and Alberic's were highly uneven in value. In the earlier part of the chronicle, where he frequently cited his authorities, we know that instead of blending two sources into a single paragraph, he included only the better one. In the thirteenth-century annals, however, he rarely alleged an authority, so we can no longer be positive

---

Romanus Sancti Angeli dyaconus cardinalis per regnum Francie, per Burgundiam et Provinciam constitutus legatus, potestative que disponenda sunt disponere intendit. Huius auctoritate Remis in crastino sancti Luce (19 October) magister Iohannes de Abbatisvilla, vir honestis moribus preditus et ad

that each paragraph was based on a single source, much less know what it was. Nonetheless, the style continues to vary from paragraph to paragraph, although within a paragraph it is consistent, which suggests that his modern annals were compiled just as the earlier ones had been. Since we suspect, then, that each paragraph comes from a different source, the reliability of each needs to be evaluated separately. Often this can amount to no more than a subjective impression, yet occasionally some verifiable fact will provide a more objective measure. Thus, of the three selections below, the first is a local chronological note of convincing particularity; but this quality is lacking in the second paragraph, which is vague and general. In such a context, we must doubt that the casualty figures are accurate (Doc. 5.2), especially since one reliable source notes a mortality as well (Doc. 2.1) and another only "bloodshed" (Doc. 3.3). The final item, by contrast, cites and faithfully paraphrases an original document, which can be verified from other sources (see note in MGH; cf. Potthast, no. 8254).

Ed.—P. Scheffer-Boichorst, MGH, SS, XXIII (1874), 674-950. The title there, *Chronica Alberici monachi Trium Fontium a monacho novi monasterii Hoiensis interpolata,* refers to a second redaction in which a monk of the Cistercian house Neufmoutier, near Huy in the Liège area, interpolated the history of his house and locality.

Text.—Doc. 5 reprints the MGH edition, pp. 916-917, 921.

Refs.—The definitive *Monumenta* introduction (pp. 631-673) superseded earlier studies, for which see Potthast, *Wegweiser,* I (1896), 29. *Repertorium fontium historiae Medii Aevi,* II (1967), 167-168. Molinier, *Sources,* no. 2521 and Introd., § 170. M. Prevost in *Dictionnaire de biographie française,* IV (1948), 294-295, s.v. "Aubry des Trois-Fontaines."

Romanus, cardinal-deacon of Sant' Angelo, who was appointed legate for all of France, Burgundy, and Provence, was determined to use his legatine power to correct those things that needed correction. By his authority, Master Jean of Abbeville, the dean of Amiens, a man of upright character and the best

predicandum optimus theologus, Ambianensis decanus, consecratur in archiepiscopum Bisuntinensem.

. . . .

2 Bituricis civitate concilium celebratum est in festo sancti Andree (30 November), Romano cardinali presidente, de statu ecclesie et Albigensium. Qui cardinalis Parisios reversus nuper tumultum fecerat maximum, quoddam privilegium magistrorum et doctorum scindendo per medium; et vulnerati fuerant duo de familia eius. Scandalum amovit et absolvendos absolvit et turbatos pacificavit.

. . . .

3 Siquidem hoc eodem anno (1228) cardinalis Romanus, a Roma regressus pro facto Albigensium et pro discordia principum Francie, misit generali capitulo Cisterciensi duo paria litterarum, quas ei miserat summus pontifex. In quibus dicitur, quod papa omnes, qui iuramento fidelitatis Frederico imperatori erant astricti, et specialiter homines regni, a sacramento absolvit et absolutos denunciavit, 2. Kalendas Augusti (31 July); et multa mala ibi publicata sunt contra eum, quod sit hostis ecclesie et discipulus Machometi.

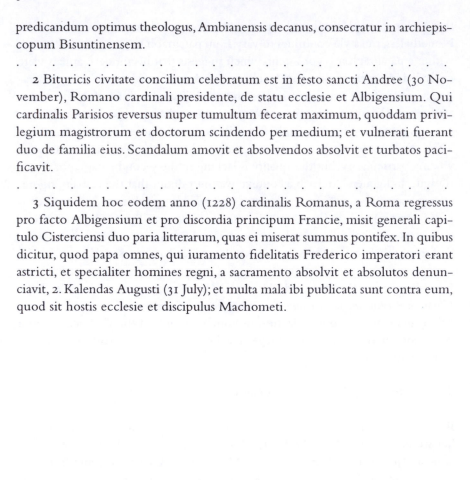

Document 6
CHRONICLE OF MS. REGINENSIS 171

The archbishops, bishops, and abbots present at Bourges are enumerated with apparent exactitude in a brief notice on the council which was published from an old chronicle by Devic and Vaissète. If correct, this testimony would alter the traditional view of the council's nature and composition, but since it conflicts with sources otherwise trustworthy (as discussed in chapter 3), its own reliability needs to be established. From what chronicle was it copied? Was the author in a position to give precise figures? Have the numerals been copied correctly? If Devic's manuscript was a late copy, does an earlier and more accurate one

theologian for preaching, was consecrated archbishop of Besançon at Reims on the morrow of St Luke's [19 October 1225].[1]

. . . .

2 In the city of Bourges a council was celebrated on the feast of St Andrew [30 November 1225] with cardinal Romanus presiding; it was about the state of the Church and of the Albigensians. The cardinal arrived from Paris, where he had recently caused the greatest commotion by tearing in half a certain privilege of the masters and doctors;[2] and two men belonging to his household were wounded. [At Bourges] he put an end to the scandal and absolved those who deserved absolution and pacified those who were stirred up.

. . . .

3 Also this same year [1228], after cardinal Romanus had returned from Rome because of the Albigensian affair and because of discord caused by the leading nobles of France, he sent to the Cistercian general chapter two similar letters that the pope had sent him. In one of these letters, dated 31 July, it was said that the pope released from their oath all those who had been bound to the emperor Frederick by an oath of fealty, and especially men of the [Sicilian] Regno, and the pope declared them to be released [from the bond of fealty].[3] And many bad things were publicly declared against Frederick, to the effect that he was an enemy of the Church and a follower of Mohammed.

1. Jean Halgrin (Allegrin) of Abbeville, archbishop of Besançon 1225–1227; also patriarch of Constantinople 1226–1227 and cardinal-bishop of Santa Sabina 1227–1238. Eubel, *Hierarchia*, I, 6, 38, 140; Maleczek, *Kardinalskolleg*, p. 191, n. 493.
2. Thus also Philip Mousket: see Doc. 4.1.
3. Cf. Potthast, nos. 8251 (5 Aug.) and 8254 (30 Aug.); Auvray, no. 233 (June–July?).

───

exist? To answer these essential questions, we must consult the manuscript that the Maurists cited as "Mss. 171. de la reine de Suède à Rome."

MS.—Easier said than done. Christina (1626–1689), the queen of Sweden who abdicated to become a Catholic convert in 1655 and, after traveling in France, retired to live the rest of her days in Rome, had accumulated a rich manuscript collection. She had not been dead a year when these 2,111 manuscripts were purchased by the Ottoboni pope, Alexander VIII, who selected 240 for his family library and placed the rest in the Vatican collections. Although some 72 were assigned to the Archivio Segreto, most form a separate series in the Apostolic Library—the *Codices Reginae Suecorum*, or for short, the *Reginenses*.

In Christina's time, the collection was arranged in a continuous series of

numbers, which was used by the Vatican librarians who drew up an initial inventory of the new accession when it was received in 1689. This classification
was not retained, however, by the new owner. After the books were rebound
and arranged by size, they were given new numbers, "which were, in fact, frequently changed," as Dom Wilmart noted darkly (p. xi). The new classification
was regarded as a provisional working arrangement during the fifty years that
the definitive catalogue was in preparation. The project was begun by Zacagnius
(curator 1692-1715) but the new *Inventario,* which is still the key to the collection, was prepared for the most part by Teolius between 1734 and 1740, and completed not later than 1751, when it was listed in a survey of the library's holdings
(idem). In the course of cataloguing, new manuscripts were inserted into the series (the last in 1740) and some old ones had their shelfmarks changed.

The history of the collection during these transitional years is shrouded in
obscurity, and particularly the shelfmark changes. Wilmart, in his modern printed
catalogue of the first five hundred *Reginenses latini,* carefully recorded and indexed the cancelled shelfmarks for every manuscript described. But for over
three-quarters of the collection, for which such a description has yet to be published, there is at present no concordance of the provisional shelfmarks employed
between the initial inventory of 1689 and the definitive one which went into
effect sometime in the 1740s. Unfortunately, the reference in Devic-Vaissète
seems to be to just such an intermediate shelfmark.

Certainly the *Mémoire,* as the editors entitled the extract from some MS.
Reginensis 171, did not come from the manuscript which has borne that mark
since at least the mid-eighteenth century. Dom Wilmart accurately described it
as a collection of the letters of Hildebert of Le Mans, and my own examination
has eliminated the possibility that the *Mémoire* might have been an unrecorded
fragment of a chronicle employed by the binder as a pastedown or flyleaf.

A more likely prospect seemed to be the manuscript that was numbered 171
in Christina's day. This is a miscellaneous collection (French, saec. xv med.) comprising twenty-six items, including two chronicles: *Chronico Martini Poloni ordinis Minorum* (fol. 131r), followed by the *Flores temporum, seu Chronicae imperiales*
(fols. 137r–203r). Both are listed in the inventory of 1689 printed by Montfaucon, but in their published form neither of the chronicles contains the *Mémoire*
(MGH, SS, XXII, 377-475, and XXIV, 230-250). The manuscript itself was located and thoroughly examined for me by Signorina Adriana Marucchi, who
reported positively that the *Mémoire* was not to be found in the corpus, although
she suggested that it might conceivably have formed part of the old binding,
which was redone under Pius IX. As she discovered from the inventory of 1689
(MS. Vat. lat. 7189), this was one of those *Reginenses* which Alexander VIII had
transferred to the *Ottoboniani,* which in turn became part of the Vatican Library

in 1751. Today MS. Ottob. lat. 2087, it still bears the ex-libris: "Ex Bibl. Seren. Reginae N. 171."

Neither the original *Reginensis* manuscript numbered 171 nor the present MS. Reg. lat. 171 contains the *Mémoire*. Two possibilities remain: either the number given by Devic-Vaissète is incorrect, or else it refers to a provisional shelfmark dating from the half-century 1690-1740 when the collection was being re-arranged in the course of perfecting the *Inventario*.

The second alternative has much to recommend it, for the authors of the *Histoire générale de Languedoc* would have consulted the collection during its transition period. The Congregation of St-Maur undertook that monumental history in 1709, but Devic and Vaissète were only assigned to the project in 1715. Of the two, Devic was familiar with the libraries of Rome, where he had spent the years 1701-1715. He may himself have come upon the passage in Rome and extracted it, for he often performed such services for fellow Maurists; or, during his years with the *Histoire,* he may have received the extract from some Roman correspondent. Whoever discovered it, we can be sure that it was a chance find because it is the only *Preuve* from the *Reginenses* in the third volume of the *Histoire* (1737); indeed, there are few, if any, contributions from other Roman collections. The actual publication was supervised by Dom Vaissète, since Devic had died three years before, and perhaps some more exact indication of provenance died with him. As it was, the Maurists left only one clue beyond the *Preuve* as printed below. In their narrative, we are told that the *Mémoire* was extracted from "une ancienne chronique," but nothing more (Devic-Vaissète, 1st ed., III, 348; 3rd ed., VI, 594).

There is always the possibility that the number given in Devic-Vaissète was never the correct one. One can try, as I have, various permutations of 171, but the *Reginenses* are rich in chronicles, many of them French ones from the Petau collection. Using both permuted numbers and the unpublished subject index, I consulted better than a dozen in June 1960 with no success, and I easily could have trebled that number had time permitted (MSS. Reg. lat. 111, 480, 507, 553, 555, 711, 733, 754, 771, 881, 897, 924, 925).

Even if I were in a position to pursue such a search indefinitely, it would be effort wasted, for eventually the subsequent volumes of the printed catalogue will complete Wilmart's list of all the *Reginenses* that have at one time or another been numbered 171. Until then, the manuscript source of the *Mémoire* remains unidentified, and the best I can hope is that this record of my aporia may lead to the identification of the fugitive piece.

Ed.—[C. Devic and J. Vaissète], *Histoire générale de Languedoc avec des notes et les pièces justificatives, composée sur les auteurs et les titres originaux et enrichie de divers monuments, par deux religieux Bénédictins de la congrégation de S. Maur,* 5 vols. (Paris,

1730-1745); 2nd edn., 10 vols. (Toulouse, 1840-1846). The third edition is usually cited in the present study: *Histoire générale de Languedoc avec des notes et les piéces justificatives, par Dom. Cl. Devic & Dom J. Vaissete,* 16 vols. (Toulouse, 1872-1904). A. Molinier revised the narrative and *Preuves* of the original vol. III (1737) for the third edition, where it occupies respectively vols. VI and VII–VIII (1879). Despite his profound knowledge of French chronicles, he provided no annotation on MS. Reg. 171, which was not included in his "Table des principaux ouvrages cités" (VIII, 2377 ff.).

On the authors, see Hoefer's *Nouvelle biographie générale,* s.v. "Vaissète, Dominique-Joseph" and "Vic, Claude de", in vols. XLV, 837-838, and XLVI, 80 (Paris, 1866). On their work, M. Lecomte, "Les Bénédictins et l'histoire de provinces aux XVIIᵉ et XVIIIᵉ siècles," *Revue Mabillon,* XVIII (1928), 48-55. See also the history of Devic-Vaissète in its companion atlas by E. Roschach and A. Molinier, *Histoire graphique de l'ancienne province de Languedoc* (Toulouse, 1904).

Text.—The text below is reproduced from the first edition (III, 299, preuve no. CLX). In addition to revised punctuation and capitalization, the 1879 edition (VIII, 815-816, preuve no. 242) alters the date to "Anno M CC XXV" with the tantalizing note, "Le ms. porte M CC XXV." Since it is unlikely that Molinier knew, much less consulted, the manuscript, he probably composed this note carelessly as a substitute for the marginal note in the 1737 edition, "*Leg.* MCCXXV," which of course was not a variant reading but only a conjectural correction by Devic and Vaissète. In place of my own emendation (*fide*), the 1737 edition indicated a presumably four-letter *lacuna* by as many periods (. . . .); nonetheless, there are *five* in the 1879 edition.

Mémoire sur le concile de Bourges.
Mss. 171. de la reine de Suède à Rome.

Anno M CC XXVI.ᵃ convocatum est concilium Bituricis à Romano tituli S. Angeli diaconi cardinali, in quo fuerunt principaliter XIV. archiepiscopi, & duo absentes, de quorum provinciis episcopi interfuerunt. Fuerunt autem omnes episcopi pariter CXIII. abbates verò D. & XX. exceptis procuratoribus; & tractatum est ibi de <fide>ᵇ comitis S. Egidii, & de terra Albigensi. Hoc anno mortuus est filius Philippi Ludovicus rex Franciae, & multi alii nobiles in terra Albigensium, & eodem anno successit ei in regnum Ludovicus filius suus habens annos .XII.

ᵃ *Leg.* MCCXXV.] *add. in marg.* ed. 1737
ᵇ fide *scripsi; lacuna literarum quatuor* ed. 1737

Refs.—The inventory of 1689 exists in two copies, today MSS. Vat. lat. 7138 and 10255: "Inventarium librorum manuscriptorum Reginae Alexandrae Christianae confectum anno 1689." Cf. the inventory printed by B. de Montfaucon, *Bibliotheca bibliothecarum,* I (Paris, 1739), 14-61.

The unpublished inventory that was completed in the 1740s may be consulted in the Vatican Library's Sala dei Manoscritti (no. 336): "Inventario dei Mss. Regin." There is also a subject index (no. 337), bound with the arms of Clement XIV (1769-1774): "Index codicum manuscriptorum latinorum reginae Suecorum." These are superseded down to MS. lat. 500 by the printed catalogue: *Codices Reginenses latini,* I–II (Vatican City, 1937-1945), ed. A. Wilmart, in the series "Bibliothecae Apostolicae Vaticanae codices manuscripti recensiti." See I, xi–xii, for the best account of the cataloguing.

For the view that the present numbers date back to November or December 1690, see G. Monticolo, "Intorno al codice Barberini XXXII, 125," *Archivio dell R. Società romana di storia patria,* XVI (1893), 503-515, esp. pp. 504-505, 508. See also his "Intorno ad alcuni antichi cataloghi della biblioteca manoscritta di Christina che si conservano nella Biblioteca Vaticano," ibid., XVII (1894), 197-226. However, Monticolo was tracing *Reginenses* only up to 1690, and thus he was hardly concerned with the subsequent half century. For further bibliography on the collection, see P. O. Kristeller, *Latin Manuscript Books Before 1600* (Munich, 1993), s.v. "Vaticano (Fondo Reginense)."

Finally, I must express my thanks to Mlle J. Vielliard, who as directorix of the Institut de Recherches et d'Histoire des Textes (Paris) communicated my inquiry to Signorina Adriana Marucchi, the Institut's agent in Rome, to whom I am deeply indebted for her detailed report, dated 27 September 1960, on MS. Ottob. lat. 2087.

I n the year 1226, a council was convoked at Bourges by Romanus, cardinal-deacon of Sant' Angelo. Chief among those present were 14 archbishops; two others were absent although bishops from their provinces were present. Altogether, however, there were 113 bishops present and 520 abbots, not counting the proctors. And the faith of the count of St-Gilles was discussed there, and the Albigensian land. This year King Louis of France, who was Philip's son, and many other nobles died in the land of the Albigensians; and the same year his twelve-year-old son, Louis, succeeded him as king.

SECTION TWO

FRANCO-PAPAL NEGOTIATIONS
PRELIMINARY TO THE CRUSADE

Document 7
LOUIS PETITIONS HONORIUS TO GRANT
HIS CONDITIONS
Late January or February 1224

Date.—Since the document bears no date, that must be reckoned from the context of events. The petition was Louis' response to proposals dispatched by Honorius after mid-December 1223, which would have taken at least a month to
reach the king (Doc. 9.4; cf. chap. 1, at n. 82), so mid-January 1224 is the earliest possible date for the petition. It was already in existence in February, when
Amaury de Montfort promised to cede Louis his rights in Languedoc if the pope
granted the petitions (Devic-Vaissète, VIII, 789; cf. chap. 1, at n. 91). Consequently, the petition dates from some time between mid-January and Amaury's
act in February. Petit-Dutaillis specified February, but it is possible that in 1224
the royal council met late in January, as it did the following year (Docs. 23-27).

MSS.—(A) Paris, Arch. nat., JJ 26, fol. 13va–vb: Register E. (B) Paris, BnF, MS.
lat. 9778, fol. 8v: Register F. Docs. 7 and 9 are an addendum in the hand of the

---

PETITIO AD PAPAM PRO REGE
QUANDO[a] IVIT[b] IN ALBIGENSIUM CONTRA HERETICOS[c]

Primo petit dominus rex quod ipse et omnes illi[d] qui cum eo ibunt in Albigesium habeant eandem indulgentiam et remissionem peccatorum quam
habent crucesignati de partibus transmarinis.

2 Item petit quod archiepiscopi Bitur', Rem', Senon', et quilibet eorum per
se habeant plenariam potestatem excommunicandi personas et interdicendi terras omnium illorum qui regnum[e] Francie inquietabunt vel turbabunt, seu personas vel terras eorum qui cum eo ibunt, sive sint de regno Francie sive extra
regnum, vel qui in regno Francie inter se moverint guerram, nisi ad mandatum
domini regis pacem fecerint vel treugam.

[a] quando] cum *Vaissète*
[b] ivit] ibit *Vaissète*
[c] Petitio—hereticos *om.* B
[d] illi] alii *Vaissète*
[e] regnum] regem *Vaissète*

original scribe; they are on a bifolium that is prefixed to the table of contents. Doc. 7, though undated, precedes Doc. 9 in both A and B. (C) Paris, BnF, MS. Baluze 8, fols. 16r–17v (transcript of A).

Ed.—Devic-Vaissète, III (1737), 292–293, preuve no. 155; VIII (1879), 792–794, preuve no. 236. Molinier supposedly revised the text from the original, but Vaissète's mistakes, noted in my apparatus, were not corrected. Moreover, Vaissète's text was inaccurately reprinted in *Rec. hist. Gaules*, XIX (1833), 750–751, which in turn was reprinted by Horoy, IV (1880), 595–598.

Refs.—Petit-Dutaillis, *Louis*, p. 460 (Catalogue des actes, no. 81), with free translation on pp. 282–283. On the registers: J. W. Baldwin, *The Government of Philip Augustus* (Berkeley and Los Angeles, 1986), pp. 412–418.

Text.—Transcribed from a photocopy of A and corrected from the original. Section numbers are supplied from the *Recueil* edition, except the last, which is my own, as is the paragraphing. B and C were collated, but as both are copies of A, I have recorded only the one substantial variant, from B.

PETITION TO THE POPE FOR THE KING WHEN HE SHALL GO
TO THE ALBIGEOIS AGAINST THE HERETICS

First the lord king requests that he and all who shall go with him to the Albigeois have the same indulgence and remission of sins that crusaders overseas have.

2 Item, he requests that the archbishops of Bourges, Reims, and Sens each have full power to excommunicate the persons and to interdict the lands of all those who disturb the peace of the kingdom of France or stir up the kingdom; and to do the same to all those who do so to the persons or lands of those who shall go with him. This applies both to those from the kingdom of France and to those who are from outside the kingdom; and also to those in the kingdom of France who make war among themselves, unless they make peace or a truce at the lord king's command.

3 Item petit dominus rex quod si qui astrinxerint se ad eundum cum eo in terram Albigesii vel ad morandum ibidem, quod predicti archiepiscopi habeant potestatem cohercendi eos per excommunicationem et interdictum ad solvendum id ad quod se astrinxerunt.

4 Item petit quod habeant potestatem excommunicandi personis[f] et interdicendi terras baronum Francie et aliorum hominum suorum qui in propriis personis cum ipso non perrexerint in Albigesium, vel si ire non possint, qui competens subsidium non fecerint ad expugnandum[g] hostes fidei et regni in Albigesium, maxime cum per hominagium[h] et juramentum teneantur domino regi ad expugnandum impugnatores regni, et nulla sit major impugnatio regni quam ista, que est de hostibus fidei et in regno, et omnes supradicte sententie relaxari non poterunt donec prius satisfactum fuerit competenter.

5 Item de treuga quam dominus papa et dominus rex Jerosolimitanus et rex Anglie petunt prorogari, vult dominus rex et petit quod ab instanti Penth'[i] in decem annos prorogetur inter se et heredes suos ex una parte et regem Anglie et heredes suos ex altera, et firmetur utrimque[j] juramento, ita quod dominus rex et heredes sui et imprisii remaneant in eadem teneura et saisina in qua sunt modo et fuerunt tempore alterius treuge. Et tantam vult habere prorogationem, pro eo quod nescit quantum durabit negotium et in ipso negotio nudabit se et regnum suum pecunia et hominibus.

6 Item petit quod habeat litteras domini pape patentes de abjudicatione comitatus Tholos' cum omnibus pertinentiis suis, ab utroque Raimundo, scilicet patre et filio et eorum heredibus in perpetuum, et totius terre de qua dictus Raimundus pater et Raimundus filius fuerunt tenentes, que est in regno domini regis, et totius vicecomitatus Biterren' et Carcasonesii[k] cum omnibus pertinentiis in regno domini regis, et omnium terrarum in eodem regno existentium eorum, qui guerreaverunt[l] aperte cum eis vel pro eis, et similiter omnium eorum qui huic negotio se opponunt vel decetero opponent, vel guerram faciunt seu decetero facient; et per predictos archiepiscopos fiat dicte abjudicationis denunciatio. Et petit dominus rex quod omnes terre predicte sibi et heredibus suis in perpetuum confirmentur, et illis quibus eis[m] dabit, si eas dare voluerit, retento sibi et heredibus suis hominagio[n] tamquam domino principali.

[f] personas A *et supralin. corr.* A1.
[g] expurgandum *Vaissète*
[h] hominagium] hommagium *Vaissète*
[i] Penth' *om. Vaissète*
[j] utrimque] utriusque *Vaissète*
[k] Carcassonensis *Vaissète*
[l] guerraverunt *Vaissète*
[m] eas *Vaissète*
[n] hommagio *Vaissète*

3 Item, the lord king requests that, if any shall obligate themselves to go with him to the Albigensians' land or to remain there, the same archbishops have the power of coercing them by excommunication and interdict to perform what they have obligated themselves to do.

4 Item, he requests that they have the power of excommunicating the persons and interdicting the lands of the barons of France and of his other men who shall not personally go with him to the Albigeois; or, if they are not able to go in person, shall not pay an appropriate subsidy for overcoming the enemies of the faith and of the kingdom in the Albigeois. This is especially justified because by homage and oath to the lord king they are bound to defend the kingdom from subversion, and nothing subverts the kingdom more than having enemies of the faith within the kingdom itself. And all the sentences mentioned above cannot be revoked unless competent satisfaction shall be made first.

5 Item, concerning the truce that the lord pope and the lord king of Jerusalem and the king of England have asked to be prolonged, the lord king wishes and requests that it be prolonged for ten years, beginning this year at Pentecost; and that it be between him and his heirs on the one hand and the king of England and his heirs on the other. And both parties shall confirm it with an oath to the effect that the lord king and his heirs and adherents shall remain in the same tenure and seisin in which they now are and were at the time of the other truce. And he greatly wishes to have a prolongation because he does not know how long the Albigensian business shall last, and in that business he shall strip himself and his kingdom of money and men.

6 Item, he requests that he have the lord pope's letters patent stating that both Raymonds, namely father and son, and their heirs forever have been deprived by judicial sentence of the county of Toulouse with everything pertaining to it; and of all land that said Raymond senior and Raymond junior held as fiefs in the kingdom of the lord king; and the entire viscounties of Béziers and Carcassonne with everything pertaining to them in the kingdom of the lord king. And let all those who openly fight on their side or for them be deprived likewise; and similarly all those who themselves oppose or in future shall oppose this business. And let the declaration of this judicial sentence be made by the aforesaid archbishops. And the lord king requests that all of the aforesaid lands be confirmed to him and to his heirs forever, and to those to whom he shall give them, if he shall wish to give them, the right of homage being reserved to himself and his heirs as principal lord.

7 Item petit sibi dari archiepiscopum Bitur' legatum, qui inter cetera habeat potestatem reconciliandi omnes illos qui ad debitam Ecclesie satisfactionem venerint, et quod° habeat legationem suam super omnes archiepiscopos et episcopos totius terre que se opponit catholice fidei in partibus illis, et omnium terrarum adjacentium que possunt cedere in utilitatem istius negotii vel impedimentum; et habeat eandem legationem quam habuit Corraudus episcopus Portuen' legatus Albig'; et fiat predicatio per totum regnum Francie pro subsidio terre Albig'.

Omnia supradicta fiant appellatione remota.

8 Item petit dominus rex quod, cum expense sint infinite et inestimabiles, ecclesia Romana provideat ei in Lx^{ta} milibus libris Parisiensibus singulis annis usque ad decem annos, que convertentur in usus illius terre.

9 Item petit quod dominus papa procuret erga imperatorem quod terre sue vicine Albigesio non noceant regi in hoc negotio nec aliquo modo negotium impediant, et si ei nocuerint vel negotium impedierint, quod de voluntate imperatoris possit dominus rex eos^p impugnare sicut alias, salvo jure imperatoris.

10 Si hec omnia supradicta facta fuerint^q domino regi, assecurata et confirmata, dominus rex ibit in propria persona in Albig' et in predicto negotio bona fide laborabit, et quando ipse in propria persona fuerit in terra Albig' et in negotio illo laboraverit^r bona fide, ipse vel heredes sui a Romana curia non capientur ad occasionem extunc in antea moram faciendi vel remanendi in terra illa vel denuo revertendi, nisi ad voluntatem suam.

11 Ad dictas siquidem petitiones faciendas et impetrandas in curia Romana, mittit dominus rex dilectos et fideles suos archiepiscopum Bitur' et^s Lingon' et Carnot' episcopos, ita quod si petitiones iste non fiant hac vice qua modo mittuntur, extunc in antea non tenebitur dominus rex ire in Albigesium, nisi voluerit.

° quod *om. Vaissète*
^p eas *Vaissète*
^q et *add. Vaissète*
^r et quando—laboraverit *om. Vaissète (homoioteleuton)*
^s et *om. Vaissète*

7 Item, he requests that the archbishop of Bourges be given to him as legate. Among other things, let the archbishop have the power of reconciling all those who shall render due satisfaction to the Church. And let his legation include all the archbishops and bishops of the land that is opposed to the Catholic faith in those parts; and let it also include those of all the adjacent lands that can help or hinder that business. And let him have the same legation that the Albigensian legate Conrad, bishop of Porto, had. And let there be preaching throughout the entire kingdom to obtain assistance for the Albigensian land.

And let all the aforesaid be granted with no possibility of appeal.

8 Item, the lord king requests that, since the expenses are immense and cannot be estimated, the Roman church provide him with sixty thousand pounds of Paris each year for ten years, which shall be used for the benefit of that land.

9 Item, he requests that the lord pope shall get the emperor to agree that his lands near the Albigeois neither do harm to the king in this business nor in any way impede it; and if they do harm to him or impede the business, the emperor has to agree that the lord king can attack them just like the others, saving the rights of the emperor.

10 If all the requests mentioned above are granted to the lord king, fully guaranteed and confirmed, the lord king will go personally to the Albigeois and work in good faith at the aforesaid business. And when he shall have been personally in the Albigeois and shall have worked in good faith at that business, he or his heirs shall not, from that time forward, be required by the Roman curia on any pretext whatsoever, either to delay returning from that land, or to remain there, or to go back there again, unless he wants to.

11 In order to make these requests and to plead for them at the Roman curia, the lord king sends his beloved and faithful subjects, the archbishop of Bourges and the bishops of Langres and Chartres. And if these requests are not granted as a result of the negotiations now entrusted to these agents, from then on the lord king shall not be held to go to the Albigeois unless he wants to.

Document 8
HONORIUS URGES LOUIS
TO RECONCILE RAYMOND
4 April 1224

Early in April 1224, Honorius decided against a new Albigensian Crusade because it would weaken support for his more cherished project of a crusade to
recover the Holy Land, which Frederick II was then promising. Accordingly, his
legate Conrad was sent back to Louis bearing this letter and a copy of Frederick's, to tell the king that his services would not be required after all. Conrad's
new instructions were that he effect a peaceful settlement in Languedoc and secure a truce between France and England, since peace in the West would turn
warriors to the East. To implement this mission, he carried four other letters,
also dated 4 April. One urged Louis to make peace with Henry III for the sake
of Frederick's crusade (Pressutti, no. 4919; the only published fragment is identical to §1 below). Supplementing this was another that instructed the French
prelates to aid the legate in persuading the king (4921). The third informed the
archbishop of Narbonne that Raymond would be pardoned if he joined the
Sixth Crusade and supported Catholicism at home. The archbishop should work
for the count's reconciliation (4922) and the prelates of Provence were to assist
him (4923).

MSS.—(A) Vatican, Arch. Segreto Vat., Serie generale de' Regesti, vol. 12, fol.
178rv: Reg. Hon. III., tom. IV, an. viii, ep. 380. (B) Paris, Arch. nat., JJ 26, fol.
122vab: Register E. (C) Paris, BnF, MS. lat. 9778, fol. 96rab: Register F. (D) Paris,

---

Honorius episcopus, servus servorum Dei, karissimo in Christo <filio>[a]
Lodowico, regi Francorum illustri, salutem et apostolicam benedictionem.[b]
   1 Petitionibus quas per venerabiles fratres nostros . . archiepiscopum Bituricen' et . . Lingonen' et[c] . . Carnoten'[1] episcopos nobis tue serenitatis devotio
destinavit, a nobis et fratribus nostris multa diligentia, sicut exposcebat negotii
magnitudo, discussis, ita quod, finali tractatu habito super illis, prefati episcopi jam

   [a] filio *scripsi, om.* D
   [b] Honorius—benedictionem D: Eidem A *(cf. ep. 379*: Lodoico regi Francorum illustri*),*
Honor' etc. Lud' Franc' regi etc. BC
   [c] ac *Duchesne*

Arch. nat., JJ 13, fol. 9rab: Albigensian Register, copied 1245~1254; best copy of the original.

Ed.—(1) A. Duchesne, *Historiae Francorum scriptores coaetanei*, V (Paris, 1649), 859, no. 17. Reprinted in *Rec. hist. Gaules*, XIX (1833), 750-751, from which it was again printed by Horoy, IV (1880), 593-597, no. 183. (2) A new transcription by C. Rodenberg in MGH, Epist. saec. XIII, I (1883), 177, no. 249. (3) Excerpts in Baronio-Theiner, XX (1870), pp. 482 and 490, ad an. 1224, nos. 13 and 39, citing ep. 380.

Excerpts from this letter were also printed by Huillard-Bréholles, *Historia diplomatica Friderici secundi*, II (Paris, 1852), 589-590, who mistakenly cited as his source another letter of the same date in the Vatican register (ep. 379; Pressutti, no. 4919), inc. *Cum cogitamus apud*, which was printed for the first time in 1994 by Neininger, pp. 556-558 (Urkunden, no. 29; cf. his Regesten, no. 186, pp. 394-395). Huillard-Bréholles' mistake was perpetuated by Horoy, who reprinted the excerpt (II, 589-590, no. 181), and by Potthast, who calendared it (7214).

Refs.—Potthast, no. 7212. Pressutti, no. 4920. Böhmer-Ficker-Winkelmann, II (1892-1894), no. 6569. F. Neininger, *Konrad von Urach* (Paderborn, 1994), pp. 395-396 (Reg. no. 186a).—Translated in P. Belperron, *La Croisade contre les Albigeois*, 2nd ed. (Paris, 1967), p. 364.—On MS. D, see Molinier in Devic-Vaissète, VII, 261-263.

Text.—Transcribed from a photocopy of A. Punctuation and capitalization normalized; section numbers and paragraphing supplied.

Honorius, bishop, servant of the servants of God, to his most beloved son in Christ, Louis, illustrious king of the French, greeting and apostolic blessing.

1 The petitions that the devotion of your serene highness sent to us through our venerable brothers archbishop [Simon] of Bourges and the bishops [Hugh] of Langres and [Gautier] of Chartres[1] have been examined by us and our brothers with great diligence, as the importance of the business required. The final negotiations about this matter had been completed, and the aforementioned bishops had already begun their journey back bearing our letter to you, while

---

1. On the embassy, see Doc. 7.11. The papal chancery usually omitted the personal names of officials and indicated the omission by two spaced dots (. .).

iter arripuerant ad te cum nostris litteris[d] revertendi, ipso archiepiscopo, qui pro quibusdam negotiis suis apud apostolicam sedem remanserat, ad huc in nostra presentia constituto, supervenerunt sollempnes nuntii karissimi in Christo filii nostri[e] .F. illustris Romanorum imperatoris semper augusti et regis Sicilie,[f] nobis per ipsos nuntios et imperiales litteras exponentis[g] fervens desiderium quod ei de Terre Sancte succursu Dominus inspiravit, ac postulantis instanter ut, cum ipse reges et principes Christianos ad id animare studeat imperialibus largitionibus et promissis, sicut plenius[h] colligere poteris ex tenore litterarum ipsarum quem tibi per venerabilem fratrem nostrum .C. Portuen' episcopum, apostolice sedis legatum, curavimus destinare, nos quoque universos Christi fideles exhortationibus et indulgentiis apostolicis ad idem excitare negotium[i] studeremus.

2 Predictum ergo legatum ad te cum festinantia dirigentes, tue serenitatis devotionem et magnificentiam[j] rogamus, monemus, et obsecramus per aspersionem sanguinis Jesu Christi, qui pro te morti crucis tradidit semetipsum, quatinus, cum pro[k] certo credatur quod[l] nobilis vir .R. filius quondam[m] .R. comitis Tolosan' magnitudinis tue potentiam adeo reformidat quod, si cognoverit te contra eum ex animo velle totis viribus tuis[n] uti, eas exspectare aliquatenus non audebit, set mandatis Ecclesie—quibus et utinam vera devotione se offert[o]—parebit juxta[p] tue beneplacitum voluntatis, ipsum regiis commonitionibus[q] et comminationibus efficaciter inducere studeas ad pacem cum Deo et ejus Ecclesia veraciter faciendam: ita quod et terra purgetur hereticis et ecclesiis ac viris ecclesiasticis congrue satisfiat de dampnis et injuriis hactenus irrogatis; et provideatur libertati ecclesiastice in futurum; et honori dilecti filii nobilis viri[r] .A. comitis Tolosani— qui, sicut et clare memorie .. pater ejus, pro servitio Dei[s] et apostolice sedis exposuit semetipsum, propter quod sibi non possumus aliqua ratione deesse—in

---

[d] nostris litteris *tr.* BC

[e] nostri *om. Duchesne*

[f] Sicilie] scilicet C

[g] exponentis] exponentes C *et corr.* C[1]

[h] plenius *om.* BC

[i] negotium] teneremus *add.* B *et expunct.* B[1]

[j] magnificentiam AD: magnificam C

[k] pro *om. Rodenberg*

[l] quod] quo C

[m] filius quondam *tr.* BC

[n] tuis *om. Duchesne*

[o] offert] offerat *corr. Duchesne*

[p] juxta AD: secundum BC

[q] commonitionibus *om.* D *et supralin. add.* D[1]

[r] nobilis viri *om.* BC

[s] Dei] ejus B, *expunct. et* Dei *suprascr.* B[1]

that archbishop, who remained at the apostolic see for certain business of his own, was still in our presence. Then solemn messengers arrived unexpectedly from our most dear son in Christ Frederick, the illustrious ever-august emperor of the Romans and king of Sicily. Through those messengers and imperial letters, he expressed to us a burning desire, which the Lord had inspired in him, to succor the Holy Land. Since he was trying to arouse the Christian kings and princes with imperial largess and promises—as you can gather from the tenor of that letter, which we are having sent to you through our venerable brother Conrad, bishop of Porto, the legate of the apostolic see—he urgently asked that to the same end we also might strive to stir up all of Christ's faithful by apostolic exhortations and indulgences.

2 Therefore we are dispatching the aforesaid legate to you in haste, and for the sake of the blood shed by Jesus Christ, who for you delivered himself to death on the Cross, we ask, recommend, and implore the devotion of your serene highness that by royal admonitions and threats you endeavor to induce the noble man Raymond, son of the late Count Raymond of Toulouse, to make peace truly and faithfully with God and his Church. For it is believed to be certain that Raymond fears the power of your greatness so much that, if he knew you sincerely meant to use all of your forces against him, he would not dare to wait very long for them but, in accordance with your wishes, would obey the orders of the Church, as he is offering to do out of hopefully true devotion. Therefore try your best to induce him by royal warnings and threats truly to make peace with God and his Church. Our conditions are: that the land be purged of heretics; that he make suitable reparations to churches and churchmen for the damages and injuries that have been inflicted on them up to now; that ecclesiastical liberty be provided for in the future; and that in the peace treaty everything possible be done to preserve the honor of our beloved son, the noble man Amaury, count of Toulouse, who like his well-remembered father [Simon], put himself at risk in the service of God and of the apostolic see, whom we cannot in consequence desert for any reason. Quickly write back to us what you plan to do about this.

ipsa pace, quantum fieri poterit, deferatur. Quod super hoc inveneris, nobis celeriter rescripturus.

3 Si enim hoc feceris—ut de rerum dispendio taceamus—multis eris causa salutis animarum et corporum ac removendo impedimentum hujusmodi discordie, quod multum potest[t] officere negotio Terre Sancte, quasi inextimabiliter[u] ejusdem terre[v] subsidio providebis; nec ex hoc majores potes[w] assequi titulos laudis et glorie quam si[x] prefatum nobilem ad viam ab invio et ad apostolice sedis mandatum solo potentie tue terrore feceris sine bellico strepitu et sanguinis effusione redire.

4 Deposcimus igitur serenitatem tuam precibus cumulatis quatinus eundem legatum tanquam personam nostram digna te ipso devotione recipiens, sic eidem, immo verius nobis in ipso, super premissis intendas quod tibi proveniat ad incrementum glorie temporalis pariter et eterne; hiis autem que idem legatus exparte nostra tibi dixerit super treugis inter te ac illustrem regem Anglie innovandis, adhibeas plenam fidem.

Dat' Laterani ii. non. Aprilis, pontificatus nostri anno octavo.[y]

[t] multum potest *tr.* BC
[u] inextimabiliter AD: inestimabiliter BC
[v] terre] sancte *add. et canc.* A
[w] majores potes *tr.* B
[x] si] sibi C
[y] Dat'—octavo BCD: Dat' ut supra A *(cf. ep. 378:* Dat' Lateran' .ii. non. Aprilis anno octavo)*

Document 9
MEMORIAL OF LOUIS VIII
REVIEWING AND ENDING THE NEGOTIATIONS
5 May 1224

Date.—The title uses an uncommon formula, "the Sunday of three weeks of Easter." What is meant is the third Sunday after Easter, when three weeks have passed since Easter Sunday. In 1224, Easter fell on 14 April, and the third Sunday thereafter was 5 May. This interpretation is confirmed by the *Gesta Ludovici VIII*, which says plainly that the assembly met on 5 May ("tertio nonas maii": *Rec. hist. Gaules*, XVII, 303). Indeed, the meaning of *Dominica trium septimanarum*

3 We will not mention how much less this plan will cost in material expenditures; but if you shall do as we ask, you will be the cause of saving many souls and bodies. And by removing the impediment of civil discord, which can greatly impede the business of the Holy Land, you will provide as it were a subsidy of inestimable value for that land. Moreover, you can attain no greater claims to praise and glory than if you make the aforesaid noble return to the path from which he has strayed, and to obedience to the apostolic see, solely by the power of the terror you cause and without the noise of battle or the shedding of blood.

4 Therefore we implore your serene highness with countless prayers that you receive our legate with the devotion due us if we were present in person. Thus you should pay attention to what he says—or really what we say through him—about what has been said above, which will bring to you an increase of glory in this life as well as the next. Moreover, place complete trust in what the same legate shall say to you on our behalf concerning the renewal of a truce between you and the illustrious king of England.

Given at the Lateran, on the day before the nones of April, in the eighth year of our pontificate.

Paschae was established from this coincidence: see Mas Latrie, *Trésor de chronologie*, col. 636. The date is erroneously given as 4 May in Devic-Vaissète, VIII, 794.

MSS.—(A) Paris, Arch. nat., JJ 26, fol. 14v: Register E; see Doc. 7, above. (B) Paris, BnF, MS. lat. 9778, fol. 9v: Register F.

Ed.—Devic-Vaissète, III (1737), 293–295, preuve no. 155; VIII (1879), 794–796, preuve no. 236. *Rec. hist. Gaules*, XVII (1818), 303–304, from Devic-Vaissète.

Refs.—Devic-Vaissète, VI (1879), 579–580. Petit-Dutaillis, *Louis*, 463 (Cat. no. 103). Neininger, *Konrad von Urach*, 400–401, Reg. no. 193.

Text.—Transcribed from a photocopy of A and corrected from the original; collated with a photocopy of B, likewise corrected from the original.

RESPONSIO QUAM DOMINUS REX FECIT EPISCOPO
PORTUEN' DOMINICA TRIUM SEPTIMANARUM PASCHE
DE AFFARIO ALBIGEII
ANNO DOMINI M° CC° XXIIII°

Noveritis quod karissimus dominus et genitor noster Ph', pie memorie rex quondam Franc' illustris, in principio non est aggressus negotium Albigesii; et quod honus illud numquam recipere voluit, quamvis multa expenderit in eodem negotio, et multi milites de regno Francie ibidem mortui sunt et multa expenderunt; et quod semel et secundo in propria persona in eadem terra pro dicto negotio, in quantum potuimus, fideliter laboravimus.

2 Et quando^a genitor noster vite sue diem ultimum clausit, dominus Portuensis venit ad nos,[1] supplicans nobis humiliter ut consilium apponeremus in negotio Albig' quia prelati Francie idem negotium aggredi volebant si assensum et voluntatem nostram super hoc haberent. Nos autem, quamvis essemus incerti de statu regni, dedimus prelatis nostris licentiam aggrediendi negotium supradictum.

3 Postea[2] idem Portuen' petiit a nobis ut consilium apponeremus in munitionibus castrorum que comes Amalr' tenebat in partibus Albig' ut illos salvo^b posset reducere qui in illis erant munitionibus ita quod morti non traderentur. Tunc nos fecimus eidem Amalrico dari decem millia marcarum de elemosina patris nostri. Tunc dictus Amalricus auxilio dicte pecunie reduxit milites et servientes qui erant in dictis munitionibus, et reddidit castra et munitiones quas tenebat in partibus illis.

4 Postea[3] venit ad nos archiepiscopus Bituricen' et episcopus Lingon', deferentes secum litteras domini pape in quibus continebatur quod dominus papa multis auctoritatibus et aliis persuasionibus nos inducere nitebatur ad hoc quod negotium istud personaliter assumeremus; et etiam viva voce nobis promiserunt ex parte domini pape et cardinalium quod thesauros Ecclesie nobis exponerent, et alia auxilia impenderent et consilia quantum secundum Deum^c facere possent. Nos autem, communicato consilio cum prelatis et baronibus nostris, petitiones quas vidimus negotio Albigesii expedire transmisimus domino pape.[4]

5 Dominus autem papa nobis mandavit per dominum Portuen' quod ipse paratus erat petitionibus nostris omnino satisfacere, cumque hoc ipsum injunctum esset domino Portuen' quod accederet ad nos et satisfaceret petitionibus nostris, supervenit nuntius domini imperatoris tot et tanta promittens et pro-

---

^a quando AB] cum *Vaissète*
^b salvo AB] salvos *Vaissète*
^c Dominum *Vaissète*

THE REPLY THAT THE LORD KING MADE TO THE BISHOP OF PORTO ON THE THIRD SUNDAY AFTER EASTER CONCERNING THE ALBIGEOIS AFFAIR
A.D. 1224

Be it known that our dearest lord and father Philip of pious memory, the former king of France, did not at first undertake the Albigeois business, and he never wanted to take on that burden. Nonetheless, he spent a great deal on that business, and many knights from the kingdom of France died there and spent a great deal there. And we worked for that business once and again in that land both faithfully and in person.

2 And when our father had completed the last day of his life, the lord Porto came to us[1] and humbly begged us that we might take counsel on the Albigeois business because the prelates of France wanted to undertake that business if they had our assent and approval on this. Although we were uncertain about the state of the kingdom, we nonetheless gave our permission to undertaking the aforesaid business.

3 Afterwards,[2] the same lord Porto requested us to take counsel concerning the fortifications of the castles that Count Amaury held in the Albigeois area, in order that he might be able to bring back to safety those who were in those forts so that they would not be left to die. Then we had ten thousand marks given to this Amaury out of the alms that our father left in his will. Then with the aid of said money, said Amaury led back the knights and soldiers who were in said forts, and he surrendered the castles and fortifications that he held in that area.

4 Afterwards,[3] the archbishop of Bourges came to us, and with him the bishop of Langres, bearing with them a letter of the lord pope, in which the lord pope tried, with many authorities and other persuasive arguments, to induce us to take on that business in person. And viva voce they also promised us on the part of the lord pope and the cardinals that they would make the treasures of the Church available to us, and that they would supply as many other aids and counsels as they could according to God. We took counsel with our prelates and barons, and in response we transmitted to the lord pope the requests that we saw would expedite the Albigeois business.[4]

5 Through the lord Porto, the lord pope declared to us that he was ready to grant our requests in every respect; and when this very task had been imposed on the lord Porto, namely that he should come to us and fulfill our requests, a

1. July 1223
2. Between July and November 1223, since the pope knew of the result by mid-December.
3. In January 1224.
4. I.e. Doc. 7.

ponens ad subsidium Terre Sancte quod oportuit dominum papam et curiam Romanam intendere negotio Terre Sancte et ad presens postponere negotium Albig', quia dominus papa et curia Romana talia promiserant domino imperatori quod nullum negotium postponerent negotio Terre Sancte.[5]

6 Preterea nobis significavit dominus papa per eumdem dominum Portuen' et per litteras suas quod si Remundus crederet quod totis viribus uteremur ad ipsum deprimendum, non auderet nos expectare, set rediret ad mandatum Ecclesie; et propter hoc nos instanter monuit et rogavit ut comminationibus et commonitionibus studeremus eum inducere ad pacem Ecclesie hereticos eliminando[d], ecclesiis et personis ecclesiasticis satisfaciendo, et libertatibus Ecclesie in posterum providendo, et cum Amalr' Tholosano comite componendo.

7 Nos autem eidem Portuen' respondimus, quod ex quo dominus papa petitiones nostras rationabiles ad negotium pertinentes ad presens exaudire nolebat, quod absoluti sumus ab honere hujus negotii; et hoc publice protestati sumus coram omnibus prelatis et baronibus Francie.

8 De pace siquidem ad quam dominus papa voluit quod induceremus comitem Reimundum comminationibus et commonitionibus, respondimus domino Portuen' quod non erat nostrum[e] examinare articulos fidei nec tractare de compositione que ad negotium fidei pertinet; set bene volumus quod ecclesia Romana, ad quam pertinet examinatio fidei, componat cum predicto Reimundo sicut viderit expedire, salvo jure nostro et salvis feodis nostris sine aliqua diminutione, ita quod eis nullum honus novum vel insolitum imponatur.

9 Ad ultimum diximus[f] eidem domino Portuen' quod de cetero ad nos de negotio Albigesii nullum verbum reportaret, a quo sumus penitus absoluti.

[d] eliminandos A *et Vaissète*
[e] nostrum (nrm) AB] necessarium *Vaissète*
[f] dicimus *Vaissète*

Document 10
THE POPE ANNOUNCES ROMANUS' LEGATION TO RAYMOND
31 January 1225

The papal chancery did not bother to keep a permanent record of many of the letters it issued concerning the settlement of what it called "the Albigensian busi-

messenger arrived unexpectedly from the lord emperor, who promised and proposed so many things and so much to help the Holy Land that the lord pope and the Roman curia felt it was only proper to concentrate their efforts on the Holy Land and, for the moment, to postpone the Albigeois business, because the promises that the lord pope and the Roman curia had made to the lord emperor were such that they could undertake no other enterprise at the same time.[5]

6 Furthermore, the lord pope indicated to us by his letter and by the same lord Porto that if Raymond believed that we would use all our forces to overcome him, he would not dare to wait for us but would obey the orders of the Church. And therefore the pope urgently recommended and asked that we endeavor by admonitions and threats to induce him to make peace with the Church by eliminating heretics, by making reparations to churches and churchmen, by providing for the liberties of the Church in the future, and by reaching a settlement with Amaury, count of Toulouse.

7 We replied to the lord Porto, however, that because the lord pope refused at present to comply with our reasonable requests pertaining to the business, we are freed from the burden of this business, and we have declared this publicly in the presence of all the prelates and barons of France.

8 As for the peace to which the lord pope wanted us to induce Count Raymond by admonitions and threats, we replied to the lord Porto that it was neither our business to examine articles of the faith nor to negotiate a settlement that pertains to the business of the faith. Since examination of the faith is the business of the Roman church, we quite properly wish it to reach a settlement with the aforesaid Raymond just as it sees fit, provided that our rights and our fiefs are in no way diminished, and that no new or unusual burden is imposed on them.

9 Finally, we said to the same lord Porto that in future he should not bear back [from Rome] a single word about the Albigeois business, which we have washed our hands of altogether.

5. For § 5, cf. Doc. 8, dated 4 April 1224.

---

ness." The most likely reason is that many of the letters no longer seemed worth preserving after Honorius had changed his Albigensian policy, and accordingly the drafts were not included in the register, which was prepared year by year. Fortunately ten of these unregistered letters, as well as eighteen other documents, were copied from drafts in the chancery not long after they were written and sent to an unknown correspondent, who received them in three installments, which he had joined together to make up a single roll—"the Albigensian Roll," as I call it for convenience. The first installment contained the instructions sent to Conrad and other papal legates in June 1221 to promote a second Albigensian crusade; the second installment documented the attempts to reconcile Raymond VII between April and September 1224; and the final one concerned the dispatch of the legate Romanus in February 1225. Thus each installment corresponds to a new phase of the curia's vacillating Albigensian policy, and accordingly was apparently intended by the curia to make the details known to its favored correspondent.

This Albigensian Roll was acquired by Etienne Baluze (1630-1718), probably late in life; after his death, it went to the royal library along with the rest of his papers and collections. There Dom Vaissète copied out about half of the letters, which he published in his *Histoire générale de Languedoc* (III, 1737), but since then the roll seems to have attracted little attention, and consequently its unique indications of curial chancery practice have been overlooked. Because I plan to publish a detailed analysis of it elsewhere,[1] I shall indicate here only its contribution to the documentation of the Council of Bourges.

Among the documents published here, seven appear in the Albigensian Roll; most of these, however, also occur in the Vatican Registers (Docs. 12, 13, 15, 17). Of the three that are unique to the Roll, two have not been published previously (16 and 17), while the third requires a new edition here to correct Vaissète's errors of transcription (Doc. 10).

The present letter preserves a number of details about Raymond's embassy: first, the names of his representatives; second, the date at which Honorius decided not to reconcile Raymond; and third, the fact that the pope did not an-

---

1. "Quelques ébauches des lettres papales conservées dans le *Rotulus de negotio albigense* (1221-1225)," forthcoming in the *Bibliothèque de l'Ecole des chartes*, CLX (2002); originally presented at the XI International Congress of Medieval Canon Law, Catania, 5 August 2000.

Honorius episcopus, servus servorum Dei,>[a] nobili viro R., filio R. quondam comitis Tolosan', spiritum consilii[1] salutarem.

Venientes ad apostolicam sedem G. vicecomitem Cavellicen', B. de Avinion',[b] P. Martin', et magistrum G.[2] nuntios tuos, viros utique sollicitos et prudentes, audiri fecimus diligenter, et hiis que tue nobis per eos misse littere continebant ac hiis que ipsi viva voce dixerunt provide ac prudenter cum diligentia intellectis, dilectum filium nostrum R(omanus), sancti Angeli diaconum cardinalem, virum inclito[c] generis et scientia morumque venustate preclarum, in regnum

ᵃ Honorius–Dei *supplevi*
ᵇ d'Avinione *Vaissète*
ᶜ inclito] & titulo *Vaissète*

nounce his decision to Raymond but instead temporized, thus leaving his options open in case Romanus could not reach a satisfactory agreement with Louis.

Date.—Scholars have uncritically accepted the year as printed in Devic-Vaissète (*anno VIIIº*) and have accordingly dated the letter 1224 n.s., but this announcement of Romanus' appointment as legate must have been written a full year later, together with his other letters of legation (Docs. 12–21). In fact, the manuscript is actually dated *anno nono*; Vaissète, however, expressed the year in roman numerals, apparently at some point dropping the fourth *I*. The error was not due to the printer, because Vaissète's marginal notation already placed the document *sub anno 1223*, which in Old Style reckoning corresponds to a date in January 1224 New Style.

MS.—(A) Paris, BnF, MS. Baluze 385, no. 239, item 19. Not included in Vat. Reg. Hon. III.

Ed.—Devic-Vaissète, III (1737), 283, preuve no. 147, § iv; VIII (1879), 775–776, preuve no. 228, § iv. Reprinted in *Rec. hist. Gaules*, XIX (1833), 745, and thence in Horoy, IV (1880), 527, no. 115.

Refs.—Devic-Vaissète, VI (1879), 579. Potthast, no. 7157. Pressutti, no. 4743, *sub anno octavo*. Petit-Dutaillis, *Louis*, p. 286. P. Belperron, *La Croisade contre les Albigeois*, 2nd ed. (Paris, 1967), p. 363. F. Neininger, *Konrad von Urach* (Paderborn, 1994), p. 211.

Text.—Transcribed directly from A. At some points, where the manuscript has been stained, the readings proved to be more distinct in a photocopy.

Honorius, bishop, servant of the servants of God, writes to the noble man Raymond, son of Raymond the former count of Toulouse, wishing him the spirit of counsel that brings salvation.[1]

Your messengers G. viscount of Cavaillon, B. of Avignon, P. Martini, and Master G.,[2] all painstaking and prudent men, came to the apostolic see and we

1. The normal salutation, "greeting and apostolic blessing," was not appropriate for Raymond because he was excommunicated; instead, the pope wishes that the count may be inspired to change his mind. Counsel was one of the seven gifts of the Holy Spirit (Isaiah xi.2).

2. The personnel of this embassy are not otherwise known. Significantly, one was a nobleman and another a *magister*, probably a canon lawyer.

Francie et Provinciam, concesso sibi plene legationis officio duximus destinandum ut que deformata sunt in partibus illis, per industriam ejus auctore Domino reformentur. Tu igitur eidem, cum ad partes illas pervenerit, sic reverenter et obedienter intendas, sicque humiliter et efficaciter acquiescas ejus salubribus monitis et mandatis, quod Dei et apostolice sedis gratiam valeas promereri. Predictos autem nuntios tuos tibi de[d] sollicita diligentia et diligenti sollicitudine reddimus commendatos.

Dat' Laterani pridie kal. Februarii, pontificatus nostri anno nono.[e]

[d] de] in *Vaissète*
[e] nono] non. A, VIII° *Vaissète*

Document 11
PROLONGATION OF THE TRUCE IN PROVENCE
[31 January 1225]

MS.—(A) Paris, BnF, MS. Baluze 385, no. 239, item 18: Albigensian Roll; see Doc. 10.

Honorius episcopus, servus servorum Dei, venerabili fratri . . archiepiscopo Narbon' salutem et apostolicam benedictionem.>[a]

Cum dilectum filium nostrum R(omanum) sancti Angeli diaconum cardinalem in regnum Francie ac in Provinciam, concesso sibi plene legationis officio, duximus destinandum ut que deformata sunt in partibus illis per ejus industriam auctore reformentur[b] Domino, fraternitatem tuam per apostolica scripta mandamus quatinus des operam cum effectu ut pax seu treuga que usque ad proximum Pascha facta est in Provincia et usque ad terminum illum et ultra inconcussa servetur ut ipse legatus terram tranquillam inveniens plenam et firmam pacem possit divina favente gratia stabilire.

<Dat' Laterani pridie kal. Februarii, pontificatus nostri anno nono.>[c]

[a] Honorius—benedictionem *supplevi*] Eidem A *(cf. Doc. 20)*
[b] auctore reformentur *tr.* A, *corr.* A1.
[c] Dat'—nono *scripsi (cf. Doc. 10)*

caused them to be heard diligently. We have studied what your letter that they brought us said and what they said viva voce with diligence, prudence, and foresight. Accordingly we are sending to the kingdom of France and to Provence our beloved son Romanus, the cardinal-deacon of Sant' Angelo, a man distinguished by noble birth, learning, and charming manners, and we are entrusting him with the office of full legation, so that those things that are corrupt there might (God willing) be reformed through his efforts. Consequently, when he arrives there, you must be so reverently and obediently attentive to him, and so humbly and effectually acquiesce to his wholesome warnings and commands that you may be able to deserve the favor of God and the apostolic see. We are sending back your aforesaid messengers and commend their painstaking diligence and diligent painstaking.

Given at the Lateran on the day before the kalends of February, in the ninth year of our pontificate.

Ed.—Unpublished.

Date.—The truce expired on 30 March 1225, Easter Day. If this undated letter were written in mid-February, when most of Romanus' letters were issued, the archbishop to whom it was addressed would have had only the four weeks of March in which to arrange an extension of the truce. Therefore it seems likely that the letter was sent earlier, most probably on 31 January, together with Doc. 10, which follows it on the Albigensian Roll.

Honorius, bishop, servant of the servants of God, to our venerable brother [Arnaud Amaury], the archbishop of Narbonne, greeting and apostolic blessing.

We have directed that our beloved son Romanus, the cardinal-deacon of Sant' Angelo, be dispatched to the kingdom of France and also to Provence, and we have appointed him to the office of full legation so that those things that are corrupt in those parts may (God willing) be reformed by his diligence. Consequently, by apostolic writ we command your fraternity that you make an effective effort to have the peace or truce that currently is in effect in Provence until next Easter be observed unbroken until that time and beyond, so that the legate, finding the land undisturbed, shall be able (God willing) to establish a full and firm peace.

Given at the Lateran on the day before the kalends of February, in the ninth year of our pontificate.

INTRODUCTION TO DOCUMENTS 12–21

PREPARATIONS FOR ROMANUS' LEGATION
February 1225

Romanus left Rome in March 1225 laden with several dozen letters, including not only his credentials and instructions but also letters to be delivered for Honorius in France. From the register's record of letters issued for the most part in February, we can reassemble the probable contents of his diplomatic pouch. Such a reconstruction is worth an excursus to elucidate the nature of Romanus' office and mission, especially since no previous legation is as well documented.

As *legatus a latere*, Romanus was furnished with letters of credence for the several authorities to whom he was sent. Just as the clergy, king, and lesser civil authorities each stood in a different relation to the pope, so also to his legate. Three letters were accordingly required to establish as many relationships, which the final section of each (inc. *Ideoque*) defined appropriately, requiring obedience from the clergy, commanding respect from the laity, and requesting the filial cooperation from the Church's eldest son. Taken together, the pair of letters to the ecclesiastical and civil authorities (Docs. 12–13) set forth the general legatine powers conferred on Romanus, and for this reason they were both to be alleged a year later as his authority to bind the papacy (Doc. 27). Since the legation included the kingdom of France, Romanus was especially commended to the king as an adviser in a third letter (Doc. 15).

Moreover, to facilitate his journey, Romanus was also provided with letters requesting safe conduct through the lands of secular lords (Doc. 16). A copy of the draft for one of these, addressed to the count of Savoy, has survived, but others may well have been issued, for the chancery was instructed to issue similar ones to any other addressees Romanus might wish, thus leaving the legate free to plan his own itinerary.

The general resources of the legate included yet another letter of introduction, addressed to ecclesiastical authorities in general rather than to those of his legation only, enjoining them to receive him "hilariter et honorifice" and to provide him with safe conduct and other necessities. Obviously, such an authorization to live and travel at the expense of any church or monastery along his route was a simple and economical means for the Roman curia to maintain an agent abroad (Doc. 17). Some expenses of legation could only be met with ready money, however, which in Romanus' case was supplied by granting him the income from a church in Rome (Doc. 18).

Although his letters of legation conferred general powers, they did not permit a legate to act in matters that canon law reserved to the pope. To exercise such powers, the legate needed a separate grant that explicitly stated the special powers conceded to him.[1] The powers conceded varied from legate to legate. In Romanus' case (Doc. 19), he was given the power to absolve those excommunicated for laying violent hands on clergy and for arson; the power to dispense those who received holy orders or celebrated Mass while excommunicated or interdicted; also to dispense clerics to study civil law; and finally, to confer benefices and other ecclesiastical dignities that were in the pope's gift because they had been vacant too long.

Romanus' credentials and finances were much the same as any legate's, but in addition to these routine documents, he received others that provided for the peculiar circumstances of his mission, as well as yet others that entrusted to him certain matters that, though unrelated to his principal business, could be better settled locally than in Rome. One specific to his mission was a matter left unfinished by his predecessor. In 1224, Honorius had assigned certain uncollected taxes to Amaury de Montfort, but Legate Conrad had been recalled before he could execute the commission, which now was passed on to Romanus.[2] To strengthen the Church in Provence, Honorius directed that while his legate was there, prelates be elected in his presence and with his counsel (Doc. 20). To the same end, Romanus was commissioned to judge the appeal of the church of Carcassonne, which apparently had not been able to agree on a new bishop (Doc. 21).[3] A major objective of Romanus' mission was to negotiate a truce between the kings of France and England. In this matter he was explicitly instructed to defend Henry's rights against Louis.[4] Moreover, he carried two letters to the French king: in one Honorius urged Louis with extreme length and eloquence to cease his aggressions and renew the truce his father had made with the English, which now was all the more desirable during the crusade in the Holy Land;[5] in the other he insisted that Louis restore the territory that he had recently conquered from the English.[6]

---

1. K. Ruess, *Die rechtliche Stellung der päpstlichen Legaten bis Bonifaz VIII.* (Paderborn, 1912), pp. 122-126, 146-150.

2. Ep. 200, 26 Feb., inc. *Dilecto filio nostro* (Pressutti, no. 5337; Potthast, no. 7371): ed. *Rec. hist. Gaules*, XIX, 767; Horoy, IV, 795-796, no. 93. The original grant was made 4 May 1224 from the twentieth levied in 1218 (Horoy, IV, 618). See R. Kay, "The Albigensian Twentieth of 1221-3," *Journal of Medieval History*, VI (1980), 307-315.

3. The previous bishop of Carcassonne, Guy, died in 1219; his successor, Clarinus (or Clarius) is first mentioned in 1226: Mas Latrie, *Trésor de chronologie*, col. 1403.

4. Ep. 187, 27 Feb., inc. *Tua novit prudentia* (Pressutti, no. 5341; Potthast, no. 7372): ed. *Rec. hist. Gaules*, XIX, 767; Horoy, IV, 796-797, no. 94.

5. Ep. 169, undated, inc. *Utinam fili karissime* (Pressutti, no. 5350; Potthast, no. 7510): ed. *Rec. hist. Gaules*, XIX, 761; Horoy, IV, 756, no. 55; fragments in Baronio-Theiner, XX (1870), 501-502, ad an. 1225, nos. 30-34. To the manuscripts listed by Pressutti, add: Florence, Bibl. Laurenziana, MS. Plut. XXV. sin. 4 (a collection of epistolary models made in the Latin East, saec. xiii 4/4), fol. 26v; see C. V. Langlois, *Notices et extraits*, XXXV (1897), 413. This letter

Heresy and peace were to be the legate's chief concerns, but other lesser commissions were also entrusted to him. Mandates to enforce a papal decision[7] and to have a deacon ordained priest[8] are of little interest, but a commission to settle the claims of Bourges to primacy over Bordeaux merits notice because the dispute was to be an issue at the Council of Bourges. When Honorius had cited the archbishop of Bordeaux to appear before him and to reply to Bourges' complaint that his primatial rights were being disregarded, the summons had been ignored and in consequence Bordeaux was fined for contumacy. Romanus was now told to collect only a nominal five percent of the fine and then to hear and terminate the dispute in France.[9] In explanation of an exceptional feature of this affair,

and the next (n. 6, below) were probably left undated so Romanus could, at his discretion, present them opportunely to further his arguments for peace, as the conclusion of this letter suggests: "Cum ergo dilectus filius noster R. S. Angeli diaconus card. A.S.L. ad regnum tuum propter hoc aliaque negotia destinemus, sic et iis quae tibi scribimus, et iis quae tibi viva voce proponet, aures tuas et animum reverenter inclines, quod nec nos, nec ipse contra te procedere, quod omnino vitare cupimus, tua faciente duritia compellamur" (ed. Baronio-Theiner, XX [1870], 502, no. 34).

6. Ep. 168, undated, inc. *Illius cui omne* (Pressutti, no. 5575, dated February 1225): ed. Petit-Dutaillis, *Louis*, pp. 516-517, no. 7, and dated "Janv. ou fév. 1225."

7. Ep. 282, addit., 23 Feb., inc. *Cum seculares viri* (Pressutti, no. 5326); "in eundem modum" to Romanus.

8. Ep. 205, 1 March, inc. *Dilectus filius magister* (Pressutti, no. 5352). This is the most recent dated letter in the series issued to Romanus.

9. Ep. 183, 25 Feb., inc. *Citatus venerabilis frater* (Pressutti, no. 5328; Potthast, no. 7367): ed. *Rec. hist. Gaules*, XIX, 766; Horoy, IV, 795, no. 92.

Document 12
LETTER OF LEGATION FOR ROMANUS
TO THE ECCLESIASTICAL AUTHORITIES
15 February 1225

MSS.—(A) Vatican, Arch. Segreto Vat., Serie generale de' Regesti, vol. 13, fol. 33rv: Reg. Hon. III, tom. V, an. ix, ep. 175. (B) Paris, BnF, MS. Baluze 385, no. 239, item 9: Albigensian Roll; see Doc. 10. (C) Paris, Arch. nat., J 428, no. 3: Trésor des chartes, Albigeois, no. 3; the original *vidimus* of 31 January 1226 (Doc. 27), which is an authenticated copy of the letter dispatched with Romanus. Cf. Doc. 13.

he was also given a memorandum to the effect that a judge-delegate of Innocent III had suspended his hearing of the case on the understanding that Bordeaux had made a counterappeal directly to the pope before the hearing had begun.[10]

Finally, we may surmise that Romanus was given a number of papal letters that he was to deliver to French addressees but which otherwise required no action on his part. Certainly while his own papers were being drawn up in February, many other French affairs were also settled,[11] and although some of the resultant twenty-one letters may have been dispatched by another courier, Romanus probably carried the bulk of them.

It took the curia the whole month of February to complete the arrangements for Romanus' mission. Meanwhile several urgent letters were dispatched to prepare for his coming. Certainly this was the case with the letter to Raymond VII (Doc. 10, dated 31 January) and probably also the one to the archbishop of Narbonne concerning the Provençal truce (Doc. 11). An early date is less likely, but not impossible, for another letter to the archbishop of Narbonne (Doc. 21) and the advance notice to Louis VIII (Doc. 14).

10. Ep. 201, 26 Feb., inc. *Cum dilectus filius* (Pressutti, no. 5338): unpublished. Despite the similar incipit, the content is unrelated to that of Doc. 16.

11. Pressutti, nos. 5284 (= Doc. 41), 5286, 5288, 5290, 5291, 5297, 5301, 5310, 5316, 5322, 5323, 5324, 5327, 5329, 5331, 5332, 5333, 5335, 5342, 5344, 5345, ranging in date from 28 Jan. to 27 Feb. Seven letters were addressed to England during the same period (5285 [= Doc. 41], 5295, 5296, 5311, 5336, 5349, 5353), but most likely they went by another messenger, who informed Henry III that Romanus was expected in France in the near future (Chaplais, *Diplomatic Documents*, no. 162 = Shirley, *Royal Letters*, no. 215; see chap. 2, above, at nn. 58–59).

Ed.—(1) Baronio-Theiner, XX (1870), 500, ad an. 1225, nos. 28–29; prints only §2, 4, and *Datum* from MS. A, with five variants from ed. 3. (2) *Rec. hist. Gaules*, XIX (1833), 764–765, from La Porte du Theil's copy of MS. A. Reprinted by Horoy, IV (1880), 781–784, no. 78, with twenty variants from ed. 3. (3) Teulet, no. 1694; transcribes MS. C almost exactly.

Refs.—Potthast, no. 7360. Pressutti, no. 5313. *Gallia Christiana novissima*, ed. J. H. Albanès and U. Chevalier, III (Valence, 1901), 360. U. Chevalier, *Regeste dauphinois*, III (Valence, 1914), no. 6762.

Text.—As the base manuscript, I have used the certified copy of the sealed original (C).

Date.—The Vatican register copy is dated 15 February (xv. kal. Mart.), but the preceding day is indicated by C, the contemporary certified copy of the bull as dispatched: xvi. kal. Mart. The discrepancy may have arisen either when the draft copy was enregistered or when the certified copy of the actual bull was made; it is also possible that the bull was dated a day earlier than the draft had anticipated. Arbitrarily, I have followed the register.

Comm.—The transcript of the draft (B) often transposes words. It is tempting to view these as reflecting an earlier state of the text, which later was stylistically

---

Honorius episcopus, servus servorum Dei, venerabilibus fratribus[a] archiepiscopis et episcopis, et dilectis filiis[b] abbatibus, prioribus, et aliis ecclesiarum prelatis in regno Francie ac in Provincia constitutis, et . . Tarentasien',[c] . . Bisuntinen', . . Ebredunen', . . Aquen', . . Arelaten', et . . Viennen' archiepiscopis et eorum suffraganeis, nec non abbatibus et aliis ecclesiarum prelatis consistentibus in diocesibus eorumdem, salutem et apostolicam benedictionem.[d]

1 "Mirabiles elationes maris"[1] sed mirabilior Dominus in excelsis, quia quantumcumque mundanarum tempestatum fluctus contra navem Petri, Ecclesiam videlicet, intumescant, quantumcumque dormire videatur Dominus in eadem, ipsam agitari procellis et fluctibus concuti permittendo, excitatus tamen suorum clamore fidelium clamantium toto corde, surgens ventis imperat atque mari, fitque magna tranquillitas ita ut videntes divinam potentiam admirentur.[2]

2 Sane miserabilis status, immo stabilis miseria Narbonen' provincie ac circumadjacentium regionum diu nos et anxietate torsit et dubietate suspendit, anxiantes quidem viam invenire ac modum quibus possemus relevare negotium pacis et fidei quod in partibus illis videtur quasi penitus corruisse, et econtrario dubitantes ne terra illa sic ex toto esset[e] in salsilaginem versa quod cassus et inanis existeret labor noster[3] et ne possemus, quantacumque culture adhibita[f] diligentia, optatos ex ea manipulos reportare, cum non videatur illi esse similis de

---

   [a] Honorius—fratribus C: *om.* A; H. ven. fr. B

   [b] et dilectis filiis C: *om.* A; ac dil. fil. B

   [c] Tarientasien' C

   [d] salutem—benedictionem *om.* AB; *in marg.* Archiepiscopis et episcopis, abbatibus, prioribus, et aliis ecclesiarum prelatis in regno Francie ac in Provincia constitutis, et . . Tarentasien' et . . Bisuntin', . . Ebredunen', . . Aquen', . . Arelaten', et . . Viennen', et eorum suffraganeis, nec non abbatibus et aliis ecclesiarum prelatis consistentibus in diocesibus eorumdem *scr.* A

   [e] ex toto esset AC: esset ex toto B

   [f] culture adhibita *tr.* B

improved before being engrossed; but if this be the case, then the transcript must have been made from a draft that differed from the one copied into the register: either the same draft in an earlier state (i.e. before engrossment) or another, earlier draft. The latter possibility is supported by the fact (not recorded in my *apparatus criticus*) that B's scribe made frequent mistakes, which he corrected by erasure (6), insertion (4), or cancellation (2). Accordingly, he may have been working from "foul" copy—difficult to read, from which a fair-copy draft was subsequently made that served as the exemplar for both the sealed originals and the register.

Honorius, bishop, servant of the servants of God, to his venerable brothers the archbishops and bishops, and to his beloved sons the abbots, priors, and other prelates of churches located in the kingdom of France and in Provence; and to the archbishops of Tarentaise, Besançon, Embrun, Aix, Arles, and Vienne and their suffragans, and also to the abbots and other prelates of churches located in their dioceses, greeting and apostolic blessing.

1 "Wonderful are the surges of the sea,"[1] but more wonderful is the Lord on high, because no matter how much the waves caused by the storms of worldly affairs increase against Peter's ship—namely the Church—and no matter how much the Lord seems to be sleeping in it and permitting it to be shaken by tempests and stricken by waves, he is nonetheless aroused by the shouting of the faithful who cry unto him with all their heart, and rising up he commands the winds and the sea, and makes a great calm, so that those who see it might marvel at the divine power.[2]

2 The miserable status, or rather the static misery, of the province of Narbonne and the regions surrounding it have indeed long tormented us with anxiety and suspended us in doubt. We have been anxious to find the way and means by which we might be able to raise up the business of peace and the faith, which seemed to have gone under almost completely in those parts. On the other hand, we have been in doubt for fear that our labor might be empty and in vain because that land may be completely turned into a salty waste,[3] and for fear that, no matter how diligently we worked the land, we might not be able to bring home from it the harvest we had hoped for, since it does not seem to be like the land of which one reads in the Bible: "For the earth that drinketh in

1. Psalm 92.4b (AV 93.3).
2. This prologue is based on Christ's stilling of the storm (Matthew viii.23-27, Mark iv.37-40, Luke viii.22-25).
3. Psalm 106.34 (AV 107.34); cf. Jeremiah xvii.6 and xxxix.6.

qua legitur: "terra, sepe venientem super se bibens imbrem et herbam gene-
rans, illis a quibus colitur oportunam accipiet benedictionem a Deo";[4] sed ei
potius de qua continuo subinfertur: "proferens autem spinas ac tribulos, reproba
est et proxima maledicto."[5] Hec enim vere est "terra deserta, invia, inaquosa,[g][6]
immo terra ferrea, terra cui celum eneum dedisse videtur Deus,[7] et ne super
illam pluant nubibus mandavisse, cum nullo himbre doctrine,[8] nullo rore gratie
sit ad ferendum fructus debitos emollita. Hec est terra que argentum reprobum[9]
videtur merito appellanda, quia et si multo sudore laboratum[h] sit et multo labore sudatum[i] ad purgationem ejusdem, frustra tamen conflavit conflator; non
est enim ejus consumpta malitia et nimia rubigo ejus de ipsa non exiit nec per
ignem, Deo terram cordis incolarum ejus, constrictam infidelitatis et malitie
gelu, occulto sed justo[j] judicio, permittente adeo indurari ut nec fomentis blan-
dimentorum nec flagellorum tormentis potuerit hactenus emolliri, eisdem sic
suos animos obfirmantibus contra Deum ut quamlibet multiplicibus attriti
flagellis renuerint accipere disciplinam; quinimmo immemores nichil esse infeli-
cius felicitate peccantium, adversus Dei Ecclesiam glorientur et in sui erroris
argumentum et confirmationem assumant quod eis videtur contra Catholicos
successisse, non attendentes filios Israel, peculiarem populum Domini, gentibus,
quas ipse Dominus oderat, succubuisse frequenter, ac demum gentes easdem,
ab ipsis omnino deletas, frustra de habitis victoriis exultasse.

3 Quantumcumque autem navis Ecclesie ipsorum fluctibus videatur,[k] Deo
permittente, concussa, nos tamen certi quod ille qui se cum ea promisit usque
ad finem seculi permansurum nec permissurum quod adversus eam prevaleant
porte mortis, eam in hujusmodi fluctuum turbatione non deseret, sed ventis et
mari, cum tempus beneplaciti ejus advenerit, imperabit, simulque sperantes
quod, quantumcumque sit ipsorum obstinata duritia et desperabilis plaga, ille
tamen qui dictatam in Ninivitas sententiam subversionis[l] misericorditer revocavit,[10] adhuc dignabitur terram ipsam rore gratie sue perfundere ac de lapidibus
illis Habrahe[m] filios suscitare.[11]

[g] invia inaquosa ABC: et inser. "Rec. hist. Gaules" cum Ps. 62.3
[h] sudore laboratum AC: sudatum labore B
[i] labore sudatum AC: laboratum sudore B
[j] justo] rasura decem litterarum et supralin. justo scr. B
[k] ipsorum fluctibus videatur AC: videatur ipsorum fluctibus B
[l] sententiam subversionis tr. B
[m] Habrahe C: Habrae A, Abrahe B

the rain which cometh often upon it, and bringeth forth herbs meet for them by whom it is tilled, receiveth blessing from God."[4] But rather it is like that land mentioned in the next verse, "which bringeth forth thorns and briars, is reprobate, and very near unto a curse."[5] For this is truly "a desert land, where there is no way, and no water";[6] indeed, it is an iron land, to which God seems to have given a heaven of brass,[7] and over which he seems to have commanded the clouds never to pour down rain,[8] since no rain of doctrine, no dew of grace has prepared it to bear the fruits it ought. This is a land that, it seems, rightly deserves to be called "reprobate silver,"[9] because the founder has cast it in vain after laboring with much sweat and sweating with much labor to purify it, since its malice is not consumed by the fire and its abundant rust is not removed. By a hidden but just judgment, God has up to now permitted the land—that is, the hearts of its inhabitants—being compacted by infidelity and frozen by malice, to be hardened to such a great extent that it cannot be softened either by the incentives of sweet talk or by the torments of whips. They have so set their minds against God that no matter how many times they have been worn down by whips, they refuse to receive discipline. Instead, not recalling that nothing is more unhappy than the happiness of sinners, they make boasts against the Church of God, and they assume it to be an argument for, and confirmation of, their error that they seem to have been successful against Catholics. They have overlooked the fact that the sons of Israel, who were the Lord's chosen people, were frequently defeated by gentiles whom the Lord himself detested; and in the end they utterly destroyed those gentiles, who exulted in vain over their victories.

3 However often the ship of the Church seems to be, with God's permission, stricken by their waves, we are nonetheless certain that he, who promised he would be with it until the ending of the world, shall not desert it amidst such turbulence of the waves, but instead in his own good time he shall command the winds and the sea. Likewise we hope that however obstinate their hardness and however severe their wound may be, nevertheless he, who mercifully revoked his declared sentence that Nineveh should be destroyed,[10] shall even now

---

4. Hebrews vi.7, with words transposed in the Latin text.

5. Hebrews vi.8.

6. Psalm 62.3 (AV 63.1).

7. Leviticus xxvi.19; cf. Deuteronomy xxviii.23.

8. Cf. Isaiah v.6

9. Jeremiah vi.30: "Call them reprobate silver, for the Lord hath rejected them" (Douay-Rheims).

10. Jonah i.1-2, iii.4-10.

4 Ecce dilectum filium nostrum R(omanum), sancti Angeli diaconum cardinalem, virum generis et morum nobilitate preclarum, constantia industriaque conspicuum, et nobis inter ceteros fratres nostros merito sue probitatis carum specialiter et acceptum, illuc providimus destinandum ut, preeunte divine pietatis auxilio, errata corrigat et deformata reformet, noxia evellat plantetque salubria, ipsamque terram, diu obsitam sentibus vitiorum et fructus iniquitatis ac amaritudinis proferentem, fructus pietatis et dulcedinis, auctore Deo, faciat germinare.

5 Et quoniam[n] auxilium carissimi in Christo filii nostri Lodowici regis Francorum illustris et regni ejus est ad hec facienda modis omnibus necessarium, aliaque negotia in regno[o] ipso habet sedes apostolica pertractare, eidem cardinali, tam in eodem regno quam in Provincia nec non in Tarentasien', Bisuntinen', Ebredunen', Aquen', Arelaten' et Viennen' provinciis, plene legationis officium duximus[p] committendum, data sibi libera potestate destruendi et evellendi, edificandi atque plantandi,[12] disponendi, ordinandi, statuendi, diffiniendi, et faciendi quecumque, secundum datam sibi a Deo prudentiam, viderit facienda.

6 Ideoque universitati vestre per apostolica scripta mandamus et districte precipimus quatinus ipsum sicut apostolice sedis legatum, immo verius nos in ipso, studentes devote recipere ac honorifice pertractare, sibique diligenter ac fideliter[q] assistentes, ipsius salubria monita et mandata recipiatis humiliter et irrefragabiliter observetis. Nos enim sententias quas rationabiliter tulerit in rebelles ratas habebimus et faciemus, auctore Deo, inviolabiliter observari.

Dat' Laterani xv.[r] kal. Martii, pontificatus nostri[s] anno nono.[t]

[n] quoniam (qm) ABC: quum *Teulet*
[o] regno] Francie *add. et canc.* B
[p] duximus] concedendum *add. et canc.* B
[q] diligenter ac fideliter] fideliter ac diligenter B
[r] xv. A] xvi C
[s] pontificatus nostri *om.* A
[t] Dat'—nono *om.* B

deign to spread the dew of his grace over that land and to raise up the sons of Abraham from those stones.[11]

4 Behold our beloved son Romanus, the cardinal-deacon of Sant' Angelo, a man outstanding for the nobility of his birth and manners, conspicuous for the diligence and persistence with which he pursues his goals, and the one among our brothers [the cardinals] whom we especially cherish and deservedly esteem for his probity. Our purpose in sending him thither is so that he may, proceeding in the spirit of godly piety, correct errors and reform corruption, and so that he may uproot the noxious and plant the wholesome, and so that he may (God willing) cause that land, which has long been covered with the briars of vice, to bear the sweet fruits of piety instead of the bitter fruits of iniquity.

5 To do this it is absolutely necessary to have the aid of our most dear son in Christ, Louis, illustrious king of the French, and of his kingdom. For this reason, and because the apostolic see has other business to transact in that kingdom, we have entrusted to the same cardinal the office of full legation both in that kingdom and in Provence, as well as in the provinces of Tarentaise, Besançon, Embrun, Aix, Arles, and Vienne, giving him free power to pull down and to uproot, to build and to plant,[12] to appoint, to ordain, to enact, to define, and to do whatsoever he sees fit to do according to the prudence given to him by God.

6 Therefore by apostolic writ we command and strictly enjoin all of you that you endeavor to receive him devoutly as legate of the apostolic see, or really to receive us in his person, and to treat him with honor; you are to assist him diligently and faithfully, and you must receive his wholesome recommendations and commands with humility and observe them without dispute. For we shall treat as valid the sentences that he inflicts with good reason on rebels, and (God willing) we shall cause them to be observed inviolably.

Given at the Lateran on the fifteenth day before the kalends of March, in the ninth year of our pontificate.

11. Matthew iii.9 and Luke iii.8.
12. Jeremiah xlv.4; cf. i.10.

Document 13
LETTER OF LEGATION FOR ROMANUS
TO THE CIVIL AUTHORITIES
13 February 1225

MSS.—(A) Vatican, Arch. Segreto Vat., Serie generale de' Regesti, vol. 13, fols. 33v–34r: Reg. Hon. III, tom. V, an. ix, ep. 177. (B) Paris, BnF, MS. Baluze 385, no. 239, item 10: Albigensian Roll; see Doc. 10. (C) Paris, Arch. nat., J 428, no. 3: Trésor des chartes, Albigeois, no. 3; the original of the *vidimus* of 31 January 1226 (Doc. 27), which is an authenticated copy of the letter dispatched with Romanus. Cf. Doc. 12.

Honorius episcopus, servus servorum Dei, dilectis filiis nobilibus viris,[a] ducibus, comitibus, baronibus, nec non rectoribus et communitatibus civitatum et castrorum in regno Francie ac in Provincia et in . . Tarentasien', . . Bisuntinen', . . Ebredunen', . . Aquen', . . Arelaten', et . . Viennen' provinciis constitutis,[b] salutem et apostolicam benedictionem.[c]

1 Cum negotia que in regno Francie ac in Provincia nobis imminent pertractanda, propter sui arduitatem virum multe constantie, multe circumspectionis exposcant, pro hiis dilectum filium nostrum R(omanum) sancti Angeli diaconum cardinalem, morum et generis nobilitate conspicuum, et de circumspectione, industria, et constantia specialiter commendabilem, providimus destinandum, concesso sibi plene legationis officio et data sibi libera potestate disponendi, ordinandi, diffiniendi,[d] et faciendi quecumque secundum datam sibi a Deo prudentiam viderit facienda.

2 Ideoque universitati[e] vestre per apostolica scripta mandamus quatinus sicut personam nostram honorifice recipiatis eundem, et ei fideliter et efficaciter assistatis in omnibus in quibus ab eo fueritis requisiti, ita quod devotionem vestram in Domino commendare possimus, nec vos aliquam difficultatem[f] incurrere secus faciendo possitis. Nos enim sententiam, quam rationabiliter tulerit in rebelles, ratam habebimus et faciemus, auctore Deo,[g] inviolabiliter observari.[h]

Dat' Laterani idibus Februarii, pontificatus nostri anno nono.[i]

---

[a] Honorius—viris: *om.* A; Ho. vi. B   [b] *in marg.* ducibus, comitibus, baronibus necnon rectoribus et communitatibus civitatum et castrorum in regno Francie ac in Provincia et Tarentasien', Bisuntin', Ebredun', Aquen', Arelaten', et Viennen' provinciis constitutis *scr.* A   [c] salutem—benedictionem *om.* AB   [d] ordinandi diffiniendi *tr.* B   [e] Ideoque universitati] *supra ras.* . . . . *(quatuor puncti) ins.* B   [f] aliquam difficultatem *tr.* C   [g] et faciemus / auctore Deo *tr. et corr.* B   [h] tulerit—observari BC: etc. A *(cf. eamdem formam in Doc. 12)*   [i] Dat'—nono: *om.* B, pontificatus nostri anno nono *om.* A

Ed.—Teulet, no. 1693; transcribes MS. C. exactly.

Refs.—Potthast, no. 7358. Pressutti, no. 5305. Baronio-Theiner, XX (1870), 500, n. 2, ad an. 1225, no. 29. *Rec. hist. Gaules*, XIX (1833), 766. Horoy, IV, 786, noted after no. 79. U. Chevalier, *Regeste dauphinois*, III (Valence, 1914), no. 6761.

Text.—Base manuscript is the certified copy of the sealed original (C), collated against a copy of the draft (B) and the register (A).

In this document, two of B's transpositions (cf. Doc. 12) can be attributed to the scribe, not his exemplar: one he himself corrected (var. g) and in the other he alters a common formula (var. d).

Honorius, bishop, servant of the servants of God, to his beloved sons the noblemen, dukes, counts, barons, and also the rectors and communities of cities and castles located in the kingdom of France and in Provence, and also in the provinces of Tarentaise, Besançon, Embrun, Aix, Arles, and Vienne, greeting and apostolic blessing.

1 We have affairs pending in the kingdom of France and in Provence that we are about to deal with, and because of their difficulty they require a man who is both persistent and circumspect. Consequently to do this we are sending our beloved son Romanus, the cardinal-deacon of Sant' Angelo, who is conspicuous for his nobility of manners and birth, and especially commendable for his circumspection, diligence, and persistence. We have entrusted him with the office of full legation and have given him free power to appoint, to ordain, to enact, to define, and to do whatsoever he sees fit to do according to the prudence given to him by God.

2 Therefore by apostolic writ we command all of you that you receive him with honor just as if he were our own person; you are to assist him faithfully and effectively in all things that you shall be required by him to do. And do this in such a manner that we can commend your devotion to the Lord, and that you cannot incur any difficulty by doing otherwise. For we shall treat as valid the sentences that he inflicts with good reason on rebels, and (God willing) we shall cause them to be observed inviolably.

Given at the Lateran, on the ides of February, in the ninth year of our pontificate.

Document 14
ADVANCE NOTICE OF THE LEGATION TO LOUIS VIII
[early February] 1225

In addition to the usual formal letter of legation (Doc. 15), Honorius also sent Louis an informal notification that the pope was sending a legate who was especially well disposed towards Louis and France (Doc. 14). This letter was intended to arrive shortly before the legate himself and was perhaps carried by the French *nuntii* who, Honorius says, could vouch for Romanus' Francophilia. Advance notification was a noncommittal means of intimating Honorius' change of plan to the king (cf. Doc. 12).

Honorius episcopus, servus servorum Dei, carissimo in Christo filio>[a] Lodovico regi Francorum illustri <salutem et apostolicam benedictionem>[b]

1 Destinaturi legatum ad regnum tuum et ad Provincie partes, in ipsius legati persona ostendimus[c] manifeste quam ad te caritatis habundantiam habeamus. Illum omnium ex fratribus nostris illuc providimus destinandum quem tibi vidimus acceptiorem utilioremque futurum, dilectus scilicet filius noster R(omanus) sancti Angeli diaconus cardinalis, qui, sicut et nos certissime novimus et nuntii tui sunt multis et evidentibus argumentis jam frequenter experti, personam tuam sincerissime[d] diligit et ad tuum ac regni tui honorem et exaltationem diligenter ac ferventer intendit.

2 Hunc ergo, cum ad te venerit—veniet autem dante Deo in proximo— curabis sereno vultu recipere ac de cunctis agendis tractare plena fiducia cum eodem.

<Dat' Laterani xv. kal. Martii, pontificatus nostri anno nono.>[e]

[a] Honorius—filio] *supplevi*
[b] salutem—benedictionem *supplevi*
[c] ostendimus] *quatuor litteras add.* A, *corr. cum quatuor punctis supra ras.* A[1]
[d] sincerissme] sincerime B, *supra lin. corr.* B[1]
[e] Dat'—nono *om.* A *et ex Doc. 15 supplevi*

MS.—(A) Paris, BnF, MS. Baluze 385, no. 239, item 13: Albigensian Roll; see Doc. 10.

Ed.—Unpublished.

Text.—Transcribed from a photocopy of A.

Date.—Doc. 14 is undated in MS. A, where it is preceded and followed by letters written in med-February. While it is possible that it was written then and dispatched immediately, two weeks before the legate's departure, I am inclined to date it earlier than the other letters of legation because it anticipates that the legate will arrive subsequently ("in proximo"). Tentatively, I have assigned it to sometime soon after 31 January, when Honorius had certainly decided to send Romanus (Docs. 10-11), on the assumption that the king would be notified as soon as possible.

Honorius, bishop, servant of the servants of God, to the most dear son in Christ, Louis, illustrious king of the French, greeting and apostolic blessing.

1 We are about to dispatch a legate to your kingdom and to Provence, and in the person of that legate we have plainly shown what an abundance of love we have for you. From all of our brothers [the cardinals], we have chosen to send thither the one whom we see shall be more acceptable and useful to you, namely our beloved son Romanus, the cardinal-deacon of Sant' Angelo, who loves your person most sincerely and who diligently and fervently is directing his efforts to the honor and exaltation of you and your kingdom, as we have long known for certain, and as your envoys have come to know recently and frequently by many plain proofs.

2 Therefore, when he comes to you—he shall come (God willing) very soon—you will want to receive him with a cheerful face and to deal with him about the whole agenda in full confidence.

Given at the Lateran on the fifteenth day before the kalends of March, in the ninth year of our pontificate.

Document 15
LETTER OF LEGATION TO LOUIS VIII
15 February 1225

MSS.—(A) Vatican, Arch. Segreto Vat., Serie generale de' Regesti, vol. 13, fol. 34r: Reg. Hon. III, tom. V, an. ix, ep. 178. (B) Paris, BnF, MS. Baluze 385, no. 239, item 12: Albigensian Roll; see Doc. 10.

Honorius episcopus, servus servorum Dei, carissimo in Christo filio>ᵃ Lodow- icoᵇ regi Francorum illustri <salutem et apostolicam benedictionem>.ᶜ

1 Inter ceteros fratres nostros, dilectusᵈ filius noster R(omanus) sancti Angeli diaconus cardinalis honorem tuum speciali affectione zelatur, sicut et nos ipsi certissime novimus et nuntii tui sunt multis et evidentibus argumentis jam frequenter experti. In tuum igitur regnum et circumstantes partes legatum, urgente multiplicium negotiorum necessitate, missuri, dictum cardinalem illuc providimus destinandum ut in hoc quoque cognoscas quam ad te habeamus habundantiam caritatis.ᵉ

2 Ideoque serenitatem tuam rogamus attentius et hortamur quatinus ipsum tanquam apostolice sedis legatum, immo verius nos in ipso sereno vultu recipias, eique dignam honorificentiam exhibens et a tuis faciens subditis exhiberi, ejus salubribus monitis et consiliis sic reverenter intendas, quod idem in dilectione tua de die in diem crescere teneatur, et nos, qui eumᶠ quadam prerogativa diligimus, caritatis devotionem regiamᵍ commendare in Domino debeamus.

Dat' Laterani xv. kal. Martii, <pontificatus nostri anno nono>.ʰ

ᵃ Honorius—filio *supplevi*
ᵇ Lodovico B, Lodowico *corr.* B¹
ᶜ illustri—benedictionem: *om.* A; salutem—benedictionem *om.* B *et supplevi*
ᵈ dilectus (dil') AB] dilectos *Rec. hist. Gaules*
ᵉ k'ritatis B
ᶠ *duas litteras add.* B, *corr. cum duos puncti supra ras.* B¹
ᵍ regiam *om. Horoy*
ʰ Dat'—nono *om.* B, pontificatus nostri anno nono *om. A et supplevi; annum ex contextu, viz. anno Registri nono, patet*

Ed.—*Rec. hist. Gaules*, XIX (1833), 766, from MS. A. Reprinted by Horoy, IV (1880), 785–786, no. 79.

Refs.—Potthast, no. 7361. Pressutti, no. 5314. Baronio-Theiner, XX (1870), 500, n. 3, ad an. 1225, no. 29.

Text.—The base text is from a photocopy of the Vatican Register (A), collated against B, for which I used both the original and a photocopy.

Honorius, bishop, servant of the servants of God, to the most dear son in Christ, Louis, illustrious king of the French, greeting and apostolic blessing.

1 Among our other beloved brothers [the cardinals], special affection makes our son Romanus, the cardinal-deacon of Sant' Angelo, zealous for your honor, as we have long known for certain and as your envoys have come to know recently and frequently by many plain proofs. Because of the pressing necessity of dealing with complex affairs, we are about to send a legate to your kingdom and adjacent areas; therefore we have caused the said cardinal to be dispatched thither so that by this choice you may know what an abundance of love we have for you.

2 Therefore with special concern we ask and urge your serene highness that with cheerful face you receive him like a legate of the apostolic see, or rather, more truly, us in him, showing him due honor and making your subjects do so too; moreover, pay such good attention to his wholesome recommendations and counsels that your love for him may grow from day to day, and that we, who have loved him longer, will be obliged to commend to the Lord your majesty's devotion of love.

Given at the Lateran on the fifteenth day before the kalends of March, in the ninth year of our pontificate.

Document 16
SAFE-CONDUCT FOR ROMANUS
TO A SECULAR LORD
[12 February 1225]

MS.—(A) Paris, BnF, MS. Baluze 385, no. 239, item 14: Albigensian Roll; see Doc. 10.

Honorius episcopus, servus servorum Dei,>[a] nobili viro comiti Sabaudie, <salutem et apostolicam benedictionem>.[b]

Cum dilectum filium nostrum R(omanum) sancti Angeli diaconum cardinalem apostolice sedis legatum in regnum Francie ac circumstantes partes pro magnis arduisque negotiis destinemus, nobilitatem tuam rogandam duximus et monemus per apostolica tibi[c] scripta mandantes quatinus eidem per terram tue dicioni subjectam ita cures in securo providere ducatu quod ad Romanam ecclesiam matrem tuam debitam devotionem te habere demonstres, et nos ad commodum et honorem tuum, cum oportunum fuerit, studiosius intendere debeamus.

<Dat' Laterani ii. idibus Februarii, pontificatus nostri anno nono.>[d]

§ In eundem modum quibus voluerit.[1]

[a] Honorius—Dei *scripsi*
[b] salutem—benedictionem *scripsi*
[c] tibi *supra lin. ins.* A
[d] Dat'—nono *scripsi (cf. Doc. 17)*

Document 17
SAFE-CONDUCT FOR ROMANUS
TO ECCLESIASTICAL AUTHORITIES
12 February 1225

MSS.—(A) Vatican, Arch. Segreto Vat., Serie generale de' Regesti, vol. 13, fol. 33v: Reg. Hon. III, tom. V, an. ix, ep. 176. (B) Paris, BnF, MS. Baluze 385, no. 239, item 11: Albigensian Roll; see Doc. 10.

Ed.—Unpublished.

Refs.—None.

Text.—Transcribed from a photocopy of A.

Date.—Presumably the same as Doc. 17, which has a similar purpose.

Honorius, bishop, servant of the servants of God, to the noble man the count of Savoy, greeting and apostolic blessing.

Since we are appointing our beloved son Romanus, the cardinal-deacon of Sant' Angelo, as legate of the apostolic see in the kingdom of France and adjacent areas to transact great and difficult business, we ask and recommend to you by apostolic writ that you provide him with safe conduct through the land subject to your authority. If you do so in such a way that you demonstrate that you have the devotion you owe to your mother the Roman church, we will be obliged to direct our efforts diligently to your advantage and honor when it shall be opportune to do so.

Given at the Lateran, on the fifteenth day before the kalends of March, in the ninth year of our pontificate.

§ Send the same form letter to whomever he [the legate] may wish.[1]

1. The last line was a note on the draft letter indicating its distribution.

Ed.—Unpublished.

Refs.—Pressutti, no. 5303. Cited by Baronio-Theiner, XX (1870), 500, ad an. 1225, no. 29, n. 1, from A. Cited by *Rec. hist. Gaules*, XIX (1833), 766, note, from La Porte du Theil; hence Horoy, IV (1880), 786, after no. 79. Potthast omits.

Text.—From photocopies; base text A, collated with B.

Honorius episcopus, servus servorum Dei, venerabilibus fratribus>[a] archiepiscopis et[b] episcopis et dilectis filiis[c] abbatibus, prioribus ac aliis ecclesiarum prelatis presentes[d] litteras inspecturis <salutem et apostolicam benedictionem>.[e]

Cum omnia nobis imminentia non possimus facere per nos ipsos, exemplo illius qui spiritus facit angelos suos[f] et eos in ministerium mittit, fratres nostros ad ea facienda dirigimus, quibus per nos ipsos intendere non valemus majora majoribus committentes. Cum ergo dilectum filium[g] nostrum R(omanum) sancti Angeli diaconum cardinalem, apostolice sedis legatum, pro magnis arduisque negotiis in Franciam et Provinciam destinemus, universitati vestre per apostolica scripta precipiendo[h] mandamus quatinus eum tanquam unam de columpnis precipuis[i] ecclesie recipientes, hilariter et honorifice pertractantes, in securo conductu et aliis necessariis ineundo et redeundo ita liberaliter provideatis eidem quod ejus vobis comparetis favorem, qui vobis esse poterit multipliciter fructuosus, et nos devotionem vestram merito commendare possimus. Alioquin sententiam quam tulerit in rebelles volumus et precipimus usque ad satisfactionem condignam firmiter observari.[j]

Dat' Laterani ii. idibus Februarii, <pontificatus nostri>[k] anno nono.[l]

[a] Honorius—fratribus *scripsi*
[b] et *om.* B
[c] et—filiis *om.* A
[d] presentem B, *supralin. corr. et quinque characteres subsequentes eras.* B [1]
[e] salutem—benedictionem *scripsi*
[f] suos *om.* A, *supra lin. ins.* A[1]
[g] filium *om.* B
[h] scripta precipiendo] mandamus *ins.* A
[i] columpnis precipuis *tr.* B; precipuis *om.* A, *in marg. ins.* A[1]
[j] quam—observari B] etc. A
[k] pontificatus nostri *scripsi*
[l] Dat'—nono *om.* B

Document 18
A ROMAN CHURCH IS GIVEN TO ROMANUS
20 February 1225

MS.—(A) Vatican, Arch. Segreto Vat., Serie generale de' Regesti, vol. 13, fol. 35r: Reg. Hon. III, tom. V, an. ix, ep. 186.

Honorius, bishop, servant of the servants of God, to our venerable brothers the archbishops and bishops and to our beloved sons the abbots, priors, and other prelates of churches who shall see this letter, greeting and apostolic blessing.

Since by ourselves we are not able to do all the things we are supposed to do, we follow the example of him who made spirits to be his angelic messengers and sends them to administer his affairs; likewise, we direct our brothers [the cardinals] to do those things that we do not have the ability to do ourselves, thus entrusting our greater affairs to our greater ministers. Because we are appointing our beloved son Romanus, the cardinal-deacon of Sant' Angelo, as legate of the apostolic see in France and Provence to transact great and difficult business, we command all of you, notifying you by apostolic writ, that you receive him as one of the principal pillars of the Church; entertain him with honor and good cheer; and provide him with safe conduct and other necessities both when he goes and when he returns. Do all this in such a way that you may gain his favor, which can be fruitful to you in many ways, and so that we can deservedly commend your devotion. In any event, we wish and command that any sentence that he shall pronounce against rebels be observed until appropriate satisfaction be rendered.

Given at the Lateran on the second day before the ides of February, in the ninth year of our pontificate.

Ed.—Unpublished.

Ref.—Pressutti, no. 5325.

Honorius episcopus, servus servorum Dei, dilecto filio>[a] R(omano) sancti Angeli diacono cardinali, apostolice sedis legato, <salutem et apostolicam benedictionem>.[b]

Cum ecclesiam sancti Stephani in Celio Monte tibi ob curie vicinitatem et commoditates alias utilem et idoneam reputemus, eam devotioni tue presentia auctoritate concedimus, ita ut cum ad sacerdotii gradum te auctore Deo promoveri contigerit, illam habeas propriam, habiturus eandem interim commendatam.[1] In cujus rei testimonium et memoriam presentes tibi duximus litteras concedendas.

Dat' <Laterani x. kal. Martii, pontificatus nostri anno nono>.[c]

[a] Honorius—filio *scripsi*
[b] salutem—benedictionem *scripsi*
[c] Laterani—nono *scripsi*] ut supra A *(cf. ep. 185, unde data supplevi)*

Document 19
VARIOUS SPECIAL POWERS FOR ROMANUS
15 February 1225

MSS.—(A) Vatican, Arch. Segreto Vat., Serie generale de' Regesti, vol. 13, fol. 34r: Reg. Hon. III, tom. V, an. ix, ep. 179. (B) Paris, BnF, MS. Baluze 385, no. 239, item 15: Albigensian Roll; see Doc. 10.

Ed.—Horoy, IV (1880), 794, no. 90, from copy of A by La Porte du Theil.

Honorius episcopus, servus servorum Dei,>[a] dilecto filio R(omano) sancti Angeli diacono cardinali, apostolice sedis legato, <salutem et apostolicam benedictionem>.[b]

Ut et tuam honoremus personam et per[c] exhibitum tibi honorem aliis con-

[a] Honorius—Dei *scripsi*
[b] salutem—benedictionem *scripsi*
[c] per *om.* B, *supra lin. ins.* B[1]

Honorius, bishop, servant of the servants of God, to our beloved son Romanus, the cardinal-deacon of Sant' Angelo, legate of the apostolic see, greeting and apostolic blessing.

Since we consider that the church of St Stephen on the Caelian Hill is suitable for you because it is near the curia and can be useful to you in other ways, by the present authority we grant it to your devotion. This is done on the understanding that if (God willing) you are promoted to the grade of priest, you may have that church as your own, but in the meantime you are to have it in trust.[1] We have caused the present letter to be granted to you as an attestation and record of this act.

Given at the Lateran on the tenth day before the kalends of March, in the ninth year of our pontificate.

1. "An individual was said to hold an ecclesiastical benefice *in commendam* [= "in trust"] when its revenues were granted to him temporarily during a vacancy." *Oxford Dictionary of the Christian Church*, ed. F. L. Cross, 3rd ed., ed. E. A. Livingstone (Oxford, 1997), p. 383.

Refs.—Pressutti, no. 5315. Baronio-Theiner, XX (1870), 500, ad an. 1225, no. 29, n. 4.

Date.—The copyist of A replaced the date of his original with an *ut supra* reference to the date given in the preceding letter (ep. 178 = Doc. 15). Pressutti accordingly dated the letter 15 February, but for no discernible reason Horoy misdated it 25 February.

Text.—The Vatican Register (A) has been taken as the base text, with variants from the Albigensian Roll (B).

Honorius, bishop, servant of the servants of God, to our beloved son Romanus, the cardinal-deacon of Sant' Angelo, legate of the apostolic see, greeting and apostolic blessing.

That we may honor your person and look after other matters by means of the honor shown to you, by the authority of the present letter we grant you free power: to absolve, according to the form prescribed by the Church, those who have incurred the canonical penalty for laying violent hands [on a cleric] or for causing fires; and to grant dispensations to those who have received holy or-

sulamus, absolvendi juxta formam ecclesie illos qui pro violenta injectione manuum seu pro commissis incendiis in canonem inciderunt, et dispensandi cum illis qui excommunicati vel interdicti receperunt ordines vel divina officia celebrarunt, necnon cum illis qui contra prohibitionem apostolicam secularium legum studio[d]1 vacaverunt, conferendi etiam dignitates et beneficia que tanto vacaverunt tempore, quod ad nos est eorum donatio devoluta, tibi presentium auctoritate concedimus liberam potestatem.

Dat' <Laterani xv. kalendas Martii, pontificatus nostri anno nono.>[e]

[d] legum studio *tr. (o supra ras.)* B
[e] Laterani—nono *scripsi*] ut supra A *(cf. ep. 178 = Doc. 15), om.* B

Document 20
ELECTIONS OF PRELATES IN PROVENCE ARE TO BE HELD IN ROMANUS' PRESENCE OR WITH HIS COUNSEL
13 February 1225

Honorius episcopus, servus servorum Dei, dilecto filio R(omano) sancti Angeli diacono cardinali, apostolice sedis legato, salutem et apostolicam benedictionem.>[a]

Quia quanto corruptior est terra Provincie, tanto est studiosius providendum ut prelati tales instituantur ibidem qui verbo et exemplo possint ad bonum alios informare, volumus ut[b] intersis prelatorum electionibus quas in Provincia te ibi existente contigerit celebrari, et ut electiones ipse cum tuo semper consilio celebrentur.

Dat' Laterani idibus Februarii, <pontificatus nostri anno nono>.[c]

[a] Honorius—benedictionem *scripsi*] Eidem AB *(cf. ep. 179)*
[b] ut A] quod B
[c] Dat'—nono *om.* B, pontificatus—nono *om.* A *et scripsi*

ders or have celebrated the divine office when they were excommunicated or interdicted; and moreover to grant dispensations to those who have been deprived by studying secular law contrary to the apostolic prohibition;[1] and also to confer dignities and benefices that have been vacant so long that giving them has devolved upon us.

Given at the Lateran on the fifteenth day before the kalends of March, in the ninth year of our pontificate.

1. In November 1219, Honorius III prohibited clerics from studying civil law at Paris and nearby places, on pain of suspension from conducting lawsuits (*causarum patrocinium*), as well as of excommunication: *Super specula* in X 5.33.28 (Friedberg, II, 868) = Pressutti no. 2270.

MSS.—(A) Vatican, Arch. Segreto Vat., Serie generale de' Regesti, vol. 13, fol. 34r: Reg. Hon. III, tom. V, an. ix, ep. 180. (B) Paris, BnF, MS. Baluze 385, no. 239, item 16: Albigensian Roll; see Doc. 10.

Ed.—(1) Baronio-Theiner, XX (1870), 500, ad an. 1225, no. 29. (2) Horoy, IV (1880), 780, no. 76, from La Porte du Theil's copy of A.

Refs.—Pressutti, no. 5306.

Honorius, bishop, servant of the servants of God, to our beloved son Romanus, the cardinal-deacon of Sant' Angelo, legate of the apostolic see, greeting and apostolic blessing.

The more corrupt the land of Provence is, the more careful one must be to see to it that the prelates who are installed there are such as can by word and example be a good influence on others. Therefore it is our will that you be present at the elections of prelates that happen to be celebrated in Provence while you are there, and that the elections themselves always be celebrated with your advice.

Given at the Lateran on the ides of February, in the ninth year of our pontificate.

Document 21
THE DISPUTED ELECTION OF A BISHOP
OF CARCASSONNE
[13 February 1225]

Honorius episcopus, servus servorum Dei, venerabili fratri . .>[a] archiepiscopo Narbon' <salutem et apostolicam benedictionem>.[b]

Noverit tua fraternitas quod causam electionis Karcasson' ecclesie, pro qua ejus procuratores ad nostram presentiam accesserunt, dilecto filio nostro R(omano) sancti Angeli diacono cardinali, legato sedis apostolice, commisisse; quod ideo[c] tibi significare curavimus ut, si forte te super hujusmodi questione adiri contigut,[d] scias illam translatam esse ad ipsius iudicium cardinalis.

<Dat' Laterani xv. kal. Martii, pontificatus nostri anno nono.>[e]

[a] Honorius—fratri . . *scripsi*
[b] salutem—benedictionem *scripsi*
[c] id'eo A
[d] contigut A *(ex 'continguo' = 'contingo')*
[e] Dat'—nono *scripsi (dies atque mensis incerti)*

Document 22
ROMANUS' REMONSTRANCES
ON DEFENDING FAWKES
St-Ouen, 20 August 1225

Although legates wrote frequently to the pope, as his enregistered replies demonstrate, yet for the thirteenth century the legate's side of the correspondence rarely has been preserved. The present letters survived because Romanus gave copies to a team of English agents, who transmitted them to the king, enclosed in their long report together with a postscript (Chaplais, *Diplomatic Documents*, nos. 182–183); the entire packet was preserved in the royal archives. The second letter (22B) is even a greater curiosity than the first (22A): its vivid glimpse into the curia's domestic politics is probably unique for the period.

MS.—(A) Paris, BnF, MS. Baluze 385, no. 239, item 17: Albigensian Roll; see Doc. 10.

Ed.—Unpublished.

Date.—Probably 13 February, as the subject is closely associated with Doc. 20. It is possible, however, that this letter was sent earlier, on 31 January, with Doc. 11, which is also addressed to the archbishop of Narbonne.

Honorius, bishop, servant of the servants of God, to our venerable brother [Arnaud Amaury], the archbishop of Narbonne, greeting and apostolic blessing.

Be it known to your fraternity that the case of the election [of a bishop] of the church of Carcassonne, for which its proctors came into our presence, has been committed to our beloved son Romanus, the cardinal-deacon of Sant' Angelo, legate of the apostolic see. Accordingly, we have taken care to let you know about this, so that if perchance you happen to be approached concerning this question, you may know that it has been transferred to the judgment of that cardinal.

Given at the Lateran on the fifteenth day before the kalends of March, in the ninth year of our pontificate.

Date and place.—Rymer placed both undated letters at the end of the series of letters dated 1224, with that year noted against each in the margin. Perhaps misled by their terminal position, Hardy conjectured the month to be December. A date in late August 1225 was first proposed by Shirley and is accepted without question by Chaplais. However, from the agents' report (Chaplais, no. 182) it is clear that they met with Romanus at St-Ouen on 19 August and again on 21 August, and that in the meantime—on 20 August—he had written to the pope and the cardinals.

Recipients.—The English agent who transmitted this copy to Henry III explained that the second letter was sent "illis cardinalibus de quibus [Romanus] confidit specialius" (Chaplais, no. 182). The recipient list therefore affords a rare indication of a coterie within the college of cardinals (not noted by Maleczek).

From the context, "Magister T.," the first recipient of Doc. 22B, does seem to be a cardinal. The only cardinal created between 1191 and 1225 with a Christian name beginning with the letter T was Thomas de Ebulo, cardinal-priest of Santa Sabina, 1216-1239. At this period he was a papal penitentiary and a frequent *auditor* of cases at the Roman curia. Moreover, Thomas was in fact a *magister*. Romanus, himself a university man, was evidently careful to address degree holders by their proper title; the one cardinal-deacon who was not a *magister* he addressed as *dominus*. See Maleczek, *Kardinalskolleg*, pp. 62, 201-203, esp. n. 568 for Thomas as *magister*; for creations after 1216, see Eubel, *Hierarchia*, I, 4.

Doc. 22B indicates six other recipients to whom copies were to be sent. This note has for the most part been overlooked, however, because Rymer omitted it. Prynne's 1672 edition is helpful in establishing the readings, which today are partly illegible. Chaplais correctly expanded the names, but without identifying the individuals. All six, like Master Thomas, were cardinals in 1225. I list them in the form they appear in the index to Maleczek's *Kardinalskolleg*: (1) Aegidius Hispanus, cardinal-deacon of SS. Cosma e Damiano, 1217-1255; (2) Pelagius, cardinal-bishop of Albano, 1213-1230; (3) Rainer de Viterbo, cardinal-deacon of S. Maria in Cosmedin, 1216-1250; (4) Petrus Capuanus *junior*, cardinal-deacon of S. Giorgio in Velabro, 1219–post 1236; (5) Hugolinus, cardinal-bishop of Ostia, 1206-1227, and subsequently Pope Gregory IX, 1227-1241; (6) Stephanus Comes, cardinal-deacon of S. Adriano, 1216-1228.

MS.—(L) London, PRO, Special Collections 1/5/17 (Ancient Correspondence, vol. V, no. 17; Royal Letters, no. 989); "Bundela litterarum in Turre London. A. 8. H. 3" (Prynne in mg.). Parchment, 200 mm long, 127 mm at top, 136 mm at bottom. Cracked and stained. Both letters are copied by one hand on a single

---

A. To the pope

D OMINO PAPE. Sanctitati vestre duxi tenore presentium intimandum quod, antequam ad me litere vestre quas mihi misistis pro facto Falkasii[a] pervenissent,[b] idem in Burgund' captus erat.   2 Quibus devote receptis et que continebantur in eis intellectis, statim illis personis scribere diligentius procuravi, per quas ipsum credebam debere restitui[c] libertati.   3 Recepi postmodum literas et nuntios ex parte regis Anglorum[d] illustris, quibus intellexi quod tam ipse rex quam fere totum rengnum Anglie per missionem[e] ejusdem F(alkasii) quam faci-

---

[a] Falkatii *Prynne*

[b] pervenissent *edd.*] pervenis***t L

[c] restitui *edd.*] resti*ui L *(cf. B § 1)*

[d] Anglorum] Angliae *Prynne et Rymer*

[e] per missionem] pro missionem L[1], per *corr.* L[1] *(cf. § B 2)*; pro missione *Prynne et Rymer*

sheet, most probably from Romanus' draft copy (whence the closing note on distribution). The copyist was probably English: hence the forms *rengnum* for *regnum* and *malingno* for *maligno*, which occur in related originals of English provenance (for instance Chaplais, nos. 182, 183, 192).

Ed.—(1), W. Prynne, *Antiquae constitutiones regni Angliae* (London, 1672), III, 59. (2) T. Rymer, *Foedera*, I (London, 1727), 274-275, ad an. 1224 (9 Hen. III); idem, I.i (The Hague, 1739), 94, collated below as "Rymer"; idem, I.i (London, 1816), 176. *Rec. hist. Gaules*, XIX, 768 n., reprints Doc. 22A only, from Rymer 1739. (4) Chaplais, *Diplomatic Documents*, I (London, 1964), 124-125, no. 184.

Refs.—Shirley, *Royal Letters*, I (1862), 264 n.; also pp. 267-269 for the occasion of the letters and the copies thereof sent to England. T. D. Hardy, *Syllabus (in English) of the Documents Relating to England and Other Kingdoms Contained in the Collection Known as "Rymer's Foedera,"* I (London, 1869), 28. Public Record Office, *Lists and Indices*, No. XV: *List of Ancient Correspondence of the Chancery and Exchequer Preserved in the Public Record Office*, by C. T. Martin (London, 1902), p. 20, and rev. ed. (New York, 1968), p. 71. The original of A was kindly examined for me by Schafer Williams in 1969; I saw it myself in 1984.

Text.—Transcribed from photographs of L (one with ultraviolet light) and corrected from the original. Because the phraseology of 22A is often repeated in 22B, lacunae can often be filled with confidence. In the apparatus, "edd." indicates a consensus of previous editors.

A. To the pope

TO THE LORD POPE. I am having the present letter written to let your holiness know that Fawkes was captured in Burgundy before your letter that you sent me on his behalf had arrived.   2 After I had received and read your letter, as a faithful servant I immediately and diligently had letters written to those persons through whom I believed Fawkes ought to be restored to liberty. 3 Subsequently I received a letter and envoys from the illustrious king of the English, from whom I learned that both the king himself and almost the whole kingdom of England are agitated and irritated by the mission that you sent on Fawkes' behalf;[1] and his enemies there are puffed up with pride because they

---

1. In early June 1225, Honorius had sent his nuncio Otto to England to intercede for Fawkes with King Henry III.

tis[f1] turbati sunt plurimum et commoti; et ipsius inimici, depressionem[g] ejusdem in hac parte[h] percipientes, elati sunt in superbiam.[i] 4 Unde videtur per hoc quod negotium pacis vel treugarum inter eundem et regem Francorum illustrem pro quo tantum Deus novit laboravi non possit effectui[j] mancipari,[k] et sic per consequens negotium Albigen' potest,[l] sicut credimus, retardari. 5 Cum itaque diebus istis propter malitias hominum[m] regum et rengnorum sint scandala[n] evitanda, cum totus mundus fere sit positus in malingno plus[o] etiam quam creditis,[p] si placet,[q] sanctitas vestra provideat quod[r] sit exinde faciendum.

B. To certain cardinals

1 MAGISTRO T(HOME). Paternitati vestre tenore presentium intimamus quod, antequam litere domini pape ad nos[a] pervenissent, quas[b] nobis pro facto Falkasii[c] destinavit, idem F(alkasius) in Burgund' captus erat, set statim post receptionem literarum ipsarum illis personis scripsimus per quas credebamus[d] ipsum debere restitui libertati.   2 Recepimus postmodum nuntios et literas ex parte regis Anglorum illustris, quibus intelleximus evidenter quod tam ipse quam fere totum[e] rengnum Angl' valde turbati sunt plurimum et commoti pro missione quam dominus papa facit in Angl'[f] super negotio[g] Falkasii[h] memorati.   3 Unde videtur per hoc quod negotium pacis vel treugarum inter duos reges pro quo tantum Deus[i] novit laboravimus non possit effectui[j] mancipari, et sic per con-

---

[f] facitis] faciatis *Prynne et Rymer*

[g] depressionem] derisionem *Prynne et Rymer*, deversionem *Williams*

[h] parte *edd.*] part* L

[i] superbiam *corr. edd. (cf. 1 Tim. 3.6)*] superbum L

[j] effectui] effectum *Rymer*

[k] mancipari *edd. (cf. B § 3)*] manci*ari L

[l] potest (pt) L] patet *Prynne et Rymer*m

[m] hominum] et *add. Prynne et Rymer*

[n] scandala *edd. (cf. B § 4)*] ****dala L

[o] plus *edd. (cf. B § 4)*] p**s L

[p] creditis L] credatis *cum dubitatione corr. Chaplais (cf. B § 4)*

[q] placet *edd. (cf. B § 6)*] *lacet L

[r] quid *Prynne*

[a] ad nos *om. Prynne et Rymer*

[b] quas *edd. (cf. A § 1)*] *s L

[c] Falkatii *Prynne*

[d] credebamus *corr. edd.*] credebimus L

[e] totum *edd. (cf. A § 3)*] **t L

[f] Angl'] Angliam *Prynne et Rymer*, Anglia *Chaplais*

[g] negotio *corr. Chaplais (super + abl.)*] ***ocii L, negotiis *Prynne et Rymer*

[h] Falkatii *Prynne*

[i] Deus *edd. (cf. A § 4)*] *eu* L *(sic leg. Chaplais)*

[j] effectui] effectum *Rymer*

have heard of his misfortunes here.   4 As a result, it seems that the negotiation of a peace or truce between the illustrious kings of England and France, for which God knows I have worked hard, cannot be brought to a successful conclusion, and in our opinion the Albigensian business can be retarded in consequence.   5 We should avoid outrageous behavior towards kings and kingdoms these days because almost the whole world is more disposed to be hostile [to the papacy] than you think. If you please, let your holiness indicate what is to be done next.

B. To certain cardinals

1 TO MASTER THOMAS. By the present letter we are letting you know that Fawkes was captured in Burgundy before the letter that the lord pope sent us on Fawkes' behalf had arrived. But immediately after receiving that letter, we wrote to those persons through whom we believed Fawkes ought to be restored to liberty.   2 Subsequently we received envoys and a letter from the illustrious king of the English, from whom we learned clearly that both the king himself and almost the whole kingdom of England are agitated and irritated by the mission that the lord pope sent to England concerning the affair of the aforesaid Fawkes.   3 As a result, it seems that the negotiation of a peace or truce between the illustrious kings of England and France, for which God knows we have

sequens negotium Albigen', prout credimus, sit quasi penitus exsufflatum.   4
Cum itaque diebus istis propter hominum malitias regum et rengnorum sint
scandala evitanda, cum totus mundus fere in malingno sit positus plus etiam
quam credatis,[k] vos et alii qui, cum estis in cameris vestris, non cogitatis hujusmodi, set, ut videtur, ecclesie Dei parantes excidium, reges et rengna non ad
devotionem ecclesie, set potius ad scandalum et discordias provocatis,   5 scientes[l] quod plurimum admiramur et multi alii commoventur quod, cum rengnum
Anglie nunc in bono statu consistat, quod[m] dominus papa et vos ad vocem unius
ad inquirendum de facto regis illius,[n] quod antea de hiis que regiam contingunt[o]
potestatem fieri non consuevit, et de statu ipsius[p] rengni et prelatorum ejusdem mandatis.   6 Et ideo, si placet, provido[q] in hac parte utentes consilio, sicut
decet, procedatis in ipso negotio, Deum solum habentes pre oculis, prout melius
videritis expedire.

Scribat[r] magistro Egidio, episcopo Alban', magistro Rayner',[s] magistro P(etro)
Capuan', episcopo Hostien'[t] <et>[u] domino S(tephano) sancti Addriani.[vw]

[k] credatis] creditis *Prynne et Rymer (cf. A § 5)*
[l] scientes] sciatis *Rymer*
[m] quod] quare *Prynne et Rymer*
[n] regis illius] Rêg illius L, Regum Angliae *Prynne et Rymer*, regis Anglie *Chaplais*
[o] contingunt] contingant *Prynne et Rymer*
[p] statu ipsius *edd.*] stat* **sius *(lacuna)* L
[q] provido *corr. Chaplais*] provide L
[r] scribat L] scribatur *male corr. Chaplais*
[s] Rapner *Prynne*
[t] Hostien'] H****** L *hodie sed* Hostien. *leg. Prynne*
[u] et *suppl. Chaplais; om. Prynne*
[v] Addriani] Albani *Prynne*
[w] Scribat—Addriani *om. Rymer*

Document 23
THE FRENCH BARONS COUNSEL LOUIS
TO CRUSADE
[29] January 1226

From the Chronicle of Tours we know that the legate and king celebrated a joint
concilium generale on the first day of the assembly—Wednesday, 28 January—and
that, "after having taken diligent counsel" at an unspecified time, the king as-

worked hard, cannot be brought to a successful conclusion. And thus in our opinion the Albigensian business may be as it were completely blown away. 4 We should avoid outrageous behavior towards kings and kingdoms these days because almost the whole world is more disposed to be hostile [to the papacy] than you and the others think. You are not aware of this when you are in your chambers [at Rome]; instead, you seem to be facilitating the downfall of God's Church by provoking kings and kingdoms to scandal and discord rather than to devotion to the Church.   5 You should realize that we are much amazed and many others are irritated that, given the present good state of the kingdom of England, you and the lord pope are with one voice questioning an act of the king, which it was not formerly the custom to do in matters touching the royal power, and that you are issuing commands concerning the state of that kingdom and its prelates.   6 Therefore, if you please, use prudent advice on the matter, as is proper, and proceed in this business just as may seem best to you, with your eyes fixed on God alone.

He wrote to Master Egidius, the bishop of Albano, Master Rainer, Master Peter of Capua, the bishop of Ostia, and to the lord Stephan of Sant' Adriano.

sumed the cross on the third day (Doc. 3.7–8). The present document memorializes the counsel of the lay barons at the time it was given (verbs in the present tense). The chronicler does not tell us what was done on the second day, but we may surmise that it was then that the king took counsel and in response received the present document from the lay barons.

Barons.—Teulet identified the twenty-nine barons as follows: (1) Philippe de France, comte de Boulogne et de Clermont en Beauvoisis; (2) Pierre Mauclerc, comte de Bretagne; (3) Robert III "Gatebled," comte de Dreux et de Braine; (4) Jean d'Oisy, seigneur de Montmirail, comte de Chartres; (5) Gui II, comte de

St-Paul; (6) Jean II, comte de Roucy; (7) Jean IV de Montoire, comte de Vendôme; (8) Mathieu II de Montmorency, connétable de France; (9) Robert de Courtenay, bouteiller de France; (10) Enguerrand III "le Grand," seigneur de Coucy; (11) Amauri de Craon, sénéchal d'Anjou; (12) Jean, seigneur de Nesle; (13) [Raoul], vicomte de Ste-Susanne; (14) Geoffroi III or IV, vicomte de Châteaudun; (15) Savari de Mauléon; (16) Thomas de Coucy; (17) Robert de Coucy; (18) Gaucher de Joigny; (19) Gautier de Rinel; (20) Henri de Sully; (21) Philippe de Nanteuil; (22) Etienne de Sancerre; (23) Renaud de Montfaucon; (24) Gui de la Roche (de Roca on seal); (25) Renaud d'Amiens; (26) Robert de Poissy; (27) Simon de Poissy; (28) Bouchard de Marly; (29) Florent de Hangest.

MSS.—(A) Paris, Arch. nat., J 428, no. 1 bis: Trésor des chartes, Albigeois, no. 1 bis; sealed original. Closely resembles Doc. 24 in format (425 × 90 mm + flap on bottom margin to secure seals) but is in another hand. (B) Arch. nat., JJ 26, fol. 327v: Register E. Copy in Paris, BnF, MS. Baluze, vol. 8, fol. 20r–v. (C) Paris, BnF, MS. lat. 9778, fol. 272ra: Register F.

P*hilippus* comes Bolonie et Clarimont*is*, comes Petrus Brit*annie*, comes Robertus Droc*ensis*, comes Carnot*ensis*, comes Sancti Pauli, comes Rociaci, comes Vindocin*ensis*, Matheus de Monte Morenc*iaco* Franc*ie* constabularius, Robertus de Corten*aio* buticularius Franc*ie*, Inger*ranus* de Cotiaco,[a] senescallus Andeg*avie*, Joha*n*nes de Nigella, vicecomes Sancte Susanne, vicecomes Castri Duni, Savar*icus* de Malo Leone, Thom*as* de Cotiaco,[a] Robertus de Cotiaco,[a] Galche*rus* de Jovigniaco, Galterus de Rinello, Henr*icus* de Soliaco, Ph*ilippus* de Nantol*io*, Steph*anus* de Sacrocesare, Ren' de Monte falcon*is*, Guido de Ruppe, Ren' de Ambian*is*, Robertus de Pissiaco, Sim*on* de Pissiaco, Boch*ardus* de Malliaco, Floren*cius* de Hangesta, omnibus ad quos littere presentes pervenerint salutem in Domino.

Noveritis quod, propter amorem Jesu Christi et fidei Christiane, necnon et honorem karissimi domini nostri Lud' regis Franc' illustris et regni, laudamus ei et consulimus ut negotium terre Albigesii sibi assumat, et promittimus, super fidem quam ei debemus, quod nos juvabimus eum bona fide, sicut dominum nostrum ligium, usque ad ipsius negotii consummationem, vel quamdiu in eo negotio laborabit.

Actum Paris' anno Domini m° cc° xxv°, mense Januario.

[a] Cociaco *Teulet*

Register copies.—Although it is pointless to record every way in which the register copies (B and C) vary from the original document (A), it may be noted that B's scribe not only freely altered word order and the spelling of place names but even omitted six barons altogether (6, 16-18, 20-21, 23, 27) as well as half of a title (*et Clarimontis*, 1). In the registers, the document is entitled: *Carta majorum de via Albig'*.

Seals.—"Scellé de vingt-neuf sceaux" noted Vaissète; but by Teulet's day, ten had been lost, though slits for attaching all twenty-nine are still visible. In 1968 wax chips had separated from many of the seals. Teulet identified the extant ones and, when possible, cited examples of those missing.

Ed.—(1) Devic-Vaissète, III (1737), 299-300, preuve no. 161; VIII (1879), 816-817, preuve no. 243. (2) Teulet, no. 1742.

Ref.—Petit-Dutaillis, *Louis*, p. 491 (no. 315).

Text from Teulet's transcript of A, verified from photographs and the original of A. Teulet's expansions of proper names are given in *italics*.

Philippe, count of Boulogne and Clermont; count Pierre of Brittany; count Robert of Dreux; the count of Chartres; the count of St-Pol; the count of Roucy; the count of Vendôme; Mathieu de Montmorency, constable of France; Robert de Courtenay, butler of France; Enguerrand de Coucy; the seneschal of Anjou; Jean de Nesle; the viscount of Ste-Susanne; the viscount of Châteaudun; Savari de Mauléon; Thomas de Coucy; Robert de Coucy; Gaucher de Joigny; Gautier de Rinel; Henri de Sully; Philippe de Nanteuil; Etienne de Sancerre; Renaud de Montfaucon; Gui de la Roche; Renaud d'Amiens; Robert de Poissy; Simon de Poissy; Bouchard de Marly; Florent de Hangest: to all to whom the present letter comes, greeting in the Lord.

Be it known to you that, because of the love of Jesus Christ and the Christian faith, and also because of the honor of our lord Louis, the illustrious king of France, and of the kingdom, we recommend and counsel that he undertake the Albigensian business. And we promise, over and above the faith that we owe to him, that we shall assist him in good faith as our liege lord until that business is completed, or as long as he shall be involved in that business.

Done at Paris, A. D. 1225, in the month of January.

Document 24
CERTIFICATION OF LOUIS' INTENTION
[30] January 1226

In this open letter the legate acknowledged that he had received the king's oath as crusader on the express understanding that Louis would be obliged to go South only once, for no longer than he wished, and at no obligation to his heirs. Since the document patently records the intentions both parties expressed during the ceremony, with verbs in a past tense, this declaration, dated *sine die*, can best be assigned to the day on which Louis took the cross. For that date we must depend on the chroniclers, who differ. The Salisbury Register gives the date as 29 January (Doc. 42.10c), but the Chronicle of Tours gives Friday, 30 January (Doc. 3.8). The latter date is to be preferred not only because the writer was closer to the events but also because he adds the weekday both for this one and the opening of the council (Doc. 3.7), thus eliminating the possibility of scribal error.

Prelates.—The superscription names Romanus, five archbishops, and eleven bishops. Teulet identifies each individual, but confuses Philippe I de Jouy, the bishop of Orléans (1221-1234), with his successor and homonym, Philippe II Berruyer (1234-1237); he has it right, however, in his annotation to Doc. 27 (his no. 1693).

R(omanus) Dei miseratione Sancti Angeli diaconus[a] cardinalis, Apostolice sedis legatus, Rem*ensis*, Bituric*ensis*, Senon*ensis*, Rothom*agensis*, Turonen-*sis* archiepiscopi, et Belvac*ensis*, Lingon*ensis*, Laud*unensis*, Noviom*ensis*, Sil-van*ectensis*, Morin*ensis*, Carnot*ensis*, Paris*iensis*, Aureli*anensis*, Alti*ssiodorensis*, Melden*sis* episcopi, omnibus ad quos littere presentes pervenerint, salutem in Domino.

1 Noverit universitas vestra quod, cum dominus noster Lud', rex Franc' il-lustris, ad honorem Dei et ad exhortationem nostram, contra Albigenses et ini-micos fidei signum crucis de manu nostri legati suscepisset, ante receptionem dixit et protestatus est quod ex ista crucis assumptione et tali voto emisso non vult nec intendit obligari ad morandum in terra Albigesii nisi quantum sibi placuerit, nec ad revertendum illuc cum inde redierit; et, quando placuerit ei de terra recedere, possit sine scrupulo conscientie, quantum ad Deum et Ecclesiam,

---

[a] diaconi *Teulet*

MSS.—(A) Paris, Arch. nat., J 428, no. 2: Trésor des chartes, Albigeois, no. 2; sealed original, in similar format (80 × 422 mm + foldup flap to secure seals) as Doc. 23 but in a different hand. (B) Arch. nat., JJ 26, fol. 328r: Register E. Copy in Paris, BnF, MS. Baluze, vol. 8, fols. 26v–27r. (C) Paris, BnF, MS. lat. 9778, fol. 272vb: Register F.

Register copies.—In the royal chancery registers, both B and C are entitled: *Transcriptum litterarum de modo obligationis.* Except for alterations and an occasional slip (*uostrum* for *nostrum* in C, § 1), the transcripts are exact.

Seals.—"Scellé de dix-sept sceaux" noted Vaissète; Teulet found six missing and most of the rest fragmentary (the wax is inferior to the quality of that used in Doc. 23). Teulet references each seal.

Ed.—(1) Devic-Vaissète, III (1737), 301, preuve no. 162, ii; VIII (1879), 818-819, preuve no. 244, ii. (2) Teulet, no. 1743.

Ref.—Petit-Dutaillis, *Louis,* pp. 491-492 (no. 316).

Text from Teulet's transcript of A, verified from photographs and the original of A. Teulet's expansions of place names given in *italics.*

Romanus by God's mercy cardinal-deacon of Sant' Angelo, legate of the apostolic see; the archbishops of Reims, Bourges, Sens, Rouen, and Tours; and the bishops of Beauvais, Langres, Laon, Noyon, Senlis, Thérouanne, Chartres, Paris, Orléans, Auxerre, and Meaux: to all to whom the present letter comes, greeting in the Lord.

1 Be it known to all of you that, when our lord Louis, illustrious king of France, received from our legate's hand the sign of the cross against the Albigensians and the enemies of the faith, he did so for God's honor and at our urging. But before he received it, he said and publicly declared that by thus taking the cross and by making such a vow he did not wish or intend to be obliged to stay in the Albigeois any longer than pleased him, nor to return there again after he had come back home. And when it should please him to depart from that land, he could go back home with a clean conscience with regard to God and the Church. And, if he should go the way of all flesh, he does not wish his heirs to be bound in any way by this taking of the cross and this vow.

redire; et heredes suos, si de eo contingeret humanitus, non vult, ex hac crucis assumptione et voto, aliquo modo teneri.

2 Nos autem attendentes pium ipsius propositum et sanam intentionem, et quod nullus ex voto nisi voluntarie obligatur, nec etiam filii ex patris voto tenentur, nos legatus signum crucis ei dedimus, non intendentes nec volentes ipsum obligari ex hac crucis assumptione nisi secundum quod ipse superius est protestatus.

Ut autem hec nota sint et inconcussa permaneant, presentibus litteris sigilla nostra fecimus apponi.

Actum Paris*ius* anno Domini m° cc° vicesimo quinto, mense januario.

Document 25
DRAFT VERSION OF THE PARIS PROMISES TO THE KING BY THE LEGATE AND FRENCH PRELATES
late January 1226

Somehow an English spy secured an advance copy of the agenda for the council that was to be celebrated at Paris on 28–31 January 1226. The original that he transmitted to London still survives and invites comparison with the documents that were the result of the Paris council. As is evident from the passages that the draft and the final versions have in common, which are indicated by *italics* in the text printed below, about half of the draft text appears unaltered in the final version. The English agent perhaps paraphrased nonessential matters (§ 1, 4–5) and certainly reproduced others practically verbatim (§ 8–10).

The draft version was changed considerably, though chiefly in the interests of clarity, precision, and style. Evidently the draft was produced by the royal chancery because it invariably refers to the king of France as "*dominus* rex," whereas the legate is only once accorded the same honorific. Thus it seems likely that many of the revisions were suggested by Romanus himself, for example the expansion of § 1 to stress Raymond's opposition to the Church (cf. Doc. 26.3). Similarly, the legate was no doubt responsible for providing a precise legal definition of the crusaders' privileges (§ 7 = Doc. 26.2). Probably there was also a touch of his diplomatic tact in removing the awkward limitation on the king's spending of the grant and leaving the matter instead to his *bona fides* (§ 6 = Doc. 26.9). Other alterations, however, touched the interests and experience of Louis VIII's secular vassals who counseled him at Paris, and these may accordingly have

2 Furthermore, we were aware that his purpose was pious and his intention sound; and that no one is obligated by a vow unless it is voluntary; and that sons are not bound by their father's vow. With this all in mind, we, the legate, gave him the sign of the cross neither intending nor wishing him to be obliged by this taking of the cross otherwise than, as stated above, he publicly declared.

That these things may be known and may remain secure, we have caused our seals to be affixed to the present letter.

Done at Paris, A. D. 1225, in the month of January.

been made at their suggestion. Thus the ambiguous term *turbatores*, for "disturbers of the peace," might include turbulent royal vassals and was altered to *invasores* (§ 2 = Doc. 26.4); and again, the clause enforcing a fine on private feudal warfare was dropped (§ 3 = Doc. 26.5).

Most noteworthy, however, is the lack of revision in the promises concerning the tenth (§ 8–10 = Doc. 26.6–8). Clearly these terms had been agreed upon well before the Paris council and were subject to only minor stylistic improvements.

Date.—With undue caution, Langlois stated that the report had been "expédié de France en 1226," that is, at any time before 31 January, on which the only firmly dated document was issued at the conference. But the phrase "in presenti" (twice repeated) indicates events that will take place "immediately" or "instantly" (Niermeyer, *Lexicon*, p. 838, s.v. "praesens," 3). Chaplais unaccountably dates the document "1225, late October," which cannot be, because it provides for the first collection of the tenth on the *next* feast ("in instanti festo") of All Saints, that is, 1 November, which could only refer to 1226, since the tenth had not even been granted in November 1225.

MS.—(A) London, PRO, Special Collections 1/57/73 (Ancient Correspondence, vol. XLVII, no. 73).

Ed.—(1) C. V. Langlois, "Notices et documents relatifs à l'histoire du XIIIᵉ et du XIVᵉ siècle," *Revue historique*, LXXXVII (1905), 58, n. (2) Chaplais, *Diplomatic Documents*, no. 191.

Text reprinted from Chaplais' edition; sections and paragraphs added.

Dominus legatus *excommunic*abit *Raymundum* in presenti qui se dicit *comitem* de *Tholose* et omnes illos qui eum adjuvabunt et *fautores suos*[1]

2 et *omnes* turbatores *regni Francie*, si fuerint *de regno* Francie vel *de extra regnum*, et faciet eos excommunicatos denunciari per totam legationem suam nec relaxabitur illa *sentencia* donec turbatores vel *guerreatores* regni *sint extra regnum* et *donec* interceptiones, *dampna et injurias* quas fecerint prius emendaverint *competenter domino regi et suis*.[2]

3 Quod si aliqui *de regno Francie guerram moverent inter se* nec *pacem facerent* vel *treugam* darent *ad mandatum domini regis*, ipse legatus excommunicaret eos donec pacem facerent vel treugam et competenter emendarent domino regi et injuriam passis factas interceptiones contra defensionem domini regis.[3]

4 Preterea transcriptum legationis sue tradet legatus domino regi sigillatum sigillo suo et sigillis archiepiscoporum, episcoporum regni Francie presentium,[4]

5 et similiter faciet apponi sigilla eorumdem archiepiscoporum et episcoporum in sentencia excommunicacionis predicta quam faciet in presenti contra Raymundum de Tholos' et fautores et coadjutores suos et omnes turbatores et invasores regni Francie.[5]

6 De auxilio quod facit ecclesia domino regi poterit facere *dominus rex voluntatem suam* de *expede*ndo illo et in terra Albig' et alibi ubi guerra moveretur eidem.[6]

7 Omnes crucesignati de Albig' et illi qui pro se mittent ibidem et terre et res eorum erunt *in protectione* sancte *ecclesie quamdiu* erunt *in servicio* ecclesie,[7] et habebunt easdem *indulgentias* et remissiones *quas habent crucesignati de* partibus transmarinis.[8]

8 Sciendum est quod *dominus rex* habebit *decimam omnium proventuum ecclesiasticorum* per totam *legationem* ipsius legati *usque ad quinquennium si tantum negocium duraverit, deductis expensis illis que proveniunt ex cultura vinearum et agrorum*,[9]

9 exceptis *Templo, Hospitali, Cisterciensi, Premonstratensi* ordinibus qui *nichil solvent de decima ista nec prelati nec clerici de familia sua qui personaliter in hoc negocio laborabunt*.[10]

10 *Fiet autem solucio decime duobus terminis, in festo omnium sanctorum et in pascha, et incipiet prima solucio in instanti festo omnium sanctorum*.[11]

In the immediate future the lord legate shall *excommunicate Raymond*, who calls himself *count of Toulouse*, and all those who help him and *his supporters*,[1]

2 and *all* who disturb the peace *of the kingdom of France*, whether they shall be *from the kingdom* of France or *from outside the kingdom*, and he shall cause them to be denounced as excommunicates throughout his entire legation, nor shall that *sentence* be canceled until those *warriors* or disturbers of the kingdom shall be outside the kingdom, and *until* they first have made amends *adequately to the lord king and his supporters* for the attacks, *damages, and injuries* they shall have made.[2]

3 If any persons *from the kingdom of France are making war among themselves* and do not *make peace* or give *a truce at the lord king's command*, the same legate shall excommunicate them until they make peace or a truce and adequately make amends to the lord king for injury suffered from attacks made contrary to the lord king's prohibition.[3]

4 Moreover, the legate shall deliver to the lord king a transcript of his letters of legation sealed with his seal and the seals of the archbishops [and] bishops of the kingdom of France who shall be present there.[4]

5 And similarly he shall cause the seals of the same archbishops and bishops to be affixed to the aforesaid sentence of excommunication which he shall presently make against Raymond of Toulouse and his supporters and helpers and all disturbers and invaders of the kingdom of France.[5]

6 Concerning the aid that the Church is granting to the lord king, *the lord king shall be able to spend it as he wishes*, both in Albigeois and elsewhere where war is waged for the same purpose.[6]

7 All the crusaders in Albigeois and those who send substitutes there, as well as their lands and goods, shall be *under the protection of holy Church as long as* they shall be *in the service* of the Church;[7] and they shall have the same *indulgences* and remissions of sins *that the crusaders* overseas *have*.[8]

8 It is a fact that *the lord king shall have a tenth of all the ecclesiastical revenues* throughout the entire *legation* of the same legate *for a five-year period, if the business shall last so long, after the expenses of viticulture and agriculture have been deducted*.[9]

9 *Exempt from paying that tenth are: the Temple, the Hospital, the Cistercian and Premonstratensian* orders; *prelates, as well as clerics of their households, who participate personally in this business.*[10]

10 *Payment of the tenth shall be made in two installments, one due at the feast of All Saints and the other at Easter. And the first payment shall be made at the next feast of All Saints.*[11]

1. § 1 = Doc. 26.3.
2. § 2 = Doc. 26.4.
3. § 3 = Doc. 26.5.
4. § 4 provides for Doc. 27.
5. The intent of § 5 is fulfilled by Doc. 26, which is so sealed and contains the excommunications in § 3-5.
6. § 6 = Doc. 26.9.
7. § 7a = Doc. 26.1.
8. § 7b = Doc. 26.2.
9. § 8 = Doc. 26.6.
10. § 9 = Doc. 26.7.
11. § 10 = Doc. 26.8.

Document 26
THE PARIS PROMISES TO THE KING
BY THE LEGATE AND FRENCH PRELATES
[30] January 1226

Of the five surviving acts associated with the council of Paris (Docs. 23-27), this is the only one for which no original has been preserved in the French royal archives. One may speculate that the sealed original was removed to substantiate the terms of the tenth of 1225 (§ 6-9) when they were disputed in 1226-1227. Before the original was lost, however, it was copied into chancery Register E, the corpus of which was completed in 1220, although additions (including Doc. 26) continued to be made until 1247 (Baldwin, pp. 413-415).

Less than a week after sealing this document, Romanus incorporated much of its tenor (§ 1-8) in his mandate to the French clergy that ordered them to pay the tenth he had just granted to the king (Doc. 28). He altered the original text occasionally to suit the new context and somewhat more to improve on the Latinity of the royal chancery. Thus C is in effect a second recension, so I have relegated its readings to the apparatus; nonetheless, it has proved useful in resolving conflicts between A and B.

Day.——None of the three copies preserves the *actum*-clause giving the date. Our document was enacted after the king had received the Cross (§ 1) but not necessarily on the same day. It would have been appropriate, however, for Church and king to exchange commitments at the time of the ceremony. A comparison of this piece with its companion documents suggests that such was in fact the case. The resemblance to Doc. 24 is marked, as both acts run in the name of the same prelates and list them in identical order. By contrast, Doc. 27 lists the prelates in another sequence, wherein seven of the sixteen names have been transposed. It is especially significant that the order of Doc. 27 corresponds more closely to the traditional order of ecclesiastical precedence: for example, Laon precedes Beauvais among Reims' suffragans. Docs. 24 and 26, then, both list the prelates improperly, which fact strongly suggests that they had a common origin. We may suspect that they were drawn up by royal clerks who were ignorant of the niceties of provincial precedence. At least the style of the date clause of Doc. 24 (lost for Doc. 26; cf. Doc. 23) is characteristic of the royal chancery: *Actum . . . anno Domini . . . mense . . .* (cf. Doc. 27 by contrast). The important point, however, is not who prepared the pair but that they were prepared together. Similarities in nonformulaic phrasing (for instance § 1) reinforce this impression. If, as I have supposed, Doc. 24 was sealed on 30 January, then its mate was most likely enacted on the same occasion.

The document incorporates at least one act that had been performed two days earlier, for the Chronicle of Tours states that Raymond was excommunicated by Romanus on 28 January (Doc. 3.7). This accounts for the anomalous formula of § 3: "excommunicavimus et excommunicatum denuntiamus" (cf. "excommunicamus" in § 4-5). Horoy mistakenly dated *all* the excommunications, and hence Doc. 26 itself, 28 January.

MSS.—(A) Paris, Arch. nat., JJ 26, fol. 328ra: Register E. Copy in Paris, BnF, MS. Baluze, vol. 8, fols. 25v–26v. (B) Paris, BnF, MS. lat. 9778, fols. 272va–vb: Register F; cf. Doc. 7. (C) Avranches, Bibl. mun., MS. 149, fol. 78v = Doc. 28 (1226), which incorporates most of Doc. 26.1-8.

Ed.—(1) Devic-Vaissète, III (1737), 300-301, preuve no. 162, i: from B; VIII (1879), 817-818, preuve no. 244, i. (2) Martène-Durand, *Thesaurus*, I (1717), 913-933: from C (see Doc. 28).

Refs.—Horoy, IV (1880), 783, n. 1. Petit-Dutaillis, *Louis*, p. 492 (no. 317). For the French royal registers, J. W. Baldwin, *The Government of Philip Augustus* (Berkeley and Los Angeles, 1986), pp. 412-418.

Text from A with paragraphs supplied; collated with B (original) and C (photograph). The draft version (Doc. 25) offers no variants that alter my text.

R(omanus),[a] Dei miseratione[b] Sancti Angeli diaconus cardinalis, Aposto-lice sedis legatus, Remen', Bituric', Senon', Rothom', Turon' archiepiscopi, Belvac', Lingonen',[c] Laudun', Noviomen', Sylva', Morin', Carnot', Parisien', Aurel', Altisiodor',[d] Melden' episcopi, omnibus presentes litteras inspecturis salutem in Domino.

1 Noverit universitas vestra quod, cum dominus noster Ludovicus, rex Franc' illustris, ad honorem Dei et fidei Christiane negotium crucis assumpserit con-tra Albigenses et[e] hereticos et pravitatem hereticam expugnandam, nos ipsum [f]regem, familiam suam, et regnum suum, et omnes qui cum eo[g] in hoc negotio ibunt et laborabunt[h] in Ecclesie protectione suscepimus quam diu fuerint in servitio Jesu Christi.

2[i] Et concessimus eisdem, auctoritate Dei omnipotentis et beatorum apos-tolorum Petri et Pauli et nostra, indulgentiam quam habent crucesignati de terra Jerosolimitana, sicut etiam continetur in Lateranen' concilio.

3 Et excommunicavimus et excommunicatum denuntiamus Raym(undum), filium Raym(undi) quondam comitis[j] Tolosan',[k] fautores, complices suos, et omnes qui consilium vel[l] auxilium[m] ei[n] dederint[o] contra Ecclesiam[p] et fidem Christianam, et regem[q] Franc', qui pro ea[r] defendenda laborat.

4 Item excommunicamus[s] omnes illos qui guerrearent vel invaderent[t] reg-num Franc', sive sint[u] de regno sive sint de extra regnum, statuentes ut a sen-

---

[a] *Titulus praemisit* B[3] *(cf. Doc. 29):* Littere R. Sancti Angeli diaconus cardinalis de domino rege Lud' et toto regno capto in protectione Ecclesie dum erit in negotio Albig' contra hereti-cis et fautores eorum, et de concessione decime per quinquennium.

[b] miseratione] divina *add.* B

[c] Turon'—Lingon' *om.* B[1] , *supra lin. inser.* B[2]

[d] Altisiodorum B

[e] et *om. Vaissète*

[f] regem] *hic extractum incipit et usque ad § 8 finem currit* C

[g] cum eo *om.* C

[h] et laborabunt] personaliter *ins.* C

[i] § *2 om.* C

[j] comitem B

[k] Tolosanum C

[l] vel] et C

[m] vel auxilium *om.* B *et Vaissète*

[n] eidem C

[o] dederint] et *add.* B

[p] Ecclesiam] Dei *add.* C

[q] et regem] contra *ins.* C

[r] eadem C

[s] excommunicamus AC: excommunicavimus B

[t] guerreabant ... invadent C

[u] sint *om.* C

Romanus, by God's mercy cardinal-deacon of Sant' Angelo, legate of the apostolic see; the archbishops of Reims, Bourges, Sens, Rouen, and Tours; the bishops of Beauvais, Langres, Laon, Noyon, Senlis, Thérouanne, Chartres, Paris, Orléans, Auxerre, and Meaux: to all who shall see the present letter, greeting in the Lord.

1 Be it known to all of you that when our lord Louis, the illustrious king of France, for the honor of God and the Christian faith took upon himself the business of the Cross against the Albigensians and heretics in order to wipe out heretical perversity, we took that king under the protection of the Church, and likewise his family and his kingdom, and all who shall go with him and work at this business, as long as they are in the service of Jesus Christ.

2 And by the authority of almighty God and the blessed apostles Peter and Paul, as well as by our own [legatine] authority, we concede to them the indulgence that crusaders to the Holy Land have, just as is provided in the Lateran council [IV, c.71].

3 And we have excommunicated, and we proclaim to be excommunicate, Raymond the son of Raymond the former count of Toulouse, his supporters and accomplices, and all who shall give him aid or counsel against the Church and the Christian faith, and against the king of France, who is working to defend them.

4 We also excommunicate all those who make war in the kingdom of France or invade it, whether they are from the kingdom or are from outside the kingdom. And we decree that they are in no way to be absolved from this sentence

tentia excommunicationis nullatenus absolvantur donec de dampnis et injuriis competentem prestent^v satisfactionem^w domino^x regi et suis, et regnum egrediantur^y illi guerreatores vel invasores qui sunt de extra regnum.

5 Item excommunicamus omnes illos qui sunt de regno Franc' qui inter se guerram moverint, nisi^z treugam vel pacem facerent^a ad mandatum domini^b regis.

6 Quia vero negotium^c istud magnum est et magnos sumptus exigit et expensas, promisimus et promittimus domino^d regi dare decimam omnium proventuum ecclesiasticorum legationis nostre usque ad quinquennium, si tantum negotium^e duraverit, deductis expensis illis que^f proveniunt ex cultura vinearum et agrorum.

7 Hospitalar'^{g} autem et Templar',^{h} Cistercienses et Premonstratenses nichil solvent^i de decima illa, nec prelati^j nec clerici^k de familia sua qui personaliter in hoc negotio laborabunt, nec alii clerici quos legatus et dominus rex^l elegerimus ydoneos ad personaliter^m laborandum in hoc negotio.^{n}

8 Fiet autem solutio decime duobus terminis per annum^o in festo Omnium Sanctorum et in Pascha. Et incipiet prima solutio in instanti festo Omnium Sanctorum.^{p}

^{v} prestant B

^{w} competentem prestent satisfactionem] satisfecerint competenter *et post* suis *ins.* C

^{x} domino] dicto C

^{y} regnum egrediantur *tr.* C

^{z} nisi ABC: nec *perperam leg. Martène*

^{a} facerint C

^{b} domini] dicti C

^{c} negotium ABC: regnum *Martène*

^{d} et promittimus domino] *om.* C *et substituit* sacro aprobante concilio Bitur' congregato eidem

^{e} tantum negotium *tr.* C

^{f} qui B

^{g} Hospitalar' A: Hospitalarum B, Hospitalarii *Vaissète*

^{h} Templar' A: Templarum B, Templarii *Vaissète*

^{i} nichil solvent *iteravit* B^1, *del.* B^2

^{j} Hospitalar'—prelati] *om.* C *et substituit* Decimam autem illam prelati non solvent

^{k} clerici *om.* C

^{l} legatus et dominus rex] nos rex predictus C; et *post* nos *ins. Martène*

^{m} personaliter] persolvendum *add.* B^1, *del.* B^2

^{n} negotio] supradicto *add.* C

^{o} per annum *om. Vaissète*; videlicet *add.* C

^{p} et in Pascha—Sanctorum *om. Vaissète et* B1. ; *signum insertionis* (//) *add. sed textum omissum non dedit* B^2; *extractum cum verbo* Sanctorum *explicit* C

of excommunication until they provide adequate satisfaction to the lord king and his supporters for damages and injuries, and until those warriors or invaders who are from outside the kingdom have departed from it.

5 We also excommunicate all those from the kingdom of France who make war among themselves, unless they make a truce or peace at the lord king's command.

6 Because this business is indeed a large one and requires great expenses and expenditures, we have promised and we do promise to give the lord king a tenth of all the ecclesiastical revenues of our legation for a five-year period, if the business shall last so long, after the expenses of viticulture and agriculture have been deducted.

7 Exempt from paying that tenth are: the Hospitalers, Templars, Cistercians, and Premonstratensians; prelates, as well as clerics of their households, who participate personally in this business; and other clerics whom the legate and the lord king shall designate as suitable for participating in this business.

8 Payment of the tenth shall be made in two installments per annum, one due at the feast of All Saints and the other at Easter. And the first payment shall be made at the next feast of All Saints.

9 Pecuniam autem illam provenientem ex illis proventibus percipiet et expendet dominus rex pro voluntate sua quam diu erit in negotio illo per se vel per suos, bona fide sicut negotium illud exegerit memoratum.[q]

Ut autem hec nota sint[r] et inconcussa permaneant, presentibus litteris sigilla nostra fecimus apponi.

<Actum Paris' anno Domini m° cc° vicesimo quinto, mense Januario.>[s]

[q] memorandum B
[r] sunt *in marg. corr.* B[2]
[s] Actum—Januario *ex Doc. 24 supplevi*

Document 27
VIDIMUS OF ROMANUS' LETTERS OF LEGATION
31 January 1226

The date leaves no doubt that Romanus' letters of legation were attested the day after Louis took the cross. Although the delivery of this document was stipulated in the agenda (Doc. 25.4), the *vidimus* differs markedly from the set of documents used at the ceremony on 30 January, which were prepared by royal clerks without due regard for episcopal precedence (see Doc. 26). The present document employs a different format, is written in an elegant hand, has improved the order of precedence, and uses a different style for the *datum*-clause. The dating formula *anno gratiae* points to an ecclesiastical, rather than the royal, chancery; it is used in Doc. 28.11-12 by the archbishop of Rouen and the bishop of Avranches.

Both the fact that this *vidimus* was specified in the agenda (Doc. 25.4) and that the sealed original was preserved in the royal archives indicate that the crown thought it expedient to have at its disposal this proof of the legate's powers over the clergy and laity (Docs. 12 and 13). It follows that the *vidimus* was drawn up to document the authority on which the grants of the previous day were based. Romanus' letters of legation establish that the legate acted for the pope in these matters, and so the papacy was bound by his promises. But the act served another interest as well, for it demonstrated that the bishops and archbishops assembled at Paris were cognizant of Romanus' letters of legation; by attesting their familiarity with the legate's credentials, the French prelates acknowledged not only that he acted on papal authority but also that he could have done so without them.

9 The lord king shall collect and spend the money resulting from these revenues as he wishes as long as he shall engage in that business in good faith, either in person or through his people, just as the aforesaid business may require.

That these things may be known and may remain secure, we have caused our seals to be affixed to the present letter.

<Done at Paris, A. D. 1225, in the month of January.>

Precedence.—The archbishops are ranged according to the dignity of their sees; most of the bishops are grouped by province: the suffragans of Reims (Laon, Beauvais, Noyon, Thérouanne, Senlis) and those of Sens (Chartres, Orléans, Auxerre, Paris, and Meaux). The exception is Langres (*Lingonensis*), a suffragan of Lyon; probably Langres should have been put first among the bishops, since his province, Lyon, takes precedence over the others. An explanation may be found in the fact that Langres also appeared among the Reims suffragans who were listed in Docs. 24 and 26 on the previous day. Most likely the royal clerks who drafted Friday's acts (see Doc. 26) guessed incorrectly that Reims province included not only Châlons on the middle course of the Marne but also Langres at the headwaters as well. Most of their misapprehensions were corrected in Saturday's list, but the misplacement of Langres was overlooked.

The presence of Langres among Reims' suffragans is an error that links the twin Docs. 24 and 26 to Doc. 27. The ameliorated list of Doc. 27 separates it from the other two, however, and we may safely assume that the improvements were made *after* Docs. 24 and 26 were drawn up, probably the next day; consequently my reasons for assigning Docs. 24 and 26 to Friday, 30 January are strengthened.

Produced in Romanus' household.—The interrelation of these three documents indicates that the drafter of the *vidimus* had the earlier pair at his disposal, but he also had Romanus' letters of legation, which would not have been in the royal archives, as they were addressed to the clergy and laity. Probably the draftsman assembled his document from sealed originals supplied by the legate, to which he added the address derived from the previous day's acts and a distinctive, Rouen-style *datum* (*anno gratiae*).

Another clue is provided by the script. The same elegant hand is used in Docs. 30 and 31, original letters that were undoubtedly written by one of Romanus' clerks. Although the style of the *datum*-clause is not the same as in Docs. 30-31, it seems likely that the *vidimus* was produced in Romanus' household.

This conclusion is confirmed by the English agent's report that the legate would deliver this document to the king *already sealed* (Doc. 25.4), which indicates that Romanus was responsible for its production.

MS.—(A) Paris, Arch. nat., J 428, no. 3: Trésor des chartes, Albigeois, no. 3; sealed original (250 × 355 mm). Only fragments remain of the sixteen seals originally appended to the *vidimus*. Teulet cites intact examples of each and identifies the prelates named. Endorsed: *littera plurimum prelatorum Franc' continens tenorem lit-*

W (ilielmus) Dei gratia Remen', . . Senon', . . Bituricen', . . Rothom' et . . Turon' archiepiscopi; . . Laudunen', . . Belvacen', . . Lingonen', . . Noviomen', . . Morinen', . . Silvanecten', . . Carnoten', . . Aurelianen', . . Autisiodoren', . . Paris',ᵃ etᵇ . . Melden' episcopi, omnibus presentes litteras inspecturis salutem in Domino.

1 Noverit universitas vestra nos inspexisse et legisse quedam rescripta apostolica, ad nos et alios prelatos et barones regni Francie et quarumdam vicinarum provinciarum directa, quorum tenorem verbo ad verbum, sicut in bullatis continetur auctenticis, duximus presentibus inserenda:

2 "Honorius episcopus, servus servorum Dei, venerabilibus fratribus archiepiscopis et episcopis, et dilectis filiis abbatibus, prioribus, et aliis ecclesiarum prelatis in regno Francie ac in Provincia constitutis, et . . Tarientasien', . . Bisuntinen', . . Ebredunen', . . Aquen', . . Arelaten', et . . Viennen' archiepiscopis et eorum suffraganeis, nec non abbatibus et aliis ecclesiarum prelatis consistentibus in diocesibus eorumdem, salutem et apostolicam benedictionem.

'Mirabiles elationes maris' . . . (= Doc. 12, Romanus' letter of legation to the ecclesiastical authorities) . . . inviolabiliter observari.

Datum Laterani xvi. kal. Martii, pontificatus nostri anno nono."

3 "Honorius episcopus, servus servorum Dei, dilectis filiis nobilibus viris, ducibus, comitibus, baronibus, nec non rectoribus et communitatibus civitatum et castrorum in regno Francie ac in Provincia et in Tarentasien', Bisuntinen',

---

ᵃ Paris' *om. Teulet*
ᵇ *ductus pennae curvus similis ad C litteram* A

terarum Honorii pape eis et baronibus Franc' missarum pro legato misso ad partes Narb'
m° cc° xxv°.

Ed.—Teulet, in note to no. 1693.

Text from A, transcribed from a photograph and verified from the original.
Teulet prints the incorporated letters separately (his nos. 1693 and 1694); in his
text of the *vidimus*, both letters are indicated by but a single phrase: "Honorius
episcopus servus servorum Dei, etc." Thus one cannot tell which letter comes
first. My text follows the order in which they occur in the manuscript. Inadvertently, Teulet omitted Paris from the enactors listed in the address of the
vidimus but did include it in his inventory of the seals.

William by the grace of God archbishop of Reims, and the archbishops of
Sens, Bourges, Rouen, and Tours; and the bishops of Laon, Beauvais, Langres, Noyon, Thérouanne, Senlis, Chartres, Orléans, Auxerre, Paris, and Meaux:
to all who shall see the present letter, greeting in the Lord.

1 Be it known to all of you that we have examined and read certain apostolic
rescripts addressed to us and to other prelates and barons of the kingdom of
France and certain neighboring provinces. We have ordered that the tenor of
these letters be inserted in the present one word for word, just as it appears in
the originals that are authenticated by the papal seal.

2 "Honorius, bishop, servant of the servants of God, to his venerable brothers the archbishops and bishops, and to his beloved sons the abbots, priors, and
other prelates of churches located in the kingdom of France and in Provence;
and to the archbishops of Tarentaise, Besançon, Embrun, Aix, Arles, and Vienne
and their suffragans, and also to the abbots and other prelates of churches located
in their dioceses: greeting and apostolic blessing.

'Wonderful are the surges of the sea' . . . [= Doc. 12, Romanus' letter of legation to the ecclesiastical authorities] . . . to be observed inviolably.

Given at the Lateran on the sixteenth day before the kalends of March, in the
ninth year of our pontificate."

3 "Honorius, bishop, servant of the servants of God, to his beloved sons the
noble men, dukes, counts, barons, and also the rectors and communities of cities
and castles located in the kingdom of France and in Provence, and also in the
provinces of Tarentaise, Besançon, Embrun, Aix, Arles, and Vienne: greeting and
apostolic blessing.

Ebredunen', Aquen', Arelaten', et Viennen' provinciis constitutis, salutem et apostolicam benedictionem.

Cum negotia que in regno Francie . . . (= Doc. 13, Romanus' letter of legation to the civil authorities) . . . inviolabiliter observari.

Datum Laterani idibus Februarii, pontificatus nostri anno nono."

4 Ne ergo super tenore rescriptorum hujusmodi aliqua dubitatio in posterum oriatur, ea fideliter transcripta sigillis nostris duximus munienda.

Datum Par' anno gratie m° cc° vicesimoquinto, ii. kal. Februarii.

We have affairs pending in the kingdom of France and in Provence . . . [= Doc. 13, Romanus' letter of legation to the civil authorities] . . . to be observed inviolably.

Given at the Lateran on the ides of February, in the ninth year of our pontificate."

4 Therefore, lest any doubt might arise in the future about the tenor of these rescripts, they were copied faithfully and we have ordered the copies to be validated by our seals.

Given at Paris in the year of grace 1225, on the second day before the kalends of February.

COLLECTION OF THE TENTH FOR THE CRUSADE

Document 28
THE LEGATE'S MANDATE TO PAY THE TENTH
5 February 1226

MS.—(A) Avranches, Bibl. mun., MS. 149, fol. 78va–vb: collection of canons and letters concerning Normandy, saec. xiii in. (latest dated entry, 1234); formerly Mont-St-Michel, MS. 249. This item was not included in Montfaucon's catalogue of the monastery's manuscripts, which though published in 1739 was drawn up in the late seventeenth century (Omont), so probably the manuscript was acquired thereafter (canceled shelfmark on flyleaf: ".I.O. / 39"), but before it was used at Mont-St-Michel by Martène and by Bessin (*Concilia Rothomagensis provinciae*), who both published extracts from it in 1717.

The core of the book is a copy of Bernard of Pavia's *Brevarium*, which was the *Compilatio prima* of decretals (fols. 7r–77v). The owner's plan was to supplement this with a collection of later decretals, which takes up much of the remaining space (fols. 79r–109r), that is now known from this manuscript as the *Collectio Abrincensis*. See S. Kuttner, *Repertorium der Kanonistik (1140–1234)*, Studi e testi, vol. 71 (Vatican City, 1937), pp. 264, 299, 335, 422.

The blank spaces before, between, and after these collections were used to transcribe a variety of documents concerning bishoprics and monasteries, mainly in the province of Rouen. Mont-St-Michel figures most prominently (8 times in Delisle's description), but there are also items from Bec (3) and St-Vincent-lez-le-Mans (1). Avranches, the diocese of Mont-St-Michel, occurs only twice, compared with Bayeux (3) and Coutances (1). Therefore a Mont-St-Michel provenance seems likely but not certain.

Between the two main collections, fol. 78 was filled with copies of nine documents, three of which concern Romanus' legation (Docs. 28, 50, and 51). They

---

Willelmus Dei gratia Abrincen' episcopus, dilecto in Christo viro religioso et honesto R(adulfo)[a] abbati Montis Sancti Mich' de periculo maris salutem in Domino. Mandatum domini legati per venerabilem patrem nostrum dominum (Theobaldus)[1] Rothomagen' archiepiscopum recepimus in hunc modum:

[a] *lacuna* A: Th. *scr. Martène*

are preceded by a petition dated 1215 and are followed by letters of Innocent III (four) and Honorius III (one); consequently, these three documents concerning Romanus form a homogeneous group.

Following the *Collectio Abrincensis* is a longer miscellany (fols. 109r–151v) in which other documents relating to papal legates are scattered: the complaint of a metropolitan chapter against the visitation of an unnamed legate (fol. 109va = Doc. 53); a copy of *Super muros* (fol. 110rb = Doc. 41); Legate Conrad's summons to the council of Sens 1223 (fol. 128vb = Doc. 49); and a letter from Romanus to the bishop of Coutances (fol. 135vb = Doc. 52).

See the description by L. Delisle in *Catalogue générale des manuscrits des bibliothèques publiques des départements* (quarto series), IV (1872), 502–506; reprinted in the octavo series, X (1889), 68–73, edited by H. Omont.

Ed.—(1) Martène-Durand, *Thesaurus*, I (1717), 913–933, "Ex ms. sancti Michaëlis in periculo maris." (2) *Rec. hist. Gaules*, XIX (1833), 765–766, in note. The contextual letters of transmission to Avranches and Mont-St-Michel are not printed. The text was taken from Martène's edition, but with a normalized punctuation. Thus only three emendations (*app. crit.,* c, f, and o) qualify this as a distinct edition. Reprinted by Horoy, IV (1880), 783–786, no. 78 (= Doc. 12), in note.

Ref.—F. Lot and R. Fawtier (eds.), *Histoire des institutions françaises au Moyen Age*, vol. III: *Institutions ecclésiastiques*, by J. F. Lemarignier et al. (Paris, 1962), livre ii by J. Gaudemet, pp. 316–317. The letter is inadvertently said to be addressed to the archbishop of Lyon instead of Rouen.

Text transcribed from photographs of A. The portions adapted from Doc. 26 are collated there.

William by the grace of God bishop of Avranches, to Radulf,[1] abbot of Mont-St-Michel in Peril of the Sea, a religious and honest man, beloved in Christ, greeting. From our venerable father and lord Theobald archbishop of Rouen, we have received the mandate of the lord legate as follows:

---

1. Radulfus II des Isles, abbot 1212–1230 (*Gallia Christiana*, XI [1759], 521–522).

Th(eobaldus) Dei gratia Rothomagen' archiepiscopus, venerabili fratri (Willelmo)[b] eadem gratia Abrincen' episcopo, salutem, gratiam, et benedictionem. Noverit fraternitas vestra quod nos litteras domini legati nuper recepimus in hec verba:

Venerabili in Christo patri Dei gratia Rothom' archiepiscopo, Rom(anus) eadem gratia Sancti Angeli diaconus cardinalis, Apostolice sedis legatus, salutem et sinceram in Domino caritatem.

1 Rex regum et Dominus dominantium Jesus Christus, qui se cum Ecclesia sua promisit usque ad finem seculi permansurum nec permissurum quod adversus eam mortis porte prevaleant, nolens eandem in fluctuum turbatione[c] deficere; in cujus manu sunt omnium[d] corda regum et quo voluerit[e] vertit illa, diebus istis ad revelationem ejusdem, que miserabiliter, peccatis nostris exigentibus, erat ab inimicis pacis et fidei depressa, mirabiliter operando, regis Francie illustris cordi, ratione sue gratie, ex alto infudit quod divina gratia faciente, negotium pacis et fidei contra hereticos terre Albigen' in se assumens ad honorem Dei et Ecclesie, crucis vivifice a nobis est caractere insignitus ad purgandam terram illam ab heretica pravitate et ad relevationem in illis partibus Ecclesie Dei, que jam esse submersa penitus videbatur; cum quo plures archiepiscopi, episcopi, comites, et barones et magnates regni Franc' crucis similiter assumpserunt <signum>.[f] Propter quod eundem [g]*regem, familiam suam, et regnum suum, et omnes qui in hoc negotio ibunt et* personaliter *laborabunt in Ecclesie protectione suscepimus quam diu fuerint in servitio Jesu Christi.*

2 *Excommunicamus et excommunicatum denuntiamus* R(aymundum) *filium* R(aymundi) *quondam comitis Tolosan',*[h] *fautores, complices suos, et omnes qui consilium et auxilium eidem dederint contra Ecclesiam* Dei *et fidem Christianam, et* contra *regem Franc', qui pro eadem defendenda laborat.*

3 *Item excommunicamus omnes illos qui guerreabunt vel invad*ent *regnum Franc', sive sint de regno sive de extra regnum, statuentes ut a sententia excommunicationis nullatenus absolvantur donec de dampnis et injuriis* dicto *regi et suis satisfecerint competenter, et egrediantur regnum illi guerreatores vel invasores qui sunt de extra regnum.*

4 *Item excommunicamus omnes illos qui sunt de regno Franc' qui inter se guerram moverint, nisi*[i] *treugam vel pacem fece*rint *ad mandatum dicti regis.*

[b] *lacuna* A: Willelmo *scr. Martène*
[c] turbationem *leg. Martène; corr. "Rec. hist. Gaules"*
[d] omnia *perperam leg. Martène*
[e] voluerit *iteravit* A; voluerit[2] *om. Martène*
[f] signum *scripsi (cf.* signum crucis *infra, § 9, et in Doc. 24.1;* insignia *Martène et* signaculum *"Rec. hist. Gaules" scripserunt*
[g] *Scriptura cursiva (§ 1–7) denotat verba quae auctor ex Doc. 26.1–8 sumpsit*
[h] Tolosanum A; Tolosani *Martène*
[i] nisi] nec *Martène*

Theobald by the grace of God archbishop of Rouen, to his venerable brother William by the same grace bishop of Avranches, greeting, grace, and blessing. Be it known to your fraternity that we recently received a letter from the lord legate in these words:

To the venerable father in Christ, the archbishop of Rouen by God's grace, Romanus by the same grace cardinal-deacon of Sant' Angelo, legate of the apostolic see, greeting and sincere affection in the Lord.

1 The king of kings and lord of lords Jesus Christ, who promised that he would continue to be with his Church until the end of the world and that he would not permit the gates of death to prevail against it, does not intend to abandon it to the raging waves. Moreover, in his hand are the hearts of all kings, and he inclines them to what he has willed. Thus a few days ago he, out of his grace, wonderfully moved the heart of the illustrious king of France in order to bring relief to his Church, which for our sins was miserably oppressed by the enemies of peace and the faith. Pouring down his grace from on high, Christ inspired the king to undertake the business of peace and the faith against the heretics of the Albigeois for the honor of God and the Church. From us he received the emblem of the life-giving Cross as a sign that he intended to cleanse that land from heretical perversity and to raise up God's Church, which in those parts now seems to have gone completely under. And with him many archbishops, bishops, counts, and barons and magnates of the kingdom of France likewise took the sign of the Cross. Consequently[2] *we took that king under the protection of the Church, and likewise his family and his kingdom, and all who shall go on this business and work at it in person, as long as they are in the service of Jesus Christ.*

2 *We have excommunicated, and we proclaim to be excommunicate, Raymond the son of Raymond the former count of Toulouse, his supporters and accomplices, and all who shall give him aid and counsel against God's Church and the Christian faith, and against the king of France, who is working to defend them.*

3 *We also excommunicate all those who are making war in the kingdom of France or are invading it, whether they are from the kingdom or are from outside the kingdom. And we decree that they are in no way to be absolved from this sentence of excommunication until they give satisfaction adequately to the said king and his supporters, and until those warriors or invaders who are from outside the kingdom have departed from it.*

4 *We also excommunicate all those from the kingdom of France who make war among themselves, unless they make a truce or peace at the said king's command.*

2. In § 1-7 *italic type* indicates words that are borrowed from Doc. 26.1-8. Slight variations are not indicated.

5 *Quia vero negotium*[j] *magnum est, et magnos sumptus exigit et expensas, promisimus,* sacro aprobante concilio Bituricis congregato, eidem *regi dare decimam omnium proventuum ecclesiasticorum legationis nostre usque ad quinquennium, si negotium tantum duraverit, deductis expensis illis que proveniunt ex cultura vinearum et agrorum.*

6 *Decimam autem illam* prelati non *solvent, nec clerici de familia sua qui personaliter in hoc negotio laborabunt, nec alii quos nos <et>*[k] *rex* predictus *elegerimus ad personaliter laborandum in negotio* supradicto.

7 *Fiet autem solutio decime duobus terminis* per annum, videlicet *in festo Omnium Sanctorum et in Pascha. Et incipiet prima solutio in instanti festo Omnium Sanctorum.*

8 Quo circa paternitatem vestram rogamus et monemus attentius, qua fungimur auctoritate mandantes, quatinus, excommunicationis sententias predictas per vestram provinciam denominari publice facientes, verbum crucis per personas discretas et litteratas nec ecclesiis honerosas[l] in eadem predicari faciatis: concedentes illis catholicis qui, crucis assumpto caractere, ad exterminium eorundem supradictorum[m] hereticorum se accinxerint, et in personis propriis laboraverint, et expensas <contulerint>;[n] necnon et illis qui non[o] in personis propriis illuc accesserint, set in suis dum taxat expensis juxta facultatem et quantitatem suam viros idoneos demonstraverint; et[p] illis similiter qui, licet in alienis expensis, in propriis tamen personis accesserint ut illa gaudeant libertate, illoque privilegio sint muniti, que accedentibus in Terre Sancte subsidium conceduntur; hujus quoque remissionis denuntiantes esse participes, juxta quantitatem subsidii et devotionis affectum, qui ad subventionem predicti negotii Jesu Christi de bonis suis congrue ministrabunt aut circa predicta consilium et auxilium impenderint oportunum.[q]

9 Monemus etiam discretionem vestram et hortamur in Domino Jesu Christo quatinus suffraganeos vestros ad hujus[r] Christi obsequium imittetis[s] ut signum crucis, tam vos quam episcopi, accipiatis pro amore illius qui pro vobis sanguinem suum fudit.

10 Sic enim studeatis in hoc opere sollicitius vigilare quod proximos ipse caritatis vestre ardor accendat, vosque preter bone fame mercedem, eternum possitis premium a Domino expectare. Scientes quod prefatus rex ad mensem post

---

[j] negotium] regnum *perperam leg. Martène*

[k] et *om.* A; *recte suppl. Martène (cf. Doc. 26.7)*

[l] honerosis A[1], *supra lin. corr.* A[1]

[m] super A: *supra scripsi cum Martène et addidi* dictorum *(cf. § 6, supra)*

[n] contulerint *scripsi cum Martène*

[o] non *perperam om. Martène; corr. "Rec. hist. Gaules"*

[p] et A: ut *Martène*

[q] oportunum] optimum *leg. Martène*

[r] hujusmodi *scr. Martène*

[s] imittetis A *(cf. § 12, infra):* invitetis *Martène*

5 *Because this business is indeed a large one and requires great expenses and expenditures, we have promised*, with the approbation of the holy council assembled at Bourges, *to give the same king a tenth of all the ecclesiastical revenues of our legation for a five-year period, if the business shall last so long, after the expenses of viticulture and agriculture have been deducted.*

6 *Exempt from paying that tenth are: the Hospitalers, Templars, Cistercians, and Premonstratensians; prelates who participate personally in this business, and those of their household; and other clerics whom we and the said king shall designate as suitable for participating in the aforesaid business.*

7 *Payment of the tenth shall be made in two installments per annum, one due at the feast of All Saints and the other at Easter. And the first payment shall be made at the next feast of All Saints.*

8 Wherefore we ask and strictly warn your paternity, commanding you by the authority that we exercise, that you cause the aforesaid sentences of excommunication to be announced publicly throughout your province. Moreover, cause the word of the Cross to be preached there by persons who are discreet, literate, and not burdensome to the churches. In the preaching, stress that eligible Catholics can enjoy the liberties, and can be protected by the privileges, that are granted to those who join in aiding the Holy Land. Three groups are eligible for this grant: (1) those who, having taken the Cross, arm themselves in order to exterminate those heretics mentioned above, and do the work in person, and pay their own way; (2) those who do not go there in person but who at least show they are worthy by how much they contribute according to their ability; and (3) likewise those who do go in person but at someone else's expense. The preachers should also announce that this remission of sins can be shared by those who provide an appropriate amount of their goods to assist the aforesaid business of Jesus Christ, or who support it with suitable aid and counsel; their remission will be proportionate to the quantity of aid and the quality of devotion.

9 We also warn your discretion and exhort you in the name of the Lord Jesus Christ that you so motivate your suffragans in this service of Christ that both you and the bishops take the sign of the Cross for the love of him who shed his blood for you.

10 May you take such pains to work diligently in this matter that the very ardor of your love may inflame your neighbors, and that you can expect to receive not only a good reputation now but also an eternal reward from the Lord.

festum Resurrectionis Dominice proximum erit Bituris personaliter cum exercitu suo, concedente <Deo>,[t] profecturus viriliter et prudenter contra hereticos supradictos. Nosque similiter tunc ibidem personaliter erimus cum eodem. Dat' Parisius nonis Februarii.[3]

11 Hujus igitur mandati <auctoritate>[u] vobis mandamus quatinus predictas sententias excommunicationis per vestram dioecesim denuntiari publice facientes,[v] verbum crucis in eadem per personas discretas, litteratas, et ecclesiis non onerosas predicari faciatis, et exponi libertatem et privilegium que eis qui crucem contra hereticos assumpserint conceduntur, fraternitatem vestram in Domino nichilominus exhortantes quatinus crucem ad predicti negotii subsidium salubriter assumatis pro amore illius qui in crucis[w] angustia nos redemit ut vestre devotionis exemplo ad predicti negotii succursum subditi vestri[x] facilius inducantur. Dat' anno gratie m° cc° xx° v°, Dominica qua cantatur "Circumdederunt me."[4]

12 Hujus itaque mandati vobis auctoritate mandamus quatinus per decanatum Abrincatinum[y] juxta formam ipsius mandati verbum crucis predicantes, in propria persona privilegium et libertatem ut predictum est exponentes,[z] necnon et predictas excommunicationis sententias publice de nuntiantes, fideles Christi ad sumendum crucis signaculum imittetis.[a] Dat' die festo Sancti Gregorii,[5] anno gratie predicto, apud Abrinc'. Valete.

[t] Deo *scripsi cum Martène*
[u] auctoritate *scripsi cum Martène (cf. § 12, infra)*
[v] facientes] faciatis *Martène (cf. § 12, infra)*
[w] crucis *scripsi cum Martène*: cruci A
[x] vestri A] nostri *Martène*
[y] Abrincatinum *scripsi cum Martène*: Abrincatino A
[z] in propria—exponentes *om. Martène*
[a] imittetis A *(cf. § 9, supra)*: invitetis *Martène*

Document 29
ROMANUS AUTHORIZES SEQUESTRATION OF DELINQUENT CHAPTERS' GOODS
17 May 1227

MSS.—(A) Paris, Arch. nat., J 1035, no. 18: sealed original; damaged by damp. (B) Paris, Arch. nat., JJ 26, fol. 327ra–rb: Register E. (C) Paris, BnF, MS. lat. 9778,

Be aware that, God willing, said king will be at Bourges in person with his army a month after the next feast of the Lord's Resurrection, ready to set out with prudence and power against the aforesaid heretics. And likewise we shall be there with him in person.

Given at Paris on the nones of February.[3]

11 By the authority of this mandate we order that you cause the aforesaid sentences of excommunication to be announced publicly throughout your diocese; that you cause the word of the Cross to be preached there by discreet and literate persons who are not burdensome to the churches; and that you have them explain the liberty and privilege that are granted to those who take up the Cross against the heretics. We likewise exhort your fraternity in the Lord that, for the love of him who redeemed us in the distress of the Cross, you take up the Cross in support of the aforesaid business, so that by the example of your devotion your subjects may more easily be induced to come to the aid of the aforesaid business. Given in the year of grace 1225 on the Sunday on which "Circumdederunt me" is sung.[4]

12 Therefore by the authority of this mandate we order that you motivate Christ's faithful to take the sign of the Cross by preaching the word of the Cross throughout the deanery of Avranches as the mandate it self specifies; and by explaining in person the privilege and liberty as has been stated above; and also by announcing the aforesaid sentences of ex communication publicly. Given on the feast day of St Gregory,[5] in the same year of grace, at Avranches. Farewell.

3. 5 February 1226.
4. Septuagesima Sunday, 16 February 1226.
5. 12 March 1226.

---

fols. 271rb–vb: Register F. (D) Paris, BnF, MS. Baluze, vol. 8, fols. 22r–24r: copy using both B and C.

Rubric in B (not C) as part of the original layout, in red ink by a hand (saec. xiii 2/4) contemporary with, but not the same as, that of the text: "*Littere Rom(ani) Sancti Angeli dyaconi cardinalis de consilio habito Bitur' a prelatis ecclesiarum super negotio Albig' et de decima per quinquennium domino regi concessa et de coactione solutionis eidem.*"

Ed.—(1) Devic-Vaissète, III (1737), 323-324, preuve no. 181, i, citing both MSS. B and C, but transcribed from C; VIII (1879), 866-868, preuve no. 267, i.

Refs.—A was calendared by H. F. Delaborde in A. Teulet et al., *Layettes de Trésor des chartes,* V: *Ancienne série des Sacs dite aujourd'hui Supplément* (Paris, 1909), p. 106, no. 324 (cf. p. ccxiii). Cited by E. Berger, *Histoire de Blanche de Castille, reine de France* (Paris, 1895), p. 96, n. 1.

R om(anus) miseratione divina Sancti Angeli diaconus cardinalis, apostolice sedis legatus, universis presentes litteras inspecturis salutem in Domino.

1 Ad relevandum negotium pacis et[a] fidei, quod penitus corruerat, et ad pravitatem hereticam evellandam terre Albigen' et circumadjacentium regionum, venerabiles patres . . archiepiscopos, . . episcopos, et alios prelatos et viros religiosos, necnon capitula ecclesiarum cathedralium legationis nostre, ut per procuratores idoneos eadem capitula in nostra presentia comparerent,[b] olim Bituris[c] specialiter evocantes, presentibus ibidem nobilibus viris R(aymundo), filio R(aymundi) quondam comitis Tholosani, et . . comite Montisfortis,

2 de pace inter ipsos nobiles primo, sicut expedire vidimus, tractavimus diligenter; sed cum non potuerit pax vel aliqua concordia inter eos cum honore Ecclesie provenire, nec idem R(aymundus) obtulerit[d] se ut debebat mandatis Ecclesie pariturum, auditis et intellectis in publicum coram omnibus supradictis que tam iidem R(aymundus) pro parte sua quam comes Montisfortis pro se proponere curaverunt,

3 predicti . . archiepiscopi, . . episcopi, viri religiosi, alii ecclesiarum prelati, et procuratores ecclesiarum cathedralium, adjurati a nobis in virtute obedientie et quod in die judicii coram omnium judice responderent si nobis super hoc secundum suas conscientias non darent consilium salutare, et nobis dederunt consilium separatim,[e]

4 quod idem R(aymundus) secundum oblata non erat aliquatenus absolvendus, sed bone memorie L(udovicum), regem quondam Francorum illustrem, induceremus modis omnibus et supplicaretur ei ab Ecclesia ut in se assumeret negotium memoratum, cum non posset per alium relevari nec terra illa purgari

---

[a] et A: ac BC
[b] comparent *Vaissète*
[c] Bituris AB: Bitur' C, Bituricis *Vaissète*
[d] obtulerit] obtulit *Vaissète*
[e] separatum *Vaissète; locus per X in margine signatus* B[2]

Text.—Because the A-text is often illegible today, B has been taken as the base manuscript; however, variants have regularly been adopted from the legible portions of A. Transcription and collation from microfilm. Vaissète's readings are cited in the apparatus only when they differ from C, which was his exemplar.

Romanus by divine mercy cardinal-deacon of Sant' Angelo, legate of the apostolic see, to all who shall see the present letter, greeting in the Lord.

1 To raise up again the business of peace and the faith, which had wholly collapsed, and to uproot the heretical perversity of Albigeois and surrounding regions, we formerly summoned these persons to Bourges: the venerable fathers the archbishops, bishops, and other prelates and men of religion, as well as the chapters of the cathedral churches of our legation, who were to appear in our presence by means of suitable proctors. Also there present were the noble men Raymond, son of Raymond the former count of Toulouse, and the count of Montfort.

2 There it seemed expedient to us that we first diligently consider whether peace could be made between those nobles, so publicly in the presence of all those named above we heard and understood both what Raymond chose to propose for his side and the count of Montfort for his. But neither peace nor any kind of agreement between them could be made with honor for the Church, and Raymond did not indicate that he was ready and willing to obey the commands of the Church, as he should have done.

3 Then the aforesaid archbishops, bishops, men of religion, other prelates of churches, and proctors of cathedral churches gave us counsel separately. We charged them to do so in virtue of obedience, and warned them that if they did not give us salutary counsel on this according to their consciences, they would answer on Judgment Day in the presence of the judge of all.

4 Their counsel was that Raymond was by no means to be absolved on the basis of what he had offered. Instead, they counseled that by every means we were to induce the late Louis, illustrious former king of France, to undertake that business, and to beg him to do so on the part of the Church, since no one

ab heretica pravitate; et si dictum negotium assumeret, daretur ei decima[f] omnium proventuum ecclesiasticorum usque ad quinquennium, si tantum duraret[g] negotium antedictum, prout in illorum consiliis in scriptis redactis et sigillatis evidenter apparet.

5 Unde secundum predictorum consilia, ad regem ipsum cum pluribus . . archiepiscopis, . . episcopis, et aliis ecclesiarum prelatis personaliter accedentes, induximus eum quantum potuimus ut in se assumeret negotium supradictum. Sed quia negotium ipsum erat desperatum omnino, et non poterat reinchoari[h] sine magnis periculis[i] laboribus et expensis nisi ei Ecclesia[j] in magno auxilio subveniret, de consilio eorumdem archiepiscoporum et episcoporum qui nobiscum presentes aderant, decimam omnium proventuum ecclesiasticorum nostre legationis usque ad quinquennium, si tantum duraret negotium,[k] concessimus dicto regi ad magnam instantiam nostram[l] et ipsorum prelatorum, immo potius inspirationem divinam ut credimus, negotium[m] assumenti,[n] sicut in nostris et ipsorum archiepiscoporum et episcoporum litteris super hoc confectis plenius continetur.[1]

6 Nos autem, hoc idem prelatis et aliis in nostra legatione constitutis per nostras[o] litteras intimantes, mandavimus ut in festo Omnium Sanctorum medietatem ipsius decime ac reliquam medietatem in Pascha nuper preteritis ipsi regi vel aliis pro eo ad mandatum nostrum solverent ad subsidium negotii antedicti.[2]

7 Et licet nullus, promissioni dicto regi facte et mandatis nostris super hoc promulgatis, se aliquatenus opposuisset, quinimmo ipsa capitula medietatem decime que solvi debuit in festo Omnium Sanctorum, quamvis non plene post mortem ipsius regis, et post Pascha partem residue medietatis voluntarie persolverunt,

8 verum quia capitula ecclesiarum cathedralium[p] quatuor provinciarum, videlicet Rem', Senon', Rothom',[q] et Tur', contra dictam promissionem regi factam de consilio procuratorum ipsorum et fere totius concilii[r] supradicti ab ipsis

---

[f] daretur ei decima A: decima daretur ei BC

[g] daretur C

[h] reinchoari A: reincooari B, revocari CD

[i] periculis] et *add.* BC

[j] ei Ecclesia] ad Ecclesiam ei C[1]; Ecclesia ei *corr.* C[2]

[k] duraret negotium *tr.* C

[l] nostri *Vaissète*

[m] negotii *Vaissète*

[n] assumenti AC: assumpti B

[o] nostras *om.* C

[p] ecclesiarum cathedralium A: *tr.* BC

[q] Rothom' *om.* C; Tur' et Rothom' *Vaissète*

[r] concilii A: consilii BC

else could raise up that business and purge that land from heretical perversity. And if he assumed that business, a tenth was to be given to him of all ecclesiastical revenues for as long as five years, if the aforesaid business lasted so long. This advice appears plainly in their counsels, which were put in writing and sealed.

5 In accordance with these counsels, we personally approached the king himself with many archbishops, bishops, and other prelates of churches, and we persuaded him as much as we were able to take on himself the aforesaid business. But because that business was altogether desperate and could not be attempted without great dangers and efforts and expenses unless the Church gave great aid to support him, on the advice of those archbishops and bishops who were present with us, we conceded to the king a tenth of all the ecclesiastical revenues of our legation for as long as five years, if the business lasted so long. We did this after the king undertook the business at the great insistence of ourselves and those prelates—or rather, we believe, by divine inspiration. This grant is more fully set forth in the letter about it that we and those archbishops and bishops wrote.[1]

6 The prelates and others within our legation were informed of this by a letter from us that ordered them to support that business by paying half of that tenth at the feast of All Saints and the other half at the Easter just now past, and by our command to make the payments to the king or to others acting for him.[2]

7 And certainly up to a point no one opposed the promise made to the king and the orders we promulgated about this; indeed, on the contrary, those chapters did voluntarily pay the half of the tenth that was due on the feast of All Saints, although not fully after the king's death, and they likewise paid part of the remaining half after Easter.

8 The payments were made only in part because, acting in contempt of God and the Church and the Christian faith, the chapters of the cathedral churches of four provinces—namely Reims, Sens, Rouen, and Tours—willfully refused to pay that tenth in full at the said two terms now past as we had ordered and had

[1] Doc. 26.
[2] Doc. 28.

etiam approbatam, ex eo maxime quod dictam decimam spontanee solvere inceperunt, in contemptum Dei et Ecclesie et fidei Christiane temere venientes, ad mandatum nostrum decimam ipsam in predictis duobus terminis jam transactis solvere ad plenum, pluries admoniti, contempserunt.

9 Ex parte regis Francorum illustris nobis est oblata[s] querela[t] quod cum clare memorie pater suus pro ipso negotio maximas expensas fecerit ac[u] ipse post mortem ipsius, et magnam multitudinem militum et servientium ibidem habuit[v] et habeat ad expugnandam hereticam pravitatem, et hec per se non possit sustinere sine auxilio Ecclesie, quod ipsa capitula sibi subtrahere[w] nitebantur, super hoc sibi deberemus, prout eidem negotio expedit et promissum et statutum fuerat, providere.

10 Nos vero considerantes quod maximum[x] Ecclesie periculum immineret et negotium destrueretur omnino si rex negotium ipsum dimitteret, ad quod[y] dimittendum suum consilium concordabat, nisi promissum sibi auxilium ab ecclesiis solveretur, attendentes nichilominus ipsorum rebellionem pariter et contemptum qui mandatis nostris parere contempnebant pro sue arbitrio voluntatis,

11 eidem regi autoritatem concessimus et potestatem ut de bonis ipsorum capitulorum cathedralium capiat[z] et saisiri faciat pro solutione decime que fieri debuit in ipsis terminis jam transactis,[a] donec ipsi de prefata decima et nobis de ipso contemptu fuerit plenarie satisfactum, ut quos timor jurisdictionis ecclesiastice a malo non revocat, saltim potestas coherceat secularis.

Actum die Lune ante ascensionem Domini, anno Domini m° cc° xx° septimo.

[s] oblata A: ablata BC, allata *Vaissète*

[t] querele C

[u] ac] ad C

[v] habuit (huit) A: habuerit BC

[w] substrahere B

[x] maximum] maximeum C[1], *corr.* C[1]

[y] quid B

[z] cathedralium capiat AB: *tr.* C[1] *et Vaissète; corr.* C[2]

[a] transactis C (*cf. § 8, supra*): transauctis B, *lacuna in* A

frequently warned them to do. They did so contrary to the said promise made to the king on the advice of their proctors and of almost the entire council [of Bourges], which was even approved by them, especially inasmuch as they began to pay the tenth of their own accord.

9 On the part of the illustrious king of France a complaint was submitted to us that declared that his late distinguished father had made immense expenditures for that business, and that he had done the same after his father's death; that he had and has a great multitude of knights and sergeants there to combat the heretical perversity, and that he himself cannot maintain them without the aid of the Church, which those chapters were trying to take away from him; and that we owed it to him to take care of this problem in a way that would expedite the business for him, just as had been promised and formally stated in writing.

10 Whereas we consider that the greatest danger threatens the Church, and that the business would be altogether ruined if the king lets that business drop, which he intends to do unless the aid promised him by the churches is paid; and likewise taking into account both their rebellion and contempt, since they refuse to obey our orders by their own willful decision;

11 we therefore have conceded to the same king the authority and power to seize and sequester goods of those cathedral chapters as a pledge for the payment of the tenth that ought to have been made at those terms already past, until those chapters fully satisfy the king concerning that tenth and also make amends to us for their contempt. Thus those who are not recalled from evil by fear of the ecclesiastical jurisdiction will at least be coerced by the secular power.

Done on the Monday before the Lord's Ascension, A. D. 1227.

Document 30
ROMANUS PROHIBITS
SANCTIONS AGAINST THE CROWN
17 May 1227

MS.—(A) Paris, Arch. nat., J 1035, no. 19: sealed original; damaged by damp. The hand is the same as in Docs. 27 and 31.

Venerabilibus in Christo patribus Dei gratia . . archiepiscopis et . . episcopis, et dilectis in Christo abbatibus, et aliis ecclesiarum prelatis, et quibuscunque aliis personis ecclesiasticis, necnon universis per nostram legationem constitutis presentes litteras inspecturis, Rom(anus), miseratione divina sancti <Angeli diaconus cardinalis, aposto>ᵃlice sedis legatus, salutem in Domino.

1 Licet de vestro, prelati, et procuratorum cathedralium ecclesiarum consilio, sicut in vestris et eorum consiliis in scriptis redactis et sigillatis <evidenter apparet,>ᵇ bone memorie Lodovico, regi quondam Francorum illustri, negotium pacis et fidei, ad extirpandam hereticam pravitatem terre Albigen' et circumadjacentium regionum, ad instantiam nostram et prelatorum, immo potius ad inspirationem divinam, ut credimus, assumenti, decimam omnium proventuum ecclesiasticorum nostre legationis, usque ad quinquennium, si tantumᶜ duraret negotium ipsum, duxerimus concedendam, prout in nostris et quorumdam vestrum, qui nobiscum presentes eratis, litteris super hoc confectis plenius continetur,

2 nullus tamen promissioniᵈ dicto regi facte ac nostris mandatis super hoc promulgatis se opposuit ullo modo. Quinimmo vos et omnes alii medietatem decime, que solvi debuit in festo Omnium Sanctorum, quamvis quidam non plene post mortem ipsius regis, et post Pascha partem residue medietatis, voluntarie solvere inceptistis,

3 verum quia capitula cathedralia quatuor provinciarum scilicet Rem', Senonen', Rothom', et Turon', contra dictam promissionemᵉ eidem regi factam,

---

ᵃ Angeli—aposto] *ex Doc. 29 suppl. Delaborde*
ᵇ evidenter apparet] *suppl. ex Doc. 29 Delaborde*
ᶜ tantum (*cf. Doc. 26.6*)] tamen *leg. Delaborde*
ᵈ promissioni A] permissioni *perperam leg. Delaborde (cf. Doc. 29.8)*
ᵉ promissionem] *locus maculatus in* A, permissionem *leg. Delaborde, sed cf. supra, § 2*

Ed.—(1) H. F. Delaborde in Teulet et al., *Layettes du Trésor des chartes,* V: *Ancienne série des Sacs dite aujourd'hui Supplément* (Paris, 1909), pp. 106-107, no. 325 (cf. p. ccxiii), from A and Vaissète's edition of Doc. 29.

Ref.—E. Berger, *Histoire de Blanche de Castille, reine de France* (Paris, 1895), p. 96, n. 2.

Text.—From Delaborde's edition, verified from a copy on microfilm. Delaborde identified only two restorations, which I have noted below in the *apparatus criticus*; I do not note the many other passages illegible today (especially almost all the text after 4).

To the venerable fathers in Christ by God's grace the archbishops and bishops, and to the beloved in Christ the abbots and prelates of other churches, and to any other ecclesiastical persons, and also to everyone living anywhere in our legation who shall see this letter, Romanus by divine mercy cardinal-deacon of Sant' Angelo, legate of the apostolic see, greeting in the Lord.

1 Those of you who are prelates and proctors of cathedral chapters gave us counsel, as plainly appears in your written and sealed counsels, to the effect that, when the late Louis, illustrious former king of France, should undertake the business of peace and of the faith, in order to eradicate the heretical perversity of Albigeois and surrounding regions, at our insistence and that of prelates—or rather, we believe, by divine inspiration—we were to concede to him a tenth of all the ecclesiastical revenues of our legation for as long as five years, if the business lasted that long, on terms that are more fully set forth in the letter written about this by us and some of you who were present with us.

2 No one, however, was opposed in any way to the promise given to the said king and to our mandates promulgated concerning this. Indeed, on the contrary, you and all the others did voluntarily begin to pay the half of the tenth that was due on the feast of All Saints, although in some cases not fully after the king's death, and likewise part of the remaining half after Easter.

3 The payments were made only in part because, in contempt of God and the Church and the Christian faith, and to the ruination of that business, the cathedral chapters of four provinces—namely Reims, Sens, Rouen, and Tours—are manifestly seen to oppose making them. They are doing so contrary to the

ab ipsis etiam approbatam, ex eo maxime quod dictam decimam spontanee solvere inceperunt, in contemptum Dei et Ecclesie et fidei Christiane ac in destructionem ipsius negotii videntur se opponere manifeste.

4 Si contigerit, propter ipsorum contumaciam, de mandato regis ipsorum bona capi vel saiziri, vobis interdicimus et districtissime prohibemus ne in prefatum regem et reginam, baillivos suos, clericos, homines et terras eorumdem, seu quoslibet alios, excommunicationis, suspensionis, vel interdicti sententias aliquas, occasione huiusmodi, per vos vel per alios aliquo modo ferre vel promulgare aliquatenus presumatis.

5 Ad majorem autem cautelam vos omnes et singulos, ex nunc, ab omni potestate ligandi, excommunicandi, interdicendi, et suspendendi, vel aliquam sententiam proferendi, propter factum hujusmodi, suspendimus et omnino privamus; ipsas etiam sententias, si quas tuleritis, decernimus irritas et inanes et ipso jure nullius esse momenti.

Actum die lune ante ascensionem Domini, anno Domini m° cc° xx° vii°.

Document 31
ROMANUS NOTIFIES THE CHAPTERS
Sens, 5 June 1227

Romanus had his own clerks who traveled with him and prepared the fair copies of his correspondence and diplomata. The present letter together with Docs. 29 and 30 can be attributed to Romanus' household with certainty. These letters enable us to assign documents written in the same or a similar curial hand to the same source. As we have already seen, Docs. 27 and 30 seem to have been written in the clear, distinctive hand of the same scribe who wrote Doc. 31, and two copies of Romanus' manifesto of 9 June 1226, issued on the eve of the siege of Avignon, are written in a hand that is similar but not identical: Paris, Arch. nat., J 428, nos. 5–6; ed. Teulet, no. 1787.

MSS.—(A) Paris, Arch. nat., J 428, no. 7 (olim no. 1928): Trésor des chartes, Albigeois, no. 7. Folded original (unfolded 90 × 173 mm; 65 × 60 mm folded) with traces of a lost seal and cord on dorso. (B) Paris, BnF, MS. Baluze 8, fol. 24r–v: copy of A ("ex archivio regio Parisiensis").

said promise made to the king, which was even approved by them, especially inasmuch as they began to pay the tenth of their own accord.

4 If it happens that, because of their contumacy, their goods are seized or sequestered by the king's command, we forbid and absolutely prohibit you to presume, either through yourselves or through others, in any way and to any extent, either to issue or to promulgate any sentences of excommunication, suspension, or interdict that are prompted by such circumstances and are directed against the aforesaid king and queen, his bailiffs, clerics, men, and their lands, or against any one else.

5 To assure your compliance, however, as of now we altogether deprive each and every one of you of, and suspend you from, all power of binding, excommunicating, interdicting, and suspending, or of publishing any sentence on account of such a deed. If you shall issue such sentences, we declare them to be null and void and hence to have no legal effect.

Done on the Monday before the Lord's Ascension, A. D. 1227.

Ed.—(1) Devic-Vaissète, III (1737), 325, preuve no. 181, iii, from MS. B ("Portefeuille de Baluze, n. 11"); VIII (1879), 869–870, preuve no. 267, iii. (2) Teulet, no. 1930, from A.

Refs.—Molinier in Devic-Vaissète, VIII (1879), 2398 (corrigenda). Auvray, at no. 230. Petit-Dutaillis, *Louis*, p. 304 (manifesto).

Date.—Baluze carelessly misread the date in A as "MCCXXVIII," and Vaissète, working from B, reproduced the error, which was eventually corrected by Teulet, Molinier, and Auvray.

Fortuna.—The presence of this document in the royal archives is curious. Evidently A is the original that Romanus sent to the archbishop of Tours, who presumably returned it to Romanus as instructed (§ 2); Romanus himself must have eventually turned it over to the royal clerks to provide them with a full record of his handling of the matter, as he evidently did also with Docs. 29 and 30.

Text from photocopy of A, verified from the original.

Venerabili in Christo patri .. Dei <gratia>[a] archiepiscopo Turon'[1] et ejus suffraganeis, Rom(anus) eadem gratia Sancti Angeli diaconus cardinalis, Apostolice sedis legatus, salutem in Domino.

1 Cum de consilio venerabilium patrum .. archiepiscoporum, episcoporum,[b] aliorum prelatorum ecclesiarum, necnon et procuratorum ecclesiarum cathedralium quos Bituris ad concilium convocavimus pro negotio fidei atque pacis, sicut in eorum consiliis in scriptis redactis et sigillatis plenius continetur,[2] bone memorie L(udovico), regi quondam Francorum illustri, concessimus[c] decimam omnium proventuum ecclesiasticorum nostre legationis usque ad quinquennium, si tantum duraret negotium memoratum, prout in nostris et aliorum prelatorum qui nobiscum presentes aderant <litteras>[d] super hoc confectis evidenter apparet, quidam minus plene solverunt, quidam contra venire presumpserunt in contemptum Dei et Ecclesie et fidei Christiane necnon etiam in destructionem negotii supradicti.

2 Ideoque paternitati vestre qua fungimur auctoritate districte precipiendo mandamus quatinus penas quas olim constituimus contra hujusmodi contemptores, sicut in litteris super hoc editis videre poteritis manifeste,[3] coram capitulis ipsis vel illis qui fuerint in capitulis, publice legi et publicari facientes, transcriptum ipsarum litterarum vel etiam ipsas litteras eis nullatenus concedatis, sed tam nostras quas ad vos mittimus quam alias statim per latorem nobis presentium remittatis.

Dat' Senon' non. Junii, anno Domini m° cc° xx° vii°.

[a] gratia *scripsi cum Baluze et Teulet*
[b] episcoporum] et *add. Teulet*
[c] cocessimus A
[d] litteras *scripsi*

Document 32
THE PARIS CHAPTER APPEALS TO THE POPE
Mid-June 1227

The taxpayers' perspective is preserved in this remarkable document. The rambling and even disjointed sentences suggest that the letter was written in haste and dispatched without much revision. Although the curia frequently received petitions such as this, it is extraordinary that one of them was transcribed into the register, which normally recorded only select outgoing letters. This appar-

To the venerable father in Christ John[1] by God's grace archbishop of Tours and to his suffragans, Romanus by the same grace cardinal-deacon of Sant' Angelo, legate of the apostolic see, greeting in the Lord.

1 To the late Louis, illustrious former king of France, we conceded a tenth of all the ecclesiastical revenues of our legation for as long as five years, if the business of the faith and of peace there lasted so long, just as appears plainly in the letter written about this by us and the other prelates who were present with us.[2] This concession was made on the counsel of the venerable fathers the archbishops, the bishops and other prelates of churches, and also of the proctors of the cathedral churches whom we convoked to a council at Bourges for the aforesaid business, just as is more fully contained in their counsels that were drawn up in writing and sealed. While some have not quite paid that tenth in full, others have presumed to withhold payment in contempt of God and the Church and the Christian faith, and also to the ruination of the aforesaid business.

2 Therefore we order your paternity, strictly commanding you by the authority that we exercise, that you cause to be read publicly and to be published in the presence of those chapters, or of those persons who shall be present in those chapters, the penalties that we formerly established against those guilty of such contempt, which you can plainly see in the letter issued concerning this.[3] By no means let them have a transcript of that letter, much less the letter itself, but by the bearer of this communication immediately send back to us both our letter that we are sending to you now and the other one.

Given at Sens on the nones of June, A. D. 1227.

1. Johannes I de Faye, archbishop of Tours 1208-1228.

[2] Doc. 26.

[3] Cf. Doc. 32.7.

---

ent anomaly is explained by the fact that the pope sent a copy of the petition to Romanus (Doc. 33.4), so it was considered outgoing correspondence.

Date.—Although the copyist of the papal register omitted the *datum*-clause of the main letter, still we can ascertain its date from the text of the letter and the context of events. The appeal of the four provinces, of which probably only the concluding passage is quoted (§ 5), furnishes a provisional *terminus post quem*: 27 May 1227. The appellant chapters relate little of the events which directly preceded their joint letter, so little indeed that one cannot be certain whether or not they knew the actual text of the legate's authorization to the crown (Doc.

29: 17 May), although the terms of their complaint suggest that they were at least acquainted with the argument and intent of the act (§ 5, "imposuit . . . Bituris"). The Paris chapter, on the other hand, relates at length how the legate unexpectedly proceeded to have their goods confiscated. Before the king's *prévôt* sequestered the capitular property, a letter from the legate was read to the canons that provided severe penalties for all who obstructed the confiscation. We can be sure this event occurred after 5 June, for the agents of the legate and king carefully complied with Romanus' instructions of that date to let no canon have a copy of his letters (Doc. 31). Since the confiscation of 5 June provoked our letter, that date must be its *terminus post*. On 18 July, Pope Gregory responded to this petition (Docs. 33-35), probably as soon as he received it. Since the trip from Paris to Rome would have taken about a month, the petition must have been dispatched from Paris in mid-June, which is accordingly our *terminus ante*. Roughly, then, these *termini* bracket the confiscation and complaint within the second week of June 1227.

LITTERE CAPITULORUM REGNI FRANCIE.

S anctissimo in Christo patri ac domino G(regorio), miseratione divina summo et universali pontifici, devoti et humiles ejus famuli P(hilippi) decanus[1] totumque capitulum ecclesie Parisien', subjectionis, devotionis, et totius obedientie plenitudinem.

1 Si populo suo reservasset Dominus alterum Jeremiam sanctificatum ab utero qui, sicut ille planxisse legitur, sciret plangere captivitatem populi sui, non tantum quadruplici set multiplici, si posset, plangeret alfabeto;[2] et merito juxta novitatem flagitii, novum excogitaret genus lamenti. Ille planxit transmigrationem populi sui ab hostibus factam, meritis peccatorum inflictam; iste plangeret calamitatem non veteris populi, set inclite Syon, de qua dictum est: "Diligit Dominus portas Syon super omnia tabernacula Jacob."[3] Calamitatem plangeret,

MSS.—(A) Vatican, Arch. Segreto Vat., Serie generale de' Regesti, vol. 14, fols. 24r–25r: Reg. Greg. IX, tom. I, an. i, ep. 134. (B) Ibid., fol. 58r: ep. 181. The scribe here began a second copy of the letter and had nearly reached the end of § 1 when he realized it was redundant; he stopped in midsentence: expl. " . . . quorum esset protegere//." (C) Vatican, Bibl. Apost., MS. Vat. lat. 7024, fols. 109v–112v ("ex Greg. ix." i.e. copied from A). (D) Paris, BnF, MS. Moreau 1184, fol. 57 (from C) and fol. 86.

Ed.—(1) Baronio-Theiner, XX (1870), 542–543, ad an. 1227, nos. 56–58 (om. § 5–8). The source is not stated, but A is cited for related letters, for instance, Doc. 33. (2) Auvray, no. 134 (= A); p. 104, no. 182 (= B: address, incipit, and explicit only).

Text from microfilm of A. C and D have not been consulted; perhaps they are the source of Auvray's occasionally egregious misreadings (e.g. *facultatem* for *potestatem*).

LETTER OF THE CHAPTERS OF THE KINGDOM OF FRANCE.

To the most holy lord and father in Christ Gregory, by divine mercy supreme and universal pontiff, his devoted and humble servants Dean Philip[1] and the whole chapter of the church of Paris send complete subjection, devotion, and entire obedience.

1 If for his people the Lord had destined another Jeremiah by sanctifying him from the womb, this man would know how to lament the captivity of his people just as the Bible says that the prophet lamented: he would lament through the alphabet not only four times but many, if he could;[2] and he would be right to think up a new kind of lament to match the novelty of the present outrageous situation. The prophet lamented the exile of his people, which was done by their enemies, although inflicted on them by reason of their sins; the new Jeremiah

---

1. Philippe de Nemours, dean of Paris since 24 February 1227, when his predecessor died; he became bishop of Châlons in 1228. His father, Ours de Bréci ("de la Chapelle") was Louis VIII's chamberlain. *Gallia Christiana*, VII, 203; Petit-Dutaillis, *Louis*, p. 445; J. W. Baldwin, *The Government of Philip Augustus* (Berkeley and Los Angeles, 1986), pp. 107–109.

2. The first four chapters of the Lamentations of Jeremiah are alphabetic acrostics, each containing twenty-two verses beginning with one of the twenty-two letters of the Hebrew alphabet,

non ab extraneis et inimicis immissam, set ab eis quorum esset protegere, non opprimere, procuratam; calamitatem plangeret que non meritis redditur, set potius ex insolentia dominationis infertur eorum quibus dicitur: "Providentes non coacte set spontanee, neque ut dominantes in clero set forma facti gregis ex animo."[4]

2 Veritas quidem ita se habet quod a domino legato totius legationis sue concilio Bituricen'[a] convocato, capitulorum ibidem nuntii pro Albigen' negotio convenerunt ut ea que in eodem concilio tractarentur seu statuerentur, capitulis suis referrent ut super eis deliberarent, nulla quidem penitus eis potestate consentiendi concessa. Cum igitur de modo subventionis negotii Albigen' eos consuleret, et ipsos ad hoc inducere niteretur quod decima bonorum Ecclesie per quinquennium solveretur si rex Ludowicus bone memorie negotium assumeret et ad idem personaliter laboraret, responderunt nuntii quod nullam habebant super hoc consentiendi potestatem,[b] nec que sibi limitata fuerant poterant excedere. Unde pro se ipsis, non pro capitulis, responderent; et bene videbatur eis quod utile erat consilium, decimam pretaxatam persolvi si rex aliter non vellet dictum negotium assumere et personaliter laborare, sine cujus presentia nullatenus, secundum quod videbatur eis, poterat negotium utiliter expediri.

3 Postmodum autem quicquid fecerit, quicquid constituerit super hoc, capitula non convenit set, tractatu cum quibusdam episcopis habito, ad regem accessit, et quod rex negotium personaliter susciperet procuravit. Cum igitur vide-rent capitula quod dominus rex Ludowicus felicis memorie pro negotio fidei tantum onus susciperet, fidei ejus fervori devotionem suam juncxerunt, non quod attenderent aliquam promissionem, que nulla in veritate precesserat, set cum gaudio animi—de pura liberalitate, ne tanto deesse negotio viderentur—dimidiam partem decime, non quidem nomine decime set obtentu subsidii, persolverunt; aliam partem et etiam majorem, si expediret, si Deus eundem regem reservasset incolomem et in eodem negotio persistentem, libenter et liberaliter soluturi.

[a] Bituris *Auvray*
[b] facultatem *Auvray*

would lament a calamity, not of God's old people, but of glorious Sion, of which it is said: "The Lord loveth the gates of Sion above all the tabernacles of Jacob."[3] He would lament a calamity not caused by foreigners and enemies, but one contrived by those whose duty it is to protect rather than to oppress; he would lament a calamity that does not repay misdeeds but rather is inflicted because lordship is being exercised arrogantly by those to whom it is said: "Taking care [of God's flock], not by constraint, but willingly: neither as lording it over the clergy, but being made a pattern of the flock from the heart."[4]

2 The truth of the matter is that when the lord legate convoked a council of his whole legation at Bourges, the nuncios of the chapters assembled there so that they might bring back to their chapters those things that were discussed or enacted in that council, in order that the chapters might deliberate about them. Absolutely no power of consenting was granted to the nuncios. Therefore when the legate consulted them concerning the kind of aid to be given to the Albigensian business, and when he tried to convince them that for this purpose a tenth of the goods of the Church should be paid for five years if the late King Louis undertook the business and participated in person, the nuncios replied that they had no power of consenting about this, and that they were not able to exceed the powers that had been set as their limits. Hence they would be speaking for themselves, not for the chapters; and it seemed clear to them that the practical plan was to pay the aforesaid tenth only if otherwise the king would not wish to undertake that business and participate in person, because they thought there was no way in which the business could be carried out effectively without his presence.

3 Afterwards, however, whatever the legate did and whatever provision he made about this, he did not convene the chapters. Instead, after having conferred with some bishops, he went to the king and got him to undertake the business in person. Therefore, when the chapters saw that the late lord King Louis had assumed such a great burden for the business of the faith, they matched the fervor of his faith with their own devotion. Thus they fully paid half of the tenth, though they did not call the payment a "tenth" but said it was "thanks to an aid"; and they paid not because they had in mind some promise, which in fact had never been made previously, but rather they did so with joyful hearts, out of pure generosity, lest they might seem to be not supporting so great a business. And they would have freely and liberally paid the other part of the tenth, which if it had been paid would have been the greater part, if God had kept the said king unharmed and persistent in that business.

3. Psalm 86 (AV 87).2 (Douay-Rheims translation).
4. I Peter v.2-3 (Douay-Rheims).

4 Rege autem defuncto, quicquid dominus legatus cum regina fecerit, quicquid constituerit, quicquid promiserit, requisita capitulorum voluntate non est
factum. Unde considerantes quod non erat in cujus manu negotium posset profi-
cere sicut prius, nullam visum est eis subesse causam quare quinque annorum
decima solveretur; maxime cum jam legatus vellet eos, sicut[c] dicebatur, ad solutionem, ut regine promiserat, compellere, eo dicente quod etiam capas nostras
daret ei;[d]5 nec regina se vellet ad certum tempus vel certum terminum[e] militum
aliquatenus obligare. Attendentes quod hoc ipsum quod de liberalitate
processerat convertebatur in obligationem, et servitutem sibi timentes in
posterum, capitula quatuor provinciarum Remen', Senonen', Turonen', et
Rothomagen', habita deliberatione et tractatu pro libertate sua servanda, potius
quam pro subventione vitanda, ne ad onus hujusmodi compellerentur, sub hac
forma sedem apostolicam appellarunt:

5 Nos capitula cathedralia provinciarum Remen', Senonen', Turonen',
et Rothomagen' et omnes de provinciis istis nobis consentientes,[6] gravatos
nos dicimus a domino legato quod, nullo speciali mandato domini pape
super hoc nobis exhibito, et nobis non consentientibus, imposuit nobis
jugum solvende decime omnium proventuum ecclesiasticorum, occasione
cujusdam ordinationis facte, ut dicitur, Bitur', cui nec consensimus nec
nobis fuit promulgata. Propter hec igitur gravamina et multa alia jam illata
et alia que timemus inferenda, nomine capitulorum predictorum et omnium de predictis provinciis nobis consentientium, sedem apostolicam ap-
pellamus; et specialiter ne nobis vel aliquibus in hoc nobis consentientibus
aliquo modo fiat coactio de solutione decime vel alicujus aliquote, personas nostras et res et beneficia et statum nostrum protectioni sedis apostolice supponentes. Et[f] ad hanc appellationem faciendam viva voce pro
nobis et omnibus aliis de diocesi Parisien' in hoc nobis consentientibus,
mittimus ad vos talem[7] presbyterum presentium portitorem. Datum anno
Domini m.° cc.° xxvii°, mense Maio, feria quarta ante Pentecosten.[8]

[c] sicuti *Auvray*
[d] ei *scripsi cum Auvray*: eis A
[e] terminum] numerum *Auvray*
[f] Et *om. Auvray*

4 Once the king was dead, whatever the legate did with the queen, whatever provisions he made, and whatever he promised was not done after ascertaining the will of the chapters. Therefore, considering that the business was no longer in the hands of one who could advance it, the chapters could see no reason why the five-year tenth should be paid; especially since the legate, as was being said, wished to compel them to pay, as he had promised the queen, he having said that he would even give her our capes;[5] and also since the queen did not wish to commit herself, even in a general way, to a fixed season or a fixed length of knight service. The chapters of the four provinces of Reims, Sens, Tours, and Rouen were well aware that what they had granted out of generosity was being turned into an obligation, and they feared that the next step would be to reduce them to servitude; therefore they conferred and discussed, not how they might avoid paying the subvention, but rather how they might preserve their liberty, lest they be compelled to bear a burden of this kind. Consequently, they appealed to the apostolic see in this way:

5 We, the cathedral chapters of the provinces of Reims, Sens, Tours, and Rouen, and all from these provinces who support us,[6] say we have been wronged by the lord legate. Without showing us any special mandate of the lord pope concerning this, and without our consent, he imposed on us the yoke of paying a tenth of all ecclesiastical revenues, which is supposedly authorized by a certain ordinance made, it is said, at Bourges, to which we never consented and which was never made known to us by public proclamation. Therefore, because of these grievances and many others already inflicted and others that we fear are about to be inflicted, we appeal to the apostolic see in the name of the aforesaid chapters and all from those provinces who support us. And we especially place our persons and property and benefices and our clerical status under the protection of the apostolic see, lest we or any of our supporters be coerced in any way to pay the tenth or any part of it. And we are sending you the priest so-and-so,[7] the bearer of the present letter, in order to make this appeal viva voce for us and for all the others from the Paris diocese who sup-

5. A hooded cloak was the distinctive dress of the cathedral chapters' canons.

6. The formulation excludes unsympathetic elements in these provinces, such as appear in Doc. 36.

7. The bearer's name has been omitted because if another agent were substituted for the one named, he would not be authorized to present the case to the curia. Curial practice, however, required that the bearer's name be included in a petition: C. R. Cheney, *From Becket to Langton* (Manchester, 1956), p. 66.

6 Unde dominus legatus ex insperato, nulla monitione premissa, hujusmodi litterarum tenorem ad capitula quatuor provinciarum transmisit.[9] De quo mandato multi et magni admirati sunt et versum est omnibus in stuporem, quoniam intemptatum est hactenus et inauditum. Unde non creduntur hujusmodi littere de amicorum suorum consilio processisse, maxime cum tunc temporis absens esset magister Petrus de Collemedio,[10] et prohibitum sit eis qui litteras detulerunt ne nobis concederetur transcriptum; quas litteras attulerunt prepositus[g] regis[11] et magister .P. Carnifex[12] in capitulum nostrum et legerunt, dicentes sibi inhibitum fuisse, cum instrumenti copia instanter iterum et iterum peteretur ne nobis vel aliis concederent transcriptum. Verba autem ultima condempnationis que pro sensu nostro potuimus capere, hec sunt, quarum sumus sensum et verba quantum potuimus fideliter prosecuti:

7 Si autem, eisdem a solutione cessantibus, pro contumacia eorum bona sive possessiones eorum a rege vel ejus mandato capi vel sessiri contigerit, interdicimus universis et singulis et districtissime prohibemus ne in terram regis vel ejus ministros, homines, aut subditos aliquam sententiam interdicti, suspensionis, vel excommunicationis propter hoc ferre,[13] vel etiam a divinis cessare, presumant. Illos autem qui hoc attemptare presumpserint, universos et singulos ineligibiles esse, et etiam ad[h] majores ordines promoveri non posse, decernimus. Insuper eos eligendi potestate privamus, ita quod eligendi potestas ad eos qui super hoc fuerint inculpabiles devolvatur. Ad majorem etiam cautelam et omnem fraudem et cavillationem evitandam, eos interdicendi, suspendendi, et excommunicandi potestate privamus; omnes sententias interdicti, suspensionis, vel excommunicati-

---

[g] prepositus *scripsi cum Auvray (cf.* idem prepositus *infra § 8):* prepositi A
[h] ad] a *Auvray*

port us in this. Given A.D. 1227, in the month of May, on the Thursday before Pentecost.[8]

6 Next the lord legate, unexpectedly and without previous warning, transmitted to the chapters of the four provinces the tenor of such a letter.[9] Many men, and great ones, marveled at that mandate, and everyone was dumbfounded, since such a thing was never before done or heard of. Hence this letter is not believed to have been based on the advice of his friends, especially since Master Peter of Collemezzo[10] was absent at that time, and since those who brought the letter to us were forbidden to let us have a transcript. The king's prévôt[11] and Master P. Carnifex[12] brought this letter to our chapter and read it, and when we urgently begged them again and again to provide us with a copy of the document, they said they were forbidden to let us or anyone else have a transcript. However, we were able to remember the letter's concluding words of condemnation by hearing them read; in the following report, we have followed the sense and the words as faithfully as we can:

7 If, because they have contumaciously stopped paying, it happens that their goods or possessions are seized or sequestered by the king or at his command, we forbid and most strictly prohibit each and every person from presuming because of this to pronounce any sentence of interdict, suspension, or excommunication on the king's land or on his ministers, men, or subjects;[13] or even to stop administering the sacraments. Each and every one of those who presume to attempt this we decree to be ineligible [for ecclesiastical preferment] and even to be incapable of being promoted to higher orders. Moreover, we deprive them of the power of election, so that the power of election devolves on those who shall not be culpable

---

8. Thursday, 27 May 1227. Berger incorrectly gives the date as 26 May (*Blanche de Castille*, p. 96, n. 3).

9. "such a letter": its nature is not stated until § 7; this use of "such" is standard but uncommon English.

10. Pietro da Collemezzo, archbishop of Rouen, 1236-1244, and cardinal-bishop of Albano, 1244-1253. *Fasti ecclesiae Gallicanae*, II: *Diocèse de Rouen*, ed. V. Tabbagh et al. (Turnhout, 1998), pp. 84-85, no. 4339.

11. Probably Jean des Vignes, prévôt (*praepositus*, provost) of Paris, 1223-1227. W. C. Jordan, *Louis IX and the Challenge of the Crusade* (Princeton, 1979), p. 224, citing L. Delisle, "Chronologie des baillis . . . ," *Rec. hist. Gaules*, XXIV (1904).

12. P. Carnifex is otherwise unknown. His title *magister* suggests a degree in canon law. Probably he was representing the bishop of Paris, whom Romanus had presumably directed to have his mandate read to the chapter (cf. Doc. 31). Under Philip Augustus, one member of the Carnifex (Fr. Bouchier = Eng. butcher) family held a fief in Pontoise and another subscribed sworn inquests at Montlhéry: *Rec. hist. Gaules*, XXIII (1894), 629 and 673-674.

13. "If, because—subjects": cf. Doc. 30.4.

onis, sique ab ipsis late fuerint, ex nunc ipso jure denuntiamus irritas et inanes.[14]

8 Post predictas litteras quatuor provinciarum capitulis a domino legato transmissas, idem prepositus et magister .P. Carnifex alias litteras regis coram nobis legerunt, que similiter ad alia capitula transmittuntur, quarum tenor opere secutus est, ita quod bona omnia universorum et singulorum occupata sunt a prepositis et ministris ipsius, et etiam ad bona patrimonialia manus suas extendunt, et in omnibus preposituris[15] et aliis ecclesie locis, nostris exclusis, custodes suos posuerunt. Ac ipse prebende que nunc temporis consueverunt dari ad modiationem pro derelictis[16] habentur; nec aliquid est eis salvum nisi infra munitionem claustri Parisien', in aliis enim locis etiam cimiteria infringuntur. Unde quia[i] nimis cohartati sunt, compelluntur[j] in exilium transmigrare, et jam sunt in deliberatione et tractatu quomodo possint civitatem exire.

9[17] Quis ista oculis siccis vobis valeat enarrare? Deficit in scribendo manus et plus fluit oculus quam calamus; quicquid calamus pingit incausto, delet oculus lacrimarum proluvio,[k] ac[l] per talem pingentis et plangentis mixturam littera convertitur in lituram. Utinam vos dominus pater sanctissime nobis alterum suscitet Jeremiam qui nobis compatiatur, et plangat et oret pro nobis, sicut dicitur in ultimo Machabeorum:"Hic est fratrum amator et populi Israel; hic est qui multum[m] orat pro populo et universa sancta civitate, Jeremias propheta Dei."[18] Ad quem autem recurrere possimus, nisi ad vos? ad quem pulsare debemus, nisi ad vos? quem prius Hostien'[19] Dominus in hostium feliciter commutavit,[20] per quod ingrediamur et egrediamur et pascua vite invenire possimus; quem Dominus providit hostiam sibi, hostem[n] diabolo, hostium gregi suo, qui estis[o] hostiarius simul et hostium: secundum quod hostium, vicarius Jesu Christi, qui dixit: "Ego sum hostium";[21] secundum quod hostiarius, successor Gregorii, cujus est

---

[i] qui *Auvray*

[j] compellentur *tacite corr. Auvray*

[k] pro luvio A: profluvio *Auvray*

[l] ac] et *Auvray*

[m] multum *om. Auvray*

[n] hostem *scripsi cum Auvray*: hostium A

[o] est *tacite corr. Auvray*

of this. As an additional precaution, and to avoid all fraud and quibbling, we deprive them of the power of interdiction, suspension, and excommunication. We declare that as of now all sentences of interdict, suspension, or excommunication, if they have been imposed by them, are automatically null and void and hence have no legal effect.[14]

8 After the above letter from the lord legate was communicated to the chapters of the four provinces, the same prévôt and Master P. Carnifex read another letter from the king in our presence, which was likewise communicated to the other chapters. The provisions of this letter were carried out with the following results. All the goods of each and every chapter are now seized by the prévôts and their agents; they even took control of patrimonial goods; and they have placed their custodians in all provostries[15] and in other ecclesiastical places, with the exception of ours. And those prebends that at present are customarily distributed by shares are considered to be derelict.[16] Nothing is safe from them unless it is inside the walls of the Paris cloister, for in other places even the immunity of cemeteries is violated, and consequently the canons here are packed in together so tightly that they are compelled to go into exile, and they are already discussing and planning how they can leave the city.

9[17] Who would be able to tell these things with dry eyes? In writing them, the hand fails and the eye flows more than the pen; whatever the pen sets down in ink, the eye deletes with a flow of tears; by such a mixture of pigment and lament is the letter turned into a blot. Oh that you, most holy lord and father, would raise up for us another Jeremiah who would suffer with us, and lament and pray for us, as is said in the last book of Maccabees: "This is a lover of his brethren, and of the people of Israel; this is he that prayeth much for the people, and for all the holy city, Jeremiah the prophet of God."[18] To whom can we have recourse, if not to you? To whom ought to we press our complaint, if not to

14. "As an additional precaution—no legal effect": cf. Doc. 30.5.

15. *Praepositura* = "church or monastery headed by a provost" (Niermeyer, *Lexicon*, 835, s.v., sense 2); in other words, one organized as a college, or chapter, consisting of members and a head. *Praepositus*, or "provost," is used here as a generalized title that includes such collegiate heads as bishops, deans, abbots, priors.

16. In Roman law, *derelictio* is "the abandonment of a thing by its owner with the intention of getting rid thereof," so that one who occupies a derelict property immediately acquires a right to it. A. Berger, *Encyclopedic Dictionary of Roman Law* (Philadelphia, 1953), 433, s.v. "derelictio."

17. For no apparent reason, Auvray encloses § 9 in quotation marks.

18. II Maccabees xv.14 (Douay-Rheims).

super gregis dominici custodiam vigilare.[22] Recte enim Hostiensi et officium hostiarii et nomen Gregorii, commutatione facta, divinitus debebatur. Ad quod hostium pulsamus et hostiarium imploramus;[p] ad vigilem respicimus, qui est virga vigiliarum,[23] ut juxta verbum Domini nobis[q] fiat: "Petite et accipietis; querite et invenietis; pulsate et aperietur vobis."[r][24] Petimus igitur ab hostiario, querimus a vigili, pulsamus ad hostium, et aperietur nobis.

[p] imploramus] et *add. Auvray*
[q] nobis *scripsi cum Auvray:* vobis A
[r] vobis *scripsi cum Auvray:* nobis A

Document 33
THE POPE'S INJUNCTION TO ROMANUS
18 July 1227

MSS.—(A) Vatican, Arch. Segreto Vat., Serie generale de' Regesti, vol. 14, fol. 22v: Reg. Greg. IX, tom. I, an. i, ep. 130. (B) Paris, BnF, MS. Moreau 1184, fols. 43 and 75.

Honorius episcopus, servus servorum Dei>[a] R(omano) Sancti Angeli cardinali, apostolice sedis legato <salutem et apostolicam benedictionem>.[b]

[a] Honorius—Dei *scripsi*
[b] salutem—benedictionem *scripsi*

you? For the Lord has happily changed you, who were formerly *Hostiensis*,[19] into a *portal*[20] through which we enter in and go out and can find the pastures of life. In you the Lord has provided an *offering* to himself, an *enemy* to the devil, a *portal* for his flock. You are at once the *porter* and the *portal*: the *portal* because you are the vicar of Jesus Christ, who said, "I am the *portal*";[21] the *porter* because you are the successor of Gregory, whose name signifies that he was to keep watch by night over the Lord's flock (*gregis*).[22] And rightly so, for it is by divine inspiration that the office of *porter* and the name "Gregory" mean the same thing, which is appropriate to *Hostiensis*. We knock at that *portal* and we implore the *porter*; we look to the watchman for help, who is the rod of vigilance,[23] that he may do unto us according to the word of the Lord: "Ask, and you shall receive; seek, and you shall find; knock, and it shall be opened to you."[24] Therefore we beg the *porter*, we ask the watchman, we knock at the *portal*, and may it be opened to us.

19. Hugolinus, cardinal-bishop of Ostia since 1206, and hence long called "Hostiensis," was elected Pope Gregory IX on 9 March 1227.

20. The rest of § 9 is based on a series of puns on the title *Hostiensis* (see the preceding note). To indicate the connections, these interrelated words are *italicized* in this translation. In medieval Latin, all the words involved begin in *host-*: *Hostiensis*, one from Ostia, the port of Rome; *hostium*, a door, gate, portal; *hostiarius*, a porter, doorkeeper; *hostis*, an enemy; *hostia*, an offering, a sacrificial victim.

21. John x.7 (Douay-Rheims).

22. Cf. Luke ii.8.

23. Perhaps "virga vigiliarum" here alludes to the *virga vigilantem* ("the rod watching") seen by Jeremiah (i.11), thus recalling the opening theme of this letter.

24. Matthew vii.7 and Luke xii.9; but for *accipietis*, John xvi.24 (Douay-Rheims).

Ed.—(1) Auvray, no. 130.

Refs.—Baronio-Theiner, XX (1870), 543, ad an. 1227, § 59. Potthast, no. 7985.

Text from microfilm of A.

Honorius, bishop, servant of the servants of God, to Romanus cardinal of Sant' Angelo, legate of the apostolic see, greeting and apostolic blessing.

1 Careful exercise of our office requires that we approve those things that are done with foresight, and that we reprove those that seem to be done improvidently.

1 Officii nostri sollicitudo deposcit ut approbemus ea que sunt provide facta, et que videntur facta improvide reprobemus.

2 Ad aures siquidem nostras incertis quibusdam rumoribus fuerat mussitando prolatum quod per quandam ordinationem Senonis editam, intolerabiliter gravaveras ecclesiam Gallican'; set rumores ipsos falsos et incredibiles reputavimus, quia nec fiducia quam de tue circumspectionis prudentia gerebamus nec merita ipsius ecclesie nos talia credere permittebant.

3 Ecce autem nos et fratres nostri Senonen' et Parisien' capitulorum recepimus litteras,[1] protestantes quod Remen', Senonen', Turonen', et Rothomagen' provinciarum capitula importabiliter gravavisti, et seriatim modum intolerabilis revera gravaminis ac mala subsecuta occasione ordinationis hujusmodi lacrimabiliter explicantes;

4 quarum tenorem tibi mittimus presentibus interclusum ut clarificato tandem oculo rationis, advertas tuum immoderatum excessum, quem hoc ipsum non mediocriter aggravat, quod ad gravamen hujusmodi non raptus subito iracundia set premissa deliberatione firmatus, sicut littere ipse insinuant, processisti. Ea enim gravamina que calore iracundie inferuntur, quasi non judicio facta, qualemqualem videntur excusationem habere; illata autem deliberato consilio gravius indigniusque feruntur.

5 Profecto, ne blandiamur tibi set ut dicamus libere quod sentimus, non credimus quod aliquis legatus apostolice sedis ita processerit quemadmodum tu fecisti, si vera sunt, quod vix credimus, que in ipsis litteris continentur. Cum enim ecclesia Gallicana post apostolicam sedem sit quoddam totius Christianitatis speculum et immotum fidei firmamentum, tu eam—sine gravi dolore nec audire nec dicere possumus—quasi hereticam, si prefate littere veritatem continent, exponere[2] presumpsisti, contempto quod ad sedem apostolicam sollempniter appellaverant, et ejus protectioni supposuerant se ac omnia bona sua. Quid enim aliud est illam exponere quam eandem hereticorum judicio judicare?

6 Ut autem hec sufficiat objurgatio, quam tamquam amica diligentis patris verbera tua debet ferre prudentia patienter, discretioni tue presentium auctoritate, in virtute obedientie, districte precipiendo mandamus quatinus ordinationem ipsam, sive quocumque alio nomine factum hujusmodi censeatur, et quicquid ex ea secutum est, omni mora et dilatione postpositis revoces, ita quod ultra tres dies post receptionem presentium, ipsa revocatio nullatenus differatur, et expresse inhibeas e contrario ne quis contra ipsa capitula vel aliquas alias personas ecclesiasticas, sive bona earum, aliquam[c] occasione predicta presumat vio-lentiam exercere; et si qua ecclesiastica bona sunt occasione hujusmodi occupata, ea restitui facias universa.

[c] aliqua *Auvray*

2 It has been brought to our attention, by unverified rumors murmured in our ears, that you have oppressed the Gallican church intolerably by a certain ordinance published at Sens. But we considered those rumors to be false and incredible because neither the faith that we have in your prudence and circumspection nor the merits of that church permitted us to believe such things.

3 But lo and behold! now we and our brothers [the cardinals] have received a letter[1] from the chapters of Sens and Paris protesting that you have unbearably oppressed the chapters of the provinces of Reims, Sens, Tours, and Rouen; and this letter tearfully lists and describes the details of a truly intolerable oppression and the subsequent evils occasioned by this ordinance.

4 We are sending you a copy of that letter enclosed in the present one, so that when the eye of reason at last sees the light, you may discover your immoderate excess, which is much worse because you have proceeded to commit this offense not in a fit of rage but with deliberate forethought, as the letter itself suggests. For those offenses that are committed in the heat of anger seem to have some sort of excuse because they were done without judgment; while those that are committed with deliberate planning are graver and more scandalous.

5 Really, not to delude you by sweet talk but to say frankly what we feel, we do not believe that any legate of the apostolic see would have acted as you have done, if the things contained in that letter are true, which we can hardly believe. For the Gallican church, almost as much as the apostolic see, is as it were the mirror of all Christianity and the unmoved firmament of the faith; and, if that letter tells the truth, you have presumed to treat this church like a heretic—though we cannot hear or say so without heavy sorrow. For you have treated with contempt the fact that they solemnly appealed to the apostolic see and placed themselves and all their goods under its protection. What difference is there between depriving them of their defenses[2] and judging them as one would heretics, who have no legal rights?

6 Your prudence ought to bear this reprimand patiently, as if it were a father's flogging for your own good. And to make it complete, by the authority of the present letter we command your discretion in virtue of obedience to carry out these precise instructions: revoke that ordinance—or whatever you want to call the instrument that did the deed—and whatever resulted from it. Do so without any delay or postponement, so that the revocation is in no way deferred more than three days after the receipt of the present letter. On the other hand, expressly prohibit anyone from using that ordinance as a pretext for presuming to use any violence against those chapters or any other ecclesiastical persons, or

1. Doc. 32, which was enregistered because a copy of it was sent to Romanus.
2. *Exponere*, "to expose" = "depriving them of their defenses," which is similar in effect to outlawry in England.

7 Sciens nos venerabilibus fratribus nostris . . Cenomanen'³ et . . Aurelianen'⁴ episcopis, et dilecto filio . . abbati de Burgo-medio Blesen'⁵ per scripta nostra mandasse ut si nostrum, quod omnino non credimus, neglexeris aut distuleris adimplere preceptum, ipsi id auctoritate apostolica exequantur.

Dat' Anagnie xv. kal. Augusti, pontificatus nostri anno primo.

Document 34
THE POPE COMMISSIONS
THREE PRELATES AS JUDGES
18 July 1227

MSS.—(A) Vatican, Arch. Segreto Vat., Serie generale de' Regesti, vol. 14, fols. 22v–23r: Reg. Greg. IX, tom. I, an. i, ep. 131. (B) Paris, BnF, MS. Moreau 1184, fol. 49.

. . CENOMANENSI EPISCOPO¹ ET CONJUDICIBUS SUIS.ª

Devotionem ecclesie Gallicane verbis extollere superfluum reputamus, cum sit devotis et claris operibus manifesta. Intellectis igitur gravaminibus que dilectus filius noster R(omanus) Sancti Angeli diaconus cardinalis, apostolice sedis legatus, Remen', Senonen', Turonen', et Rothomagen' provinciarum capitulis per ordinationem quandam Senonis editam,² ac postmodum eis per suas

---

ª episcopo *scripsi cum Auvray*: episcopis A *(cf. Doc. 33.7)*

their goods. And if any ecclesiastical goods were occupied on such a pretext, cause all of them to be restored without exception.

7 Know that our venerable brothers the bishops of Le Mans[3] and of Orléans[4] and our beloved son the abbot of Bourgmoyen-lèz-Blois[5] have been ordered by our writ to carry out these instructions by apostolic authority if you neglect or delay to do so, which we can hardly believe will happen.

Given at Anagni, on the fifteenth day before the kalends of August in the first year of our pontificate.

3. Mauritius, bishop of Le Mans, 1216-1231.
4. Philippus, bishop of Orléans, 1221-1234.
5. Notre Dame du Bourgmoyen-lèz-Blois was an Augustinian house in the diocese of Chartres. By mid-1227 its abbot was Roger, who is attested by a charter of 1226. His predecessor, Richard, was elected in 1225 but soon resigned, seemingly because his position became untenable after a papal commission, appointed at his request to investigate the murder of Hervé, the previous abbot, had severely punished the canons involved. *Gallia Christiana*, VIII, 1391-1392; Pressutti, no. 5440 (11 April 1225).

Ed.—(1) Auvray, no. 131.

Ref.—Not in Potthast's *Regesta*.

Text from microfilm of A. I give the register rubric instead of attempting a reconstruction of the address.

TO THE BISHOP OF LE MANS AND HIS COJUDGES.[1]

We think it would be a waste of words to praise the devotion of the Gallican church, since this is already manifest by its devout and famous works. Therefore, when we learned of the oppressions that our beloved son Romanus, cardinal-deacon of Sant' Angelo, legate of the apostolic see, is said to have

1. See Doc. 33.7, above.
2. See Docs. 29-30, above.

litteras intimatam,[3] dicitur intulisse, tacti fuimus dolore cordis intrinsecus et grandi ammiratione commoti, pensantes quam sit indecens et indignum ut qui sunt in apostolice sedis devotione precipui, per eam novo oppressionis genere contra sua merita videantur oppressi.

2 Unde ipsum legatum litterarum asperitate nostrarum ut decuit redarguimus, et eidem continuo dedimus in virtute obedientie firmiter in preceptis[4] ut ordinationem ipsam, sive quocumque alio nomine factum hujusmodi censeatur, et quicquid ex ea[b] secutum est, omnino revocet sine mora, ita quod ultra tres dies post receptionem litterarum nostrarum, revocatio ipsa nullatenus differatur, et expresse inhibeat ne quis contra ipsa capitula vel aliquas alias personas ecclesiasticas, sive bona ipsarum, aliquam[c] occasione predicta presumat violentiam exercere; et si qua ecclesiastica bona sunt occasione hujusmodi occupata, ea restitui faciat universa.

3 Ideoque discretioni vestre per apostolica scripta mandamus quatinus, si legatus ipse nostrum, quod omnino non credimus, neglexerit adimplere preceptum, aut forte ad presentiam nostram regrediens terminos fuerit sue legationis egressus, vos id auctoritate apostolica exequentes, ordinationem ipsam, quocumque censeatur vocabolo, denuntietis penitus irritam et inanem;   4 ac inhibeatis expresse ne quis ea occasione presumat ecclesiastica bona invadere vel turbare, quoslibet qui secus attemptare presumpserint a presumptione hujusmodi, monitione premissa, per ecclesiasticam censuram,[d] appellatione postposita, compescentes; et compellentes nichilominus ad reddendum, si qui forte occasione jamdicta aliqua de bonis ecclesiasticis occuparunt,   5 nec permittatis ullatenus impediri quin illi qui voluerint, libere valeant ad nostram venire presentiam, personas et bona eorum ac aliorum clericorum de provinciis supradictis auctoritate apostolica defendentes et conservantes illesa, molestatores eorum districtione simili efficaciter compescendo, auctoritate conservationis hujusmodi, quamdiu nobis placuerit duratura.

6 Quod si non omnes <hiis exequendis potueritis[e] interesse, duo vestrum ea nichilominus exequantur>[f]

Dat' <Anagnie xv. kal. Augusti, pontificatus nostri anno primo>.[g]

[b] eo *Auvray*

[c] aliqua *Auvray*

[d] ecclesiasticam censuram *tr. Auvray*

[e] potueritis] nequiveritis *in alterna formulae versione:* Cheney, "Letters of Pope Innocent III," *p. 195*

[f] hiis—exequantur *supplevi ex* Cheney, loc. cit.: Quod si non omnes etc., duo vestrum etc. A

[g] Anagnie—primo *supplevi ex Doc. 33:* Dat' ut supra A

inflicted on the chapters of the provinces of Reims, Sens, Tours, and Rouen through an ordinance formerly published at Sens[2] and afterwards made known to them by his letters,[3] we were touched inwardly with heartfelt sorrow and were struck with great amazement because we thought how improper and undeserved it was that those who were outstanding in devotion to the apostolic see should be oppressed contrary to their merits by this new kind of oppression.

2 Therefore we sent that legate a sharp reprimand, as was proper, and in the same letter we firmly instructed him in virtue of obedience[4] to revoke that ordinance—or whatever one wants to call the instrument that did the deed—and whatever resulted from it. And he is to do so without delay, so that the revocation will in no way be deferred more than three days after the receipt of our letter. Moreover, he is expressly to prohibit anyone from using that ordinance as a pretext for presuming to use any violence against those chapters or any other ecclesiastical persons, or their goods. And if any ecclesiastical goods were occupied on such a pretext, he is to cause all of them to be restored without exception.

3 Therefore, if that legate shall have neglected to implement our instructions, or perhaps shall have gone beyond the boundaries of his legation on his way back to our presence, by apostolic writ we command your discretion that you, acting by apostolic authority, are to declare that ordinance, or whatever it is called, to be completely null and void. 4 And you are expressly to prohibit anyone from using that ordinance as a pretext for presuming to invade or disturb ecclesiastical goods. Anyone at all who wrongfully shall have presumed to attempt this, you are first to warn and then to restrain from such presumption by ecclesiastical censure, even if they appeal. Similarly, you are to compel them to restore any ecclesiastical goods that they may happen to have occupied on the pretext mentioned above. 5 Nor are you to permit those who wish to come into our presence to be impeded in any way; but in order that they may do so freely, by apostolic authority defend and preserve unharmed their persons and goods and those of other clerics of the aforesaid provinces. In order to enforce this preservation, a similar, legally valid punishment is authorized to restrain those who molest them, which is to last as long as we please.

6 If all of you are not able to be present to carry out these instructions, they may nonetheless be carried out by two of you.

Given at Anagni on the fifteenth day before the kalends of August, in the first year of our pontificate.

3. See Doc. 31, above.
4. The rest of § 2 repeats Doc. 33.6 *mutatis mutandis.*

Document 35
THE POPE NOTIFIES THE CHAPTERS
OF HIS INJUNCTION
[18] July 1227

Documents 33 and 34 were the executive instruments of Gregory's response; the present letter informs the appellant chapters of these acts, and at the same time it seeks to placate the aggrieved parties with an extravagant display of sympathy.

Date.—The register copy lacks a *datum*-clause. Potthast conjectured a date some time in the latter half of July (15-31), but surely the letter was written *after* Docs. 33 and 34, both of which it quotes (below, *app. font.*, nn. 1 and 3), and hence not before 18 July. With Auvray, I guess that it was written on the same day as the others; doubtless all three were dispatched by the same courier.

Distribution.—Just as the register omits the *datum*-clause, so also it fails to state to whom copies were sent *in eodem modo*. The text refers to Doc. 32 as an ap-

---

REMENSI ET ALIIS CAPITULIS.

Presentate pagine Senonen' et Parisien' capitulorum tenor exhibitus amarissime mirre fasciculum nobis, de novo in cruce carnis et patibulo spiritus immolatis, exhibuit, qui ita paginam cordis nostri inaudite turbationis calamo et nove amaritudinis atramento conscripsit quod scripturam nec lugubris mentis gemitus nec lacrimarum fluvius oblitterare valet,[a] quam nostro animo, quasi ungue adamantino novo cudendi genere, stilus exarati doloris impressit. Quomodo lugens valeat consolari merentem dolensve delinire dolores, cum contraria suis curentur oppositis, non est facile repperire. Nemo querat ab amaricato quod sapiat, ab exasperato quod mulceat, quia exterminantur in verbis[b] mella dulcedinis ubi totum pectus occupat vis doloris.

2 Principium principis incliti quondam regis Lodowici[c] clare memorie, negotium pacis et fidei fideliter promoventis, Ecclesie matri sue attulit risum et gaudium; set emule mortis fato miserando subtractus, risum in luctum convertit, gaudium in lamentum, totumque negotium quod felicibus Deo auctore pro-

---

[a] valet (val&) A: valeat *Raynaldus et Auvray*
[b] in verbis A: in \<amara\> verba *Raynaldus*; in \<amaris\> verbis *Auvray*
[c] Ludovici *Raynaldus et Auvray*

peal by the chapters of the province of Sens, including Paris (§ 1); but the rubric in the register indicates a broader distribution, to the Reims cathedral chapter "and the others," presumably including all the chapters of the four provinces that appealed to Romanus (Doc. 32.5: Reims, Sens, Tours, and Rouen).

MSS.—(A) Vatican, Arch. Segreto Vat., Serie generale de' Regesti, vol. 14, fol. 23rv: Reg. Greg. IX, tom. I, an. i, ep. 133. (B) Paris, BnF, MS. Moreau 1184, fols. 53 and 80.

Ed.—(1) By Raynaldus in Baronio-Theiner, XX (1870), 543, ad an. 1227, § 59–60 (= § 1-5 below, explicit *sine mora*), incorrectly identified as "Ep. CXXX." (2) Auvray, no. 133.

Ref.—Potthast, no. 7986.

Text from microfilm of A. I give the register rubric instead of attempting a reconstruction of the address.

TO REIMS AND THE OTHER CHAPTERS.

When the tenor of the exceedingly harsh pages of the chapters of Sens and Paris came to our attention, it produced within us a virtual book about sacrifices on the cross of the flesh and on the new gibbet of the spirit. With the pen of unprecedented disturbance of mind and with the ink of new bitterness, it inscribed on the page of our heart writing that neither the groans of a grieving mind nor the flow of tears can obliterate; by gouging, a stylus of sorrow impressed that writing on our mind as if by a new kind of engraving with an adamantine nail. It is not easy to discover how a mourner can console the one he is mourning for, or how one who is grieving can describe griefs, since contraries are cured by their opposites. Nobody asks someone who has a bitter taste in his mouth what would taste good to him, or someone who is irritated what would soothe him, because when the whole mind is under the influence of sorrow, "sweet" and "pleasant" are nothing but words.

2 When that prince of princes, the renowned Louis, former king, of illustrious memory, faithfully promoted the business of peace and the faith, he brought joy and laughter to his mother the Church; but when, by a deplorable destiny, death's jealousy took him away, the laughter was changed to mourning, the joy to lamentation, and the whole business that, with God's help, he had been pro-

movebatur auspiciis, mortis sue gladio graviter vulneravit; set successione prolis obducta, vulneris cicatrice reviguit quasi,[d] et spem futuri fructus preteritis laboribus penitus non ademit.

3 Verum, quod dolentes referimus, verendum est ne novum infortunium negotio pacis et fidei sic infortunate succedat ut scintillam spei que in cleri devotione remanserat, flatus exorte malignitatis extinguat. Sed absit quod hoc negotium unius culpa perimat, pro quo tot martyrum sanguis sub altare Dei voce indefessa clamat; presertim cum potius pro ecclesiastica libertate tuenda quam pro negotii subventione vitanda, duxeritis appellandum. Recognoscimus siquidem et fatemur quod ecclesia Gallicana post apostolicam sedem quoddam totius Christianitatis est speculum et immotum fidei firmamentum, utpote que in fervore fidei Christiane ac devotione apostolice sedis non sequitur alias set, ut cum earum pace dixerimus, antecedit; cujus devotionem verbis extollere superfluum reputamus cum sit claris operibus manifesta.

4[1] Intellectis igitur gravaminibus vobis a dilecto filio nostro R(omano) Sancti Angeli diacono cardinali, apostolice sedis legato, per ordinationem quandam Senonis editam irrogatis, tacti dolore cordis intrinsecus et gravi admiratione commoti, eundem legatum litterarum asperitate nostrarum ut decuit redarguimus, et ei continuo dedimus in virtute obedientie firmiter in preceptis ut ordinationem ipsam, sive quocumque alio nomine factum hujusmodi censeatur, omnino revocet sine mora, ita quod revocatio ipsa ultra tres dies post receptionem litterarum nostrarum nullatenus differatur, et expresse inhibeat ne quis contra vos seu alias personas ecclesiasticas, sive bona ipsarum aliquam,[e] occasione predicta presumat violentiam exercere; ac restitui faciat universa, si qua, occasione jamdicta, sunt de bonis ecclesiasticis occupata.

5 Denique, volentes vobis et aliis quos hoc negotium tangit plenius providere, venerabilibus fratribus nostris[2] . . Cenomanen' et . . Aurelianen' episcopis, et dilecto filio . . abbati de Burgo-medio Blesen' per scripta nostra mandavimus ut,[3] si cardinalis ipse nostrum, quod omnino non credimus, neglexerit vel distulerit adimplere preceptum, aut forte ad presentiam nostram regrediens terminos[f] fuerit sue legationis egressus, ipsi id auctoritate apostolica exequentes, ordinationem contra vos Senonis editam ac vobis postmodum ipsius legati litteris intimatam, denuntient penitus irritam[g] et inanem; et expresse inhibeant ne quis ea occasione presumat ecclesiastica bona invadere vel turbare, quoslibet qui secus attemptare presumpserint, a presumptione hujusmodi compescentes

[d] reviguit quasi *tr. Raynaldus et Auvray*
[e] aliqua *Auvray*
[f] termino *Auvray*
[g] irratam *Auvray*

moting auspiciously was wounded gravely by the sword of his death. But the succession of his offspring, like new skin growing over a wound, has somewhat restored the business, so that the hope has not completely perished that past labors will bear future fruit.

3 But now, sad to say, it is to be feared that a new misfortune may unfortunately overtake the business of peace and of the faith, namely that a blast arising from stinginess may extinguish the spark of hope that remained in the devotion of the clergy. But God forbid that one person's fault should destroy this business for which the blood of so many martyrs calls with unwearied voice at the foot of God's altar; especially since you made your appeal, not in order to avoid supporting the business, but rather in order to defend ecclesiastical liberty. We recognize and acknowledge that the Gallican church, almost as much as the apostolic see, is as it were the mirror of all Christianity and the unmoved firmament of the faith,[1] inasmuch as it is not second to other churches but—we speak with all due respect to them—it surpasses them in fervor of the Christian faith and devotion to the apostolic see; hence we think words would be wasted in praising its devotion, since this is already manifest by its famous works.[2]

4[3] Therefore, when we learned of the oppressions that our beloved son Romanus, cardinal-deacon of Sant' Angelo, legate of the apostolic see, imposed on you through an ordinance formerly published at Sens, we were touched inwardly with heartfelt sorrow and were struck with great amazement. Consequently, we sent that legate a sharp reprimand, as was proper, and in the same letter we firmly instructed him in virtue of obedience to revoke that ordinance—or whatever one wants to call the instrument that did the deed. And he is to do so without delay, so that the revocation will in no way be deferred more than three days after the receipt of our letter. Moreover, he is to expressly prohibit anyone from using that ordinance as a pretext for presuming to use any violence against you or any other ecclesiastical persons, or their goods. And if any ecclesiastical goods were occupied on such a pretext, he is to cause all of them to be restored without exception.

5 Furthermore, because we wished to make fuller provision for you and others whom this matter concerns, by our writ we have commanded our venerable brothers the bishops of Le Mans and Orléans and our beloved son the abbot of Bourgmoyen-lèz-Blois that if that cardinal of ours shall have neglected or delayed implementing our instructions, or perhaps shall have gone beyond the boundaries of his legation on his way back to our presence, they, acting by apostolic authority, are to declare that ordinance, or whatever it is called, which was

---

1. "the Gallican—faith": cf. Doc. 33.5.
2. Cf. Doc. 34.1.
3. *Mutatis mutandis* 4 reproduces the tenor of Doc. 34.1-2 (cf. Doc. 33.6).

^h et compellentes nichilominus ad reddendum, si qui forte occasione iamdicta aliqua de bonis ecclesiasticis occuparunt, nec impedire permittant quin illi qui voluerint, libere valeant ad nostram venire presentiam, personas et bona eorum ac aliorum clericorum de dictis provinciis defendentes et conservantes illesa, molestatores eorum efficaciter compescendo, auctoritate conservationis huiusmodi quamdiu nobis placuerit duratura.^h

6 Firmiter denique gerimus in proposito facere omnia que pro conservatione vestri honoris ac status secundum Deum et honestatem viderimus facienda.

<Dat' Anagnie xv. kal. Augusti pontificatus nostri anno primo.>^i

^h-h et compellentes—duratura *om. Auvray*
^i Dat'—primo *ex Doc. 33 supplevi*

Document 36
TWO BISHOPS ENGAGE TO PAY THE TENTH FOR THE SENS CHAPTERS
August 1227

MSS.—(A) Paris, Arch. nat., J 428, no. 8 (*olim* no. 1940): Trésor des chartes, Albigeois, no. 8; original (175 × 185 mm), with two seals; formerly folded twice crosswise. Endorsed: *Littere .G. archiepiscopi Senon' et .G. episcopi Carnoten' de subventione facienda pro negotio Albigesii m° cc° xxvii°.* (B) Paris, BnF, MS. lat. 9778, fol. 188ra: Register F. (C) Paris, BnF, MS. Baluze 8, fol. 24r–v: copy citing "Ibid.

G(alterus), Dei gratia Senon' archiepiscopus,[1] et G(alterus), eadem gratia episcopus Carnoten',[2] omnibus presentes litteras inspecturis, salutem in Domino.

published against you at Sens and afterwards made known to you by that legate's letters, to be completely null and void. And they are expressly to prohibit anyone from using that ordinance as a pretext for presuming to invade or disturb ecclesiastical goods. Anyone at all who wrongfully shall have presumed to attempt this, they are to restrain from such presumption, and similarly they are to compel restitution of any ecclesiastical goods that may have been occupied on the pretext mentioned above. Nor are they to permit those who wish to come into our presence to be impeded in any way; but that such persons may do so freely, they and their goods and those of other clerics of the aforesaid provinces are to be defended and preserved unharmed. In order to enforce this preservation, a legally valid punishment is authorized to restrain those who molest them, which is to last as long as we please.

6 Finally, we intend to do everything that seems to us ought to be done according to God and decent conduct in order to preserve your honor and status.

Given at Anagni on the fifteenth day before the kalends of August, in the first year of our pontificate.

---

211. verso," although this does not correspond to any foliation in B or to fol. 211v in Register E (Paris, Arch. nat., JJ 26).

Ed.—(1) Martène-Durand, *Vet. script. coll.*, I (1724), 1212–1213, "Ex ms. Colbertino," probably MS. B; (2) Devic-Vaissète, III (1737), 324–325, preuve no. 181, ii; VIII (1879), 868–869, preuve no. 267. (3) Teulet, no. 1942.

Text from A; transcribed from microfilm and verified from the original; a few select variants from copies.

Walter,[1] by the grace of God archbishop of Sens, and Walter,[2] by the same grace bishop of Chartres, to all who shall see the present letter, greeting in the Lord.

1. Galter(i)us Cornut, archbishop of Sens, 1222–1241.
2. Galter(i)us O.S.B., bishop of Chartres, 1219–1234.

1 Notum facimus quod nos, pro utilitate ecclesiarum nostrarum et pro conservanda pace et indempnitate ipsarum, et ne impediatur succursus negotii pacis et fidei in terra Albigen', karissimo domino nostro Lud(ovico)[a] regi Franc' illustri et nobilissime domine Bl(anche) regine, matri ejus, promisimus nos soluturos eis vel heredibus eorum singulis annis usque ad quadriennium,[b] si negotium terre Albigesii tantum duraverit, in manu domini regis vel heredum suorum mille et quingentas librarum[c] Parisien' pro capitulis ecclesiarum cathedralium provincie Senonen'; ita quod unusquisque in solidum teneatur, set, uno solvente, alter liberabitur.

2 Et ad hoc faciendum obligamus personas nostras et bona nostra, et ecclesias etiam nostras et successores nostros, de assensu etiam et auctoritate venerabilis patris domini Rom(ani) Sancti Angeli diaconi cardinalis, apostolice sedis legati; ita etiam quod, si de altero nostrum infra predictum spatium aliquid humanitus contigerit, reliquus ad solutionem totius predicte summe nichilominus teneatur, et bona sua et ecclesie illius qui decesserit erunt obligata, et successores etiam eadem obligatione tenebuntur.

3 Solutio autem hujus pecunie fiet in duobus terminis: medietas videlicet in festo Omnium Sanctorum et medietas in Pascha; et fiet Parisius apud Templum; et fiet in instanti festo Omnium Sanctorum prima paga.

In cujus rei testimonium, presentes litteras sigillis nostris confirmamus.
Actum Parisius anno Domini m° cc° xx° septimo, mense Augusti.[d]

[a] Lud' A: *om.* B *et Baluze, Martène, Vaissète, et Teulet*
[b] quinquennium *Baluze*
[c] libras *Baluze, Martène, Vaissète, et Teulet*
[d] Augusto *Martène*

Documents 37 and 38
HOW THE POPE APPROVED THE TENTH
August—November 1227

Doc. 37: William of Andres.—In 1084 the Benedictine monastery of Andres was established in Artois between Guines and Ardres (diocese of Thérouanne, later Boulogne). Originally subject to Charroux Abbey near Poitiers, the monks of Andres won the right to elect their own abbot in 1207, and their independence was assured when the pope abrogated the veto power of Charroux in 1211. As abbot they chose William, the monk who had negotiated the separation, and he ruled them for twenty-three years (1211–1234). Late in life he compiled a

1 We make it known that, for the utility of our churches, and in order to preserve their peace and immunity, and lest assistance to the business of peace and of the faith in Albigeois be impeded, we have promised to our lord Louis, illustrious king of France, and to the most noble lady Queen Blanche, his mother, that we shall pay them or their heirs fifteen hundred pounds paris every year for up to five years, if the Albigensian business shall last so long. This payment is being made for the chapters of the cathedral churches of the province of Sens; it is to be paid directly to the lord king or his heirs; and it is understood that each of us is liable for the full amount, so that if one pays it all, the other is released from the obligation.

2 And to insure that this is done, we pledge our persons and our goods, and also obligate our churches and our successors, with the assent and by the authority of the venerable father the lord Romanus, cardinal-deacon of Sant' Angelo, legate of the apostolic see. This is done on the understanding that if one of us should die or be otherwise incapacitated within the aforesaid period, the other one is nevertheless obligated to pay the whole of the aforesaid sum, and the goods and church of the deceased are likewise obligated, and even his successors shall be bound by the same obligation.

3 The payment of this money shall be made in two installments, namely half at the feast of All Saints and half at Easter; and it shall be made at the Temple in Paris; and the first payment shall be made this year on the feast of All Saints.

In witness thereof, we confirm the present letter with our seals. Done at Paris, A. D. 1227, in the month of August.

---

chronicle that was primarily the history of his community, in which his own career of lawsuits and travels filled the latest and longest chapter. The affairs of Andres occupied the foreground in his plan, but to provide a chronological framework of extramural events, he interspersed brief notices often borrowed from earlier chronicles. The events of his own lifetime, however, including those which are our concern, he chronicled himself. Our events, however, were no longer fresh in his mind, for he had forgotten that the tithe was originally imposed for five years; he must have derived his four-year figure from the pope's decision (Doc. 39), which was only concerned with the unpaid balance. Nonetheless, the chronicler's indignation had not cooled: Andres had been subject to the tax, and its abbot still identified with the chapters opposing Romanus and the royalists—"nostre universitatis hostibus" (§ 4).

Ed.—(1) L. d'Achery, *Spicilegium*, IX (1669), 338-671; 2nd ed., II (1723), 781-871. (2) A partial but improved text by Dom Brial, reprinted in *Rec. hist. Gaules*, XVIII (1822), 568-583. (3) Second complete edition by J. Heller, MGH, SS, XXIV (1879), 690-773.

Text.—The excerpts below are substantially the same in all three editions: Achery, pp. 655-656; Brial, p. 580; Heller, pp. 766-767. I reproduce Heller's text.

Refs.—Heller's introduction (pp. 684-690) is the most thorough, Daunou's notice remains adequate: *Hist. litt. France*, XVIII (1835), 131-134. Slight, but useful for relations with other chronicles: Molinier, *Sources*, no. 2518; cf. 2519, 2193. *Repertorium fontium historiae Medii Aevi*, V (1984), 291.

Doc. 38: John Longus.—Abbot William's chronicle was hardly known outside the walls of Andres, save by one far more popular chronicler, who died just a century and a half after William. This was John Longus, native of Ypres, who could, like his surname, have been either Flemish or Walloon, either *Lang* or *Long*. Like William, he was abbot (1366-1384) of a Benedictine house in Thérouanne diocese, but his was one famous and far older—the abbey of St-Bertin. For this monastery, with its long tradition of chronicling, Abbot John prepared a community history much like that of Andres in conception, into which he nonetheless incorporated a wealth of regional history that gave it wider appeal. Longus died when his project had only reached the annal for 1294, but continuators carried it on progressively down to 1483, and in one form or another it was much copied (twenty-two manuscripts).

Among the many sources used for this St-Bertin chronicle, Longus adapted passages from the work of his counterpart at Andres, which may have passed into his hands after Andres was destroyed by the English in 1351. The parallel passages below demonstrate his tendency to stylistic simplification, mainly through periphrasis. The MGH edition displays typographically how the chronicler reworked his sources, but below I have indicated only Longus' three substantive additions (in *italics*). How did he, some hundred and fifty years after the events, come by this new but accurate information? St-Bertin, like Andres, lay in the appellant province of Reims, so he would not have had to travel far to seek a copy of the chapters' appeal (Doc. 32), which names the four provinces; yet he could hardly have had access to our source for the defection of Sens from their number (Doc. 36). That detail Longus may have either learned explicitly from some unknown source or inferred from a known one, such as the papal decision, which lists only three provinces (Doc. 39, of which the chapters surely received a version). But perhaps he needed no clue other than William of Andres' indication that the archbishop, as royal agent in the case, was the legate's fellow traveller (Doc. 37.4).

Ed.—(1) First and only complete edition in Martène-Durand, *Thesaurus*, III (1717), 442-776. (2) Extracts in *Rec. hist. Gaules*; our passage in XVIII (1822), 579-580, from an inferior manuscript, according to Holder-Egger, pp. 746-747. (3) The core of the work was elaborately edited by O. Holder-Egger, MGH, SS, XXV (1880), 747-866, with competent introduction (pp. 736-747); our text at pp. 834-835.

Text reprinted from Holder-Egger's edition.

Refs.—*Repertorium fontium historiae Medii Aevi*, VI (1990), 351-352. Molinier, *Sources*, no. 1782. Mansi, who knew only Longus' version, demonstrated with unwonted erudition that Sens did not withdraw its appeal until *after* the king's death: annotation in Baronio-Theiner, XX (1870), 542-545, ad an. 1227, no. 61, n. 1.

Doc. 37
William of Andres

Anno Domini 1226. Romanus di-aconus cardinalis, apostolice sedis legatus, in Gallias venit; qui inter cetera que correxit in Morinensi diocesi quam plures sacerdotes ob incontinentie vitium gravi correptione corripuit.

2 Convocavit autem Bituricas epis-coporum ac aliorum prelatorum, sed et procerum, grande concilium, ubi de Albigensi heresi confutanda tractatum est et ordinatum. Ludovicus rex et multi nobiles tam episcoporum quam procerum admonitu domini legati cum ipso legato ad Albigenses cruce signati ad solvendum votum se preparant et disponunt.

. . . .

3 Anno Domini 1227. . . . Romanus apostolice sedis legatus, qui, invitis fere omnibus prelatis et subditis Gallicani orbis et reclamantibus et contra eum appellantibus, bona ecclesiarum et monasteriorum in favorem regis et suorum per quatuor annos decimari preceperat:

Doc. 38
John Longus

Dominus Romanus Sancti Angeli dyachonus cardinalis, apostolice sedis legatus, in Gallias venit, et inter cetera que in partibus istis egit, in dyochesi Morinensi quam plures sacerdotes ob incontinencie vicium gravi punicione corripuit.[1]

. . . .

2 Romanu cardinalis, apostolice sedis legatus, hoc eodem anno Domini 1226, grande consilium tam baronum quam prelatorum convocavit in civitate Bituricensi, in quo de Albigencium heresi confutanda fuit ordinatum. In hoc consilio rex Francie et multi nobiles cum ipsomet legato cruce signati sunt. . . .

. . . .

3 Romanus apostolice sedis legatus supra in Bituricensi consilio in auxilio regis Francie bona ecclesiarum ad quatuor annos decimari preceperat, invitis et reclamantibus, immo eciam appellantibus fere omnibus Galliarum prelatis *et specialiter quatuor provinciarum Remensis, Senonensis, Bituricensis*[2] *et Turonensis; sed Senonensis ab appellacione sua cito recessit;*

Doc. 37
William of Andres

Doc. 38
John Longus

Anno Domini 1226. Romanus, cardinal-deacon and legate of the apostolic see, came to Gaul. Among other things that he corrected in the diocese of Thérouanne, he punished many priests with a heavy punishment on account of the sin of incontinence.

The lord Romanus, cardinal-deacon of Sant' Angelo and legate of the apostolic see, came to Gaul, and among other things that he did in those parts, in the diocese of Thérouanne he punished a great many priests with a heavy punishment on account of the sin of incontinence.[1]

. . . .

2 At Bourges he convoked a great council of bishops and other prelates, as well as of lay magnates. How to destroy the Albigensian heresy was discussed there and decided. Exhorted by the lord legate and accompanied by him, King Louis and many nobles, both bishops and lay magnates, prepared and organized themselves to fulfil their vow as crusaders against the Albigensians.

2 In this same year of the Lord 1226, Cardinal Romanus, legate of the apostolic see, convoked a great council of both barons and prelates in the city of Bourges, in which it was decided how to defeat the Albigensian heresy. In this council the king of France and many nobles, together with the legate himself, took the Cross . . .

. . . .

. . . .

3 A. D. 1227. . . . Romanus, the legate of the apostolic see, ordered that for four years the goods of churches and monasteries were to pay a tithe in favor of the king and his men. Almost all the prelates and subjects of the Gallican world were unwilling; they protested and they appealed against him.

3 At the council of Bourges mentioned above, Romanus, the legate of the apostolic see, ordered that for four years the goods of churches were to be tithed to help the king of France. Almost all the prelates of Gaul were unwilling and protested; indeed, they even appealed, *and especially those of the four provinces of Reims, Sens, Bourges,*[2] *and Tours; but Sens quickly withdrew its appeal.*

1. Next, reforms at St-Bertin by Romanus and the abbot are related at length.
2. The chronicler is mistaken; for "Bourges" read "Rouen" (cf. Doc. 32.4-5).

4 mortuo rege, comite Sancti-Pauli occiso, et maxima multitudine procerum diversis mortibus defunctis, per generale capitulum Cisterciense transitum faciens et inde secum Cisterciensem et Clarevallensem abbates et quosdam episcopos et abbates quos creaverat, necnon et Senonensem archiepiscopum, qui in favorem regine eum sequebantur, ducens, omnibus personis Gallicane ecclesie sibi contrariis mala quidem minatur et contra eos peiora machinatur, et ita cum suis complicibus et nostre universitatis hostibus quasi victor Romam revertitur.

4 et mortuo rege, rediens ad curiam, secum ducens Senonensem archiepiscopum, *qui ab appellacione sua recesserat,* ac abbates Cisterciensem et Clarevallensem, quos ipse creaverat et quosdam alios, omnibus Gallicane ecclesie sibi contrariis minas fortes inferens; sed nil ob hoc desistunt alii.

5 Sequuntur eum e vestigio sollempnes nuntii de singulis urbibus ab universitate electi, qui multa quidem expenderunt, sed nichil omnino profecerunt, excepto eo, quod post multiplices repulsas et tam a curia quam a suis vicinis et emulis perpessas iniurias promissam decime summam per quatuor annos ad centum milia librarum Turonensis monete taxari impetraverunt.

5 Sequti sunt itaque eum e vestigio ad curiam nuncii *trium provinciarum cum appellacione sua;* qui multas perpessi iniurias et expensas, nichil omnino profecerunt, nisi quod dicte decime quadriennes ad sommam centum milium librarum Turonencium taxari impetrarunt; sicque redierunt.

4 The king died, the count of St-Pol was killed, and a very great multitude of lay magnates died in various ways. After that the legate returned to Rome like a victor with his accomplices and the enemies of our coalition. Along the way he stopped at the Cistercian general chapter and added the abbots of Cîteaux and Clairvaux to his retinue, which included certain bishops and abbots whom he had created and the archbishop of Sens; they all followed him to support the queen. He kept threatening bad things indeed against all persons of the Gallican church who opposed him, and against them he was contriving worse things.

5 In his footsteps followed solemn nuncios who were chosen by the coalition to represent the several cities. Although they spent a great deal, they accomplished next to nothing, except that, after suffering many rebuffs and injuries, not only from the curia but also from their neighbors and rivals, their petition was granted for the tithe to be assessed at the agreed [annual] sum of one hundred thousand pounds tours for four years.

4 After the king died, Romanus returned to the curia, leading with him the archbishop of Sens, *who had withdrawn from his appeal,* and the abbots of Cîteaux and Clairvaux, whom he himself had created, and some others. He kept making strong threats against all persons of the Gallican church who opposed him, but in no way did they give up because of this.

5 And so nuncios *of the three provinces* followed in his footsteps to the curia *with their appeal.* Although they suffered many injuries and expenses, they accomplished next to nothing, except that their petition was granted for the said four-year tithe to be assessed at the [annual] sum of one hundred thousand pounds tours; and thus they returned.

Document 39
GREGORY IX INFORMS THE KING
THAT THE CHAPTERS MUST PAY THE TENTH
13 November 1227

MSS.—(A) Vatican, Arch. Segreto Vat., Serie generale de' Regesti, vol. 14, fol. 44v: Reg. Greg. IX, tom. I, an. i, ep. 154. (B) Ibid., vol. 19, fol. 87r (811): Reg. Greg. IX, post an. xii, ep. 438, where it stands first in a documentary appendix on the peace negotiations between Louis IX and Raymond VII in 1229. This text was not recopied from A, however, since its registrar (another hand) was un-

Honorius episcopus, servus servorum Dei, karissimo in Christo filio Lodoico>[a] . . illustri regi Francie,[b] <salutem et apostolicam benedictionem>.[c]

1 Cum dilectus filius noster R(omanus) Sancti Angeli diaconus cardinalis tunc apostolice sedis legatus in concilio Bituris pro negotio pacis et fidei convocato consilium accepisset quod si clare memorie rex Francie pater tuus negotium ipsum[d] sibi assumeret, decimam omnium ecclesiasticorum proventuum sue legationis usque ad quinquennium, si tantum duraret negotium, offerret eidem.[1]

2 Et rex ipse divinitus inspiratus assumpsisset negotium supradictum. Idem legatus ei obtulit et promisit usque ad predictum tempus, si negotium tantum duraret, decimam memoratam expendendam pro voluntate sua quamdiu per se vel per suos, sicut negotium exigeret, illud curaret[e] prosequi bona fide.[2]

3 Cum autem hujusmodi facto legati quedam capitula trium provinciarum, Remen' videlicet Turonen' et Rothomagen', se opposuerint, et ne compellerentur dictam decimam solvere ad sedem apostolicam pro se et sibi adherentibus duxerint appellandum;

4 nos, auditis super hoc quibusdam capitulorum procuratoribus et cardinale predicto, considerato etiam[f] quod pro tam evidenti necessitate et tam utili ne-

[a] Honorius—Lodoico *scripsi (cf. Doc. 8)*
[b] *rubrica om.* B
[c] salutem—benedictionem *scripsi*
[d] ipsa C
[e] procuraret B
[f] etenim C, *Raynaldus et Auvray*

aware of A's existence, as is evident from his marginal note that B could be added to the end of the first year's register as ep. 181 (see Auvray, II, 1267, n. 1). (C) Paris, BnF, MS. Moreau 1185, fol. 162rv (58).

Ed.—(1) Raynaldus in Baronio-Theiner, XX (1870), 544, ad an. 1227, § 61; from A. (2) Auvray, no. 155; from A. (3) Auvray, no. 4782; from B, giving only incipit and explicit.

Ref.—Potthast, no. 8053.

Text from microfilms, based on A, collated with B and C.

Honorius, bishop, servant of the servants of God, to his most beloved son in Christ, Louis, illustrious king of the French, greeting and apostolic blessing.

1 When our beloved son Romanus cardinal-deacon of Sant' Angelo was legate of the apostolic see, he convoked a council at Bourges for the business of peace and of the faith. There he received the counsel that if your father, the well-remembered king of France, took that business upon himself, the legate should offer him a tenth of all the ecclesiastical revenues of his legation for five years, if the business were to last so long.[1]

2 And the king himself, being divinely inspired, did undertake the aforesaid business. The same legate offered and promised him the tenth mentioned above for the aforesaid time, if the business were to last so long, and the tenth was to be spent as the king wished as long as he took care to pursue that business in good faith, either in person or through his people, just as that business might require.[2]

3 This act of the legate was opposed, however, by certain chapters of three provinces, namely of Reims, Tours, and Rouen, and they instituted an appeal to the apostolic see lest they be compelled to pay the said tenth.

4 Concerning this appeal, we have heard several proctors of the chapters and the aforesaid cardinal. We also have taken into consideration that, both for evident necessity and for business serving the interests of God's Church, the said

1. See Doc. 29.1–5, above.
2. See Doc. 26.9, above

gotio Ecclesie Dei dictus legatus tum[g] jure legationis statuere vel ordinare potuit quod expedire videbat, tum etiam ex eo quod specialem potestatem ab ecclesia Romana receperat ordinandi et statuendi quecumque, secundum datam
sibi a Deo prudentiam, videret[h] negotio expedire;[3]

5 ordinationem ipsius ex ordine legitimam et sanctam ex causa, necnon et
promissionem factam regi de consilio pene totius Bituricen' concilii, de fratrum
nostrorum consilio duximus approbandam, et non solum firmam set ratam et
gratam habemus eandem; volentes et statuentes auctoritate presentium ut tibi,
secundum dictam promissionem a memorato legato eidem[i] patri tuo factam,
decima integre persolvatur.

Dat' Laterani idibus Novembris, pontificatus nostri anno primo.

[g] tunc C
[h] viderit C *et Auvray*
[i] eidem *om. Auvray*

legate was not only empowered by the general rights of legation to enact or ordain what seemed expedient to him, but he also had received from the Roman church the specific power of ordaining and enacting whatever seemed to him, according to the prudence given to him by God, might expedite the business.[3]

5 Therefore, on the advice of our brothers, we have approved his ordinance as being legitimate from first to last and as being holy in motivation, and likewise we have approved the promise made to the king on the advice of almost the whole council of Bourges, and we not only confirm it but also declare it to be valid and pleasing. By the authority of the present letter, we wish and establish that the tenth be fully paid to you in its entirety, according to the said promise made by the above-mentioned legate to your father.

Given at the Lateran on the ides of November, in the first year of our pontificate.

3. See Doc. 12.5, above.

PROPOSALS FOR FINANCING PAPAL GOVERNMENT

Document 40
GERALD OF WALES ON HENRY VI'S PROPOSAL
1196

The proposal for a financial reform of the Roman curia that was considered at Bourges was only the latest and last attempt to endow the papal bureaucracy with a regular income by setting aside for papal appointees a fixed number of benefices in every major church. The idea originated in a proposal made by Emperor Henry VI to the effect that one prebend in every cathedral should be put at the pope's disposal. The scheme was under consideration when Henry died in 1197 and nothing more was heard of it for almost two decades. Then, at the Fourth Lateran Council, Innocent III suggested that the Roman church receive a tithe of each cathedral's revenues, but finding little support for the plan, he did not make an issue of it. Some ten years later the proposal was made in its third and final form by Honorius III, who in his bull *Super muros* (Doc. 41) reverted to the suggestion of 1196 that the subsidy consist of benefices, but now each church was to contribute not one but two. Because Honorius' bull was formally discussed in France and England, his version of the proposed reform was common knowledge and is attested by a variety of sources (Docs. 1.6 ff., 2.2, 32–35). By comparison, little is known of the earlier proposals, for both are reported together in a single source that unfortunately is not altogether trustworthy.

That source is Gerald of Wales' *Speculum Ecclesiae*, a work of the garrulous archdeacon's extreme old age, for he was almost seventy when he completed it shortly before the opening of the Fourth Lateran Council. In the chapter reprinted below, he recounted the offer Henry had made some twenty years before, to which he added, a year or so later, a brief account of the similar plan put forth by Innocent at the recent council. If the report had come from a sober, matter-of-fact chronicler such as Richard de Mores (Doc. 2), it would be accepted today without question, since everything in the chapter itself accords with what little is known of the attendant circumstances. However, those who know Gerald's volatile character from his more famous writings can never trust him implicitly as an accurate and objective reporter. Sometimes he is thoroughly reliable, to be sure, but then again he is not. When his statements cannot be controlled from other sources, their evaluation must be a delicate and uncertain business. The case that concerns us has already been the subject of a monographic investigation by Volkert Pfaff, who was disposed to accept Gerald's testimony as substantially correct. This conclusion seems justified, but not always by Pfaff's arguments; the present notice therefore will be concerned not so much with the facts, which may be found in his treatise, but rather with their interpretation. Gerald himself is too well known to require a lengthy introduction—those who have not made his acquaintance may do so in the voluminous literature of which a selection is cited in the endnote below—but his competence as a witness in the present case must be set forth and qualified.

According to Pfaff's reconstruction of the negotiations of 1196-1197, the proposal was not made public, so Gerald could have learned of it only via some member of the imperial court or the Roman curia. The known facts strongly suggest that the latter was indeed his source. In connection with his disputed election as bishop of St David's, Gerald spent about twelve months in Rome between November 1199 and April 1203, when memory of Henry's proposal would still have been fresh among the *curiales*. Gerald himself has left abundant evidence of his familiarity with the cardinals and even the pope. Since ecclesiastical anecdotes were a staple of his conversation, some knowledgeable friend during an exchange of stories may well have added this one to the visitor's repertory. In short, there is every likelihood that Gerald learned his story at the curia. The informant would appear to have been reliable, for Pfaff and Baaken have shown that the account agrees with what is known of Henry's last years (see chapter 6, text between nn. 63 and 71, above).

About the details one can be less sure. Gerald must have heard the story some years before he wrote it down circa 1215. His most recent visit to Rome was in early 1207 as a pilgrim; his extended stay at the curia ended in 1203. At the other extreme, almost twenty years separate the event from the completion of the account in 1215. Moreover, the author was an accomplished raconteur and facile rhetorician whose imagination lightly glossed over gaps in his memory or information. One may readily suspect that Henry's plan was not precisely as reported by Gerald; but his inaccuracies must be few, however, since the chapter for all its verbosity contains no more than a few lines of positive data, most of which could easily be remembered over the course of many years. The only questionable passage is the description of the proposal itself (§ 3), the vagueness of which is more likely to have been in Gerald's mind than in Henry's plan. Yet even here the basic idea is simple enough, and of it Gerald must have been sure: in every cathedral the best benefice is to be held by a member of the Roman curia. If Gerald's account of just how the distribution was to be made is somewhat confusing, one may recall that the plan of 1225 was also misunderstood in such details. Gerald's story, then, must be read for what it is: an anecdote recalled in outline after a lapse of many years and fleshed out by much rhetoric and perhaps a little imagination. The latter is most evident in the lengthy exposition of the emperor's motives (§ 2), which Pfaff uncritically accepted as a reliable report (pp. 40-43) rather than a fictive reconstruction, as it certainly must be.

★ ★ ★

Gerald's reliability concerning this anecdote is greatly increased by two further considerations. First, this is not just any anecdote; instead, it is the centerpiece of his whole massive *Speculum Ecclesiae*. Second, it was intended to be read by Innocent III and his *curiales*, who, as the original source of the anecdote, would know whether he was telling the truth. If they discounted the anecdote, then the whole *Speculum Ecclesiae* would have been pointless. In these circumstances, Gerald must have indeed been certain of his facts since so much depended on their accuracy.

This argument is based on my published reconstruction of the development of the *Speculum Ecclesiae* (see bibliography below); here it will suffice to summarize the conclusions of that study.

Since circa 1187, Gerald had been collecting examples of ways in which monks, especially Benedictines and Cistercians in England and Wales, failed to observe their own monastic rules. Probably his intention was simply to satirize monastic laxity in the hope that shame would induce reform. In the spring of 1212, he began composing a work based on this material, which was well advanced when he heard the news that on 19 April 1213 Innocent III had issued a summons to the Fourth Lateran Council with the intention of reforming the Church. Gerald realized that now his scandalous anecdotes might document the need for closer supervision of Benedictine monasteries, and accordingly he included a recommendation that each order should institute a system of visitation based on the Cistercian model (*Spec. Eccl.* II.29).

At the same time, Gerald decided to enlarge his work to include the secular clergy as well, and to reflect this wider scope he now titled the book *Speculum Ecclesiae*. All the new material was collected in the fourth and final distinction, which Gerald declared was by far the most important part of his work (I.pr, in *Opera*, IV, 14). Significantly, its principal proposal was to revive Henry VI's plan to provide the Roman church with an adequate income (IV.19 = Doc. 40). Previous chapters led up to this thesis, first by recalling the great dignity and antiquity of the Roman church, "mother and mistress of all the other churches" (IV.1–10), and then by explaining how it had been impoverished by the barbarian invaders who had deprived it of Constantine's ample endowment, and in consequence Rome was forced to live at the expense of other churches. But Rome was only demanding her due, Gerald argued, since all things spiritual belong to the pope just as secular princes possess all temporalities (IV.13), so it is unjust to accuse Rome of greed.

Chapter 19 culminates the argument with the revelation that Rome's chronic poverty might have been ended had Henry's plan been adopted. The emperor's premature death is lamented, and the section closes with bitter reflections on the insecurity of our human condition. In Gerald's original design, the valedictory rhetoric of § 6 was doubtless intended to mark the close of the section on Rome; with chapter 20, he leaves Rome and moves on down the hierarchy for a sketchy and inconsequential inspection of the archbishops, bishops, and lower clergy.

By the spring of 1215, Gerald had completed the first redaction of his *Speculum* and presented one copy of it to the Hereford cathedral chapter and another to Archbishop Stephen Langton. From Gerald's account of the plan of 1196 (§ 4) we can be sure that he knew that the common consent of the donors was required by canon law, and by giving a copy of his proposal to the Hereford chapter, which would be represented at the council, he probably was hoping to persuade its proctors to champion his idea there. Langton, more obviously, could also be a powerful proponent of the plan.

The Fourth Lateran Council completed its work on 30 November 1215, and by early 1216 Gerald had learned how his proposals had fared. The canon on monastic chapters was all that he had hoped for,[1] but the council did nothing to benefice the curia. He determined to revise his *Speculum* accordingly. The Hereford copy was recalled and the anticlimactic *notandum* (§ 7) was appended to IV.19, as well as a note of triumph at II.29.[2] This second redaction, which was completed by late summer 1216, was eventually followed by a third, in which Gerald revised the preface at some time between 1220 and his death circa 1223.

When the *Speculum Ecclesiae* is read in the light of this new chronology, a set purpose can be discerned that informs the apparent disorder of the work. What began as a satiric collection of monastic anecdotes was converted into a publicist work by adding a judicious recommendation for monastic visitation and by composing an elaborate argument for a general subsidy for the Roman church. Viewed in this context, the revelations made in the chapter printed below are seen to be the crux of the entire work. Gerald must indeed have been sure of his story to have made it the keystone of his reform program, and thus we can accept it as authentic.

MS.—London, BL, MS. Cotton Tiberius B. xiii (siglum L in apparatus), which is badly damaged by fire at this passage (Liebermann; Brewer's ed., pp. vii, xi–xiii). On the manuscript and its history see Hunt, "Preface," pp. 189–193; he assigns the hand to "the early thirteenth century" (p. 191).

---

[1] Conc. Lateran. IV, c. 12 *In singulis regnis* (X 3.35.7), ed. A. García y García, *Constitutiones concilii quarti Lateranensis una cum commentariis glossatorum* (Vatican City, 1981), pp. 60–62. On the application of its provisions, see M. Maccarrone, *Studi su Innocenzo III* (Padua, 1972), pp. 246–262.

[2] *Speculum Ecclesiae* II.29, in *Opera*, IV, 93–94; a more accurate transcript in MGH, SS, XXVII, 418.

Ed.—(1) J. S. Brewer in *Giraldi Cambrensis Opera*, Rolls Series, no. 21, 8 vols. (London, 1861-1891), in vol. IV (1873), 1-354 (dist. 4, c. 19 at pp. 301-305). (2) The whole of c. 19 appears among the extracts from Gerald, ed. R. Pauli, with an improved text of Brewer's edition collated by F. Liebermann against the manuscript (L), in MGH, SS, XXVII (1885), 395-421; our passage (as printed below, with Pauli's apparatus) at pp. 419-421. (3) The first folios (1r–4v) ed. R. H. Hunt, "The Preface to the 'Speculum Ecclesiae' of Giraldus Cambrensis," *Viator*, VIII (1977), 189-213, at pp. 204-213. Brian Golding is preparing a new edition of the *Speculum Ecclesiae*.

Gerald: Select biobibliography.—J. Conway Davies, "Giraldus Cambrensis 1146-1946," *Archaeologia Cambrensis*, XCIX (1946-1947), 85-108, 256-280; Michael Richter, *Giraldus Cambrensis: The Growth of the Welsh Nation* (Aberystwyth, 1972); Robert Bartlett, *Gerald of Wales, 1146–1223* (Oxford, 1982); and Brynley F. Roberts, *Gerald of Wales*, Writers of Wales (Cardiff, 1982). F. M. Powicke's portrait conveys the spirit of the man and his age, but it is neither documented nor altogether accurate in detail: "Gerald of Wales," *Bulletin of the John Rylands Library*, XII (1928), 389-410, reprinted in his *Christian Life in the Middle Ages and Other Essays* (Oxford, 1935), pp. 107-129. For a psycholiterary approach, G. Misch, "Die autobiographische Schriftstellerei des Giraldus Cambrensis," in his *Geschichte der Autobiographie*, III.2 (Frankfurt a. M., 1962), 1297-1479. Michael Richter, "Gerald of Wales: A Reassessment on the 750th Anniversary of his Death," *Traditio*, XXIX (1973), 379-390. Gerald's story is best told at book length

---

DE ROMANI PRINCIPIS HENRICI NOSTRIS DIEBUS IMPERANTIS PROPOSITO[a] NOBILI, PER QUOD ET INOPIAM SEDIS ROMANE SUBLEVARE ET CUPIDITATIS NOTAM PURGARE PARABAT.

Propter has et similes suggillationes et insultationes curie sacre tam verbis quam scriptis minus discretis minusque circumspectis, salva tamen pace maiorum,[1] irrogatas Henricus, Fretherici filius, qui Sicilie regnum et Apulie Romano nostris diebus imperio potenter adiecit et ad pristinam subiectionem, mediante nimirum matrimoniali vinculo et plurimum ad hoc opitulante, revocavit, filiali pietate pariter et dilectione, materne satis laudabiliter in hoc compassus erumpne, nisibus totis ac studiis in hunc modum delere curavit.

[a] proposito] posito L

in his own words, however, or in H. E. Butler's admirable translation: *The Auto-biography of Giraldus Cambrensis* (London, 1937). Older scholarship is summarized by A. B. Emden, *A Biographical Register of the University of Oxford to A.D. 1500* (Oxford, 1957-1959), I, 117-118. For more recent bibliography, consult the biographies cited above; also *Dictionary of the Middle Ages*, V (1985), 420-421.

Speculum Ecclesiae.—Above all, see Hunt's edition of the preface, cited above. Brewer wasted thirty-two pages in a ponderous, mid-Victorian introduction to monkery (*Opera*, IV, xiii–xliv), which casts hardly a glimmer of light on the *Speculum*. For Gerald as a critic of monasticism, see rather D. Knowles, *The Monastic Order in England*, 2nd ed. (Cambridge, Eng., 1949), pp. 663-674; also Brian Golding, "Gerald of Wales and the Monks," *Thirteenth Century England*, V, ed. P. R. Coss and S. D. Lloyd (Woodridge, 1995), pp. 53-64. These studies pay little or no attention to distinction 4; only its c. 19 has been thoroughly monographed: V. Pfaff, *Kaiser Heinrichs VI. höchstes Angebot an die römische Kurie (1196)*, Heidelberger Abhandlungen zur mittleren und neueren Geschichte 55 (Heidelberg, 1927), pp. 1-83, citing earlier literature (pp. 38-39). The imperial-papal negotiations have since been studied in greater detail by G. Baaken, "Die Verhandlungen zwischen Kaiser Heinrich VI. und Papst Coelestin III. in den Jahren 1195-1197," *Deutsches Archiv für Erforschung des Mittelalters*, XXVII (1971), 457-513. The present notice is based on my article, "Gerald of Wales and the Fourth Lateran Council," *Viator*, XXIX (1998), 79-93.

THE PROPOSAL OF HENRY, THE ROMAN EMPEROR WHO RULED IN OUR TIME, BY WHICH HE WAS PREPARING BOTH TO RELIEVE THE ROMAN SEE'S POVERTY AND TO ELIMINATE ITS NOTORIOUS CUPIDITY.

In our time Frederick's son Henry added the kingdom of Sicily and Apulia to the Roman Empire and recalled that kingdom to its original subjection [to the Empire] with a show of strength that was certainly made possible and greatly aided by his marriage [to the heiress]. At this time mockery and insults were being inflicted on the papal curia, both in writing and by word of mouth, and they were becoming less discreet and less circumspect, though not directed against the very highest officials.[1] Moved equally by filial piety and affection, Henry laudably enough pitied the mother church's distress at this situation, and with every effort and thought he undertook to put an end to it in the following way.

1. Gerald has given examples in the chapter just before this one.

2 Videns enim et animadvertens, propter patrimonium beati Petri, tam a principibus, qui id tueri deberent, quam a ceteris, undique direptum et penitus indefensum, dictam aviditatis et avaritie notam ex summa penuria et rerum usualium inopia provenire, quia terras et opida prediaque perampla, a Constantino ecclesie collata et a decessoribus suis iniuriose sublata, restituere nec voluit nec alios per Ytaliam modernis diebus ad restituendum ablata universa propter ignaviam aut inpotentiam compellere valuit, saltem in ecclesiasticis et spiritualibus remediabile subsidium adhibere curavit. Considerans enim et mente revolvens, indecens valde et incongruum esse filias long lateque <per[b]> orbem fid<eliu>m terrenis opulentiis abundare, matremque tamen inopem et egenam existere, menbraque divitiis affluere deliciisque florere, capud autem utriusque carens tamquam aridum et marcidum penitusque fere desolationi datum, animo disposuit statuendumque firma ratione decrevit,

3 quatinus per imperii sui totius amplitudinem cunctis metropolitanis ecclesiis et singulis meliorem canonicam papa de cetero propriam haberet et iure perpetuo possideret necnon et in aliis ecclesiis pontificalibus, maioribus scilicet et opulentioribus, singulis singulas ad rerum temporalium copiam eidem honorifice ministrandam. Ad hoc etiam, ut in singulis ecclesiis simplicibus episcopalibus singulis cardinalibus iuxta gradus et ordinis dignitatem necnon et capellanis ac clericis in capella domini pape ministrantibus eiusque obsequiis iugiter assistentibus tot prebende tantique redditus annui specialiter assignarentur, quot quantique ad decus et decorem domus Domini basiliceque principalis et beati Petri cathedralis, quam Christus ipse gloriosam in terris tamquam sponsam suam pretioso sanguine suo redemptam et honorabilem in oculis hominum ac venerabilem esse volebat, ad plenum, ut decuit, sufficere possent.

4 Ad instar autem imperii cetera per orbem regna catholica, convocatis ad hoc consiliis universalibus, et persuasibilibus magnorum virorum eloquiis, ad generalem dicto beneficio consensum applicandum[c] firmoque munimine roborandum citra difficultatis omnis aut dilationis obstaculum, Domino desuper inspirante favorem, indici possent.

5 <O[d]> quam nobile factum quamque subtiliter atque salubriter excogitatum, si tamen felici fuisset effectui mancipatum, menbris nimirum minime gravatis aut nullum prorsus ob hoc in detrimentum datis, verum ex sociali tante celsitudinis solatio multum honoratis et emendatis, capite vero principali sum

---

[b] *codex enim multis locis incendio mutilatus est*
[c] aplic. *abbr.* L
[d] *litteras initiales scriba omisit ut variis coloribus exararentur*

2 Henry had observed that the notorious greed and avarice [of the Roman curia] was the result of extreme poverty and lack of the necessities of life, because the patrimony of St Peter had been plundered in every respect, both by the rulers who ought to defend it and by others, and it was wholly unprotected from them. Constantine had given the church lands and towns and estates that were more than ample, all of which had wrongfully been taken away by his successors, and Henry neither wished to restore them nor, either out of cowardice or lack of power, was he able to compel others throughout modern Italy to restore everything they had taken. Instead he wanted to remedy the situation by providing a subsidy derived from ecclesiastical and spiritual goods. For after giving the matter considerable thought, it seemed to him to be extremely unbecoming and unfitting that throughout the length and breadth of the Christian world daughter churches abounded in earthly opulence while their mother was poor and destitute; and that the members were affluent with riches and overflowing with delights, while the head lacked both of these and instead was, as it were, arid, drooping, and given over almost entirely to desolation. Therefore Henry made up his mind and, having good reason for his decision, he decided

3 that throughout his entire broad empire, the pope would in future have the best canonry in each and every metropolitan church and would possess it by perpetual right; moreover, that he would have the same from other pontifical churches, namely the greater and wealthier ones, so that each and every one would do the pope honor by contributing to his supply of temporal things. Similarly, in all the plain and simple episcopal churches, prebends and annual incomes would be specifically assigned to each of the cardinals according to their grade and order, and also to the chaplains and clerics who serve in the chapel of the lord pope and constantly assist in his services. As many prebends and as much income would be assigned as is needed for the honor and beauty of the principal house and basilica of the Lord and the cathedral of St Peter, which Christ himself wished to be glorious on earth as his bride redeemed by his precious blood and to be honorable and venerable in the eyes of men.

4 Following the example of the Empire, the other kingdoms of the Catholic world could be convoked for this purpose to universal councils and, inspired by the Lord, could be persuaded by the unanimous advice and eloquence of great men to give general consent to this beneficent plan, and they could make their decision public by a valid document that would establish it firmly against any obstacle of difficulty or delay.

5 If this plan had been brought to a successful conclusion, O what a noble deed, so subtly and usefully thought out, would have been done! Certainly the members would hardly be oppressed or even sustain any loss from this; indeed, they would be much honored and improved by joining together to give com-

moque menbrorum omnium vertice propter mundane opulentie pariter et excellentie gloriam tante maiestati, Deo disponente, dignam ac debitam decorato decenter et exornato. Porro dum princeps ad hoc propositum operis exhibitione complendum totis nisibus anelaret ad Urbem, matrem urbium omnium atque magistram, maturius ob hoc accelerando, infecto negotio tam utili quidem et tam honesto, omine sinistro quidem et infausto in ipsis viridis iuvente diebus et annis immaturis mortis intempestive morsu crudeli rebus, proh dolor! humanis exemptus est.

6 Mirum autem mentibus humanis forte videri posset, quod ecclesie Romane, cui gloriam in terris quandoque contulit inmensam, tantum decus eidem inminens et tamquam in ianuis iam existens pius et misericors Deus Deique filius sponse sue, quam ex mera gratia et incomparabili clementia redemit sibi quoque[e] proprio pretiosoque sanguine fuso comparavit, tamquam minus in hoc articulo misericors, subitis huiuscemodi casibus et inopinatis deperire permisit, nisi quoniam nichil in terris stabile, nichil umquam perdurabile divina potentia stabilivit. Verum res humanas omnes nunc ab imis ad summa, nunc a summis ad ima quasi iuxta rote volubilitatem vicissim aut scandere videas aut descendere sursumque rupi subito seu demitti. Nec dissimiliter, quia sors hominis varia firmoque gradu stare nescia semper adversis pervertit prospera, semper amaris miscet et mutat dulcia. Unde etsi diuturni[f] <. . .> valle lacrim<arum . . .>licitas, iuxta Sapienti<s eloqui>um: "Semper extrema gaudii luctus occupat."[2] Circumspecte nimirum ille, qui conspicit omnia quique suaviter et sapienter disponit universa, manuum suarum ordinavit opera sicque a supernis civibus celestique militia distinxit et discrevit hec infima,[g] ut ibi cuncta stabilia, cuncta iocunda cunctaque perpetua et fine carentia, hic e diverso cuncta labilia, cuncta lugubria cunctaque transitoria et exitum amarum finemque letalem et lamentabilem expectantia; quatinus a mundanis istis momentaneis et amaritudine plenis ad eterna bona et gaudio plena, ubi nichil amarum, nichil adversum, nichil varium, sed inmutabile, sed delectabile, sed perdurabile totum, totis viribus et nisibus mens humana consurgat. Et iuxta salutiferam Pauli doctrinam,[3] quia non habemus hic manentem civitatem neque mansionem diuturnam, futuram inquiramus et permanentem. Unde et metricos sapientis cuiusdam[4] versus hos, similem sententiam exprimentes, hic apponere preter rem non putavimus:

[e] sibi quoque] sibique *corr. Brewer*
[f] *iterum lacunae incendio ortae*
[g] hec infima] hic infirma *corr. Brewer*

fort to so great an eminence. On the other hand, the head, which is chief of all the members and their highest crown, would (God willing) be properly embellished and adorned by reason of the worthy and due glory of worldly wealth being joined to that of such an excellent majesty. Such a fine and useful plan was still incomplete, and in order to bring it to a conclusion through his own intervention, Henry was striving with all his might to get to the City, the mother and mistress of all cities, and hence was hurrying as fast as he could, when alas! by a stroke of bad luck he was cut off from things human by the untimely bite of cruel death while in the vigor of youth and not yet mature in years.

6 Perhaps it can seem astonishing to human minds that a compassionate and merciful God and the son of God would permit his bride, whom he redeemed for himself out of pure grace and incomparable clemency, and whom he also purchased by shedding his own precious blood, to be ruined by sudden and unexpected events of this sort just when so much honor was expected for, and (so to speak) had almost arrived at the gates of, the Roman church, on which God had from time to time conferred such immense glory on earth. The most likely explanation is that divine power ordained that nothing on earth should be stable, that nothing should ever endure. For you see all human affairs, like the turning of a wheel, are either rising from the bottom to the top, or falling from the top to the bottom, so that what has been lifted up is suddenly thrust down or shattered. Similarly, because human fortune is changeable and unable to remain the same for very long, it always perverts prosperity into adversity, and always mixes the bitter with the sweet. Hence felicity is not of long duration in this vale of tears, according to the saying of Solomon: "Mourning taketh hold of the end of joy."[2] Undoubtedly God, who sees all things simultaneously and who has disposed every thing wisely and agreeably, arranged the works of his hands circumspectly and thus distinguished and separated things here below from heavenly citizens and celestial soldiers. Accordingly, there in heaven all things are stable, delightful, and continuous without end; while here on earth, all things are unstable, mournful, transitory, and can expect a bitter end and a deadly and deplorable conclusion. Thus the human mind by all its powers and efforts can rise up from these momentary, mundane things full of bitterness to eternal goods and full joy, where there is nothing bitter, nothing disagreeable, nothing changing, but where everything is immutable, delectable, and everlasting. And according to the health-giving teaching of Paul, because we do not have an abiding city here or a lasting abode, let us seek a permanent one that is to come.[3] The same point has been made in the verses of a certain wise man,[4] which can appropriately be quoted here:

2. Proverbs xiv.13b (Douay-Rheims).
3. Hebrews xiii.14.
4. Actually Gerald himself: see his *Opera*, I, 354, ed. Brewer.

Semper adest homini quo pectoris ima gemiscant,
Ne possit plena pros<peritate fruit>.
<Gaudia> nunc <luctu, nunc mutat amara secun>dis,
Versans <humanas sors> inopina vices.
<Sola ve>nire solent et vix et sero secunda,
Et simul et subito semper amara fluunt.
Ergo, ubi nil varium, nil vanum nilve nocivum,
Sint ibi fixa tibi spes, amor atque fides.

7 Notandum hic quoque,[5] quod his ultimis diebus nostris in concilio Lateranensi a papa Innocentio III. magnifice celebrato, ab universis nempe fidelium
orbis finibus undique tam remotis quam propinquis cum diligentia multa convocato et prelatorum ecclesie maiorum, tam abbatum scilicet quam episcoporum, pre ceteris cunctis a tempore beati Petri consiliis fecundissimo, dictus papa
ad relevandam[h] Romane sedis inopiam vigilantem, ut fertur, curam adhibuit,
adeo ut de cunctis et singulis cathedralibus per orbem ecclesiis redditibus largi-
tione fidelium ample locupletatis decimam partem ecclesia Romana perciperet[i]
sibique in posterum irrefragabiliter appropriaret, totis nisibus elaboravit. Sed cleri
universi conciliique parte maiori et magis auctentica consensum ad hec nullatenus prestare volente, minus in hoc profecit nec desiderium suum iuxta
propositum et animi conceptum effectui mancipare prevaluit.

[h] relevandam] revelandam L
[i] perciperet] percipiet L

Document 41
THE PROPOSAL OF HONORIUS III
Super muros Jerusalem
28 January 1225

Honorius' request for prebends was never enregistered; none of the actual bulls
dispatched have survived, but the text is known from contemporary copies made
of the letters addressed to the French and English prelates. The French version
was copied only once, on the flyleaf of a canonistic collection (Av); the English
one was twice transcribed in the Salisbury register (Sa and Sb) and also inserted
into the annal for 1225 that was added to a chronicle written at Crowland Abbey
and which survives in three manuscripts (ACM). Despite the absence of both a

When a man groans from the bottom of his heart,
The possibility of enjoying full prosperity is always present.
Now joy changes to mourning, now bitterness to prosperity,
As human fortune alternates unexpectedly.
Good things are apt to come reluctantly and too late,
While troubles always come suddenly and all together.
Therefore fix your faith, hope, and charity there
Where nothing is harmful, changeable, or in vain.

7 It is also to be noted here[5] that just recently Pope Innocent III magnificently celebrated a Lateran council to which with much diligence he convoked the Church's greater prelates, namely both abbots and bishops, who came from everywhere in the Christian world, both far and near. It was the most fruitful council held since the time of St Peter. It is reported that said pope took vigilant care to relieve the poverty of the Roman see; he made every effort to elaborate a plan for that purpose, namely that the Roman church would collect and irrevocably appropriate to itself for the future a tenth part of the revenues of each and every cathedral church throughout the world, which had come from the abundant donations of the faithful. But because all the clergy and the part of the council that was larger and of greater authority were by no means willing to consent to these things, he made little progress in the matter and was not able to carry into effect his plan as he had conceived and proposed it.

5. Gerald inserted a similar note in *Speculum Ecclesiae* II.29.

Vatican register copy and sealed originals, there seems little reason to question the authenticity of the copies. As is well known, the papal registers included only those letters that would be required for future reference. Apparently, by the time the register for Honorius' ninth year was compiled, the curia recognized that the scheme was dead once and for all, so no record of it was kept. In consequence, we cannot determine from the chancery record whether copies *in eodem modo* were, as the *Relatio* has Romanus suppose (Doc. 1.17), also transmitted to Spain and the Empire.

Of the extant copies, none could with any likelihood have been transcribed directly from the bull itself, for neither the annalist's Fenland monastery nor the Salisbury chapter, nor even Mont–St–Michel, would possess the authentic original of the bull brought from Rome. Rather, the text would have been diffused in each nation by the legate or nuncio from his exemplar. We cannot be sure that official copies were ever distributed in France. The French proctors at Bourges knew the proposal only as a rumor until Romanus produced the letter (Doc. 1.7-8), and as the bull was addressed only to the prelates of the French church, the chapters may not have received copies even then. Transcripts were almost certainly provided for the representatives of the English chapters, however, so that each of them might consider the proposal and return a reply in May 1226 (Doc. 42.3). Thus we may fairly assume that our English manuscripts were at best copied from the transcripts borne home by the proctors, or perhaps from copies supplied by the nuncio to the prelates to whom the letter was in fact addressed (see figure 3).

Which copy is best? Consequently, it is not surprising that the English copies present a better text than the French one. The Mont-St-Michel manuscript (Av) contains some obvious blunders: for example, it omits an important qualification: "ad commodum *animarum*" (§ 1, var. j), turns bad-talking tongues into big-talking ones (§ 2, v), and reads *ville* where the context clearly calls for papal *bulle* (§ 5, k)).

    The English tradition is evidently better than the French, but the editor must still decide which of the three English versions is best to use as the base text. In fact, any one of them would do, for all three traditions are fairly accurate, but I have preferred that of the "Barnwell" chronicle (A) because its scribe was sparing of abbreviations and his work was carefully corrected (though these and other corrections are usually not recorded in the variants). Altogether, AMC disagree with the consensus AvSaSb only six times, and except for an accidentally omitted passage (§ 6, var. t), the differences are minor. Moreover, A presents only four peculiar readings, i.e. scribal errors (§ 1, i and o; § 3, t; § 4, x)). By contrast, the Salisbury register copies have less to recommend either of them. They both derive from a common exemplar (Sigma), as is evident from the five instances when Sa and Sb agree against AAvCM. Sigma was a slightly less reliable copy than A, reading, for example, *quod* for *quid* three times (§ 2, s–u), *magni* for *un-amini* in a stock phrase (§ 3, s), and *moneat* for *moveat* (§ 7, h). Moreover, each Salisbury scribe departed frequently from his exemplar (see readings of Sa or Sb alone in the *apparatus criticus*), so neither offers as accurate a base text as A.

MSS.—(A) London, College of Arms, MS. Arundel 10, fol. 104ra–vb: England, saec. xiii. The so-called "Barnwell" chronicle, of which this is the only manuscript, incorporated the full text of *Super muros* in its continuation of the Crowland chronicle's annal for 1225. See Doc. 44.2 for the context; also the prolegomena there for bibliography on the Barnwell chronicle and its subsequent use by Walter of Coventry (C).

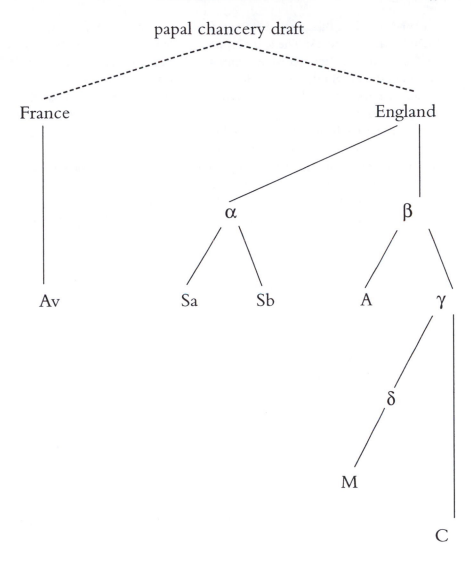

papal chancery draft

France

England

α

β

Av

Sa

Sb

A

γ

δ

M

C

A = London, College of Arms, MS. Arundel 10 ("Barnwell" chronicle)
Av = Avranches, Bibl. mun., MS. 149 (Mont-St-Michel)
C = Cambridge, Corpus Christi College, MS. 175 ("Walter of Coventry")
M = Magdalen College, Oxford, MS. lat. 36
S = Trowbridge, Wiltshire Co. Record Office, D 1/1/1 (2 copies in Salisbury Register)

FIGURE 3. Stemma of *Super muros Jerusalem*

(Av) Avranches, Bibl. mun., MS. 149, fol. 110rb: Mont-St-Michel, saec. xiii (bibliography at Doc. 28). The letter is one of eighteen items copied by various hands on two folios (109r–110v) of a quire that had been left blank after the conclusion of the canonistic *Collectio Abrincensis* (fols. 79r–109ra), on which see S. Kuttner, *Repertorium der Kanonistik (1140–1234)*, Studi e testi, 71 (Vatican City, 1937), pp. 299, 467. The next quire begins with the glossed text of *Digest* 50.16 in a format distinctly different from the long double columns of our quire. Thus it appears that fol. 110 was at one time the last leaf in a work bound separately. In a column of 63 lines, the text of *Super muros* fills the first 51. The same hand completed the column with an extract "Ex Registro Jnnocentii secundi" and may also have written, in smaller characters, the preceding item, a letter from Gregory I to Augustine of Canterbury. These letters immediately adjacent to *Super muros* illustrate the miscellaneous nature of the addenda to the *Collectio Abrincensis*. Most are papal letters concerning Normandy or England, including two related to Romanus' legation (Docs. 52 and 53).

(C) Cambridge, Corpus Christi College, MS. 175, fols. 164r–165v (175 by mistake): England, ca. 1300. Walter of Coventry's copy of the continuation of the Crowland annal for 1225, to which has been added a paragraph for 1226 (also in M but not A). See Doc. 44 for details.

(M) Oxford, Magdalen College, MS. lat. 36, fol. 196r–v: ca. 1270. Like A and C, a copy of the continuation of the Crowland annal for 1225, plus a paragraph for 1226 (as in C). See Doc. 44 for details.

(S) Trowbridge, Wiltshire County Record Office, D 1/1/1, *olim* Salisbury Diocesan Registry: MS. Vetus registrum ecclesie Sarum ("The Register of St. Osmund"), two copies of Doc. 41: (Sa) in 1226 at MS. pp. 108b–109b = fols.

H onorius[a] episcopus, servus servorum Dei,[b] venerabilibus fratribus archiepis-copis et[c] episcopis et dilectis filiis universis ecclesiarum prelatis per regnum Anglie[d] constitutis, salutem et apostolicam benedictionem.

1 Super muros Jerusalem custodes positi, quanto eminentiorum speculam dignitatis ascendimus,[e] tanto imminentiori[f] debito sollicitamur officii ut vigi-lanti custodia nobis et aliis vigilemus—nobis quoque[g] per meritum, aliis per ex-

---

[a]*littera initialis om.* M, *suppl. marg.* M[1]   [b]episcopus—Dei] etc. Av   [c]et *om.* CM
[d]Francie Av   [e]attendimus Av   [f]in eminentiori Av   [g]quoque] quidem Sb

54vb–55rb, double columns, in a hand different from the entries preceding and following this item; (Sb) in 1229 at MS. pp. 137-138 = fol. 69r–v, on long lines in a bookhand. See Doc. 42 for an analysis of the two passages and their context (Sa = § 1, Sb = § 6).

Ed.—(1) From Av: Martène-Durand, *Thesaurus*, I (1717), 929-931, "Ex ms. sancti Michaëlis in periculo maris" (not always accurate; see *app. crit.*, below). Reprinted by Mansi, *Supplementum*, II (1748), 922; thence into Mansi, XXII (1778), 1217-1220. Also reprinted in the bullaria: *Bullarum, privilegiorum ac diplomatum Romanorum pontificum amplissima collectio*, ed. C. Cocquelines, III.i (Rome, 1740), 238-239, no. 75; thence in *Bullarum, diplomatum et privilegiorum sanctorum Romanorum pontificum Taurinensis editio*, III (Turin, 1858), 404, no. 75. Another reprint with emendations in *Rec. hist. Gaules*, XIX (1833, reprinted 1880), 763-764; whence Horoy, IV (1880), 766-769, no. 66. (2) From Sb: D. Wilkins, *Concilia Magnae Britanniae et Hiberniae* (London, 1737), I, 558-559. (3) From C (A and M collated): *Memoriale fratris Walteri de Coventria*, ed. W. Stubbs, Rolls Series, no. 58, 2 vols. (London, 1872-1873), II, 274-276. (4) From Sa: *Vetus registrum Sarisberiense alias dictum Registrum s. Osmundi episcopi; The Register of St. Osmund*, ed. W. H. Rich Jones, Rolls Series, no. 78, 2 vols. (London, 1883-1884), I, 366-369, with a reference to the Sb-text at II, 45. The transcription is occasionally faulty.

Refs.—Potthast, nos. 7349 (France) and 7350 (England). Pressutti, nos. 5284-5285. Böhmer-Ficker-Winkelmann, *Regesta Imperii*, V (1892), no. 6598. Powicke-Cheney, *Councils & Synods*, II.i (Oxford, 1964), 155, n. 1.

Honorius, bishop, servant of the servants of God, to the venerable brothers the archbishops and bishops, and to all the beloved sons the prelates, of the churches located in the kingdom of England, greeting and apostolic blessing.

1 Placed as watchmen on the walls of Jerusalem, the higher we climb up the watchtower of hierarchy, the more anxious we are about the ever more imposing responsibilities of office. We must keep vigilant watch over the watchman, both for ourselves and for others. We do this for ourselves for the sake of merit, so that the purity of our conscience may be maintained in the sight of God the most high; for others we do it for the sake of example, so that our reputation

emplum—quatinus[h] in conspectu altissimi conscientie puritas conservetur et in facie proximi[i] fame integritas non ledatur. Multum enim cedit ad commodum animarum[j] ut et[k] conscientiam fama non deserat et famam conscientia contemptui[l] non exponat. Sed potius mutuis promoveantur suffragiis et mutuis sibi promotionibus suffragentur, propter quod in vestibus Aaron mala punica cum tintinnabulis dependebant.[1] Porro dum attentius[m] quid honus honoris exposcat, quid sarcina dignitatis[n] desideret,[o] multa nos[p] cura sollicitat, multe[q] sollicitudinis urgemur instantia qualiter Deo satisfaciamus et homini, et si non ut volumus et debemus, saltem pro ut permittimur et valemus.

2 Sane multos multotiens et audivimus et vidimus murmurantes[r] propter expensas quas venientes ad sedem apostolicam faciebant. Scimus autem quid[s] ex talibus inferebat presumptio detractorum, quid[t] labia dolosa, quid[u] lingua mali loqua[v] presumebant, cum nonnulli[w] sermones in publico[x] molientes[y] et inmittentes[z] periculosius[a] jacula in occulto, Romanam mordere niterentur[b] ecclesiam,[c] parati non solum ea que rigor[d] justitie sed etiam que judicium equitatis nec non[e] benignitatis gratie[f] consummabat, suis oblocutionibus[g] depravare, presertim apud eos qui aures prurientes habebant[2] et gratis[h] erectas ad malum. Illos quoque in talibus experti sumus frequenter[i] offendere[j] qui missi procurare negotia, dum ea que illis ad necessarias deputabantur expensas suis voluptatibus applicabant, ad miserabile mendacii subsidium[k] recurrentes, alienis manibus[l] impingebant que[m] proprie defraudaverant.[n]

3 Quia vero in hiis[o] contra sedem apostolicam detractoribus[p] obrepebat occasio, et ecclesiis ecclesiarumque[q] prelatis nec non et aliis videbatur imminere gravamen, cum fratribus nostris diligentem[r] curavimus habere tractatum quo studio, qua cautela secundum Deum et hominem inveniremus in talibus salubrem provisionis effectum; et tandem, pro ut Domino placuit, communi et unanimi[s] deliberatione consilii, rem non novam nec inexcogitatam[3] a predecessoribus nos-

---

[h]quatinus] quamvis Sa   [i]proximi CMSaSb: proxime A, proprie Av   [j]animarum *om.* Av   [k]ut et *tr.* Sa   [l]contempni Av   [m]attendimus Av   [n]dignitatum Av [o]desiderat A   [p]nos *om.* Sa   [q]multe] multe nos Av   [r]murmurantis Sb   [s]quid Av: quod A, *corr.* quid A[1]; quod CMSaSb   [t]quid AAv: quod CMSaSb   [u]quid AAv: et quod CMSa, et Sb   [v]maliloqua ACMSb: magniloca Av, magniloqua *scripsit Martène (deinde Stubbs!),* magnililoqua Sa, *corr.* Sa[1]   [w]nonnullos Sb   [x]in publico ACMSaSb *et Martène:* impublico Av   [y]molientes] monstrantes Av   [z]inmittentes] mittentes Av   [a]periculosius *om.* Sa   [b]mordere niterentur *tr.* Av   [c]niterentur ecclesiam *tr.* CM   [d]rigor] vigor *Martène*   [e]nec non] et *add.* C   [f]et gratie Sb, gratia Av   [g]loquutionibus Av   [h]gratis et Sa, graves et Av   [i]frequenter *post* talibus Av   [j]ostendere Av   [k]mendacii subsidium *tr.* Av   [l]manibus] manibus *cancell. et* moribus *suppl. marg.* Av[1], *et sic leg. Martène*   [m]que] quod Av   [n]defraudarant ASaSb   [o]hiis] que *add.* CM   [p]detractionis Av   [q]ecclesiarum Av, *praem. et supra lin.* Av[1]   [r]diligenter Av   [s]magni SaSb

may be unblemished in the view of the neighbors. For one of our chief concerns is the benefit of souls, so that reputation should not neglect conscience and conscience should not expose reputation to contempt. But instead they should be promoted by supporting one another and supported by promoting one another, because on Aaron's vestments pomegranates alternated with bells.[1] Furthermore, much care makes us anxious because we are aware of what the weight of honor demands, what the burden of office requires, and we are urged by the pressure of great anxiety to find the means whereby we can satisfy both God and man, and if not as we wish and ought, at least as we are permitted and are able.

2 To be sure we have frequently heard and seen many who grumble about the expenses incurred by those who come to the apostolic see. However, we know that much of this grumbling is inspired by the arrogance of detractors and by the presumption of deceitful lips and evil tongues, since there are some who are trying to wound the Roman church by casting dangerous darts in private, although in public they utter more soft and pleasant words. By their reproaches, they are always ready to misrepresent not only those judgments that are based on strict justice but also those that are tempered with equity, generosity, and grace; they appeal especially to those whose ears itch[2] to hear evil whether it is justified or not. In our experience, such grumbling frequently also comes from those representatives who are sent to the curia on business; the money entrusted to them for their necessary expenses, they spend on luxuries, and then they justify their expenditures by a pathetic lie, claiming that what they themselves have embezzled was paid to someone else at the curia.

3 Because an astute stratagem is required to deal with these detractors of the apostolic see, and because a complaint from churches and their prelates, and also from others, seems to be imminent, we have taken the trouble to discuss diligently with our brothers [the cardinals] how we might discover an effective remedy for such grumbling that would be agreeable to God and man. At last it has pleased God that, after deliberating together and agreeing unanimously, we have adopted a proposal that is neither new nor unknown[3] to our predeces-

1. According to Exodus xxviii.33–35, embroidered pomegranates and golden bells alternated on the border of the high priest's ephod, which was first worn by Aaron.
2. II Tim. iv.3.
3. Cf. *Codex Justinianus* 3.1.14: "Rem non novam neque insolitam. . . . "

tris sumus aggressi, volentes quod illi salubri consilio providerunt[t] efficaci opere consummare, videlicet:

4 ut ad opus sedis apostolice in singulis cathedralibus ecclesiis et aliis prebendalibus, prebende singule[u] reserventur,[v] et interim donec id fiat, competentes in eisdem[w] redditus assignentur.[x] In monasteriis vero et ceteris regularibus domibus[y] ac[z] collegiatis ecclesiis, nec non de bonis episcoporum, secundum facultates suas constituantur certi redditus pro prebendis,[a]

5 quorum proventus in commune recepti, tam in nostras quam in[b] fratrum nostrorum necessitates, nec non capellanorum,[c] cancellarie,[d] hostiariorum, aliorumque sedis apostolice officialium convertantur[e] ut sic provideatur[f] nostris in vite necessariis et gratis omnibus omnia pro quibuscumque negotiis venientibus[g] ministrentur, nec sit qui per se vel[h] alium expresse vel aliquid tacite[i] exigat, vel etiam oblata sponte[j] recipiat, preter bulle[k] redditum consuetum. Quod si quis Gieziticus[l,4] tante cupiditati animum[m] audebit exponere, quod contra prohibitionis nostre rigorem manus ad munus quantumcumque gratuitum presumat extendere,[n] tante pene duritie subjacebit quod preter publice confusionis obprobrium, culpam in pena cognoscet.

6 Quis igitur frater gratie, quis devotionis filius, quis Sponsi et sponse dilectus, ad[o] hujusmodi statum ecclesie consilio et auxilio non assurget? An non licet, non decet, non expedit ut sic filie dexteram[p] porrigant ad subsidia matris que occupationibus[q] multis et magnis involvitur pro necessitatibus filiarum?[r] Nonne id[s] quam plures ecclesiarum prelati magnique testimonii viri tempore generalis concilii suadebant? Nonne ad id toto videbantur desiderio aspirare? Tunc tamen sedes apostolica distulit, ne videretur ad hoc concilium evocasse.[t]

7 Ne igitur tam pii, tam[u] sancti propositi consumatio retardetur, per quod[v] multum[w] crescere poterit decor ecclesie Dei multaque subtrahi occasio detrahendi, universitatem vestram monemus, rogamus et exortamur[x] in Domino per apostolica scripta vobis mandantes quatinus ad executionem provisionis hujusmodi[y] tam in cathedralibus quam aliis,[z] ut dictum est, ecclesiis[a] impendatis[b] sic[c]

---

[t]providerunt CMSaSb: providerant A, providerent Av   [u]prebende singule tr. Av   [v]reserventur AvSaSb: serventur ACM   [w]eis Av   [x]assignetur A   [y]regularibus domibus tr. Av   [z]ac aliis Av   [a]pro prebendis] prebendas Av, add. tacite aequantes Martène   [b]in om. Av   [c]capellorum nec non Av   [d]cancellariorum ACM   [e]convertatur ASaSb [f]et provideantur Av   [g]negotiis venientibus tr. Av   [h]per add. AvCM   [i]aliquid tacite tr. AvCM   [j]sponte ablata tr. Av, oblata corr. Av[1]   [k]bulle] ville Av   [l]Gieziticus ACSa: Gyeziticus M, Gyeziacus AvSb   [m]animam Av, aîm CM   [n]quod contra—presumat extendere] om. Av   [o]ad Av] et substit. Martène   [p]dextram Av   [q]preocupationibus ACM [r]filiorum Av   [s]idem ACM   [t]convocasse SaSb; Nonne ad id—concilium evocasse om. ACM   [u]pii tam om. ACM   [v]quod om. CM   [w]multum om. Av   [x]hortamur SaSb [y]hujusmodi] huius SaSb   [z]in aliis AvCM   [a]ecclesiis post aliis tr. Av   [b]impendentes Av   [c]sic] sic et SaSb

sors, and it is our wish that the beneficial plan that they worked out can now be put into effect.

4 The plan is this: In each and every cathedral church, and in any other church that has prebends, one prebend is to be set aside for the use of the apostolic see. And in the meantime, until this arrangement can be implemented, the income from these prebends is to be assigned to duly qualified persons. However, [in cases where there are no prebends, namely] in monasteries and other houses living under a rule, and in collegiate churches, and also from the goods of bishops, instead of a prebend a given part of the income is to be set aside for this purpose, the amount of which is to be determined by the resources available.

5 The proceeds are to be paid into a common fund that will be used to pay for both our necessary expenses and those of our brothers [the cardinals], as well as those of chaplains, chancery officials, doorkeepers, and other officials of the apostolic see. Thus the necessities of life would be provided for us and all services would be performed gratis for everyone coming on any kind of business. Except for the customary payment for the bull, no one would demand anything either for himself or for anyone else, either expressly or in any way tacitly, and no one would even receive anything that was offered spontaneously, except the customary payment for the bull. If anyone, like Giezi,[4] should dare to display a soul of such greed that, contrary to our stern prohibition, he would presume to extend his hand for a gratuitous reward of any kind, he shall be subjected to such harsh punishments that he will recognize how wrong he was not only by the shame of public humiliation but also by the punishment itself.

6 Therefore what friendly brother, what devout son, what beloved of the Bridegroom and the bride would not improve the condition of the Church by his counsel and aid? Is it not legitimate, proper, and expedient that the daughters lend a hand to aid their mother, who is preoccupied with providing for the daughters' necessities in many and important ways? At the time of the general council did not a great many ecclesiastical prelates and men of great reputation favor this plan? Were they not seen to long for it as their heart's desire? At that time, however, the apostolic see deferred the proposal lest it seem that the council had been called for that purpose.

7 The implementation of such a pious and holy proposal should not be delayed any longer, since through it the decorum of God's Church can be much increased and many an opportunity for disparaging remarks can be removed. Therefore we advise, ask, and exhort all of you in the Lord by apostolic writ or-

4. The prophet Elisha's servant Giezi (AV Gehazi) enriched himself by seeking and receiving payment for a cure effected by his master; as punishment, he was afflicted with leprosy: IV Kings v.20-27. The form *Giezeticus* ("simoniac") is attested from England ca. 1143 (Latham).

opem^d et^e operam efficacem quod interprete facto monstretur quantum vos domus Domini^f decor alliciat, quantum Sponsi et sponse amor accendat, quantum^g multorum relevatio moveat,^h quantumque^i utilitas generalis inducat.

8 Ceterum cum ad relevanda ecclesiarum onera et prelatorum gravamina^j pro ut possumus intendamus, de prebendis clericis Romanis, vel ab apostolica sede^k concessis duximus^l providendum ut postquam fuerint predicta^m completa, cum eas^n vacare contigerit, ad proprias ecclesias revertantur, ne si successive conferantur extraneis, sicut aliquando consuevit, filiis ecclesiarum qui continuo servitio resident redderentur inutiles^o et utilitate^p quodammodo^q fierent aliene.

Datum Laterani v^o kal. Februarii, pontificatus nostri anno nono.^r

^d opem ACM: operem Sa, opere AvSb   ^e et Av] ut *substit. Martène*   ^f domus Dei vos Av, domus domini vos CM   ^g quantam Av, quantum *emend. Martène*   ^h moveat ACM: moneat AvSaSb   ^i quantumque SaSb: quantamque Av, quantumque *emend. Martène*, quantum ACM   ^j prelatorum gravamina *tr.* AvSa   ^k aliis ab sede apostolica Av   ^l concedendum *add. et expunct.* C   ^m supradicta Av   ^n eas AMSaSb: ea C, eos Av   ^o in utiles Av   ^p voluntate Av   ^q quo ad minus ACM   ^r ix. A, ix^o. Sb

---

Document 42
THE SALISBURY REGISTER
Entries made in 1226 and 1229

MS.—Trowbridge, Wiltshire County Record Office, D 1/1/1, *olim* Salisbury Diocesan Registry: MS. Vetus registrum ecclesie Sarum ("The Register of St Osmund"), 263 × 182/190 mm. Two passages: (Sa) § 1-4 at MS. fols. 54vb–55vb = pp. 108b–110b; (Sb) § 5-13 at fols. 68v–71r = pp. 136-141. By accident, the leaf of pages 139/140 was passed over in the medieval foliation, which Wordsworth recovered chemically, so the four leaves now paged 135-142 were once foliated: lxviij, lxix, (lxix *bis*), lxx. The Rolls edition closed that gap (old fol. lxix *bis* = ed. fol. 70), and consequently from fol. 70 onwards, its citations are one number ahead. For convenient reference, I shall cite by the Rolls system.

This volume deserves a thorough codicological analysis. The Rolls editor left no physical description of the codex and drew no conclusions from the arrangement of the quires and their contents. When the manuscript was rebound in 1896, Christopher Wordsworth drew up a diagrammatic "anatomy," as he called it, which is now inserted in the volume itself. The following observations are

dering that you devote such influence and effective effort to carrying out this program, both in cathedral churches and in the others mentioned above, that it will be evident from the result how much you care for the decorum of the Lord's house, how much the love of the Bridegroom and bride excites you, how much the prospect of lifting of many burdens motivates you, and how much the common welfare persuades you.

8 Moreover, since we intend to relieve churches of their burdens and to remedy the complaints of prelates as much as we can, we have made a new regulation concerning prebends granted to Roman clerics or by the apostolic see: after the aforesaid program has been implemented, when such prebends happen to become vacant, they shall revert to their own churches. Otherwise, if they were conferred on a succession of foreigners, as has sometimes been the practice, they would be rendered useless to the sons of the churches who reside there to provide continuous service and, with respect to their usefulness, such prebends would become, so to speak, alienated.

Given at the Lateran on the fifth day before the kalends of February, in the ninth year of our pontificate.

---

based on that analysis and my own examination of the manuscript in 1984. They should suffice to place our document in context and may also serve to renew interest in the mysteries of this complex codex.

(Sa) The first of our passages occurs in a quire that was conceived as an independent unit and was probably at one time a separate brochure. It is a quaternion, lettered H in Wordsworth's collation (MS. fols. 48-55 = pp. 95-110; ed., I, 337-370). Quire H was begun as a transcript of the charters in the custody of the chapter's chamberlain, excepting those stored in the treasury, as the initial title indicates: "Transcripta cartarum ecclesie de Hegtredebyrie et prebende Sarum, que apud camerarium sunt, preter eas que in Thesauro Sar'." The first eleven pages of the quire are filled with documents concerning prebendal churches of the chapter. Most date from the twelfth century but several from 1219 provide the *terminus post quem*, since another dated 1262 is a later addition. This series took up only two-thirds of the quire, ending on fol. 53r; five pages remained blank.

In the course of the 1220s, this space was filled with copies of papal bulls and related letters, which form four distinct groups. (i) Fols. 53v–54r were written on long lines, as had been the practice of the original scribe. The first document, a 1214 bull of Innocent III confirming John's concession of free elections to the English church (53v = p. 106), is the only entry with no apparent relation to prebends, which is the general subject of the quire. It is followed by "Transcripta privilegiorum abbatis de Abendon contra ecclesiam Sarum" (54r = p. 107), namely four letters of Honorius III, all dated 1224, which confirm certain exemptions from diocesan jurisdiction. Appended is the abbot's statement that he believes the terms have for the most part been observed in the diocese of Salisbury. These Abingdon documents seem to have been placed here because they concern rights due to Salisbury prebendal churches from the lands held by the abbey in the diocese.

(ii) Fols. 54va–55rb (pp. 108a–109b) contain three more letters from Honorius, written in double columns, the format that is used for the remaining pages of the quire. The first two (1224, 1219) concern the common fund (*communa*) of the resident canons; the third is *Super muros* itself (Doc. 41 = Doc. 42.1), which is written in a slightly different hand from the two others (fols. 54vb–55rb = pp. 108b–109b). All three are explicitly concerned with the chapter's prebends, and consequently they found a place in this particular quire, even though the first and last also appear elsewhere in the register.

(iii) On fols. 55rb–vb (pp. 109b–110b) yet another hand added four letters transmitted by the bishop to his chapter, which form an appendix to *Super muros*. Two are citations to hear the nuncio make the proposal in January 1226 and to give him a reply in May; the others are from the nuncio himself, who demanded therein his procuration money and a list of would-be pluralists (Doc. 42.2-4).

(iv) Just enough room was left on the last column of the quire (55vb = p. 110b) for a later hand to add an undated note on pasture rights disputed between an abbot and a rector.

From the foregoing description, we may surmise that *Super muros* was included in quire H because the subject of that cartulary quaternion, which originally had been charters concerning prebendal churches, had by extension become documents touching any aspect of prebendal income. Two accessory factors may also have attracted it thither. The quire already contained four letters from Honorius that had recently been copied there, and the scribe now had three more. Why not keep them all together? The space was available and the subject compatible with the existing contents. After *Super muros* had been entered, it in turn attracted the next entry because two of the bishop's letters concerned that bull. There was some justification for keeping Poore's letters together because all concerned Otto's nunciature as well as the chapter's income. No single principle of classification predominated: one consideration might govern the grouping of letters into a batch and quite another would determine where that group was to be enregistered. Subject, author, or date could form the basis for association. Thus the original plan of the collection was soon submerged in a cluster of interlocking associations, which in practice probably facilitated data retrieval by providing multiple avenues of approach.

(Sb) The context of the second passage is apparent even in the printed edition. Sb forms part of the series of annals for the years 1217-1228, which fills quires KL (fols. 60r–80v = pp. 119-160; ed., II, 3-105). The text, written in a careful bookhand on long lines, is divided into sections, each introduced by its *paragraphus*. A typical annal begins "Anno gratie MCCXVIII°" and subsequent entries open with the formula "Eodem anno." In short, the work was cast in the characteristic format of contemporary annalistic chronicles. The content also is more proper to a chronicle than to a cartulary or formulary. The compiler conceived his work as a record of the great events in the life of his chapter, and accordingly the documents he inserted were chosen for their historic interest. Commonplace charters needed only for legal reference were relegated to other quires of the Salisbury Register; this section served another purpose, and in truth may at one time have been bound separately. That at least would seem to be the inference from the fact that when the manuscript was rebound in 1896, Wordsworth noted a series of binder's signatures i–ix for quires A–J, which did not continue through the remaining quires K–N.

The title *Historia translationis veteris ecclesiae beatae Mariae Sarum ad novam*, which Rich Jones adapted from a marginal note to the first entry (ed., II, 3, n.) and used to describe the contents of quires KLM as a whole, properly belongs only to the early annals. The chronicle as a whole might better be entitled, "The New Salisbury Annals," for the series seems to have been conceived as a continuing record of a new era in the history of Salisbury. The turning point unquestionably was the relocation of the see, but since diocesan history was traditionally divided according to episcopates, the chronicle of New Sarum was begun with the arrival of her builder, Bishop Richard Poore, in 1217. Because the series closes abruptly with his departure in 1228, it might be argued that his pontificate is the true subject of the work, but far from being the hero of the story, the bishop stands remote from the narrative, which is told from the canons' point of view.

The first annal describes Richard's translation from Chichester; his building program fills the opening pages of Annus 1218; but towards the end of that annal the chronicle undergoes a significant change. With the first use of the *eodem anno* formula, the narrative abruptly shifts from the bishop and his building to a series of miscellaneous entries. Only at this point does the annalistic character of the work emerge. The reason for this mutation is not hard to guess, for the first of the annalistic entries records how William de Wanda became a canon of Salisbury—the very man whom Rich Jones quite plausibly identified as the author of these annals (II, x). Patently they begin in earnest with Wanda's arrival; by way of prologue he seems to have included those earlier events that were necessary for an understanding of his times.

The chronicle begins with the first leaf of quire K (fol. 6or = p. 119); it is interrupted by the insertion of several recycled leaves in other hands (fols. 63-66 = pp. 125-132) and resumed again, in Wanda's hand, with the annal for 1225, continuing through 1228 and all of quire L (fols. 67r–80v = pp. 133-160). In short, Doc. 42.5-13 (= Sb) comes from Wanda's annals for 1225 and 1226.

Although the register still presents many problems of codicogenesis, enough has been said to provide a context for the Sb version of the *Super muros* affair, which in fact marks a shift of interest on the part of the compiler. The building of the new cathedral had been the focus of the earlier annals, but when the narrative resumes in 1225, after recounting the first service in the church, the annalist straightaway found a new theme in taxation and representation, which remained uppermost through the next nine folios (67v–75v), for no sooner was the threat of *Super muros* met than the chapters were asked for a royal subsidy, the sixteenth of 1226, and before the year was out, a papal subsidy as well. The fiscal theme was no *idée fixe* but simply reflected the changing concerns of the chapter, which in 1227 occupied itself with less momentous matters, while in the year following events took a new turn with the canonization of Osmund, the translation of Richard Poore to Durham, and the selection of his successor. Indeed, at 1228 the chronicle loses its annalistic character in a profusion of documents concerning the induction of Bishop Bingham, to which quire M forms an appendix.

Therefore Sb appears in a series of annals 1225-1228 that were probably composed in 1229, while Sa comprises the ante- and penultimate entries in a cartulary quaternion, which were probably transcribed at some time in 1226. A date not far removed from the events is indicated by the fact that a marginal annotator could recall when the citations had been received (§ 2-3). As a base text for those sections that both passages have in common, Sa is to be preferred because the transcript is earlier and hence presumably closer to the original. Furthermore, the Salisbury annalist did not hesitate to improve on the style of his original and, as may be seen in the variants, in one instance he blundered egregiously (§ 3, var. o, *non exempti* for *exempti*). Both previous critical editions, by Major and Cheney, have also preferred Sa, although their reasons are not stated. Despite its inferior textual authority, the Salisbury chronicle is nonetheless an invaluable source for its unique reports.

Ed.—(1) Wilkins, *Concilia*, I (1737), 558-559: § 5-7, 10, 13. (2) W. H. Rich Jones, *Vetus registrum Sarisberiense alias dictum Registrum s. Osmundi episcopi; The Register of St. Osmund*, Rolls Series, no. 78, 2 vols. (London, 1883-1884): Sa at I, 366-373; Sb at II, 45-54. (3) K. Major, *Acta Stephani Langton Cantuariensis archiepiscopi, A. D. 1207–1228*, Canterbury and York Society, 50 (Oxford, 1950), p. 99, no. 79 (§ 2, "Stephanus . . . memorato" with vars. from § 8) and p. 102, no. 83 (§ 3, "Stephanus . . . Augustini Cantuariensis" with vars. from § 9). (4) Powicke-Cheney, *Councils & Synods*, II.i, 156-158: § 2 as no. i without vars. from § 8; § 3 as no. iii, emended once from § 9; § 11 as no. iv, omitting the final clause.

Refs.—The sections printed by Major and Cheney are accompanied by historical commentary. Only Rich Jones describes the codex: his introductions give a superficial account (I, ix–xii; II, vii–x), which can be supplemented with additional codicological details gleaned from his apparatus. See also G. R. C. Davis, *Medieval Cartularies of Great Britain: A Short Catalogue* (London, 1958), no. 867. The manuscript is briefly described in: *Diocese of Salisbury. Guide to the Records of the Bishop, the Archdeacons of Salisbury and Wiltshire, and Other Archidiaconal and Peculiar Jurisdictions* . . ., ed. Pamela Stewart (n.p., 1973), p. 1.

Text.—Transcribed below from a microfilm of the manuscript S: Sa = fols. 54vb–55vb = pp. 108b–110b (ed., I, 366-373); Sb = fols. 68v–71r = pp. 136-141 (ed., II, 45-54); full text of § 1 and 6 in Doc. 41, of § 12 in Doc. 1. Distinctive paragraphing has been adopted to display graphically the nested character of the citation mandates. The scribe of Sa corrected his work, and these corrections have often been followed tacitly.

Honorius[a] episcopus, servus servorum Dei, venerabilibus fratribus archiepis-copis et episcopis et dilectis filiis universis ecclesiarum prelatis per regnum Anglie constitutis, salutem et apostolicam benedictionem. —Super muros Jerusalem custodes positi . . . (= Doc. 41) . . . et utilitate quodammodo fierent aliene. —Datum Laterani v. kal. Februarii, pontificatus nostri anno nono.

2 [Iste littere venerunt circa principium Adventus Domini.[1]][b] (Summons to the council at London on 7 January 1226.)[c]

    R(icardus) divina permissione Sar' ecclesie minister humilis viro venera-bili et dilecto filio W(illielmo) decano Sar', salutem, gratiam et benedic-tionem. —Mandatum domini London' suscepimus in hec verba:

        Venerabili fratri et amico in Christo karissimo R(icardo) Dei gratia Sar' epis-copo, E(ustachius) divina permissione London' ecclesie minister humilis, salutem in Domino sempiternam. —Mandatum domini Cant' suscepimus in hec verba:

S(tephanus) Dei gratia Cant' archiepiscopus, totius Anglie primas, et sancte Romane ecclesie cardinalis, venerabili fratri E(ustachio) eadem permissione Lond' episcopo, salutem in Domino. —Fraternitati vestre[d] mandamus quati-nus omnes suffraganeos nostros vocetis ut veniant Lond' in crastino Epiphanie Domini, et vocent decanos cathedralium ecclesiarum et archidiaconos suos, ab-bates etiam[e] et priores conventuales ut similiter Lond' veniant audituri manda-tum domini pape termino memorato.

        Huius igitur auctoritate mandati vobis mandamus quatinus dictis die et loco secundum formam prescriptam compareatis.

    Vos igitur secundum formam prescriptam presentiam vestram dictis die et loco exhibeatis. Valete.

3 [Ista duo paria litterarum sequentium (sc. § 3–4) venerunt Dominica in Quin-quagesima.[2]][f] (Summons to the council at London on 3 May 1226.)[g]

    R(icardus) divina permissione Sar' ecclesie minister humilis venera-bilibus viris et dilectis in Christo filiis domino[h] W(illielmo) decano et capitulo Sar', salutem, gratiam et Dei[i] benedictionem. —Mandatum domini Lond' episcopi[j] suscepimus in hec verba:

[a] Sa = § 1–4
[b] *Nota marg.* Sa
[c] Sa = § 2, Sb = § 8 *infra*
[d] tue Sb
[e] abbates etiam] et abbates Sb
[f] *Nota marg.* Sa
[g] Sa = § 3, Sb = § 9 *infra*
[h] in Christo filiis domino *om.* Sb
[i] Dei *om.* Sb
[j] episcopi *om.* Sb

Honorius, bishop, servant of the servants of God, to the venerable brothers the archbishops and bishops and to all the beloved sons the prelates of churches located in England, greeting and apostolic blessing. —Placed as watchmen on the walls of Jerusalem . . . [a copy of *Super muros* = Doc. 41].

2 *This letter came at about the beginning of the Lord's Advent.*[1] [Summons to the council at London on 13 January 1226.]

> Richard by divine permission humble minister of the church of Salisbury, to the venerable man and beloved son William, dean of Salisbury, greeting, grace, and blessing. —We have received a mandate from the lord [bishop of] London that reads as follows:

>> To the venerable brother and dearest friend in Christ Richard by the grace of God bishop of Salisbury, Eustace by divine permission humble minister of the church of London, greeting and everlasting life in the Lord. —We have received a mandate from the lord [archbishop of] Canterbury that reads as follows:

Stephen by the grace of God archbishop of Canterbury, primate of all England, and cardinal of the holy Roman church, to the venerable brother Eustace by the same permission bishop of London, greeting in the Lord. —We command your fraternity that you summon all our suffragans to come to London on the morrow of the Lord's Epiphany. And they are to summon the deans of their cathedral churches and their archdeacons, as well as the abbots and conventual priors, to come likewise to London in order to hear the lord pope's mandate on the aforesaid date.

>> Therefore by the authority of this mandate we command you that you are to appear on the said day and at the said place according to the procedure stated above.

> Therefore you are to present yourself according to the procedure stated above on the said day and at the said place. Farewell.

3 *The following pair of two letters came on Quinquagesima Sunday.*[2] [Summons to the council at London on 3 May 1226.]

> Richard by divine permission humble minister of the church of Salisbury, to the venerable men and beloved sons in Christ William, the lord dean, and the Salisbury chapter, greeting, grace, and God's blessing. —We have received a mandate from the lord bishop of London that reads as follows:

---

1. First Sunday in Advent 1225 = 30 November. Noted in the margin.
2. Quinquagesima Sunday 1226 = 1 March. Again, noted in the margin.

Venerabili in Christo fratri et amico karissimo R(icardo) Dei gratia Sar'
episcopo, E(ustachius) eadem gratia Lond' ecclesie minister humilis salutem
in Domino sempiternam.   —Mandatum domini Cant' in hec verba suscepimus:[k]

S(tephanus) Dei gratia Cant' archiepiscopus, totius Anglie primas, et sancte
Romane ecclesie cardinalis, venerabili fratri E(ustachio) eadem gratia Lond' episcopo salutem in Domino.   —Mandamus vobis quatinus pro officii vestri
debito faciatis vocari omnes episcopos, abbates non exemptos a nobis, et omnes
priores, et omnes decanos cathedralium ecclesiarum et prebendalium, et omnes
archidiaconos. Et significetis singulis capitulis ut mittant procuratores, tam
videlicet ecclesiarum cathedralium[l] quam prebendalium et monasteriorum et
aliarum domorum religiosarum ac collegiatarum,[m] in virtute obedientie et sub
pena[n] suspensionis eis districtius iniungentes ut intersint London' concilio quod
erit Dominica post Pascha qua cantatur "Misericordia Domini."[3] Et significetis
omnibus predictis ut interim deliberent et plene instructi veniant ad respon-
dendum nuntio domini pape super petitione quam fecit ex parte domini pape;
et hoc faciant omni occasione et dilatione postpositis. Ut autem sciatis qui sint
abbates exempti[o] a nobis, eos vobis duximus nominandos, videlicet abbas sancti
Albani, abbas Westmonasterii, abbas sancti Edmundi, abbas sancti Augustini
Cant'.

> Huius igitur auctoritate mandati, vobis mandamus quatinus[p] dictis die et loco
> prefato intersitis concilio; omnes insuper superius nominatos secundum for-
> mam eiusdem mandati vocandos citari faciatis ut, sub pena superius expressa,
> plene instructi eisdem die et loco prefato intersint concilio.

Huius igitur auctoritate mandati, vobis mandamus quatinus formam
suprascriptam, quantum in vobis est, exequamini. Valete.

4 (§ 3 was accompanied by a second letter from the bishop of Salisbury to
his dean and chapter, transmitting to them two mandates received from the
legate: (a) a request that they pay the procuration money that was the legate's
due; and (b) an order to the bishop to submit a list of all persons in his diocese
who had sought a dispensation to hold more than one benefice.)

. . . .

[k] suscepimus *post* Cant' Sb
[l] eccl. cath. *tr.* Sb
[m] ac collegiatarum *om.* Sb
[n] pena] interminatione Sb
[o] abbates exempti] non *inser.* Sb
[p] quatinus *om.* Sa, *corr. marg.* Sa².

To the venerable brother in Christ and dearest friend Richard by the grace of God bishop of Salisbury, Eustace by the same grace humble minister of the church of London, everlasting life in the Lord.   —We have received a mandate from the lord Canterbury that reads as follows:

Stephen by the grace of God archbishop of Canterbury, primate of all England, and cardinal of the holy Roman church, to the venerable brother Eustace by the same grace bishop of London, greeting in the Lord.   —We command you that *ex officio* you issue a summons to all the bishops, to all the abbots not exempt from our jurisdiction, and to all priors, all deans of cathedral and prebendal churches, and all archdeacons. And indicate to all the chapters that they are to send proctors, namely both from cathedral churches and from prebendal ones, and from monasteries and other monastic and collegiate houses. And strictly enjoin them in virtue of obedience and under pain of suspension that they are to attend the council at London that will take place on the Sunday after Easter on which "Misericordia Domini" is sung.[3] And indicate to all the aforesaid that they are to deliberate in the meantime and come fully instructed to reply to the lord pope's nuncio concerning the petition that he has made on the part of the lord pope; and let them do this without delay whatever the circumstances. So you may know which abbots are exempt from our jurisdiction, we are providing you with the following list: the abbot of St Albans, the abbot of Westminster, the abbot of St Edmond's, the abbot of St Augustine's Canterbury.

By the authority of this mandate, we command that you attend the aforesaid council on the said day and at the said place. Moreover, all the above named who ought to be summoned you are to have cited according to the procedure stated above, so that they appear fully instructed at the aforesaid council on the same day and at the same place, or else they will incur the penalties expressed above.

By the authority of this mandate, we command that you carry out the procedure stated above to the best of your ability. Farewell.

4 [§ 3 was accompanied by a second letter from the bishop of Salisbury to his dean and chapter, transmitting to them two mandates received from the legate: (a) a request that they pay the procuration money that was the legate's due; and (b) an order to the bishop to submit a list of all persons in his diocese who had sought a dispensation to hold more than one benefice.]

. . . .

3. Psalm 32 (AV 33).5b, the introit for the second Sunday after Easter.

5 Ante Natale,^{q} circa Adventum Domini, per litteras domini Cant'[4] citati fuerunt omnes episcopi Anglie et abbates et priores et decani cathedralium ecclesiarum et archidiaconi ut London' in octabis Epiphanie (13 January 1226) convenirent audituri mandatum domini pape eis per Octonem subdiaconum, de quo supra mentio facta est,[5] proponendum, cujus continentia talis est.

6 (A second copy of *Super muros*: see § 1.)

7 (Account of the council at London, 13 January 1226.) Eo die comparente London' in ecclesia beati Pauli magna multitudine cleri, lecte fuerunt apostolice predicte litere; sed tunc temporis accesserat dominus Cantuar' ad dominum regem apud Merleberg' visitaturus eum in egritudine sua. Et propter absentiam ipsius, et quorumdam episcoporum qui regi assistebant, nichil inde actum fuit.

8 A domino archiepiscopo autem forma^r citationis facta talis erat.

R. divina permissione Sar' . . . —Fraternitati tue mandamus . . . (the second copy [Sb] of the summons to the January council: see § 2) . . . exhibeatis. Valete.

9 Postea vero in Quinquagesima sequenti venit alia citatio ab archiepiscopo ad episcopum Lond', et per eum ad alios, sub hac forma:

R. divina permissione Sar' . . . —Mandamus vobis quatinus pro officii vestri debito . . . (the second copy [Sb] of the summons to the May council: see § 3) . . . . exequamini. Valete.

. . . .

10 (Because this section of the register is arranged in strictly chronological order, five entries pertaining to events between January and May 1226 precede the account of the second council.)

a (The death of Earl William Longespée, 10 January 1226.)

b (Abbot-elect installed at Reading, 15 March.)

c Eodem anno, iiii^{to} kalendas Februarii (29 January), suscepit Ludowicus, rex Francie, crucem a manu magistri Romani, sancte Romane ecclesie cardinalis, tunc temporis in Francia legati; et multi cum eo milites et magnates de regno Francie cum eo cruce signati sunt ad expugnandum comitem Tholosanum, quem idem legatus in concilio Bituricensi judicavit esse sismaticum et hereticum. Postea vero, mense Maio, quinto idus Maii (11 May), profectus est idem rex Francie cum magna multitudine crucesignatorum ad expugnandam terram predicti comitis, et predictus legatus cum eo. Eodem anno, circa festum sancti Martini, mortuus est idem rex.

d (Death of Hugh *de Templo*, canon of Salisbury, 12 April.)

e (Declaration concerning the prebend that Hugh's death left vacant.)

---

^{q} Sb = § 5–13

^{r} A domino—forma] Forma" autem" a domino archiepiscopo" Sb *cum signa transpositionis*

5 Before Christmas, about [the beginning of the season of] the Lord's Advent, all the bishops of England, and the abbots, priors, deans of cathedral churches, and archdeacons were summoned by a letter of the lord Canterbury[4] to convene at London on the octave of Epiphany [13 January 1226] so they might hear the lord pope's mandate that was to be proposed by the subdeacon Otto, which was mentioned above,[5] the contents of which were as follows.

6 [A second copy of *Super muros* (Doc. 41): see § 1.]

7 [Account of the council at London, 13 January 1226.] When a great crowd of clergy convened at London in St Paul's church on that day, the aforesaid apostolic letter was read. But at that time the lord Canterbury had gone to the king at Marlborough to visit him because he was sick. And because of his absence, and that of several other bishops who were attending the king, nothing was done at that time.

8 The form of the citation made by the lord archbishop was as follows: [a second copy of the summons to the January council: see § 2].

9 Afterwards, on the next Quinquagesima Sunday, another citation came from the archbishop to the bishop of London, and through him to the other bishops, which ran as follows: [a second copy of the summons to the May council: see § 3].

. . . .

10 [Because this section of the register is arranged in strictly chronological order, five entries pertaining to events between January and May 1226 precede the account of the second council.]

a [The death of Earl William Longespée, 10 January 1226.]

b [Abbot-elect installed at Reading, 15 March.]

c In the same year, on the fourth day before the kalends of February [29 January], King Louis of France received the cross from the hand of Master Romanus, cardinal of the holy Roman church, who was at that time legate in France. And many knights and great men of the kingdom of France were signed with the cross along with the king. Their mission was to conquer the count of Toulouse, whom the same legate in the Council of Bourges had judged to be a schismatic and a heretic. Afterwards, in the month of May, on the fifth day before the ides of May [11 May], the same king set out with a great number of crusaders to conquer the land of the aforesaid count, and the aforesaid legate went with him. In the same year, about the feast of St Martin [11 November], the same king died.

d [Death of Hugh *de Templo*, canon of Salisbury, 12 April.]

e [Declaration concerning the prebend that Hugh's death left vacant.]

4. Cf. above, § 2 = § 8, below.
5. Sb, p. 134, ed. Rich Jones, II, 40, s.a. 1225.

11 (Account of the council at London, 3 May 1226.) Anno ab incarnatione Domini m. cc. xxvi., Dominica ii[a] post Pascha qua cantatur "Misericordia Domini," summonitum fuit concilium in ecclesia beati Pauli apud Lond' ut ibidem responderent domino pape super petitione quam fecerat per Octonem nuntium suum, sicut supra notatum est. Eodem autem Octone versus curiam Romanam profecto, tenuit dominus Cantuar' concilium in quo fuit ei ab omnibus universaliter negatum quod prius fuerat a domino papa petitum, iuxta formam responsionis quam habuit legatus Francie in concilio quod celebravit apud Bituricas, que quidem forma legitur esse huiusmodi:

12 Convenerunt ad concilium ... (the *Relatio de concilio Bituricensi* as printed above in Doc. 1.2-17) ... quod minime creditur posse provenire.

13 (Death of the bishop of Durham, 1 May 1226.) Ad istud concilium quod factum fuit Lond' proficiscens cum magna festinatione episcopus Dunolmensis, Ric(ardum) de Marisco, apud burgum sancti Petri obitu[s] arreptus est.

[s] obitu *emend. Rich Jones*] obiter Sb

Document 43
THE ANNALS OF ROGER WENDOVER
composed 1226~1232

The Benedictine monks of St Albans were exceptionally well situated to observe English affairs in the later Middle Ages, for their house was but a day's journey from London on the principal route to the north.[1] Early in the thirteenth century, this house began to keep a particularly well-informed and detailed chronicle, which was continued sporadically for three centuries. From time to time it was recopied and recast, both at St Albans and elsewhere, giving rise to a confusing variety of versions, which in their modern printed form fill no less than twenty-nine volumes of the Rolls Series. As there was no attempt to preserve the work of any contributor intact, the relation of the individual authors to the work as a whole was like that found today in an encyclopedia that practices a policy of continuous revision, under which signed articles may be rewritten at any time by the editor and may also borrow tacitly from earlier edi-

1. R. Vaughan, *Matthew Paris* (Cambridge, Eng., 1958), p. 11.

11 [Account of the council at London, 3 May 1226.] In the year 1226 from the Lord's incarnation, on the second Sunday after Easter, on which is sung "Misericordia Domini," a council was convoked in St Paul's church at London so that there they might respond to the lord pope concerning the petition that he made through his nuncio Otto, as is noted above [§ 9]. However, since the same Otto had set out for the Roman curia, the lord Canterbury held the council. In it everyone unanimously gave him a negative response to what had been previously requested by the lord pope, and this response was modeled on the one given to the legate of France in the council that he celebrated at Bourges, which reads as follows:

12 [The *Relatio de concilio Bituricensi* as printed above in Doc. 1.2-17.]

13 [Death of the bishop of Durham, 1 May 1226.] While travelling in great haste to that council in London, the bishop of Durham, Richard Marsh, died at Peterborough.

---

tions. In effect, it is misleading to think of Roger Wendover as the author of one chronicle, Matthew Paris of another, and Thomas Walsingham of a third. Each in his day was in charge of the St Albans chronicle and molded the materials at hand with editorial license. In short, this chronicle was a living text that had no one definitive form but rather successive and even parallel versions.

The modern historian who wishes to work from those sources that were closest to the events must untangle the several skeins of this tradition, since to read the chronicle as it was originally set down, one must trace the process of revision through its successive stages back to the earliest recoverable form. In the case of the annals for 1225-1226, from which Doc. 43 is drawn, there can be no doubt that Roger Wendover was their author, but as his work does not survive in its original form, we must consult two later versions, each independent of the other. Fortunately, both agree in all that is important for the historian, but when one or the other has improved on the style of the original, we cannot be sure what Wendover actually wrote. To make this situation clear, it will be necessary to introduce not only Wendover and his successor, Paris, but also the manuscripts that transmitted their works.

★ ★ ★

The origins of the St Albans chronicle are shrouded in mystery. After three generations of controversy, the most that can be said is that both Wendover and Paris
drew on an earlier compilation. "This, it seems, could have been a manuscript
of some early compilation called the *Flores historiarum* and perhaps extending
only to 1066, which was used by Roger Wendover as the basis for the early part
of his chronicle, and used again by Matthew Paris in the preparation of" his work
bearing the same title.[2] Who compiled that work and what it contained will
probably never be known, for the earliest surviving version of the St Albans
chronicle is the one prepared by Roger Wendover between 1220 and 1236.

We meet our annalist for the first time when he is already in the middle of
his career. No later than 1217 he had been sent to administer St Albans' dependent house at Belvoir, but during a formal visitation of that priory late in
1219, the abbot of St Albans received complaints that Prior Roger was wasting
the goods of that cell "in prodigalitate incircumspecta."[3] Several months later
the prodigal prior was accordingly recalled to St Albans, where he remained to
lavish the last sixteen years of his life on the compilation of a chronicle that extended from Creation down to his own time. When he died in May 1236, the
narrative had reached at least the end of April 1234, if not July 1235; it was continued from wherever he stopped by Matthew Paris.[4]

As the title *Flores historiarum* suggests, Wendover himself considered his work
to be a compilation rather than an original composition, but the historical value
of such a work will of course depend on the compiler's sources. Down to at least
the annal for 1201, Roger's material was entirely derived from earlier chroniclers
whose works have come down to us, and for those years the *Flores* consequently
has no independent value. At the other extreme are the annals for the years
during which Wendover was actively compiling his history. This material he
gathered himself, and although he incorporated documents when they were available, most of the narrative was a report in his own words of the news of the day

2. Vaughan, *Matthew Paris*, pp. 96–97, with diagram. For yet another chronicle, which was
copied at St Albans ca. 1220, just at the time Wendover was beginning to compile his history, see *The Chronicle attributed to John of Wallingford*, ed. R. Vaughan as *The Camden Miscellany, Vol. XXI* in the Camden Third Series, vol. XC (London: Royal Historical Society, 1958).
Later additions to the same manuscript are published in the *English Historical Review*, LXXIII
(1958), 66–77. There is no longer reason to believe, as Luard did, that Wallingford, alias Johannes de Cella, St Albans' abbot 1195–1214, ever wrote this or any other chronicle: see
Vaughan, pp. 22–23. See also biographies of "John de Cella" and "John of Wallingford" in Russell's *Dictionary* (1936), pp. 59 and 79, with supplement in the *Bulletin of the Institute of Historical Research*, XIX (1942), 99.

3. *Gesta abbatum monasterii Sancti Albani*, ed. H. T. Riley in *Chronica monasterii S. Albani*,
Rolls Series, no. 28, IV, i (1867), 270, 274.

4. Where Wendover stopped is still, I think, an open question: see n. 16, below.

as he had heard it. It is generally agreed that beginning at the latest with the accession of Henry III (1216), Wendover's chronicle is a contemporary record of events as they were known at St Albans. Between these two extremes lies the troubled reign of John, which had already become a legend when Roger turned to history, and students of that reign have long debated what his sources may have been and whether their testimony can be considered as strictly contemporary with the events.[5]

Fortunately, Wendover was actively collecting material when our councils of 1226 were held in nearby London, so we are not surprised to find that he preserves the fullest account both of these proceedings and of Otto's mission in general. He was not only close to the scene but also intensely interested in the exercise of papal power in England. Indeed, the antagonism to the Roman curia that is so evident in the annals of Matthew Paris is hardly less marked in Wendover's work.[6] This interest must have governed his selection of material, but to judge by his alterations of Doc. 1, he was more concerned to improve the style than to impose his prejudices.[7] In reading Doc. 43, it should be remembered that these annals may have been written seven years or more after the events, for the annal for 1227 did not reach its present form until after 1232,[8] but the interval could not have been more than ten years, since Wendover died in 1236.

5. E.g. F. M. Powicke, "Roger of Wendover and the Coggeshall Chronicle," *English Historical Review*, XXI (1906), 286–296, and more recently, H. G. Richardson and G. O. Sales, *The Governance of Mediaeval England from the Conquest to Magna Carta* (Edinburgh, 1963). A. Gransden, *Historical Writing in England*, regards Wendover as "a primary authority" after the annal for 1202 (pp. 359–360).

6. In passing I cannot resist noting a curious, though admittedly irrelevant, family connection to the Roman curia. Richard of Wendover, canon of St Paul's, London, and probably identical with the medical writer Ricardus Anglicus, was personal physician to Pope Gregory IX between 1237 and 1241, just after Roger's death. Richard's relation to Roger is suggested not only by their common name but also by the physician's attachment to St Albans, to which he gave a reliquary cross that he had received as a legacy from Gregory. See Russell, *Dictionary*, pp. 123–124.

7. At one point Wendover did impute cunning to the legate, who, he says, dismissed the proctors at Bourges "in dolo" (Doc. 1.6, var. d).

8. In the annal for 1227, the bishops of Winchester and Exeter are reported to have departed on a crusade, "qui peregrinationis suae votum fere per quinquennium laudabiliter compleverunt" (ed. Luard, III, 127). In 1226 Wendover had not yet put the finishing touches on the 1221 annal, and in 1227 he was still working on the year 1217: Liebermann, ed. cit., p. 10, nn. 13–16. If Wendover continually retouched his work, as we know Paris did, the evidence for these dates of compilation may actually be nothing more than marginal additions to an annal composed several years earlier. The crucial phrases do in fact look to me suspiciously like interpolations. Since they are also found in B, they must have appeared in the *b*-recension for which Wendover himself was responsible.

Roger's historical work was continued and revised by his successor, Matthew Paris, who around 1243 began to revise Wendover's text for transcription into a new volume (B),[9] for which he also composed annals through May 1259, within a month of his death. He came to call this fullest version of the St Albans annals his "greater chronicle," to distinguish it from two lesser ones that are essentially abridgements of the *Chronica majora*. One bore the traditional St Albans title *Flores historiarum*, while the other was somewhat inappropriately known as the *Historia Anglorum*.

Matthew's reputation as an historian—he is widely regarded as the greatest of medieval chroniclers—rests chiefly on the two dozen annals he composed, which are the most extensive narrative of the period. We are not concerned here with Paris the author, however, but with Paris the editor, and about this little can be said with certainty, at least as regards Wendover's chronicle. From Vaughan's painstaking studies we know how Paris revised his own work, but as we shall see upon turning to the manuscripts, one cannot be certain that every variation of his version of the *ow*-recension does in fact represent a change introduced by Paris; indeed, from the collation of Doc. 1, it is evident that Paris sometimes preserved Wendover's original wording, which was later altered in the *ow*-recension. The retouched passages in Doc. 43, whoever was responsible for them, are few in number and of no historical importance, so we may attribute the substance of the present document to Wendover, remembering only that subsequently it was polished, presumably by other hands. Both Wendover and Paris, however, frequently improved the Latin style of documents that they incorporated in their chronicles, as is evident from the *apparatus criticus* to Doc. 1.

MSS.—As we have seen, Wendover was one of the first in his monastery to compile a history. His successors recopied his compilation, revised it, and drew upon it for new compilations. Today we know Wendover's text only through two revised versions, for the original recension (*b*) has not survived. One of the altered versions was made by Matthew Paris for his *Chronica majora* (B) and the other, done by an unknown hand, is here simply called the *ow*-recension. When these two versions disagree, usually there is no means of telling with certainty which preserves the original reading. The passage edited in Doc. 1 is an important exception, because in that case sources outside the Wendover-Paris tradition provide a third witness that can break the deadlock. For most of Wendover's chronicle, however, including the portion edited below, there is no third source to reveal the original reading. In this predicament, two courses are open to the

9. H. E. Hilpert, *Kaiser- und Papstbriefe in den Chronica majora des Mattaeus Paris* (Stuttgart, 1981), pp. 27-36.

editor: either he can proceed by educated guesswork to emend his texts after the fashion of a humanistic virtuoso, or he can print one version in the text and record the variants from the other in the apparatus. The latter course, which for the most part has been used here, leaves the decision to the reader. Such an edition must be used with caution and deliberation. Happily, there are few doubtful passages in the present text and none that seriously affect the sense. The reader is warned, however, that when the text is in doubt, the variants should always be consulted.

In using this text, it is therefore absolutely necessary that the reader have the manuscripts and their relationships firmly in mind. What is essential for an understanding of the Wendover-Paris annals for 1225-1226 is accordingly presented below. By no means is this offered as a complete description of the intricate interrelationships of the St Albans chronicle: only those facts which are relevant to the text of Doc. 43 are presented. A general view of the tradition can be found in Vaughan's monograph, which I have followed here unless otherwise noted (see especially pp. 21-30). Figure 4 illustrates both the chronological and the stemmatic relationships of the manuscripts;[10] the following descriptions summarize the conclusions on which it is based.

(*b*) Now lost, this manuscript is the earliest recension of Wendover's chronicle now discernible from the collation of surviving manuscripts.[11] Presumably the copy was made before Wendover's death in May 1236; certainly the book was in existence circa 1250 when Paris used it as the basis for B. Since *b* extended at least as far as the annal for 1228, our passage was evidently included.[12]

(B) Cambridge, Corpus Christi College, MS. 16. The oldest surviving witness to Wendover's original *b*-text is not a copy of Wendover's chronicle but rather the revised version of it that Matthew Paris incorporated into his *Chronica majora*, of which B is the oldest manuscript containing our passage (fols. 61r–63r). B was written in the St Albans scriptorium by several hands, but with the exception of § 1-2, Doc. 43 is in the hand of Paris himself.[13] The annal for 1250 was copied into B early in 1251,[14] but Wendover's text might have been revised and transcribed into B at any time during the preceding fifteen years: a date in

10. For more complete stemmata, see Vaughan, *Matthew Paris*, pp. 29 and 97. The symbols used here are Vaughan's, except that I have used lower-case italic letters to distinguish both hypothetical codices *b* and *ow* (Vaughan's *b* and *OW*).

11. In annals before 1066, Vaughan detected traces of a yet earlier recension (*a*), which he plausibly suggested may have been Wendover's source (pp. 96-98).

12. Vaughan, p. 28.

13. Vaughan, p. 51.

14. Vaughan, pp. 49-77.

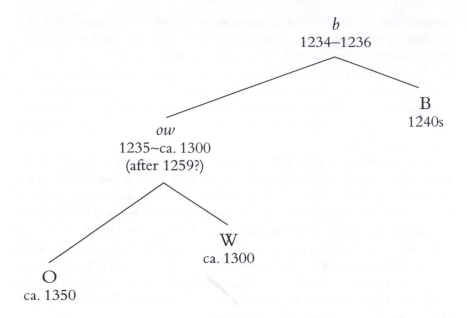

B = Cambridge, Corpus Christi College MS. 16 (Matthew Paris' *Chronica majora*)
O = London, BL, MS. Cotton Otho B. v (Roger Wendover's *Flores historiarum*)
W = Oxford, Bodleian Library, MS. Douce 207 (Roger Wendover's *Flores historarum*)

FIGURE 4.   The manuscript tradition of Document 43

the early 1240s seems most likely to me. Paris, like Wendover before him, was fond of improving the Latin prose of the materials he appropriated. Occasionally in Doc. 1 we can be sure that he altered the *b*-text,[15] but in Doc. 43 one cannot be certain whether the B-variants, here largely relegated to the apparatus, represent the original reading of *b* or an alteration introduced by Paris. In judging between B and W readings, it should be remembered that B is a half century older than W and stands stemmatically closer to *b*, from which it was copied directly.

(*ow*) This manuscript, now lost, was like B a revised version of *b* made at St Albans. Because the last annal ended in July 1235, it is not impossible that Wendover himself prepared this revision before his death in May 1236, and the OW-text derived from this version has been attributed to Wendover by his editors

15. Because B sometimes preserves the true reading in Doc. 1: § 7, var. x (*subversio*); § 8, t (*reciperet*); and § 13, s (*quod*).

without reserve. Elsewhere, I have argued that, since Paris based his revision on a *b*-text, *ow* could have been copied at any time between 1235 (its last annal) and circa 1300, when it was used as the exemplar of W.[16] Since W, the earliest copy of *ow*, was made ca. 1300, there is no reason to believe that *ow* was completed before Wendover died in 1236: it could have been written at any time during the next two generations. In other words, Wendover's modern editors may well have been mistaken in believing that OW readings represent the actual words of their author. That this is so cannot, of course, be demonstrated conclusively, for it is always possible that the *ow*-recension was in fact made as early as 1235 but that Paris for some reason or other used the *b*-text instead. Although the second alternative seems less likely to me, I shall only insist here that a reading peculiar to OW can no longer with any assurance be attributed to Roger Wendover.

(W) Oxford, Bodleian Library, MS. Douce 207 (Doc. 43 on fols. 188r–190rb). The oldest extant copy of the *ow*-recension of Wendover's *Flores historiarum*, complete except for a few lacunae which must be supplied from B, this book was copied at St Albans about 1300.[17] Unfortunately, the most widely accepted view of the textual tradition of the St Albans chronicle was framed by Luard in the mistaken belief that W was written "about the middle of the 13th century."[18] This early date encouraged him to ascribe the *b*-text to a putative predecessor of Wendover and to mistake *ow* as Wendover's original recension. Progressively this reconstruction has been eroded by Powicke, Galbraith, and Vaughan, until, by the hypothesis suggested above, the last vestige now comes into doubt. But even if the *ow*-recension can no longer be ascribed with confidence to Wendover, still W remains the best base text for an edition of Wendover's *Flores* because it seems, with the reservations noted above, to represent a state of the text prior to Paris' improvements.

16. "Wendover's Last Annal," *English Historical Review*, LXXXIV (1969), 779-785. My conclusions were rejected by Hilpert, pp. 23-27, but he was not able, however, to exclude the possibility I raised, that *ow* may have been written after Paris' death in 1259. The point now at issue is which hypothesis is simpler: to account for certain discrepancies, Hilpert would posit a second *b*-recension (*b₁*), whereas I would assume a later date for *ow*. Either way, the controversy has little relevance for Doc. 43, except that while the question remains open, one cannot attribute OW readings to Wendover himself with complete confidence.

17. In 1866, Madden dated the script quite correctly as "close of the thirteenth century": *Historia Anglorum*, Rolls Series, no. 44, vol. I, p. lxxi. Liebermann followed him in this (ed. cit., p. 18), but a slightly later date "circa 1300" was preferred by the Bodleian *Summary Catalogue of Western Manuscripts*, ed. F. Madden et al., IV (1897), 555, no. 21781. The later date has been confirmed by V. H. Galbraith: see Powicke, *Proceedings of the British Academy*, XXX (1944), p. 148, n. 2.

18. *Chronica majora*, I (1872), xiii. On Luard's critics, see Vaughan, pp. 22-23.

(O) London, British Library, MS. Cotton Otho B. v. Like W, this is a copy of *ow*, but one written a half century later (circa 1350).[19] The codex survived the fire at Ashburnham House in 1731 with a loss of five leaves and extensive damage to the edges of those remaining. Occasionally it preserves better readings than W, but these are offset by its errors, so it is of no greater textual authority than W, which makes a more convenient base text in view of the damaged state of O.

Ed.—From the foregoing it should be clear that Wendover's original *b*-text is for the most part beyond recovery. Instead we have two later versions of equal authority (B vs. OW), each of which has been edited several times.

(i) The *ow*-recension has twice been edited, though both editions, which purport to be transcripts of W, are contaminated with tacit B-text readings. (1) The fullest text, omitting only the annals before A. D. 447, was printed by H. O. Coxe, librarian of the Bodleian: *Rogeri de Wendover Chronica, sive Flores historiarum*, English Historical Society, 4 vols. (London, 1841-1842) and Appendix (1844)—Doc. 43 in vol. IV (1842), 107-125. (2) For the annals after 1154, the Coxe text was supposedly revised from W and collated against O by H. G. Hewlett, *Rogeri de Wendover liber qui dicitur Flores historiarum*, Rolls Series, no. 84, 3 vols. (London, 1886-1889)—Doc. 43 in vol. II (1887), 289-306. The deficiencies of both the Coxe and Hewlett editions were exposed by W. H. Stevenson in a scathing review of the latter's first volume: *English Historical Review*, III (1888), 353-360. (3) Select passages from W were reliably edited by F. Liebermann with an important preface in MGH, SS, XXVIII (1888), 1-73: at p. 52 are fragments from Doc. 43.11-12 (= Doc. 1.1-2) and 17 "Et hiis . . . secuturi." (4) Powicke-Cheney, *Councils & Synods*, II.i (1964), 156-167, transcribes Doc. 43.6-9, from W.

(ii) Although Paris's *Chronica majora* has been printed many times, properly speaking there have been only two editions. (1) In 1571, Archbishop Parker lent his name to an edition done by an unknown hand. The text was drawn from various manuscripts, the best one (B) being used for the annals of 1225-1226. Parker's editor emended the Latinity of his text freely and tacitly. In 1640, when this text was being reprinted for the third time, the London printer engaged William Wats to improve the text. This he did, not by altering the corrupt Parker text, which was merely reprinted, but by adding collations from the manuscripts, thus preserving some readings which would otherwise have been lost, notably from O.[20]

From the Parker text, Doc. 1 was reprinted by Labbe-Cossart, XI (1671), 292-294, whence Mansi, XXII (1778), 1215-1218. Doc. 43, including 11-12, was printed from

19. Vaughan, p. 21.

20. See Hardy, *Descriptive Catalogue*, III, 110-111. Before Wats, the Parker text was twice reprinted in Zurich (1589, 1606) and again at London in 1684.

the 1640 edition (pp. 325–331) in *Rec. hist. Gaules*, XVII (1818), 762–766. Other extracts are noticed by Potthast, *Wegweiser*, I (1896), 778–779 and 981.

(2) For all practical purposes, the Parker text was replaced by H. R. Luard's edition: *Matthaei Parisiensis, monachi Sancti Albani Chronica majora*, Rolls Series, no. 57, 7 vols. (London, 1872–1883)—Doc. 43 in vol. III (1876), 97–111, from B, with variants from OW. This is the only edition in which the two recensions of Wendover can be compared.

(iii) **Descendants of B.**—Paris produced two abridgements of his greater chronicle, as well as several copies of it. None are of any value in establishing the Wendover *b*-text, so they have not been considered in the discussion above. As neither abridgement has any independent historical value, a reference to each will suffice to signal their existence.

(1) The *Historia Anglorum*, ed. F. Madden, Rolls Series, no. 44, 3 vols (London, 1866–1869), from British Library MS. Royal 14. C. vii. A shorter, reworked version of Doc. 43 appears in vol. II (1866), 275–285. That this passage was derived from the text of B, as Vaughan argues (pp. 61–65), I confirmed by a collation of the printed text and Doc. 43.

(2) A *Flores historiarum* that was once ascribed to the fictitious Matthew of Westminster but is now known to be the work of Paris himself was edited by H. R. Luard, Rolls Series, no. 95, 3 vols. (London, 1890), from Manchester, Chetham Library, MS. 6712, the earlier part of which was written at St Albans before 1265. For this abridgement, Paris summarized the whole of Doc. 1 in a single sentence; from Doc. 43 he retained much of § 3–9 and reduced § 16–17 to a sentence each (II, 182–186). On the work, see Vaughan, chapter 6.

Bibliography.—The most thorough study to date is Richard Vaughan, *Matthew Paris*, Cambridge Studies in Medieval Life and Thought, n.s., vol. 6 (Cambridge, Eng., 1958), with extensive bibliography. More convenient as an introduction, though corrected by Vaughan in important respects, is V. H. Galbraith, *Roger Wendover and Matthew Paris*, Glasgow University Publications, 61 (Glasgow, 1944), reprinted in his collected essays: *Kings and Chroniclers* (London: Variorum, 1982), item X. Galbraith should be read in conjunction with F. M. Powicke, "The Compilation of the *Chronica Majora* of Matthew Paris," *Proceedings of the British Academy*, XXX (1944), 147–160. Antonia Gransden, *Historical Writing in England c. 550 to c. 1307* (Ithaca, N. Y., 1974), chap. 16, pp. 356–379. Hans-Eberhard Hilpert, *Kaiser- und Papstbriefe in den Chronica majora des Matthaeus Paris*, Publications of the German Historical Institute London, vol. 9 (Stuttgart, 1981).

The older literature is founded on the editors' prefaces in the Rolls Series, notably those by Luard and Madden, to which should be joined the now generally dated remarks by T. D. Hardy, *Descriptive Catalogue of Materials relating to the*

History of Great Britain and Ireland, Rolls Series, no. 26 (preface of vol. III devoted to Wendover and Paris, as are notices at pp. 79 and 110). Of more enduring value, however, are Liebermann's Latin prefaces to MGH, SS, XXVIII (1888), 1-20, 74-106, and 456-462.

Biographies of Paris and Wendover by William Hunt, based on Luard, in the *Dictionary of National Biography*, XLIII (1895), 207-213, and LX (1899), 250-252. Better notices by J. C. Russell, *Dictionary of Writers of Thirteenth Century England*, Special Supplement no. 3 to the *Bulletin of the Institute of Historical Research* (London, [1936]), pp. 83-84, 146-147. M. M. Chibnall, "Roger of Wendover," *New Catholic Encyclopedia*, XII (1967), 551. B. Merrilees, "Matthew Paris" in *Dictionary of the Middle Ages*, VIII (1987), 229-230. K. Schnith, "Matthaeus Paris" and "Roger Wendover" in *Lexikon des Mittelalters*, VI (1992), 399, and VII (1994), 944-945.

Text.—The present edition takes W as its base, which has been transcribed from a microfilm copy. The orthographic peculiarities of W have been preserved but

---

U T MAGISTER OTHO PRO NEGOTIIS DOMINI PAPE IN ANGLIAM VENERIT. Eodem anno (1225) magister Otho, domini pape nuntius, in Angliam veniens pro magnis ecclesie negotiis Romane,[a] regi litteras presentavit. Sed rex, cognito litterarum tenore, respondit quod solus non potuit diffinire, nec debuit, negotium quod omnes clericos et laicos generaliter totius regni tangebat. Tunc per consilium Stephani, Cant' archiepiscopi, datus est dies a rege in octavis Epiphanie (13 January) ut, convocatis omnibus clericis et laicis, super prefato negotio tunc tractarent apud Westmonasterium, et ibidem fieret[b] quod justum singulis videretur.

2 UT IDEM OTHO FALCASIUM REGI PACIFICARE LABORAVERIT. Eodem tempore magister Otho ex parte domini pape regem Anglie humiliter rogavit ut Falcasio sibi reconciliato uxorem cum terris et omnibus rebus amissis ad integrum restitueret, et ipsum, qui patri suo et sibi in werra sua tam fideliter servierat, pura, ut decebat, diligeret caritate. Ad hoc quoque respondit rex quod propter proditionem manifestam ab omni clero et populo regni per judicium curie sue ab Anglia fuerat in exilium pulsus, et licet regni cura specialiter ad ipsum spectare videretur, debet leges[c] quidem et bonas regni consuetudines observare. Hec autem cum audisset magister Otho, cessavit ulterius de Falcasio sol-

[a] negotiis Romane *tr.* B
[b] fieret] fuerat B
[c] leges] legis B

the text has been normalized in accordance with my general principles (see above, pp. 267-277), thus eliminating such forms as *hyatus, laycos, sullevare,* and *tantumdem;* forms given as alternate spellings in the *Oxford Latin Dictionary,* however, have not been changed. The base text has been collated with, and revised from, a photocopy of B; variants from O are derived from Luard's apparatus.

Translation.—Wendover's chronicle is the only one of our sources that has previously been translated into English: *Roger of Wendover's Flowers of History,* trans. J. A. Giles, Bohn's Antiquarian Library (London, 1849), with Doc. 43 on pp. 461-462 (§ 1-2) and pp. 466-475 (§ 3-17), including the *Relatio de concilio Bituricensi* (Doc. 1) on pp. 470-473. My translation attempts a more precise and modern idiom.

How MASTER OTTO CAME TO ENGLAND ON THE POPE'S BUSINESS. In the same year [1225] Master Otto, the lord pope's nuncio, came to England on important business for the Roman church, and he delivered a letter to the king. But when the king learned the gist of the letter, he replied that he alone neither could nor should decide a matter that touched all the clergy and laity of the whole kingdom in general. Then, on the advice of Stephen archbishop of Canterbury, a day was set at the octave of Epiphany [13 January] on which all the clergy and laity would assemble at Westminster and discuss the aforesaid matter, after which he would do there what seemed just to everyone.

2 HOW THE SAME OTTO WORKED TO RECONCILE FAWKES TO THE KING. At the same time, on the pope's behalf, Master Otto humbly requested that Fawkes be reconciled to the king, and that the king would then return his wife to him, together with the lands and all the things that he had lost just as they were before, and would cherish him with unalloyed love, since he had so faithfully served the king and his father in their wars. To this the king replied that because of manifest treason he had been sent off into exile from England by all the clergy and people of the kingdom acting through the judgment of the king's court; and although the administration of the kingdom seemed to be especially the king's business, he surely ought to observe the laws and good customs of the realm. When Master Otto heard this, he stopped bothering the king any more about Fawkes. Then the same Otto took two marks of silver from all the con-

licitare regem. Tunc idem Otho cepit ab omnibus ecclesiis Anglie conventualibus, nomine procurationis, duas marcas argenti. Et sciendum est quod tempore
quo magister Otho venit in Angliam, dominus papa misit nuntios per orbem
universum, exactiones ubique indebitas exigens, sicut inferius dicetur (§ 4-5,
below; cf. § 15).

. . . .

3 QUOMODO DOMINUS PAPA PREBENDAS SIBI DARI EXEGERIT. Anno Domini
m° cc° xxvi. rex Henricus ad natale Domini celebravit festum suum apud Win-
toniam, presentibus quibusdam episcopis et magnatibus multis. Sollempnitate
itaque peracta, profectus est rex apud Merlebergiam, ubi gravi infirmitate cor-
reptus per dies multos ibi[d] desperatus jacebat.

4 (Council at London, 13 January 1226) Venit interea terminus consilii[e] ad
festum sancti Hylarii[1] apud Westmonasterium prefixus,[f] ubi rex cum clero et
magnatibus regni comparere debuerat ut domini pape mandatum audiret. Multis igitur in loco prefato congregatis episcopis cum aliis prelatis et laicorum
turbis, magister Otho, domini pape nuntius, de quo habita est mentio superius
(§ 1-2), litteras aperte coram omnibus recitavit

5 in quibus idem papa allegavit scandalum sancte Romane ecclesie et obprobrium vetustissimum, notam scilicet concupiscentie, que radix dicitur omnium
malorum, et in hoc precipue quod nullus potest aliquod negotium in Romana
ecclesia[g] expedire nisi cum magna effusione pecunie et exhibitione donorum.[h]
"Sed, quoniam scandali hujus et infamie Romana paupertas causa est, debent
omnes[i] matris inopiam sublevare et patris[j] ut filii naturales quia, nisi a vobis et
aliis viris bonis et honestis dona reciperemus, deficerent nobis necessaria vite,
quod esset omnino Romane incongruum dignitati. Ad istud itaque scandalum
penitus eradicandum, per consilium fratrum nostrorum sancte Romane ecclesie cardinalium, quandam providimus formam cui, si volueritis consentire, a
scandalo matrem vestram poteritis liberare et in curia Romana sine donorum
obsequio exhibitionem justitie obtinere. Forma autem provisa hec est: Petimus
in primis ab omnibus ecclesiis cathedralibus duas nobis prebendas exhiberi, unam

---

[d] multos dies ibi B, ibi *cancell.* B[1]
[e] consilii] concilii B
[f] prefixus: prefixi BOW, *recte corr. supralin.* B[1]
[g] ecclesia BOW: *expun. et* curia *marg.* B[1]
[h] exhibitione donorum *tr.* B
[i] omnes *om.* B
[j] et patris *om.* B

ventual churches of England on the pretext that it was procuration money. And it is to be noted that at the time that Master Otto came to England [in September 1225], the lord pope sent nuncios throughout the whole world who everywhere called for taxes that were not his due, just as is said below [§ 4-5, below; cf. § 15].

. . . .

3 HOW THE LORD POPE DEMANDED THAT HE BE GIVEN PREBENDS. In the year 1226 at Christmas, King Henry kept his feast at Winchester with some bishops and many magnates present. When the celebration was over, the king went to Marlborough, where he was stricken with a serious illness and lay there for many days in critical condition.

4 [Council at London, 13 January 1226.] Meanwhile the time came for the council at Westminster, which was scheduled for the feast of St Hilary.[1] The king was supposed to be present there with the clergy and magnates of the kingdom in order to hear the lord pope's mandate. When many bishops accordingly assembled there together with other prelates and crowds of laymen, Master Otto, the pope's nuncio who was mentioned above [§ 1-2], publicly read the letter aloud in the presence of all.

5 In his letter, the pope declared there was a scandal concerning the holy Roman church that was a reproach of long standing, namely a reputation for greed, which is said to be the root of all evils, especially because no one can transact any business at the Roman church without spending money lavishly and presenting many gifts.[2] "But because Rome's poverty is the cause of this scandal and infamy, like dutiful children everyone ought to alleviate their mother's and father's lack of wealth, because unless we receive gifts from you and other good and honorable men, we shall lack the necessities of life, which would be altogether inconsistent with Roman dignity. And so, in order to completely eliminate this scandal, on the advice of our brothers the cardinals of the holy Roman church, we have adopted a proposal by which, if you agree, you can free your mother from scandal and obtain justice at the Roman curia without having to make gifts. This is our proposal: We request first of all that two prebends be presented to us from each cathedral church, one from the bishop's share of the property and the other from the chapter's. A similar twofold contribution is to be made by those monasteries in which the abbot and the convent each

1. Strictly speaking St Hilary's feast is 13 January, but because the octave of Epiphany also falls on that day, celebration is sometimes transferred to 14 January (e.g. Mas Latrie, *Trésor de chronologie*, col. 461). Wendover, however, treats Hilary's feast as interchangeable with the octave of Epiphany (cf. § 1).

2. Although Wendover passes from indirect to direct discourse at this point, he is still paraphrasing rather than quoting the bull *Super muros* (cf. Doc. 41).

de portione episcopi et alteram de capitulo. Et similiter in cenobiis ubi diverse sunt portiones abbatis et conventus, a conventibus quantum pertinet ad unum monachum, equali facta distributione bonorum suorum, et ab abbate tantundem."

6 His in hunc modum propositis, persuasit ex parte domini pape magister Otho ut consentirent prelati, allegans supradicta commoda que in litteris continentur. Hec autem omnia audientes episcopi et ecclesiarum prelati qui personaliter interfuerunt, divertentes seorsum ad colloquium,[k] cum super rebus propositis diutius deliberassent, responsum suum in ore magistri Johannis, Bedefordensis archidiaconi,[3] communiter posuerunt. Qui veniens in presentia magistri Othonis per hec verba respondit:

7 "Domine, ista, que nobis proponitis, regem Anglie specialiter tangunt, generaliter vero omnes ecclesiarum patronos regni. Tangunt etiam[l] archiepiscopos et eorum suffraganeos, necnon universos[m] Anglie prelatos. Cum ergo rex, propter infirmitatem, et archiepiscopi, nonnulli[n] episcopi et alii ecclesiarum prelati sint absentes, in eorum absentia vobis respondere non possumus nec debemus quia si id facere presumeremus, in prejudicium omnium absentium fieret prelatorum."

8 Et his dictis, venit Johannes Marescallus[4] et alii nuntii regis ad omnes prelatos qui de rege baronias tenebant in capite,[o] districte inhibentes ne laicum feodum suum Romane ecclesie obligarent, unde a servitio sibi debito privaretur.

9 Hec autem cum magister Otho intellexisset, statuit his qui aderant diem ibi in media Quadragesima,[5] dum ipse procuraret regis adventum et absentium prelatorum ut tunc negotium sortiretur effectum. Sed illi, absque regis et aliorum qui absentes erant assensu, prefixum diem admittere noluerunt, unde singuli ad propria sunt reversi.

· ·

10 QUOD MAGISTER OTHO FALCASIUM REGI RECONCILIARE STUDUERIT.[6]
Venit eodem tempore ad regem Anglorum magister Otho, domini pape nun-

---

[k] colloquium BW (O *deest*): *expun. et* colloquendum *marg.* B[1]
[l] etiam *om.* B
[m] universos] innumeros B
[n] nonnulli] etiam *add.* B
[o] capite BW: destinati *add. marg.* B[1]

have their own share; the convent's share is to be that of one monk, which is to be determined by dividing the value of the property equally among the monks, and the abbot's share is to be the same amount."

6 After making this proposal, Master Otto, speaking on the lord pope's behalf, urged the prelates to consent, and he stressed the advantages that were noted in the letter cited above. When they had heard him out, the bishops and ecclesiastical prelates who were present in person went off by themselves to discuss the matter privately, and after they had deliberated on the proposal for a long time, they designated Master John, archdeacon of Bedford,[3] as their spokesman. He went to Master Otto and gave this response for them all:

7 "Lord, what you have proposed to us touches the king of England in particular, and in fact it touches in general all of the kingdom's patrons of churches. It also touches the archbishops and their suffragans, as well as all the prelates of England. Therefore, since the king is absent because of sickness, and the archbishops, some bishops, and other prelates of churches are also absent, we ought not and can not reply to you in their absence, because if we were to presume to do so, it would be prejudicial to all of the absent prelates."

8 After this speech, John Marshal[4] and other spokesmen for the king came to all the prelates who held baronies in chief from the king, strictly forbidding them to assign their lay fiefs to the Roman church, because the king would in consequence be deprived of service that was his due.

9 When Master Otto had taken this all in, he adjourned the council until a day in the middle of Lent,[5] at which time all those present were to return, and he himself would see to it that the king and the absent prelates were present, so that the unfinished business might be completed. But those present refused to agree to the proposed date without the assent of the king and the others who were absent. And thus everyone went home.

. . . .

10 HOW MASTER OTTO TRIED TO RECONCILE FAWKES TO THE KING.[6] At the same time Master Otto, the lord pope's nuncio, came to the king of the English.

3. Master John of Houton, archdeacon of Bedford 1218-1231, then of Northampton 1231-1246 (both in the diocese of Lincoln): John Le Neve, *Fasti Ecclesiae Anglicanae, 1066–1300*, rev. ed. by Diana E. Greenway, vol. III (London, 1977), pp. 42, 31-32.

4. John Marshal (1170?–1235), first baron Marshal of Hingham and grand-nephew of William Marshal I, earl of Pembroke; for a summary of his long career in royal service, see *Dictionary of National Biography*, XII (1917), 1106-1108.

5. Strictly speaking, Mid-Lent (*mi-carême*) was the fourth Sunday in Lent, which in 1226 fell on 29 March.

6. In § 10, Wendover repeats but somewhat rephrases § 2.

tius, petens ex parte ejusdem pape ut, Falcasio sibi reconciliato, uxorem, terras, possessiones ad integrum ei et omnes redderet res sublatas. Cui rex respondit quod ob proditionem manifestam ab omni clero et populo regni ab Anglia sententialiter est expulsus perpetuo exilium subiturus, quam sententiam non potuit, nisi vellet venire contra regni antiquas consuetudines, infirmare. Hec cum audisset, magister Otho regem ulterius sollicitare cessavit. Et his ita gestis, misit idem Otho litteras suas ad omnes ecclesias cathedrales per Angliam sive conventuales, exigens procurationes debitas nuntiis Romanis, ita quod nulla procuratio numerum quadrainta excederet solidorum.

11 (= Doc. 1.1W) DE CONCILIO BITURICENSI CUI PRESEDIT ROMANUS FRANCORUM LEGATUS. Hoc eodem tempore venit magister Romanus ad partes Gallicanas a domino papa missus ut ibi legationis officio fungeretur. Quo cum pervenisset, fecit convocare regem Francorum cum archiepiscopis, episcopis et clero Gallicano ad concilium, cum comite Tholosano, pro quo principaliter[p] ad partes illas idem legatus[q] missus fuerat, sicut sequens relatio declarabit.

12 "Convenerunt igitur apud Bituricam civitatem . . . (Wendover's version of the *Relatio de concilio Bituricensi*, collated in Doc. 1.2-17) . . . quod credidit provenire non posse."

13 QUOD MAGISTER OTHO ROMAM INVITUS REDIERIT. Eodem anno (1226), cum magister Otho, domini pape nuntius, tempore Quadragesimali ad Northanhumbriam profecturus et procurationes desideratas exacturus, Norhamtonam usque pervenisset, venerunt ad eum, Cantuariensi archiepiscopo procurante, littere domini pape, in quibus continebatur expressum ut statim visis litteris Romam veniret, ejus potestate penitus enervata. Obliquo igitur oculo litteris inspectis, demisso vultu eas projecit in ignem, atque ilico proposito mutato, clitellis vacuis confusus ab Anglia recessit,[r] injuncto Stephano, Cant' archiepiscopo, sicut erat in litteris domini pape expressum, ut, convocatis rege et omnibus Anglie prelatis, responsum eorum super negotio pro quo idem Otho missus fuerat domino pape transmittere non omittat.

14 (Council at London, 3 May 1226) Magistro igitur Othone Anglia a tergo salutata,[s] Stephanus, Cant' archiepiscopus, vocatis ad concilium cunctis apud Westmonasterium post Pascha[t] quos negotium tangebat, recitari fecit litteras suprascriptas de beneficiis Romane ecclesie conferendis coram rege et prelatis Anglie, qui ad ejus vocationem plene convenerant. Sed, illis auditis ac diligen-

[p] principaliter] specialiter B
[q] idem legatus *om.* B
[r] confusus *post* recessit *tr.* B
[s] Anglia . . . salutata OW: Angliam . . . salutante B
[t] post Pascha] cunctis *perperam add.* W (*dittographia*)

On the pope's behalf, Otto requested that Fawkes be reconciled to the king, and that the king would then return to him his wife, lands, undiminished possessions, and everything that had been snatched from him. To this the king replied that because of manifest treason Fawkes had been banished from England under a sentence of perpetual exile that was imposed by all the clergy and people of the kingdom, and the king declared that he was not able to annul that sentence unless he wanted to act contrary to the ancient customs of the realm. When Master Otto heard this, he stopped bothering the king any more about Fawkes. After this, the same Otto sent his letters to all the cathedral and conventual churches in England, demanding that they pay him the procurations due to Roman nuncios, with the proviso that no procuration should exceed the amount of forty shillings.

11 [= Doc. 1.1W] CONCERNING THE COUNCIL OF BOURGES, WHICH WAS PRESIDED OVER BY ROMANUS, LEGATE OF THE FRENCH. About this same time, Master Romanus was sent by the lord pope into Gaul to act as his legate there. On his arrival, he summoned the king of the French and also the archbishops, bishops, and Gallican clergy to a council, together with the count of Toulouse, which was the main reason that the legate had been sent to that country, as the following account will show.

12 [Here Wendover inserts his version of the *Account of the Council of Bourges*, which is collated above with the other versions in Doc. 1.2–17.]

13 HOW MASTER OTTO RETURNED TO ROME UNWILLINGLY. During Lent in the same year [1226], the lord pope's nuncio, Master Otto, was making his way to Northumberland, and all along the route he was collecting the procurations he longed for, when he came to Northampton. There he received the lord pope's letter, issued at the request of the archbishop of Canterbury, that entirely revoked his power as nuncio and expressly stated that as soon as he saw the letter he should return to Rome. While reading the letter he kept glancing askance, and then with a depressed look he threw it into the fire and immediately changed his plans, so that in dismay he left England with empty saddlebags. In accordance with express instructions in the lord pope's letter, Otto ordered Stephen archbishop of Canterbury to convoke the king and all the prelates of England and without fail to inform the lord pope of their response concerning the business on which Otto had been sent.

14 [Council at London, 3 May 1226.] When Master Otto had accordingly saluted England with his backside, Stephen archbishop of Canterbury summoned everyone whom the business touched to a council at Westminster after Easter. There he caused the letter about gifting benefices to the Roman church, which was described above, to be read aloud in the presence of the king and the prelates of England, who had duly assembled at his summons. But when they

ter intellectis, singuli singulos ad risum movebant super concupiscentia Romanorum, qui illud morale non intelligunt, videlicet,

Quod facit virtus,[u] non copia, sufficientem;

Et non paupertas, sed mentis hiatus, egentem.[7]

15 Tunc rex, convocatis seorsum prelatis et quibusdam magnatibus, hoc archiepiscopo dedit[v] responsum: "Ista que[w] suadet nobis dominus papa, universam Christianitatis latitudinem respiciunt, et quoniam nos quasi in extremis orbis constituti sumus partibus, cum viderimus qualiter cetera regna erga tales se habuerint exactiones, dominus papa, cum ab aliis regnis habuerimus exemplum, in obsequiis suis[x] nos inveniet aliis[y] promptiores." Et hiis dictis, concessa est omnibus licentia recedendi.

16 QUOD MOTIO MAGNA FACTA EST SUPER COMITEM THOLOSANUM. Per idem tempus facta est predicatio in partibus Gallicanis a legato Romano generalis ut omnes qui possent arma movere se cruce signarent super comitem Tholosanum et populum ejus, qui omnes heretica feditate dicebantur infecti. Ad ejus quoque predicationem multitudo maxima prelatorum et laicorum crucis signaculum susceperunt, plus metu regis Francorum et[z] legati quam zelo justitie inducti. Videbatur enim multis abusio ut hominem fidelem Christianum infestarent, precipue cum constaret cunctis cum[a] in concilio nuper apud civitatem Byturicam habito multis precibus persuasisse legato ut veniret ad singulas terre sue civitates inquirens a singulis articulos fidei, et si quempiam contra fidem inveniret sentientem catholicam, ipse secundum judicium[b] sancte ecclesie justitie ex eis plenitudinem exhiberet, et si civitatem aliquam inveniret rebellem, ipse pro posse suo eam cum habitatoribus suis ad satisfactionem compelleret. Pro se ipso autem optulit, si in aliquo deliquit, quod se fecisse non recolit,[c] plenam Deo et sancte ecclesie satisfactionem ut fidelis Christianus, et si legatus vollet,[d] etiam fidei examen subire. Hec quoque omnia legatus contempsit, nec potuit comes catholicus gratiam invenire nisi pro se et heredibus suis hereditatem suam deserens abjuraret.

17 Rex vero Francorum ad ejusdem legati exhortationem cruce signatus noluit expeditionem bellicam promovere nisi litteris prius a domino papa im-

---

[u] facit virtus OW: virtus reddit B

[v] dedit B: dedere OW

[w] Ista que B: inquiunt *inser.* OW

[x] suis *om.* B

[y] aliis *om.* B

[z] et] vel favore B

[a] cum] eum B

[b] judicium BO: *perperam om.* W

[c] recolit] recoluit B

[d] legatus vollet] legat vellet B

had heard and understood it, they were provoked to laugh among themselves at the greed of the Romans, who did not understand the moral expressed in this couplet:

> Virtue, not abundance, makes one sufficient,
>
> And not poverty, but a greedy mind, makes one needy.[7]

15 After the king had conferred privately with the prelates and some of the magnates, he gave this response to the archbishop: "The proposal that the lord pope recommends to us is one that concerns the whole wide world of Christianity, and inasmuch as we are located in almost its most remote part, we shall wait to see how the other kingdoms respond to these demands; when the other kingdoms have set us an example, the lord pope will find us more well disposed than others to comply with his wishes." After this speech, everyone was granted leave to depart.

16 THE GREAT MILITARY EXPEDITION AGAINST THE COUNT OF TOULOUSE. About the same time, the legate Romanus had it preached throughout Gaul that everyone who could bear arms should take the sign of the Cross against the count of Toulouse and his people, who were all said to be infected with a filthy heresy. At his preaching an immense number of prelates and laymen received the sign of the Cross, but they were led to do so more by fear of the king of the French and the legate than by zeal for righteousness. For to many it seemed an abuse that they should attack a faithful Christian man, especially since his position had been made known to everyone at the council that had been held recently at the city of Bourges. There, with many pleas, Raymond had tried to persuade the legate to come to each of the cities of his land to inquire into the articles of their faith. And if the legate should find anyone who held opinions contrary to the Catholic faith, the count promised that he himself would exact full justice from them according to the judgment of holy Church, and if any city refused to obey, he would do all that he could to compel that city and its inhabitants to give satisfaction. For himself, however, Raymond offered to give full satisfaction to God and holy Church as a faithful Christian if he had failed to do his duty in any way, which he did not recall having done, and also to undergo an examination of his faith if the legate wished. But the legate had no use for all these offers, nor was this Catholic count able to gain favor unless he would take an oath for himself and his heirs forsaking his inheritance.

17 At the exhortation of the same legate, the king of the French was himself signed with the Cross, but he refused to mount a military expedition unless the

---

7. Marbod of Rennes (d. 1123), *De ornamentis verborum*, cap. 8 (Migne, *Pat. Lat.*, CLXXI, 1689), identified by Dorothea Weber (Vienna): "Ergo facit virtus . . ." Wendover substituted "Quod" for "Ergo" to fit his sentence; his metrics were improved by Paris.

petratis ad regem Anglorum inhibitoriis ne sub pena excommunicationis regem Francorum inquietaret vel arma contra eum moveret de aliqua terra quam in presenti possidebat sive juste sive injuste dum idem rex esset in servitio suo et ecclesie Romane ad exterminandum hereticos Albigenses et eorum fautorem et complicem comitem Tholosanum. Sed eidem regi, ad exaltationem fidei, consilium impendere et auxilium^e non tardaret. Et his ita gestis, rex Francorum Lodowicus et legatus omnibus cruce signatis diem statuerunt peremptorium ut in ascensione Domini apud Lugdunum cum equis et armis sub pena excommunicationis convenirent, ipsos ad expeditionem propositam secuturi.

^{e} impendere *post* auxilium *tr.* B

Document 44
THE FENLAND CONTINUATION OF THE CROWLAND ANNAL FOR 1225
1226

Two dozen annals covering the years 1202–1225 have long been cited as the "Barnwell chronicle" because they appear in a manuscript that once belonged to Barnwell Priory, just outside Cambridge. In this and other manuscripts, the series directly follows Roger of Hoveden's annals for the years 1181–1201, and therefore some have preferred to describe it as a continuation of Hoveden. Most commonly, however, these annals are cited as "Walter of Coventry" because the text has been edited under the title *Memoriale fratris Walteri de Coventria*.

Today the text of these annals is preserved in at least five manuscripts as one segment of a composite world chronicle. The origin of this compilation is a complex puzzle for which I have proposed a solution elsewhere; here I shall summarize my conclusions with particular reference to the brief entries that comprise Doc. 44. (See figure 5.)

Alpha is the lost archetype of this tradition. It appears to have been written at the Benedictine abbey of Peterborough because it was used there by two later compilers: the *Liber niger*, or Black Book, of Peterborough (N), and the annals of Spalding (S), a Benedictine house eight miles north of Peterborough.

lord pope issued a letter prohibiting the king of the English under pain of excommunication from disturbing him or making war against him concerning any
land that he presently possessed, either justly or unjustly, while the king of France
was in the service of the pope and the Roman church for the purpose of ex-
terminating the Albigensian heretics and their supporter and accomplice, the
count of Toulouse. Instead, the king [of England] should not delay to lend counsel and aid to the king of the French for the exaltation of the faith. After this
was done, Louis king of the French and the legate set a deadline for all the crusaders; under pain of excommunication, they were to assemble with their horses
and arms at Lyon on the Lord's Ascension, in order to follow them on the proposed expedition.

Alpha contained a composite chronicle that began at Creation with the
chronicle of Marianus Scotus as continued by Florence of Worcester down to
1131, occasionally interspersed with paragraphs from William of Malmesbury;
next, the chronicle by Henry of Huntington supplied the annals 1131-1154. To
fill in the gap between his sources, the Alpha compiler composed his own brief
annals 1155-1169; then for the years 1170-1177, he transcribed the *Gesta regis
Henrici*, ascribed to Benedict of Peterborough. Next, he closed another gap with
original annals 1177-1180, and concluded his compilation with the annals of
Roger of Hoveden for 1181-1201.

The Peterborough monk who assembled Alpha was no mere compiler, however; he himself took up the story where Hoveden, his last source, stopped in
1201. For the next twenty-three years, from 1202 down to the siege of Bedford
in June 1224, he composed "the best, the fullest and most sophisticated annals"
written in England for that period (Gransden, p. 318). Stubbs judged this to be
"one of the most valuable contributions in existence to the history of that eventful period" (ed. cit., II, vii). More recently, J. C. Holt characterized particular annals as "most perceptive" and "surprisingly accurate and sympathetic" (pp. 223,
215). This anonymous monk of Peterborough accordingly ranks among the
greatest medieval chroniclers. His original composition, which has mistakenly
been attributed to Walter of Coventry or to Barnwell Priory, can more accurately be called "the Peterborough annals 1202-1224."

The Alpha annalist was apparently preparing to continue his account, for documents from the latter half of 1224 and from 1225 were appended to Alpha,
where they were used by N and S.

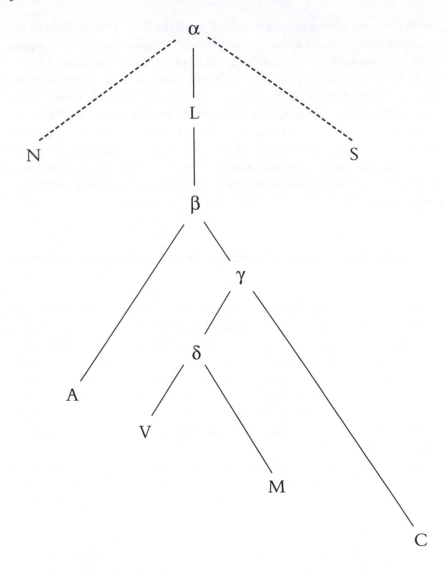

A = London, College of Arms, MS. Arundel 10 ("Barnwell" chronicle)
C = Cambridge, Corpus Christi College, MS. 175 ("Walter of Coventry")
L = London, BL, MS. Add. 35,168 (Crowland annals)
M = Magdalen College, Oxford, MS. lat. 36
N = London, Society of Antiquaries, MS. 60 (Black Book of Peterborough)
S = London, BL, MS. Cotton Claudius A. v (Spalding annals)
V = London, BL, MS. Cotton Vitellius E. xiii

FIGURE 5.   Stemma of "Walter of Coventry" (C) and related manuscripts

(L) London, British Library, MS. Add. 35,168. Less than a year after the completion of Alpha, a copy of it was made for the Benedictines at Crowland Abbey, eight miles south of Peterborough. The redactor of L completed the annal for 1224, inserting the documents that had been appended to Alpha and providing narrative continuity; he also supplied other materials that dated from the second half of 1225, the latest being a papal letter written in August. The result was the "Crowland annals."

Beta is a lost manuscript, the existence of which is indicated by a continuation of L's 1225 annal (Doc. 44.1-4) that is found in all of Beta's descendants (ACMV). Since the Beta continuation records the beginning of the *Super muros* crisis but not its conclusion, it was probably written in the early months of 1226, before the council of London in May (§ 5). The redactor eliminated the annals *ante Christi natum* and began instead with the Incarnation. Beta's provenance is unknown, but it does not seem likely to have been made for either Peterborough or Crowland, which both had recent copies of the text; the nearby Benedictine houses of Spalding and Thorney, also in the Fen country, are more plausible destinations. For want of a better name, I have called Beta "the Fenland continuation of the Crowland annals."

Gamma was the earliest copy of Beta, probably made in 1226, since it continued the Beta text by adding a single paragraph (§ 5) on the council concerning *Super muros* that was held at London on 3 May 1226. Gamma's redactor found another, easier way to reduce the bulk of the pre-1202 text: he simply started copying Beta at A. D. 1002. This solution proved to be an acceptable compromise, which was maintained in CMV.

(A) London, College of Arms, MS. Arundel 10. A second copy of Beta was made ca. 1233. Like Beta, its chronicle began with the Incarnation, but the annals before 1202 were drastically abridged; thereafter they are complete, and to them the compiler added his own continuation for 1226-1232. Because this was the earliest copy Stubbs knew of the Peterborough continuation of Hoveden, he mistook it for the archetype; moreover, because the manuscript had once belonged to Barnwell Priory, he assumed that it was written there and accordingly named it the "Barnwell chronicle." Actually it was written for some other, unfortunately unknown, house; when it came to Barnwell sometime before 1268, entries concerning its new home had to be added in the margins.

Delta was a copy of Gamma, made in the second quarter of the thirteenth century. Its existence is established by slight variants that show that, while V and

M have certain readings in common, still neither could have been copied from the other.

(V) London, British Library, MS. Cotton Vitellius E. xiii. Written in the 1250s, this is the oldest extant witness to the Gamma recension, but its text was badly damaged in the Cottonian fire of 1731 and Stubbs did not collate its considerable fragments for his edition of C.

(M) Oxford, Magdalen College, MS. lat. 36. Written about a generation after V (ca. 1270), this plain quarto volume preserves a *complete* copy of the CMV annals 1002–1226, inasmuch as C is slightly abridged and V is mutilated. Stubbs recorded the principal variants in his edition of C. A Yorkshire provenance is faintly suggested by a list of books "ex dono fratris Ricardi de Knesall," who came from the parish of Kneesall near Nottingham, in the medieval diocese of York.

(C) Cambridge, Corpus Christi College, MS. 175. This is the manuscript that Stubbs printed in its entirety in the Rolls Series as "The Historical Collections of Walter of Coventry." For the most part, it is an accurate copy of Gamma, except that occasionally the text is very slightly abridged. The script is late thirteenth century; internal evidence suggests a date not long after 1293. The title is based on an inscription, *"Memoriale fratris Walteri de Coventria,"* which probably just means that Brother Walter of Coventry donated the book. But Walter of Coventry is otherwise unknown, and his house as well, except that *frater* suggests a mendicant rather than a monastic establishment.

The development of this chronicle shows the reaction of the English monastic clergy to *Super muros*. The bull and its reception in France was the sole subject of the long Beta continuation (Doc. 44.1–4), and the only purpose of the paragraph Gamma added (§ 5) was to record the conclusion of the crisis. Evidently the affair was a major concern for the Fenland monasteries where the chronicle originated and circulated, just as it was for the Salisbury chapter (Doc.

Harum[a] bajulus litterarum pro Falcasio fuit Otho, domini pape subdiaconus et capellanus, litteras archiepiscopis,[b] episcopis et clero Anglie alias, immo alienas,[1] quia ut videbatur a rege et regno, clero et populo, libertates et jura non

[a] *littera initialis om.* A, *suppl. marg.* A[1]
[b] et *add.* C

42). Moreover, the fact that copies of *Super muros* and the *Relatio* were widely disseminated suggests that the clergy summoned to the council of London in May 1226 were provided with documentation to inform the preliminary discussions enjoined on them by the citation mandate, which required that they "deliberate in the meantime and come fully instructed to reply to the lord pope's nuncio" (Doc. 42.3). That these lengthy documents were preserved long after the crisis had passed indicates not only the growing importance attached to legal precedents but also the determination to minimize financial subsidies.

MSS.—(A) London, College of Arms, MS. Arundel 10, fols. 103vb–105vb; (C) Cambridge, Corpus Christi College, MS. 175, fols. 174vb–176ra; (M) Oxford, Magdalen College, MS. lat. 36, fols. 196r–197v.

Ed.—(1) An inferior edition appeared in *Rec. hist. Gaules*, XVIII (1822), 164-187. (2) *Memoriale fratris Walteri de Coventria: The Historical Collections of Walter of Coventry*, ed. W. Stubbs, Rolls Series, no. 58, 2 vols. (London, 1872-1873), II, 274-279. Transcribes C with select variants from A and M.

Refs.—A. Gransden, *Historical Writing in England c. 550 to c. 1307* (Ithaca, N.Y., 1974), pp. 339-345. J. C. Holt, *Magna Carta*, 2nd ed. (Cambridge, Eng., 1992). R. Kay, "Walter of Coventry and the Barnwell Chronicle," *Traditio*, LIV (1999), 141-167.

Text.—The passages edited below were Beta's "Fenland" continuation of the Crowland annal for 1225, with the exception of § 5, which was added later in the Gamma recension. Accordingly, the text of § 1-4 has been transcribed from a photocopy of A, the earliest extant manuscript containing this passage, and collated with photocopies of C and M. Stubbs reported no variants from V for this document and I have not used the manuscript. The V-text breaks off with the word "Remis" (Doc. 1.7).

The bearer of this letter to help Fawkes was the lord pope's subdeacon and chaplain, Otto; he also brought another letter addressed to the archbishops, bishops, and clergy of England, which indeed could be called an "alien" letter[1]

---

1. The chronicler is playing feebly on the similarity of the words *alias* ("another") and *alienas* ("alien").

tantum auferentes, immo potius[c] penitus alienantes, bulla intonante apostolica sub hac forma: -

2 "Honorius[d] episcopus, servus servorum Dei, venerabilibus fratribus archiepiscopis et[e] episcopis et dilectis filiis universis ecclesiarum prelatis per regnum Anglie constitutis, salutem et apostolicam benedictionem.   —Super muros Jerusalem custodes positi . . . (= Doc. 41) . . . et utilitate quo ad minus fierent aliene.   —Datum Laterani v° kal. Februarii, pontificatus nostri anno ix."[f]

3 (= Doc. 1.1A, repeated here in context:) Cum[g] autem talia vel prossus[h] similia per universarum terrarum spatia pontifici summo[i] subjecta prius essent promulgata—et "quicunque ea audierunt, tinnierunt[j] ambe aures eorum"[2]— legatus quidam, Romanus nomine, a Roma directus in Galliam,[k] concilium celebravit apud Lugdunum Gallie.

4 "Convenerunt igitur ad capitulum . . . (the "Fenland" version of the *Relatio de concilio Bituricensi*, collated in Doc. 1.2-17) . . . quod minime creditur posse provenire."[3]

5 Dictus[l] idem Otho, domini pape nuntius, apud Londonias concilio convocato in xv. dies post Pascha, litterisque apostolicis ibidem coram rege Henrico et comitibus atque baronibus coramque archiepiscopo et ejus suffraganeis et clero recitatis,[m] responsum est ex parte regis et cleri quod, etiam si alia regna domini pape petitioni assentirent in prebendis et redditibus curie Romane solvendis, regnum Anglie de jure ab hujusmodi exactione deberet esse immune, ratione recognitionis facte per Johannem regem patrem suum Innocentio summo pontifici, cui regnum Anglie subjecit et Hiberniam, scilicet[n] pro Anglia dcc. marcas et pro Hibernia ccc. marcas per annum. Cumque cerneret regnum et clerum unanimi assensu sibi resistere, infecto negotio recessit, et non multos post[o] dies, litteris domini pape acceptis, repatriavit.

---

[c] potius AC: *om.* M
[d] *littera initialis om.* AM, *suppl. marg.* A[1] M[1]
[e] et *om.* CM
[f] nono CM
[g] Cum C: *littera initialis om.* AM, *suppl. marg.* A[1] M[1]; Dum *scripsit Stubbs!*
[h] prorsus CM
[i] pontifici summo *tr.* CM
[j] tinnuerunt A (*perf. in* −ui *perperam*)
[k] directus *post* Galliam *iteravit* C
[l] *littera initialis om.* M, *suppl. marg.* M[1]
[m] recitatis AM: recitans C
[n] scilicet *om.* M
[o] multos post *tr.* M

because it seemed to be not only taking away privileges and rights from the king and kingdom, but more precisely actually *alienating* them altogether. The apostolic bull thundered thus:

2 [The text of *Super muros Jerusalem* follows; see Doc. 41 above.]

3 [= Doc. 1.1A, repeated here in context:] Because the same or a very similar letter was being promulgated in all the lands subject to the pope—and the ears of everyone that heard it tingled[2]—a certain legate, Romanus by name, who had been sent to France from Rome, celebrated a council at Lyon.

4 [The "Fenland" version of the *Account of the Council of Bourges*, which is collated above in Doc. 1.2-17.][3]

5 That same Otto, the lord pope's nuncio, summoned a council at London on the fifteenth day after Easter [Monday, 4 May 1226], and there the apostolic letter was read aloud in the presence of King Henry and the counts and barons, and in the presence of the archbishop and his suffragans and clergy. The response, given for the king and the clergy, was that even if other kingdoms agreed to the lord pope's petition to have prebends and revenues paid to the Roman curia, the kingdom of England ought by right to be immune from an exaction of this sort, because of the recognition his father King John had made to Pope Innocent, to whom he subjected the kingdom of England and Ireland as well, namely seven hundred marks for England and three hundred for Ireland [were to be paid as annual tribute to the papacy]. And when Otto perceived that the government and the clergy were unanimously agreed to resist the proposal, he did not press the matter but left it unfinished, and not many days later he received a letter from the lord pope and went back home.

2. Cf. I Reg. (AV I Sam.) iii.11.

3. In some versions of the "Fenland" chronicle, this document is the last item in the text, but § 5 was added ca. 1226 in the Gamma recension, which was Walter of Coventry's source.

SECTION FIVE

MONASTIC PROVINCIAL CHAPTERS

Document 45
INNOCENT III ESTABLISHES
MONASTIC CHAPTERS-GENERAL AND VISITORS
Fourth Lateran Council, 1215

Innocent III crowned his energetic years of administration with the greatest of the reforming councils of the medieval Latin Church.[1] The public sessions of the council, held in the Lateran basilica during November 1215, did not deliberate over the reform of the Church, however.[2] The seventy canons, for which the Fourth Lateran Council is chiefly remembered, were prepared secretly, recited in public session, and approved as read.[3] How they were prepared remains something of a mystery.

As was common in medieval conciliar legislation, the Lateran statutes were cast in the form of authoritative prescriptions made by the council's head and approved by its members.[4] The enacting clause leaves no doubt that the voice of authority is that of Innocent alone, speaking with the plural of majesty: "sicut olim aperte distinximus et nunc sacri approbatione concilii confirmamus . . ." (c. 8). Thus it is not surprising that contemporary copies of the canons frequently bear a title in which the Lateran legislation is credited to Innocent alone.[5] Certainly the pope was ultimately responsible for the decrees he ordained in the council; doubtless, too, they were drafted by his curia; but the council also had its role to play, albeit a supporting one.

Assembled in public session, the council expressed its collective approval of the proposed legislation, as such phrases in the canons as "sacro approbante concilio" (c. 47) testify. This, however, was a solemn, ceremonial formality which invited neither debate nor dissent. More important but less known are the legislative procedures by which the statutes were formulated. That they were the product of the council and not merely imposed upon it appears from the *rubri-*

1. The most recent general account is R. Foreville, *Latran I, II, III et Latran IV*, Histoire des conciles oecuméniques, 6 (Paris, 1965).

2. See the anonymous description of the public proceedings, edited with commentary by S. Kuttner and A. García y García, "A New Eyewitness Account of the Fourth Lateran Council," *Traditio*, XX (1964), 115-178.

3. Ibid., pp. 164-165.

4. On metropolitans as conciliar legislators, see my unpublished doctoral dissertation, "The Making of Statutes in French Provincial Councils, 1049-1305" (University of Wisconsin, Madison, 1959); cf. *Dissertation Abstracts*, XX (1959), 1004 (L.C. card no. Mic 59-3006).

5. Examples in A. García [y] García, "El concilio IV de Letrán (1215) y sus comentarios," *Traditio*, XIV (1958), 484-502, at p. 486; also Kuttner-García, "Fourth Lateran Council," p. 164.

cella prefixed to the Lateran decrees in Innocent's own register:"Sequuntur multe ordinationes per diversa capitula *facte* et ordinate in dicto concilio . . . "[6] No doubt the pope took counsel in some way with the assembled prelates, although the mechanics of the process are now obscure. In the summons to Lateran IV, the bishops were instructed to ascertain what reforms were needed and to bring their recommendations in writing to the council.[7] Innocent, too, had his proposals on which the prelates were consulted, for in at least one instance an unfavorable response caused him to abandon a reform he had desired.[8] In general, then, we may be sure that the members of the council participated in the shaping of the statutes as counsellors to their lord the pope. If the legislation of Lateran IV was prepared by commissioners and debated by the fathers before being submitted to Innocent for his final disposition, as was the practice at later general councils, no trace of the process has survived.

Concerning c. 12 itself, we have the contemporary report of Gerald of Wales, who was not present at the council, and it contains no hint of how the statute was framed: he says simply that "in the Lateran council . . . it was provided by God's grace."[9]

Text.—The text of the canons promulgated at Lateran IV has long been uncertain. Innocent's register, the obvious place to look for a reliable copy, has disappeared. Most of the statutes were of course incorporated into the *Decretals of Gregory IX* (1234) but, inasmuch as the compilers had papal sanction to alter the texts of their materials, the result must be regarded as a second, authorized redaction.[10] Before the Gregorian codification, the original conciliar text had circulated both independently and in the decretal collection known as the *Compilatio quarta*, in which Innocent's letters and statutes were selected and systematically organized shortly after his death by the canonist Johannes Teutonicus for

6. A. Theiner, *Vetera monumenta Slavorum meridionalium historiam illustrantia*, I (Rome, 1863), 63, no. 14.

7. Mansi, XXII (1778), 961e–962a: "Interim vero et per vos ipsos, et per alios viros prudentes, universa subtiliter inquiratis, quae correctionis aut reformationis studio indigere videntur, et ea fideliter conscribentes, ad sacri concilii perferatis examen. . . . "

8. Doc. 40.7 and n. 1, above; cf. R. Kay, "Gerald of Wales and the Fourth Lateran Council," *Viator*, XXIX (1998), 79–93, at p. 84.

9. *Speculum Ecclesiae*, II.29, ed. J. S. Brewer in *Giraldi Cambrensis Opera*, 8 vols., Rolls Series, no. 21 (London, 1861–1891), IV, 93–94 (variants from MGH, SS, XXVII, 418): "nuper, his ultimis nostris diebus, in Concilio Lateranensi a Papa Innocentio III. cum multa solemnitate, multaque tam episcoporum quam abbatum ab universo fidelium orbe convocatorum ad haec (hoc) et collectorum numerositate celebrato, per capitula singulis in regnis semel in triennio uno in loco tenenda, et (per) visitatores annuo more officientium ad singula coenobia destinandos, salubre remedium per Dei gratiam est provisum."

10. Friedberg, II, xii; Doc. 45 = *Decretales Gregorii IX*, 3.35.7 (ed., II, 600–601).

use in schools and courts of law.[11] Even before this appeared, canonistic commentaries had been made on the text of the Lateran statutes, which must be extremely close to the original when found conjoined with these earliest comments.[12] In addition to these various branches of the canonistic tradition of the Lateran text, some twenty other early copies of the decrees survive. The conciliar collectors, from Crabbe in 1538 down to the *Conciliorum oecumenicorum decreta* of 1962, based their several editions on a few isolated manuscripts and the work of their predecessors.[13] Nothing even approaching a reliable text was avail-

11. *Quinque compilationes antiquae*, E. A. Friedberg (Leipzig, 1882), p. xxxiii; Doc. 45 = 4 Comp. 3.12.2 (ed., p. 143).

12. Commentaries by Johannes Teutonicus, Vincentius Hispanus, and Damasus in *Constitutiones concilii quarti Lateranensis una cum commentariis glossatorum*, ed. A. García y García (Vatican City, 1981).

13. For manuscripts and editions, see García, "El concilio," pp. 484, 488-489. The edition by C. Leonardi in *Conciliorum oecumenicorum decreta*, ed. G. Alberigo et al., 2nd ed. (Freiburg: Herder, 1962), is based on earlier conciliar collections, but with useful bibliography for each canon; the 4th ed. (Bologna: Dehoniane, 1991) refers to García's edition but simply reprints Leonardi's text (pp. 226-271).

<CONCILII QVARTI LATERANENSIS CONSTITUTIONES>

Constitutio xii

In singulis regnis siue prouinciis fiat de triennio in triennium, saluo iure diocesanorum pontificum, commune capitulum abbatum atque priorum abbates proprios non habentium, qui non consueuerunt tale capitulum celebrare, ad quod uniuersi conueniant prepeditionem canonicam non habentes, apud unum de monasteriis ad hoc aptum,

2 hoc adhibito moderamine ut nullus eorum plus quam sex euectiones et octo personas adducat.

3 Aduocent autem caritatiue in huiusmodi nouitatis primordiis duos Cisterciensis ordinis uicinos abbates ad prestandum sibi consilium et auxilium opportunum, cum sint in huiusmodi capitulis celebrandis ex longa consuetudine plenius informati. Qui absque contradictione duos sibi de ipsis associent quos uiderint expedire; ac ipsi quatuor presint capitulo uniuerso, ita quod ex hoc nullus eorum auctoritatem sibi prelationis assumat unde, cum expedierit, prouida possint deliberatione mutari.

able until the appearance of the definitive critical edition of the statutes and their early commentators by García y García in 1981, from which I reproduce the twelfth canon here.[14] I have paragraphed the text according to the *divisiones* established by Panormitanus that form part of the medieval ordinary apparatus to the *Decretals of Gregory IX* (my edition, Lyons, 1548).

Translation.—Italian translation of c. 12 by A. N. Alberigo in *Conciliorum oecumenicorum decreta,* ed. G. Alberigo et al.; 4th ed. (Bologna, 1991), pp. 240-241; English translation in *Decrees of the Ecumenical councils*, ed. Norman P. Tanner, 2 vols. (London, 1990), I, *240-*241. I have consulted both usefully while making my own version from García's slightly better text.

14. See n. 12, above; c. 12 at pp. 60-62. I am indebted to Professor García's publishers for permission to reproduce this text. The punctuation and orthography of García's edition have been retained unaltered.

CONSTITUTIONS OF THE FOURTH LATERAN COUNCIL
Constitution 12

Every three years, in every kingdom or province, saving the right of diocesan bishops, let there be held a general chapter of those abbots, and of those priors who do not have their own abbot, who do not customarily celebrate such a chapter. With the exception of those persons who have a canonical impediment, they all should assemble at one of the monasteries that is suitable for the purpose,

2 and they should show moderation, so that no one brings more than six horses and eight persons.

3 To inaugurate this innovation, in the spirit of brotherhood let them invite two nearby Cistercian abbots to lend them timely counsel and aid, since the Cistercians are more experienced because it has long been their custom to hold such chapters. The two Cistercian abbots are without opposition to select as their associates two of the others who seem to them to be appropriate; and these four are to preside over the whole chapter in such a way that none of them assumes

4 Huiusmodi uero capitulum aliquot certis diebus continue iuxta morem Cisterciensium celebretur, in quo diligens habeatur tractatus de reformatione ordinis et obseruantia regulari,

5 et quod statutum fuerit, illis quatuor approbantibus, ab omnibus inuiolabiliter obseruetur, omni excusatione, contradictione ac appellatione remotis,

6 prouiso nichilominus ubi sequenti termino debeat capitulum celebrari.

7 Et qui conuenerint uitam ducant communem, et faciant proportionaliter simul omnes communes expensas, ita quod, si non omnes poterint in eisdem, saltem plures simul in diuersis domibus commorentur.

8 Ordinentur etiam in eodem capitulo religiose ac circumspecte persone que singulas abbatias eiusdem regni siue prouincie non solum monachorum set etiam monialium, secundum formam sibi prefixam, uice nostra studeant uisitare, corrigentes et reformantes que correctionis et reformationis officio uiderint indigere, ita quod si rectorem loci cognouerint ab amministratione penitus amouendum, denuncient episcopo proprio ut illum amouere procuret, quod si non fecerit, ipsi uisitatores hoc referant ad apostolice sedis examen.

9 Hoc ipsum regulares canonicos secundum ordinem suum uolumus et precipimus obseruare.

10 Si uero in hac nouitate quidquam difficultatis emerserit quod per predictas personas nequeat expediri, ad apostolice sedis iudicium absque scandalo referatur, ceteris irrefragabiliter obseruatis que concordi fuerint deliberatione prouisa.

11 Porro diocesani episcopi monasteria sibi subiecta ita studeant reformare ut, cum ad ea predicti uisitatores accesserint, plus in illis inueniant quod commendatione quam quod correctione sit dignum, attentissime precauentes ne per eos dicta monasteria indebitis honeribus aggrauentur, quia sic uolumus superiorum iura seruari, ut inferiorum nolimus iniurias sustinere.

12 Ad hec districte precipimus tam diocesanis episcopis quam personis que preerunt capitulis celebrandis ut per censuram ecclesiasticam, appellatione remota, compescant aduocatos, patronos, uicedominos, rectores et consules, magnates et milites seu quoslibet alios ne monasteria presumant offendere in personis aut rebus; et si forsan offenderint, eos ad satisfaciendum compellere non omittant, ut liberius et quietius omnipotenti Deo ualeant famulari.

authority over the others, and consequently they can be replaced if necessary after mature deliberation.

4 Such a chapter is to be celebrated continuously for a set number of days, as is the custom of the Cistercians, and in it the reformation of the order and the observance of the rule is to be diligently discussed.

5 What has been enacted with the approval of the four is to be observed inviolably by all, with no excuses, contradictions, or appeals allowed.

6 Moreover, it is to be decided where the chapter is to be celebrated next time.

7 Those who attend should lead a common life and together share all common expenses proportionately. If they cannot all live in the same house, at least let groups of them stay together in several houses.

8 At the same chapter let there be appointed religious and prudent persons who are to make it their business to visit on our [the pope's] behalf all the abbeys of their kingdom or province, and not only the houses of monks but also of nuns. In accordance with a prescribed form, they are to correct and reform those things that seem to require correction and reform. If they discern that the superior of a place needs to be relieved altogether of administrative duties, they should notify that person's own bishop, so he can attend to the matter himself; if he does not, then the visitors are to refer the case to the apostolic see for review.

9 We wish and command canons regular to observe this constitution according to their order.

10 In making this innovation, if any difficulty emerges that cannot be resolved by the aforesaid persons, it is to be referred without scandal to the judgment of the apostolic see; but other matters, for which provision was made after general agreement in discussion, are to be observed without dispute.

11 Moreover, diocesan bishops should try to reform the monasteries subject to them, so that when the aforesaid visitors come there, they will find more that is worthy of praise than of correction. Bishops should take every possible precaution not to encumber their monasteries with undue burdens, because just as we wish the rights of superiors to be observed, so we do not wish the injuries of inferiors to be tolerated.

12 To facilitate this innovation, we strictly command both diocesan bishops and the persons who preside at the celebration of the chapters to use nonappealable ecclesiastical censure to restrain those who presume to offend monasteries by harming either their persons or their goods, including such offenders as advocates, patrons, vidames, rectors and consuls, magnates and knights, or anyone else. If perchance they do commit such offenses, let the ecclesiastical officials named above not neglect to compel them to make amends, so that the monks may be able to serve the omnipotent God with greater freedom and peace.

Document 46
HONORIUS III IMPLEMENTS A GENERAL CHAPTER FOR BENEDICTINES OF REIMS PROVINCE
20 December 1224

MSS.—(A) Vatican, Arch. Segreto Vat., Serie generale de' Regesti, vol. 13, fols. 23r–24r: Reg. Hon. III, tom. V, an. ix, ep. 128. (B) Paris, BnF, MS. Moreau 1183, p. 88 (copy of A for La Porte du Theil, 1776~1786).

Ed.—Horoy, IV (1880), 747–753, no. 51, from B.

Refs.—Pressutti, nos. 5233 (20 Dec. 1224, to Reims bishops) and 5240 (24 Dec. 1224, to Reims Benedictine abbots and priors).

Text.—From A, with special thanks to James Powell, who provided a photocopy.

Honorius episcopus, servus servorum Dei, dilectis filiis>[a] . . Sancti Remigii Remen'[1] et . . de Macheriis Attrebaten' dioc'[2] abbatibus, <salutem et apostolicam benedictionem>.[b]

<Honorius episcopus, servus servorum Dei, venerabilibus fratribus>[c] . . Remensi archiepiscopo[3] et suffraganeis ejus,[d] <salutem et apostolicam benedictionem.>[e]

1 Sapientia[f] que ex ore prodit altissimi, cujus delicie sunt esse cum filiis hominum inter eos habitatura,[g] in ipso sibi paradisum voluptatis plantavit, claustrum videlicet regularium. . . .

[a] Honorius—filiis *scripsi*
[b] salutem—benedictionem *scripsi*
[c] Honorius—fratribus *scripsi*
[d] In eodem modo scripta est . . Remen' archiepiscopo et suffraganeis ejus, usque "decorem" *et § 9b add.* A
[e] salutem—benedictionem *scripsi*
[f] Sapientiam *Horoy*
[g] habitura *Horoy*

Hungary.—*Sapientia* was later used to form a Benedictine chapter in Hungary: on 13 Feb. 1225, Honorius addressed the bull to the archbishops of Gran and Kalocza (Potthast, no. 7359; Pressutti, no. 5309); it is known only from an original, ed. G. Fejér, *Codex diplomaticus Hungariae ecclesiasticus ac civilis*, III.ii (Budapest, 1829), p. 19.

Compilatio quinta.—The canonist Tancred included an extract of *Sapientia* in his original version of the *Compilatio quinta* (compiled by or before 2 May 1226), as attested by five manuscripts: K. Pennington, "The French Recension of Compilatio tertia," *Bulletin of Medieval Canon Law*, n.s., V (1975), 53-71, Appendix I: "Extravagantes in Compilatio quinta" (pp. 67-69). Most of the seventeen known manuscripts of the *Quinta* (which became obsolete with the publication of the *Liber extra* in 1234) omit this decretal, as is noted in E. Friedberg's edition, *Quinque compilationes antiquae* (Leipzig, 1882), p. 177, ad 3.20.2. See Leonard E. Boyle, "The Compilatio quinta and the Registers of Honorius III," *Bulletin of Medieval Canon Law*, n.s., VIII (1978), 9-19, at pp. 14-16; reprinted as item XI in his *Pastoral Care, Clerical Education and Canon Law, 1200–1400*, Collected Studies Series, 135 (London: Variorum, 1981). See also chapter 8, nn. 43-44, above.

Honorius, bishop, servant of the servants of God, to the beloved sons [Peter] abbot of St-Remi[1] at Reims and [Eligius] abbot of Marchiennes[2] in the diocese of Arras, greeting and apostolic blessing.

Honorius, bishop, servant of the servants of God, to the venerable brothers [William] the archbishop of Reims[3] and his suffragans, greeting and apostolic blessing.

1 God, whose delight is to be with the sons of men, himself planted a paradise of pleasure for himself—namely a cloister of monks living according to a rule—so that the wisdom that proceeds from the mouth of the Highest might

1. Peter "the Lame" of Nogent, abbot 1212-1236: *Gallia Christiana*, IX (1751), 235.

2. There is some mistake here because *de Maceriis* = Mézières, a Benedictine priory (not abbey) in the diocese of Reims (not Arras = *Atrebatensis*), and subject to Mouzon (Cottineau, II, 1841). According to *Gallia Christiana* III, in the diocese of Arras there were two abbeys with names beginning with the letter M: (1) *Marchianense* = Marchiennes, a Benedictine house near Douay, and (2) *Mareolum* = Maroëul-lez-Arras, better known as St-Amand, a house of Augustinian canons regular, near Tournai. Since Doc. 46 is directed to Benedictines, Marchiennes is most likely the intended recipient. M. Maccarrone correctly identified the recipient as the abbot "di Marchiennes di Arras" without explanation: *Nuovi studi su Innocenzo III* (Rome, 1995), p. 30. In Dec. 1224 the house had a new abbot, Eligius: *Gallia Christiana*, III (1715), 298.

3. Guillaume de Joinville, 1219-1226: Mas Latrie, *Trésor de chronologie*, col. 1470.

2 Unde felicis recordationis Innocentius papa predecessor noster de rehedificatione ac cultu sepedicti paradisi sollicitus, sacro generali statuit approbante concilio[4] ut "in singulis regnis sive provinciis de triennio in triennium, salvo jure diocesanorum pontificum fieret commune capitulum abbatum atque priorum abbates proprios non habentium, qui non consueverunt tale concilium celebrare, ad quod universi prepedimentum non habentes canonicum convenirent apud unum de monasteriis ad hoc aptum"[5] tractaturi de ipso in statum pristinum reformando. . . .

3 Verum operante illo cujus invidia mors intravit[h] in mundum, quod non sine amaritudine mentis referimus, ex constitutione predicta in memorato concilio habita parum adhuc aut nichil utilitatis provenit; eo quod abbates et priores abbates proprios non habentes neglexerunt ad hujusmodi capitulum convenire, ac hii qui presidere debebant[i] eidem cogendi rebelles non sunt visi habere aliquam potestatem, et sic usquemodo in stercore suo computruere jumenta[6] et Mhoab in suis fetibus requievit.[7]

4 Licet igitur facta videatur desperabilis plaga ejus,[8] scientes tamen quod non est abbreviata manus Domini ut salvare non possit, et excoquere scoriam ejus ad purum, necnon auferre omne stagnum illius ac restituere judices ejus ut prius fuerunt et consiliarios sicut antiquitus,[9] compatiendo[j] ex intimo cordis super contritione Joseph,[10] adhuc curationi ejus duximus insistendum, discretioni vestre per apostolica scripta mandantes quatinus apud monasterium Sancti Remigii Remen' hoc anno convocantes[k] capitulum, abbates et priores non habentes abbates proprios tam exemptos quam non exemptos Remen' provincie qui non consueverunt hujusmodi celebrare capitulum venire ad illud, dummodo non sint impedimento canonico prepediti, monitione premissa per censuram ecclesiasticam sublato cujuslibet contradictionis et appellationis obstaculo compellatis, et advocatis caritative duobus Cist' ordinis vicinis abbatibus,[11] procedatis

[h] introvit A
[i] debeant *Horoy*
[j] compatientes *Horoy*
[k] ad *inser. Horoy*

dwell among them. . . . [In an elaborate analogy, a Benedictine monastery is compared at length—over a thousand words—to the biblical garden of Eden. Corrupted now by wealth and royal favor, monks have departed from Benedict's Rule and instead prefer forbidden fruits. When visitors (*angeli pacis*) sent by the pope failed to reform corrupt houses, it was evident that another cure had to be found.]

2 Consequently the well-remembered Pope Innocent, our predecessor, being concerned to rebuild and care for the paradise of which we have been speaking, made this statute with the approbation of the general council:[4] "Every three years, in every kingdom or province, saving the right of diocesan bishops, let there be held a general chapter of those abbots, and of those priors who do not have their own abbot, who do not customarily celebrate such a chapter. With the exception of those persons who have a canonical impediment, they all should assemble at one of the monasteries that is suitable for the purpose."[5] There they should deliberate on how to restore that paradise to its original state. . . . [The anticipated good results are described in terms of the analogy developed in § 1.]

3 In fact, up to now little or nothing useful has resulted from this statute issued in that council, which we cannot report without bitter thoughts: the devil must be at work here, by whom death entered into the world. Results have been few because abbots, and priors not having their own abbots, have failed to assemble at such a chapter, and those who are supposed to preside there do not seem to have any power to compel rebels to obey. And thus "the beasts have rotted in their dung"[6] and "Moab has rested in his filth."[7]

4 Although the wound that has been made seems incurable,[8] we know, however, that the hand of the Lord is not so short that he is unable to cure it; he can purge its impurities until it is pure and also remove all its stagnant parts. Did the Lord not restore his judges as they were before and his counsellors as of old?[9] And did he not have compassion in his inmost heart for Joseph's desperate plight?[10] Therefore, still intent on curing this wound, by apostolic writ addressed to your discretion, we command that this year you are to convoke at St-Remi in Reims the abbots, and priors not having their own abbots, both exempt and nonexempt, of Reims province, who are not accustomed to celebrate this kind of chapter. And, provided that they are not hindered by a canonical impediment, after first warning them, you are to compel them to come to it by ecclesiastical

---

4. IV Lateran Council, c. 12 *In singulis* = Doc. 45.
5. See Doc. 45.1, the text of which is repeated here with insignificant variants.
6. Joel i.17 (Douay-Reims).
7. Jeremiah xlviii.11.
8. Jeremiah xv.18.
9. Isaiah i.26.
10. When Joseph was unjustly imprisoned (cf. Genesis xxxix.21).

in celebratione capituli Deum habentes pre oculis juxta constitutionem concilii memorati;

5 eadem censura facturi que in eo deliberatione provida fuerint ordinata firmiter observari; et reddituri Domino, in cujus conspectu[l] omnia nuda sunt et aperta, in extremo die districti examinis rationem, si omnem sollicitudinem, et diligentiam que circa correctionem, et reformationem ordinis, ac visitationem cenobiorum adhibende fuerint neglexeritis adhibere.

6 Ut autem que statuta fuerint magis teneantur memoriter et serventur, volumus et mandamus ut hujusmodi capitulum in singulis regnis sive provinciis annis singulis celebretur,

7 concessa eis qui ad presidendum annis futuris capitulis celebrandis fuerint ordinati, convocandi abbates et priores predictos, et cogendi rebelles appellatione postposita, simili potestate;

8 adicientes[m] ut si visitatores qui fuerint in eodem ordinati capitulo aliquos exemptos invenerint deponendos, id apostolice sedi non differant nuntiare, in ceteris juxta formam sepedicti concilii processuri; si forte convertatur Dominus et ignoscat, et relinquens post se benedictionem, gloriam Libani det deserto et Carmeli decorem.

9a Ecce presentibus ostendimus regularibus semetipsis ut a quo, in quid, et per quod ceciderint, videant, recogitent, et intelligant, ac cum Magis offerentibus Domino munera, per aliam viam in suam reverti studeant regionem.[12]

9b Quocirca universitati vestre per apostolica scripta precipiendo mandamus[n] quatinus rectores monasteriorum vestrarum diocesum quos visitatores predicti vobis a suis locis denuntiaverint amovendos, singuli vestrum in sua diocesi, sublato cujuslibet contradictionis et appellationis[o] obstaculo, non differant amovere. Alioquin poteritis non immerito formidare quod minus jurisdictionis vobis relinquantur[p] in eis quam habuistis hactenus et habetis.

Dat' Laterani viiii. kal. Januarii, <pontificatus nostri>[q] anno nono (24 Dec. 1224).

Dat' Laterani xiii. kal. Januarii, <pontificatus nostri>[q] anno nono (20 Dec. 1224).

[l] aspectu *Horoy*
[m] adjacentes *Horoy*
[n] precipiendo mandamus *tr. Horoy*
[o] appellationis et contradictionis A[1], *corr.* A[2]
[p] relinquatur *Horoy*
[q] pontificatus nostri *scripsi*

censure, since the obstacle of any kind of contradiction or appeal has been re-moved. Then, having "in the spirit of brotherhood invited two nearby Cister-cian abbots,"[11] proceed to celebrate the chapter according to the statute of the aforesaid council, keeping your eyes fixed on God.

5 Those things that, after prudent deliberation, are ordained in that chapter are to be firmly observed under penalty of incurring the same censure. And if you are negligent in employing all the care and diligence that ought to be em-ployed in the correction and reformation of the order and in the visitation of monasteries, you will be accountable to the Lord, in whose sight all things are open and plain, when you are strictly examined on the last day.

6 So that these statutes shall be remembered better and observed more, we wish and command that a chapter of this kind be celebrated in each kingdom or province every year.

7 Moreover, to those who are appointed to preside over chapters to be cel-ebrated in future years, we concede the same power of convoking the aforesaid abbots and priors, and of compelling rebels, even if they appeal.

8 In addition, if the visitors who are appointed in this chapter shall find any exempt abbots or priors who ought to be deposed, they should notify the apos-tolic see immediately; in other cases they are to proceed in the manner pre-scribed by the aforesaid council. If perchance the Lord should turn away his wrath and forgive, and leave his blessing behind him, he would give glory to the wilderness of Lebanon and decency to that of Carmel.

9a Behold! By the present letter we have shown monks the truth about themselves, so that they may see, rec-ognize, and understand for what rea-son, in what way, and by what means they have been wounded; and so that, like the Magi bearing gifts to the Lord, they may seek to return home by another road.[12]

9b Wherefore we command all of you by apostolic writ, enjoining that you do not delay in removing the heads of monasteries whom the afore-said visitors shall have informed any one of you are to be removed from their places in your diocese, since the obstacle of any kind of contradiction or appeal has been removed. Other-wise you have good reason to dread that less jurisdiction over them may be relinquished to you than you have had up to now and still have.

Given at the Lateran on the ninth day before the kalends of January, in the ninth year of our pontificate [24 December 1224].

Given at the Lateran on the thir-teenth day before the kalends of Janu-ary, in the ninth year of our pontificate [20 December 1224].

11. Doc. 45.3 = Lateran Council IV, c. 12.
12. Matthew ii.12.

Document 47
HONORIUS III REITERATES HIS ORDER
TO BISHOPS WHO OPPOSE
MONASTIC CHAPTERS AND VISITORS
3 November 1225

Honorius episcopus, servus servorum Dei, venerabilibus fratribus>[a] [. . archiepiscopo Remensi[1] et suffraganeis ejus],[b] <salutem et apostolicam benedictionem>.[c]

1 <C>um[d] ex officio vestro[e] religionem fovere[f] teneamini, et in suavi ejus odore conveniat delectari, oportet vos sollicitudinem et diligentiam adhibere ut in provincia vestra nec ordinis reformatio nec excessuum correctio postponatur, cum religionis cultum nunquam melius foveri[g] contingat quam correctis excessibus et ordine in quibus reformatione indiget reformato.

2 Verum non sine grandi ammiratione audivimus quod cum per litteras nostras[2] vobis duxerimus injungendum ut amoveatis abbates vestre ditioni subjectos qui per generale capitulum vel visitatores ipsius vobis nuntiantur aliquando amovendi, nec[h] volentibus celebrare capitulum aut excessus corrigere resistatis, sicut in eisdem litteris plenius continetur, tales vos exhibuistis in facto hujusmodi, quo non alia nisi que sunt Christi queruntur, ut non augmentum set detrimentum ordinis, et non animarum salutem set periculum videamini affectare.

3 Quia vero graviter in hoc delinquitis et sanguis delinquentium debet de manu vestra requiri, sive impediatis tantum bonum sive detractetis super hoc facere quod debetis, fraternitati vestre monemus per apostolica vobis scripta sicut iterum sic attentius in virtute obedientie districte precipiendo mandantes quatinus, in iteratione mandati plenius intelligentes mandatoris affectum, in nullo vos opponatis volentibus celebrare capitulum et corrigere delinquentes.

[a] Honorius—fratribus *scripsit Horoy*
[b] . . archiepiscopo—ejus *in margine* A
[c] salutem—benedictionem *scripsit Horoy*
[d] *initialis littera rubra om.* A
[e] vestro] nostro *Horoy*
[f] fovere] favere *Horoy*
[g] foveri] faveri *Horoy*
[h] nec] vel *Horoy*

MSS.—(A) Vatican, Arch. Segreto Vat., Serie generale de' Regesti, vol. 13, fol. 104r: Reg. Hon. III, tom. V, an. x, ep. 145. (B) Paris, BnF, MS. Moreau 1183, fols. 267r–268v (copy of A for La Porte du Theil, 1776~1786).

Ed.—Horoy, IV (1880), 942-943, no. 48, from B.

Refs.—Pressutti, no. 5708.

Text from A, collated with Horoy's edition.

Honorius, bishop, servant of the servants of God, to the venerable brothers [William] archbishop of Reims[1] and his suffragans, greeting and apostolic blessing.

1 Since you are required *ex officio* to promote the monastic life, and it is becoming to be delighted by its pleasant perfume, it is proper for you to employ solicitude and diligence so that neither the reformation of the monastic order nor the correction of its excesses is delayed in your province, inasmuch as there is no better way to promote the monastic life than by correcting excesses and reforming the order in those matters that require reformation.

2 By our previous letter,[2] to which we refer you for details, we enjoined you to remove the abbots under your control whom the general chapter or its visitors once instructed you to remove, and we also enjoined you not to resist those who wish to celebrate a chapter or correct excesses. It is indeed not without great amazement that we have heard that you have shown by your conduct in this matter, which concerns nothing but the Christian life, that you seem to favor harming the order rather than improving it, and endangering souls rather than saving them.

3 You are indeed sinning greatly, whether you are impeding so much good or are omitting to do what you ought to do about this, and the blood of those who in consequence are also delinquent ought to be required at your hand. Therefore by apostolic writ we warn your fraternity again, this time more emphatically, since you will know what we desire more fully because we are repeating the command, and we strictly instruct you and in virtue of obedience command that you in no way oppose those who wish to celebrate a chapter and to correct delinquents.

1. Guillaume de Joinville, archbishop of Reims 1219-1226.
2. Doc. 46.

4 Subjectos etiam ditioni vestre abbates qui per capitulum vel visitatores vobis amovendi fuerint nuntiati, curetis absque more dispendio amovere, ita quod videatur vobis sicut esse debet acceptum quod in provincia vestra cultus religionis per reformationem ordinis et animarum profectus per correctionem excessuum procuratur.

5 Alioquin cum tantum inobedientie vitium palpandum decetero non existat, et dignum sit et conveniens ut in quo quis probatur delinquere puniatur, formidare poteritis ne jurisdictionem quam in abbatibus vobis subjectis habetis generali eorum capitulo et visitatoribus concedamus, cum aliis honorem vestrum dare potius volueritis quam nobis in hac parte humiliter obedire.

Datum Reate iii. non. Novembris, <pontificatus nostri anno decimo>.[i]

---

[i] pontificatus—decimo *scripsit Horoy*

4 Without delay see to the removal of the abbots subject to your control whom the chapter or visitors instructed you to remove, so that it seems welcome to you, as it ought to be, that the monastic life should be maintained in your province by reforming the order and profiting souls by correcting excesses.

5 Furthermore, since so great a sinful habit of disobedience ought not to be condoned in future, and since it is fit and proper that one be punished when his guilt has been proven, you should fear lest we concede to the general chapter and visitors the jurisdiction that you have over the abbots subject to you because you shall have chosen to give your honor to others rather than to obey us in this matter humbly.

Given at Rieti, on the third day before the nones of November, in the tenth year of our pontificate.

SECTION SIX

MISCELLANEOUS

Document 48
HONORIUS III MANDATES CAPITULAR
REPRESENTATION AT PROVINCIAL COUNCILS
25 February 1217

This document is a landmark in the development of representative government. In the ancient world, democracy was not possible for units larger than the city-state because it was not feasible to assemble all the citizens of a province, kingdom, or empire. It did not occur to the Greeks and Romans that a constituency could be represented by a few of its members; that idea, which now seems obvious, was slowly evolved in the thirteenth century from concepts derived from Roman law that originally had applied to private law, rather than to public, constitutional law.

This development was traced in detail by Gaines Post in his *Studies in Medieval Legal Thought* (Princeton, 1964). The fundamental concept is expressed by Justinian's legal maxim, "Quod omnes similiter tangit, ab omnibus comprobetur" (*Cod.* 5.59.5.2): everyone whose rights are similarly affected by a legal action should meet together and approve it in common. By 1200, lawyers understood this to mean that new taxes could not be imposed without the participation of the taxpayers in the decision-making process. The question was how this could be accomplished expeditiously on a large scale. The answer was suggested by the way in which Roman law provided for a corporation to be represented in court by an agent (*procurator* = proctor) empowered to act for his principal, as we would say, with "power of attorney."

The simplest form of representation was to assume that the head of a corporation could act for the whole body; for example, that a king could speak for his kingdom, a bishop for his diocese, a mayor for his city. This power was occasionally made explicit by formally granting the head *ad hoc* powers to act for the members (Post, pp. 86-88). But this did not fit the legal realities of canon law because, in the course of the twelfth century, many cathedral chapters came to have property rights of their own, distinct from those of the bishop. Accordingly, in 1215 when Innocent III wanted to impose a new tax to support a crusade, the principle of *quod omnes tangit* led him to summon proctors from each cathedral chapter to attend the Fourth Lateran Council. This was a portentous precedent but it remained to be seen whether it would become a general practice in church councils.

The test case came the next year, in 1216, when the chapters of the province of Sens insisted on their right to participate in a provincial council. All that is known of the incident is the summary of the chapters' complaint, "that you [the archbishop] have refused to admit to your deliberations their proctors who were recently summoned to a comprovincial council, even though some things are usually treated in such councils that are known to pertain to these chapters" (Doc. 48.2). Apparently the archbishop did not want to admit the proctors to deliberations that did not concern them; he had invited them so they would be available if needed, but when the council met, he decided that their participation was not necessary. The chapters appealed to the pope, arguing that if they were invited, they should be admitted to the deliberations. Honorius agreed with them, and although later canonists considered that proctors might be excluded from certain confidential proceedings, still this decree established the general principle that *representatives*, in the modern sense, would normally be included in the deliberations of ecclesiastical assemblies. At the least they had the right to be heard there, although at this time it was unclear whether they could actually veto an action by withholding their consent (Kemp, *Counsel and Consent*, pp. 41–48).

This decretal, then, is a milestone on the long road to parliamentary democracy because here, for the first time, constituents gained the legal right to participate in assemblies through their representatives, not on an *ad hoc* basis at the discretion of the convoker, but as a regular, normal entitlement. This arrangement later provided the model for corporate representation in secular assemblies, such as the English parliament, which developed in the next hundred years; these, in turn, eventually gave rise to modern representative government.

MSS.—(A) Vatican, Arch. Segreto Vat., Serie generale de' Regesti, vol. 9, fol. 76r: Reg. Hon. III, tom. I, an. i, ep. 290. (B) Paris, BnF, MS. Moreau 1178, fols. 269r–270r (copy of A made for La Porte du Theil, 1776~1786). (C) Troyes, Trésor de la cathédrale: sealed original preserved there, saec. xvii in.; present location unknown. (D) Paris, Arch. nat., L 239, no. 31 (*olim* no. 28): original, "Dat' Lateran' v. kal. martii, pontificatus nostri anno primo."

Ed.—(1) Horoy, II, 291, no. 238, from B. (2) Extract from C in Jean Rochette, *Décisions de plusieurs questions et différens qui se présentent journellement, tant ès cours ecclésiastiques que séculières sur matières bénéficiales de mariages, preuve, appellations, circonstances et dépendances*, 3rd ed. (Troyes, 1614), fol. 134. Text reprinted by Kemp (1961), p. 43, n. 4.

Refs.—Potthast, *Regesta*, no. 7796 (an. 1216~1227) and 25822 (25 Feb. 1217). Pressutti, no. 373 (25 Feb. 1217). Barbiche, no. 154 (MS. D). For the date, see Eric W. Kemp, "The Origins of the Canterbury Convocation," *Journal of Ecclesiastical His-*

tory, III (1952), 132–143, at p. 133, and his *Counsel and Consent* (London, 1961), pp. 43–44. On the decretal's significance, see Gaines Post, *Studies in Medieval Legal Thought: Public Law and the State, 1100–1322* (Princeton, 1964), pp. 235–236.

Decretalist redactions.—In addition to the original version referred to above, the text of this decretal was subsequently modified for inclusion in successive collections of legal texts. What amounts to a second, official redaction was prepared by the Bolognese canonist Tancred as part of his *Compilatio quinta*, a collection of the decretals of Honorius III, which that pope commissioned and, on 2 May 1226, formally promulgated (5 Comp. 3.8.1 = lib. 3, title 8 *De his que fiunt vel conceduntur a prelatis sine consensu capituli*, c.1). Tancred's text was printed as *Quinta compilatio epistolarum decretalium Honorii III. p. m.*, ed. Innocentius Cironius (Toulouse, 1645), p. 197; reprinted, Leipzig, 1726, and Vienna, 1761; modern condensed edition by E. Friedberg, *Quinque compilationes antiquae* (Leipzig, 1882), p. 171.

In 1234, this and many other canons in Tancred's *Compilatio quinta* were incorporated into the *Decretales Gregorii IX* (3.10.10, ed. Friedberg, II, 205–206). The compiler, Raymond of Penyafort, neglected to indicate which pope had issued the decretal, so for a long time it was attributed to Innocent III. Raymond

---

Honorius episcopus, servus servorum Dei, venerabilibus fratribus . . archiepiscopo Senonen'[1] et suffraganeis ejus, salutem et apostolicam benedictionem>].[a]

1 [b]Et si menbra corporis [c]Christi, quod est ecclesia, non omnia unum actum habeant sed diversos, secundum illius beneplacitum qui distributor gratie multiformis prout voluit in ipso corpore posuit unumquodque, ipsa tamen menbra efficiunt unum corpus, ita quod non potest oculus dicere manui "tua opera non indigeo" aut caput pedibus "non estis michi necessarii," sed multomagis que videntur menbra corporis infirmiora esse necessaria sunt, quandoquidem omnia secundum temperationem divinam[d] in idipsum sollicta esse debent ut non sit scisma in corpore quod in vinculo pacis servare debet spiritus unitatem.

2 Hec idcirco premisimus quia[e] provincie vestre capitula cathedralia suam[e]

[a] Honorius—benedictionem D: Archiepiscopo Senonen' et suffraganeis ejus *in marg.* A; Honorius III etc. Venerabilibus fratribus archiepiscopo Sen' et suffraganeis etc. *Rochette*
 [b-b] Et si menbra—cupientes et *om. Rochette*
 [c] Christi quod est ecclesia—premisimus quia *om.* X
 [d] divnam A, *corr.* A[1].
 [e] vestre capitula cathedralia suam] Senonensis capitula cathedralium ecclesiarum X

also introduced still further alterations into the text. In his edition of the *Corpus iuris canonici*, Friedberg distinguishes Tancred's text from Raymond's but did not consult the Vatican register.

Date.—The *datum*-clause was omitted from the canonistic redaction, so Potthast (1874) and Friedberg (1881) simply dated the decretal to the pontificate of Honorius III (1216~1227); the correct date was first given in Pressutti's calendar of Honorius' register (1895) and was corroborated by Kemp (1961). Rochette (1614) supplied the year as "*1216*"; presumably he was reckoning in Old Style, as Honorius' first year began in July 1216. The original reported by Barbiche (1975) confirms the register date.

Text.—The Latin text printed below is in effect the *editio princeps* of the Vatican register copy (A), transcribed from microfilm, and collated with a photocopy of D. Variants from Friedberg's edition of the second redaction are indicated by the siglum **X** (= *Liber extra* = *Decretales Gregorii IX*); the edition of Lyons 1548 agrees with Friedberg's text.

Honorius, bishop, servant of the servants of God, to the venerable brothers [Peter] archbishop of Sens[1] and his suffragans, greeting and apostolic blessing.

1 Although the members of Christ's body, which is the Church, do not have one function but diverse ones, according to the gracious purpose of him who, distributing grace in as many forms as he wished, placed every single member in the body itself, these members do, however, make up one body, so that the eye cannot say to the hand "I don't need what you do" or the head to the feet "you aren't necessary to me." Still more important, the weaker members of the body seem to be necessary, inasmuch as, mindful of the interdependence established by God between the parts, all of them ought to be vigilant that there be no schism within the body, which ought to preserve unity of spirit in the bond of peace.

2 The reason we have made these prefatory remarks is that the cathedral chapters of your province have transmitted to us their complaint that you have refused to admit to your deliberations their proctors who were recently summoned to a comprovincial council, even though some things are usually treated

---

1. Petrus de Corbeil, archbishop of Sens 1200–1222.

ad nos querimoniam transmiserunt quod vos[f] procuratores ipsorum[g] nuper ad comprovinciale[h] concilium convocatos ad tractatum vestrum[i] admittere noluistis,[j] [k]licet nonnulla soleant in huiusmodi tractari conciliis que ad ipsa noscuntur capitula pertinere, quare nostram audientiam appellarunt.

3 Sane nos, auditis que ipsorum nuntii super hiis proponere voluerunt, et intellectis nichilominus litteris quas nobis super eodem curastis negotio destinare ad nostre provisionis arbitrium provide recurrendo, tractatum exinde cum fratribus nostris habuimus diligentem,[l] dolentes super huiusmodi turbatione dissidii, et amputare a vobis in posterum similis dissentionis materiam cupientes; et[b] utique[k] nobis et eisdem fratribus nostris concorditer visum fuit[m] ut ipsa capitula[n] ad huiusmodi concilia invitari debeant[o] et eorum nuntii ad tractatus[p] admitti, maxime super illis que capitula ipsa[q] contingere dinoscuntur.

4 [r]Ideoque volumus et presentium vobis auctoritate mandamus quatinus id decetero sine disceptatione servetis, [s]in hiis et aliis exhibentes vos vestris subditis favorabiles et benignos ut, pastoris nomen operibus exequentes nec quasi "dominantes in clero sed facti forma gregi ex animo,"[2] cum apparuerit princeps pastorum inmarcessibilem glorie coronam merito percipere debeatis; et ipsi subditi, vestre benignitatis mansuetudine provocati, vobis—cum omnis anima subdita esse debeat sublunioribus potestatibus[3]—reverentiam et obedientiam humilem et devotam studeant exhibere; quatinus capite menbris et menbris capiti digna vicissitudine obsequentibus corpus scismatis detrimenta non sentiat sed connexum in caritatis unitate consistat.[s]

Datum Laterani v. kal. Martii, pontificatus nostri anno primo.[r]

[f] vos] archiepiscopus Senonensis et eius suffraganei X
[g] ipsorum] eorum X
[h] comprovinciale] provinciale X
[i] vestrum] eorum
[j] noluistis] noluerunt X
[k-k] licet nonnulla—cupientes et utique *om.* X
[l]diligentem AD: diligenter X
[m] fuit] est *Rochette;* utique—fuit] Visum fuit nobis et fratribus nostris X
[n] ipsa capitula *tr.* X
[o] invitari debeant *tr.* X
[p] tractatus] tractatum X
[q] capitula ipsa *tr.* X
[r] Ideoque—anno primo *om.* X
[s-s] in hiis—unitate consistat *om. Rochette*

in such councils that are known to pertain to these chapters, which is why they appealed to us.

3 First of all we heard what their nuncios wanted to bring to our attention about all this, and we were no less attentive to the letter that you sent us about the matter, in which you prudently left the decision up to our discretion. Next, to be sure, we diligently discussed the matter with our brothers [the cardinals] because we were saddened by the disturbance such disagreement has caused, and because we desire to help you by eliminating the cause of similar dissension in the future. And it certainly seemed to us, and our brothers were in complete agreement, that those chapters ought to be invited to such councils and their nuncios admitted to the deliberations, especially those about matters that evidently concern the chapters themselves.

4 Therefore we wish and by the authority of the present letter we command that in future you follow this procedure without dispute. In this and other matters, show yourselves to be favorable and friendly to your subjects, so that by being shepherds in deed and not in name only, "neither as lording it over the clergy, but being made a pattern of the flock from the heart,"[2] when the chief of the shepherds shall appear, you deservedly ought to gain a crown of everlasting glory. And in response to your courteous friendliness, your subjects should do their best to give you reverence and humble, loyal obedience, since every soul ought to be subject to the sublunary powers.[3] Thus, when the head gives the members their due and they give the head its due, the body shall not experience the ravages of schism but will remain whole in the unity of love.

Given at the Lateran, on the fifth day before the kalends of March, in the first year of our pontificate.

2. I Peter v.3 (Douay-Rheims).
3. Cf. Romans xiii.1.

Document 49
SUMMONS TO A LEGATINE COUNCIL AT SENS
[2] June 1223

This document has received much attention because of Conrad's sensational reference to a Cathar "pope" in the Balkans with subordinates operating in Spain. Here it is included as an example of how a papal legate summoned a council of French prelates.

Provenance.—It is problematic when and where this document was issued. In discussing these problems, one should be aware that all our witnesses are derived from the Rouen archiepiscopal chancery, as is self evident for manuscripts A and B and is expressly stated in the case of C. It is unclear whether A was sent directly to Mont-St-Michel or, as in the case of the analogous Doc. 28, to the bishop of Avranches; the bishop of Séez received B, which was copied into his register, which we know from an eighteenth-century transcript; Roger Wendover probably worked from a copy made either from the letter received at Rouen or, more likely, from one distributed by the archbishop, that is, just like A. Thus the text in each case is at least two removes from the original, and probably more; all this recopying accounts for many of the differences between our several witnesses.

Date.—Errors have crept into the dates given in all three manuscripts, and there is no consensus on how the discrepancies should be resolved. Neininger ably summarizes the discussion but leaves the question open. Three dates are stated in the text; if we examine them in turn, however, proceeding from the most secure to the least, a probable answer can be formulated.

(a) The summons is for a council to meet at Sens "on the octave of the [feast of the] apostles Peter and Paul next to come" (§ 4). In 1223, this would be on *Thursday*, 6 July. The following year, 1224, which Zimmermann assumed was intended,[1] seems less probable because 6 July falls on a Saturday, which would be awkward and unusual if, as seems likely, the proceedings were to extend over several days. More decisively, there is chronicle evidence that the council did in fact meet just as Philip Augustus was dying in July 1223.[2]

---

1. H. Zimmermann, *Die päpstliche Legation in der ersten Hälfte des 13. Jahrhunderts* (Paderborn, 1913), p. 77.

2. Ralph of Coggeshall, *Chronicon Anglicanum*, ed. J. Stevenson, Rolls Series, no. 66 (London, 1875), p. 195: "in octobas apostolorum Petri et Pauli"; Guillaume le Breton, *Philippidos* XII.543–548, ed. H. F. Delaborde in *Oeuvres de Rigord et de Guillaume le Breton*, 2 vols. (Paris, 1882–1885), II, 368. See also Neininger, *Konrad von Urach*, Register, no. 157.

(b) Archbishop Theobald transmitted the citation mandate to his suffragans on 8 June 1223 ("vi. id. Junii"). This *datum*-clause appears only in A. Unfortunately, Martène mistakenly transcribed *Junii* as *Julii*, so the date seemed to be 10 July 1223, which made it appear that a council called for 6 July could not meet until 1224. But a re-examination of the manuscript shows that 8 June 1223 is securely the correct date.

(c) It is harder to be sure when the legate issued his citation mandate. Both B and C give the date as 2 July (vi. non. Julii), which is patently impossible for a council about to meet on 6 July. But A also gives a date that is impossible— "ui° nonas Junii"—because there are only *four* nones in June. Consequently, several emendations of the roman numeral in A have been proposed: perhaps the Rouen scribe's exemplar read "iu" (2 June) or perhaps, as was first suggested by Dossat,[3] "iii" (3 June). To decide between the two, we must consider where the summons was issued.

Place.—Where was Legate Conrad on 2 and 3 June 1223? His whereabouts on 2 June is well attested by a charter that he issued then while staying at the abbey of St-Pourçain in the diocese of Clermont.[4] Thus our summons, *Dum pro sponsa*, would seem to have been issued the next day, on 3 June. Its *datum*-clause (§ 4) has two variant readings of the place: Wendover-Paris reads "Data Planium" (C) and the Mont-St-Michel version is "Datum Provin." (A), while B omits the place altogether. Most scholars have concluded that the A-version is correct and have identified "Provin." as Provins, roughly between Paris and Troyes in the département Seine-et-Marne (Luard, Dossat, Neininger). While this is not impossible, since Provins-en-Brie was sometimes called *Provinum* in Latin, still other forms were more commonly used, such as *Pruviniacum, Provignum, Provisina civitas, Proynum, Pruvignum, Pruvinensis, Pruvinum,* or *Pruvinum Senonum*.[5] But it is plainly impossible that Conrad was there on 3 June 1223, because he certainly could not have travelled the 170 miles from St-Pourçain to Provins in one day, or even two.[6]

3. Y. Dossat, "Un Evêque cathare originaire de l'Agenais: Vigouroux de la Bacone," *Bulletin philologique et historique (jusqu'à 1610)*, année 1965 (Paris, 1968), pp. 623-639, at p. 637, n. 2; reprinted in his *Eglise et hérésie en France au XIIIe siècle* (London, 1982), no. XIII.

4. Neininger, *Konrad von Urach*, Register, no. 152: charter sealed by Conrad, now Rodez, Archives départementales, G 578 ("Datum apud Sanctum Portianum, anno Domini M° CC° XX°III°, IIII nonas iunii").

5. *Orbis Latinus: Lexikon lateininischer geographischer Namen der Mittelalter und der Neuzeit* ("Graesse-Benedict-Plechl"), ed. H. Plechl, 3 vols. (Braunschweig, 1972), III, 213.

6. M. N. Boyer, "A Day's Journey in Mediaeval France," *Speculum*, XXVI (1951), 597-608, concludes that, except for couriers, the daily rate would hardly exceed 35 miles.

Consequently, one must look instead for a nearby place to which *Data Planium* refers. Most likely it would be a religious house, where the legate usually stayed, and in France there were over a dozen such with *Plan-* as the initial element of the name;[7] however, none of the ones listed by Cottineau is within a hundred miles of St-Pourçain. One possibility was suggested by Savini: the Augustinian abbey of Plain-Pied-sur-Avron (*de Plano Pede*),[8] near Bourges and hence north of St-Pourçain by about 75 miles, which would be a journey of about two days.[9] Savini also suggested another, less likely possibility: about 75 miles *south* of St-Pourçain is the Benedictine abbey of St-Flour, which is some ten miles distant from an upland plain, "de la Planèze."

But it seems improbable that the legate sealed a charter early on 2 June at St-Pourçain, then rode for all that day and the next, and still had the time and energy after the journey to draft and indite *Dum pro sponsa* after arriving at his destination late on 3 June. Hence there does not seem to be any place that could be called *Planium* where Conrad might have been the day after his undoubted presence at St-Pourçain on 2 June. Instead, it would seem that the place name in the *datum*-clause of his summons was somehow unintelligible in the copy received at Rouen, which was the exemplar for all three of our versions. My conjecture, therefore, is that Conrad simply remained at St-Pourçain and that the *datum* of his letter was something like *Portian'* (*p* with a crossed stem + 5 minims, which might be misread as *Prouin'* if written closely).

If we assume, then, that Conrad was at St-Pourçain on both 2 and 3 June, which day is more likely to have been intended by the erroneous "ui. nonas Junii"? The earlier date seems preferable because it allows slightly more time for the letter to be carried to Rouen and for the preparation there of the archbishop's letter of transmission.

To summarize: Legate Conrad most likely issued his citation mandate on 2 June 1223 at St-Pourçain, for a council to meet at Sens on 6 July; Archbishop Theobald transmitted copies of the summons to his subordinates on 8 June.

MSS.—(A) Avranches, Bibl. mun., MS. 149, fol. 128vb (this item in a hand different from those before and after it): *olim* Mont-St-Michel, MS. 249, a collection of canons and of letters concerning Normandy, saec. xiii in. (see Doc. 28,

---

7. Cottineau, *Répertoire*, III, 339.

8. Savino Savini, *Il catarismo italiano ed i suoi vescovi nei secoli XIII e XIV* (Florence, 1958), p. 81. He does not document these forms, but *Orbis Latinus* gives "Planipedes" and two related forms, as well as others derived from *plenus* (III, 161). "Plein-Pied" in *Gallia Christiana*, II (1720), 186; but "Plainpied" in the Index generalis, s. v. "Plenus-pes." Cottineau lists the house s.v. "Plaimpied, *Pleni pedis*, St-Martin."

9. Neininger, *Konrad von Urach*, Register, no. 155.

above). (B) Steinfeld Abbey (Westphalia): MS. register of Gervase, bishop of Séez 1220-1228. The Steinfeld collection was dispersed in the aftermath of the French Revolution and this manuscript has not been located. An earlier redaction of Gervase's letters was made in 1219 or 1220, apparently at the point when he gave up the abbacy of Prémonté for the bishopric of Séez; the second redaction contains letters as late as 1227, and thus was expanded to cover his years as bishop: see C. R. Cheney, "Gervase, Abbot of Prémonté: A Medieval Letter-writer," *Bulletin of the John Rylands Library, Manchester*, XXXIII (1950-1951), 25-56, at pp. 46-47; reprinted in his *Medieval Texts and Studies* (Oxford, 1973), pp. 242-276, at pp. 263-264. (C) An abridged version in Roger Wendover, *Flores historiarum*, ed. H. G. Hewlett, Rolls Series, no. 84, vol. II (1887), pp. 78-79; and repeated with stylistic improvements by Matthew Paris (see Doc. 43, above, for discussion of manuscripts and editions). Like A and B, this Wendover-Paris version was derived from the summons sent to Rouen: "Contra quem [antipapam] C. Portuensis episcopus et in partibus illis Apostolicae sedis legatus, Rothomagensi archiepiscopo scripsit in haec verba: "Venerabilibus patribus . . . " (Paris, *Chronica majora*, ed. Luard, III, 78).

Ed.—(1) The earliest printed version was the St Albans extract (C), in Matthew Paris, *Chronica majora*, ed. Matthew Parker (London, 1571); 2nd ed. by W. Wats (London, 1640); 3rd ed. by H. R. Luard, Rolls Series, no. 57, III (1876), 78-79; 4th ed. by F. Liebermann, MGH, SS, XXVIII (Hanover, 1888), p. 51. (2) From MS. A in Martène-Durand, *Thesaurus*, I (1717), 901-903. (3) From MS. B in Charles Louis Hugo, *Sacrae antiquitatis monumenta historica, dogmatica, diplomatica*, I (Estival, 1725), 115-117.

In his conciliar *Supplementum* (II [1748], 918-920), Mansi reprinted (2) with variants from (3), to replace the text that Labbe-Cossart (XI.i [1671], 288-289) had derived from (1) and which subsequent conciliar collectors had repeated (Hardouin 1714 and Coleti 1730). Mansi's 1748 text was reprinted in his *Amplissima collectio*, XXII (1778), 1203-1206.

Refs.—Christine Thouzellier, *Un Traité cathare inédit du début du XIIIe siècle d'après le "Liber contra Manicheos" du Durand de Huesca*, Bibliothèque de la Revue d'histoire ecclésiastique 37 (Louvain, 1961), pp. 30-32, n. 5. Falko Neininger, *Konrad von Urach* (Paderborn, 1994), pp. 374-375, no. 153, dated "1223 [vor Juni 8], Provins." Both provide further bibliography.

Text.—The base is MS. A, which has been transcribed from microfilm. This base has been collated with, and often corrected from, Hugo's edition of B and Luard's edition of C.

Th(eobaldus)[ab1] Dei gratia Rothom' archiepiscopus,[c] venerabilibus fratribus omnibus suffraganeis suis[d] salutem, gratiam, et benedictionem.[e] Litteras venerabilis patris C(onradi)[2] Portuen' et sancte Rufine episcopi,[f] apostolice sedis legati, recepimus in hec verba:

2 Venerabilibus patribus[g] Dei gratia Rothom' archiepiscopo[h] et ejus suffraganeis, [i]abbatibus, prioribus, decanis, archidiaconis, capitulis in Rothom' provincia constitutis, C(onradus) ejusdem miseratione Portuen' et sancte Rufine episcopus, apostolice sedis legatus,[i] salutem in Christo Jesu.[j]

3 Dum pro sponsa veri[k] crucifixi vestrum cogimur auxilium implorare,[l] potius compellimur lacerari singultibus et plorare.... (The legate relates at length why he is summoning the council: the pope of the Cathari in the Balkans has sent his legate into Languedoc, where he is establishing Catharist bishops and churches, and prompt countermeasures must be taken.)

. . . .

4 Hinc est quod vos[m] monemus instantius,[n] rogamus[o] attentius, et per aspersionem[p] sanguinis Jesu Christi propensius[q] obsecramus, [r]auctoritate domini pape qua fungimur in hac parte districte precipientes, quatinus veniatis Senon' in octavis[s] apostolorum Petri et Pauli proximo[t] futuris, ubi et[u] alii prelati Francie[v] favente Domino congregabuntur, parati consilium dare <d>e negotio predicto[w] et cum aliis qui ibidem[x] aderunt providere super negotio Albig';[y] alioquin inobedientiam vestram domino pape curabimus significare.[z] Datum P<ortia>n' <iv>[o] non. Junii.[a]

5 [b]Hujus auctoritate mandati vobis mandamus predicta die Senon' personaliter intersitis. Eccetis[c] etiam eadem auctoritate omnes abbates, priores, decanos, archidiaconos, et capitula vestrarum diocesum ut ibidem conveniant eadem die attentius provisuri, et[d] negotium istud ita

---

[a] G. Roth' episcopus suffraganeis suis *pro titulo praemisit* B; Theobaldus—in hec verba *om.* C
[b] Th. A: G. B   [c] Rothom' archiepiscopus *tr.* B   [d] suis *om. Martène*   [e] benedictionem B *(recte: cf. Doc. 28)*: honorem A   [f] episcopi B *et Martène*: episcopus A *(cf. § 2)*   [g] patribus BC *(recte: cf. Doc. 28)*: fratribus A   [h] Rothom' archiepiscopo *(recte: cf. Doc. 28)* C: *tr.* AB   [i-i] abbatibus—legatus *om.* C; episcopis *add. Paris (sed non Wendover)* C   [j] in domino Jesu Christo C   [k] veri CB: veii (?) A, veri *corr. marg.* A[1].   [l] implorare AC: postulare B   [m] vos B: nos A   [n] Hinc—instantius *om.* C   [o] igitur *add.* C   [p] aspirsionem B   [q] propensius BC *et Martène*: perpensius A   [r] atque *praem.* B   [s] octavis BC: oct' A, octava *Martène*   [t] proxime B   [u] etiam *Martène*   [v] Francie AC: futuri B   [w] dare <d>e negotio predicto: dare super negotio [predicto *supralin.* A[1].] Albig' [enegotio predicto A, *expunct.* A[1].] A; dare negotio predicto B; dare in negotio predicto C; enegotio *emendavi*   [x] ibidem AC: tunc B   [y] super negotio Albig' BC: *om.* A *(sed vide notam w supra)*   [z] significari B   [a] Datum—Junii: Datum Provin' (prouin') vi[o] non. Junii A; Datum vi. Nonas Julij 1223 B; Data Planium 6 Non. Iulii C; *emendationes in praefatione explicavi*   [b] Huius auctoritate—Junii *om.* BC   [c] Eccetis: accersatis *glossavit Martène*   [d] et A: ut *Martène*

Theobald[1] by the grace of God archbishop of Rouen, to all the venerable brothers his suffragans, greeting, grace, and blessing. We have received a letter from the venerable father Conrad[2] bishop of Porto and Santa Rufina, legate of the apostolic see, the text of which follows:

2 To the venerable fathers by the grace of God the archbishop of Rouen and his suffragans, and to the abbots, priors, deans, archdeacons, and chapters located in the province of Rouen, Conrad by the mercy of God bishop of Porto and Santa Rufina, legate of the apostolic see, greetings in Christ Jesus.

3 We are forced to implore your aid for the bride of the upright one crucified, or rather we are compelled to be racked with sobs and to utter cries of pain. . . . [The legate relates at length why he is summoning the council: the pope of the Cathari in the Balkans has sent his legate into Languedoc, where he is establishing Catharist bishops and churches, and prompt countermeasures must be taken.]

. . . .

4 Hence it is that we urgently warn you, more intently ask you, and the more readily beseech you for the sake of the blood shed by Jesus Christ, ordering you by the lord pope's authority that we exercise in these parts, that you are to come to Sens on the octave of the apostles Peter and Paul next to come, where (God willing) the other prelates of France will be gathered together, and you should be prepared to give counsel concerning the aforesaid business and, with the others there present, to take steps to deal with the Albigensian business. Otherwise we shall take care to report your disobedience to the lord pope. Given at St-Pourçain, on the fourth day before the nones of June.

5 By the authority of this mandate we command you to be present in person at Sens on the day stated. Also by the same authority summon all the abbots, priors, deans, archdeacons, and chapters of your diocese to convene there properly prepared on that day. And do your best

1. Theobaldus d'Amiens, archbishop of Rouen 1222-1229. In a note, Hugo identified the archbishop G. of his text as Gaufridus (Godefredus), whose pontificate began in 1111 and lasted seventeen years (as Hugo correctly states), but he accordingly died in 1128 (Mas Latrie, *Trésor de chronologie*, col. 1476), not in 1228, the date Hugo gives.

2. Conrad von Urach, cardinal-bishop of Porto and St Rufina, papal legate in France 1219-1223.

fideliter exequi studeatis ne a Domino Jesu Christo, cujus fides in periculo constituta est, in districto examine propter hoc puniri debeatis et
ne a domino papa possitis de negligentia seu inobedientia reprehendi.
Datum anno gratie m° cc° xx° iii°, vi° id. Junii.[be]

[e] Junii A: Julii *Martène*

Document 50
LOUIS VIII ASKS ROMANUS TO ENFORCE
DEBTORS' OATHS
[1226]

Strange to say, this letter is not included in Petit-Dutaillis' catalogue of the acts
of Louis VIII. Yet it could hardly have been written in the name of the infant
Louis IX in the later years of Romanus' legation (1226-1229), since *this* King
Louis addresses Romanus as "his most dear and special friend," which does describe the relationship between Romanus and Louis VIII (Docs. 14.1 and 15.1).
Dom Martène drew the same conclusion, as his title for the piece indicates, but
he did not state his reasons.

   From this letter, it appears that some time ago Louis had asked Romanus to
prevent debtors from disavowing their obligations before ecclesiastical judges on
the pretext that usury was involved. Romanus had deferred immediate action
by referring the royal request to the pope, and now the king is asking the legate
to act on the matter on his own initiative, if only *ad interim*. Most likely Louis
had grown impatient when the pope failed to respond—as in fact he never did,
judging from Honorius' registers.

   A closer reading reveals Romanus attempting to satisfy his sometimes conflicting obligations to enforce canon law and to accommodate the king. In the
letter, Louis specifies that the ecclesiastical judges involved were not only the
ordinary authorities of the church in France but also judges-delegate appointed
by Romanus. When the king wanted Romanus to restrict the powers of both
kinds of judges, the legate could have done so by virtue of his broad, discre-
tionary powers (Doc. 12) but apparently he decided to procrastinate instead and
referred the matter to Rome. Thus he was able to preserve the normal operation of canon law in general, and to back up his subordinates in particular, without impeding the crusade by losing the king's good will.

to carry out that business, lest you deserve to be punished because of this when you are strictly examined by Jesus Christ, whose faith is now endangered; and also lest you can be censured by the lord pope for negligence or disobedience. Given in the year of grace 1223, on the sixth day before the ides of June.

Date.—The letter was written several months at the least after Romanus' arrival at the royal court in April 1225; Louis's death on 8 November 1226 provides the *terminus ante*. A date in 1226 seems likely, given the lengthy probable sequence of events leading up to the letter: the creditors appeal to the legate; he appoints judges–delegate; the case is heard with due process; the debtors complain to the crown; Louis asks the legate for a remedy; he refers the proposal to Rome; then an immediate response would have taken two months, and Louis probably waited considerably longer before addressing this follow-up letter to Romanus.

Occasion.—Although it is tempting to view this letter as evidence of a general royal policy of enforcing debtors' obligations, more likely the crown's concern was more specific. For instance, it was in Louis' reign that Lombard bankers were established in Paris under royal protection;[1] furthermore, the crown had a special obligation to help the Rouennais collect their debts: in January 1224, Louis advised his officials that those in debt to citizens of Rouen would be forced by the king to go there and pay their debts.[2] Although either one of these commitments could have led Louis to intervene with Romanus, it seems most likely that his concern arose from a specific case. In May 1226 Louis declared that as far as the crown was concerned, Raoul Guiton and his heirs were forever acquitted of any accusation or pretext of usury,[3] the apparent purpose of which was to waive the crown's right to confiscate the property of a usurer.[4]

1. Petit-Dutaillis, *Louis*, pp. 417–418.

2. Petit-Dutaillis, *Louis*, p. 457 (Register, no. 62, January 1224), ed. L. Delisle, *Cartulaire normand*, no. 777, from a *vidimus* of 1270. Petit-Dutaillis states that this act confirms an article of the royal charter of 1207 (p. 421, n. 2), but the act itself appears to be *de novo*.

3. Petit-Dutaillis, *Louis*, p. 499 (Register, no. 374, May 1226), ed. Delisle, *Cartulaire normand*, no. 355: "Quod nos Radulfum Guiton et heredes suos de uxore sua desponsata, quos habet ad presens, quittamus in perpetuum, quantum ad nos pertinet, de omni accusatione et occasione usure. . . . " The privilege goes on to grant Raoul the right to provide a suitable dowry for his niece.

4. *Medieval France: An Encyclopedia*, ed. W. W. Kibler et al. (New York, 1995), p. 942.

Significantly, the Guiton family was prominent in Avranches,[5] which would explain why this document was preserved at the nearby monastery of Mont-St-Michel. Probably Raoul Guiton was first found guilty of usury by a local ecclesiastical judge ordinary and that decision was upheld on appeal by the legate's judges-delegate. In addressing the legate, Louis seems to have been concerned to forestall similar cases rather than to reverse the decision against Raoul.

5. Delisle, *Cartulaire normand*, note to no. 62. Cf. Chevalier, *Topo-bibliographie*, I (1894), 1370, and *Bio-bibliographie*, I (1905), 1994: in 1423 Jean Guiton was "capitaine de Mont-St-Michel."

L ud(ovicus) Dei gratia Franc' rex karissimo et speciali amico suo Rom(ano) Sancti Angeli diacono cardinali, apostolice sedis legato, salutem et sincere dilectionis affectum.

1 Ad vestram notitiam pervenire <credimus>[a] quod in quibusdam regni nostri partibus usque adeo quorumdam excrevit malitia quod, cum sub sacramenti vel fidei religione ad certum terminum suis sint creditoribus obligati, paulo ante terminum coram judicibus delegatis a vobis seu ordinariis suos conveniunt creditores, liberatione petita pro eo quod asserant[b] contractus quibus obligantur[c] continere usuras. Unde contingit interdum quod creditores per hujusmodi fraudem creditum suum amittere compelluntur,[d] et quandoque eis invitis differtur solutio in terminum longiorem.

2 Proinde dilectionem vestram rogamus quatinus per vestras dignemini litteras prohibere ne qui judices ordinarii seu delegati a vobis quemlibet audiant contra fidem prestitam[1] vel sacramentum proprium venientem,[e] set potius debitores ad observandum juramentum auctoritate vestra compellant, et postea si quas actiones adversus creditores suos se habere confidunt, eis secundum juris ordinem liceat experiri.

3 Meminimus enim vos super hoc ipso scripsisse domino pape ad petitionem nostram.

[a] credimus *scripsi cum Martène*
[b] asserant] afferant *perperam leg. Martène*
[c] obligentur *Martène*
[d] compellantur *Martène*
[e] vincentem *Martène*

The document is included here to illustrate the legate's priorities and modus operandi, so I have not attempted to explicate it in the wider context of contemporary credit operations and the problem of usury.[6]

MS.— (A) Avranches, Bibl. mun., MS. 149, fol. 78rb; *olim* Mont-St-Michel MS. 249. See Doc. 28 for further analysis. This document is the second of three letters related to Romanus' legation, all entered on the same blank folio (the others are Doc. 28 and Doc. 51).

Ed.—(1) Martène-Durand, *Thesaurus*, I (Paris, 1717), 935, from A, under the title: *Epistola Ludovici VIII. regis Francorum ad Romanum sedis apostolicae legatum.*

Text transcribed from a microfilm of A.

6. See, for example, Kathryn L. Reyerson, "Les Opérations de crédit dans la coutume et dans la vie des affaires à Montpellier au Moyen Age: Le problème de l'usure," *Diritto comune e diritti locali nella storia dell'Europa: Atti del Convegno di Varenna (12–15 giugno 1979)* (Milan, 1980), pp. 189–209.

Louis by the grace of God king of France, to his dearest and special friend Romanus cardinal-deacon of Sant' Angelo, legate of the apostolic see, greeting and the affection of sincere love.

1 We believe it has come to your notice that in some parts of our kingdom the evil of some persons has grown to such an extent that, when they are obligated by a sanction based on their oath or their good faith to repay their creditors at a given date, a little before the deadline they have their creditors appear before your judges-delegate or their ordinary ecclesiastical judges, where they plead to be freed from their obligation on the grounds that they claim that the contracts by which they are obligated involve usury. Whence it sometimes happens that by a fraud of this kind the creditors are restrained from collecting what they have loaned, inasmuch as contrary to their wishes payment is deferred to some more distant date.

2 Consequently we ask you as a friend to deign by your writ to prohibit judges ordinary or delegated by you from hearing anyone who is obstructing the operation of a guarantee of good faith[1] or of an oath proper; but instead have them compel debtors to observe their oaths by your authority, and after they have paid, if they are confident that they have any actions against their creditors, they can have them tried in conformity with proper legal procedure.

3 We recall that at our request you wrote to the lord pope about this.

1. In Roman law, interest could be promised by a simple agreement (*usurae ex pacto*), which a judge might enforce if it was "connected with a contract governed by good faith (*contractus bonae fidei*)": Adolf Berger, *Encyclopedic Dictionary of Roman Law* (Philadelphia, 1953), 753, s.v. "usurae ex pacto."

Document 51
ROMANUS EXEMPTS A PRIORY
FROM LEGATINE PROCURATIONS
1226

In this document, procuration refers to an annual cash contribution to support a papal legate that was paid by the ecclesiastical corporations of his legation, namely by cathedral chapters, monasteries, priories, and cathedral churches. The amount was large enough to be burdensome: four marks a year was the usual rate for a legate in thirteenth-century England. Custom determined which houses had to pay procurations there, and this document shows that the same was true in Normandy. Similar but lesser payments were exacted to support visitations by archbishops and bishops, which occurred more frequently, if not regularly as required by law.

With this background, the story of the present document emerges clearly. Romanus had entrusted the collection of the procurations that were his due to the episcopate, and the bishop of Bayeux had in turn delegated the task to his archdeacon. But in their diocese, the Benedictine priory of Torteval felt it was not obliged to pay this legatine procuration because it customarily did not pay procurations to either the bishop of Bayeux or the archbishop of Rouen when they visited the priory. Consequently, while the legate was in Normandy in 1226, at Avranches he was petitioned to grant the priory an exemption. Romanus of course did not know what the custom was, so he satisfied the petition by instructing the archdeacon of Bayeux that, if the custom was as Torteval had stated, he was not to require payment and was to cease any legal action he might have begun to force payment. The legate was careful to stipulate that

---

R om(anus) miseratione divina Sancti Angeli diaconus cardinalis, apostolice sedis legatus, dilecto in Christo .R.[1] archidiacono Bajoc' salutem in Domino.

Cum sicut accepimus in prioratu de Torta Valle[2] Bajoc' diocesis archiepiscopi vel episcopi procurationes aliquas non consueverint aliquando percipere[a] vel habere, nolentes quod ex facto nostro eis in posterum aliquod prejudicium generetur, discretioni vestre, auctoritate qua fungimur, mandamus quatinus, si est ita, ab ipso

[a] pecipere A

he did not mean this action to create a precedent, thereby leaving his successors free to collect legatine procurations even though Torteval was exempt from episcopal ones.

The document affords our only insight into the financing of Romanus' legation. Like his counterparts in England, Romanus delegated the collection of his procuration money to the bishops of his legation, and probably a new procuration was collected every year for the duration of the legation. In 1226 the papal procuration system was by no means fixed, and this document provides a rare glimpse of how it functioned. As in England, it was as yet unclear precisely what corporations were liable to pay the tax, and Romanus was not prepared to establish a precedent. Nevertheless, Romanus' practice did become standard some decades later. His leniency with Torteval was good public relations and perhaps spared him the reputation for avarice that dogged legates to England.

MS.—(A) Avranches, Bibl. mun., MS. 149, fol. 78rb; *olim* Mont–St–Michel MS. 249; for details, see above, Doc. 28. This document is one of three related to Romanus' legation that were copied together in the same column; the others are Docs. 28 and 50.

Ed.—(1) Martène–Durand, *Thesaurus*, I (1717), 935–936, under the title, *Romani legati epistola ad R. archidiaconum Bajocensem, ut procurationes non exigat a priore de Tortavalle.*

Refs.—K. Ruess, *Die rechtliche Stellung der päpstlichen Legaten bis Bonifaz VIII.*, Görres-Gesellschaft, Sektion für Rechts- und Sozialwissenschaft, 13 (Paderborn, 1912), pp. 188–204. W. E. Lunt, *Financial Relations of the Papacy with England to 1327* (Cambridge, Mass., 1939), pp. 532–570.

Text from a microfilm of A.

Romanus by divine mercy cardinal-deacon of Sant' Angelo, legate of the apostolic see, to the beloved in Christ R.[1] archdeacon of Bayeux, greeting in the Lord.

We understand that customarily no archbishop's or bishop's procurations have ever been collected or acquired from the priory of Torteval[2] in the diocese of Bayeux. Although by our action we do not intend to establish any precedent concerning them in the future, by the authority we exercise we command that, if the

1. Papal letters mention an archdeacon R. of Bayeux in 1217 and 1219, but in 1221 the office was held by one T. (Pressutti, nos. 498, 1828, 2978, 2984).

2. Notre Dame de Torteval (*Tortavallis*), a Benedictine priory dependent on the monastery of St-Etienne de Caen; in the diocese, and near the city, of Bayeux. Cottineau, *Répertoire*, II, 3175.

prioratu nomine procurationis nostre nichil exigas vel requiras; et si forte propter hoc contra ipsum in aliquo est processum, auctoritate nostra studeas revocare.

Datum Abrinc' anno Domini m° cc° xx° vi°.

Document 52
A CONCUBINARY PRIEST IS SENT TO ROMANUS
[1226]

Since the time of the Gregorian reform, the Church had insisted that priests should be celibate, and consequently that they should not have female bedmates (*concubinaria*), or concubines, and those who persisted were most commonly deprived of their benefices. In 1208 Guala, the papal legate to France, laid down a much more severe penalty: once such priests had been duly warned they were to be excommunicated automatically (*latae sententiae*) by the authority of Guala's legatine constitution rather than at the discretion of their bishop.[1] Guala's canon was poorly drafted, however, for it failed to specify who was to reconcile the excommunicates. Normally only the pope or his legate could absolve one whom a papal legate had excommunicated, which would greatly complicate the process of reconciliation; consequently he was asked to clarify the matter when he issued his constitutions in a longer version. His intention, Guala explained, was that concubinary priests were to be reconciled by the archbishop of their province, while for other offenses against his constitutions, the local bishop would suffice.[2] This interpretation indicates that by his innovation Guala meant to make the reconciliation of concubinary priests more difficult than previously had been the case, but not impossibly difficult. Although his interpretation was regularly appended to the longer, later version of his constitutions, unfortunately it did not become associated with the shorter, earlier version that the province of Rouen took to be authoritative.

This misunderstanding created a series of problems in the province of Rouen, as offenders had to go to Rome for absolution, and it took a series of papal interventions to rectify the situation. In 1222, Honorius III granted Archbishop Theobald the power to absolve those concubinary priests in his province who were excommunicated by Guala's sentence and to impose an appropriate

---

[1.] Constitutio Galae, c. 1, ed. Pontal (see below, *app. font.*, n. 2).

2. See text in *app. font.*, n. 2, below.

case is as stated above, you neither exact nor demand from this priory anything termed a procuration for us. And if perchance this priory has in any way been proceeded against because of this, make it your business to revoke it by our authority.

Given at Avranches in the year of the Lord 1226.

---

penance on them.[3] But there were further complications: within a year, Theobald complained that in his archdiocese many priests who were excommunicated by Guala's sentence were nevertheless administering the sacraments, and "so great a multitude was involved that it would be immensely expensive for them all to go to the apostolic see," so Honorius directed him to "do what shall seem to you to be useful for their [spiritual] health."[4] A year later, the same power was granted to all the bishops of Rouen province in response to allegations not only of the expense of going to Rome but also of the danger of the journey and the physical disabilities of the excommunicates. The dilemma was that they endangered their own souls if they continued to serve their churches, but if they were removed, suitable replacements could not be readily found.[5]

From the present document, it appears that the bishop of Coutances had duly reconciled the concubinary priest C. after he had incurred excommunication under Guala's canon. The problem was that the man had subsequently relapsed, and Bishop Hugh was not quite sure what to do in that case, which had not been raised previously; although he had suspended the offender and deprived him of his benefice, Hugh did not know what penance to impose before lifting the excommunication, so he passed his problem on to the legate. The complexity of the case accounts for its preservation as a canonistic curiosity in Avranches 149, and the copyist's wry motto implies that Rome, by reserving to itself jurisdiction in such petty matters, is only getting here what it asked for.

3. Pressutti 4150 (19 Nov. 1222), ed. Horoy, IV, 244, no. 22: "juxta formam Ecclesiae absolvendi, injuncta eis poenitentia competenti. . . . "

4. Pressutti 4601 (9 Dec. 1223), ed. Horoy, IV, 474, no. 55: "facias, quod ipsorum saluti videris expedire. . . . "

5. Pressutti 5179 (26 Nov. 1224), ed. Horoy, IV, 719-720, no. 32: "asseritis," Honorius wrote the bishops, "perplexitatem non modicam incurreritis, cum praedicti [concubinarii clerici] non possint in suis ecclesiis sine animarum periculo deservire, et si amoveretis eosdem alii idonei de facili reperiri non possent, et multi ex eis propter viarum pericula, suorum debilitatem corporum, et expensarum defectum ad nos venire nequeant absolutionis beneficium petituri. . . . Nos . . . mandamus, quatenus singuli vestri [sc. episcopi] hujusmodi dioecesis suae clericis secundum formam Ecclesiae beneficium absolutionis impendant et cum eis faciant super aliis, prout animarum suarum saluti viderint expedire."

Date.—Tentatively I assign the incident to the year 1226, when Romanus visited Avranches (Doc. 51), but it could have taken place at any time during his legation (1225-1229), since additions were made to MS. A as late as 1234.

MS.—(A) Avranches, Bibl. mun., MS. 149, fol. 135vb; *olim* Mont-St-Michel MS. 249; for details, see above, Doc. 28. The recto of this folio contains legal extracts; the verso is mostly filled with miscellaneous items: an account of Berengar's retraction, another of Charlemagne's coronation; then a new hand fills the last ten lines with the present item, preceded by this note: "Johannes Crisostomus super Matheum: Omnes res per quascunque causas nascitur, per easdem dissolvitur" (an appropriate motto for a case arising from Guala's excommunication *latae sen-*

DOMINO LEGATO.

R(omano) divina gratia Sancti Angeli diacono cardinali et apostolice sedis legato, <Hugo>[a1] eadem gratia Const' ecclesie minister humilis, salutem et obedientiam debitam et devotionem.

Noverit discretio vestra quod cum C. presbiter, lator presentium, incidisset in canonem a domino Gal(e)[3] cardinale quondam apostolice sedis legato in concubinarios promulgatum,[2] ipse coram nobis concubinariam abjuravit; et postea, instigante diabolo, sicut ex confessione ejus in jure facta cognovimus, passus est recidivum. Unde ipsum ad vos transmittimus suspensum ab ordine et beneficio ut cum eo agatis secundum quod salutem anime sue districtioni[b] vestre visum fuerit expedire. Valete.

[a] R. *perperam leg.* A
[b] districtionic (*littera* e *semiformata?*) A, *corr.* A[1].

tentiae). A canonistic summa begins on the next folio. In other words, Doc. 52 has no significant manuscript context.

Ed.—Unpublished.

Refs.—H. C. Lea, *History of Sacerdotal Celibacy in the Christian Church*, 2 vols. (New York, 1907), I, 410-411. E. Vodola, *Excommunication in the Middle Ages* (Berkeley, 1986), pp. 28-32, for excommunication *latae sententiae*. C. D. Fonseca, "A proposito della 'Constitutio Gale' del 1208," *Studia Gratiana*, XIII (1967), 45-55.

Text transcribed from a microfilm of A.

TO THE LORD LEGATE.

To Romanus by divine grace cardinal of Sant' Angelo and legate of the apostolic see, H.,[1] by the same grace humble minister of the church of Coutances, greeting, due obedience, and devotion.

Your discretion is to be informed that when C., a priest and the bearer of the present letter, transgressed the canon[2] that was promulgated against concubinary priests by the lord cardinal Guala,[3] former legate of the apostolic see, the same priest abjured his concubine in our presence. And later by the devil's instigation, he suffered a relapse, as we learned from his confession, which was lawfully made. He has been suspended from his priestly order and deprived of his benefice; consequently, I am sending him to you so that you may do what seems to your sense of strictness will expedite the health of his soul. Farewell.

1. Hugo de Morville was certainly bishop of Coutances from 1208 to 1238: see documents cited in *Gallia Christiana*, XI (1759), 878-880.

2. The legatine constitution of Guala consists of ten (sometimes seven) canons promulgated in his name without either date or place: Mansi, XXII (1778), 763-766; J. F. Pommeraye, *Sanctae Rotomagensis ecclesiae concilia* (Rouen, 1677), p. 208, notes that the Rouen synodal contains the short version (seven canons). New edition in O. Pontal, *Les Statuts synodaux français du XIIIᵉ siècle*, I (Paris, 1971), 98-99. Three manuscripts cited by Pontal also give Guala's oral interpretation of c. 1, concerning concubinary priests, but inexplicably she gives only the *incipit* (p. 43). The full text, from Paris, BnF, MS. lat. 14593, fol. 36va-b: "Sicut autem ab ipsius ore G(alli) domini accipimus illi qui incidunt in primum articulum, scilicet presbiteri et clerici tenentes fornicarias, non possunt absolvi nisi a suis archiepiscopis tantum. In sequentibus articulis possunt absolvere episcopi, set quisque in sua diocesi; Parisien' vero omnes scolares Parisien'."

3. Guala (Gal[l]a, Gal[l]o) Bicchieri, in 1208 cardinal-deacon of Santa Maria *in Porticu* and bishop-elect of Vercelli; later cardinal-priest of St Martin *tituli Equiti*. See Maleczek, *Kardinalskolleg*, pp. 141-146. He was commissioned legate to France on 29 May 1208 and completed his mission in January 1209: H. Zimmermann, *Die päpstliche Legation in der ersten Hälfte des 13. Jahrhunderts* (Paderborn, 1913), p. 41. Most recent life by C. D. Fonseca in *Dizionario biografico degli italiani*, X (1968), 314-324, s.v. "Bicchieri, Guala."

Document 53
THE ROUEN CHAPTER RECUSES ROMANUS
[September] 1227

This rare and fascinating document has gone unnoticed because it was not itemized in the published descriptions of MS. Avranches 149.[1] It is a complaint, which could only be addressed to the pope, against an unnamed legate whom the complainants are seeking to disqualify from judging them. This appears from their thesis that they consider the legate to be "suspect," which according to canon law meant they could challenge, or "recuse," the competence of their judge.[2] Although the document bears no indication of date or place and identifies none of the parties, nonetheless it does provide us with enough clues to determine its historical context.

To begin, the complainants are collectively the cathedral chapter of an *archbishop*, "who is our head and an integral part of the body of this church" (§ 4). Since most of the documents in MS. Avranches 149 relate to the province of Rouen (namely Docs. 28, 49-52), the metropolitan church referred to is probably that of Rouen. Our first clue is that the archbishop in question was present at the time of the legate's inquest (§ 2) and at the time of writing he had departed for the curia (§ 4). The other clue is that when the legate first arrived, he was particularly upset about "this church's interdict" (§ 5). Accordingly, if we can find an interdict at Rouen that was shortly followed by the archbishop's departure for Rome, that should supply the context for this document.

Both of these circumstances were present at Rouen in the late summer of 1227. Archbishop Theobald had been quarreling with local crown officials over his right to take timber from the forest of Louviers. The dispute escalated until in July 1227 the archbishop appeared before a royal court at Vernon and declared that the king had no jurisdiction over him in either spiritual or feudal matters. When Theobald maintained this position somewhat later at an assembly of crown vassals, on their advice the king confiscated the archbishop's worldly

1. *Catalogue générale des manuscrits des bibliothèques publiques des départements*, quarto series, IV (Paris, 1872), 504 = octavo series, X (1889), 71: fol. 109v ff., 6 cols. of "Lettres de papes et fragments divers intéressant l'histoire de Normandie et d'Angleterre." For both editions, L. Delisle printed Taranne's 1841 description unaltered.

2. X 2.28 *de appellationibus, recusationibus, et relationibus*, ed. Friedberg, II, 409-443, e.g. cc. 27, 43, 61 (II, 419, 425, 437). The concept of the *iudex suspectus* is derived from Roman law: see Linda Fowler, "Recusatio iudicis in Civilian and Canonist Thought," *Studia Gratiana*, XV (1972), 717-786.

goods. In response, the archbishop assembled his bishops[3] and on their advice placed an interdict on "all the domains and castles the king had in his archiepiscopate, excepting cities." All this comes from the *Chronicon Rotomagense*, which continues: "and therefore he [Theobald] lived in exile; having set out for the Roman curia, he was detained at Reims by sickness, and he sent to the Roman curia."[4] The chronicle goes on to tell how the quarrel was subsequently settled in the archbishop's favor,[5] but that need not concern us, for we already have the two required elements: an interdict and an archbishop who has set out for Rome. Our document tells what happened at Rouen between the declaration of the interdict and the archbishop's departure.

The suspect legate was, of course, Romanus. Since May 1227, as we have seen in chapter 5, he was engaged in a dispute over the payment of the Albigensian tenth, which was to culminate in his departure for Rome, probably in September because he attended the annual Cistercian chapter at Cîteaux (Doc. 37.4), which customarily met in that month. Since Theobald had confronted the king at Vernon in July, and then again later, his subsequent council approving the interdict could not have taken place much earlier than 1 September.[6] Thus the legate's objectionable visit to Rouen must have taken place soon thereafter, early in September 1227.

Upon hearing of the interdict, then, Romanus hurried to Rouen in a state of exasperation. For months his efforts to prolong the crusade and to support the

---

3. This assembly should be added to the already considerable list of Rouen provincial councils omitted from the conciliar collections: see R. Kay, "Mansi and Rouen: A Critique of the Conciliar Collections," *Catholic Historical Review*, LII (1966), 155-185.

4. Luc d'Achery, *Spicilegium*, 2nd ed. (Paris, 1723), III, 613-614; "Fragmentum ex Chronico MS. Ecclesiae Rotomagensis," at p. 614: "Unde Archiepiscopus habito tractatu cum Episcopis suis, omnia dominia & castella, quae Rex habebat in Archiepiscopatu suo, interdicto conclusit, exceptis tantummodo civitatibus, & inde exulavit ad Curiam Romanam profecturus, & infirmitate detentus Remis, & misit ad Curiam Romanam." The source is the *Chronicon Rotomagense*, on which see *Repertorium fontium historiae Medii Aevi*, III (Rome, 1970), 430-431, and esp. L. Delisle in *Histoire littéraire de la France*, XXXII (1898), 194-188. D'Achery's fragment is printed *inter alia* in *Rec. hist. Gaules*, XXIII (1876), 332-333.

5. The settlement, which Romanus effected after returning from Rome, is given in his open letter dated 21 October 1228: printed in Martène-Durand, *Vet. script. coll.*, I (Paris, 1724), 1226, from Paris, Arch. nat., JJ 26, fol. 235v (Register E). On 23 August 1228 Gregory IX had commissioned him to settle the dispute (Auvray, no. 216).

6. Given the rapid succession of events, Theobald must have convoked the council well in advance, probably after returning from Vernon in July. An autumn council was mandated by canon law (Gratian, *Decretum* D.18 c.2-4, ed. Friedberg, I, 54), but a generation later Rouen provincial councils occasionally met in late August or early September (3 Sept. 1265, 30 Aug. 1267), though later dates in September or even October were more usual (Kay, "Mansi and Rouen," pp. 175-176).

regency of Queen Blanche had been undermined by the chapters' refusal to pay the tenth; during August he had succeeded in detaching Sens from the coalition, and now he apparently attempted to pressure the chapters of Rouen province "by defamation, suspension, excommunication, and appropriation of benefices" (§ 5). On top of this came the interdict, and for Romanus it was the last straw: soon after arriving in Rouen, he assembled the canons and vented his anger by scolding and threatening them "publicly in his sermon, with laymen present" (§ 3, 5). Probably Romanus' visitation never did result in any reforms, partly because they were forestalled by the archbishop's absence and partly because the legate had to break off his inquiry and himself leave for Rome in order to defend his treatment of the delinquent chapters: by 13 November the pope had heard the case and rendered his judgment (Doc. 39).

Because Romanus' visit to Rouen was prompted by the interdict, probably his main purpose was to have it lifted, which required negotiation with Theobald rather than the chapter; when the archbishop proved intractable and set off for Rome, the legate soon followed him. The legate's visitation of the chapter and province was secondary, then; but because he had to be in Rouen to deal with the interdict, he took the opportunity to pressure the chapter into abandoning its appeal against the tenth. All he accomplished was to goad the canons into yet another complaint against him.

For the present study, the chapter's complaint provides unique evidence of Romanus' high-handed treatment of uncooperative subordinates. One might

---

Habemus dominum legatum suspectum multis rationibus.

1 Una est quia excessit in inquirendo, timemus ne excedat corrigendo.

2 Alia est quia promisit se facturum correctionem de consilio domini archiepiscopi. Et, cum diu post inquisitionem factam, dominus archiepiscopus presens fuerit, nec dominus legatus aliquid correxerit; modo captata eius absentia, cum non possit uti eius consilio nec nos eius defensione si opus esset, videlicet corrigere, unde habemus eum suspectum.

3 Alia est ratio quia ipsa die inquisitionis, cum inquisitio fieret, antequam sciret vel audiret deposita, publice in sua predicatione coram laicis minatus est nobis et diffamavit nos.

4 Item, dominus archiepiscopus, qui caput nostrum est et de integritate corporis huius ecclesie, iam appellavit facto, arripiendo iter ad curiam; et nos illius appellationis sumus participes, cum ipse stet in curia pro se et ecclesia sua.

5 Item, multos spirituali in hac ecclesia et quamplures in aliis gravavit eccle-

have guessed as much from other sources (for example Doc. 32), but his bully-ing sermon described here leaves no room for doubt. Other aspects of his char-acter emerge as well: the energy with which he responded to the interdict; the opportunism with which he made the most of his presence in Rouen; and above all, his tendency to react intemperately when faced with insubordination.

MS.—(A) Avranches, Bibl. mun., MS. 149, fol. 109va; *olim* Mont-St-Michel MS. 249. See Doc. 28 for further analysis. Adjacent items are unrelated to this one: before, in the same hand, a letter from the *officialis* of the bishop of Salisbury to his counterpart at Winchester; after, in another hand, an abbot is informed of his faults (by a legate?), *incipit* "Derelictionis (?) maxime ignorantie quam re-supine ad modum extitit. . . . "

Ed.—Unpublished.

Refs.—Elie Berger, *Histoire de Blanche de Castille, reine de France* (Paris, 1895), pp. 101-102. G. J. Campbell, "The Attitude of the Monarchy toward the Use of Ec-clesiastical Censures in the Reign of Saint Louis," *Speculum*, XXXV (1960), 535-555, at pp. 538-539. R. Kay, "Romanus and Rouen: A Papal Legate's Tainted Visitation in 1227," *Annales de Normandie*, LI (2001), 111-119.

We consider the lord legate to be suspect for many reasons. One reason is that because he was excessive in inquiring, we fear that he may be excessive in correcting as well.

2 Another reason is because he promised that he would do the correcting with the counsel of the lord archbishop. And, when the lord archbishop was present for a long time after the inquiry was completed, the lord legate did not correct anything. But now that his absence has been secured, since the legate cannot use his counsel and we his defense if there be any need for correction, we therefore consider the legate to be suspect.

3 Another reason is because, on the very day of the inquiry, when the inquiry had not yet taken place, before he knew or had heard the depositions, he threat-ened and defamed us publicly in his sermon, with laymen present.

4 Also, the lord archbishop, who is our head and an integral part of the body of this church, has in fact already appealed, having set off in haste for the curia; and we are participants in that appeal, since in the curia he represents himself and his church.

siis, diffamando, suspendendo, excommunicando, beneficiis spoliando. Et maxime totam hanc ecclesiam gravavit vehementer de interdicto huius ecclesie in primo suo ingressu. Et ideo difficultas introitus nos facit timere ne durior sit exitus.

6 Item, alias privatas et familiares habemus rationes quas in audientia superioris loco suo et tempore proponemus.

5 Also, he has oppressed many spiritual persons in this church and very many in other churches by defamation, suspension, excommunication, and appropriation of benefices; and above all, when he first arrived he oppressed this whole church exceedingly on account of this church's interdict. And the difficulty at his arrival therefore makes us fear that his departure may be even more difficult.

6 Also, we have private and confidential reasons that we shall state orally to a superior at the time and place of his choice.

BIBLIOGRAPHY

MANUSCRIPTS

This list includes all manuscript materials cited.

Avranches, Bibl. mun., MS. 149 (*olim* Mont-St-Michel, MS. 249): Docs. 26, 28, 41, 49–53.

Berlin, Deutsche Staatsbibliothek, MS. Phillipps lat. 145: Chronicle of Tours; Doc. 3.

Bern, Bürgerbibliothek, MS. 22: Chronicle of Tours; Doc. 3.

Cambridge, Corpus Christi College, MS. 16: Matthew Paris, *Chronica majora*; Docs. 1, 43, 49.

———, MS. 175: Walter of Coventry: Docs. 1, 41, 44.

Cambridge, Trinity College, MS. 993: Abingdon Chronicle; chap. 6.

Laon, Arch. dép. Aisne, G 1850: chap. 2.

London, BL, MS. Add. 35,168: Crowland annals; Doc. 44.

———, MS. Cotton Tiberius A. x: Dunstable annals; Doc. 2.

———, MS. Cotton Tiberius B. xiii: Gerald of Wales; Doc. 40.

———, MS. Cotton Claudius A. v: Spalding annals; Doc. 44.

———, MS. Cotton Otho B. v: Wendover's *Flores historiarum*; Docs. 43, 49.

———, MS. Cotton Vitellius E. xiii: proto "Walter of Coventry"; Doc. 44.

———, MS. Royal 14. C. vii: Paris' *Historia Anglorum*; Doc. 43.

London, College of Arms, MS. Arundel 10: "Barnwell" chronicle; Docs. 1, 41, 44.

London, PRO, Special Collections 1/5/17 (Ancient Correspondence, vol. V, no. 17); Doc. 22.

———, Special Collections 1/57/73 (Ancient Correspondence, vol. XLVII, no. 73): Doc. 25.

London, Society of Antiquaries, MS. 60: Black Book of Peterborough; Doc. 44.

Manchester, Chetham Library, MS. 6712: "Matthew of Westminister"; Doc. 43.

Oxford, Bodleian Library, MS. Douce 207: Wendover's *Flores historiarum*; Docs. 1, 43, 49.

Oxford, Magdalen College, MS. lat. 36: proto "Walter of Coventry"; Docs. 1, 41, 44.

Paris, Arch. nat., J 428, no. 1 bis (*olim* no. 1742): Doc. 23.

———, J 428, no. 2 (*olim* no. 1743): Doc. 24.

———, J 428, no. 3 (*olim* nos. 1693 and 1694): Docs. 12, 13, 27.

———, J 428, no. 7 (*olim* no. 1928): Doc. 31.

———, J 428, no. 8 (*olim* no. 1940): Doc. 36.

———, J 1035, no. 18: Doc. 29.

———, J 1035, no. 19: Doc. 30.

———, JJ 13: Register of the Trésor des chartes; Doc. 8.

———, JJ 26: Delisle's Register E, compiled in 1220, with supplements to 1276; *olim* Colbert MS. 2670; Regius MS. 8408; Docs. 1, 7, 8, 9, 23–24, 26, 29.

Paris, BnF, MS. Baluze 8: Draft conciliar collection; Docs. 7, 23–24, 26, 29, 31, 36.

———, L 239, no. 31: Doc. 48.

———, MS. Baluze 385, no. 239: Albigensian Roll; Docs. 10–17, 19, 20, 21.

————, MS. franç. 4963: *Chronique rimée* of Philip Mousket; Doc. 4.

————, MS. lat. 934: chap. 3.

————, MS. lat. 4991: Doc. 3.

————, MS. lat. 9778: Delisle's Register F, copied from E ca. 1247; *olim* Colbert MS. 2669; Regius MS. 9852/3: Docs. 7, 8, 9, 23, 24, 26, 29, 36.

————, MS. lat. 12768: chap. 4.

————, MS. lat. 14591: chap. 2.

————, MS. lat. 14593: Paris synodal statutes; Doc. 52.

————. MS. Moreau 1178: copy made for La Porte du Theil (1776~1786) of Register of Honorius III, an. 1: Doc. 48.

————, MS. Moreau 1183, idem, Honorius III, an. 9-11: Docs. 46, 47.

————, MS. Moreau 1184: idem, Gregory IX, an. 1-3: Docs. 32-35.

————, MS. Moreau 1185: idem, Gregory IX, an. 1-2: Doc. 39.

Rodez, Arch. dép. Aveyron, G 578: charter of Conrad von Urach; Doc. 49.

Sens, Bibl. mun., MS. 9: chap. 3.

Steinfeld Abbey (Westphalia): Register of Bishop Gervase of Séez: Doc. 49.

Trowbridge, Wiltshire County Record Office, D 1/1/1 (*olim* Salisbury Diocesan Registry): Salisbury Register; Docs. 1, 41, 42.

Troyes, Trésor de la cathédrale: Doc. 48.

Vatican, Arch. Segreto Vat., Serie generale de' Regesti, vol. 9 (Reg. Hon. III, tom. I, an. i): Doc. 48.

————, vol. 12 (Reg. Hon. III, tom. IV, an. viii): Doc. 8.

————, vol. 13 (Reg. Hon. III, tom. V, an. ix): Docs. 12-13, 15, 17-20, 46-47.

————, vol. 14 (Reg. Greg. IX, tom. I, an. i): Docs. 32-35, 39.

————, vol. 19 (Reg. Greg. IX, tom. VI, an. xii): Doc. 39.

Vatican, Bibl. Apost., MS. Vat. lat. 7024: Doc. 32.

————, MS. Vat. lat. 700: chap. 2.

————, MS. "Reginensis 171": Doc. 6.

PRINTED WORKS

This list includes all the printed works cited in chapters 1-8 and in the List of Abbreviations; however, most of the works cited in the prolegomena to Docs. 1-53 are *not* included here.

Achery, Luc d'. *Spicilegium, sive Collectio veterum aliquot scriptorum qui in Galliae bibliothecis delituerant.* 2nd ed. 3 vols. Paris, 1723; reprint, Farnborough: Gregg, 1967.

Alberigo. See *Conciliorum oecumenicorum decreta.*

Alloing, L. "Belley (diocèse de)." *DHGE,* VII (Paris, 1933), 886-902.

Andrieu, Michel, ed. *Le Pontifical romain au Moyen-Age.* 4 vols. Studi e testi, 86-88 and 99. Vatican City, 1938-1941.

Annales monastici. Ed. H. R. Luard. Rolls Series, no. 36. 5 vols. London, 1864-1869.

Atlas zur Kirchengeschichte: Die christlichen Kirchen in Geschichte und Gegenwart. Ed. Jochen Martin. Freiburg i. B., 1970.

Auvray, Lucien, et al., eds. *Les Registres de Grégoire IX (1227-1241).* Bibliothèque des écoles françaises d'Athènes et de Rome, 2nd ser., no. 9. 4 vols. Paris, 1890-1955.

Baaken, Gerhard. "Die Verhandlungen zwischen Kaiser Heinrich VI. und Papst Coelestin III. in den Jahren 1195-1197." *Deutsches Archiv für Erforschung des Mittelalters,* XXVII (1971), 457-513.

———, ed. See *Regesta Imperii.*

Babey, Pierre. *Le Pouvoir temporel de l'évêque de Viviers au Moyen Age.* Paris, 1956.

Baier, Hermann. *Päpstliche Provisionen für niedere Pfründen bis zum Jahre 1304.* Vorreformationsgeschichtliche Forschungen, 7. Munster i. W., 1911.

Baldwin, John W. *The Government of Philip Augustus: Foundations of French Royal Power in the Middle Ages.* Berkeley and Los Angeles, 1986.

———. *Masters, Princes and Merchants: The Social Views of Peter the Chanter & His Circle.* 2 vols. Princeton, 1970.

Baluze (Baluzius), Etienne. *Concilia Galliae Narbonensis.* Paris, 1668.

Barbiche, Bernard, ed. *Les Actes pontificaux originaux des Archives nationales de Paris.* Vol. I: *1198-1261.* Commission internationale de diplomatique (C. I. S. H.), Index actorum Romanorum pontificum ab Innocentio III ad Martinum V electum, vol. I. Vatican City, 1975.

Barker, Ernest. *The Dominican Order and Convocation: A Study of the Growth of Representation in the Church During the Thirteenth Century.* Oxford, 1913.

Baronius (Baronio), Caesar, et al., eds. *Annales ecclesiastici a Christo nato ad annum 1571.* Ed. Augustin Theiner. 37 vols. Bar-le-Duc, 1864-1874.

Barraclough, Geoffrey. "The Making of a Bishop in the Middle Ages: The Part of the Pope in Law and Fact." *Catholic Historical Review,* XIX (1933), 275-319.

———. *The Medieval Papacy.* New York, 1968.

————. *Papal Provisions: Aspects of Church History Constitutional, Legal, and Administrative in the Later Middle Ages.* Oxford, 1935.

Belperron, Pierre. *La Croisade contre les Albigeois et l'union du Languedoc à la France (1209–1249).* 2nd ed. Paris, 1967.

Benedict XIV. See Lambertini.

Benson, Robert L. *The Bishop-elect: A Study in Medieval Ecclesiastical Office.* Princeton, 1968.

Benzinger, Josef. *Invectiva in Romam: Romkritik im Mittelalter vom 9. bis zum 12. Jahrhundert.* Historische Studien, Heft 404. Lübeck and Hamburg, 1968.

Berger, Adolf. *Encyclopedic Dictionary of Roman Law.* Transactions of the American Philosophical Society, n.s., XLIII, pt. 2. Philadelphia, 1953.

Berger, Elie. *Histoire de Blanche de Castille, reine de France.* Bibliothèque des écoles françaises d'Athènes et de Rome, fasc. 70. Paris, 1895.

Berlière, Ursmer. "Le Cardinal Mathieu d'Albano." *Revue bénédictine*, XVIII (1901), 113–140 and 280–303.

————. "Les Chapitres généraux de l'ordre de S. Benoît." *Revue bénédictine*, XVIII (1901), 364–398, and XIX (1902), 38–75, 268–278, and 374–411. [Reprinted in his *Mélanges d'histoire bénédictine*, IV (Maredsous, 1902).]

————. "Les Chapitres généraux de l'ordre de S. Benoît avant le IVᵉ concile de Latran (1215)." *Revue bénédictine*, VIII (1891), 255–264.

————. "Les Chapitres généraux de l'ordre de Saint Benoît du XIIIᵉ au XVᵉ siècle." *Revue bénédictine*, IX (1892), 545–557.

————. *Documents inédits pour servir à l'histoire ecclésiastique de la Belgique*, I. Maredsous, 1894.

————. "Honorius III et les monastères bénédictins, 1216–1227." *Revue belge de philologie et d'histoire*, II (1923), 237–265 and 461–484.

————. "Innocent III et la réorganisation des monastères bénédictins." *Revue bénédictine*, XXXII (1920), 22–42 and 145–159.

————. "Notes pour servir à l'histoire des monastères bénédictins de la province de Reims." *Revue bénédictine*, XI (1894), 36–38 and 136–138.

Berlioz, Jacques. *"Tuez-les tous, Dieu reconnaîtra les siens": Le Massacre de Béziers (22 juillet 1209) et la croisade contre les Albigeois vus par Césaire de Heisterbach.* Portet-sur-Garonne, 1994.

Bernard of Clairvaux. *De consideratione ad Eugenium papam.* In *S. Bernardi Opera*, ed. J. Leclercq and H. M. Rochais, vol. III. Rome, 1963.

————. *Five Books on Consideration: Advice to a Pope.* Trans. John D. Anderson and Elizabeth T. Kennan. Cistercian Fathers Series, no. 37. Kalamazoo, 1976.

Bessin, Guillaume, ed. *Concilia Rothomagensis provinciae.* Rouen, 1717.

Bible. *Biblia sacra vulgatae editionis.* Ed. C. Vercellone. Rome, 1861; reprint, Paris, 1891.

————. *The Holy Bible containing the Old and New Testaments and the Apocrypha, Translated by His Majesty's Special Command* [i.e. the Authorized Version of King James I, A.D. 1611].

————. *The Holy Bible Translated from the Latin Vulgate.* Reims, 1582, and Douai, 1609. Revised by R. Challoner [1749–1750]; reprint, New York, 1899.

Bliss, W. H. *Calendar of Entries in the Papal Registers Relating to Great Britain and Ireland.* 11 vols. London, 1893–1921.

Bloch, Marc. *Feudal Society.* Trans. L. A. Manyon. London, 1961.

Bock, F. "Originale und Registereinträge zur Zeit Honorius III." *Archivio paleografico italiano*, II–III (1956-1957), no. 1, pp. 101-116.

Böhmer, Johan Friedrich. *Regesta Imperii*. Bd. IV, Abt. iii: *Die Regesten des Kaiserreiches unter Heinrich VI.* 2nd ed. by Gerhard Baaken. Cologne, 1972.

————. ————. Bd. V: *Jüngere Staufer: 1198–1272.* Ed. by J. Ficker, E. Winkelmann, and F. Wilhelm. 3 vols. Innsbruck, 1881-1901.

Bossuat, Robert. *Manuel bibliographique de la littérature française du Moyen Age.* Melun, 1951. — *Supplément (1949–1953).* Paris, 1955. —*Second supplément (1954–1961).* Paris, 1961.

————, et al., eds. *Dictionnaire des lettres françaises:* [vol. I] *Le Moyen Age.* 2nd ed. by G. Hasenohr and M. Zink. Paris, 1992.

Bouquet, Martin, et al., eds. *Recueil des historiens des Gaules et de la France; Rerum Gallicarum et Francicarum scriptores.* 24 vols. Paris, 1738-1904.

Boussard, Jacques. "Ralph Neville, évêque de Chichester et chancelier d'Angleterre (+ 1244) d'après sa correspondance." *Revue historique,* CLXXCVI (1935), 217-233.

Boyer, Marjorie Nice. "A Day's Journey in Mediaeval France." *Speculum,* XXVI (1951), 597-608.

Boyle, Leonard E. "The Compilatio quinta and the Registers of Honorius III." *Bulletin of Medieval Canon Law,* n.s., VIII (1978), 9-19. [Reprinted as item XI in his *Pastoral Care, Clerical Education and Canon Law.*]

————. *Pastoral Care, Clerical Education and Canon Law, 1200–1400.* Collected Studies Series, 135. London: Variorum, 1981.

Branner, Robert. *The Cathedral of Bourges and Its Place in Gothic Architecture.* 2nd ed. by Shirley Prager Branner. Architectural History Foundation books, no. 13. New York, 1989.

Bréhier, Louis. "Brienne (Jean de)." *DHGE,* X (Paris, 1912), 698-709.

Brevarium Romanum. 4 vols. New York: Benziger, 1943. [1914 revision of 1568 edition; 4th ed., 1928.]

Brial, M. J. J. "Hélinand, moine de Froidmont: Sa vie." *Hist. litt. Fr.,* XVIII (Paris, 1835), 87-103.

Brown, Jacqueline, and William P. Stoneman. *A Distinct Voice: Medieval Studies in Honor of Leonard E. Boyle, O. P.* Notre Dame, 1997.

Brundage, James A. *Medieval Canon Law and the Crusader.* Madison, 1969.

Bruns, T., ed. *Canones apostolorum et conciliorum saeculorum IV. V. VI. VII.* Bibliotheca ecclesiastica, ed. A. Neander. Berlin, 1839; reprint, Turin, 1959.

Brussel, Nicolas. *Nouvel examen de l'usage général des fiefs de France pendant le XIe, le XIIe, le XIIIe et le XIVe siècle, pour servir à l'intelligence des plus anciens titres du domaine de la couronne.* 2 vols. Paris, 1727.

Bullarum, diplomatum et privilegiorum sanctorum Romanorum pontificum Taurinensis editio. . . . ["*Bullarium magnum Romanum.*"] 26 vols. Turin, 1857-1885.

Bullarum, privilegiorum ac diplomatum Romanorum pontificum amplissima collectio. Ed. Charles Cocquelines and Hieronymus Mainardi. 6 vols. Rome, 1739-1762.

Burchardi praepositi Urspergensis chronicon. 2nd ed. Ed. Oswald Holder-Egger and Bernard von Simson. MGH, Scriptores rerum Germanicarum, o.s., 16. Hanover, 1916.

Caesarius of Heisterbach. *The Dialogue of Miracles.* Trans. H. von E. Scott and C. C. Swinton Bland. 2 vols. New York, 1929.

————. *Dialogus miraculorum*. Ed. J. Strange. 2 vols. Cologne, 1851.

Caillemer, E. "Des Conflits entre l'église de Lyon et l'église de Rouen relativement à la primatie." *Mémoires de l'Académie des sciences, belles-lettres et arts de Lyon, Sciences et lettres*, 3rd ser., XIII (1913), 353-387.

Cambridge Medieval History. Ed. J. B. Bury et al. 8 vols. Cambridge, 1911-1936.

Canivez, Joseph Marie, ed. *Statuta capitulorum generalium ordinis Cisterciensis ab anno 1116 ad annum 1786*. 4 vols. Bibliothèque de la Revue d'histoire ecclésiastique, fasc. 9-14B. Louvain, 1933-1941.

Carpenter, D. A. *The Minority of Henry III*. Berkeley and Los Angeles, 1990.

Cartellieri, Alexander. *Philipp II. August, König von Frankreich*. 4 vols. Leipzig, 1899-1922.

Catholic Encyclopedia. Ed. C. G. Herbermann et al. 16 vols. New York, 1907-1914.

Cazel, Fred A., jr. "Financing the Crusades." In *A History of the Crusades*. 2nd ed. by Kenneth M. Setton. Vol. VI. Madison, 1989. Pages 116-119.

Chaplais, Pierre, ed. *Diplomatic Documents Preserved in the Public Record Office*, vol. I: *1101-1272*. London: Her Majesty's Stationery Office, 1964.

Charay, Jean, et al. *Petite histoire de l'église diocésaine de Viviers*. Aubenas-en-Vivarais, 1977.

Chartularium Universitatis Parisiensis. See Denifle.

Cheney, C. R. *English Synodalia of the Thirteenth Century*. Oxford, 1941.

————. *Episcopal Visitation of Monasteries in the Thirteenth Century*. 2nd ed. Manchester, 1983.

————. *From Becket to Langton*. Manchester, 1956.

————. "A Letter of Pope Innocent III and the Lateran Decree on Cistercian Tithe-paying." *Cîteaux: Commentarii Cistercienses*, XIII (1962), 146-151. [Reprinted in his *Medieval Texts and Studies*, pp. 277-284.]

————. *Medieval Texts and Studies*. Oxford, 1973.

————. *The Papacy and England, 12th-14th centuries: Historical and Legal Studies*. Collected Studies Series, 154. London: Variorum, 1982.

———— and Mary G. Cheney, eds. *The Letters of Pope Innocent III (1198–1216) Concerning England and Wales: A Calendar with an Appendix of Texts*. Oxford, 1967.

Chevalier, Cyr Ulysse Joseph, ed. *Répertoire des sources historiques du Moyen Age: Bio-bibliographie*. 2nd ed. 2 vols. Paris, 1905-1907.

————. ————: *Topo-bibliographie*. 2 vols. Montbéliard, 1894-1903.

————. *Regeste dauphinois, ou Répertoire chronologique & analytique des documents imprimés et manuscrits relatifs à l'histoire du Dauphiné, des origines chrétiennes à l'année 1349*. 7 vols. Valence, 1913-1926.

Choffel, Jacques. *Louis VIII le Lion: Roi de France méconnu, roi d'Angleterre ignoré*. Paris, 1983.

Chronicle of Tours. See Salmon.

Chronicon Cluniacensis coenobii [*Chronicon Cluniacense*]. In *Rec. hist. Gaules*, XVIII, 742-743.

Chroniques de Saint-Martial de Limoges. Ed. Henri Duplès-Agier. Société de l'histoire de France. Paris, 1874.

Clarke, Maude V. *Medieval Representation and Consent: A Study of Early Parliaments in England and Ireland, with Special Reference to the "Modus tenendi parliamentum."* London, 1936.

Clément, Ambroise. "Conrad d'Urach, de l'ordre de Cîteaux, légat en France et en Allemagne." *Revue bénédictine*, XXII (1905), 232-243, and XXIII (1906), 62-81, 373-391.

Cocquelines. See *Bullarum*.

Codex Justinianus. Ed. Paul Krueger. Berlin, 1880.

Conciliorum oecumenicorum decreta. Ed. G. Alberigo et al. 2nd ed. Freiburg: Herder, 1962.

————. ————. 3rd ed. Bologna: Istituto per le scienze religiose, 1973.

————. ————. 4th ed. Bologna: Dehoniane, 1991.

————. ————. See also Tanner.

Congar, Yves M. J. "Quod omnes tangit, ab omnibus tractari et approbari debet." *Revue historique de droit français et étranger*, 4th ser., XXXVI (1958), 210-259.

Corpus iuris canonici [with *Glossa ordinaria*]. 3 vols. Lyon: Apud Hugonem & haeredes Aemonis à Porta, 1548-1549.

Cottineau, Laurent H., and Grégoire Poras. *Répertoire topo-bibliographique des abbayes et prieurés*. 3 vols. Macon, 1935-1970.

Coulet, Noël. *Les Visites pastorales*. Typologie des sources du Moyen Age occidental, ed. L. Genicot, fasc. 23 (A-IV.1*). Turnhout, 1977.

Crosby, Everett U. *Bishop and Chapter in Twelfth-Century England: A Study of the* Mensa episcopalis. Cambridge Studies in Medieval Life and Thought, 4th ser., no. 23. Cambridge, Eng., 1994.

Cross, F. L., ed. *The Oxford Dictionary of the Christian Church*. 3rd ed. by E. A. Livingstone. Oxford, 1997.

Cuissard, Charles. "Election de Guillaume de Bussi, évêque d'Orléans, et principaux actes de son épiscopat (1238-58)." *Mémoires de la Société archéologique et historique de l'Orléanais*, XXV (1894), 561-620.

d'Achery. See Achery.

Dammertz, Viktor. *Der Verfassungsrecht der benediktinischen Mönchskongregationen in Geschichte und Gegenwart*. Kirchengeschichtliches Quellen und Studien, 6. St Ottilien, 1963.

Delisle, Léopold, ed. *Cartulaire normand de Philippe-Auguste, Louis VIII, Saint Louis et Philippe-le-Hardi*. Mémoires de la Société des antiquitaires de Normandie, 2nd ser., vol. 6 (vol. 16 of the collection). Caen, 1852; reprint, Geneva: Mégariotis, 1978.

Denholm-Young, Noël. *Richard of Cornwall*. New York, 1947.

Denifle, Heinrich, and E. Châtelain, eds. *Chartularium Universitatis Parisiensis*. 4 vols. Paris, 1891-1899.

Dereine, C. "Chanoines (dès origines au XIIIᵉ s.)." *DHGE*, XII (Paris, 1950), 353-405.

[Devic, Claude, and Joseph Vaissète.] *Histoire générale de Languedoc . . . par deux religieux Bénédictines de la congrégation de S. Maur*. 1st ed. 5 vols. Paris, 1730-1745.

Devic, Claude, and Joseph Vaissète. *Histoire générale de Languedoc*. 3rd ed. [by A. Molinier et al.] 16 vols. Toulouse, 1872-1904; reprint, Osnabruck, 1973.

Dictionary of National Biography. Ed. Leslie Stephen and Sidney Lee. 22 vols. 3rd ed. London, 1968.

Dictionary of the Middle Ages. Ed. Joseph Reese Strayer. 13 vols. New York, 1982-1989.

Dictionnaire de biographie française. Ed. J. Balteau et al. 19 vols. to date. Paris, 1930-.

Dictionnaire de droit canonique. Ed. R. Naz. 7 vols. Paris, 1935-1965.

Dictionnaire d'histoire et de géographie ecclésiastiques. Ed. Alfred Baudrillart. 27 vols. to date. Paris, 1912—.

Dizionario biografico degli italiani. Ed. A. M. Ghisalberti. 54 vols. to date. Rome, 1960-.

Donovan, Joseph P. *Pelagius and the Fifth Crusade.* Philadelphia, 1950.

Duchesne, André, ed. *Historiae Francorum scriptores coaetanei.* . . . 5 vols. Paris, 1636-1649.

Duchesne, Louis. *Fastes épiscopaux de l'ancienne Gaul.* 2nd ed. 3 vols. Paris, 1907-1915.

[Dunstable Annals.] *Annales prioratus de Dunstaplia (A. D. 1–1297).* In *Annales monastici,* ed. H. R. Luard. Rolls Series, no. 36, vol. III. London, 1866.

Dupont, André. "Les Comtes de Toulouse et le Vivarais (Xme - fin XIIme siècle." *Bulletin annuel de l'Ecole antique de Nîmes,* n.s., V (1970), 75-94.

Ellis, Clarence. *Hubert de Burgh: A Study in Constancy.* London, 1952.

Ellis, Matthew. "Landscape and Power: The Frangipani Family and Their Clients in the Twelfth-century Roman Forum." In *The Community, the Family and the Saint: Patterns of Power in Early Medieval Europe,* ed. Joyce Hill and Mary Swan. International Medieval Research. Turnhout, 1998. Pages 61-76.

Eméric-David, T. B. "Robert, dauphin d'Auvergne." *Hist. litt. Fr.,* XVIII (Paris, 1835), 607-615.

Enciclopedia dantesca. 6 vols. Rome, 1970-1978.

Eubel, Conrad, ed.. *Hierarchia Catholica Medii Aevi (1198–1431).* Vol. I. 2nd ed. Munster i. W., 1898.

Evans, Austin P. "The Albigensian Crusade." In *A History of the Crusades,* vol. II: *The Later Crusades, 1189–1311,* ed. Robert Lee Wolff and H. W. Hazard. 2nd ed. by Kenneth M. Setton. Madison, 1969. Pages 277-324.

Fabre. See *Liber censuum.*

Fasti ecclesiae Gallicanae: Répertoire prosopographique des évêques, dignitaires et chanoines de France de 1200 à 1500, II: *Diocèse de Rouen.* Ed. Vincent Tabbagh et al. Turnhout, 1998.

Fawtier, Robert. *The Capetian Kings of France: Monarchy & Nation (987–1328).* London, 1960.

Ferraris, F. L. *Prompta biblioteca canonica.* 8 vols. Paris: Migne, 1852-1857.

Figueira, Robert C. "Papal Reserved Powers and the Limitations on Legatine Authority." In *Popes, Teachers, and Canon Law in the Middle Ages,* ed. James Ross Sweeney and Stanley Chodorow. Ithaca, 1989. Pages 191-211.

Fletcher, R. A. *Saint James's Catapult: The Life and Times of Diego Gelmírez of Santiago de Compostela.* Oxford, 1984.

Foreville, Raymonde. *Latran I, II, III et Latran IV = Histoire des conciles oecuméniques,* ed. Gervais Dumeige, vol. VI. Paris, 1965.

Forey, Alan. *Military Orders and Crusades.* Collected Studies Series, 432. Aldershot, Hants.: Variorum, 1994.

———. "The Military Orders and Holy War against Christians in the Thirteenth Century." *English Historical Review,* CIV (1989), 1-24. [Reprinted as item VII in his *Military Orders and Crusaders.*]

———. *The Military Orders from the Twelfth to the Early Fourteenth Centuries.* Toronto, 1992.

Fransen, Gérard. "L'Ecclésiologie des conciles médiévaux." In *Le Concile et les conciles: Contribution à l'histoire de la vie conciliaire de l'Eglise,* [ed. O. Rousseau]. Chevetogne, 1960. Pages 125–141.

Friedberg, Emil (Aemilius), ed. *Corpus iuris canonici.* 2 vols. Leipzig, 1879-1881.

———. *Quinque compilationes antiquae.* Leipzig, 1882.

Gallia Christiana in provincias ecclesiasticas distributa. Edited by the Benedictines of the Congregation of St-Maur and (vols. XIV-XVI) by B. Hauréau. 16 vols. Paris, 1715-1865.

Gallia Christiana novissima: Histoire des archevêchés, évêchés et abbayes de France accompagnée des documents authentiques recueillis dans les registres du Vatican et les archives locales. Ed. J. H. Albanès and U. Chevalier. 7 vols. Montbéliard and Valence, 1899-1920.

García y García, Antonio. "El concilio IV de Letrán (1215) y sus comentarios." *Traditio*, XIV (1958), 484-502.

———, ed. *Constitutiones concilii quarti Lateranensis una cum commentariis glossatorum.* Monumenta iuris canonici, series A, vol. 2. Vatican City, 1981.

Gatien-Arnould, A. F. "Hélinand: Son rôle à l'université and dans la ville de Toulouse, en l'année 1229." *Revue de Toulouse et du Midi de la France*, XX (1866), 287-302 and 345-356.

Gaudemet, Jean. "Unanimité et majorité (Observations sur quelques études récentes)." In *Etudes historiques à la mémoire de Noël Didier*, publiées par la Faculté de droit et des sciences économiques de [l'Université de] Grenoble. Paris, 1960. Pages 149-162.

Gebhardt, Bruno. *Handbuch der deutschen Geschichte.* 9th ed. by Herbert Grundmann. Vol. I. Stuttgart, 1970.

Gerhoch of Reichersberg. *De investigatione antichristi.* Ed. Ernst Sakur. MGH, Libelli de lite, III. Hanover, 1897. Pages 304-395.

Gesta Innocentii III. Migne, *Pat. Lat.*, CCXIV.

Gibbs, Marion, and Jane Lang. *Bishops and Reform, 1215–1272, with Special Reference to the Lateran Council of 1215.* Oxford, 1934.

Gilchrist, John. "Visitation, canonical, history of." *New Catholic Encyclopedia*, XIV (1967), 718-719.

Goering, Joseph. "Robert Grosseteste at the Papal Curia." In *A Distinct Voice: Medieval Studies in Honor of Leonard E. Boyle, O. P.*, ed. Jacqueline Brown and William P. Stoneman. Notre Dame, 1997. Pages 253-276.

Gransden, Antonia. *Historical Writing in England c. 550 to c. 1307.* Ithaca, N. Y., 1974.

Gratian. See Friedberg and *Corpus iuris canonici.*

Greenway, Diana E., ed. *Fasti Ecclesiae Anglicanae, 1066–1300,* IV: *Salisbury.* London, 1991.

Gregory IX. See Auvray.

Guillaume. See William.

Habig, M. A., ed. *St. Francis of Assisi: Writings and Early Biographies; English Omnibus of the Sources for the Life of St. Francis.* 4th ed. Quincy, Ill., 1991.

Haigneré, Daniel, and O. Bled, eds. *Les Chartes de Saint-Bertin d'après le "Grand chartulaire" de Dom Charles-Joseph Dewitte, dernier archiviste de ce monastère.* 4 vols. St-Omer, 1886-1899.

Handbook of British Chronology. 2nd ed. by F. M. Powicke and E. B. Fryde. Royal Historical Society Guides and Handbooks, no. 2. London, 1961.

———. 3rd ed. by E. B. Fryde et al. Royal Historical Society Guides and Handbooks, no. 2. London, 1986.

Hardy, Thomas Duffus, ed. *Rotuli litterarum clausarum in Turri Londinensi asservati.* 2 vols. Record Commissioners. London, 1833-1844.

Haskins, Charles Homer. *Studies in the History of Mediaeval Science.* Harvard Historical Studies, no. 27. Cambridge, Mass., 1924.

Hauck, Albert. *Kirchengeschichte Deutschlands.* 5th ed. 5 vols. Leipzig, 1904-1920.

Heckel, R. von. "Studien über die Kanzleiordnung Innocenz' III." *Historisches Jahrbuch,* LVII (1937), 258-289.

Hefele, Carl Joseph, and Jean Leclercq. *Histoire des conciles d'après les documents originaux.* 11 vols. Paris, 1907-1952.

Henricus de Segusio (Hostiensis). *In primum (sextum) Decretalium librum commentaria.* Venice, 1581; reprint, Turin, 1965.

Histoire lit(t)éraire de la France. Ed. A. Rivet et al. 42 vols. to date. Paris, 1733–.

Historia Compostellana. In Migne, *Pat. Lat.,* CLXX.

Hoefer, J. C. F. *Nouvelle biographie générale.* 46 vols. Paris, 1854-1866.

Holt, J. C. *Magna Carta.* 2nd ed. Cambridge, Eng., 1992.

Honorius III. See Horoy and Pressutti.

Horoy, César Auguste, ed. *Honorii III Romani pontificis opera omnia.* 5 vols. Medii Aevi bibliotheca patristica, vols. 1-5. Paris, 1879-1882.

Hostiensis. See: Henricus de Segusio.

Hourlier, Jacques. *Le Chapitre général jusqu'au moment du Grand Schisme: Origines—Développement—Etude juridique.* Paris, 1936.

Huillard-Bréholles, J. L. A., ed. *Historia diplomatica Friderici secundi.* 6 vols. Paris, 1852-1861.

Innocent III. *Die Register Innocenz' III.* Ed. Othmar Hageneder et al. Osterreichische Akademie der Wissenschaften, Publikationen des historischen Instituts beim österreichischen Kulturinstitut in Rom, Abt. 2, Reihe 1. 6 vols. to date. Vienna, 1964-.

———. See Cheney.

Iung, Nicolas. "Concile." In *Dictionnaire de droit canonique,* III (1942), 1268-1301.

Ivo of Chartres. *Epistolae.* In Migne, *Pat. Lat.,* CLXII.

Jacobatius, Dominicus. *Tractatus de concilio.* In Mansi, vol. 0. Paris, 1903.

John of Salisbury. *Policraticus.* Ed. C. C. J. Webb. 2 vols. Oxford, 1909.

Jordan, William Chester. *Louis IX and the Challenge of the Crusade: A Study in Rulership.* Princeton, 1979.

Kay, Richard. "'Ad nostram praesentiam evocamus': Boniface VIII and the Roman Convocation of 1302." In *Proceedings of the Third International Congress of Medieval Canon Law, Strasbourg, 3–6 September 1968.* Monumenta Iuris Canonici, Series C, vol. 4. Vatican City, 1971. Pages 165-189.

———. "The Albigensian Twentieth of 1221-3." *Journal of Medieval History,* VI (1980), 307-315.

———. *Dante's Christian Astrology.* Middle Ages Series. Philadelphia, 1994.

———. *Dante's Swift and Strong: Essays on* Inferno *XV.* Lawrence, Kans., 1978.

———. "An Eyewitness Account of the 1225 Council of Bourges." In *Collectanea Stephan Kuttner,* II = *Studia Gratiana,* XII (1967), 61-80.

———. "Gerald of Wales and the Fourth Lateran Council." *Viator,* XXIX (1998), 79-93.

———. "Innocent III as Canonist and Theologian: The Case of Spiritual Matrimony." In *Pope Innocent III and his World,* ed. John C. Moore. Aldershot, Hants, 1999. Pages 35-49.

———. "The Making of Statutes in French Provincial Councils, 1049-1305." Ph.D. diss., University of Wisconsin. Madison, 1959. [Cf. *Dissertation Abstracts,* XX (1959), 1004; L.C. card no. Mic 59-3006.]

———. "Mansi and Rouen: A Critique of the Conciliar Collections." *Catholic Historical Review*, LII (1966), 155-185.

———. "Quelques ébauches des lettres papales conservées dans le *Rotulus de negotio albigense* (1221-1225)." *Bibliothèque de l'Ecole des chartes*, CLX (2002) [forthcoming]. [Study of Paris, BnF, Baluze MS. 385, no. 239.]

———. "Romanus and Rouen: A Papal Legate's Tainted Visitation in 1227." *Annales de Normandie*, LI (2001), 111-119.

———. "A Study of the Council of Bourges (1225)." M. A. thesis. University of Wisconsin. Madison, 1954.

———. "Walter of Coventry and the Barnwell Chronicle." *Traditio*, LIV (1999), 141-167.

———. "Wendover's Last Annal." *English Historical Review*, LXXXIV (1969), 779-785.

———, ed. and trans. *The Broadview Book of Medieval Anecdotes.* Peterborough, Can., 1988.

Kemp, Eric W. "The Canterbury Provincial Chapter and the Collegiality of Bishops in the Middle Ages." In *Etudes d'histoire du droit canonique dédiées à Gabriel Le Bras*, I. Paris, 1965. Pages 184-201.

———. *Counsel and Consent: Aspects of the Government of the Church as Exemplified in the History of the English Provincial Synods.* The Bampton Lectures for 1960. London, 1961.

———. "The Origins of the Canterbury Convocation." *Journal of Ecclesiastical History*, III (1952), 132-143.

Kibler, W. W., et al., eds. *Medieval France: An Encyclopedia.* New York, 1995.

Kibre, Pearl. *Scholarly Privileges in the Middle Ages: The Rights, Privileges, and Immunities of Scholars and Universities at Bologna, Padua, Paris, and Oxford.* Mediaeval Academy of America Publication no. 72. Cambridge, Mass., 1962.

Kienzle, Beverly M. "Deed and Word: Hélinand's Toulouse Sermons, I." In *Erudition at God's Service: Studies in Medieval Cistercian History, XI*, ed. John R. Sommerfeldt. Cistercian Studies Series, no. 98. Kalamazoo, 1987. Pages 267-275.

Kirchner, Joachim, ed. *Scriptura Latina libraria.* Munich, 1955.

Kristeller, Paul Oscar. *Latin Manuscript Books before 1600: A List of the Printed Catalogues and Unpublished Inventories of Extant Collections.* 4th ed. by S. Kramer. MGH, Hilfsmittel no. 13. Munich, 1993.

Krueger, Paul. See *Codex Justinianus.*

Kuttner, Stephan. "Notes on the Presentation of Text and Apparatus in Editing Works of the Decretists and Decretalists." *Traditio*, XV (1959), 452-464.

———. *Repertorium der Kanonistik (1140–1234).* Studi e testi, 71. Vatican City, 1937.

——— and Antonio García y García. "A New Eyewitness Account of the Fourth Lateran Council." *Traditio*, XX (1964), 115-178.

——— and Beryl Smalley. "The 'Glossa Ordinaria' to the Gregorian Decretals." *English Historical Review*, LX (1945), 97-105.

Labbe, Philippe, and Gabriel Cossart, eds. *Sacrosancta concilia.* 18 vols. Paris, 1671-1672.

Lacger, L. de. "La Primatie et le pouvoir métropolitain de l'archevêque de Bourges au XIIIᵉ siècle." *Revue d'histoire ecclésiastique*, XXVI (1930), 45-60 and 268-330.

Lambertini, Prospero (Pope Benedict XIV). *De synodo dioecesano.* 2 vols. Ferrara, 1760.

Langlois, C. V. "Le Fonds de l'*Ancient Correspondence* au *Public Record Office* de Londres." *Journal des savants*, n.s., II (1904), 380-393 and 446-453.

————. "Notices et documents relatifs à l'histoire du XIIIe et du XIVe siècle." *Revue historique*, LXXXVII (1905), 55-79.

Langosch, Karl, ed. *Vagantes Dichtung*. Sammlung Dietrich, 316. Bremen and Leipzig, 1968.

Latham, R. E., ed. *Revised Medieval Latin Word-list from British and Irish Sources*. London, 1965.

Laurent, Jacques, ed. *Cartulaires de l'abbaye de Molesme, ancien diocèse de Langres, 916–1250*. Recueil de documents sur le nord de la Bourgogne et le midi de la Champagne. 2 vols. Paris, 1907-1911.

Lecoy de la Marche, A. *La Chaire française au Moyen Age*. 2nd ed. Paris, 1886.

Leff, Gordon. *Paris and Oxford Universities in the Thirteenth and Fourteenth Centuries: An Institutional and Intellectual History*. New York, 1968.

Lehmann, Paul. *Die Parodie im Mittelalter*. 2nd ed. Stuttgart, 1963.

Le Nain de Tillemont, Louis Sebastian. *Vie de Saint Louis, roi de France*. Ed. J. de Gaulle. 6 vols. Société de l'histoire de France, vols. 47, 50, 53, 55, 57, 66. Paris, 1847-1851.

Le Neve, John. *Fasti Ecclesiae Anglicanae, 1066–1300*. Rev. ed. by Diana E. Greenway. Vol. III. London, 1977.

[*Liber censuum*.] *Le "Liber censuum" de l'église romaine*. Ed. Paul Fabre and Louis Duchesne. Bibliothèque des écoles françaises d'Athènes et de Rome, 2nd ser., no. 6. 3 vols. Paris, 1889-1952.

Limoges, St-Martial de. See *Chroniques*.

Lot, Ferdinand, and Robert Fawtier, eds. *Histoire des institutions françaises au Moyen Age*. 3 vols. Paris, 1957-1962.

Luchaire, Achille. *Manuel des institutions françaises: Période de Capétiens directs*. Paris, 1892.

Lunt, William E. "The Consent of the English Lower Clergy to Taxation during the Reign of Henry III." In *Persecution and Liberty: Essays in Honor of George Lincoln Burr*. New York, 1931. Pages 117-169.

————. *Financial Relations of the Papacy with England to 1327*. Mediaeval Academy of America Publication no. 33 = Studies in Anglo-papal Relations during the Middle Ages, 1. Cambridge, Mass., 1939.

————, ed. and trans. *Papal Revenues in the Middle Ages*. 2 vols. Records of Civilization, no. 19. New York, 1934.

Maccarrone, Michele. "Le costituzioni del IV concilio Lateranense sui religiosi." In his *Nuovi studi su Innocenzo III*, pp. 1-45. [Reprinted from *Dizionario degli istituti di perfezione*, V (Rome, 1975), 474-495.]

————. *Nuovi studi su Innocenzo III*. Ed. R. Lambertini. Nuovi studi storici, 25. Rome, 1995.

————. "Il IV concilio lateranense." *Divinitas*, V (1961), 270-298.

————. "Riforme e innovazioni di Innocenzo III nella vita religiosa." In his *Studi su Innocenzo III*, pp. 223-337. [Revised from *Rivista di storia della Chiesa*, XVII (1962), 29-72.]

————. *Studi su Innocenzo III*. Italia sacra, 17. Padua, 1972.

Madaule, Jacques. *The Albigensian Crusade: An Historical Essay*. Trans. Barbara Wall. New York, 1967.

Mahn, J. B. *L'Ordre cistercien et son gouvernement des origines au milieu du XIIIe siècle (1098–1265)*. 2nd ed. Paris, 1982.

Mai, Angelo, ed.. *Spicilegium Romanum*. 10 vols. Rome, 1839-1844.

Maisonneuve, Henri. *Etudes sur les origines de l'Inquisition.* 2nd ed. L'Eglise et l'Etat au Moyen Age, no. 7. Paris, 1960.

Maitland, F. W. *Roman Canon Law in the Church of England.* London, 1898.

Major, Kathleen, ed. *Acta Stephani Langton Cantuariensis archiepiscopi, A. D. 1207–1228.* Canterbury and York Society, 50. Oxford, 1950.

Maleczek, Werner. *Papst und Kardinalskolleg von 1191 bis 1216: Die Kardinäle unter Coelestin III. und Innocenz III.* Publikationen des historischen Instituts beim österreichischen Kulturinstitut in Rom, Abt. 1, Bd. 6. Vienna, 1984.

Mann, Horace K. *Lives of the Popes in the Middle Ages.* Vols. XII–XIII. London, 1925.

Mansi, Giovanni Domenico, ed. *Sacrorum conciliorum nova et amplissima collectio.* 31 vols. Florence/Venice, 1759-1798; reprint, with continuation (vols. 0 + XXXII-LIII) ed. L. Petit and J. B. Martin, Paris/Arnhem: Welter, 1901-1927.

———. *Sanctorum conciliorum et decretorum collectio nova, seu collectionis conciliorum . . . supplementum.* 6 vols. Lucca, 1748-1752.

Mantello, F. A. C. "'Optima Epistola': A Critical Edition and Translation of Letter 128 of Bishop Robert Grosseteste." In *A Distinct Voice: Medieval Studies in Honor of Leonard E. Boyle, O. P.,* ed. Jacqueline Brown and William P. Stoneman. Notre Dame, 1997. Pages 277-301.

Map, Walter. *De nugis curialium.* Ed. M. R. James. In *Anecdota Oxoniensia,* Mediaeval and Modern Series, part XIV. Oxford, 1914.

Martène, Edmond, and Ursin Durand, eds. *Thesaurus novus anecdotorum.* 5 vols. Paris, 1717.

——— and Ursin Durand, eds. *Veterum scriptorum et monumentorum historicorum, dogmaticorum, moralium amplissima collectio.* 9 vols. Paris, 1724-1733.

Mas Latrie, L. de. *Trésor de chronologie d'histoire et de géographie pour l'étude et l'emploi des documents du Moyen Age.* Paris, 1889; reprint, Turin, 1962.

Matthew Paris. See Paris.

Meersseman, Gilles Gérard. "Etudes sur les anciennes confréries dominicaines: IV. Les Milices de Jésus-Christ." *Archivum fratrum praedicatorum,* XXIII (1953), 275-308.

Migne, Jacques Paul, ed. *Patrologiae cursus completus . . . series Latina.* 221 vols. Paris, 1841-1864.

Missale Romanum. 7th ed. New York: Benziger, 1949. [1920 revision of 1570 edition.]

Molinier, Auguste. "Catalogue des actes de Raimond VI & de Raimond VII, comtes de Toulouse." In Devic-Vaissète, VIII (1879), 1940-2008.

———. "Catalogue des actes de Simon et d'Amauri de Montfort," *Bibliothèque de l'Ecole des chartes,* XXXIV (1873), 153-203, 445-501.

———. *Les Sources de l'histoire de France dès origines aux guerres d'Italie (1494).* Les Sources de l'histoire de France depuis les origines jusqu'en 1815, ed. A. Molinier et al., Part I = Manuels de bibliographie historique, 3-5. 6 vols. Paris, 1901-1906.

Mollat, Guillaume. "Bénéfices ecclésiastiques." *DHGE,* VII (1934), 1237-1270.

———. "Bénéfices ecclésiastiques en Occident." *Dictionnaire de droit canonique,* II (1937), 407-449.

Moore, John C., ed. *Pope Innocent III and his World.* Aldershot, Hants., 1999.

Müller, Eugène. *Analyse du cartulaire, des statuts, etc. de Notre-Dame de Senlis, 1041–1395.* Senlis, 1904.

Müller, Wolfgang. *Huguccio: The Life, Works, and Thought of a Twelfth-century Jurist.* Studies in Medieval and Early Modern Canon Law, 3. Washington, D.C., 1994.

Munz, Peter. *Frederick Barbarossa: A Study in Medieval Politics.* Ithaca, N.Y., 1969.

Neininger, Falko. *Konrad von Urach (+1227): Zähringer, Zisterzienser, Kardinallegat.* Quellen und Forschungen aus dem Gebiet der Geschichte, n.s., 17. Paderborn, 1994.

New Catholic Encyclopedia. 16 vols. New York, 1967-1974.

Niermeyer, J. F. *Mediae Latinitatis lexicon minus.* Leiden, 1984.

Norgate, Kate. *The Minority of Henry the Third.* London, 1912.

Nowak, Kristi Oddsen. "Fawkes de Bréauté." Ph.D. diss., Stanford University. Stanford, Calif., 1974.

Orbis Latinus: Lexikon lateinischer geographischer Namen der Mittelalter und der Neuzeit ["Graesse-Benedict-Plechl"]. Ed. H. Plechl. 3 vols. Braunschweig, 1972.

Painter, Sidney. *William Marshal: Knight-errant, Baron, and Regent of England.* Baltimore, 1933.

Pantin, W. A., ed. *Documents Illustrating the Activities of the General and Provincial Chapters of the English Black Monks, 1215-1540.* Camden Third Series, 45. London, 1931.

Paravicini Bagliani, Agostino. *Cardinali di curia e "familiae" cardinalizie dal 1227 al 1254.* 2 vols. Italia Sacra, 18-19. Padua, 1972.

Paris, Matthew. *Chronica majora.* Ed. H. R. Luard. Rolls Series, no. 57. 7 vols. London, 1872-1883.

———. *Historia Anglorum.* Ed. F. Madden. Rolls Series, no. 44. 3 vols. London, 1866-1869.

———. *The Illustrated Chronicles of Matthew Paris: Observations of Thirteenth-century Life.* Trans. and ed. Richard Vaughan. Cambridge, Eng., 1993.

Paro, G. *The Right of Papal Legation.* The Catholic University of America, Studies in Canon Law, no. 211. Washington, D.C., 1947.

Partner, Peter. *The Lands of St Peter: The Papal State in the Middle Ages and the Early Renaissance.* Berkeley and Los Angeles, 1972.

Patent Rolls of the Reign of Henry III Preserved in the Public Record Office, A.D. 1216–1225. London, 1901.

Pène, J. L. *La Conquête du Languedoc: Essai de critique et d'histoire.* Nice, 1957.

Peter Abelard, Letters IX-XIV. Ed. Edmé R. Smits. Gronigen, 1983.

Peters, Edward. *The Shadow King: "Rex inutilis" in Medieval Law and Literature, 751–1327.* New Haven, 1970.

Petit-Dutaillis, Charles. *Etude sur la vie et le règne de Louis VIII (1187–1226).* Bibliothèque de l'Ecole des hautes études, fasc. 101. Paris, 1894.

———. *The Feudal Monarchy in France and England from the Tenth to the Thirteenth Century.* Trans. E. D. Hunt. London, 1936.

Pfaff, Volkert. *Kaiser Heinrichs VI. höchstes Angebot an die römische Kurie (1196).* Heidelberger Abhandlungen zur mittleren und neueren Geschichte, Heft 55. Heidelberg, 1927.

Pissard, Hippolyte. *La Guerre sainte en pays chrétien: Essai sur l'origine et le développement des théories canoniques.* Paris, 1912.

Pommeraye, Jean François, ed. *Sanctae Rotomagensis ecclesiae concilia.* Rouen, 1677.

Pontal, Odette, ed. and trans.. *Les Statuts synodaux français du XIIIe siècle, précédés de l'historique du synode diocésain depuis ses origines,* vol. I: *Les Statuts de Paris et le Synodal de l'Ouest (XIIIe siècle).* Collection de documents inédits sur l'histoire de France, Section de philologie et d'histoire jusqu'à 1610, 8vo ser., vol. 9. Paris: Bibliothèque nationale, 1971.

Post, Gaines. "Parisian Masters as a Corporation, 1200-1246." *Speculum*, IX (1934), 421-445. [Reprinted in his *Studies*, pp. 27-60.]

——. *Studies in Medieval Legal Thought: Public Law and the State, 1100–1322.* Princeton, 1964.

Potthast, August, ed. *Regesta pontificum Romanorum inde ab a. post Christum natum MCXCVIII ad a. MCCCIV.* 2 vols. Berlin, 1874-1875.

——. *Bibliotheca historica Medii Aevi: Wegweiser durch die Geschichtswerke des europäischen Mittelalters bis 1500.* 2nd ed. 2 vols. Berlin, 1896.

Powell, James M. *Anatomy of a Crusade, 1213–1221.* Middle Ages Series. Philadelphia, 1986.

——. "Honorius III and the Leadership of the Crusade." *Catholic Historical Review*, LXIII (1977), 521-536.

——. "Innocent III and Petrus Beneventanus: Reconstructing a Career at the Papal Curia." In *Pope Innocent III and His World*, ed. John C. Moore. Aldershot, Hants., 1999. Pages 51-62.

Powicke, F. M. *King Henry III and the Lord Edward: The Community of the Realm in the Thirteenth Century.* 2 vols. Oxford, 1947.

——. *Stephen Langton.* Oxford, 1928.

—— and C. R. Cheney, eds. *Councils & Synods, with Other Documents Relating to the English Church*, vol. II: *A. D. 1205–1313*, part i: *1205–1265.* Oxford, 1964.

Pressutti, Pietro, ed. *Regesta Honorii Papae III.* 2 vols. Rome, 1888-1895.

Queller, Donald E. *The Office of Ambassador in the Middle Ages.* Princeton, 1967.

Raine, James, jr., ed. *The Historians of the Church of York and its Archbishops.* Rolls Series, no. 71. 3 vols. London, 1879-1894.

——. *The Register, or Rolls, of Walter Gray, Lord Archbishop of York.* Surtees Society, o.s., vol. 56 for 1870. London, 1872.

Ralph of Coggeshall. *Chronicon Anglicanum.* Ed. J. Stevenson. Rolls Series, no. 66. London, 1875.

Recueil des historiens des Gaules et de la France. See Bouquet.

Regesta Imperii. See Böhmer.

Repertorium fontium historiae Medii Aevi. 8 vols. to date. Rome: Istituto storico italiano per il Medio Evo, 1962–.

Rhein, André. *La Seigneurie de Montfort en Iveline depuis son origine jusqu'à son union au duché de Bretagne (X^e-XIVe siècles).* Mémoires de la Société archéologique de Rambouillet, 8vo ser., vol. 22. Versailles, 1910.

Richard de Mores. See [Dunstable Annals].

Rigaldus, Odo (Eudes Rigaud). *Regestrum visitationum archiepiscopi Rothomagensis; Journal des visites pastorales d'Eudes Rigaud, archevêque de Rouen MCCXLVII—MCCLXIX.* Ed. T. Bonnin. Rouen, 1852.

——. *The Register of Eudes of Rouen.* Trans. Sydney M. Brown. Records of Civilization, no. 72. New York, 1964.

Robinson, I. S. *The Papacy 1073–1198: Continuity and Innovation.* Cambridge Medieval Textbooks. Cambridge, Eng., 1990.

Robinson, J. Armitage. "Convocation of Canterbury: Its Early History." *Church Quarterly Review*, LXXXI (1915), 81-137.

Rocquain, F. *La Cour de Rome et l'esprit de reforme avant Luther.* 3 vols. Paris, 1893-1897.

Rodenberg, C., ed. *Epistolae saec. XIII e regestis pontificum Romanorum selectae per G. H. Pertz.* MGH, Epist. saec. XIII. 3 vols. Berlin, 1883-1894.

Roger Wendover: See Wendover.

Rony, A. "Saint Jubin, archevêque de Lyon, et la primatie lyonnaise." *Revue d'histoire de l'église de France*, XV (1929), 409-430.

Roquebert, Michel. *L'Epopée cathare.* 5 vols. Toulouse/Paris, 1970-1998.

Roschach, Ernest, and Auguste Molinier, eds. *Histoire graphique de l'ancienne province de Languedoc.* Toulouse, 1904.

Rotuli litterarum clausarum in Turri Londinensi asservati. Ed. Thomas Duffus Hardy. 2 vols. Record Commissioners. London, 1833-1844.

Ruess, Karl. *Die rechtliche Stellung der päpstlichen Legaten bis Bonifaz VIII.* Görres-Gesellschaft, Sektion für Rechts- und Sozialwissenschaft, no. 13. Paderborn, 1912.

Runciman, Steven. *A History of the Crusades.* 3 vols. 2nd ed. Cambridge, Eng., 1955.

————. *The Medieval Manichee: A Study of the Christian Dualist Heresy.* Cambridge, Eng., 1947.

Russell, Frederick H. *The Just War in the Middle Ages.* Cambridge Studies in Medieval Life and Thought, 3rd ser., vol. 8. Cambridge, Eng., 1975.

Russell, Josiah Cox. *Dictionary of Writers of Thirteenth Century England.* Special Supplement no. 3 to the *Bulletin of the Institute of Historical Research*. London, [1936].

Rymer, Thomas [and Robert Sanderson], eds. *Foedera, conventiones, literae, et cujuscunque generis acta publica, inter reges Angliae et alios quosvis imperatores, reges, pontifices, principes, vel communitates.* 2nd ed. 20 vols. London, 1726-1735.

————. ————. 3rd ed. by George Holmes. 10 vols. The Hague, 1739-1745.

———— et al., eds. ————. 4th ed. 4 vols. London, 1816-1869.

[Salisbury Register]. *Vetus registrum Sarisberiense alias dictum Registrum s. Osmundi episcopi; The Register of St. Osmund.* Ed. W. H. Rich Jones. Rolls Series, no. 78. 2 vols. London, 1883-1884.

Salmon, A., ed. *Recueil des chroniques de Touraine.* Collection de documents sur l'histoire de Touraine, vol. 1 = Bulletin trimestriel de la Société archéologique de Touraine, no. 1. Tours, 1854.

Salter, H. E., ed. *Chapters of the Augustinian Canons.* Oxford Historical Society, o.s., vol. 74 = Canterbury and York Society, vol. 29. Oxford, 1922.

Savio, Giulio. *Monumenta onomastica romana Medii Aevi (X-XII sec.).* 4 vols. Rome, 1999.

Sayers, Jane E. "Centre and Locality: Aspects of Papal Administration in England in the Later Thirteenth Century." In *Authority and Power: Studies on Medieval Law and Government Presented to Walter Ullmann on His 70th Birthday*, ed. Brian Tierney and Peter Linehan. Cambridge, Eng., 1980. Pages 115-126. [Reprinted as item I in her *Law and Records*.]

————. *Innocent III: Leader of Europe, 1198-1216.* The Medieval World. London, 1994.

————. "The Judicial Activities of the General Chapters." *Journal of Ecclesiastical History*, XV (1964), 18-32 and 168-185. [Reprinted as item V in her *Law and Records*.]

————. *Law and Records in Medieval England: Studies on the Medieval Papacy, Monasteries and Records.* Collected Studies, no. 278. London: Variorum, 1988.

————. *Papal Government and England during the Pontificate of Honorius III (1216-1227).* Cambridge Studies in Medieval Life and Thought, 3rd ser., vol. 21. Cambridge, Eng., 1984.

Schmitz, Philibert. *Histoire de l'ordre de Saint-Benoît*. 7 vols. Maredsous, 1942-1956.

Schneider, Herbert, ed. *Die Konzilsordines des Früh- und Hochmittelalters*. MGH, Ordines de celebrando concilio. Hanover, 1996.

Schneyer, J. B., ed. *Repertorium der lateinisches Sermones des Mittelalters für die Zeit von 1150–1350*. Beiträge zur Geschichte der Philosophie und Theologie des Mittelalters: Texte und Untersuchungen, Bd. 43. 11 vols. Münster i. W., 1969-1990.

Schoeck, Richard J. "Medieval Lawyers and the Red Mass: Towards a History of the Mass of the Holy Ghost." *Saint Louis University Law Journal*, V (1958), 274-279.

Schreiber, Georg. *Kurie und Kloster im 12. Jahrhundert*. 2 vols. Kirchenrechtliche Abhandlungen, nos. 67-68. Stuttgart, 1910.

Setton, Kenneth M., ed. *A History of the Crusades*. 2nd ed. 6 vols. Madison, 1969-1989.

Shirley, Walter Waddington, ed. *Royal and Other Historical Letters Illustrative of the Reign of Henry III*. Rolls Series, no. 27. 2 vols. London, 1862-1866.

Sieben, Hermann Josef. *Die Konzilsidee des lateinischen Mittelalters (847–1378)*. Konziliengeschichte, ed. Walter Brandmüller. Paderborn, 1984.

Smith, Cyril Eugene. *The University of Toulouse in the Middle Ages: Its Origins and Growth to 1500 A. D.* Milwaukee, 1958.

Somerville, Robert. *Pope Alexander III and the Council of Tours (1163): A Study of Ecclesiastical Politics and Institutions in the Twelfth Century*. Publications of the Center for Medieval and Renaissance Studies, UCLA, no. 12. Berkeley and Los Angeles, 1977.

Southern, Richard W. *The Making of the Middle Ages*. New Haven, 1953.

Strayer, Joseph Reese. *The Albigensian Crusades.*. New York, 1971.

———. ———. 2nd ed. by Carol Lansing. Ann Arbor, 1992.

———. *Medieval Statecraft and the Perspective of History*. Princeton, 1971.

———, ed. See *Dictionary of the Middle Ages*.

Sumption, Jonathan. *The Albigensian Crusade*. London and Boston, 1978.

Sutherland, Stuart. *The International Dictionary of Psychology*. 2nd ed. New York, 1996.

Tangl, M. *Die päpstlichen Kanzleiordnungen von 1200–1500*. Innsbruck, 1894.

Tanner, Norman P., ed. *Decrees of the Ecumenical Councils*. 2 vols. London: Sheed and Ward, 1990. [Text of *Conciliorum oecumenicorum decreta*, 3rd. ed. (1973) with English translation and notes.]

Teulet, Alexandre, et al., eds. *Layettes du Trésor des chartes*. 5 vols. Archives nationales, Inventaires et documents. Paris, 1863-1909.

Thomas Aquinas. *Summa theologiae*. Ed. P. Caramello. Turin: Marietti, 1952.

Thomassin, Louis. *Vetus et nova ecclesiae disciplina circa beneficia et beneficiarios*. 3rd ed. (1st Latin). 3 vols. Paris, 1691.

Thomson, Rodney M. "The Origins of Latin Satire in Twelfth Century Europe." *Mittellateinisches Jahrbuch*, XIII (1978), 73-83. [Reprinted as item XI in his *England and the 12th-Century Renaissance*, Collected Studies, no. 620 (Aldershot, Hants.: Variorum, 1998).]

———. See *Tractatus Garsiae*.

Thorndike, Lynn. *Michael Scot*. London, 1965.

———, ed. and trans. *University Records and Life in the Middle Ages*. Records of Civilization, no. 38. New York, 1944.

Thouzellier, Christine. *Un Traité cathare inédit du début du XIIIe siècle d'après le "Liber contra Manicheos" de Durand de Huesca.* Bibliothèque de la Revue d'histoire ecclésiastique, fasc. 37. Louvain, 1961.

Thrupp, Sylvia L., ed. *Change in Medieval Society: Europe North of the Alps, 1050–1500.* New York, 1964.

Tierney, Brian. *Foundations of the Conciliar Theory: The Contribution of the Medieval Canonists from Gratian to the Great Schism.* Cambridge Studies in Medieval Life and Thought, n.s., 4. Cambridge, Eng. 1955.

————. "The Idea of Representation in the Medieval Councils of the West." In his *Rights, Laws and Infallibility in Medieval Thought.* Collected Studies, no. 578. Aldershot, Hants.: Variorum, 1997. Item XI.

———— and Peter Linehan, eds. *Authority and Power: Studies on Medieval Law and Government Presented to Walter Ullmann on His 70th Birthday.* Cambridge, Eng., 1980.

Tillmann, Helene. *Papst Innocenz III.* Bonn historische Forschungen, 3. Bonn, 1954.

Tractatus Garsiae, or The Translation of the Relics of SS. Gold and Silver. Ed. and trans. Rodney M. Thomson. Textus minores, vol. 46. Leiden, 1973.

Van Cleve, Thomas C. "The Crusade of Frederick II." In *A History of the Crusades.* Vol. II. 2nd ed. by Kenneth M. Setton. Madison, 1969. Pages 429-462.

————. *The Emperor Frederick II of Hohenstaufen: "Immutator Mundi."* Oxford, 1972.

————. "The Fifth Crusade." In *A History of the Crusades.* Vol. II. 2nd ed. by Kenneth M. Setton. Madison, 1969. Pages 377-428.

Vaughan, Richard. *Matthew Paris.* Cambridge Studies in Medieval Life and Thought, n.s., vol. 6. Cambridge, Eng., 1958.

————, ed. and trans. See Paris, Matthew.

Vendeuvre, Jules. *L'Exemption du visite monastique: Origines; concile de Trente; législation royale.* Thesis, Faculté de droit, Université de Dijon. Dijon, 1906, and Paris, 1907.

Vincent, Nicholas. *Peter des Roches: An Alien in English Politics, 1205–1238.* Cambridge Studies in Medieval Life and Thought, 4th ser., no. 31. Cambridge, Eng., 1996.

Wakefield, Walter L. *Heresy, Crusade and Inquisition in Southern France, 1100–1250.* London, 1974.

Waley, Daniel. *The Papal State in the Thirteenth Century.* London, 1961.

Walter of Coventry. *Memoriale.* Ed. William Stubbs. Rolls Series, no. 58. 2 vols. London, 1872-1873.

Wendover, Roger. *Chronica, sive Flores historiarum.* Ed. H. O. Coxe. English Historical Society. 4 vols. London, 1841-1842.

————. *Rogeri de Wendover liber qui dicitur Flores historiarum.* Ed. H. G. Hewlett. Rolls Series, no. 84. 3 vols. London, 1886-1889.

————. *Roger of Wendover's Flowers of History.* Trans. J. A. Giles. 2 vols. Bohn's Antiquarian Library. London, 1849.

Weske, Dorothy Bruce. *Convocation of the Clergy: A Study of Its Antecedents and Its Rise with Special Emphasis upon Its Growth and Activities in the Thirteenth and Fourteenth Centuries.* London, 1937.

Wilkins, David, ed. *Concilia Magnae Britanniae et Hiberniae.* 4 vols. London, 1737.

William (Guillaume) of Nangis. *Chronique latine de Guillaume de Nangis de 1113 à 1300, avec les continuations de cette chronique de 1300 à 1368*. Ed. Hercule Géraud. 2 vols. Société de l'histoire de France. Paris, 1843.

William (Guillaume) of Puylaurens. *Chronique / Chronica Magistri Guillelmi de Podio Laurentii*. Ed. and trans. Jean Duvernoy. Sources d'histoire médiévale. Paris, 1976.

Yunck, John A. "Economic Conservatism, Papal Finance, and the Medieval Satires on Rome." *Mediaeval Studies*, XXIII (1961), 334-351. [Reprinted in *Change in Medieval Society*, ed. Sylvia L. Thrupp (New York, 1964), pp.72–85.]

Zimmermann, Heinrich. *Die päpstliche Legation in der ersten Hälfte des 13. Jahrhunderts*, Görres-Gesellschaft, Veröffentlichungen der Sektion für Rechts- und Sozialwissenschaft, 17. Paderborn, 1913.

INDEX

The scope of this index includes primarily the text of chapters 1–8; also included are notable matters in the footnotes and in the prolegomena to the documents. References to postmedieval scholars, however, have not been indexed. To avoid needless repetition, the text of the documents has not been indexed, although the principal subjects of each have been noted. The following abbreviations are used: abp = archbishop; bp = bishop; chap. = chapter; doc. = document; prov. = province; st = saint.

abbots: 93–94
Abelard: 163
Abingdon, chronicle: 197
absence from council: 222
absolution: 253, 367
absolutism: 256
acolyte: 184
Ad liberandum: 190
Adhemar of Chabannes: 113
adjournment: 220, 223
advowson: 222
Aegidius Hispanus, cardinal: 372
Agde, bp: 11, 13, 18, 26
Agen, bp: 26
agents: 28, 32, 34–36, 40, 50-52, 65–66, 137, 210, 222–223, 370, 382, 394
Aimeric de Thouars: 62
Aix,
 abp: 55
 canon of: 8
 location: 86
 prov.: 5, 7, 83, 85, 87
Alberic of Trois-Fontaines: 81-82, 202, 307; doc. 5
Albi: 1, 80
 location: 86
Albigensian crusade I: 2, 6
Albigensian crusade II: 5–6, 9, 147–150, 173, 231, 255, 259
 negotiations for: 71-75; docs. 7, 9
Albigensian Roll: 341-342
Albigensian tenth of 1226–1229: 135, 256–258
 abbots protest: 149, 155
 coalition against: 152–174
 collection of: 147–174; docs. 28–39
 granting: 115–146; docs. 25–26

imposing: 147–148
 terms of: 142–145
Albigensian twentieth of 1221-1223: 7–9, 12, 14, 18, 72, 143–144
Albigensians: 1, 22
Alexander III, pope: 182
Alexander IV, pope: 43
Alexander VIII, pope: 320
Amanianus de Grisinhac, abp Auch: 89–90
Amaury de Montfort: 1, 4, 6, 8–10, 13, 15, 17–20, 25, 27, 36, 104–105, 115–116, 118, 121- 127, 129, 135, 138, 141, 258, 291, 326, 347
 his case at Bourges: 122–123
Amiens: 203
Anagni: 49
Andres: 242, 444, 446, 461
Angers: 58
Angoulême, bp: 91
Anjou: 63
Antioch: 241
antipopes: 213
appeal: 20, 54, 153, 158–159, 161, 163, 168, 176–177, 207, 244, 307; docs. 32, 53
Aquitaine: 33–34, 36–37, 60, 63, 68, 70, 110
archbishop-legates: 12–13, 15, 71, 143
archdeacon: 93–94, 184, 191, 218, 221, 554
Aristotle: 47–48, 257
Arles: 73
 abp: 26-27, 55
 location: 86
 prov.: 5, 7, 85, 87
Arnaud Amaury, abp Narbonne: 90, 120
Arras, 242
 bp: 106, 147, 245
 diocese: 527
assemblies, modern: 212

Auch,
    abp: 26, 89–90, 107–110, 170
    location: 86
    prov.: 7, 85, 87
auditor litterarum contradictarum: 184
Augustine of Canterbury, St: 472
Augustine of Hippo, St: 47
Augustinian canons: 59, 168, 194, 234, 290, 527;
    see also canons
Auterive: 152
Auvergne: 15
Auxerre: 294
    bp: 147
avarice: 148, 179–181, 213, 228, 308, 555; doc. 40
Avignon: 5, 9, 73, 142, 150, 174, 258, 307
    location: 86
    bp: 91–92, 170
Avranches: 169, 400, 552, 554
    bp: 147

bailiffs: 210
baillis: 210
Baldwin IX, pseudo: 62
Balkans: 16, 544
bankers, Lombard: 551
Bar, count of: 151–152
Barnwell chronicle: 277, 468; doc. 44
barons of France: doc. 23
Bartholomew of Carcassonne: 16
Bath, bp.: 28
Bayeux,
    bp: 554
    location: 86
Bazas, bp: 92
Beaucaire: 3–4, 117
Beaulieu: 69
Beauvais, bp: 125, 147
Bec: 400
Bedford : 64, 221
Belley, bp: 92
Belvoir: 492
Benedict XII, pope: 249
Benedict of Peterborough: 511
Benedictines: 230, 233–234, 236–237, 245,
        248–249, 256, 460, 490; doc. 46
    in England: 239, 249
    in Reims prov.: 241–246
benefices: 46, 162, 181, 183–184, 186, 194, 222,
        252, 369, 556
Berengar: 558
Bernard of Clairvaux: 176

Bernard of Pavia: 400
Bertrand, cardinal: 4, 7–8, 10
Besançon,
    abp: 5, 91, 170, 202
    location: 86
    prov.: 5, 85, 87
Béziers: 3, 11, 120, 152
    bp: 1, 13
    viscount: 20, 27, 105; *see also* Raymond-Roger
Bitius, master: 185
Blanche of Castille: 41, 150–152 160, 167, 170,
        173–174, 258, 562
blessings: 178–179
Blois: 165
Bologna: 47, 49, 113, 248
Bonaventura,
    family: 39–40; *see also* de Papa
    Nicholas: 39
    Peter: 39, 46
    Romanus, vestiarius Urbis: 40
    See also Romanus, cardinal
Bordeaux: 33
    abp: 5, 54, 59, 90–91, 109–110, 348
    location: 86
    prov.: 12, 85, 87, 132–133
Bouchier family: 161
bourgeoisie: 305, 308
Bourges,
    abp: 5, 18, 20–21, 54, 59, 71, 80, 107–111, 113,
        132, 139–140, 143, 348
    cathedral: 111–112
    council, 1214: 79
    council, 1225: *passim*; docs. 1–6
        abps at: 89–91
        bps at: 91–93
        composition of: 83–107
        counsel at: 128–135
        date of: 80–81
        laymen at: 104–106
        location of: 86
        organization of: 77–114
        president: 78–79
        proctors at: 94–95
        purpose of: 1, 82–83
        results not announced: 134
        seating at: 107–111
        size of: 106–107
        summons to: 77–107
    prov.: 85, 87, 242, 247
    rendezvous at, May 1226: 80, 148, 160
    St-Etienne: 111–112

Bourgmoyen at Blois: 165; docs. 33–35
Bouvines: 6
Brevarium Romanum: 113
bribery: 66, 178, 192, 212
Brittany: 69
    count of: 151–152; *see also* Peter de Dreux
Burchard of Ursberg: 177, 181
bureaucracy: 177, 199
Burgundy: 65, 75, 84–87, 92
Bury, St Edmond's: 224

Cahors: 105
Cambrai,
    bp: 147, 247
    diocese: 242
Campagna: 40-42
canons: 193–194, 237, 245; *see also* Augustinian
    and St-Victor
Canterbury,
    abp: 102–103, 111, 198, 205, 215, 217, 220, 227,
        229, 273; *see also* Stephen Langton
    location: 86
    prov.: 217, 220, 224–225, 228, 239
    St Augustine's: 224
Capannace: 188
capes: 161, 163
Capua: 188–189
Carcassonne: 3, 11, 15, 18–19
    bp: 58, 92, 170, 347; doc. 21
    viscount: 20
cardinals: 184, 195
    assault on: 252
    counsel of: 164, 172
Carmina Burana: 180
Carnifex, Magister P.: 161–162
Carpentras, bp: 26
Carta caritatis: 235
Carthusians: 235
cartulary: 479–481
Castelnaudary: 11
Catalonia: 113
Catania: 34, 73, 142
Cathars: 1, 16, 544
Cavaillon,
    bp: 91
    viscount: 27
Celestine III, pope: 85, 188, 257
Celestine IV, pope: 43
celibacy: 556
cemetaries: 163
Cencius de Papa: 40

Cencius Savelli: 177, 185–186, 188
cens: 178
ceremonial, conciliar: 112–114
cession: 11, 13
Châlons-sur-Marne, 316
    bp: 125
    location: 86
chamberlain: 184
Champagne: 316
    count of: 105, 125, 151–152; *see also* Thibault
chancery: 157, 184, 195, 386, 392–393, 544;
        see also fees
chaplain: 46, 49, 184, 195
chapters: 95–96, 193, 210
    appellant: doc. 35
    delinquent: docs. 29, 31
    general, monastic: 233–250; docs. 45–46
Charlemagne: 125, 306, 558
Charroux: 444
Chartres: 46
    bp: 21, 147, 153, 166; doc. 36
    location: 86
Chichester, bp.: 28, 481; *see also* Ralph Neville
Childeric III: 2
Chinon: 62, 151
Christina, queen of Sweden: 319
churches, pontifical: 187
Cistercians: 5, 7, 9, 17, 46, 144, 153, 169–170,
        234–235, 237–240, 242–243, 247–248, 316,
        460, 561
Cîteaux: 90, 102, 169–170, 235, 561
    location: 86
civil service: 199
Clairvaux: 21, 169–170
Clarendon: 219
Clément familiy: 166
Cluny: 234
    chronicle of: 134, 205
Cluse: 59
coalition: 156–158, 161, 163, 165, 171
collect: 113–114
Collectio Abrincensis: 400–401
collegiate church: 194, 225
colloquium. See Montpellier
Cologne, prov.: 5, 85
commendam, benefice in: 367
Comminges, count of: 4
Compilatio quinta: 248, 527, 540
complaints: 192
Compostela, abp: 179, 182; *see also* Diego
        Gelmirez

conciliarism: 145
concubinage: 58, 168, 195; doc. 52
Condom: 89
confirmation, papal: 137
congregations: 249
Conrad von Urach, cardinal: 9, 12–13, 15–17,
    21–24, 36, 40, 42, 44, 52, 71, 77–79, 82,
    100, 102–103, 115, 141, 170, 173, 332, 339,
    342, 347, 401; doc. 49
consecration: 202
consent: 132, 152, 154, 159–160, 172, 192, 201, 204,
    209, 214, 248, 461
    nonvoluntary: ix, 101, 160
    voluntary: 95, 196
Conserans, bp: 92
Constantine: 460
consultation: 256
contempt: 155
contributions, private: 148
convocation of clergy: 99
council,
    comprovincial: 225, 228–229, 538
    general: 79, 140, 145, 230, 376
    legatine: 78
    plenary: 79
    provincial: 98, 100, 131, 133, 145, 209, 221–223,
        231; doc. 48
counsel: 208–209, 218, 521; doc. 23
    written: 131–133, 154, 159, 206
Coutances,
    bp: 169, 401, 557, 559; see also Hugh de Morville
    location: 86
Cremona: 91
crossbowmen: 307
Crowland: 468
    annals: doc. 44
Crusade V: 7–8, 21, 73, 75, 97
    twentieth for: 190
Crusade VI: 15, 22, 29–31, 35, 37, 164, 332, 347
Crusade VII: 74, 143
crusaders,
    obligations of: 141
    status of: 6, 20, 36, 73, 141–142
Cum ex officio vestro: 247; doc. 47
Cum hii qui: 198
custodians: 162

Damasus: 239–240
Dante: 44
dean: 93–94; see also Paris
debtors: 58; doc. 50

Decretals of Gregory IX: 239, 246, 257, 521,
    527, 540
Denmark: 236
de Papa family: 39–40
deposition: 247–248
Diego Gelmírez, abp Santiago: 179
dispensation: 367
dispersion: 163
Dominic, St: 164
doorkeepers: 195
draft: 393, doc. 25
due process: 119, 164, 172, 256
Dunstable Annals: 63–64, 115, 126, 215, 225,
    228–230, 252, 307; doc. 2
Durham, bp: 226, 482, 491

Ea que pro religionis: 246
échevins: 305
election, episcopal: 54, 90, 162, 170, 211, 459;
    doc. 21
Elne, bp: 92
Embrun,
    abp: 55
    location: 86
    prov.: 5, 7, 83, 85, 87
Empire: 3, 30, 34, 73, 150, 183, 187, 191, 209,
    213, 258
endowment: 194
England, English: passim
esprit laïque: 308
Essex, earl of: 62
ethics: 48
Etienne de Bourbon: 48
Etsi membra corporis: 12, 84, 98–99, 102, 175, 201,
    206, 218
excommunication: 1, 5, 8, 20, 29, 71–74, 117, 134,
    138–139, 142, 148, 164–165, 233, 252–253,
    347, 369, 387, 556–557
exempt monasteries: 224, 236, 238, 240, 243
Exeter, bp: 493
exheredation: 10, 13, 74, 141
expense accounts: 192
exposition en proie: 2, 5–6

factions, Roman: 213
familiaritas: 51
Fanjau: 28
Farfa: 236
Fawkes de Bréauté: 64–66, 208, 216, 501,
    505–507, 515; doc. 22
fees, chancery: 178, 181, 195–196

Fenland: 79, 216, 229, 468; doc. 44
feudal war: 37, 148, 258
fiefs: 74, 222–223, 252, 258, 274, 560
financial reform: chaps. 6–7; doc. 40
Flanders: 30, 62, 306
    count of: 125
    countess of: 124
Florence of Worcester: 511
Foigny: 242
Foix, count of: 4, 5, 27, 104; *see also* Roger-
    Bernard
Folco of Marseille: 170
France, French: *passim*
    barons: doc. 23
Francis, St: 164–165
Franciscan Rule: 164
Frangipani family: 40–41; *see also* Romanus
Frederick I, emperor: 188-189
Frederick II, emperor: 15, 21, 23, 29–31, 33–34,
    73, 91, 142, 151, 164, 231, 258, 319, 332
frontispiece: 111, 216
fund, common: 195–196, 212

Garonne: 33
Garsias de l'Ort, abp Auch: 89
Gascony: 30, 33, 63, 68, 87
Gaul: 92, 108
Geoffrey Craucumb: 28
Gerald of Wales: 186–191, 196, 236, 266, 521;
    doc. 40
Gerhoch of Reichersberg: 180-181
Germany: 22, 30, 33, 87, 163, 183, 258
Gervase of Tilbury: 124
gifts: 59, 195, 198–199, 212
Gilbertines: 235
gîte (gist): 106, 210
Glandèves, bp: 92
Glossa ordinaria: 98–99
grammarian: 97
Gran, abp: 527
Grandmontines: 235
Gratian's *Decretum*: 47, 96, 133, 250
Great Schism: 213
Gregorian reform: 176, 194, 556
Gregory I, pope: 47, 472
Gregory VII, pope: 109
Gregory IX, pope: 41–43, 46, 51, 82, 143, 146,
    152–153, 158–159, 161, 163–166, 171–173,
    183, 230, 248–249, 255, 372, 493; docs.
    32–35, 39
Guala Bicchieri, cardinal: 58, 169, 556–557, 559

Guiton family: 552
Guy de Montfort: 32, 35, 138

Hélinand: 45, 47, 60, 179
Heloise: 163
Henry III, king of England: 20, 28, 33–34, 46,
    57, 60, 62, 64–67, 69–70, 72, 91, 142,
    150–151, 215–217, 227–229, 231, 258,
    332, 493
Henry V, emperor: 188
Henry VI, emperor: 40, 186–189, 196, 257;
    doc. 40
Henry, king of Romans: 33, 142
Henry of Huntington: 511
Henry of Villeneuve, bp Auxerre: 147
Hereford, chapter of: 190, 461
heresy and heretics: 1–3, 10, 13–14, 22, 32,
    118–120, 122, 257
Herodotus: 265
Hildebert of Le Mans: 320
Hohenstaufen: 43, 255
Holy Land: 2, 5, 7, 21–24, 30–31, 34, 347
Holy Spirit, Mass of: 112–113
Honnecourt: 242–243
Honorius III, pope: 1, 4–8, 10, 13–18, 20–24,
    26–32, 34–35, 41, 48, 50–51, 55–56, 59–61,
    65–70, 72, 74, 83, 85, 98–99, 100, 102,
    116–117, 120, 123, 127, 137, 140, 160, 164,
    170, 174–175, 179, 181–182, 184–185,
    189–191, 197, 201, 205–208, 210–211, 216,
    222, 225, 227, 229–231, 233–234, 239, 242,
    245–246, 248–253, 255–259, 401, 458, 480,
    556–557; docs. 7–8, 10–21, 41, 46, 48; *see*
    also Cencius Savelli
Hospitallers: 2, 144
host, feudal: 148
Hugh IX of Lusignan, count of La Marche: 151
Hugh Beroard, abp Arles: 27
Hubert de Burgh: 61, 64
Hugh de Morville, bp Coutances: 559
Hugh de Templo: 488
Huguicio Lombardus: 185
Hungary: 30, 183, 527
hypocrisy: 179

In medio ecclesie: 248
In singulis regnis: 234, 243, 246–249; doc. 45
    commentaries on: 239–241
    implementation of: 238, 241–246
    origin of: 237–239
income: 177, 185, 193–194

indulgences: 5–6
inelegibiles: 162
infamy: 252
injunction: 153, 164; docs. 33–35
Innocent II, pope: 472
Innocent III, pope: 1–2, 6, 9–10, 25, 40–41, 47, 97–98, 103, 164, 175, 178, 184–187, 190, 193, 196, 205, 213, 234, 236, 249, 255–257, 401, 480, 538; docs. 40, 45
Innocent IV, pope: 43, 221, 230–231, 251, 256–257
inquisition: 41–42, 49
    papal: 119, 173
insubordination: 31
interdict: 20, 71–72, 369, 561–562
Investiture Contest: 179
Ireland: 241
Isidore of Seville: 114
Italy and Italians: 30, 163, 183, 199, 231
Ivo of Chartres: 178, 195

James of Aragon: 4
Jean of Abbeville, abp Besançon: 91, 202–203
Johannes de Cella: 492
Johannes Teutonicus: 239–241, 244–245, 521
John, cardinal: 185
John of Bedford: 94
John de Brienne, king of Jerusalem: 22, 30, 34, 63–64
John Chrysostom, St: 558
John de Colonna: 185
John, king of England: 6, 33, 64, 229, 257, 480, 493
John of Houton, archdeacon of Bedford: 221–222, 229
John Longus: 105, 169–170; doc. 38
John Marshal: 220, 223
John le Romeyn, Roman noble: 185
John of Salisbury: 180
John of Wallingford: 492
Jouarre abbey: 58
judges-delegate: 41, 43, 58, 110, 251, 550; docs. 33–35
jurisdiction: 233–234, 237, 240–241, 244–245, 247, 251
justiciar: 35

Kalocza, abp: 527

La Marche, count of: 69, 151–152; *see also* Hugh IX
La Réole: 33, 63–64, 68
La Roche au Moine: 6
La Souterraine: 105

Langres, bp: 18, 20–21, 125, 139, 147, 393
Laon: 46
    bp: 125, 147
    cathedral: 58
Largentière: 27
Lateran III, council: 82, 186, 213
Lateran IV, council: 2–3, 6, 8, 10, 14, 28, 32, 82–83, 97–98, 100, 107, 111–114, 119, 122, 141, 175, 186, 190–191, 193, 233–239, 255–257, 458, 460–461, 538; doc. 45
law, civil: 347, 369
laymen: 220–222, 228, 238
Lectoure, bp: 91
legalism: 256–257
legation, letters of: 114; docs. 12–13, 15, 27
legatus
    a latere: 53, 140, 174, 346
    natus: 71, 140
legislation: 520
Le Mans,
    bp: 165; docs. 33–35
    location: 86
Lescar, bp: 91
Liber censuum: 85, 177, 185, 198
Limoges: 59, 89
    bp: 147
    chronicle of: 89, 104, 205
    council, 1031: 113
    St-Martial: 89
Limoux: 152
Lincoln,
    bp: 28, 62–63; *see also* Robert Grosseteste
    diocese: 221
litigation: 177, 180, 192
liturgy: 112, 210, 221, 253
living: 177
Llywelyn, prince of N. Wales: 57
Lodève, bp: 11, 13, 113
logic: 47, 257
Loire: 36–37
Lombards and Lombardy: 236, 246, 551
London: 227
    bp: 62, 217, 224–225
    council, Jan. 1226: 78, 93–94, 208, 215, 217–224, 229, 485, 488
    council, May 1226: 78, 95, 99, 102–103, 201, 209, 2 15, 224–231, 272–274, 480, 485, 489, 491, 517
    council, 1237: 99, 111, 216, frontispiece
    council, 1240: 99
    council, 1245: 230
    council, 1246: 99

location: 86
St Paul's: 219, 221–222
Louis VIII, king of France: 1, 6, 8, 17–19, 21–24,
    26, 28, 32–33, 35, 37, 40–41, 50–52, 56, 58,
    60–61, 63–65, 67–69, 71–74, 80–81,
    105–106, 116–117, 129–131, 134–136, 138,
    141–142, 145, 147–152, 165, 167, 172–174,
    227, 252, 258, 294, 307, 509; docs. 7–9,
    14–15, 23–26, 50
Louis IX, king of France: 74, 143, 150, 171, 550,
    560; doc. 39
Louis the Bavarian, emperor: 213
Louviers: 560
Luxeuil: 59, 169
Lyon: 57, 150
    abp: 5, 79, 107–111
    council, 1245: 230, 257
    location: 86
    prov.: 85, 87, 276

Mâcon, bp: 92
magister: 161, 185, 221
Maguelonne, bp: 13, 15, 18
Maimonides: 48
Mainz, prov.: 5
Manichaeans: 1
Mantes: 17
Marborough: 215, 222
Marches: 236
Marchiennes: 243, 527
Margaret of Austria: 33
Marianus Scotus: 511
Marittima: 40–42
mark, silver: 180, 226
Marlborough: 219
Marmande: 8, 120
Marseilles: 5
Martin, papal nuncio: 230–231
Matilda, countess of Tuscany: 188
Matthew of Albano: 235
Matthew Paris: 105, 108, 111, 124, 183, 230–231,
    265, 270–271, 274, 545; doc. 43; frontispiece
Maugio. See Melgueil
Maurists: 265, 321
Mazan: 43
Meaux: 41, 113, 173
    bp: 7, 58
Melgueil: 15, 18
Melun: 63, 122, 307
    council, 1216: 98
    council, Nov. 1225: 70, 105, 136–37
mercenaries: 33

Messina: 187
Mézières: 527
Michael Scot: 48
Missale Romanum: 113
Mohammed: 319
Montauban: 3
Montecassino: 236
Montfort family: 9; see also Amaury, Guy, and
    Simon
Montpellier: 5, 19, 25
    colloquia at: 25–27, 29, 31–32, 36, 90, 104–105,
        117–123, 126–127, 174, 259
    council, 1211: 2
    location: 86
Montpensier: 150
Mont-St.-Michel: 147, 400, 468, 544, 552, 527
    location: 86
Muret: 2

Narbonne: 3–4, 11, 18–19
    abp: 19, 21, 23–26, 90, 107–110, 170, 319, 332,
        349; doc. 11
    duke: 104, 125
    location: 86
    prov.: 7, 55, 85, 87, 92
nationalism, proto: 213
necessity: 166, 172, 255, 257
negligence: 240-241
nepotism: 185
Nîmes: 9
    bp: 11, 18, 26
nonresidence: 182
Normandy and Normans: 63, 154, 176, 546
Northampton: 221, 227
Northumberland: 227
notaries: 184
Notitia dignitatum: 109–110
Noyon, bp: 7, 125, 147
nuncio: 98, 101–103, 130, 207, 216, 220, 223–224,
    231; see also spokesman

oaths: doc. 50
obedience: 127
Odo Rigaldus, abp Rouen: 250
omens: 149
Order of the Faith, Militia of: 9
orders, liturgical: 112, 221, 253
Orient: 183
Orléans: 58
    bp: 165, 380; docs. 33–35
orphans: 259
Osmund, St: 482

Ostia: 431
  cardinal-bp of: 164
Otto of Tenengo, papal nuncio: 64–67, 99, 102,
    184, 201, 203, 215–217, 219–227, 228–229,
    480, 493, 501, 507, 515–516; frontispiece
outlawry: 252

P. Carnifex, magister: 161–162
Palermo: 34
Paris: 16, 46, 57, 79, 163, 306
  bp: 161, 250-252
  chapter: 157–158, 161–162; doc. 32
  chancellor of: 251
  council of,
      May 1224: 23–24
      July 1223: 16, 62, 70
      Jan. 1226: 70, 136–146, 155; docs. 23–27
      March 1226: 147
      May 1225: 61, 70
  dean of: 130–131, 158–161, 164; doc. 32
  location: 86
  masters of: 104, 205, 233, 250-253
  prévôt of: 161–162
  treaty of, 1229: 4, 49, 74, 123, 173–174, 259
  university of: 47, 52, 58, 169, 253, 250, 291
pars, maior et sanior: 191
Paschal II, pope: 109
patrimony: 162–163
  of St Peter: 42–43, 177, 258
patronage: 177, 181, 222, 231
Péan Gâtineau: 295
peers of France: 123–126
Pembroke, earl of: 62
penitentiary, papal: 184
Péronne: 62
Perpignon, bp: 170
Peter Ameil, abp Narbonne: 90
Peter of Capua, cardinal: 372
Peter de Dreux, count of Brittany: 151
Peter la Papa: 63
Peter des Roches: 30
Peter's pence: 178
Peterborough: 226, 491; doc. 44
  location: 86
petition: 197
Philip II Augustus, king of France: 3–4, 6–7,
    11, 13–18, 33, 64, 122, 124, 151, 166, 258,
    306, 544
Philip Mousket: 22, 40, 104, 115, 117; doc. 4
Plain-Pied-sur-Avron: 546
plena potestas: 97, 101, 103

plenitudo potestatis: 2, 13, 182, 192, 196, 244, 250,
    255–257
Poitiers, bp: 92
Poitou: 32–33, 35, 50, 60, 62–64, 67–70, 142
pontificale: 112–113, 253
pope, relatives of: 184
Porto, cardinal-bp of: 41–43, 173
postponement: 209
power of the purse: 145
preaching: 31, 141, 148,
prebendal churches: 194, 196, 224, 480
prebends: 186, 189, 193–194, 202, 205, 210, 231,
    503–505; docs. 40–41
precedence: 107, 386, 393; see also primacy
Premonstratensians: 144, 194, 235
prévôt: 161, 163, 210, 420
primacy: 107–111, 348
priors: 93–94, 218
private law, analogy to: 103
proctors: 78, 82–84, 88, 92, 97–98, 130–131, 175,
    206–208, 214, 218, 224–225, 231, 246, 276,
    468, 538; doc. 48
  instructed: 102–103, 225
  suitable: 103, 159
procurations: 46, 111, 210, 214, 226–227; doc. 51
procurator: 103
propaganda, council as: 135
Provence: 14, 54, 73, 85–87, 211; docs. 11, 20
  clergy of: 55
  marquisate of: 4, 150
provinces, rank of: 87
Provins: 545
provisions, papal: 181–185, 197–198, 231

Quod omnes tangit, maxim: 98–99, 145, 172, 190,
    205, 221–222, 229–230, 538

Rain., chaplain: 46, 49
Rainer de Viterbo, cardinal: 372
Ralph Neville, bp Chichester: 210
Raoul Guiton: 551–552
ratione peccati: 255, 258
Raymond VI, count of Toulouse: 1–2, 4, 10, 20,
    73–74, 90, 118–119, 122
Raymond VII, count of Toulouse: 1–20, 23–29,
    31, 34, 36, 41, 43, 49, 56, 69, 74, 81, 90,
    104–105, 115, 117–118, 121–123, 125, 127,
    129, 134–135, 138–139, 149, 151–152,
    173–174, 205, 258, 271–272, 274, 291, 349,
    509; docs. 8, 10
  his case at Bourges: 117–22, 206, 209

reconciliation of: 3, 24, 26, 116–117
ultimatum to: 126–128
Raymond of Penyafort: 540
Raymond-Roger Trencavel jr., viscount of
  Béziers: 105
Reading: 488
reconciliation: 253; doc. 8; *see also* Raymond VII
recusation: 168; doc. 53
Reformation, Protestant: 175, 179
regalian rights: 162
Reginensis chronicle: 81, 83, 88–89, 94–95, 104,
  106; doc. 6
Regno: 176, 187, 258
Reims: 100, 561
  abp: 5, 71, 109–110, 124–125, 139–140, 143, 147,
    195, 241, 244, 247; *see also* William de
    Joinville
  chapter: 438
  conference, Oct. 1225: 201–205, 207
  diocese.: 527
  location: 86
  monastic chapters: 153, 161, 171, 239, 241–248
  prov.: 12, 85, 87, 144, 238, 247, 447; doc. 46
  provost of: 59, 169
  St-Remi: 241, 243
Relatio: 79–80, 89–90, 92, 94, 104–105, 107,
  109–111, 115, 122, 127, 175, 201–202,,
  204–209, 212, 225, 230–231, 468; doc. 1
religion, men of: 93–94
renaissance, twelfth-century: 257
representation: 95–101, 175, 192, 225, 231; doc. 48
  by head: 192, 218, 283, 538
reputation: 192
reservations: 205, 212
reserved powers: 53
restitutions: 25, 120
rhetoric: 214, 459
Rhone: 3–4, 10, 14, 20, 34, 36, 55, 73, 142, 150
Ricardus Anglicus, physician: 493
Richard of Cornwall: 70, 72, 142
Richard de Mores: 290, 458
Richard Poore, bp Salisbury: 481
Richard of Wendover:, physician : 493
Rieti: 245
Robert, dauphin of Auvergne: 48
Robert of Clari: 305
Robert of Courson, cardinal: 79
Robert Grosseteste, bp Lincoln: 183, 193
Robert, bp Troyes: 246
Rochester, bp: 63
Roger-Bernard, count of Foix: 104

Roger of Hoveden: 510–511
Roger Wendover: 80, 93–94, 105, 107, 109, 115,
  120, 124–126, 197, 203, 216–220, 226–227,
  229–231, 270–272, 274, 278–279, 291,
  544–545, 547; doc. 43
Romanus Bonaventura/Frangipani, cardinal: 1,
  29, 34–35, 37, 39–57, 82–83, 85, 93,
  100-104, 107, 110-111, 112–118, 121–123,
  125, 127, 130-136, 138, 140–142, 144–147,
  157–158, 160, 162, 165–175, 179, 191, 195,
  201, 203, 206–207, 210-211, 213–214, 217,
  220, 230–231, 233, 245–247, 250–253,
  257–259, 468, 507; docs. 10, 22, 24–36,
  50-53
  legation,
    preparations for: 346–370
    map of: 86
Rome: 21, 42, 57, 165, 177, 187, 212–213
  St John Lateran: 177
  St Peter's: 43, 187, 130
  St Stephan: doc. 19
  Sant' Angelo in foro piscium: 41
  vicarius urbanus: 50
Rouen: 236, 546, 551
  abp: 5, 58, 78, 102, 107–110, 139, 147, 168, 250,
    544, 554; doc. 53; *see also* Odo Rigaldus
    and Theobald
  chapter: 60, 153, 562; doc. 53
  council, Aug. 1227: 561
  location: 86
  monastic chapters: 153, 161, 171
  prov.: 58, 85, 87, 100, 144, 242, 247, 556–557,
    560
  Romanus at: 168–169
Rule of St Benedict: 234

Sacramentary, Gregorian: 113
sacrilege: 252
safe-conduct: 81, 105, 346; docs. 16–17
St Albans: 86, 224, 271, 490, 492
  location: 86
St-Amand: 527
St-Bertin: 59, 169, 446–447
  location, 86
St David's, bp: 459
St-Flour: 15, 546
  location: 86
St-Gilles: 5, 104
St-Michel at Cluse: 59
St-Omer: 65
St-Ouen: 370

St-Pierre d'Audembourg: 30
St-Pierre at Uzerche: 59
St-Pol-de-Leon, bp: 91
St-Pourçain: 16, 545–546
St-Quentin: 242–243
St-Victor, canons-regular of: 194, 235
St-Vincent-lez-le-Mans: 400
Saladin tithe: 7
Salisbury: 273, 468
    bp: 28, 102, 224, 227; *see also* Richard Poore
    location: 86
    officialis: 276
    Register: 81, 107–108, 217–219, 221, 225–226,
        228, 230–231, 274, 277, 380; doc. 42
Salzburg, prov.: 5
Sancho, Don: 5
San Germano: 29–30
sanctions: 156, 162; doc. 30
Sapientia que ex ore: 243–245, 247–248, 253; doc. 46
satire: 179–181, 212, 461
Savoy: 346
Saxony: 235
Scandinavia: 183
schism: 213–214
schools, cathedral: 186; *see also* grammarians *and*
        theologians
scribe: 184
seals: 58, 132, 251, 379, 381, 394–395, 406, 414
secrecy: 128–129, 134, 272, 276, 539
Séez, bp: 544, 547
senate, Roman: 133
sénéchausées: 150
seniority: 133
Senlis: 46
    bp: 18
Sens: 113, 562
    abp: 5, 71, 100, 107–110, 139–140, 143, 147, 153,
        166, 169–170, 447, 538; doc. 36; *see also*
        Walter Cornut
    council, 1223: 16, 77–79, 82, 93, 100, 115, 401;
        doc. 49
    location: 86
    prov.: 85, 87, 98, 144, 246–247, 538
        chapters: 153, 161, 166–167
sequestration: 153–163, 165; docs. 29–32
sermons: 47–48, 112, 114, 138, 141, 168
Sicily: 30
Simon de Montfort: 2–6, 10, 28, 32, 90, 122
Simon de Senlis: 210
Simon de Sully, abp Bourges: 80
sixteenth of 1226: 482
Spain: 4, 92, 96, 183, 191, 209

Spalding: 510
spokesman (*prolocutor*): 88, 94, 208, 220–221, 229
Spoleto: 42, 236
Stephan Comes, cardinal: 372
Stephen Langton, abp Canterbury: 190, 215,
        217–218, 223–225, 228, 231, 251, 461
Stephen Lucy: 28
Stratford: 61
Subiaco: 236
submissions: 149–150
subsidy: 1, 11–12, 20, 23, 84, 143
Summa providentia principis: 252
summons: 77, 102, 521; doc. 49
Super muros Jerusalem: 80, 87–88, 99, 175, 233,
        246–247, 253, 257, 271, 273, 276, 458, 489;
        chaps. 7–8; doc. 41
    analysis of: 191–199
    at Bourges: 205–214
    in England: 214–231
    in France: 201–214
    implementation of: 204–205
    merits of: 198
    publication of: 203, 208
    rejection of: 201–231
Sweden: 242
synod, diocesan: 96, 209

Tancred: 248, 527, 540
Tarbes-Bigorre, bp: 89–90, 170
Tarentaise: 87
    abp: 5, 55
    location: 86
    prov.: 5, 85, 87
Tarragona, prov.: 85
tax: 9, 72, 74–75, 84, 96, 100, 130, 135, 190
    collection: 12, 143
    collectors, papal: 164, 173, 210–211
    exemption: 144–145
Templars: 2, 9, 144
Terracina: 40
Theobald, abp Rouen: 545, 556–557; doc. 53
theologians: 98
Thérouanne: 59
    diocese: 168, 444
Thibault, count of Champagne: 105
Thomas of Chopham: 276
Thomas de Ebulo, cardinal: 50, 68, 372
Thomas Walsingham: 491
Thouars: 62–3, 68, 151
    viscount: 62
tithe: 190
Tivoli: 188

Torronet: 170
Torteval priory: doc. 554
Toulon, diocese: 85
Toulouse: 1–5, 9, 16, 120, 125, 149–150
  bp: 16, 170
  council, 1229: 44–45, 133, 173
  count of: 104, 125
  location: 86
  university of: 41. 49, 173
Tournai: 304, 306
  location: 86
Tournus: 243
Tours,
  abp: 5, 139, 417
  Chronicle of: 61–63, 68, 70, 81, 88, 95, 104, 119,
    122, 128, 138–141, 143–145, 148–149, 155,
    160, 167, 172, 206–208, 214, 233, 241,
    246–247, 250-253, 376, 380; doc. 3
  council, 1163: 107
  Marmoutier: 295
  prov.: 91, 109–111, 144, 185, 276
  St-Martin: 294–295
Trent, council of: 142, 234
Trier, abp: 5
Trois-Fontaines: See Alberic
truce: 19–20, 22, 25 , 34, 67–70, 73, 142, 347, 349;
    doc. 11
Tuscany: 42

unanimity: 132
Uzerche: 59

Uzès, bp: 18

Vernon: 560-561
vicar: 50
vidimus: 348, 356, 551; doc. 27
Vienne,
  abp: 5,: 7
  prov.: 85, 91
Villehardouin: 305
visitation: 59–60, 460; docs. 45, 53
Viterbo: 9
Viviers: 27–29, 32, 43
  bp: 15

Wales: 460
Walter of Coventry: 79, 266, 272, 277; doc. 44
Wendover. See Roger and Richard
Westminster: 61
widows: 259
William Amanieu, abp Bordeaux: 90-91
William of Andres: doc. 37
William de Joinville, abp Reims: 527
William Longespée, earl: 488
William de Wanda: 481–482
Winchester,
  bp: 493
  officialis: 276

Yolande of Brittany: 69
Ypres: 446